The Ultimate Childproofing Home Guide

Infant/Non-mobile: **(Birth - 6 months)**
Infant Crawl/Roll: **(5 months - 1 year)**
Toddler/Pre-school: **(1 year - 4 years)**
School-age: **(5 years - 6+ years)**

Artemis Hootenanny

EVERPRESENT
North America Inc.
Copyright © 2025
ISBN: 979-8-9924367-0-9

Copyright © 2025

All rights reserved. No part of this publication may be reproduced, distributed, or transmitted in any form or by any means, including photocopying, recording, or other electronic or mechanical methods, without the prior written permission of the publisher, except in the case of brief quotations embodied in critical reviews and certain other noncommercial uses permitted by copyright law.
Published by Everpresent North America Inc.
First Edition: June 2025
UltimateChildproofingguide.com
Soft Cover: ISBN: 979-8-9924367-0-9

From the Author

This book is packed with detailed information, and I'll admit it might sometimes feel a bit overwhelming. But here's the thing, **you don't need to implement every single tip or suggestion**. Instead, think of it as a resource to heighten your awareness. Use your best judgment and keep the key ideas in mind as you go about childproofing your space. The goal is to help you spot potential hazards that might otherwise go unnoticed, not make you worry about everything.

Childproofing is about taking reasonable precautions and not living in constant fear. The steps you take will give you peace of mind, knowing that you've created a safer environment for your kids. Minimizing regrets starts with being proactive. After all, your children are your top priority, and there's no need to cut corners when it comes to their safety.

That said, **it's essential to strike a balance**. You don't want to overprotect or shelter your kids from every little bump or bruise. These are natural parts of growing up and learning. Instead, take the necessary steps to protect them from severe dangers while allowing them to explore, grow, and experience life. Your role is to create a safe space where they can do that freely.

Disclaimer

The information provided in this book is intended to serve as a general guide to childproofing and promoting safety in your home. While the author and publisher have made every effort to ensure the accuracy and completeness of the information contained herein, they make no guarantees, warranties, or representations, either express or implied, concerning the safety, efficacy, or appropriateness of any of the methods, products, or suggestions described in this book. Childproofing is a complex and nuanced task; what may be appropriate and effective in one situation may not be in another. It is the reader's responsibility to assess the unique circumstances of their home and to exercise due diligence, caution, and common sense in implementing any childproofing measures. The reader is strongly encouraged to consult with a professional childproofing expert or other qualified professionals to ensure the safety of their home environment. The author and publisher disclaim all liability for any injuries, losses, or damage that may result from the use or misuse of the information in this book, and they shall not be held responsible for any errors, omissions, or inaccuracies in the content. Remember, no book can replace the personalized advice and expertise of a certified professional in child safety. Your child's safety is of the utmost importance, and we urge you to prioritize it above all else. This disclaimer emphasizes the reader's responsibility to approach childproofing with caution and seek professional advice, helping to protect the author and publisher from potential liability. It also underscores the importance of prioritizing the safety of children in all circumstances.

Acknowledgments

I am incredibly grateful to Lori. From the beginning, her role as a mother and a creative thinker has been at the heart of this project. Lori brought to the table her deep experience as a parent and an intuitive understanding of what truly matters when protecting children. Her insights, grounded in real-life challenges and triumphs, have shaped this book in ways that go beyond words.

Lori's creative spark and hands-on approach have enriched every chapter. She has an uncanny ability to see practical solutions where others see problems, and her suggestions are always thoughtful and actionable. Whether it was coming up with ideas for making safety tools more accessible or providing real-life examples that would resonate with readers, Lori consistently offered perspectives that added layers of meaning and practicality to the advice within these pages. Her contributions were not just helpful, they were transformative.

But beyond her ideas, Lori's unwavering dedication to child safety truly inspired me. Her passion for ensuring every home can be a safer place for children has driven this entire project. She has tirelessly shared her knowledge, always intending to empower parents and caregivers to make informed, thoughtful choices about their children's well-being. Lori's commitment to this cause was a constant reminder of the importance of this work, and her belief in its potential fueled my motivation at every step.

Thank you, Lori, for your boundless creativity, your wisdom, and, most of all, your unshakable support throughout this journey. You were more than a contributor; you were a partner in bringing this book to life. Your passion for child safety shines through every page, and this book is as much a reflection of your influence as it is of my work. I am deeply honored to have had you by my side in this endeavor, and I will always be grateful for your role in shaping its success.

Preface

Welcome to the enchanted realm of "Childproofing Wonderland", where every nook and cranny holds a secret, and every corner whispers tales of mischief and wonder! As you turn the pages of this tomb of wisdom, you'll embark on a quest, armed with a shield of knowledge and a sword of wit, to create a castle safe for your tiny princes and princesses. In the bustling kingdom of Parenthood, where sleep is scarce, and coffee is treasured, our little ones, with twinkling eyes and boundless energy, explore, tumble, and occasionally bump into things. They are curious explorers, fearless warriors, and imaginative creators, living in a world where furniture becomes towering mountains and carpets transform into deep, mysterious oceans.

However, amidst laughter and play, the kingdom has its dragons. These fire-breathing monsters are the hidden dangers lurking in your home, disguised as innocent-looking objects, waiting for a moment of distraction to cause chaos. But fret not, dear adventurer, for this book is your magical scroll, revealing the spells and incantations needed to tame these beasts and shield your offspring from harm. With a sprinkle of humor and a dash of love, we've crafted a guide that is as entertaining as it is informative. Each chapter is a treasure trove of tips and tricks designed to navigate you through the labyrinth of childproofing with ease and confidence. We cover everything from the living room to the kitchen, from the bathroom to the magical attic, leaving no stone unturned.

Table of Contents
Childproofing Chronicles

1. Foyer/Main Entrance 5
2. Living Room/Family Room 18
3. Kitchen 92
4. Dining Room 167
5. Hallways/Stairways 172
6. Children's Bedroom 184
7. Children's Bathroom 210
8. Parents and Guest Bedrooms 222
9. Parents Bathroom 231
10. Nursery 238
11. Children with Diverse Needs 270
12. Laundry Room 275
13. Home Office/Den 283
14. Sunroom/Patio 294
15. Attic 299
16. Panic/Safe Room 305
17. Prayer/Meditation Room 313
18. Game/Recreation/Fitness Room 315
19. Theater/Entertainment Room 333
20. Hobby/Scrapbooking/Sewing Room 336
21. Unfinished Basement/Furnace/Water Heater 338
22. Rooftop Terrace 346
23. Garage 352
24. The Yard 375
25. Wild Animals 473
26. Holidays 475
27. Grandparents/Caretakers 510
28. Child Internet Safety 513
29. Intruder and Child Abduction Protection 515
30. Government Agencies 518
Conclusion 520
Ultimate Childproofing Checklist 521

Book Introduction

The joy of watching a child explore, learn, and grow within the home is one of the most rewarding experiences for any parent. There's something magical about seeing your little one take their first wobbly steps, touch everything in sight with wide-eyed curiosity, and begin to understand the world around them. However, with this excitement comes an undeniable reality: with exploration comes risk. Children, especially those between the ages of 0-6, are like tiny adventurers navigating a home with potential hazards they had no idea existed.

According to the Centers for Disease Control and Prevention, **a staggering 8.7 million children are treated in emergency departments for unintentional injuries every year**, and many of these incidents happen right in the comfort of their own homes. That statistic is more than just a number; it's a reminder of how quickly a routine day can take a dangerous turn. The home, with all its corners, edges, and seemingly innocent everyday objects, can present many hidden dangers for young children. The risks are everywhere, from the sharp edges of coffee tables to the irresistible allure of household cleaners.

Poisoning Incidents Are Alarming. Approximately **500,000 children** under the age of 6 are treated in emergency rooms annually due to accidental poisoning, with medications and household cleaners being the top culprits. (Source: American Association of Poison Control Centers (AAPCC) - National Poison Data System) For new moms and parents, those numbers can be downright terrifying. The space that's supposed to be your family's safe haven can sometimes feel more like a maze of accidents waiting to happen. It's overwhelming. You constantly scan the room, wondering if you've missed something that could lead to a bump, bruise, or worse. But here's the good news: the more you know, the more empowered you'll feel to turn your home into the safe, nurturing environment it's meant to be.

This book is designed to be your trusted companion as you embark on the journey of childproofing. We know the challenges you face, and we're here to guide you every step of the way. Through expert insights, practical tips, and an easy-to-follow guide to common household dangers, we'll help you identify the areas that need attention and show you how to address them. But more than that, we want to give you peace of mind. Childproofing isn't just about installing locks or moving fragile items out of reach, it's about creating a space where your child can freely explore, learn, and thrive, with you feeling confident in their safety.

Let's work together to ensure that every step, crawl, and reach for the unknown is met with confidence and protection. From the nursery to the kitchen, from the playroom to the bathroom, you'll find the tools and tips you need to stay one step ahead of your child's boundless curiosity. With a little preparation, your home can be a place where the joy of childhood meets the security of thoughtful, loving parenting.

"Within these walls, no harm shall reach the little feet that run free." – Artemis

|Ch. 1| Foyer/Main Entrance

Introduction: Childproofing a foyer is a pivotal step in creating a safe home environment, especially when there are young children around. The foyer, the initial entry point into the home, often experiences high traffic and can sometimes become slippery, posing a significant risk for little ones prone to slips and falls. It is imperative to implement strategies that reduce the risk of accidents and foster a secure and child-friendly zone. Each aspect plays a crucial role in enhancing safety, from utilizing anti-slip coatings and quality mats to establishing a safe footwear policy and ensuring adequate lighting. Educating children on the potential hazards and encouraging safe behavior in the foyer can go a long way in preventing accidents. As you embark on the journey of childproofing your foyer, remember that the goal is to create a space that harmoniously blends safety with functionality, offering peace of mind and a secure environment for your family.

Testimonial: *I'll never forget the moment our energetic little Julia, full of life and curiosity, took a fall in our foyer. She was running, as toddlers do, and slipped on the smooth, shiny floor, leaving her with a bruised knee and so many tears. Seeing her in pain, even over a small injury, hit me hard as a mother. It made me realize that we hadn't thought to childproof this high-traffic area. A simple non-slip mat could have given her the traction she needed, and corner guards on the furniture might have softened her fall. Better lighting would have helped her avoid the wet spot that caused her to slip in the first place.*

After that day, I took steps to make our foyer a safe place for her to explore and play. Childproofing is about more than just locks and cabinet latches—it's about ensuring every space in your home, even the ones you don't immediately think of, is safe for your little one. Now, I always encourage other parents to think of places like the foyer when childproofing their homes, so they can avoid the scare we had. It's all about creating a home where our kids can be free to explore without unnecessary risks.

– Anna R. (Mother of 2)

Foyer/Main Entrance
→ Infant/Non-mobile: (Birth - 6 months)
→ Infant crawl/roll: (5 months - 1 year)
→ Toddler/Pre-school: (1 year - 4 years)
→ School-age: (5 years - 6+ years)

Clean Yourself Immediately

Maintaining impeccable hygiene is paramount when caring for a child, especially newborns and infants. Their developing immune systems make them particularly susceptible to germs and infections. Showering or washing up thoroughly before handling your child is a crucial preventative measure.

Routine tasks like diaper changing and feeding require meticulous attention to hygiene. Washing your hands before and after these activities can significantly reduce the risk of contaminating the baby's area. Germs can easily irritate sensitive skin, making it essential to maintain a clean environment.

Creating a comfortable and positive bonding experience is vital for a child's development. Practicing proper hygiene fosters a sense of trust and security. **If you are feeling unwell, it's advisable to avoid handling the child to prevent the transmission of illness.**

To ensure a safe environment for your baby, encourage everyone to wash their hands before touching them. Regularly sanitizing commonly touched items, such as toys, pacifiers, and door handles, is also essential. By taking these precautions, you can safeguard your child's health and create a secure, hygienic space for their upbringing.

Foyer/Main Entrance
Infant/Non-mobile: (Birth - 6 months)
→ Infant crawl/roll: (5 months - 1 year)
→ Toddler/Pre-school: (1 year - 4 years)
→ School-age: (5 years - 6+ years)

Tables/Stands

Small tables, often used for keys or mail, can be dangerous for young children who might bump into them, leading to injuries. It's essential to identify and pad surfaces that are at the right height to harm a child, such as coffee tables for infants or kitchen tables for older toddlers. Various safety padding options are available, from corner guards to elasticized bumpers. Whichever you choose, ensure its securely attached to prevent choking hazards. By focusing on these details, you can create a safe, enjoyable environment for your child to explore. (For details refer to living room **pg. 24**

► *According to the CPSC, each year in the U.S., **around 2,400 young children (aged 0–6) are treated in emergency rooms for injuries caused by tables and stands tipping over**. These incidents make up nearly 40% of all furniture tip-over cases. Preschoolers. Especially ages 1–4, are most at risk, frequently suffering head injuries, fractures, and crushed limbs from what seems like harmless household furniture.*

Foyer/Main Entrance
Infant/Non-mobile: (Birth - 6 months)
Infant crawl/roll: (5 months - 1 year)
→ **Toddler/Pre-school: (1 year - 4 years)**
→ **School-age: (5 years - 6+ years)**

Loose Picture Frames

Picture frames, especially those loosely placed on tables, pose a hidden danger in homes with inquisitive toddlers. Young children have a high risk of these frames being knocked over, and their sharp corners can cause injuries. Additionally, the glass in these frames can shatter if dropped, intensifying the hazard. To ensure child safety, consider wall-mounting frames or using adhesive methods like Velcro strips or Fun-Tak to secure free-standing frames on surfaces. While displaying memories adds warmth to a home, prioritizing safety ensures a risk-free environment for children to explore. Let's work towards a house that's both aesthetically pleasing and safe for our young ones.
(For details refer to living room **pg. 38**)

Foyer/Main Entrance
Infant/Non-mobile: (Birth -6 months)
Infant crawl/roll: (5 months - 1 year)
→ **Toddler/Pre-school: (1 year - 4 years)**
→ **School-age: (5 years - 6+ years)**

Slippery Floors

Approximately **230,000 children** ages 0-4 are treated in US emergency departments each year for fall-related injuries. *According to the Centers for Disease Control and Prevention (CDC) and the National Electronic Injury Surveillance System (NEISS)

In our quest for childproofing and safety, it's essential to be mindful of our surroundings, even in areas we might not initially think of as potential hazards. Take a moment to check for any areas with sagging floors, as these can accumulate water over time, creating slip hazards, especially for little feet running around.

To further prevent slipping accidents, ensure you have a **doormat** in place, especially during wet weather or when your pet comes indoors with muddy paws. Standing water can quickly turn into a slipping hazard, and a doormat helps trap excess moisture and debris, keeping your floors safer for everyone.

While cleaning your home, be cautious when using furniture polish on your console or other wooden surfaces. Splatters of polish, especially when using lemon-scented products, can inadvertently make the floor as smooth and slick as the table, increasing the risk of accidental slips. So, take your time and clean mindfully, wiping away any excess polish that may have found its way to the floor.

Finally, **staying alert** is crucial to avoiding accidental falls. Children can be quite energetic and unpredictable, so being attentive to their movements and surroundings can go a long way toward preventing accidents.

Foyer/Main Entrance
Infant/Non-mobile: (Birth - 6 months)
Infant crawl/roll: (5 months - 1 year)
→ **Toddler/Pre-school: (1 year - 4 years)**
→ **School-age: (5 years - 6+ years)**

Secure Throw Rugs

Throw rugs and doormats, especially on hardwood or laminate floors, can be slip hazards, especially if they move or bunch up. While adults might navigate these with caution, children running around might not be as careful. To prevent accidents, it's vital to secure these mats with tape, especially near potentially dangerous areas like the top of stairs. Using the correct adhesive ensures mats stay put without damaging

the floor. By securing your rugs and mats, you prioritize safety, making your home safer for everyone. Childproofing is in the details, and a well-secured mat can make all the difference. (For details refer to living room **pg. 29**

Notes:

Foyer/Main Entrance
Infant/Non-mobile: (Birth - 6 months)
Infant crawl/roll: (5 months - 1 year)
→ **Toddler/Pre-school: (1 year - 4 years)**
→ **School-age: (5 years - 6+ years)**

Coat Access

Coat racks, although functional for hanging outerwear, can pose unexpected dangers that we shouldn't overlook. These racks are often designed to be top-heavy, making them prone to tipping over with even a slight force applied. The sharp hooks they feature can also become hazardous, particularly for small children who may accidentally run into them or pull on their coats.

The risks don't stop there. **Coat pockets might contain items that are not safe for children**, and it's challenging to inspect every pocket thoroughly. Lighters, tobacco products, or unlabeled medicines might be lurking, presenting potential dangers to curious hands.

Of course, we can't realistically plan to frisk our guests whenever they hang their coats. So, to eliminate any potential hazards and prioritize everyone's safety, it's best to **utilize the closet for coat storage instead**. Using a coat storage closet creates a controlled and secure space where any potentially harmful items are kept out of reach of curious little ones. Additionally, closets provide stability and **eliminate the risk of a top heavy coat rack tipping over.**

Testimonial: *"I used to think I had everything under control. I mean, I'd childproofed the house, right? But then, during a family get-together, my little explorer decided to go on an adventure. They climbed up on a chair and started digging through a guest's jacket. Turns out, there were some pills in the pocket. Luckily, they weren't dangerous, but it was a major wake-up call. From then on, we've been extra careful. We keep all jackets and coats locked up in a closet, out of reach. It's a small change, but it makes a big difference."*

- Sarah, (Mother of two)

Foyer/Main Entrance
Infant/Non-mobile: (Birth - 6 months)
Infant crawl/roll: (5 months - 1 year)
→ **Toddler/Pre-school: (1 year - 4 years)**
→ **School-age: (5 years - 6+ years)**

Tripping Hazards

Loose shoes and random stuff scattered at the doorway can be an unexpected tripping hazard, particularly when rushing into the house or carrying something bulky inside. A simple misstep can lead to an unfortunate accident. To ensure a safe and clutter-free entrance, it's best to designate a specific spot for shoes.

Consider keeping **discarded shoes in a closet or storage bin near the doorway.** This simple act enhances the overall tidiness of your home and reduces the risk of tripping over them.

If you have the space, **a bench with room underneath is an excellent solution**. This way, both kids and adults can comfortably sit down to put on or take off their shoes. Once done, the shoes can be neatly tucked away out of sight and out of the way, ensuring a clear pathway for everyone.

Maintaining a designated spot for shoes creates an organized and safe entryway that welcomes family and guests. Whether it's the mad dash to get ready for school or the arrival of friends for a gathering, your entrance will be free from potential hazards, and everyone can focus on the warm greetings and memorable moments ahead

---

► *According to a study published in the American Journal of Emergency Medicine,* ***approximately 12,300 patients were treated in U.S. emergency departments for rug-related injuries.***

Foyer/Main Entrance
Infant/Non-mobile: (Birth - 6 months)
→ **Infant crawl/roll: (5 months - 1 year)**
→ **Toddler/Pre-school: (1 year - 4 years)**
→ **School-age: (5 years - 6+ years)**

Sneaker Odor/Bacteria

When it comes to taking care of your sneakers, there are a few essential points to consider. One common issue is unpleasant odors, which are often caused by lingering bacteria in the soft, foamy insert. To combat this, you can try spraying the inside with a good disinfectant or sprinkling some baking soda to absorb the moisture and odor. For more thorough cleaning, gently washing them can work wonders in refreshing your favorite pair.

To ensure the **longevity of your sneakers** and maintain proper foot support, it's advisable to alternate the shoes you wear day after day. This practice helps prevent early arch breakdown and ensures that your sneakers stay in top-notch condition for a more extended period.

When purchasing new sneakers, it's vital to choose the right size. Shoes that are too big or too small can lead to discomfort, blisters, and potential foot issues, especially for growing kids. Children's feet grow rapidly, so it's essential to measure their feet regularly and get them properly fitted shoes to ensure both comfort and safety during their active playtime.

Notes: (i.e. Audit your footwear)

Foyer/Main Entrance
Infant/Non-mobile: (Birth - 6 months)
Infant crawl/roll: (5 months - 1 year)
→ **Toddler/Pre-school: (1 year - 4 years)**
→ **School-age: (5 years - 6+ years)**

Secure Doors

Childproofing doorknobs in your home is crucial to prevent children from accessing dangerous areas or getting locked in rooms. Different doorknobs require specific safety measures. For lever handles, install locks that require dual-action to open, use a Door Monkey, or create DIY solutions with rubber bands to restrict movement. For round doorknobs, use knob covers or Grip 'n Twist covers that are difficult for toddlers to operate. For oval or egg-shaped knobs, use custom covers or childproofing straps to prevent easy access. Additionally, pinch guards and door alarms should be installed, and children should be educated about the dangers of unsupervised access to certain rooms. These strategies will help create a safe and secure environment for children in your home. (For details refer to hallway/stairway **pg. 173**)

Foyer/Main Entrance
Infant/Non-mobile: (Birth - 6 months)
Infant crawl/roll: (5 months - 1 year)
→ **Toddler/Pre-school: (1 year - 4 years)**
→ **School-age: (5 years - 6+ years)**

Screen Doors

Screen doors are a wonderful addition to many homes, allowing fresh air to circulate while keeping pests out. However, they can pose certain risks for households with young children.

Sturdy Screen Material: Upgrade to a more durable screen material that can withstand pushes and pulls from curious little hands. Consider materials like pet-resistant screens, which are tear and puncture-resistant.

Door Closers: Install a pneumatic or hydraulic door closer. This ensures the door closes slowly, reducing the risk of it slamming on a child's fingers. Adjust the tension so the door doesn't close too quickly.

Safety Latches: Install a high latch or bolt out of the reach of children to prevent them from opening the door and wandering outside unsupervised. Consider adding a secondary latch as an added precaution.

Clear Visual Indicators: Sometimes, children, especially toddlers, may not recognize the screen and might walk or run into it. Place decals or stickers at their eye level to give them a clear visual indication that the screen door is closed.

Reinforce Bottom Section: Consider adding a kick plate or a more solid material to the bottom section of the screen door. This prevents children from pushing through or tearing the screen at its most vulnerable point.

Door Alarms: Install a door alarm that sounds when the door is opened.

Finger Pinch Guards: These are foam or rubber devices that attach to the edge of the door, preventing it from closing all the way and pinching little fingers.

Regular Maintenance: Regularly inspect the screen for any tears or weak points. A small tear can quickly become a larger hole that a child could push through. Ensure all latches, bolts, and alarms are in working order.

Education and Supervise: As with all childproofing measures, the best prevention is supervision. Always keep an eye on your child when they're near the screen door. Teach older children the importance of being gentle with the screen door and its potential risks.

<u>**Foyer/Main Entrance**</u>
Infant/Non-mobile: (Birth - 6 months)
Infant crawl/roll: (5 months - 1 year)
→ **Toddler/Pre-school: (1 year - 4 years)**
→ **School-age: (5 years - 6+ years)**

Foyer Closet

The foyer closet is often overlooked when it comes to childproofing, but it can be a treasure trove of hazards for curious little ones, from heavy coats and bags that can topple over to small objects like keys or tools that can be choking hazards. It's essential to make this space as safe as possible.

Install a Childproof Door Lock: Opt for a high-quality childproof lock that is out of reach of your child. This prevents them from opening the closet without adult supervision. (Refer to Hallway/Stairs pg. 164)

High Shelves for Small Objects: Place small objects like keys, batteries, or small tools on the highest shelf. Labeled bins with secure lids should be used for these small items to ensure they are out of reach and out of sight.

Hooks for Bags and Purses: Install hooks high up for bags and purses that may contain hazardous items like medications or sharp objects. Make sure the hooks are securely anchored to the wall to prevent them from being pulled down.

Store Heavy Items Low and Back: Place heavy items like boots or bags at the bottom of the closet and as far back as possible. This lowers the center of gravity, making it less likely for items to topple over if the closet is opened.

Relocate Hazardous Materials: If you store any cleaning supplies or chemicals in the foyer closet, relocate them to a higher, locked cabinet. Always keep these items in their original containers to prevent confusion and possible poisoning.

Store Sharp Objects Safely: If you have items like umbrellas with pointed tips or other sharp objects, make sure they are stored so that the sharp end is not accessible. Use protective covers for umbrella tips and hooks that hold them horizontally, out of reach.

Rotate Seasonal Items: Keep only current seasonal items in the foyer closet to minimize clutter and potential hazards store off-season items like heavy winter coats or summer beach gear in a separate, less accessible closet.

Regularly Update and Inspect: As your child grows and becomes more adventurous, periodically update and inspect the closet to ensure it remains safe. Make it a habit to check the closet's childproofing measures at the beginning of each season when you're rotating out seasonal items.

Foyer/Main Entrance
→ **Infant/Non-mobile: (Birth - 6 months)**
→ **Infant crawl/roll: (5 months - 1 year)**
→ **Toddler/Pre-school: (1 year - 4 years)**
→ **School-age: (5 years - 6+ years)**

SMOKE DETECTORS

These devices should be installed on every floor, especially near sleeping areas, to provide timely alerts during fires. Regularly test the batteries, replace them bi-annually, and immediately attend to any chirping sounds as they indicate low battery power. Keeping the detectors dust-free ensures their optimal functionality. If your detectors are wired, a periodic flashing light suggests they're working. Detectors with visual and tactile alerts are advisable for households with hearing-impaired members. Remember, a well-maintained smoke detector not only safeguards your home but also provides peace of mind, ensuring a safe environment for your family. (For detail refer to kitchen **pg. 142**)

Foyer/Main Entrance
→ **Infant/Non-mobile: (Birth - 6 months)**
→ **Infant crawl/roll: (5 months - 1 year)**
→ **Toddler/Pre-school: (1 year - 4 years)**
→ **School-age: (5 years - 6+ years)**

CARBON MONOXIDE DETECTORS

According to the Centers for Disease Control and Prevention (CDC), **over 20,000 Children are hospitalized from exposure every year.** Carbon monoxide (CO) is a colorless, odorless gas that poses a silent yet deadly threat from the incomplete combustion of household appliances. To combat this, it's essential to install CO detectors near bedrooms and living spaces, regularly test them, and ensure fuel-burning appliances are well-maintained and ventilated. The flame color in appliances can signal their condition, with an orange flame indicating potential issues. It's also crucial to inspect flues for blockages, which can lead to CO buildup, and ensure grills, especially horizontal ones, are childproofed and placed away from flammable materials. Proper ventilation throughout the home is vital, and appliances should be regularly checked for safety. Landlords are responsible for providing working detectors and maintaining electrical and gas systems. If you use attic fans, ensure proper roof ventilation to prevent CO infiltration. Never leave cars running in garages to avoid CO risks. Adhering to these guidelines, it ensures a safe environment, turning your home into a secure haven for your family. (For details refer to kitchen **pg. 143**)

Foyer/Main Entrance
→ **Infant/Non-mobile:** (Birth - 6 months)
→ **Infant crawl/roll:** (5 months - 1 year)
→ **Toddler/Pre-school:** (1 year - 4 years)
→ **School-age:** (5 years - 6+ years)

Key Concerns

Keys serve a multitude of purposes, from unlocking doors and cabinets to accessing cars and gun safes. However, as versatile as they are, keys can pose significant risks to children if not handled cautiously. Keeping keys out of reach is essential to prevent children from accessing potentially dangerous items that could lead to accidents or injuries. Imagine a child with access to keys; they could unknowingly get into situations with severe consequences, such as ingesting harmful substances, accessing firearms, or attempting to drive a car. To prevent any unwanted mishaps, **it's crucial to store your keys on wall hooks or in a secure location that is inaccessible to children**.

Another important consideration is the **presence of lead** in both house and car keys, which is often mixed in with the brass. Lead poisoning is a serious health concern, particularly for young children. Exposure to lead can lead to mental impairment, behavioral issues, hyperactivity, seizures, comas, and even death. To protect your children from lead exposure, it's essential to keep keys away from them. Babies and young children can absorb lead through their skin or accidentally ingest it by putting keys in their mouths. Always wash your hands thoroughly with soap and water to minimize potential risks if you need to handle keys.

Foyer/Main Entrance
Infant/Non-mobile: (Birth - 6 months)
Infant crawl/roll: (5 months - 1 year)
Toddler/Pre-school: (1 year - 4 years)
→ **School-age: (5 years - 6+ years)**

Backpack Weight

Attention to backpack weight and carrying method is essential to ensuring that children maintain good posture and avoid potential musculoskeletal issues. The American College of Sports Medicine highlights the impact of heavy backpacks on a child's posture, making it crucial to take appropriate preventive measures.

To prevent **posture problems**, the weight of a child's backpack should not exceed 10 percent of their body weight. You can calculate this by multiplying your child's weight in pounds by 0.10, which will give you the maximum recommended backpack weight in pounds.

Consider using a **rolling backpack** as an effective solution to eliminate the weight burden. Rolling backpacks allow children to pull their belongings instead of carrying them on their backs, reducing strain on muscles and joints.

Encourage your child to **vary how they carry their backpack** each day to avoid placing excessive strain on the same muscles and joints. For example, they can carry it over their left shoulder one day, the right shoulder the next, and entirely on their back the third day. This rotation can help distribute the load more evenly, reducing the risk of overuse injuries.

When taking the backpack off, **teach your child to shrug both straps** off simultaneously to avoid unnecessarily torquing the spine. This method minimizes strain and ensures a safe and comfortable removal of the backpack.

Foyer/Main Entrance
Infant/Non-mobile: (Birth - 6 months)
Infant crawl/roll: (5 months - 1 year)
→ **Toddler/Pre-school: (1 year - 4 years)**
→ **School-age: (5 years - 6+ years)**

Umbrellas: An Often-Overlooked Safety Measure

Annually, approximately 1,000 children are injured by umbrellas and canes, including pokes and entanglements. (Source: U.S. Consumer Product Safety Commission (CPSC) - Umbrella Safety) Umbrellas, often considered mundane household items, can pose a significant safety risk to young children. Their pointed ends and intricate mechanisms can cause accidental injuries. To create a safe home environment, it is essential to have childproof umbrellas.

One effective way to minimize the risk is to store umbrellas in a secure, out-of-reach location. High shelves, locked closets, or designated umbrella holders are ideal options. This prevents children from accessing umbrellas unsupervised and potentially injuring themselves. Additionally, choosing umbrellas with rounded tips and child-friendly designs can further reduce the likelihood of accidents. **These features mitigate the risk of punctures or other injuries caused by sharp edges.**

Educating children about the proper handling and use of umbrellas is also crucial. Teach them to use only umbrellas when necessary and be mindful of their surroundings. Emphasize the importance of holding umbrellas with both hands and avoiding running or playing with them. By instilling these safety guidelines, parents can empower their children to use umbrellas responsibly and minimize the risk of accidents.

|Ch 2| Living Room/Family Room

Introduction: The living room, often the heart of a home, is a hub of family activity. While it's a space for relaxation and bonding, it also presents numerous hazards for young explorers. This chapter delves into the essential steps to transform your living room into a safe haven for children. We cover everything from securing heavy furniture and electronics to ensuring cords and small decorative items are out of reach. We'll also discuss the importance of non-slip rugs, fireplace safety, and the safe storage of potential hazards. By the end of this chapter, you'll be equipped with practical knowledge to make your living room both cozy and child-friendly, ensuring peace of mind as your little ones play and grow.

Testimonial: *One day, little Jack was having a blast in the living room, his giggles echoing through the house. But in a blink, those giggles turned into tears. He'd tripped on a loose rug and bonked his head on the sharp corner of our coffee table. My heart dropped as I ran to him, seeing a nasty bump forming on his forehead. In that moment, I realized our "safe" living room wasn't so safe after all.*

Looking back, I can't believe we didn't do anything more to protect him. If we'd just secured the rug and put corner guards on the furniture, Jack wouldn't have gotten hurt. We've since fixed everything, from securing rugs to anchoring furniture and using those protective corner things. We even made a special play area just for him. Now, I watch him play without a worry in the world, and I wish we'd done all this sooner.

Childproofing isn't just a good idea, it's a must. It's about making our homes safe and loving places for our kids to grow.

- Sara T. (Mother of 4)

Living Room/Family Room
→ **Infant/Non-mobile: (Birth - 6 months)**
→ **Infant crawl/roll: (5 months - 1 year)**
→ **Toddler/Pre-school: (1 year - 4 years)**
→ **School-age: (5 years - 6+ years)**

Fireplace

Over 1,000 children are injured each year from accidents involving fireplaces, candles, and other open flames in the (U.S. Source: National Fire Protection Association (NFPA) - Fire Statistics.)

Establishing Protective Barriers

Safety Fences: Installing a baby safety fence around the fireplace effectively keeps curious toddlers at bay. Ensure it is sturdy and tall enough to deter climbing attempts.

Glass Doors: Opt for heat-resistant glass doors that can function as a barrier to open flames. Ensure they're securely anchored and positioned at a safe distance to prevent any stray sparks from reaching them. Chimney Maintenance and Safety

Annual Sweeping: Creosote, a byproduct of burning wood, accumulates in chimneys and can ignite, causing dangerous chimney fires. An annual sweep by a professional ensures this build-up is removed.

Vent Checks: Regularly inspect vents for blockages or damage. A well-ventilated chimney effectively draws out smoke and gases, reducing indoor pollution.

Carbon Monoxide Monitoring

Strategic Placement: Install carbon monoxide detectors in proximity to the fireplace and key areas throughout your home. This gas is undetectable by human senses, making these alarms vital.

Regular Testing: To ensure detectors are always operational, test them monthly and replace batteries as recommended by the manufacturer.

Safety Measures for Hearth and Surroundings

Padding: The hearth, especially if made of stone or brick, can be a hazard for falls. Use specialized hearth padding or soft cushions to mitigate injury risks.

Tool Storage: Fireplace tools, while essential for maintaining a fire, can be hazardous in a child's hands. Store them securely, preferably in a locked cabinet or hung high out of reach.

Fire Safety Education

Awareness Sessions: Talk to your children regularly about the dangers associated with fire. Use appropriate age language and visuals to make the lessons impactful.

Safe Practices: Emphasize the importance of not playing with or near the fireplace. This includes keeping toys, books, and other personal items away from the hearth.

Glass Door Considerations

Temperature Monitoring: The glass can get extremely hot even with safety barriers. Consider installing a temperature indicator or using an infrared thermometer to monitor the heat.

Safety Labels: Place warning labels or stickers to remind children and adults that the glass can be hot and to deter them from touching it.

Living Room/Family Room
Infant/Non-mobile: (Birth - 6 months)
→ **Infant crawl/roll: (5 months - 1 year)**
→ **Toddler/Pre-school: (1 year - 4 years)**
→ **School-age: (5 years - 6+ years)**

FLOOR LAMPS

Though practical and stylish, floor lamps can present safety hazards, particularly the torchiere style that directs light upwards. These lamps have earned their torch-like name due to their potential to cause fires when knocked over. The combination of an unstable base and the presence of electricity makes them a significant risk in any home.

A common cause of accidents with torchiere floor lamps is their **top-heavy design**. A slight bump or collision with furniture, pets, or even energetic children can cause the lamp to tip over. Once on the ground, the hot bulb or other electrical components can encounter flammable materials, leading to a potentially devastating fire.

To protect your home and loved ones, it is essential to take precautions when using floor lamps. Choose lamps with a stable and sturdy base, ideally with a broad **footprint to prevent tipping**. Additionally, position floor lamps away from high-traffic areas where they are more likely to be bumped or knocked over.

When selecting a torchiere floor lamp, consider models with protective barriers around the bulb area, which can help prevent direct contact with flammable materials in case of a fall. Ensure that the **lampshade is securely attached** to the lamp to minimize the risk of it becoming a potential fire hazard.

Regularly inspect and maintain your floor lamps to ensure that all electrical components are in good working condition. If you notice any loose parts or signs of wear, refrain from using the lamp until it is repaired or replaced.

Living Room/Family Room
Infant/Non-mobile: (Birth - 6 months)
→ **Infant crawl/roll: (5 months - 1 year)**
→ **Toddler/Pre-school: (1 year - 4 years)**
→ **School-age: (5 years - 6+ years)**

Standing Fans

Annually, approximately **2,500 children** are injured by electric fans, including cuts from blades and electrical hazards. (Source: National Electronic Injury Surveillance System (NEISS) – CDC) Standing fans, while essential for comfort, especially during warmer months, can pose potential hazards to young children. Their curiosity and natural inclination to explore can lead them to these fans, making it crucial for parents and guardians to ensure their safety.

Placement and Positioning

Elevated Surfaces: Position the fan on a tall piece of furniture or a dedicated fan stand that is out of the reach of children.

Room Selection: If feasible, operate the fan in rooms where children are less likely to be unsupervised, such as a home office, master bedroom, or an adult-only lounge.

Distance from Play Areas: Ensure that the fan is placed far from children's play zones or areas where they frequently move about. Safety Enhancements and Accessories

Robust Fan Guards: Invest in high-quality fan guards with smaller gaps, which ensure tiny fingers can't slip through.

Stable Base: Ensure the fan's base is sturdy to prevent it from being easily tipped over. Some fans come with broader bases or weighted bottoms for added stability.

Cord Management: Use cord organizers or covers to keep the fan's electrical cord out of sight and reach, preventing tripping or tugging hazards.

Maintenance and Regular Checks

Blade Inspection: Inspect the fan blades for any signs of wear, damage, or loosening. A malfunctioning blade can be a hazard.

Cleaning Routine: Dust and debris can affect the fan's efficiency and pose a fire risk if the motor overheats. Regularly clean the blades, front and back grills, and motor area and ensure it is free from dust.

Electrical Safety: Check the fan's plug and cord for fraying or damage. Consider repairing or replacing the fan if any part of the electrical system seems compromised.

Education and Supervision

Safety Discussions: Engage in age-appropriate discussions with children about the dangers of fans. Use simple terms to explain why they shouldn't touch or play near them.

Active Monitoring: Even with precautions in place, there's no substitute for active supervision. Always be present and attentive when a standing fan is in operation, and children are nearby.

Safety Drills: Conduct occasional safety drills, teaching children what to do if they ever find themselves too close to a fan or if they notice something amiss.

Living Room/Family Room
Infant/Non-mobile: (Birth - 6 months)
→ **Infant crawl/roll: (5 months - 1 year)**
→ **Toddler/Pre-school: (1 year - 4 years)**
→ **School-age: (5 years - 6+ years)**

Tables and Stands

When childproofing a home, tables pose a significant risk—especially if they are at or near a child's head height. **Any table shorter than 36 inches should be considered a potential hazard** for head injuries, so it's important to take preventive steps to make them safer. One of the most effective ways to reduce injury risk is by using safety padding. There are a variety of childproofing products available, including corner guards, long padded strips, and elasticized bumpers. These help soften sharp edges and corners that a child could bump into. When using padding, always make sure it is securely attached according to the manufacturer's instructions so that it doesn't come loose during everyday activity or play.

In addition to padding, consider securing the table to the wall. While it might seem unnecessary for smaller tables, anchoring furniture can prevent tipping if a child tries to pull up on or climb the table—a surprisingly common behavior in curious toddlers. Another **important step is to remove any small items from the table that could present a choking hazard**. Items like figurines, coins, beads, and other knick-knacks should be placed well out of reach or removed entirely from the space.

Keeping the tabletop clear of clutter also goes a long way in preventing accidents. A clutter-free surface reduces the chance of trips and falls, and it helps children understand that tables are not play areas. While physical safeguards are essential, it's also crucial to teach your child about safety. Have age-appropriate conversations about why they shouldn't climb on tables or touch certain items that might be within reach. Early education helps reinforce good habits and boundaries.

Before purchasing corner guards, take a moment to measure the table's corners so you know what size and shape will fit best. Look for corner guards made from soft, non-toxic materials to ensure safety, especially if your child is in a teething stage and likely to chew on things. If you prefer, long padded strips or elastic bumpers can also be effective for smaller tables, just make sure they fit well and are firmly in place.

After installing any padding or bumpers, inspect them regularly. Check that nothing has come loose and that the materials aren't damaged or peeling. If anything looks worn or insecure, replace it right away to maintain a safe environment. Lastly, stay aware of your child's developmental stages. As they become more mobile, more curious, and more capable of climbing, you may need to adjust your childproofing strategy to meet their evolving abilities.

Living Room/Family Room
Infant/Non-mobile: (Birth - 6 months)
Infant crawl/roll: (5 months - 1 year)
→ **Toddler/Pre-school: (1 year - 4 years)**
→ **School-age: (5 years - 6+ years)**

Record Player and Records

Spin control: Keep your record player in a spot that is out of reach. If it's on a low shelf, it can be too tempting. A record player may seem like a spinning ride to a toddler, and vinyl records could become flying frisbees.

Dust cover closed: Use a dust cover or invest in one if yours is missing. A curious child's fingers won't be able to poke, push, or turn the needle into a record-scratching disaster.

Records stored high: Vinyl records should be stored vertically on a high shelf, in a locked cabinet, or at least out of easy reach. If they get to them, your records may soon resemble abstract art.

<u>**Living Room/Family Room**</u>
Infant/Non-mobile: (Birth - 6 months)
Infant crawl/roll: (5 months - 1 year)
→ **Toddler/Pre-school: (1 year - 4 years)**
→ **School-age: (5 years - 6+ years)**

Table edges

More than 500,000 children are treated for injuries caused by sharp edges and corners of furniture and household items annually in the U.S. (Source: Centers for Disease Control and Prevention (CDC) – WISQARS)

Consider the height of the tables: Tables that are at a child's head height pose a significant risk for head injuries. If the table is less than 36 inches tall, you should take steps to childproof it. A child can easily bump their head on the table while climbing on it or playing nearby.

Use safety padding: There are a variety of safety padding options available, such as corner guards, long padded strips, and elasticized bumpers. Corner guards are a good option for protecting a table's sharp corners. Long padded strips can be used to protect the edges of a table. Elasticized bumpers are a good option for tables with curved edges.

Secure the table to the wall: This will prevent the table from tipping over if a child climbs on it. You can use a table anchor or a safety strap to secure the table to the wall.

Remove any objects that could be a choking hazard, including small items such as figurines, coins, and beads. Children can choke on these small objects if they put them in their mouths.

Keeping the table clear of clutter will make it less likely for a child to trip and fall. Clutter can also make it difficult for a child to see the table, which could lead to them bumping into it.

Teach your child about the dangers of tables: Explain to your child that they should not climb on tables or play with the objects on them. This will help them understand the risks involved and make them less likely to do it.

Inspect the padding regularly. Make sure it is still firmly in place and not damaged. If it is damaged or loose, it could become a choking hazard.

Replace the padding if it is damaged or loose.

Be aware of your child's development: As your child gets older and more mobile, you may need to take additional steps to childproof your home. For example, you may need to move the table to a higher location or remove the padding if your child is old enough to understand the dangers.

<u>Living Room/Family Room</u>
→ **Infant/Non-mobile: (Birth - 6 months)**
→ **Infant crawl/roll: (5 months - 1 year)**
→ **Toddler/Pre-school: (1 year - 4 years)**
School-age: (5 years - 6+ years)

Candles

No candlelit chaos: Put candles on high shelves where they can't be reached. To a child, a candle looks like a delicious ice cream cone or an irresistible item to grab. Don't let that happen!

Flameless is fabulous: Seriously, flameless candles exist and are unique. They have the same glow, but there is no fire, no wax drips, and no toddlers mimicking their first bonfire dance.

Hot wax, no thanks: If you must have real candles, always supervise, and never leave them lit around children. Also, consider using a hurricane glass cover that protects the flame (and the child) from easy access.

Living Room/Family Room
Infant/Non-mobile: (Birth - 6 months)
Infant crawl/roll: (5 months - 1 year)
→ **Toddler/Pre-school: (1 year - 4 years)**
→ **School-age: (5 years - 6+ years)**

Fish Tanks

While a fish tank may seem like a relatively safe addition to your home, certain precautions must be taken to ensure the well-being of both your child and your aquatic pets.

Secure Placement: Choose a sturdy and stable surface for the fish tank, such as a stand or table designed for aquariums. Ensure that the tank is placed away from high-traffic areas and areas where children frequently play.

Lid or Cover: Use a secure lid or cover to prevent curious hands from reaching inside the fish tank. Choose a lid specifically designed for your tank size and style.

Aquarium Stand: If you are using an aquarium stand, ensure it is securely assembled and designed to support the tank's weight. Some stands come with built-in cabinets that can provide additional storage and protection.

Anchor Tank and Stand: Use heavy-duty furniture safety straps (metal cords) or wall anchors designed to secure large objects. These can be found in hardware stores and are specifically made to prevent tipping. Use a stud finder to locate the wall studs. Anchoring into a stud ensures the tank is securely fastened to a solid part of the wall. Install the straps or brackets on the back of the fish tank stand and the wall. Follow the manufacturer's instructions for proper installation. Once installed, gently test to ensure the tank does not move or tip. The straps should hold the tank firmly in place.

Electrical Cord Management: Keep the cords for filters, heaters, and lighting organized and out of reach. Use cord organizers to secure cords along the back of the tank or the stand.

Childproof Outlet Covers: If there are electrical outlets near the fish tank, install childproof outlet covers to prevent children from tampering with the cords or attempting to plug/unplug devices.

Heavy Objects and Decorations: Choose decorations and ornaments that are securely placed and cannot be easily dislodged by a child. Avoid using sharp or small objects that could potentially be a choking hazard.

Safe Tank Accessories: Ensure that any tank accessories, such as air pumps or bubbling decorations, are correctly installed and secured to prevent them from being pulled into the tank.

Water Quality Maintenance: Regularly monitor and maintain the tank's water quality to ensure the health of your fish. Avoid using chemicals or treatments that could be harmful if accidentally ingested by a child.

Child-Friendly Fish: Select fish species known to be compatible with families and not aggressive. Research and choose fish that are less likely to cause harm or stress to each other or children.

Educational Supervision: Teach your child about the fish tank and the importance of not touching or putting hands inside. Explain that fish are delicate and need a calm environment.

Proper Aquarium Cleaning: When cleaning the tank, use child-safe cleaning products and ensure that no cleaning residue is left behind. Rinse thoroughly before reintroducing fish.

Cover Power Strips: If you have a power strip near the tank, consider using a cover or organizer to prevent children from accidentally tampering with it.

Emergency Preparedness: Keep an emergency kit that includes water treatments, fishnets, and other supplies for quick response to tank issues.

Regular Monitoring: Continuously observe your child's interactions with the fish tank and correct any unsafe behavior promptly.

Living Room/Family Room
Infant/Non-mobile: (Birth - 6 months)
→ **Infant crawl/roll: (5 months - 1 year)**
→ **Toddler/Pre-school: (1 year - 4 years)**
→ **School-age: (5 years - 6+ years)**

Unfinished Furniture

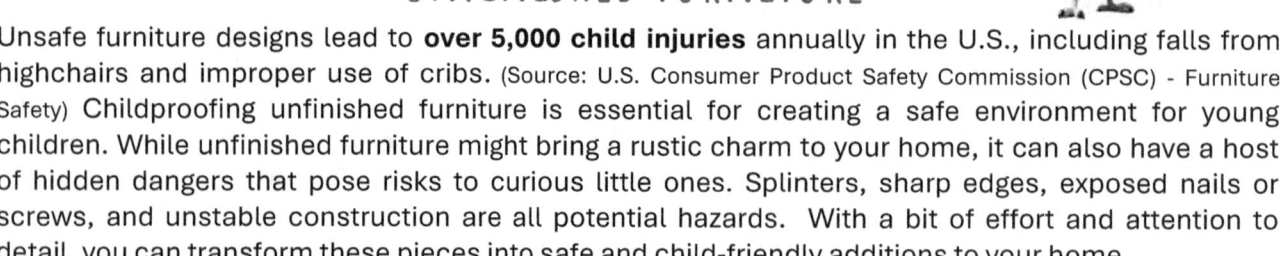

Unsafe furniture designs lead to **over 5,000 child injuries** annually in the U.S., including falls from highchairs and improper use of cribs. (Source: U.S. Consumer Product Safety Commission (CPSC) - Furniture Safety) Childproofing unfinished furniture is essential for creating a safe environment for young children. While unfinished furniture might bring a rustic charm to your home, it can also have a host of hidden dangers that pose risks to curious little ones. Splinters, sharp edges, exposed nails or screws, and unstable construction are all potential hazards. With a bit of effort and attention to detail, you can transform these pieces into safe and child-friendly additions to your home.

Let's start with one of the most important steps: **Sanding**. Unfinished furniture often has rough surfaces that can cause splinters, and those tiny, hidden splinters are a big concern for young children who like to touch and feel everything. Carefully and thoroughly sand every surface of the furniture, paying particular attention to the edges and corners. Make sure to smooth out any areas that are rough or sharp. Use fine-grit sandpaper for a polished finish to ensure that no wood fibers are left sticking up that could lead to splinters.

Choose water-based, non-toxic sealants, varnishes, or paints that are specifically designed for use around children. The sealant will create a protective layer over the wood, reducing the chances of splinters. Next up is **sealing the wood**. Once you've sanded the furniture smoothly, the next step is to apply a child-safe wood sealant or non-toxic paint. This is not only to enhance the look of the furniture but al and ensuring that the surface is safe to touch.

This step also helps to prevent moisture from warping the wood over time, which could create new hazards. Another critical element of childproofing unfinished furniture is addressing **loose parts and sharp edges**. If the furniture has any exposed nails, screws, or bolts, make sure they are securely fastened. You don't want a loose screw to come loose in your child's hands--or worse, in their mouth. Additionally, padding or corner protectors will soften any sharp edges or corners. These simple accessories can be found in most baby-proofing kits and are an easy way to prevent painful bumps and bruises.

Stability is another important factor to consider. Unfinished furniture may not be as sturdy as finished, mass-produced pieces, especially if it is handmade or an older item. Wobbly or easily tipped furniture is a significant hazard, especially for toddlers who love to pull themselves up or climb. Secure the furniture to the wall using anchors or anti-tip straps to prevent tipping. This step is crucial for taller pieces like bookshelves, dressers, or cabinets, which can be more prone to toppling over if climbed on. By anchoring the furniture securely, you drastically reduce the risk of it falling over if your child decides to use it as a makeshift jungle gym.

Finally, **inspect regularly.** Even after you've taken all these precautions, it's a good idea to check the furniture for any wear and tear regularly. Look for any new rough spots, loose screws, or other potential hazards that might develop over time. Keeping an eye on the condition of the furniture ensures that it remains safe for your child as they grow.

By sanding, sealing, securing, and regularly inspecting your unfinished furniture, you're taking important steps to eliminate potential risks. These childproofing measures protect your child from injuries and allow them to explore their home safely, giving you peace of mind as they roam and play.

▶ *According to the U.S. Consumer Product Safety Commission (CPSC),* **unfinished wooden furniture** *may look natural and charming, but it hides surprising dangers for toddlers. Rough edges can splinter into skin, causing infection or joint inflammation, and over a quarter of fractures in under-2s come from falls off low tables and stands.* **U.S. data shows 250,000 kids sustain furniture-related injuries each year**. *Many of them cuts and head bumps. Revealing that an unpolished piece can quickly turn into a hidden hazard.* (Source: PubMed)

Living Room/Family Room
Infant/Non-mobile: (Birth - 6 months)
Infant crawl/roll: (5 months - 1 year)
→ **Toddler/Pre-school: (1 year - 4 years)**
→ **School-age: (5 years - 6+ years)**

Secure Throw Rugs

Annually, **over 20,000 children** slip and fall due to loose rugs and mats, leading to fractures, sprains, and head injuries. (Source: Centers for Disease Control and Prevention (CDC) – WISQARS)

Ensuring a slip-free environment in homes, especially with hardwood or laminate flooring, requires special attention to throw rugs and doormats. These seemingly harmless additions can quickly become hazards if not properly secured.

Potential Risks

Shifting and Bunching: Mats can move, especially under energetic little feet, leading to potential trips and falls.

Wet Entrances: Mats can become incredibly slippery when wet, posing a risk for both adults and children.

Safety Measures

Secure Taping: Use strong, double-sided tape to keep mats firmly in place. Ensure full coverage, especially on the edges, to prevent corners from flipping up.

High-Traffic Areas: Prioritize areas like entrances, hallways, and bathrooms where foot traffic is frequent.

Special Attention Near Elevated Surfaces: The risk is greater if your main door is near cellar stairs or other elevated areas. A misstep could have severe consequences. Always ensure mats near such areas are doubly secure.

Adhesive Recommendations

Follow Manufacturer's Guidelines: Always use recommended adhesives for optimal results.

Residue-Free Adhesives: Choose tapes that won't leave a sticky residue, ensuring your floors remain pristine.

Living Room/Family Room
Infant/Non-mobile: (Birth - 6 months)
Infant crawl/roll: (5 months - 1 year)
→ **Toddler/Pre-school: (1 year - 4 years)**
→ **School-age: (5 years - 6+ years)**

Antique Furniture

Antique furniture certainly holds a special allure, but it's essential to approach these cherished pieces with caution when it comes to child safety.

Antique furniture often wasn't designed with child safety in consideration, and some of its features can present potential hazards for young children.

Cribs from past eras, with head-entrapping spaces, trunks that can inadvertently slam down on fingers, and old sewing machines that start with a simple press of the pedals, all require careful consideration in a home with children.

Furniture Placement: If you have valuable antique furniture, consider placing it in a safer room or storing it until your children are older and can supervise it responsibly. Alternatively, ensure that these pieces are kept in areas that are not accessible to children to prevent accidents.

Non-Intrusive Measures: If you wish to preserve the authenticity of your antique furniture without altering it, take extra precautions to ensure it is not within reach of children. Use baby safety gates or create designated child-free zones in your home.

Lead-Based Paint Concerns: Be cautious of antique furniture that might have been painted with lead-based paint, which can pose health risks. Refrain from attempting to strip such paint yourself, as this can release harmful particles. Instead, consider painting it with non-toxic paint and sealing it to prevent any potential lead exposure.

Expert Consultation: If you're unsure about the safety of your antique furniture, it's wise to seek advice from an antique dealer or appraiser who can offer specialized guidance on preservation and safety measures.

You can enjoy the beauty and history of your antique furniture while ensuring your family's safety. Let's work together to create a harmonious home where your cherished antiques and child safety coexist, allowing you to enjoy both your beloved furniture and the well-being of your children.

Living Room/Family Room
Infant/Non-mobile: (Birth - 6 months)
→ **Infant crawl/roll: (5 months - 1 year)**
→ **Toddler/Pre-school: (1 year - 4 years)**
→ **School-age: (5 years - 6+ years)**

Anchor Taller Furniture!

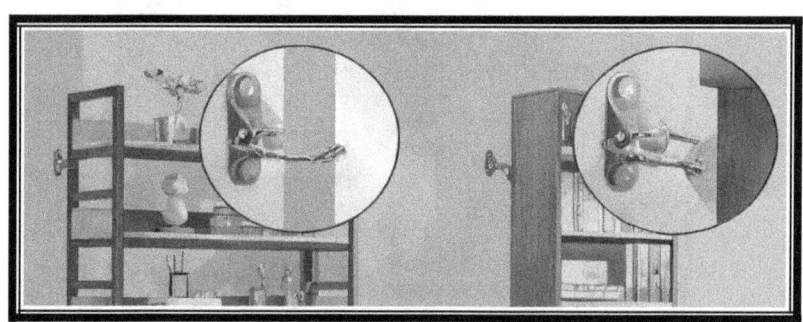

__Why Anchoring is Non-Negotiable__
Approximately **300 children die each year in the U.S. from furniture tip-overs**, such as bookshelves and dressers, emphasizing the need for anchoring heavy furniture to walls. (Source: American Academy of Pediatrics (SAP) - Safe Home Environment) Anchoring tall furniture is not just a recommendation; it's an absolute must when childproofing your home. Children are naturally curious and love to climb, pull, and explore every corner of the house. While wonderful to watch, this sense of adventure can quickly become dangerous if heavy furniture is not properly secured. The risk of furniture tipping over is frighteningly real, and the consequences can range from serious injuries to tragic fatalities.

__Statistical Urgency__
The numbers speak for themselves. According to the U.S. Consumer Product Safety Commission, **a child is sent to the emergency room every 30 minutes** due to a furniture or TV tip-over. This is not just a rare occurrence; it's an alarmingly common problem affecting families nationwide. What's even more sobering is that these incidents are preventable. Proper anchoring can drastically reduce the risk of your child being hurt by toppling furniture.

Types of Furniture That Require Anchoring

It's not just tall or oversized furniture that needs to be anchored. Any piece that a child might climb or pull on can pose a hazard if it's not secured.

Bookshelves: A bookshelf can look like the perfect climbing structure to a child. Bookshelves can easily tip over when a child tries to climb the lower shelves or pull on them to stand. Secure both the top and middle sections of the bookshelf to wall studs, ensuring that the entire unit is stable and can't be pulled forward.

Dressers and Chests of Drawers: The drawers of a dresser are particularly tempting for young climbers. They can shift the center of gravity when opened, making the dresser unstable. Use heavy-duty metal straps to anchor dressers to the wall. Ensure the straps can support not only the weight of the furniture but also the weight of whatever's inside the drawers.

Entertainment Centers/Media Console: These units are often top-heavy, especially when loaded with electronics like TVs and gaming systems. Entertainment centers should be anchored securely to prevent tipping, and you should also anchor the TV separately for added safety.

Anchoring Methods

Anchoring furniture is a straightforward process, but different methods are available depending on the type and size of the furniture. Each method has its considerations, and it's important to choose the right one for the specific piece of furniture you're anchoring.

Wall Straps are the most common and versatile option for anchoring furniture. Made of strong metal or heavy-duty fabric, wall straps can secure almost any piece of furniture. The key is to make sure they are anchored to wall studs, not just drywall, for maximum strength.

L-Brackets: L-brackets are a great option for heavier or bulkier furniture pieces. These brackets are attached both to the furniture and to the wall using long, sturdy screws. This method is ideal for large bookcases or entertainment centers that need extra stability.

Furniture Cables: (Recommended) Particularly useful for securing TVs, furniture cables are designed to keep heavy items from toppling over. The cable should be pulled tight and anchored into a wall stud. In addition to TV stands, they can also be used for lighter furniture pieces.

Floor Anchoring: Some pieces can be anchored to the floor for extra stability, particularly with narrow-based furniture. This is an excellent option for homes with uneven floors or exceptionally tall, wobbly furniture. Floor brackets are screwed into the floorboards to provide maximum stability.

Maintenance and Regular Checks

Anchoring furniture is not a set-it-and-forget-it task. Over time, the anchors can loosen due to natural wear and tear or the movement of the furniture.

Monthly Inspections: Make it a monthly habit to inspect all the furniture anchors. Check for loose screws or straps and tighten or replace them if necessary. This regular maintenance can help prevent accidents before they happen.

Post-Relocation Re-anchoring: If you decide to move a piece of anchored furniture to another room, you'll need to re-anchor it from scratch. Anchors are specific to the spot where they are installed, and moving furniture without securing it in its new location can leave it vulnerable to tipping.

Landlord and Renter Considerations
Anchoring furniture might seem tricky for renters, especially if their lease agreement discourages modifications to walls. However, safety should always be a priority.

> **Talk to Your Landlord:** Before drilling holes into the walls for anchors, have a conversation with your landlord. Explain that anchoring is a necessary childproofing measure to ensure your family's safety. Many landlords will understand and agree to these adjustments, especially when you emphasize the non-negotiable nature of childproofing.

> **Temporary Anchoring Solutions:** If permanent anchors aren't an option, there are temporary, less invasive solutions available, such as adhesive wall straps or furniture anchors that don't require screws. However, these are often less secure than traditional methods, so use them with caution and only for lighter pieces of furniture.

You are doing far more than just making your home childproof you're actively preventing life-threatening accidents. The peace of mind that comes from knowing your home is safe for your child is invaluable. In the grand scheme of childproofing, anchoring tall furniture is one of the most important steps you can take. It's a small task that yields huge safety benefits, ensuring your child's environment is safe and a place where they can explore and play without unnecessary risks.

In short, anchoring is non-negotiable. It's not just about safety; it's about protecting lives.

▶ *According to the American Academy of Pediatrics,* ***a child is rushed to the emergency department at least once every single hour of every single day with injuries from furniture or TV tip-overs. Specifically,*** *77% of all tip-over deaths from 2000 to 2019 involved kids under the age of six.*

Living Room/Family Room
Infant/Non-mobile: (Birth - 6 months)
Infant crawl/roll: (5 months - 1 year)
→ **Toddler/Pre-school: (1 year - 4 years)**
→ **School-age: (5 years - 6+ years)**

Playpens

Playpens are generally viewed as a safe space for babies and toddlers, providing you with peace of mind while your child is securely contained. However, it's crucial to prioritize safety when using a playpen.

The playpen's base should be firm and flat. Avoid adding extra mattresses or thick blankets, as these can pose suffocation risks. If using a sheet, ensure it fits snugly over the playpen's mattress or pad. Regularly inspect the playpen for any signs of wear and tear. Check the mesh sides for any holes or loose threads that could pose a risk of entanglement or strangulation.

Toys are essential for your child's playpen environment, but they must be chosen with care. Avoid toys with small parts that could be swallowed or pose a choking risk. Steer clear of toys with long cords or strings, which can pose strangulation risks. As your child grows and becomes more active, be cautious about leaving large toys in the playpen, as they can be used as steppingstones for adventurous toddlers trying to climb out.

While playpens are helpful for parents, they should never replace supervision. Always keep an eye on your child, even when they're in the playpen. It's essential to remember that while playpens can offer a safe play environment, they are not a substitute for the watchful eyes of a caregiver.

Living Room/Family Room
Infant/Non-mobile: (Birth - 6 months)
Infant crawl/roll: (5 months - 1 year)
→ **Toddler/Pre-school: (1 year - 4 years)**
→ **School-age: (5 years - 6+ years)**

Lead Paint

Lead paint poses a significant health risk, especially for homes built before 1978, when lead-based paint was prevalent. Understanding the dangers of lead exposure is crucial for protecting your family's health. Studies have shown that exposure to high levels of lead can have severe consequences on the nervous system and can lead to a range of health issues, particularly in children.

Children, especially those under the age of 6, are particularly **vulnerable to lead poisoning** because their bodies absorb lead more readily than adults. The effects of lead poisoning can be long-lasting and can include damage to the brain, seizures, delayed growth, learning disabilities, behavioral problems, and hearing loss.

In severe cases, lead poisoning can result in coma, convulsions, and, tragically, spontaneous death. Identifying lead exposure early is crucial to prevent or mitigate its harmful effects on your child's health.

One potential indicator of lead exposure is if a sibling or playmate has been diagnosed with **high blood lead levels**. In such cases, it's also essential to have your child tested for lead exposure, as they may have been exposed to the same environmental hazards.

If you suspect that your child may have been exposed to lead, seek medical advice immediately. A healthcare professional can conduct blood lead level testing to determine if there is any cause for concern and provide appropriate guidance and treatment.

By being proactive and informed, you can take steps to prevent lead exposure and create a safe and healthy environment for your family. Regularly inspect your home for lead-based paint, take necessary precautions, and stay aware of any potential risks. Together, we can work towards a safer, lead-free future for our children.

► *Approximately 500,000 children aged 1–5 in the U.S. have elevated blood lead levels (≥5 µg/dL), with many cases linked to lead-based paint and contaminated dust in older homes. (Childrenshospital.org)*

Living Room/Family Room
Infant/Non-mobile: (Birth - 6 months)
→ **Infant crawl/roll: (5 months - 1 year)**
→ **Toddler/Pre-school: (1 year - 4 years)**
→ **School-age: (5 years - 6+ years)**

Cannabis Vapes and Weed

Safe Storage of Cannabis Products

When it comes to childproofing your home, one area that often gets overlooked is the safe storage of cannabis products. Whether you use cannabis for medical or recreational purposes, it's critical to ensure that these items are stored securely and kept out of reach of children. The potential dangers of accidental exposure to cannabis, especially for young children, are genuine, ranging from mild disorientation to severe poisoning. Here's how to create a child-safe environment while responsibly managing cannabis products in your home.

Safe Storage: Keep Cannabis Products Secure

One of the most important rules is simple: **store all cannabis products in a locked, childproof container**. Whether it's cannabis flowers, edibles, oils, or vapers, the key is to ensure that children cannot access these items.

> **High and Locked:** Store the locked container in a high place, well out of reach of curious little hands. A high-up locked cabinet provides double protection, ensuring that even the most determined child can't get into something they shouldn't.
>
> **Discrete Storage:** Consider storing cannabis products in an area where they are not easily visible or accessible to children. This not only reduces temptation but also keeps these items out of sight and mind.

Child-Resistant Packaging: Seal Products Properly

Cannabis products, much like medications, should be stored in **child-resistant packaging**. Many cannabis products today are required by law to be sold in childproof containers, but the responsibility doesn't end there. After each use, ensure you properly seal the containers to ensure they remain childproof.

> **Double-Check Seals:** Always double-check that the packaging is securely sealed after each use. Even the best child-resistant packaging won't do its job if it's not closed properly.
>
> **Resealable Bags and Tins:** Some cannabis products come in resealable packaging. Be vigilant about making sure the zippers or lids are completely closed, as even a partially open package can invite an accident.

Clear Labeling: Avoid Confusion

One of the biggest risks with cannabis products, especially edibles, is that they can look like everyday food items such as candy, cookies, or gummies. To avoid dangerous mix-ups, make sure all cannabis products are **clearly labeled**.

Distinct Labels: Use bold, visible labels that identify the product as cannabis, so there's no room for confusion. This can prevent someone from accidentally consuming it, especially in a busy household.

Avoid Tempting Displays: Never leave vapes, edibles, or cannabis products where children can mistake them for everyday snacks. A colorful gummy might look like a fun treat to a child, but it's anything but safe in their hands.

Education: Teach Older Children and Teens

Education is key to preventing accidental exposure or misuse of cannabis products. As your children get older, talk to them about the dangers of cannabis use, especially when unsupervised. Explain to them why it's not safe for them to access or consume these products.

Age-Appropriate Conversations: Tailor the conversation to your child's age. For younger children, you might simply explain that cannabis is a product for adults and can make children sick. For teens, a more detailed conversation about the risks of cannabis use, especially in unsupervised situations, is essential.

Open Communication: Make sure your children feel comfortable asking questions and know why you keep certain products locked away. The more informed they are, the less likely they are to seek out these items out of curiosity.

Out of Sight: Keep Cannabis Use Private

If you use cannabis products, whether smoking, vaping, or consuming edibles, it's essential to do so away from children. **Never use cannabis in front of children**, as it can increase their curiosity about the product and may lead them to try and access it when you're not around.

Private Use: Use cannabis in a private space where your children won't see you. This not only keeps the behavior out of sight but also minimizes the risk of secondhand smoke exposure if you're smoking or vaping.

Model Safe Behavior: By keeping your use discreet and out of sight, you're setting an example of responsible behavior that your children can learn from as they grow older.

Poison Control Information: Be Prepared for Emergencies

Despite the best efforts to childproof your home, accidents can happen. If a child ingests cannabis, it's critical to act fast. **Keep the phone number for poison control readily available** in case of an emergency and familiarize yourself with the steps to take in the event of accidental ingestion.

Emergency Contacts: Post the poison control phone number in a visible location, like on the refrigerator, and ensure that all caregivers in the household know how to respond in an emergency.

Call Poison Control Immediately: If you suspect your child has ingested cannabis, don't wait to see if symptoms develop—call poison control immediately for guidance and seek emergency medical attention.

Dispose of Cannabis Products Safely

When disposing of vapes, edibles, or any other cannabis product, ensure that you do so in a way that children cannot access them. **Throwing cannabis products into a regular trash can could pose a**

risk if a child rummages through it.

> **Secure Disposal:** Use child-resistant garbage bags or bins that can be secured to prevent little hands from getting in. Better yet, place discarded products in a sealed container before disposing of them.
>
> **Environmental Consideration:** When disposing of cannabis products, consider both child safety and environmental impact. Look for local guidelines on safe disposal methods, especially for items like vapes that may contain hazardous materials.

Reducing the Risks at Home

By following these steps, you're taking proactive measures to reduce the risks associated with cannabis products in the home. Properly stored, labeled, and out of sight creates a safer environment for your family.

As a parent or caregiver, you have the responsibility to ensure that your home is comfortable and safe for your children. **Childproofing cannabis products** is an important part of that effort, and with thoughtful practices, you can significantly reduce the potential hazards they pose. This way, you can enjoy peace of mind knowing that your home is a safe space for everyone.

Living Room/Family Room
Infant/Non-mobile: (Birth - 6 months)
Infant crawl/roll: (5 months - 1 year)
→ **Toddler/Pre-school: (1 year - 4 years)**
→ **School-age: (5 years - 6+ years)**

Loose Picture Frames

Loose picture frames displayed on tables can be a hidden hazard in your home, especially when you have curious toddlers in their grabbing and reaching phase. It only takes a moment for an enthusiastic little explorer to knock down a picture frame accidentally, and the sharp corners on these frames can lead to severe injuries, especially to their delicate heads.

Many picture frames are made of fragile materials; if they fall, the glass can shatter, creating an even more dangerous situation. It's essential to take proactive measures to prevent such accidents and protect your little ones. One effective way to childproof your picture frames is by **securing them to the wall**. Wall-mounted frames eliminate the risk of them being knocked over entirely. Use sturdy picture hooks or screws to securely anchor the frames in place, ensuring they are out of reach of your curious toddlers.

If you have free-standing frames that you'd like to keep on tables or shelves, you can still make them safer by fastening them down. Adhesive Velcro strips or Fun-Tak can work wonders in maintaining the frames firmly attached to the table's surface. This simple yet effective solution ensures that the frames stay in place even if little hands get a bit too curious. While showcasing your cherished memories through picture frames adds a personal touch to your home, safety should always be a top priority.

By **securing these frames to the wall or using fastening methods**, you'll prevent potential accidents and create a child-friendly environment where your little ones can explore without unnecessary risks.

Living Room/Family Room
Infant/Non-mobile: (Birth - 6 months)
→ **Infant crawl/roll: (5 months - 1 year)**
→ **Toddler/Pre-school: (1 year - 4 years)**
→ **School-age: (5 years - 6+ years)**

Recliner/Rocking Chairs

Due to their numerous moving parts, recliners can be a source of unexpected hazards. The speed at which they open and close poses a risk of entrapment for heads, hands, and arms, making them potentially dangerous for both children and pets. To assess the squishing risk, a simple test using a pencil can be conducted. If the pencil snaps under pressure, it indicates that a finger could also be at risk of injury.

Furthermore, some recliners have areas underneath where little ones can crawl, potentially getting stuck or injured. To prevent this, it's essential to fasten fabric or a barrier behind the footrest to block access and ensure a safe environment for children.

These chairs can also become **tipping hazards when reclined**, especially if children or pets try to climb on or play around them. To avoid potential accidents, always check the stability and position of the recliner before using it or letting children near it.

It's vital to remember that young **children should never operate recliners**. These pieces of furniture often require a level of dexterity and strength that young ones may not possess. Always keep recliner controls out of reach of children to avoid any unintended adjustments. While recliners offer comfort and relaxation for adults, it's crucial to remain vigilant and take appropriate precautions to ensure the safety of children and pets in the household. Regularly inspect the recliner for potential hazards and follow the manufacturer's proper use and maintenance guidelines. By doing so, you can create a secure environment where everyone can enjoy the benefits of a recliner without unnecessary risks.

Traditional rocking chairs can provide a cozy and relaxing experience, especially when rocking a baby to sleep. However, it's crucial to be aware of potential hazards that can arise from their design. The curved edges of rocking chairs may pose a threat to toes and fingers, especially for young children who may not be fully aware of the risks. Supervising children closely when they are near rocking chairs and teaching them to keep their hands and feet away from moving parts is essential.

Another concern with traditional rocking chairs is **the gap between the spindles on the arms and the backrest**. If the gaps are wide, a child's limb or head can get trapped, leading to injuries. To prevent such accidents, choose rocking chairs with narrow gaps or consider adding safety cushions or covers to reduce the risk of entrapment.

Children's curious nature may lead them to attempt to climb on rocking chairs, not realizing the potential danger of being thrown off when the chair starts rocking. To avoid accidents, it's important to educate children that rockers are meant for sitting only and should not be used as play structures.

When using a rocking chair with a baby, follow safety guidelines and hold the baby securely to avoid mishaps. Keep the rocking chair on a stable surface and away from edges or obstacles that could cause it to tip over.

By being aware of these potential hazards and taking appropriate safety measures, you can enjoy the comfort and charm of traditional rocking chairs while ensuring the safety of your little ones. Remember to teach children about the proper use of rocking chairs and supervise their interactions with these pieces of furniture to create a safe and enjoyable environment for everyone in the household.

Platform rockers may seem safer than traditional rocking chairs, as they cannot tip back. However, it is essential to be aware of potential hazards associated with their design. While platform rockers do not have the risk of tipping, the gliding motion can still pose a danger to little arms.

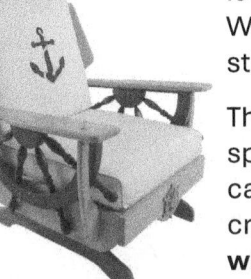

The area between the seat and the base of the platform rocker often has spindles or bars that allow for gliding motion. Unfortunately, these spindles can create gaps where a child's arm or fingers may become caught and crushed during gliding. To prevent such accidents, **it's crucial to be vigilant when children are around platform rockers** and closely supervise their interactions with the chair.

To enhance safety, consider using cushions or fabric covers that cover the gaps between the spindles, reducing the risk of entrapment. Additionally, **teach children not to place their hands or arms in the areas between the seat and the base of the rocker**. If possible, choose platform rockers with narrower gaps between the spindles to further minimize the risk.

As with any furniture piece, **educating children about safe usage** is important and setting clear rules for interacting with platform rockers. Avoid leaving children unattended near the rocker, especially if they are at an age where they may be curious and explore the chair's moving parts.

By being mindful of the potential hazards and taking appropriate precautions, you can continue to enjoy the comfort and convenience of platform rockers while ensuring the safety of your children. Always prioritize safety when choosing furniture and create a safe environment where your little ones can play and grow without unnecessary risks.

Platform Rocker with Side Panels: The perfect blend of safety and comfort! With this product, you can enjoy the soothing gliding motion without the risk of tipping, tossing, or unexpected crunching sounds. It's the ideal spot to snuggle up and unwind, creating a cozy space for relaxation.

One of the standout features of this platform rocker is its sturdy design, ensuring stability during use. You can rest assured that it won't tip over, providing peace of mind while you enjoy your leisure time.

However, like with any furniture, it's important to maintain safety awareness. Before settling into the rocker, make it a habit to double-check that no one, especially small children or pets, is standing directly behind you. This precaution helps prevent any accidental collisions or mishaps.

The platform rocker's side panels add an extra layer of safety, creating a more enclosed and secure space. The side panels enhance the chair's aesthetics and act as a protective barrier, reducing the risk of limbs or objects becoming caught in the gliding mechanism.

To enhance safety further, you can place the platform rocker in a designated area away from high-traffic zones or play areas where children may be running around. Always supervise young children when they are near the rocker to ensure they interact with it safely.

The platform rocker with side panels is a fantastic addition to any home, providing a comfortable and safe seating option for all family members. With its innovative design and focus on safety, you can relish the soothing gliding motion without any worries. So go ahead, snuggle up, and let the relaxation begin!

▶ *Since 1980, the U.S. Consumer Product Safety Commission has recorded **at least 8 fatalities** and several serious injuries to children under five caused by entrapment in recliner mechanisms One investigation from 1980–1985 alone confirmed **3 deaths and 2 brain injuries** in toddlers aged 12–30 months who became caught under footrests*

Living Room/Family Room
Infant/Non-mobile: (Birth - 6 months)
→ **Infant crawl/roll: (5 months - 1 year)**
→ **Toddler/Pre-school (1 year - 4 years)**
→ **School-age: (5 years - 6+ years)**

Couch Slipcover

In a home where little ones are bustling about, every detail counts when it comes to safety. Couch slip covers. Often overlooked, can be a potential hazard if not adequately childproofed.

Fabric Quality

Hypoallergenic: Choose hypoallergenic fabrics to prevent any skin irritations or allergic reactions.

Durability: Choose durable materials that can withstand the wear and tear of children's activities without fraying or tearing easily.

Proper Measurement

Custom Fit: Consider getting a custom-fitted slipcover to ensure there are no loose ends or excess fabric that could pose a tripping hazard.

Anti-Slip Features: Look for slipcovers with anti-slip features to prevent the cover from sliding off, which could potentially cause accidents.

Design Considerations

No Dangling Accessories: Avoid slipcovers with dangling accessories like tassels or fringe, which can be a choking hazard.

Secure Stitching: Ensure that the stitching is safe and robust to prevent small parts from coming loose.

Hygiene

Easy to Clean: Choose slipcovers that are easy to clean and maintain to ensure hygiene and prevent the growth of bacteria and molds.

Stain-Resistant: Consider stain-resistant fabrics to maintain cleanliness, mainly to avoid the buildup of harmful bacteria from food spills.

<u>**Living room**</u>
Infant/Non-mobile: (Birth - 6 months)
Infant crawl/roll: (5 months - 1 year)
→ **Toddler/Pre-school: (1 year - 4 years)**
→ **School-age: (5 years - 6+ years)**

Check Furniture Cushions for Small Choking Hazards

Children are naturally curious, constantly exploring their surroundings with little understanding of potential dangers. Furniture around the home often harbors hidden perils that can pose significant risks to these young adventurers. Items such as medications can be extremely hazardous if ingested, given their potent formulations not suited for a child's delicate system. Similarly, small objects like batteries, often found in television remotes or clocks, can be a choking hazard, blocking airways and causing severe distress. Sharp objects like pins, needles, or even glass items stored in furniture can lead to painful injuries and infections if not handled appropriately. Furthermore, heavy objects stored in upper drawers can cause furniture to tip over if a child attempts to climb, leading to crushing injuries. Therefore, it is imperative to meticulously childproof all storage units in the home, ensuring that potential dangers are mitigated to create a safe and nurturing environment for children in this critical age group.

► ***ALSO***, *loose foam beads or cushion fillings inside bean bags and soft furniture aren't just messy, they're dangerous.* ***The CPSC has recorded fatalities in children when these tiny pellets escaped through tears and caused choking or airway blockage.*** *Since any small piece that fits through a 1¼-inch cylinder is a serious choking hazard for toddlers, cushion fillings rank among unexpected yet real dangers in everyday furniture.*

Living Room/Family Room
Infant/Non-mobile: (Birth - 6 months)
Infant crawl/roll: (5 months - 1 year)
→ **Toddler/Pre-school: (1 year - 4 years)**
→ **School-age: (5 years - 6+ years)**

Travel Trunks

With their vintage charm and sturdy build, old-style travel trunks can be a delightful addition to any room. However, when it comes to childproofing, these trunks present unique challenges.

Lid Safety

Hinges and Stoppers: Older trunks often come with heavy lids that can slam shut. Install soft-close hinges or lid support hinges to prevent sudden closures that could injure tiny fingers or hands.

Locks and Latches: Vintage trunks often have old-fashioned locks and latches. Ensure these are either removed or secured in a locked position to prevent curious fingers from getting pinched or trapped. Interior Hazards

Deodorize and Clean: Old trunks can have a musty smell or even mold. Clean the interior thoroughly and use natural deodorizers like baking soda to ensure a fresh environment.

Smooth Surfaces: The interior might have splinters or rough patches. Sand down any rough areas and consider lining the trunk with a soft fabric or felt to protect against scratches.

Exterior Edges and Corners

Corner Protectors: Vintage trunks often have metal corners that can be sharp. Attach soft corner protectors to prevent injuries from accidental bumps.

Stabilize Metal Clasps and Decorative Elements: Ensure that any metal clasps, handles, or decorative elements are securely attached. If they're loose, either attach them firmly or remove them to prevent choking hazards.

Stability and Positioning

Anti-Tip Measures: If the trunk is tall, anchor it to the wall using furniture straps to prevent it from tipping over.

Floor Grippers: Place non-slip pads or grippers underneath the trunk to prevent it from sliding or moving unexpectedly, especially on smooth floors.

Repurposing with Safety in Mind

Transform into a Soft Seating Area: Add a cushioned top to the trunk, turning it into a seating area. This adds functionality and reduces the risk of the lid being opened frequently.

Storage for Non-Hazardous Items: If you're using the trunk for storage, ensure it only contains child-safe items. Avoid storing small objects, chemicals, or anything potentially harmful.

Education and Supervision

Teach Boundaries: Educate your children about the trunk's history and importance, teaching them to treat it with respect. Make them aware of potential dangers and establish boundaries.

Regular Checks: Periodically inspect the trunk for any wear and tear or new hazards, especially if it's frequently used.

Living Room/Family Room
→ Infant/Non-mobile: (Birth - 6 months)
→ Infant crawl/roll: (5 months - 1 year)
→ Toddler/Pre-school: (1 year - 4 years)
→ School-age: (5 years - 6+ years)

Vacuuming Importance

Childproofing a home goes beyond merely securing cabinets and covering electrical outlets; it encompasses creating an environment that's safe from all potential hazards, including those that might be lurking within our floors. Vacuuming, often seen as a mere cleaning routine, plays a pivotal role in ensuring child safety. With their innate curiosity, young children spend a significant amount of time on the floor, exploring their surroundings. This makes them particularly vulnerable to small objects like coins, toy parts, or even food crumbs, which can pose serious choking hazards. Regular vacuuming helps in promptly removing these small items, reducing the chances of curious little hands finding and ingesting them. Sidenote, **over 7,000 children** are injured annually by vacuum cleaners, including entanglement of cords and suction hazards. (Source: U.S. Consumer Product Safety Commission (CPSC) - Vacuum Cleaner Safety)

Carpets and rugs can trap a myriad of allergens, such as dust, pet dander, and pollen. For infants and toddlers, who often have more sensitive respiratory systems, these allergens can trigger allergic reactions or exacerbate conditions like asthma. Vacuuming, especially with devices equipped with HEPA filters, effectively removes these allergens, promoting a healthier indoor environment for children.

Food particles left on the floor can also **attract pests**, leading to potential infestations. These pests can carry diseases or cause allergic reactions. Regular vacuuming ensures that food residues are effectively removed, minimizing the risk of pest-related issues.

While vacuuming might seem like a simple chore, its implications for child safety are profound. It's integral to childproofing, ensuring that the environment where our children play, crawl, and explore is as safe and clean as possible. By recognizing the importance of vacuuming and making it a regular part of household maintenance, parents take a significant step towards creating a home that nurtures and protects their little ones.

Benefits of HEPA filters (High-Efficiency Particulate Air)

Improved Air Quality: HEPA filters are designed to trap and retain 99.97% of particles as small as 0.3 microns. This includes dust mites, pollen, pet dander, mold spores, and even some bacteria and viruses. By capturing these microscopic particles, HEPA filters prevent them from being released back into the air, resulting in cleaner and healthier indoor air quality.

Allergy and Asthma Relief: HEPA filters can be a game-changer for individuals who suffer from allergies or asthma. The ability to capture allergens and irritants ensures that those with sensitivities can breathe easier and experience fewer allergy or asthma symptoms.

Pet Hair and Dander Removal: Pet owners often struggle with managing pet hair and dander in their homes. HEPA filters effectively capture tiny particles, reducing allergens and making it easier to maintain a pet-friendly living space.

Elimination of Fine Particles: Standard vacuum filters may pick up larger debris, but they often release smaller particles back into the air. HEPA filters excel at trapping even the tiniest particles, making them ideal for homes with young children or people with respiratory conditions.

Prevention of Dust Recirculation: Traditional vacuum cleaners can inadvertently recirculate dust and allergens as they clean, leading to recontamination of previously cleaned areas. HEPA filters prevent this recirculation, ensuring a thorough and effective cleaning process.

Efficient Capture of Pet Odors: HEPA filters can also trap and remove pet odors, keeping your home smelling fresh and clean even with furry friends around.

Ideal for Allergen-Prone Environments: HEPA-filtered vacuums are particularly beneficial for homes with individuals who are more susceptible to allergens, such as young children, the elderly, or those with compromised immune systems.

Prevention of Cross-Contamination: For those concerned about cross-contamination between different areas of the home, HEPA filters act as a barrier, preventing particles from traveling between rooms during the vacuuming process.

HEPA filters in vacuums not only provide deep and thorough cleaning but also contribute to a healthier living environment by removing airborne allergens and pollutants. With their ability to capture even the tiniest particles, HEPA-filtered vacuums offer numerous advantages that benefit the overall well-being of your household.

► *According to the U.S. Consumer Product Safety Commission (CPSC), vacuum cleaners can pose various hazards to children.* **Annual Injuries: An estimated 3,300 children under age 5 are treated in US emergency rooms each year for vacuum cleaner-related injuries.**

Living Room/Family Room
Infant/Non-mobile: (Birth - 6 months)
→ **Infant crawl/roll: (5 months - 1 year)**
→ **Toddler/Pre-school: (1 year - 4 years)**
→ **School-age: (5 years - 6+ years)**

Carpet Concerns

Choosing the right carpet for your home involves more than just aesthetics and comfort; it's a decision that has significant implications for your health and well-being.

Understanding the Risks

Carpets can emit harmful fumes known as volatile organic compounds (VOCs), affecting indoor air quality, and leading to health issues.

Chemicals Involved: Certain carpets may contain hazardous substances such as ethyl benzene, formaldehyde, styrene, and acetone.

Health Effects: Prolonged exposure to these chemicals can cause headaches, nausea, respiratory irritation, and more severe health problems.

Specific Chemical Concerns: One chemical, p-dichlorobenzene, has been linked to fetal abnormalities in animal testing and can cause nerve damage and respiratory issues in humans.

Choosing the Right Carpet

Opt for Low VOC Carpets: Look for carpets labeled as low VOC options. These carpets release fewer harmful chemicals into the air, improving indoor air quality.

Consider Natural Fiber Carpets: Carpets made from natural fibers like wool or sisal tend to have lower VOC emissions. Ensure that the backing and adhesives used are also low in VOCs.

Proper Ventilation During Installation: Ensure good ventilation during and after carpet installation to disperse any lingering VOCs.

Ask for Green Label Plus Certification: Carpets with this certification meet strict criteria for low VOC emissions, making them a reliable indicator of a healthier carpet option.

The choice of carpeting in your home is not merely a design decision; it's a matter of health and safety. By understanding the potential risks and making informed choices, you can enjoy the comfort and beauty of carpets without compromising the well-being of your loved ones. Whether it's opting for low VOC carpets, investing in a HEPA filter vacuum cleaner, or ensuring proper ventilation, these steps can make a significant difference in the safety and comfort of your living space. Let's prioritize health in every aspect of our home, starting from the ground up.

<u>**Living Room/Family Room**</u>
Infant/Non-mobile: (Birth - 6 months)
Infant crawl/roll: (5 months - 1 year)
→ **Toddler/Pre-school: (1 year - 4 years)**
→ **School-age: (5 years - 6+ years)**

Space Heater Safety

Each year, **more than 1,800 children** suffer burns or fires caused by portable heaters. (Source: National Fire Protection Association (NFPA) - Heater Safety) While space heaters provide warmth and comfort during colder months, they can also pose significant risks, especially in homes with young children. Childproofing a space heater is essential to ensure that the warmth it brings doesn't come at the cost of safety.

<u>Placement is Key</u>

Stable Ground: Always place the space heater on a flat, stable surface to prevent it from tipping over. Avoid placing it on tables or elevated surfaces where children might be tempted to reach for it.

Away From Traffic: Position the heater in a location where it's less likely to be bumped into or knocked over, such as a corner of the room.

Distance from Flammables: Ensure there's at least a 3-foot clearance between the heater and any flammable materials, including curtains, furniture, and bedding.

Safety Features

Tip Over Protection: Opt for heaters that have an automatic shut-off feature if they tip over. This feature is invaluable in homes with active children or pets.

Overheat Protections: Heaters with this feature will automatically turn off if they get too hot, reducing the risk of fires.

Cool-to-Touch Exteriors: Some modern heaters are designed to remain cool outside, even when operating. This feature can prevent burns if a child accidentally touches the heater.

Operational Precautions

Supervision: Never leave a space heater unattended when children are present. If you need to leave the room, even for a short period, turn off the heater.

Educate: As children grow, teach them about the dangers associated with space heaters. Make them understand that it's not a toy and should not be touched.

Cord Management: To prevent tripping hazards, keep cords out of walkways. Consider using cord covers or cord management systems to keep them organized and out of reach.

Additional Safety Measures

Safety Barrier: Consider setting up a safety gate or barrier around the heater. While this might seem excessive, it provides an added layer of protection, ensuring curious toddlers can't get too close.

Regular Maintenance: Ensure your heater is in good working condition. Clean it regularly to prevent dust build-up, which can be a fire hazard, and check for any signs of wear or damage.

While space heaters are incredibly useful, their potential risks can't be overlooked. By implementing these detailed childproofing measures and being vigilant about their use, you can enjoy the warmth they provide while ensuring the safety of your little ones. Let's create a cozy and safe environment for the entire family.

► *Portable space heaters aren't just cozy. They're risky. Hotter than 392°F and able to tip easily, these heaters cause an **estimated 2,300 burn injuries annually in preschoolers (ages 0–6).** Combined with nearly 1,700 annual heater-related fires. **Leading to 160 injuries and 80 deaths.** They pose a hidden hazard in everyday comfort zones.* (University of Chicago Medicine)

Living Room/Family Room
Infant/Non-mobile: (Birth - 6 months)
→ **Infant crawl/roll: (5 months - 1 year)**
→ **Toddler/Pre-school: (1 year - 4 years)**
→ **School-age: (5 years - 6+ years)**

Extension Cord Concerns

Extension cords may seem harmless but pose serious risks to young children. Tripping over cords can lead to fractures, lacerations, contusions, or sprains, while frayed cords can cause electrical burns.

Replace frayed cords: Discard any damaged cords and replace them with new ones to prevent electrical shocks.

Temporary use only: Use extension cords temporarily and avoid overloading them, as this can lead to hazards.

Use polarized cords for polarized appliances: Match polarized appliances with polarized cords to ensure proper grounding and reduce the risk of electric shock.

Safety closures for outlets: Cover unused outlets with safety caps or electrical tape to prevent children from contacting live circuits.

Properly insert plugs: Ensure plugs are fully inserted into outlets to avoid any exposed prongs.

Unplug properly: When unplugging, pull from the plug itself, not the cord, to avoid damage.

Three-wire extension cords for three-prong plugs: Never remove the third prong, as it's a safety feature to prevent shock and electrocution.

Angled extension cords: Use these for tight spaces to avoid damaging cords.

Check for overheating: If the plug and cord feel warm or the plastic is softening, replace the extension cord immediately.

Avoid tripping hazards: Never run cords under carpets, rugs, or radiators, and don't staple or nail cords in place, as this can damage the protective covering.

Additional safety measures include not overloading extension cords, using power strips with caution, and using heavy-duty cords for high-wattage appliances. Use specific outdoor extension cords designed to withstand weather conditions for outdoor tools.

Living Room/Family Room
Infant/Non-mobile: (Birth - 6 months)
Infant crawl/roll: (5 months - 1 year)
→ **Toddler/Pre-school: (1 year - 4 years)**
→ **School-age: (5 years - 6+ years)**

Electrical Outlet Safety

Each year, **more than 15,000 children** are injured by inserting objects into open electrical outlets, resulting in shocks and burns. (Source: National Electronic Injury Surveillance System (NEISS) – CDC)

Outlet covers: Install outlet covers or safety caps on all electrical outlets within the reach of children. These covers are designed to fit securely over the outlets, making it difficult for little fingers to access the electrical openings. Various types of outlet covers are available, including sliding covers, spring-loaded covers, and hinged covers. Choose ones that are child-resistant yet easy for adults to use when needed.

Tamper-resistant outlets: Consider replacing standard outlets with tamper-resistant ones, also known as childproof outlets. These outlets have built-in safety shutters that automatically close the electrical openings when not in use. To insert a plug, equal pressure must be applied to both sides of the outlet, preventing children from inserting objects into the slots and reducing the risk of electric shock.

Sliding plate covers: Another option is to install sliding plate covers that automatically slide back into place when a plug is removed from the outlet. These covers provide continuous protection and are convenient for adults to use when using electrical devices.

No Outlet plugs/caps: Research also shows that 100% of 2–4 year olds were able to remove some types of plastic outlet caps in under 10 seconds.

Cord concealers: Use cord concealers or cord organizers to keep cords and cables out of your child's reach. These adhesive strips help secure cords along walls and prevent them from dangling, reducing the risk of children pulling on them. **Furniture placement:** Position furniture strategically to cover lower outlets, making them less accessible to young children. However, be cautious with furniture that children may climb, as they could gain access to higher outlets.

Educate your child: Teach your child about electrical safety and explain that outlets are not safe to touch. Use simple language and visuals to convey the message effectively. Encourage them to come to you if they have any questions about electrical appliances or outlets.

Regular inspections: Regularly inspect all wall plugs and childproofing measures to ensure they are still practical and in good condition. Replace any damaged or worn-out outlet covers or plugs promptly.

Power strip safety: If you use power strips, ensure they have covers or childproofing features to shield the outlets from curious fingers. Secure the power strip in a location that is inaccessible to your child.

(Bonus) Travel Safety: When traveling or visiting other places, bring along outlet caps or plugs to temporarily childproof unfamiliar outlets.

You can significantly reduce the risk of electrical accidents and create a safer environment for your child to explore and play. Childproofing is an ongoing process, so stay vigilant and adapt your precautions as your child grows and becomes more curious about their surroundings.

► *The Electrical Safety Foundation International (ESFI) reports approximately 2,400 children are treated annually in emergency rooms for injuries related to electrical outlets. States that 89% of these injuries involve children under age 6.* ***Research also shows that 100% of 2–4 year olds were able to remove some types of plastic outlet caps in under 10 seconds.***

Living Room/Family Room
Infant/Non-mobile: (Birth - 6 months)
→ **Infant crawl/roll: (5 months - 1 year)**
→ **Toddler/Pre-school: (1 year - 4 years)**
→ **School-age: (5 years - 6+ years)**

Use a Cord Concealment Device

Cord concealment systems are more than just aesthetic solutions; they are essential tools for ensuring safety in homes with multiple electronic devices. These systems give a neat appearance and significantly reduce potential hazards.

Key Benefits and Considerations

Safety Enhancement: By organizing and hiding cords, these systems prevent accidents like tripping or entanglement, which is especially vital in areas with numerous cables, such as entertainment centers and home offices.

Entertainment Centers: These areas typically have a variety of electronics, including TVs, gaming consoles, and speakers. This can result in a maze of cords that can attract the curiosity of children and pets. Using a cord concealment system ensures that these cords remain out of sight and reach, reducing the risk of injuries or damage to devices.

Home Offices: Offices often have devices like computers, printers, and chargers, which can lead to potential cord clutter. Tangled cords pose tripping hazards and make it challenging to identify specific cords. A concealment system neatly organizes the cords, ensuring easy identification and reducing risks.

Variety of Designs: Cord concealment systems are available in different designs, such as cord covers, cable raceways, and sleeves. These designs allow for organized bundling, reducing tangling and ensuring easy access when needed. Many also come with adhesive backings or mounting options for secure attachment.

Selection Criteria: When choosing a system, consider its capacity and size. Ensure it can accommodate all your cords. Opting for durable, flame-retardant materials adds an extra layer of safety.

Incorporating cord concealment systems in areas with electronic devices ensures a tidy, organized space while prioritizing safety. Regular checks and adjustments, combined with educating family members about the significance of a clutter-free environment, can further enhance the safety of your living space.

Living Room/Family Room
Infant/Non-mobile: (Birth - 6 months)
Infant crawl/roll: (5 months - 1 year)
→ **Toddler/Pre-school: (1 year - 4 years)**
→ **School-age: (5 years - 6+ years)**

Install Power Strip Covers

Each year, **more than 10,000 children** are injured by power strips and surge protectors, including electrical shocks and fires. (Source: National Electronic Injury Surveillance System (NEISS) – CDC) Childproofing your power strip is indeed essential to keep your little explorers safe from potential electrical hazards.

Secure your power strip: Use adhesive strips or mounting brackets to attach your power strip to a wall or furniture firmly. This will prevent it from being easily moved or pulled by curious hands, reducing the risk of accidental unplugging or tripping over cords.

Choose a surge protector: Opt for a power strip that also serves as a surge protector. This added feature protects your devices from power surges and adds an extra layer of safety by automatically shutting off power in case of an electrical fault or overload.

Keep cords organized: Use cord management accessories, such as cable clips or cord covers, to keep cords neatly bundled and out of the way. Tangled cords can be tempting for children to pull or play with, so keeping them organized will minimize their curiosity.

Check for damage: Regularly inspect your power strip and cords for any signs of wear or damage. Replace any frayed or damaged cords immediately, as exposed wires can pose a significant electrical hazard.

Educate your children: Take the time to teach your children about electrical safety. Explain the dangers of playing with power strips and cords and emphasize that they should never touch them without adult supervision.

Unplug unused devices: Encourage the habit of unplugging devices when they are not in use. This conserves energy and reduces the risk of electrical accidents, especially if the devices have small buttons or switches that curious little fingers might fiddle with.

Parental supervision: While childproofing is essential, nothing beats good old-fashioned parental supervision. Keep an eye on your children when they are in areas with power strips and educate them about the importance of staying safe around electrical outlets and devices. You can create a safe environment for your children to explore and play, giving you peace of mind and ensuring their safety as they grow and discover the world around them. Childproofing is not just a one-time task; it requires ongoing attention and adjustments as your child grows and becomes more curious and adventurous. Stay vigilant and keep your little ones safe from electrical hazards!

Living Room/Family Room
Infant/Non-mobile: (Birth - 6 months)
Infant crawl/roll: (5 months - 1 year)
→ **Toddler/Pre-school: (1 year - 4 years)**
→ **School-age: (5 years - 6+ years)**

Secure Empty Lamp Light Sockets

Childproofing an empty light bulb socket in a lamp is essential to protect curious children from potential electrical hazards. When a bulb burns out or is removed for any reason, the exposed socket can become a point of interest for little hands, posing risks of electrical shock.

Steps to Childproof an Empty Light Bulb Socket

Unplug the Lamp: Before addressing the empty socket, always start by unplugging the lamp to ensure there is no active current, eliminating the immediate risk of electrical shock.

Socket Safety Caps: Small, non-conductive caps are designed to fit securely into an empty light bulb socket. After unplugging the lamp, insert the safety cap into the socket. It should fit snugly, preventing children from touching the inner components.

Regular Inspections: Safety caps can loosen or degrade over time. Periodically check to ensure the cap remains securely in place and replace it if it shows any signs of wear.

Educate Children: While physical safeguards are crucial, it is equally important to educate children about the dangers associated with electrical items. Teach them the importance of not touching lamps, especially the inside of sockets, whether they are covered or not.

Consider a Lamp Upgrade: If a particular lamp frequently has an empty socket or is within easy reach of children, consider replacing it with a model with built-in safety features or is less accessible to young hands.

Placement Matters: Ensure the lamp is positioned in a stable location, away from edges or high-traffic areas. This reduces the chance of it being knocked over by children

---

► ***Every year, more than 21,000 preschoolers (under age 6) in the U.S. are treated in emergency rooms after inserting fingers or objects into empty lamp sockets or outlets.** Over 80% are in the toddler-to-preschool range, and many snacks, playtime, and kitchen moments involve curious hands meeting live terminals, often leading to painful burns and shocks. (ESFI, Elictrical Saftey Foundation International)*

Living Room/Family Room
Infant/Non-mobile: (Birth - 6 months)
→ **Infant crawl/roll: (5 months - 1 year)**
→ **Toddler/Pre-school: (1 year - 4 years)**
→ **School-age: (5 years - 6+ years)**

Small and Button Batteries

Young children can easily put small button batteries in their mouths. According to John Hopkins Medicine, there has been an average of **3,500 button battery ingestions per year**, and the incidence has increased in the last decade. Childproofing small batteries is of paramount importance due to the serious risks they pose when ingested or mishandled by children. Small batteries, especially button batteries, can cause severe internal injuries if swallowed, and their compact size makes them particularly attractive to curious little hands.

Secure Storage: Store batteries, especially spare ones, in a secure container or drawer with a childproof latch. Ensure this storage location is out of reach and out of sight of children.

Battery Operated Devices: For devices that use small batteries, ensure the battery compartment is secure. Some devices come with screw-secured compartments, which are ideal. If the compartment isn't secure, consider using strong tape to keep it closed or keep the device away from children.

Immediate Cleanup: If a battery leaks or is damaged, clean it up immediately. Wear gloves and ensure the area is well-ventilated, as battery acid can be harmful. Dispose of damaged batteries properly and keep them away from children.

Educate and Supervise: Talk to your children about the dangers of batteries. Make sure they understand never to put them in their mouths or play with them. Always supervise children when they're using battery-operated toys or devices.

Prompt Disposal: Dispose of old or unused batteries promptly and safely. Due to their hazardous components, many localities have specific disposal or recycling procedures for batteries.

Be Alert to Symptoms: If you suspect a child has swallowed a battery, seek emergency medical attention immediately. Symptoms might include coughing, drooling, discomfort, or a decline in appetite, but sometimes there may be no symptoms at all.

Battery Covers: Consider purchasing battery covers or cases. These are designed to hold batteries securely, preventing children from accessing them quickly.

Additionally: Over 10,000 children are injured annually by mishandling remote controls, including electrical shocks and swallowing small parts. (Source: National Electronic Injury Surveillance System (NEISS) – CDC)

<u>Living Room/Family Room</u>
→ **Infant/Non-mobile: (Birth - 6 months)**
→ **Infant crawl/roll: (5 months - 1 year)**
→ **Toddler/Pre-school: (1 year - 4 years)**
→ **School-age: (5 years - 6+ years)**

Loud Noise Concerns

According to the Centers for Disease Control and Prevention (CDC), being aware of loud noises and high volumes is essential to protecting the delicate ears of young children and preventing potential hearing damage. Children's ears are more sensitive than those of adults, and prolonged exposure to loud sounds can have detrimental effects on their hearing health.

Awareness of Noise Levels: Always be conscious of the volume when playing music, watching TV, or using any electronic devices. It's easy to underestimate how loud a volume might be for a child, even if it seems acceptable to an adult.

Limit Exposure: If you're in an environment where loud noises are unavoidable, such as a construction site or a busy street, limit the time your child spends there. Shorter durations can reduce the risk of hearing damage.

Use of Protective Gear: If you anticipate being in a loud environment, consider using protective gear like noise-cancelling headphones/earmuffs for your child. Many child-sized headphones/earmuffs are available that are designed to effectively reduce harmful noise levels.

Monitor Toy Volume: Some toys can be surprisingly loud. Regularly check the volume levels of electronic toys, and if possible, set them to a lower volume or put tape over the speaker to dampen the sound. **Educate on Safe Listening:** As children grow and begin using headphones or earbuds, teach them about safe listening practices. Encourage them to keep the volume at a safe level and take regular breaks to protect their ears.

Regular Hearing Checks: Schedule regular hearing check-ups for your child. Early detection of any hearing issues can lead to better outcomes and interventions.

By taking these measures, parents can ensure that their children's hearing is protected from potential harm. It's crucial to create an environment where children can explore and learn without being exposed to harmful noise levels. Let's prioritize their auditory health and ensure a safe and sound environment for them to thrive in.

<u>**Living Room/Family Room**</u>
Infant/Non-mobile: (Birth - 6 months)
Infant crawl/roll: (5 months - 1 year)
→ **Toddler/Pre-school: (1 year - 4 years)**
→ **School-age: (5 years - 6+ years)**

Know What Your Child Is Watching

Childproofing your home extends beyond physical safety measures; it also encompasses ensuring that the content your children consume, both visually and audibly, is age-appropriate and beneficial for their development. In today's digital age, children are exposed to a vast array of content on TV, radio, and social media, making it crucial for parents to be vigilant about what their children are watching and listening to.

Parental Controls: Modern televisions and streaming platforms often have parental control settings. Use these features to restrict access to inappropriate content based on age ratings or specific themes.

Educate and Discuss: Engage with your children about what they watch and listen to. Open discussions can help them understand the difference between fiction and reality and provide context for any confusing or mature themes they might encounter.

Co-Viewing and Co-Listening: Whenever possible, watch TV shows or listen to radio programs with your children. This not only allows you to gauge the appropriateness of the content but also offers opportunities for bonding and discussion.

Set Viewing Limits: Limit the amount of time your children spend in front of the TV or listening to the radio. Encourage other activities like reading, outdoor play, or family games to ensure a balanced routine.

Review Content: Before allowing your children to watch a new TV show or listen to a new radio station, preview the content yourself. This will give you a clear idea of its suitability for your child's age and maturity level.

Use Trusted Platforms: Opt for platforms and channels that are known for producing child-friendly content. Many streaming services offer kids' profiles that only display age-appropriate content. It's not just about restricting access but also about educating and guiding them to make informed choices as they grow. Create a safe media environment where our children can learn, be entertained, and develop a healthy relationship with technology.

<u>**Living Room/Family Room**</u>
→ **Infant/Non-mobile:** (Birth - 6 months)
→ **Infant crawl/roll:** (5 months - 1 year)
→ **Toddler/Pre-school:** (1 year - 4 years)
→ **School-age:** (5 years - 6+ years)

Insects and Pests

There are **over 200,000 cases** of insect and animal bites among children annually in the U.S., with allergic reactions posing serious health risks. (Source: Centers for Disease Control and Prevention (CDC) - Venomous Bites and Stings)

Mosquitoes

Mosquitoes are not only irritating but can also pose serious health risks. Their ability to transmit various diseases makes them a significant public health concern. Malaria alone affects hundreds of millions of people worldwide, with a high mortality rate, particularly among young children in Africa.

Mosquito repellents: When outdoors, use insect repellents containing DEET, picaridin, or lemon eucalyptus oil. Apply the repellent to exposed skin and clothing as directed on the product label.

Wear protective clothing: When venturing outdoors during mosquito-prone hours, such as dusk and dawn, wear long-sleeved shirts, long pants, socks, and closed-toe shoes to minimize skin exposure.

Screen your home: Inspect and repair any damaged window screens to keep mosquitoes from entering your home. Use screen doors to ensure proper ventilation without inviting the pesky insects inside.

Eliminate standing water: Mosquitoes lay their eggs in stagnant water, so remove any sources of standing water around your home, such as in flowerpots, buckets, or gutters.

Use mosquito nets: When camping or sleeping outdoors, consider using mosquito nets to create a protective barrier against these biting insects.

Educate yourself: Stay informed about mosquito-borne diseases prevalent in your area and take necessary precautions to reduce the risk of exposure.

Consider natural repellents: Some essential oils, such as citronella, lavender, and peppermint, can act as natural mosquito repellents. Use candles, diffusers, or lotions containing these oils to keep mosquitoes at bay.

Optimize outdoor spaces: Use fans or create airflow in outdoor areas to discourage mosquitoes, as they are weak fliers and struggle in windy conditions.

Attract natural predators: Encourage the presence of natural mosquito predators like bats, dragonflies, and birds in your garden by providing suitable habitats.

You can reduce the chances of mosquito-borne illnesses and enjoy your time outdoors more comfortably. Remember, a little preparation can go a long way in protecting yourself and your loved ones from these tiny terrors.

Houseflies

Flies may seem harmless, but they can indeed carry harmful bacteria and diseases, making them a potential health hazard. To keep them at bay and protect your family, consider these additional measures.

Maintain good hygiene: Regularly clean your living spaces, kitchen, and dining areas to remove food crumbs and spills that attract flies. Wipe down surfaces and dispose of garbage promptly, especially in warmer months when flies are more active.

Properly seal food containers: Store food in airtight containers to prevent flies from accessing and contaminating your food.

Keep outdoor areas clean: Flies can breed in decaying organic matter, so regularly clean up fallen leaves, grass clippings, and pet waste in your yard.

Install fly screens: In addition to repairing any existing window screens, consider installing fly screens on doors and windows to create a physical barrier that keeps flies out while still allowing ventilation.

Use natural repellents: Certain essential oils, such as citronella, lavender, and eucalyptus, have repellent properties that can help keep flies away. Use oil diffusers or sprays with these scents in your home.

DIY fly traps: Use simple household items like vinegar, dish soap, and plastic bottles to create fly traps. Place these traps strategically around your home to catch and reduce the fly population.

Minimize outdoor attractions: If you enjoy outdoor activities and picnics, cover food and drinks with mesh covers to keep flies away. Use fans or citronella candles to deter flies from gathering.

Avoid attracting flies: Limit the use of strong-scented cleaning products, perfumes, and lotions, as these may attract flies.

Proper waste disposal: Ensure that outdoor trash bins are covered and away from living spaces to prevent flies from congregating around them.

Regular pest control: If flies become a persistent problem, consider contacting a pest control professional to address the issue safely and effectively.

Bedbugs

Bedbugs have made a resurgence in recent years, and it's essential to be vigilant in identifying and addressing infestations. Here are some tips for dealing with bedbugs effectively.

Inspect your furniture: Bedbugs can hide in mattresses and cracks and crevices of furniture, such as bed frames, nightstands, and couches. Regularly inspect these areas for any signs of infestation.

Launder and vacuum frequently: Wash your bedsheets, pillowcases, and clothing regularly in hot water to kill any bedbugs or eggs. Vacuum your mattress, furniture, and carpets frequently to remove bedbugs, eggs, and droppings.

Use a mattress encasement: Consider using a mattress encasement that is specifically designed to prevent bedbugs from entering or escaping. These encasements are tightly woven and provide extra protection for your mattress.

Be cautious when traveling: Bedbugs can hitch a ride in your luggage, so be cautious when staying in hotels or traveling. Inspect your hotel room for any signs of bedbugs before unpacking.

Avoid second-hand furniture: Be cautious when purchasing second-hand furniture, as bedbugs could be hiding within. Inspect used furniture thoroughly before bringing it into your home.

Seal cracks and crevices: Seal any cracks or crevices in your walls, baseboards, and furniture to reduce potential hiding spots for bedbugs.

Heat treatment: Heat treatment is an effective way to eliminate bedbugs and their eggs. Consult a professional exterminator who specializes in heat treatment for bedbug infestations.

Follow professional advice: If you suspect a bedbug infestation, contact a professional exterminator immediately. They can assess the extent of the infestation and recommend the most appropriate treatment plan.

Keep a clean and clutter-free environment: Reduce clutter in your home, as it provides fewer hiding spots for bedbugs. A clean and organized living space makes it easier to identify and address any potential infestations.

Remember that bedbug infestations can be challenging to eliminate, and early detection and prompt action are crucial. If you notice any signs of bedbugs or experience unexplained bites, immediately protect yourself and your family from these bothersome pests.

Fleas

Contrary to popular belief, flea infestations are not solely a problem for pet owners. Fleas are opportunistic parasites that can easily make their way into your home through various means. Whether you have pets or not, it's essential to be aware of the potential risks and take preventive measures to keep these pesky pests at bay.

Fleas are attracted to warmth and movement, which makes them readily latch onto humans when we're outdoors and then follow us inside. They are particularly common in areas with high humidity or in regions where pets frequently roam.

Regularly inspect your home: Look for any signs of fleas, such as tiny dark specks or bites on your skin. Also, check your pet's fur for fleas and flea dirt, which appear as black or brown specks that resemble ground black pepper.

Vacuum frequently: Vacuum your floors, carpets, and upholstery regularly to remove flea eggs, larvae, and adults. Remember to dispose of the vacuum bag in an outdoor trash bin immediately to prevent fleas from reinfesting your home.

Wash bedding and linens: Wash your bedding, linens, and clothes in hot water to kill any fleas or eggs that may be present. High heat is effective at eliminating fleas at all life stages.

Treat your pets and home simultaneously: If you have pets, ensure they are on regular flea prevention treatments. However, remember that treating your pets alone may not be enough to address a flea infestation. You must also treat your home and outdoor areas to break the flea life cycle and prevent re-infestation.

Seek professional help if needed: If you have a severe or persistent flea infestation, consult with your veterinarian or call a professional exterminator. They can provide effective solutions to eliminate fleas and offer guidance on preventive measures.

Be cautious when traveling: Fleas can be present in various environments, so be cautious when traveling or spending time in places where fleas may thrive. Avoid sitting or lying on the ground in outdoor areas that may have fleas.

Bees and Wasps

Childproofing against bees and wasps is essential, especially during warmer months when these insects are most active. While bees and wasps play vital roles in our ecosystem, their stings can be painful and, for some children, can trigger severe allergic reactions. Ensuring that our homes and gardens are safe from these potential threats is crucial to providing a secure environment for our little ones to play and explore.

- **Regular Inspections:** Periodically check the outside of your house, deck, and garden, especially children's play areas, for nests. Bees might build hives in trees or shrubs, while wasps often favor gutters, eaves, or even underground.
- **Limit Attractants:** When eating outdoors, ensure that food and drinks are covered. The scent can attract these insects. Also, make sure to clean up immediately after any outdoor meals.
- **Dress with Care:** While floral and bright patterns are adorable, they can attract bees. Opt for neutral or light-colored clothing for your kids when they're playing outside.
- **Stay Calm and Educate:** Teach children not to swat at bees or wasps. Instead, instruct them to stay calm and slowly move away from the area.
- **Secure Trash Bins:** Ensure outdoor trash cans have tight-fitting lids. Leftover foods, especially sweet ones, can attract bees and wasps.
- **Natural Deterrent:** Consider planting plants that repel bees and wasps, such as marigolds, citronella, and eucalyptus.
- **Immediate Response:** If your child is stung, it's essential to monitor them for any signs of an allergic reaction, such as difficulty breathing, and seek medical attention immediately if needed.

Parents can significantly reduce the risks associated with bees and wasps. It's all about creating a balance where children can enjoy the outdoors, and nature can thrive, ensuring that our gardens remain places of joy, discovery, and safety.

Brown Recluse and Black Widow

Childproofing against brown recluse and black widow spiders is crucial. These arachnids are known for their venomous bites, which can cause severe reactions, especially in children. Their bites can lead to skin necrosis, systemic symptoms, or, in rare cases, life-threatening conditions.

Identification

Brown Recluse: Recognizable by its violin-shaped marking on its back and its six eyes (most spiders have eight). They are usually tan to dark brown.

lack Widow: Identified by its shiny black color and the distinctive red hourglass shape on its abdomen.

Childproofing Measures

Regular Cleaning: Dust and vacuum regularly, especially in corners, under furniture, and other secluded areas where spiders might hide.

Reduce Clutter: Keep basements, garages, and attics clutter-free. These spiders prefer dark, undisturbed areas.

Seal Entry Points: Check for cracks in the foundation, and gaps in windows or doors, and repair any torn screens.

Wear Gloves: When reaching into areas that have been undisturbed for a while, like storage boxes or garden sheds, always wear gloves.

Check Clothing and Shoes: Check for spiders before wearing them, especially if they've been left on the floor or in a garage.

Educate Children: Teach them to recognize these spiders and understand the importance of not touching or playing with them.

Ensuring your home is safeguarded against brown recluse and black widow spiders is vital for the safety of your children. By taking proactive measures, regularly inspecting your living spaces, and educating your family, you can significantly reduce the risks associated with these venomous spiders and ensure a safer environment for your loved ones.

Fire Ants

Childproofing against fire ants is essential, especially in regions where these aggressive insects are prevalent. Fire ant stings can be extremely painful and, in some cases, can lead to severe allergic reactions. Their venom causes a burning sensation, which is how they got their name. For children, who often play outdoors and might inadvertently disturb a fire ant mound, the risk is even higher.

Identification

Appearance: Reddish-brown to black, fire ants are small but can be identified by their aggressive behavior and the mounds they build.

Mounds: Dome-shaped and can appear almost anywhere, from open fields to playgrounds.

Childproofing Measures

Regular Yard Inspection: Periodically check your yard for new mounds, especially after rainfall.

Immediate Treatment: If you spot a mound, treat it immediately using recommended ant baits or insecticides.

Avoidance: Teach children to recognize fire ant mounds and to avoid playing near them.

Wear Protective Clothing: When playing outside in areas known for fire ants, children should wear closed-toe shoes and socks.

Immediate Action: If bitten, clean the area with soap and water to prevent secondary infections. Cold compresses can reduce pain and swelling.

Seek Medical Attention: If your child shows signs of an allergic reaction, such as difficulty breathing, swelling of the face or mouth, or dizziness, seek medical attention immediately.

Fire ants pose a significant threat, especially to curious children exploring the outdoors. By staying vigilant, treating mounds promptly, and educating our young ones about the dangers, we can create a safer environment for them to play and grow. It's our responsibility to ensure that the joys of outdoor play aren't overshadowed by the menace of these tiny aggressors.

Cockroaches

Childproofing against cockroaches is essential for your child's physical well-being and overall health. Cockroaches are known carriers of various diseases and can trigger allergies and asthma in children. Their droppings, shed skins, and even the roaches themselves can contaminate food sources and play areas.

Prevention

Seal Entry Points: Regularly inspect your home for cracks, holes, and gaps, especially in areas like the kitchen and bathroom. Seal any potential entry points to prevent cockroaches from infiltrating.

Regular Cleaning: Ensure that all food crumbs and spills are cleaned up immediately. Vacuum and sweep regularly to remove food particles.

Proper Food Storage: Store all food items, including pet food, in airtight containers. Avoid leaving food out overnight.

Manage Garbage: Empty trash bins regularly and ensure they are sealed properly. Store garbage bins away from entry points.

Treatment

Professional Pest Control: If you notice a cockroach infestation, consider hiring a professional pest control service to handle the situation safely and effectively.

Natural Repellants: Consider using natural repellents like bay leaves or cucumber slices in areas where cockroaches are commonly found.

Safe Use of Pesticides: If using pesticides, ensure they are out of reach of children and pets. Follow label instructions carefully and consider using gel-based baits that can be placed in inaccessible areas.

Cockroaches are more than just a nuisance; they pose genuine health risks, especially to our young ones. By taking proactive measures in prevention and treatment, we can ensure a cleaner, healthier living environment for our children, free from the threats posed by these persistent pests.

Ticks

Ticks are troublesome pests that can transmit a range of diseases, so proper precautions must be taken when dealing with them. If you discover a tick attached to the skin of yourself or your child, it's important to handle the situation carefully and take appropriate measures to prevent illness.

Step-by-Step Guide on How to Safely Remove a Tick

Remain calm. First and foremost, stay calm and avoid panicking. While ticks can carry diseases, **not every tick is infected**, and **prompt removal** can significantly reduce the risk of transmission.

Use **fine-tipped tweezers** to grasp the tick as close to your skin's surface as possible. Be sure to **avoid squeezing or crushing the tick**, as this may cause it to regurgitate its stomach contents, potentially increasing the risk of disease transmission.

Using a **steady, upward motion**, gently pull the tick away from your skin. **Do not twist or jerk the tweezers**, as this may cause the tick's mouth parts to break off and remain embedded in your skin.

After removal, **clean the bite area and your hands** with rubbing alcohol, an iodine scrub, or soap and water to prevent infection.

If you're concerned about potential illness, **save the tick** for identification. Place it in a small container or sealed plastic bag, and bring it to your **pediatrician or local health department** for evaluation.

Over the next few weeks, **monitor the bite site for any signs of a rash or unusual symptoms**. Early detection of illness is key.

Remember, **prevention is the best defense** against ticks and the diseases they may carry. When spending time outdoors, especially in grassy or wooded areas, take the following precautions:

- **Cover up** by wearing long-sleeved shirts and long pants to minimize skin exposure.
- **Use insect repellents** containing DEET, picaridin, or other EPA-approved ingredients.
- **Treat your clothing with permethrin**, a tick repellent that remains effective even after several washes.
- **Perform regular tick checks** on yourself, your children, and your pets after spending time outdoors.

Mice and Rats

Childproofing against mice and rats is essential to ensure the safety and health of your children.

These rodents pose direct physical threats and carry diseases that can be harmful to children

Understanding the Threat: Mice and rats are attracted to homes for food, water, and shelter. Once inside, they can contaminate food sources, chew through wires (posing fire hazards), and spread diseases. Children, with their innate curiosity, might attempt to touch or play with these creatures, risking bites or exposure to pathogens.

Seal Entry Points

Cracks and Holes: Regularly inspect your home's exterior and interior for cracks, holes, or gaps. Seal them using caulk, steel wool, or other appropriate materials.

Doors and Windows: Ensure that doors and windows close tightly. Consider installing door sweeps and repairing any torn screens.

Safe Food Storage

Containers: Store food, especially grains and cereals, in airtight containers.

Clean-Up: Promptly clean up food spills and crumbs. Ensure that dining areas are cleaned after every meal.

Regular Home Maintenance

Trash: Use garbage cans with tight-fitting lids and empty them regularly.

Clutter: Reduce clutter, especially in basements, attics, and garages, as these can provide hiding spots for rodents.

Safe Rodent Control

Traps: If using traps, opt for enclosed bait stations or electric traps that are child safe. Place them in areas inaccessible to children.

Avoid Poison: Refrain from using rodenticides, as they can be extremely harmful if ingested by children. If you must use them, ensure they are in child-resistant bait stations and out of reach.

Professional Help: If you suspect a significant infestation, consider hiring a professional pest control service to handle the issue safely.

Educate Your Children: Teach your children never to touch or approach mice or rats. Explain the potential dangers in age-appropriate terms.

Regular Inspection: Look for signs like droppings, gnaw marks, or nests. Address any signs of infestation promptly.

It's essential to be proactive, regularly inspect your home, and take immediate action if you notice any signs of these rodents. Keeping your home rodent-free not only ensures the safety of your children but also contributes to a healthier living environment for the entire family.

Living Room/Family Room
→ **Infant/Non-mobile: (Birth – 6 months)**
→ **Infant crawl/roll: (5 months – 1 year)**
→ **Toddler/Pre-school: (1 year – 4 years)**
→ **School-age: (5 years – 6+ years)**

House Plants

In the lush corners of many homes, a vibrant collection of houseplants add a touch of nature's splendor, purifying the air and bringing life to indoor spaces. However, amidst their beauty lies a hidden danger, especially for the little adventurers who are keen to explore every nook and cranny.

Keep Bugs at Bay (and Away from Little Hands!)

Indoor plants bring life and beauty into your home, but let's be real, they can also invite some not-so-welcome guests: bugs! Whether there are gnats buzzing around or ants sneaking in, it's important to take steps to keep your plants bug-free, especially if you've got a little one exploring. Here's your ultimate guide to childproofing your indoor plants while keeping insects at bay and ensuring your curious child stays safe.

Start with the Right Plants: Bug-Resistant and Kid-Safe

First things first, choosing the right plants can save you a lot of hassle. Some plants are more likely to attract bugs, while others are naturally resistant. You also want to make sure the plants are safe for kids, just in case your little explorer gets too curious.

Bug-Resistant Indoor Plants: Plants like spider plants, bamboo palms, Boston ferns, and areca palms are less likely to attract bugs and are great choices for indoor spaces. These plants are hardy and low maintenance, which means fewer watering mistakes and fewer bug invasions. Plus, they're safe for kids in case any leaves end up in tiny hands.

Plants to Avoid: Avoid plants that attract insects, such as basil, mint, or cilantro. These are more prone to attracting aphids, gnats, and other pests, especially if kept indoors. Also, be cautious of plants that are toxic to children, like **Philodendrons**, **Pothos**, or **Peace Lilies**. They're beautiful but better off kept out of reach or substituted with kid-friendly alternatives.

Keep Plants Clean and Bug-Free

Bugs love plants, especially ones that aren't properly cared for. Dirty or dusty plants are more likely to attract pests like spider mites, aphids, and mealybugs. Regular cleaning of your plants will help keep insects from settling in and spreading.

Regular Leaf Cleaning: Once a week, gently wipe down the leaves with a damp cloth to remove dust and prevent pests from getting comfortable. If you notice any bugs, like tiny webs or sticky residue on the leaves (a sign of aphids or scale insects), it's time to take action. A simple solution of mild dish soap and water can be sprayed onto the leaves to get rid of these pests safely.

Check for Pests Regularly: Remember to look under the leaves, where pests love to hide. If you spot any crawling critters, nip them in the bud by isolating the plant and treating it with a natural insecticide like neem oil. Neem oil is safe for children and pets but deadly for bugs, disrupting their life cycles and keeping your plants pest-free.

Out of Reach, Out of Trouble: Keep Plants Away from Little Hands

If you've got a curious child who loves to explore everything including the soil and leaves of your plants, you'll want to make sure those plants are out of reach.

Hanging Planters: Hanging plants are a stylish and practical solution. Suspended from the ceiling or high shelves, they're completely out of reach from little ones. **Spider plants** and **philodendrons** do well in hanging baskets and add a lovely touch to any room.

High Shelves and Plant Stands: Another option is to place plants on high shelves or tall plant stands. Just make sure the shelf is stable, so there's no risk of the whole thing tipping over. Succulents and small palms do well on shelves, adding a green touch without taking up floor space.

Room Dividers or Baby Gates: If moving plants up high isn't an option, consider using room dividers or baby gates to section off an off-limits plant area. This is especially useful for larger plants like fiddle leaf figs or rubber trees that can't be moved easily but still need protection from tiny hands.

Cover the Soil: A Bug Barrier and Dirt Deterrent

Soil is like a playground for bugs (and kids who love to dig), so keeping it covered can prevent both insects and curious fingers from causing trouble.

Decorative Rocks or Pebbles: One of the easiest and most aesthetically pleasing ways to cover the soil is by adding a layer of decorative rocks or pebbles. Not only do they look great, but they also create a barrier that makes it harder for bugs like fungus gnats to lay eggs in the soil. Plus, it'll deter your child from trying to "garden" in your houseplant pot.

Bark Chips or Moss: Another option is to cover the soil with **bark chips** or **moss**. These materials make it more difficult for bugs to burrow and discourage kids from digging around in the dirt. Moss adds a soft, natural look to your plant pots, while bark chips are an excellent deterrent for bugs and create a clean appearance.

Fine Mesh Screens: If you're looking for an invisible solution, you can place a **fine mesh screen** over the soil. This acts as a bug barrier, keeping pests out of the soil while still allowing water and air to flow freely. Your child won't even notice it, but it'll keep both bugs and hands away from the dirt.

Use Child-Safe Pest Control

Despite your best efforts, bugs might still show up, and when they do, you'll want to use pest control that's safe for your child, your pets, and the environment.

Neem Oil: This all-natural insecticide is one of the best options for indoor plants. Safe for humans and pets, neem oil works by interfering with insects' life cycles, stopping them from reproducing. A spray of neem oil mixed with water will keep pests like aphids, mealybugs, and spider mites at bay without any harmful chemicals.

Diatomaceous Earth: This is a powder made from fossilized remains of tiny aquatic organisms. It's harmless to people and pets but lethal to insects. Sprinkle **food-grade diatomaceous earth** on the surface of the soil to kill bugs like ants, gnats, and beetles. It's safe, natural, and effective.

DIY Soap Spray: For a simple, safe bug killer, mix a small amount of **mild dish soap** with water and spray it on plants when you notice pests. This will suffocate insects like aphids and spider mites without harming your child or the environment.

Water Wisely: Don't Overdo It

Overwatering plants not only drown their roots but also create a bug paradise. Fungus gnats and other pests love moist environments, so learning to water your plants properly is key to preventing an infestation.

Water the Right Way: Let the top inch or two of soil dry out between waterings to discourage bugs from settling in. Make sure your pots have **good drainage**, so water doesn't pool at the bottom, creating a perfect breeding ground for pests.

Use Self-Watering Pots: These can help you avoid overwatering by providing a steady supply of moisture to the plant without soaking the soil. They also keep the surface dry, which is less attractive to bugs.

Teach Kids About Plant Safety

Kids are curious by nature, and while you can't always stop them from getting into everything, teaching them about plant safety can go a long way.

Make it a Fun Lesson: Turn plant care into a learning experience! Explain to your child why plants are important and how to touch them gently (or better yet not touch them at all). You can even give them their own small, safe plant to take care of—something durable like a **spider plant** or **succulent**—so they feel included.

Plant Helpers: Create a "plant helper" role for your child, where they can assist with watering or wiping down leaves. This will not only teach them responsibility but also make them more mindful of how to interact with plants.

Ensure your indoor plants stay bug-free and safe for your little one and your home. With the right balance of placement, care, and kid-safe pest control, your home will be a beautiful green oasis without any unwanted six-legged guests. Happy childproofing!

► According to the American Association of Poison Control Centers (AAPCC) , *Approximately **33,000 calls are made annually to poison control centers in the U.S. concerning children ingesting plant parts.** The majority of these cases involve toddlers who explore their surroundings by placing objects in their mouths.*

Dieffenbachia (Dumb Cane)

Toxicity: This plant harbors a secret weapon, calcium oxalate crystals. These tiny crystals, invisible to the naked eye, can unleash a fiery sensation in the mouth, making swallowing a Herculean task, and causing swelling if ingested.

Symptoms: Imagine a sudden burst of fiery dragons in one's mouth, causing a fierce battle with the taste buds. The aftermath is a scene of oral irritation, a waterfall of drooling, and a volcanic eruption of vomiting.

► *According to the American Association of Poison Control Centers, each year in the U.S., houseplants account for around **102,000 poison-control calls** involving children under six, leading to approximately **11,700 visits to doctors or Ers**. And about **150 of those are severe cases** requiring hospitalization. It's proof that even 'harmless' greenery can quickly turn into a childcare hazard.*

Philodendron

Toxicity: The Philodendron shares the same defense mechanism as Dieffenbachia. It is a master of disguise, hiding its potent calcium oxalate crystals within its lush green leaves.

Symptoms: Ingesting this plant can be likened to a spicy culinary experiment gone wrong, causing a swelling orchestra to play on the lips, tongue, and throat, accompanied by a symphony of vomiting and diarrhea.

Pothos (Devil's Ivy)

Toxicity: This plant, also known as Devil's Ivy, is a siren in the plant world. Enticing with its beautiful leaves, it hides insoluble calcium oxalates that can unleash a fiery storm in the mouth.

Symptoms: The encounter with this plant can feel like a dance with the devil, causing a fiery tango of intense burning and irritation in the mouth, lips, and tongue, leaving a trail of oral discomfort in its wake.

Oleander

Toxicity: The Oleander is the dark sorcerer of the plant kingdom, with every part of it holding a deadly potion. Even a small nibble can unleash a torrent of toxins, wreaking havoc on the body.

Symptoms: Ingesting this plant can set off a cascade of catastrophic events, including a volcanic eruption of vomiting, a tidal wave of diarrhea, a plummeting heart rate, and in severe cases, it can usher the victim into the arms of death.

ZZ Plant

Toxicity: This plant is like a fortress in the plant world, harboring calcium oxalate crystals within its thick leaves, ready to defend itself against a painful onslaught if ingested.

Symptoms: A bite into this plant can feel like an ambush, causing a sudden attack of oral irritation, a siege of pain, a barrage of drooling, and sometimes a volcanic eruption of vomiting.

Peace Lily

Toxicity: Despite its serene name, the Peace Lily hides a fiery secret within its elegant leaves a reservoir of calcium oxalate crystals ready to strike at unsuspecting invaders.

Symptoms: Falling prey to this plant can feel like a betrayal of trust, causing a fiery rebellion in the mouth, with the lips, tongue, and mouth rising in painful protest.

While all these plants add a splash of greenery and a breath of fresh air to our homes, they harbor secrets that can pose dangers to our little explorers. By transforming our homes into botanical sanctuaries, we must also weave a tapestry of safety and awareness. Let's educate ourselves and our children, creating a harmonious living space where curiosity meets safety. Always have a beacon of help ready. The contact information for poison control centers, and be prepared to seek medical attention swiftly if the adventure takes a dangerous turn.

Living Room/Family Room
Infant/Non-mobile: (Birth - 6 months)
→ **Infant crawl/roll: (5 months - 1 year)**
→ **Toddler/Pre-school: (1 year - 4 years)**
→ **School-age: (5 years - 6+ years)**

Plastic Artificial House Plants

Artificial plants are a fantastic way to add greenery to your home without the hassle of watering or worrying about bugs. But, like anything else in a house with kids, they come with their own set of safety concerns. While they don't need the same care as real plants, artificial plants can still pose risks if they're not properly childproofed. Here's how to keep your little one safe while still enjoying the low-maintenance beauty of faux greenery.

Choose High-Quality, Non-Toxic Materials

Not all artificial plants are created equal. Some are made with cheap plastics or materials that could be harmful if chewed on or inhaled. When shopping for artificial plants, look for ones that are made from **non-toxic materials**. Many high-quality artificial plants are now labeled as safe for homes with children and pets.

Avoid small, detachable parts: Choose plants with leaves and stems that are securely attached to avoid choking hazards. Some lower-quality plants might have small, detachable pieces that could become a problem if your child decides to play with them.

Look for BPA-free and PVC-free options: If possible, choose artificial plants made without harmful chemicals like BPA and PVC, which are common in cheap plastics. These materials are safer for curious kids who may touch or mouth the plants.

Stabilize Plants to Prevent Tipping

Kids are natural explorers, and there's a good chance your artificial plants will be pulled, tugged, or used as a climbing prop at some point. To avoid accidents, make sure your artificial plants are stable and won't tip over.

Heavy planters: Use heavy pots or planters to keep artificial plants grounded. A plant that tips easily can be a safety hazard, especially if your child tries to grab or lean on it.

Weighted bases: Some artificial plants come with lightweight bases. If that's the case, you can add weight to the bottom by placing heavy rocks or sand inside the pot. This will help keep the plant sturdy and less likely to fall over when nudged or pulled.

Place Plants Out of Reach

If your child is still in the "everything goes in the mouth" phase, consider placing artificial plants out of reach. Even though artificial plants don't require water, they can still be a target for curious hands and mouths.

Use high shelves or hanging planters: If the plant is small enough, place it on a high shelf or use a hanging planter to keep it out of your child's reach. This is especially helpful if your child tends to pull at leaves or chew on things.

Wall-mounted plants: Consider using wall-mounted planters or artificial plant frames. These keep the plants secure on the wall, away from little ones who might want to "garden" indoors.

Avoid Plants with Small, Loose Parts

Some artificial plants, particularly ones with intricate details, may have small, loose parts like fake berries, flowers, or detachable leaves. These can be a choking hazard if your child gets a hold of them.

Check for loose parts: Before placing an artificial plant in a child-accessible area, inspect it for any small pieces that could come off. If you find any, either secure them with a strong adhesive or choose a different plant.

No fake fruit: Avoid artificial plants that feature small fake fruits or berries, which might look like real food to a child and pose a choking risk.

Secure Plants with Adhesive or Brackets

If your child loves to grab and pull at everything, you might want to consider securing larger artificial plants to the floor or wall to prevent accidents.

Adhesive strips or putty: You can use strong adhesive strips or museum putty to secure the base of your artificial plants to the floor or furniture. This will make it harder for your child to knock the plant over or drag it around the house.

Brackets for larger plants: For taller artificial plants, consider using discreet wall brackets to secure them in place. This is particularly useful for large plants that could become dangerous if they fall over.

Teach Boundaries

While you can't childproof everything, teaching your child that artificial plants are for looking, not touching, can go a long way.

Simple rules: Create simple rules about where they can play and what they can touch. For example, designate certain areas of the house where plants are out of bounds.

Supervised exploration: Let them explore the plants under supervision and explain that these are decorations, not toys. Over time, they'll learn (hopefully!) that plants aren't part of their toy collection.

Regularly Inspect Plants

Even artificial plants can wear down over time, especially with kids and pets in the house. Regularly check your artificial plants for wear and tear, such as loose parts or fraying.

Tighten or replace loose pieces: If you notice any leaves or flowers starting to come loose, reattach them with a strong adhesive or replace the plant if necessary.

Clean regularly: Wipe down your artificial plants with a damp cloth to keep them dust-free. This not only keeps them looking fresh but also prevents dust buildup, which can be a respiratory irritant for children with allergies.

Childproofing plastic plants isn't difficult, but it's important to keeping your home a safe and fun place for both your kids and your decor. After all, the only thing better than a house filled with greenery is one where everyone big and small—can thrive safely!

Living Room/Family Room
→ **Infant/Non-mobile: (Birth - 6 months)**
→ **Infant crawl/roll: (5 months - 1 year)**
→ **Toddler/Pre-school: (1 year - 4 years)**
→ **School-age: (5 years - 6+ years)**

Combination of Air Fresheners and Ozone Concerns

Air fresheners and ozone generators are popular products used to improve indoor air quality and eliminate unpleasant odors. However, it's necessary to be cautious when using them, especially in households with children. Let's delve into the risks associated with these products and the precautions you should take to ensure your family's safety.

Air Fresheners

Many air fresheners, including sprays, plug-ins, and scented gels, contain chemical compounds that emit fragrance to mask unpleasant odors. While these products can create a pleasant ambiance, some of the chemicals they release may pose health risks, particularly if used excessively or in poorly ventilated areas.

Risks

Inhalation: Prolonged exposure to certain chemicals in air fresheners can lead to respiratory irritation and exacerbate existing respiratory conditions, such as asthma or allergies.

Ingestion: Children, especially toddlers and young kids, are naturally curious and may be tempted to taste or swallow air freshener products. Ingesting these chemicals can be harmful and cause adverse reactions.

Precautions

Read Labels: Look for air fresheners labeled as "non-toxic" or "natural" with fewer synthetic chemicals. Avoid products with harmful ingredients, such as phthalates and formaldehyde.

Ventilation: When using air fresheners, ensure proper ventilation by opening windows and allowing fresh air to circulate, reducing the concentration of chemicals in the air.

Placement: Keep air fresheners out of reach of children and pets to prevent accidental ingestion or exposure.

Limited Use: Avoid excessive use of air fresheners and use them only when necessary to minimize exposure to potentially harmful chemicals.

Ozone Generators

Ozone generators are devices that produce ozone, a powerful oxidizing gas, to remove odors and eliminate indoor pollutants. While ozone can effectively neutralize odors and some contaminants, it can also be harmful when present in high concentrations.

Risks

Respiratory Irritation: Ozone can irritate the respiratory system and lead to coughing, throat irritation, and shortness of breath, especially for individuals with asthma or other respiratory conditions.

Ozone Poisoning: Inhaling high levels of ozone can lead to ozone poisoning, which can cause severe respiratory distress and other health issues.

Precautions

Limited Usage: Ozone generators should only be used in unoccupied spaces to avoid direct exposure to ozone. Turn off the generator before entering the room.

Safe Levels: Ensure that the ozone generator is used within safe limits, as recommended by the manufacturer. Exceeding these limits can lead to hazardous levels of ozone in the air.

Ventilation: Adequate ventilation is crucial when using ozone generators to help disperse the ozone and reduce exposure.

Professional Use: If ozone generators are used for odor removal or purification, consider hiring professionals who are trained to handle the equipment safely.

Living Room/Family Room
Infant/Non-mobile: (Birth - 6 months)
→ **Infant crawl/roll: (5 months - 1 year)**
→ **Toddler/Pre-school: (1 year - 4 years)**
→ **School-age: (5 years - 6+ years)**

Potpourri Concerns

Potpourri, with its alluring scents and decorative appeal, can indeed pose potential dangers to children if not handled and stored properly.

Choking Hazard: Many potpourri mixes contain small decorative items like beads, stones, or shells that are attractive to young children. These items can present a choking hazard if ingested, especially for infants and toddlers who tend to explore the world through their mouths.

Gastrointestinal Blockage: Swallowing larger pieces of potpourri or its components can lead to gastrointestinal blockage, which can cause discomfort and require medical attention.

Toxic Substances: Potpourri oils and liquid refreshers used to rejuvenate the scent can contain harmful chemicals if ingested. Some may contain essential oils that, when ingested, can cause irritation or poisoning.

Respiratory Irritation: The fumes from burning potpourri or using potpourri oil warmers can irritate a child's respiratory system, particularly those with asthma or respiratory sensitivities. Prolonged exposure to these fumes may lead to breathing difficulties and discomfort.

Precautions: Store potpourri and its components in a secure container, out of reach of young children, and avoid displaying them in areas accessible to curious hands. Supervise the use of potpourri-related products, especially when burning potpourri or using oil warmers. Ensure that children are not exposed to the fumes.

Safe Alternatives: If you wish to enjoy the scents of potpourri without the associated risks, consider using alternative methods like essential oil diffusers or scented candles. These can offer pleasant aromas without the decorative hazards.

Educate Your Child: Teach your child about the potential dangers of potpourri and why it's essential not to touch or consume it. Encourage open communication and assure them they can approach you if they come across potpourri or any other potential hazards.

Regular Inspection: Periodically check the potpourri and its container for any broken or small pieces that may pose a choking risk. Discard any damaged components immediately.

<u>**Living Room/Family Room**</u>
Infant/Non-mobile: (Birth - 6 months)
Infant crawl/roll: (5 months - 1 year)
→ **Toddler/Pre-school: (1 year - 4 years)**
→ **School-age: (5 years - 6+ years)**

Sliding Glass Door

Ensuring children's safety around sliding glass doors is vital, and implementing several precautionary measures can significantly reduce risks. These measures include installing door finger guards to prevent pinched fingers and applying safety film to the glass to avoid injuries from shattered glass. Establishing barriers or railings, utilizing childproof locks, and enhancing visibility with stickers or decals can further safeguard young ones. Additionally, educating children about the potential dangers and supervising them in these areas are crucial steps. Incorporating door alarms and anti-lift devices can provide extra security, alerting adults to any unauthorized access. Regular maintenance of the doors, including timely repairs and inspections, is essential to maintain a safe environment. By adopting these strategies, parents can foster a secure space for children to grow and explore without the risk of accidents associated with sliding glass doors. (For details refer to kitchen **Pg. 93**)

▶ According to the American Academy of Pediatrics or the Centers for Disease Control and Prevention. *In the U.S., over **58,000 door-related injuries** occur annually in children ages 0–4, and around **20,000 kids under 18** are treated each year for glass door or window injuries. This means that **thousands of preschoolers**, even in familiar home spaces, suffer from sliding glass door impacts, cuts, fractures, and even partial amputations every year.*

Living Room/Family Room
Infant/Non-mobile: (Birth - 6 months)
Infant crawl/roll: (5 months - 1 year)
→ **Toddler/Pre-school: (1 year - 4 years)**
→ **School-age: (5 years - 6+ years)**

Window Blind String Concerns

Each year, **more than 1,000** suffer strangulation or entanglement injuries from window blind cords in the U.S., emphasizing the need for cordless window treatments. (Source: Safe Kids Worldwide - Strangulation Hazards)

    Cordless Blinds or Curtains: Consider using cordless blinds or curtains to eliminate the risk of entanglement. Cordless options are increasingly available and provide a safe alternative for homes with young children. Each year, approximately **3,000 children** are injured by window treatments such as drapes and curtains, including strangulation and falls. (Source: Safe Kids Worldwide)

    Shorten and Secure Cords: If cordless blinds are not an option, ensure that window blind cords are safely out of reach. Shorten the cords and secure them to the wall using a cord cleat or tie-down device. Keep the cords taut to prevent any loops or dangling cords that could be hazardous.

    Retrofit with Safety Devices: Consider retrofitting older blinds with safety devices such as cord cleats, cord tensioners, or cord wraps. These devices can help to keep cords securely in place and prevent accidental pulling or tangling.

    Position Furniture Wisely: Arrange furniture away from windows and blinds to prevent children from climbing and accessing the cords. Keep cribs, beds, and play areas away from blinds and windows.

    Supervise and Educate: Supervise children when they are in rooms with window blinds and educate them about the potential dangers of blind cords. Teach them not to play with the cords and explain why they should stay away from them.

Use Safety Kits: Consider using safety kits designed specifically for window blind cords. These kits often include cord wraps, cord stops, and other safety devices to secure and manage the cords safely.

Inspect and Maintain Blinds: Regularly inspect blinds for any signs of wear, fraying, or damage to the cords. Replace or repair any damaged cords immediately.

Be mindful of Older Blinds: If you move into a new home or apartment with older blinds that lack safety features, prioritize updating them or using temporary solutions like cord cleats until safer blinds can be installed.

Advocate for Safer Blinds: Be an advocate for child safety by spreading awareness of the dangers of blind cords and encouraging others to take appropriate precautions.

Remember that window blind cord safety is an ongoing process, especially as children grow and explore their environment. Regularly reassess and update your safety measures to ensure your child's well-being and minimize potential hazards. By following these guidelines, you can create a safer living space for your little ones and prevent accidents related to window blind cords.

<u>Living Room/Family Room</u>
Infant/Non-mobile: (Birth - 6 months)
Infant crawl/roll: (5 months - 1 year)
→ **Toddler/Pre-school: (1 year - 4 years)**
→ **School-age: (5 years - 6+ years)**

Consider Installing Shatter Proof Windows

Opting for Plexiglass or shatterproof glass over regular glass can significantly enhance safety in different environments.

Increased Impact Resistance: Plexiglass and shatterproof glass are engineered to be much stronger than regular glass, making windows highly resistant to impacts. This is especially valuable in high-traffic areas, homes with active children or pets, schools, and public spaces prone to accidental bumps and knocks.

Reduced Risk of Breakage: The durability of Plexiglass and shatterproof glass means they are less likely to crack or break even under considerable pressure or stress. This can be particularly advantageous in areas with heavy machinery, recreational spaces, or construction sites, where accidents can occur.

Safer for Play Areas and Children's Rooms: Using Plexiglass or shatterproof glass in play areas and children's rooms provides an added layer of safety. In the event of rough play or accidental collisions, these materials are less likely to break and cause harm to children.

Enhanced Security: In commercial settings, businesses can improve security by using Plexiglass or shatterproof glass in windows and doors. These materials make it more difficult for intruders to break in, providing an additional level of protection.

Impact-Resistant Windows and Doors: In regions prone to severe weather, such as hurricanes or tornadoes, using Plexiglass or shatterproof glass in windows and doors can help protect homes and buildings from flying debris and other hazards.

Reduced Injury Risk: Unlike regular glass, Plexiglass, and shatterproof glass do not shatter into sharp and dangerous pieces when broken. This significantly reduces the risk of injury, making them a safer choice for various applications, including public spaces and sports facilities.

Versatile Applications: Plexiglass and shatterproof glass can be used in a wide range of applications, including windows, doors, skylights, displays, signage, protective barriers, and even eyewear. Their versatility makes them suitable for both residential and commercial settings.

Easy Maintenance: Plexiglass and shatterproof glass are easy to clean and maintain, making them practical choices for busy environments such as restaurants and retail stores.

Eco-Friendly Option: Plexiglass is a form of acrylic plastic, which is more environmentally friendly than traditional glass manufacturing processes.

By opting for Plexiglass or shatterproof glass, individuals and businesses can significantly enhance safety and minimize potential hazards. Whether protecting children at play, ensuring the safety of public spaces, or fortifying against extreme weather conditions, these materials offer valuable safety benefits, providing peace of mind to homeowners, businesses, and facility managers alike.

Living Room/Family Room
Infant/Non-mobile: (Birth - 6 months)
Infant crawl/roll: (5 months - 1 year)
→ **Toddler/Pre-school: (1 year - 4 years)**
→ **School-age: (5 years - 6+ years)**

French Door Concerns

Child Safety Locks: Install child safety locks on French doors to prevent your child from opening them without your knowledge. These locks can be placed at the top or bottom of the doors and may require a key or a specific action to unlock, ensuring that only adults can operate them.

Doorknob Covers: Consider using doorknob covers, which are affordable and easy to install. These covers fit over the doorknob and prevent children from turning it, effectively keeping the doors securely closed.

Safety Gates: Safety gates can be installed at the entrance of the French doors to restrict access for families with very young children. They are especially useful in areas where close supervision might be challenging.

Window Film: Adding shatter-resistant window film to the glass of the French doors can reduce the risk of injury in case of an impact. The film holds the glass together, minimizing the chances of dangerous shards scattering in the event of an accident.

Keep Keys Out of Reach: If your French doors have locks that require a key to unlock, ensure that the keys are kept out of reach of children. Consider using a keychain or a high shelf for safekeeping.

Supervision and Education: While childproofing measures are essential, nothing replaces the importance of supervision and education. Teach your child about the hazards associated with opening doors without an adult present and encourage them to seek your assistance when needed.

Proper Door Maintenance: Regularly inspect the French doors to ensure they are functioning correctly. Fix any loose hinges, handles, or locks promptly to maintain their effectiveness in childproofing.

Avoid Placing Furniture Near Doors: Be cautious when positioning furniture near the French doors. Children might use it as a climbing aid to reach the doorknobs or locks. Keep furniture away from the doors to eliminate this potential risk.

Secure Blind or Curtain Cords: If your French doors have blinds or curtains with cords, make sure to secure them out of your child's reach. Use cord cleats or tie-down devices to keep the cords safely out of the way.

You can create a secure environment for your child and have peace of mind knowing that they are protected from potential hazards associated with French doors. Remember that ongoing supervision and communication are essential in keeping your child safe.

> ► *Each year in the U.S., the equivalent of* **tens of thousands of toddlers and preschoolers, many under age 4, are injured by glass-panel doors like French or patio doors.** *A 1999–2008 study published in the journal Injury Prevention found that 41% of all door-related injuries occurred in children aged 4 or younger. Hospital reviews note that glass doors can cause deep lacerations damaging nerves or arteries. In real-world incidents, simple moments like running into an unmarked door have led to emergency room visits and even surgery.* (Consumer Product Safety Commission)

Living Room/Family Room
Infant/Non-mobile: (Birth - 6 months)
Infant crawl/roll: (5 months - 1 year)
→ **Toddler/Pre-school: (1 year - 4 years)**
→ **School-age: (5 years - 6+ years)**

Window Air Conditioner Concerns

Annually, **more than 2,500 children** are injured by window air conditioners, including falls and electrical hazards. (Source: Centers for Disease Control and Prevention (CDC) – WISQARS)

Regular Maintenance: Inspect and maintain the AC unit regularly to ensure that it is functioning correctly and safely. Check for any loose or damaged parts and promptly repair or replace them.

Install a Window Lock: In addition to using a window guard, consider installing a window lock to secure the window in a closed position when the AC unit is in use. This prevents children from accidentally opening the window and accessing the unit.

Use a Window Air Conditioner Bracket: For added stability, consider using a window air conditioner bracket that attaches the AC unit to the window frame. This helps prevent the unit from tipping or falling, especially in the event of an accidental push or bump.

Secure Window Blind Cords: If there are window blinds or curtains near the AC unit, ensure that the cords are safely secured and out of reach of children. Loose cords can pose a strangulation risk.

Use Window Stops: Window stops or wedges can be installed to limit the window's opening to a safe level. This prevents children from accidentally opening the window wide enough to reach the AC unit.

Keep Remote Controls out of Reach: If the AC unit comes with a remote control, keep it out of the reach of children. Consider storing it in a designated place when not in use.

Supervise Around the AC Unit: Always supervise children when they are in the vicinity of the window AC unit. Educate them about the potential dangers and remind them not to touch or play with the unit.

Secure Window Blinds or Curtains: If the AC unit is located near blinds or curtains, make sure they are properly secured to avoid tangling or entanglement hazards.

Use Childproof Window Locks: Childproof window locks or window guards can be installed to prevent children from opening the window themselves. These locks require an adult to unlock or release the window for safe operation.

Teach Emergency Procedures: Teach older children how to safely operate the AC unit and what to do in case of an emergency, such as overheating or unusual noises.

Being proactive in childproofing your window AC unit, you can create a safer environment for your child and have peace of mind knowing that potential hazards are minimized. Always prioritize safety and vigilance to ensure your child's well-being around household appliances and fixtures.

Living Room/Family Room
Infant/Non-mobile: (Birth - 6 months)
→ **Infant crawl/roll: (5 months - 1 year)**
Toddler/Pre-school: (1 year - 4 years)
School-age: (5 years - 6+ years)

NO BABY WALKERS

Baby walkers may appear to be a convenient aid for parents to assist their infants in learning to walk, but it's crucial to recognize the significant dangers they pose to children.

Delayed Motor Skills Development: Contrary to popular belief, baby walkers can delay the development of essential motor skills, as they do not allow infants to learn proper balance and weight distribution needed for independent walking.

Stair-Related Injuries: The mobility of baby walkers can lead to falls down stairwells or over ledges, resulting in severe injuries. The speed and unpredictability of movement can make it difficult for parents to react quickly enough to prevent accidents.

Lack of Supervision: Even with attentive parents, it can be challenging to constantly monitor a child in a baby walker. This lack of supervision may lead to accidents or dangerous situations.

Accessibility to Hazards: Baby walkers can grant access to hazards that are typically out of reach for crawling infants. For instance, children in walkers may reach sharp objects, toxic cleaning products, or electrical outlets, increasing the risk of injuries or poisoning.

Burns and Scalds: Baby walkers can allow babies to access hot surfaces or liquids that they would not normally be able to reach, leading to burns or scalds.

Strain on Legs and Hips: Baby walkers can place stress on an infant's legs and hips, potentially leading to discomfort or developmental issues.

Use on Uneven Surfaces: Using baby walkers on uneven surfaces, such as patios or driveways, can be especially dangerous, as they may tip over or become unstable.

Safety Standards and Regulations: Due to safety concerns, some countries have banned or strictly regulated the sale and use of baby walkers.

Safer Alternatives: Instead of using baby walkers, consider alternatives that promote safe exploration and development, such as stationary activity centers, playpens, or simply allowing your child to learn to walk at their own pace without aids.

Parents can prioritize their child's safety and well-being during this crucial developmental stage by understanding the risks associated with baby walkers and opting for safer alternatives. Always consult with pediatricians and child safety experts for guidance on appropriate aids and childproofing measures.

- *According to Consumer Report. 2021–2023: An estimated **2,467 injuries per year involving baby walkers, jumpers, or exercisers** were treated in U.S. emergency departments for children under 5 years old. 2023: **Over 3,000 injuries** were reported from baby walkers, jumpers, and exercisers combined. 2014–2023: Baby walkers or jumpers accounted for **34,558 nursery equipment injuries**, ranking 9th among nursery products.*

Living Room/Family Room
Infant/Non-mobile: (Birth - 6 months)
→ **Infant crawl/roll: (5 months - 1 year)**
→ **Toddler/Pre-school: (1 year - 4 years)**
→ **School-age: (5 years - 6+ years)**

Money Concerns

While money is an essential part of our daily lives, it poses unexpected hazards to young children. Coins can be especially dangerous for curious toddlers who are still in the phase of exploring the world through their mouths.

Choking Hazard: The most immediate risk money presents is choking. Coins are just the right size to become lodged in a child's airway. Their shiny appearance and easy-to-grasp size make them particularly attractive to little ones, increasing the risk of ingestion.

Toxicity Concerns: Some coins contain metals that can be toxic if ingested. Prolonged contact with or swallowing certain coins can lead to metal poisoning, which can have serious health implications.

Bacterial Transmission: Money changes hands frequently and can carry a multitude of germs. Children who handle money and then touch their mouths or eyes can be exposed to a range of bacteria and viruses.

Injury from Sharp Edges: While not as common, paper money or damaged coins can have sharp edges that might cut or scratch the skin.

To ensure safety, keep money out of children's reach, regularly clean and sanitize storage areas, and educate older siblings about safeguarding it from their younger siblings.

Living Room/Family Room
Infant/Non-mobile: (Birth - 6 months)
Infant crawl/roll: (5 months - 1 year)
→ **Toddler/Pre-school: (1 year - 4 years)**
→ **School-age: (5 years - 6+ years)**

Hidden Dangers of Knickknacks

Knickknacks, with their intriguing designs and colors, often captivate the attention of many, especially young children. However, beneath their decorative charm lie potential risks that parents and caregivers should be aware of.

Choking Hazards: Due to their small size, children might mistake Knickknacks for toys, placing them in their mouths. This poses a significant choking risk, especially for toddlers.

Injury Risks: Some Knickknacks may have sharp edges or parts that can break off, leading to cuts or other injuries.

Safety Measures

Elevated Placements: Keep decorative items on higher shelves or surfaces well out of your child's reach.

Childproof Cabinets: If stored in cabinets, ensure they are equipped with childproof locks to prevent curious hands from accessing them.

Regular Inspection: Periodically check areas where children play or spend time to ensure no small items have been left within their grasp.

Education: Talk to children about the difference between toys and decorative items. Emphasize the importance of not putting unfamiliar objects in their mouths.

While Knickknacks add aesthetic appeal to our homes, it's essential to recognize and mitigate the risks they pose to young children. By implementing safety measures and fostering open communication, we can ensure a harmonious balance between a beautifully decorated home and a safe environment for our little ones.

► *From 1995 to 2015, **over 750,000 U.S. children under age 6 were treated in emergency rooms after swallowing small household items like figurines,** coins, or beads, an average of 100 incidents per day. Research shows these objects, especially spherical ones, are among the most likely to dangerously block a toddler's airway.* (Foreign-body ingestions of young children treated in US emergency departments)

|Ch. 3| Kitchen

Introduction: The kitchen, often referred to as the heart of the home, is a bustling hub of activity, filled with enticing aromas, intriguing gadgets, and the promise of delicious meals. Yet, for all its warmth and allure, it also presents a myriad of potential hazards, especially to curious little ones. From sharp utensils to hot surfaces and from toxic cleaning agents to easily accessible cabinets, the kitchen can be a veritable minefield for children. As we delve into this chapter, we will explore comprehensive strategies and practical tips to transform your kitchen into a safe haven, ensuring that your child's exploratory adventures don't turn into dangerous misadventures. Let's embark on this essential journey of safeguarding the space where family memories are often made, ensuring it remains a place of joy, bonding, and safety.

Testimonial: *When we moved into our new home, the kitchen was the highlight for me. I loved its modern design, never imagining it could become a danger zone for my two-year-old, Lily. One evening, as I was preparing dinner, Lily managed to climb onto a chair and reach for a pot handle, spilling hot soup on herself. The terror in her eyes and her cries still haunt me. Thankfully, after a trip to the ER, her burns healed, but I couldn't shake the guilt for not anticipating this. I wish I had childproofed the kitchen sooner—securing pot handles, using the back burners, and installing stove guards. I now understand how crucial it is to make even the most familiar spaces safe. My hope in sharing this is that other parents take steps to childproof their kitchens, protecting their little ones from avoidable accidents.*

- Emma R. (Mother of 2)

Kitchen
Infant/Non-mobile: (Birth - 6 months)
Infant crawl/roll: (5 months - 1 year)
→ **Toddler/Pre-school: (1 year - 4 years)**
→ **School-age: (5 years - 6+ years)**

Sliding Glass Doors

Children's safety around sliding glass doors is crucial, and taking the right precautions can make all the difference.

Door Finger Guards: Kids' curious fingers can easily get caught in a glass door's sliding mechanism, leading to painful pinched fingers. Install door finger guards or stoppers to prevent the door from closing completely, creating a safe gap for little hands.

Safety Glass: Sliding glass doors are often made of standard glass that can shatter into dangerous shards if broken. Consider replacing or adding a safety film to the glass that holds the pieces together upon impact, reducing the risk of injuries from broken glass.

Barriers or Railings: If the sliding glass door leads to a balcony, deck, or patio, install a sturdy barrier or railing to prevent accidental falls. Make sure the railing has vertical bars close enough together to prevent a child from squeezing through.

Childproof Locks: Ensure that the sliding glass door has a lock that is high enough to be out of reach of little hands. Childproof locks or latches can prevent young children from opening the door without adult supervision.

Visibility Stickers or Decals: Sliding glass doors can sometimes be difficult for children to see, leading to accidental collisions. Apply colorful stickers or decals at a child's eye level to increase visibility and prevent collisions.

Supervision and Education: Always supervise young children around sliding glass doors and educate them about the potential dangers. Teach them not to play with the door and explain the importance of safety rules.

Door Alarms: Consider installing a door alarm that sounds when the sliding glass door is opened. This can serve as an extra safety measure, alerting you if your child attempts to open the door without your knowledge.

Anti-Lift Devices: To enhance security, install anti-lift devices on the sliding glass door track to prevent unauthorized lifting of the door from the outside.

Regular Maintenance: Regularly inspect the sliding glass door, tracks, and locks for any signs of wear and tear. Replace or repair any damaged components promptly to ensure the door functions safely.

Always be vigilant and keep in mind that childproofing is an ongoing process as your child grows and explores their surroundings. A little precaution and attention can go a long way in preventing accidents and ensuring the well-being of your little ones.

<u>Kitchen</u>
Infant/Non-mobile: **(Birth - 6 months)**
Infant crawl/roll: **(5 months - 1 year)**
→ **Toddler/Pre-school: (1 year - 4 years)**
→ **School-age: (5 years - 6+ years)**

Kitchen Island

With their blend of functionality and aesthetic appeal, kitchen islands have become a centerpiece in many modern homes. However, their prominence and accessibility from all angles introduce a set of safety concerns, particularly for households with young explorers. Approximately **150,000 children**

are treated for burns and scalds from hot foods and beverages each year in the U.S., often occurring during meal preparation or consumption. (Source: American Burn Association (ABA) - Burn Statistics)

Risks

360-Degree Access: Kitchen islands' all-around accessibility means that tools like sharp knives and hot surfaces are within easy reach of children. While this design is convenient for cooking, it can inadvertently invite curious hands to potential dangers.

Drawers as Steps: Many islands come equipped with drawers, which toddlers might perceive as steps. This can lead to them climbing the island, increasing the risk of falls or accessing items they shouldn't.

Mobile Islands: There is the added risk of movement for islands on wheels. Children's fingers or toes could get trapped, leading to painful pinches or more severe injuries.

To counter these risks

Use Rear Burners: When cooking, prioritize the burners further away from the edges. This minimizes the chances of children accidentally touching hot surfaces.

Safety Locks: Use childproof locks to equip drawers, especially those containing hazardous items like knives. This simple measure can prevent many potential accidents.

Maintain a Clutter-Free Zone: Keeping the kitchen island and its vicinity clear reduces tripping hazards and ensures a safer environment.

Above all, supervision remains paramount. Always ensure an adult is present and vigilant when children are in the kitchen. Educating your children about potential dangers and establishing kitchen safety rules can further reinforce safe behaviors.

While kitchen islands offer convenience and style, they also come with responsibilities. By recognizing and addressing these safety concerns, families can enjoy the benefits of their kitchen island without compromising the safety of their youngest members.

▶ *Kitchen islands, central to family life, double as hidden hazards for little ones. Falls from islands contribute **significantly to the 2.5 million annual fall related ER visits in children under 5**, while the kitchen remains the top site for burns. 20–30% are caused by contact with hot objects like pots and pans.*

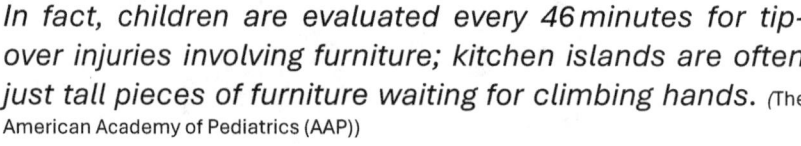

In fact, children are evaluated every 46 minutes for tip-over injuries involving furniture; kitchen islands are often just tall pieces of furniture waiting for climbing hands. (The American Academy of Pediatrics (AAP))

Kitchen
Infant/Non-mobile: (Birth - 6 months)
Infant crawl/roll: (5 months - 1 year)
→ **Toddler/Pre-school: (1 year - 4 years)**
→ **School-age: (5 years - 6+ years)**

Hydro Garden

Growing fresh herbs in your kitchen is a delight, but tiny hands don't mix well with delicate greens or electric setups.

> **Secure any electric components:** If your hydroponic garden has lights or water pumps, make sure all cords are tucked away with cord organizers or clips. Consider a cord cover to prevent curious fingers from yanking anything.
>
> **Create a barricade:** Place the hydro garden on a counter that is out of reach or use a small, clear guard to shield the plants and equipment from little hands.
>
> **Choose a plant-safe barrier:** You can use mesh or a fabric barrier that allows light through but prevents kids from accessing the garden.
>
> **Use non-toxic plants:** If your child reaches a leaf or two, ensure the plants are non-toxic. Stick to familiar kitchen herbs that won't harm a child if ingested.

Kitchen
Infant/Non-mobile: (Birth - 6 months)
→ **Infant crawl/roll: (5 months - 1 year)**
→ **Toddler/Pre-school: (1 year - 4 years)**
→ **School-age: (5 years - 6+ years)**

Tablecloths Vs. Placemats

Setting your table with a tablecloth or placemats adds both practicality and aesthetics. When childproofing dining areas, each option has its benefits and potential risks, especially with young children. Let's explore both to find the better choice for families with little ones.

Tablecloths

Risks

Pulling Hazard: Scald burns result in **over 2,500 hospitalizations of children** annually in the United States, often occurring in the kitchen or bathroom. Source: American Burn Association (ABA) - Burn Incidence Statistics Young children, especially toddlers, might be tempted to pull on the edges of tablecloths. This can cause dishes, hot beverages, or other items to tip over, posing a risk of burns or injuries.

Tripping Hazard: A tablecloth hanging too low can become a tripping hazard for children as they move around the table.

Prevention

Secure Fasteners: Consider using tablecloth clips or weights to secure the cloth, reducing the risk of it being pulled off.

Shorter Length: Opt for tablecloths that don't hang too low, minimizing tripping hazards.

Placemats

Risks

Chewing and Biting: Some children might be tempted to chew or bite on the edges of table mats, especially if they're teething.

Slipping: If not appropriately secured, mats can slide off the table or be thrown by little hands, potentially taking dishes or utensils with them.

Prevention

Non-Toxic Materials: Ensure that the table mats are made of non-toxic, BPA-free materials, especially if children might chew on them.

Anti-Slip Backing: Choose place mats with anti-slip backing to prevent them from easily moving or sliding off the table.

Which is Better? Place mats generally present fewer risks than tablecloths. They are typically more stable, don't have hanging edges that can be pulled or tripped over, and can be easily cleaned. While tablecloths offer a more traditional and sometimes elegant look, place mats are the safer choice from a childproofing perspective.

▶ *Though no national registry logs 'tablecloth pull' injuries, experts estimate tens of thousands of related injuries each year: about* **10,000 high-chair falls** *alone involve kids yanking items like placemats or hot plates, and over* **560,000 tip-over injuries.** *Including those from pulling cloths, affect children under six. Even a simple placemat slipping underfoot has led to broken bones in toddlers. (Nationwide Children's Hospital)*

Kitchen
Infant/Non-mobile: (Birth - 6 months)
Infant crawl/roll: (5 months - 1 year)
→ **Toddler/Pre-school: (1 year - 4 years)**
→ **School-age: (5 years - 6+ years)**

Garbage/Recycling Cans

Childproofing your garbage and recycling cans is crucial to child safety in the home. Children are naturally curious and may not understand the potential hazards associated with these containers.

Choose childproof lids: Opt for garbage and recycling can lids that are specifically designed to be difficult for a child to open. Look for options with locking mechanisms or lids that require a certain amount of force to open. These features can prevent your child from accidentally accessing the contents and potentially encountering harmful or sharp objects.

Keep cans out of reach: Store your garbage and recycle cans in a location that is not easily accessible to your child. Consider placing them in a locked cabinet or in a room that is off-limits to children. You can prevent your child from interacting with the cans without adult supervision.

Educate your child: Take the time to explain to your child the dangers associated with playing with garbage and recycling cans. Teach them that these containers are not toys and should never be touched or opened without an adult present. Reinforce the importance of following safety rules and respecting boundaries.

Properly dispose of hazardous materials: Be diligent in disposing of hazardous materials like cleaning products, batteries, and electronics. Keep these items out of the reach of children and ensure they are disposed of following local regulations. Some communities offer specialized recycling programs for hazardous waste disposal, so be sure to take advantage of these resources.

Supervise and monitor: Even with childproof lids and proper storage, it's crucial to supervise your child's interactions with garbage and recycling cans. Accidents can still happen, so being present and attentive can prevent potential mishaps.

Create a safe recycling area: If your child is old enough to help with recycling, create a designated and secure area for them to participate in. Use bins that are child-friendly and place them away from potentially hazardous materials.

You can significantly reduce the risk of accidents and injuries related to garbage and recycling cans. Remember, it's essential to prioritize your child's safety and take proactive steps to create a secure environment at home.

<u>Kitchen</u>
Infant/Non-mobile: (Birth - 6 months)
Infant crawl/roll: (5 months - 1 year)
→ **Toddler/Pre-school: (1 year - 4 years)**
→ **School-age: (5 years - 6+ years)**

Footstool Concerns

Footstools can be helpful additions to homes but also present potential dangers to young children if proper safety precautions are not taken. One of the primary concerns with footstools is stability. An unstable or wobbly footstool can easily tip over when a child tries to use it, leading to injuries like bumps, bruises, or even more severe harm. To mitigate this risk, it's crucial to choose a footstool that is sturdy and has a wide, stable base.

Additionally, **the height of the footstool is important** to consider. A footstool that is too high for a child can make it challenging for them to use safely. They may struggle to climb onto it or lose their balance while standing on it, increasing the likelihood of a fall. Parents should select footstools with a height appropriate for their child's age and size, ensuring they can comfortably and safely use them.

Another aspect of footstool safety is **weight capacity**. Children may be tempted to carry items like toys or books onto the footstool with them. It's essential to ensure that the footstool can support the child's weight and any additional items they might bring. Check the weight limit specified by the manufacturer and adhere to it to prevent accidents.

Supervision is paramount as with any furniture or equipment involving young children. Parents should teach their children how to use the footstool safely, emphasizing the importance of using it for its intended purpose and not as a plaything. Never leave children unattended while they are using the footstool to reduce the risk of accidents.

In addition to the safety tips mentioned earlier, parents can also consider using footstools with **non-slip surfaces** to provide better traction for little feet. If the footstool has any sharp edges or corners, padding or covers can be added to make it safer for children.

By remembering these safety tips when choosing and using footstools, parents can minimize the risks and ensure their children remain safe while using these handy pieces of furniture. Remember, childproofing is an ongoing process, and vigilance is essential to keeping children safe in every aspect of their environment.

Kitchen
→ Infant/Non-mobile: (Birth - 6 months)
→ Infant crawl/roll: (5 months - 1 year)
→ Toddler/Pre-school: (1 year - 4 years)
→ School-age: (5 years - 6+ years)

Importance of Unplugging Appliances

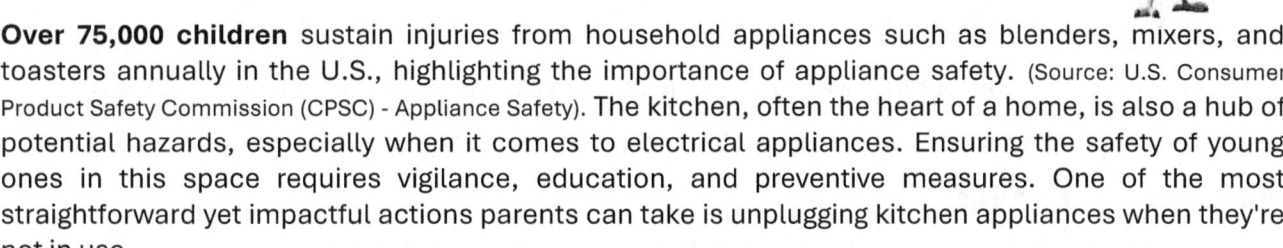

Over 75,000 children sustain injuries from household appliances such as blenders, mixers, and toasters annually in the U.S., highlighting the importance of appliance safety. (Source: U.S. Consumer Product Safety Commission (CPSC) - Appliance Safety). The kitchen, often the heart of a home, is also a hub of potential hazards, especially when it comes to electrical appliances. Ensuring the safety of young ones in this space requires vigilance, education, and preventive measures. One of the most straightforward yet impactful actions parents can take is unplugging kitchen appliances when they're not in use.

Electrical Safety: Children, with their innate curiosity, may fiddle with cords or buttons, leading to potential electrical shocks or burns. Simply unplugging eliminates the risk of a child accidentally turning on an appliance or getting shocked.

Prevention of Accidental Operations: Kids may unknowingly switch on appliances, leading to unintended operations. This is especially concerning with devices like toasters or blenders. Keeping appliances unplugged ensures they remain inactive, even if a child manages to turn them on.

Overheating and Fire Hazards: Even when not in active use, some appliances might overheat or malfunction if left plugged in for prolonged periods. Unplugging reduces the chances of electrical faults, thereby minimizing fire risks.

Reduced Chemical Exposure: Appliances like ovens might emit residual fumes when recently cleaned or after cooking certain foods. Keeping them unplugged and ensuring they are not accidentally turned on reduces the risk of children being exposed to these potentially harmful fumes.

Educational Benefits: Incorporating the habit of unplugging ensures safety and provides an opportunity to educate children. Parents can instill a sense of responsibility and awareness in their young ones by explaining the reasons and dangers. This proactive approach safeguards the present and equips children with knowledge for the future.

The act of unplugging kitchen appliances, while simple, plays a pivotal role in creating a child-safe environment. It's a proactive measure that, combined with education and supervision, ensures the kitchen remains a place of joy, learning, and safety for the entire family.

<u>Kitchen</u>
Infant/Non-mobile: (Birth - 6 months)
Infant crawl/roll: (5 months - 1 year)
→ **Toddler/Pre-school: (1 year - 4 years)**
→ **School-age: (5 years - 6+ years)**

Charging Area (Phones, Tablets, Etc...)

Out of Reach, Out of Harm's Way

High placement: Place charging stations on high shelves or countertops that are out of reach.

Cord management: Secure cords against the wall or furniture with cord covers or cable clips to prevent tripping hazards.

Electrical Safety

Outlet covers: Install outlet covers to prevent children from inserting objects into sockets.

Surge protectors: Use surge protectors to limit the risk of electrical shocks.

Preventative Measures

Supervision: Always supervise children around electrical outlets and cords.

Education: Teach children about the dangers of electricity and the importance of avoiding cords and outlets.

Additional Tips

Cordless charging: Consider using wireless charging pads for a cleaner and safer solution.

Charging station: Invest in a dedicated charging station with built-in cord management and safety features.

Regular checks: Regularly inspect the charging area for any damage to cords or outlets.

Specific Kitchen Considerations

Countertop clutter: Keep the countertop clear of clutter to prevent children from climbing on or reaching for cords.

Hot appliances: Be mindful of hot appliances like stoves and ovens when charging stations are placed.

Kitchen
Infant/Non-mobile: (Birth - 6 months)
→ **Infant crawl/roll: (5 months - 1 year)**
→ **Toddler/Pre-school: (1 year - 4 years)**
→ **School-age: (5 years - 6+ years)**

Kitchen Floor Safety

Small objects: Each year, approximately **2,000 children** under the age of 5 die in the U.S. from choking on food or small objects. (Source: National Safety Council (NSC) - Injury Facts) Young children have a natural curiosity and may pick up and put small objects in their mouths. Items like coins, beads, or even pet food can pose a choking hazard. To prevent such accidents, parents should regularly sweep or vacuum the floor to keep it clear of these small items. Additionally, it's crucial to teach children about the dangers of putting objects in their mouths and supervise them closely during playtime.

Slippery surfaces: Children are often active and may run or play on smooth or wet surfaces, such as hardwood or tile floors. This can lead to slips and falls, potentially causing injuries. Parents can use area rugs with non-slip backing in high-traffic areas or play zones to address this concern. Non-slip mats can also be placed near sinks or bathtubs to prevent slipping during water play. Providing slip-resistant footwear for children can further reduce the risk of accidents on slippery floors.

Sharp objects: If left on the floor, sharp objects like broken glass can cause cuts or puncture wounds. Regularly inspecting the floor for debris or hazards and promptly cleaning up or repairing the area can prevent accidents. It's also important to keep tools and sharp objects securely stored in locked cabinets or drawers, out of the reach of children.

Electrical cords: Electrical cords can be both a tripping hazard and an enticing plaything for young children. Parents should keep cords organized and out of the way to address this danger. Using cord covers or hiding cords behind furniture can prevent children from pulling on them or tripping over them. Additionally, securing cords with clips or ties can help keep them safely out of reach.

Parents can significantly reduce floor-related dangers through these straightforward precautions and consistent vigilance, fostering a safe place for their children to discover and roam. Continual efforts to childproof living areas, coupled with staying updated on potential threats, are pivotal in safeguarding the health and happiness of young children.

Kitchen
Infant/Non-mobile: (Birth - 6 months)
Infant crawl/roll: (5 months - 1 year)
→ **Toddler/Pre-school: (1 year - 4 years)**
→ **School-age: (5 years - 6+ years)**

Refrigerator Safety

Childproofing a refrigerator is like setting up a high-tech security system for the most mysterious vault in your home where the treasures of milk, cheese, and leftover pizza are kept!

The Lockdown

Magnetic Locks: Install childproof magnetic locks on the fridge doors. These are like secret agents, completely invisible until you need them. With a unique magnetic key, you can unlock the fridge, but your little one will think it's sealed by magic.

Strap It Up: Add an adjustable strap lock for extra security. It's like adding a seatbelt to your fridge, because safety first, right?

Handle the Handles

Handle Covers: Slip-on handle covers that require a two-handed twist to open can make sure that only someone with the strength of an adult can access the goodies inside.

Sticker Decoys: Decorate the fridge with funny stickers, but make sure to place them strategically right over the handle! Your child will be too busy trying to peel off the stickers to figure out how to open the door.

Top Shelf Shenanigans

Rearrange the Food: Keep all the tempting, snackable items (like yogurt and juice boxes) on the top shelves, out of reach. Place the broccoli and other less desirable foods on the bottom shelf. It's a win-win!

Disguise the Treats: Put treats in containers labeled with something boring, like "Mom's Kale Smoothies" or "Dad's Broccoli Snacks." Trust me, no child is going to dig into those!

Door of Danger

Fridge Mats: Use non-slip fridge mats that are easy to clean. They not only keep spills under control but also reduce the temptation to pull everything off the shelves.

Sensor Alarm: Install a fridge door alarm that goes off if the door is left open for too long. It's like having a bouncer at the fridge—no unauthorized entries allowed!

Ice Concerns

Ice Dispenser Lock: If your fridge has an ice or water dispenser, install a childproof lock on it. Little ones are fascinated by the magic of ice cubes, and before you know it, you'll have an indoor skating rink!

Remove Temptations: If the lock isn't enough, consider temporarily turning off the water supply to the dispenser or disabling it. Better safe than soggy!

The Great Shelf Escape

Shelf Guards: Install guards on the shelves to prevent items from being pulled out. These can be clear barriers that still allow you to see everything but stop those little hands from grabbing the goods.

Sliding Trays: Use sliding trays for easy access to food, but with a twist—make sure the trays lock in place when not in use. This way, your child can't yank them out and create a mini avalanche of food.

A Couple More Points

Creative Distraction: Add a magnetic chalkboard or whiteboard to the front of the fridge. Your child can draw or write while you cook, keeping them entertained and away from the fridge's treasures.

Fridge Guard Pets: Place some cute fridge magnets shaped like animals or monsters on the door. Tell your child they are the fridge guardians who keep the food safe from mischievous hands. It's a little white lie that works wonders!

By turning your refrigerator into a fortress, you ensure that your little one stays safe, and your food remains exactly where you left it unless, of course, it mysteriously vanishes in the middle of the night. (But that's a whole different childproofing challenge!)

Kitchen
Infant/Non-mobile: (Birth - 6 months)
Infant crawl/roll: (5 months - 1 year)
→ **Toddler/Pre-school: (1 year - 4 years)**
→ **School-age: (5 years - 6+ years)**

Breast Milk Safety

Breast milk is a natural and highly nutritious source of food for infants. It is generally safe and provides numerous health benefits for babies. However, to ensure breast milk safety, there are some guidelines and best practices that breastfeeding mothers should follow, according to the Centers for Disease Control and Prevention (CDC):

Clean Hands and Containers: Always wash your hands thoroughly with soap and water before expressing or handling breast milk. Store expressed milk in clean containers, bottles, or breast milk storage bags.

Proper Storage: Store breast milk in clean, BPA-free bottles or bags. Label each container with the date and time of expression to ensure you use the oldest milk first.

Refrigeration and Freezing: Breast milk can be safely stored in the refrigerator for up to four days at a temperature of 32-39°F (0-4°C). If you need to store it longer, freezing is an option. Frozen breast milk is safe for up to six months in a regular freezer (0°F or -18°C) or up to 12 months in a deep freezer (-4°F or -20°C).

Avoid Microwaving: Never microwave breast milk, as it can cause hot spots and destroy valuable nutrients. Instead, thaw frozen milk by placing the container in warm water or using a bottle warmer.

Gentle Thawing: If you have frozen breast milk, gently swirl the container to mix the separated layers. Do not vigorously shake the milk, as it can damage its components.

Avoid Adding Fresh Milk to Frozen Milk: Try to avoid adding freshly expressed milk to already frozen milk, as it can shorten the storage time for the combined batch.

Temperature Checks: Always check the temperature of the milk before feeding it to your baby. It should feel lukewarm, not hot.

Handling and Feeding: Use freshly expressed or thawed breast milk within two hours at room temperature. If it has been at room temperature for two hours or more, discard it.

Breast Pump Hygiene: If you use a breast pump, follow the manufacturer's instructions for cleaning and sterilization. Keeping the breast pump clean is essential to prevent contamination of expressed milk.

Alcohol and Medication: Be mindful of alcohol consumption and any medications you might be taking, as these substances can pass into breast milk and affect your baby.

Illness: If you have an infectious illness (e.g., flu, cold, etc.), consider consulting a healthcare professional before continuing breastfeeding. Breastfeeding can usually continue, but some precautions might be necessary.

Kitchen
→ **Infant/Non-mobile: (Birth - 6 months)**
→ **Infant crawl/roll: (5 months - 1 year)**
Toddler/Pre-school: (1 year - 4 years)
School-age: (5 years - 6+ years)

Baby Formula

According to The Food and Drug Administration (FDA) When it comes to baby formula, childproofing goes beyond just keeping it safe and stored, it's about ensuring that your little one doesn't accidentally turn into a mini chemist, mixing up concoctions that could rival a mad scientist's lab! Here's a creative and detailed guide to keeping baby formula safe, secure, and out of tiny hands.

The Storage- Fort Knox

High and Dry: Store baby formula in an airtight container on a high shelf, well out of reach. Make sure the shelf is inside a locked cabinet or pantry. You're creating a tiny, fortified vault without unauthorized access.

Double Seal Security: Use containers with double lids, one with a screw-top and an inner seal. This way, even if a curious little one gets into the pantry, they'll need some severe dexterity to get to the formula.

The Disguise

Container Camouflage: Hide the formula in a plain, boring container labeled something like "Mom's Protein Powder" or "Flour." Kids are smart, but they're not likely to find interest in something that sounds like adult stuff.

False Bottom Containers: You can even use a container with a false bottom. Place some uncooked pasta or rice on top and hide the formula underneath. It's like creating a secret compartment for your baby's most precious sustenance!

Measuring Safety

Lockable Measuring Spoons: Use measuring spoons with lockable handles. This ensures that even if your little one gets their hands on it, they won't be able to measure out any formula. No formula mixing without adult supervision!

Pre-Portioned Packs: Prepare pre-portioned formula packs in advance, sealed and stored in a childproof container. This way, you're not only making life easier for yourself, but you're also ensuring that only the correct amount of formula is available at any given time.

Mixing and Measuring

High-Tech Mixing Station: If you're using an automatic formula maker, ensure it's placed on a high countertop and unplug it when not in use. Consider placing a childproof lock on the power cord or the outlet to prevent little hands from turning it on.

Hidden Away: For manual mixing, store all mixing tools, like bottles and water, in a high, secure cabinet. You can also use a lockable kitchen drawer to keep all the necessary tools out of reach.

The Formula Lockdown

Smart Locks: Install smart locks on cabinets where you store formula or mixing tools. These can be controlled via an app, meaning only you or authorized users can unlock the cabinets when it's time to feed.

Invisible Locks: Use magnetic locks that are hidden inside the cabinets. They're invisible to curious eyes, and only the unique magnetic key can unlock the secrets within.

Creative Distraction

Formula Guard Toy: Place a fun, interactive toy on top of the formula container. Make it a ritual that the toy "guards" the formula, allowing access only when it's time to eat. This adds an element of fun while keeping things safe.

Secret Recipe Game: Turn formula mixing into a secret recipe game only you know how to play. Kids love games and will be more interested in watching you "create" the formula than trying to do it themselves.

The Final Flourish

Routine Ritual: Establish a feeding routine that's as regular as clockwork. This way, your baby associates feeding time with a specific time of day, reducing the likelihood that they'll try to access the formula on their own.

Distraction Stations: Set up a distraction station nearby with their favorite toys or books. This keeps them occupied while you prepare the formula, ensuring their attention is diverted from the "forbidden" area.

By being creative and proactive, you ensure that your baby's formula stays secure, and your little one stays safe from accidental spills, messes, or worse—unsupervised formula mixing! Your kitchen becomes a well-oiled machine where feeding time is both safe and stress-free, keeping your baby happy and healthy.

Kitchen
Infant/Non-mobile: (Birth - 6 months)
→ **Infant crawl/roll: (5 months - 1 year)**
→ **Toddler/Pre-school: (1 year - 4 years)**
→ **School-age: (5 years - 6+ years)**

Salmonella

Salmonella is a type of bacteria that can cause illness in humans, and young children are at a higher risk due to their developing immune systems.

Wash hands frequently: Encourage children to wash their hands regularly with soap and warm water. Ensure they wash their hands before handling food, using the bathroom, and playing outside. Handwashing is one of the most effective ways to prevent the transmission of bacteria.

Cook food thoroughly: When preparing meals, ensure that all food, especially meat, poultry, and eggs, are cooked thoroughly to kill any potential salmonella bacteria. Use a meat thermometer to check that the internal temperature of the food has reached a safe level to ensure it is fully cooked.

Store food properly: Promptly store cooked food in the refrigerator or freezer to prevent bacteria from multiplying. Avoid leaving perishable food items at room temperature for an extended period, as this can create an environment for bacteria growth. Discard any food that has been left out for more than two hours.

Clean surfaces and utensils: Regularly clean all kitchen surfaces and utensils with hot, soapy water, especially after handling raw meat, poultry, or eggs. Proper cleaning helps eliminate any potential cross-contamination and reduces the risk of salmonella transmission.

Avoid cross-contamination: To prevent cross-contamination, use separate cutting boards and utensils for raw meat, poultry, and eggs. Keeping these items separate from other foods helps minimize the risk of spreading bacteria to other ingredients.

Educate children about food safety: Teach children about the importance of food safety and hygiene practices. Explain why following these guidelines is essential to prevent illness and keep themselves and others healthy.

Creating a safe and hygienic environment will protect children from potential foodborne illnesses and promote good health and well-being. Remember, proper food handling and hygiene are essential for every family member's safety, especially for young children whose immune systems are still developing.

► *According to the FDA, The annual Impact in the U.S.: The Centers for Disease Control and Prevention (CDC) estimates **approximately 1.35 million cases of salmonellosis occur each year** in the United States, resulting in 26,500 hospitalizations and 420 deaths. According to the CDC, High-Risk Age Group: Children under 5 years old are particularly vulnerable. In a 2024 outbreak linked to backyard poultry, **43% of the infected individuals were under the age of 5.***

Kitchen
Infant/Non-mobile: (Birth - 6 months)
Infant crawl/roll: (5 months - 1 year)
→ **Toddler/Pre-school: (1 year - 4 years)**
→ **School-age: (5 years - 6+ years)**

Stove Safety

The kitchen, the stove stands as a central figure, often drawing the curiosity of little explorers. However, it is also a source of potential dangers for children aged 0-6 years. Here, we delve deep into the various strategies and tools that can be employed to childproof a stove effectively, ensuring a safe environment for your children to grow and learn.

Understanding the Risks: Before we delve into the specifics, it's essential to understand the potential risks associated with stoves. These appliances can be a source of burns, fire hazards, and even gas leaks if not properly secured. Children, with their innate curiosity, might attempt to turn knobs, reach for pots, or play with the stove, unaware of the dangers they pose.

Installing Stove Guards and Knob Covers

Stove Guards: These are barriers that prevent children from reaching pots and pans on the stove. They are generally easy to install and remove, making cleaning and maintenance hassle-free. Opt for guards made of heat-resistant materials to prevent melting or warping. Ensure the guard is tall and wide enough to prevent children from reaching over or around it.

Knob Covers: These are protective covers that prevent children from turning stove knobs. Consider transparent covers to allow adults to see the knob positions easily. Ensure the covers can be easily removed by adults in case of emergencies.

Maintaining a Safe Distance

Creating a Safety Zone: Establish a **"no-go" zone** around the stove.

Visual Cues: Use visual cues like floor mats or tape to delineate the safety zone.

Supervision: Always supervise children when they are in the kitchen, especially during cooking times. Safe Cooking Practices

Using Back Burners: Whenever possible, **use the back burners** to keep hot pots and pans out of reach of little hands.

Handle Positioning: Always turn the pot and pan handles towards the back of the stove to prevent children from pulling them down.

Stable Cookware: Use stable cookware to prevent tipping and spilling of hot contents.

Emergency preparedness

Fire Safety

Teach children about the dangers of fire and what to do in case of a fire emergency.

Fire Extinguisher: Keep a fire extinguisher nearby and ensure all adults know how to use it.

Emergency Numbers: Have emergency numbers readily available and teach older children how to call for help.

Caregivers can significantly reduce the risk of accidents and injuries associated with stoves. Remember, the goal is to foster a space where children can explore safely, nurturing their curiosity without compromising their well-being. Let's work together to create homes where safety and joy coexist harmoniously.

The Dangers of using an oven to heat your home

The kitchen is a hub of activity in many homes, filled with tools and appliances designed for cooking and baking. However, when it comes to heating, the oven should never be used as a substitute for a proper heating system. At the same time, it might seem like a quick solution during cold spells, using an oven to heat your home poses significant risks, especially when children are present.

Carbon Monoxide Risk

Gas Ovens: When left open and on for extended periods of time, gas ovens can produce carbon monoxide, an odorless and colorless gas. Inhalation can lead to carbon monoxide poisoning, which can be fatal, especially for young children with developing respiratory systems.

Ventilation Issues: Even if your home has good ventilation, prolonged use of an oven for heating can accumulate this harmful gas.

Fire Hazards

Flammable Objects: Kitchens often contain flammable items like paper towels, dishcloths, and wooden utensils. These types of items should be kept away from the oven. Never lay towels on top of the stove.

Overworking the Appliance: Ovens are not designed to run continuously. Extended use can cause them to overheat, leading to potential malfunctions and fire risks.

Burns and Injuries

Accessible to Children: Never leave the oven door open when children are around. Children might touch the open oven door out of curiosity or try to climb it, leading to severe burns.

Tripping Hazards: An open oven door can be a tripping hazard, especially for toddlers still mastering walking.

Inefficiency: Ovens are not designed to heat large spaces or entire homes. Using them in this manner is energy-inefficient and can lead to a spike in gas or electricity bills.

Education: Teach older children about the dangers of ovens and the importance of not playing near or with them. While the warmth of an oven might seem inviting, the risks associated with using it as a heating source far outweigh the temporary comfort it provides. For the safety of your children and everyone in the household, it's essential to invest in proper heating solutions and always prioritize childproofing measures in the kitchen.

<u>Kitchen</u>
→ **Infant/Non-mobile: (Birth - 6 months)**
→ **Infant crawl/roll: (5 months - 1 year)**
Toddler/Pre-school: (1 year - 4 years)
School-age: (5 years - 6+ years)

Highchair Safety

Highchairs are a common and essential baby product found in households with young children. However, parents and caregivers must understand the importance of securely strapping a child into a highchair to prevent potential safety concerns. Annually, **over 200,000 children** are injured by furniture and fixtures, including falling from highchairs, climbing on furniture, or being pinched by drawers and cabinets. (Source: Centers for Disease Control and Prevention (CDC) – WISQARS)

Falling Out: Active young children can easily wiggle or move around while seated in a highchair, and not being properly strapped in can lead to accidental falls. Falling from a highchair can result in injuries such as bruises, bumps, or more severe injuries like head trauma.

Slipping Down: Without proper strapping, children may slip down or slide off the highchair's seat. This can lead to discomfort and the risk of getting stuck in awkward positions, causing distress and possible injuries.

Accessing Hazardous Items: Burns from Hot Liquids and Steam Scald burns result in **over 2,500 hospitalizations of children** annually in the United States, often occurring in the kitchen or bathroom. (Source: American Burn Association (ABA) - Burn Incidence Statistics)

When not securely strapped into a highchair, children may have more freedom to reach out and grab items within their reach. This can include hot drinks, sharp utensils, or other dangerous objects on the dining table, leading to burns, cuts, or other injuries.

Difficulty Feeding: Choking Hazards Lead to Tragedy. Each year, approximately **2,000 children** under the age of 5 die in the U.S. from choking on food or small objects. (Source: National Safety Council (NSC) - Injury Facts)

Without being securely strapped into the highchair, a child may have trouble maintaining an upright and stable position for feeding. This can result in messy feeding sessions, poor eating habits, and an increased risk of choking hazards.

To ensure a child's safety when using a highchair, it's essential to strap them in properly before each use. Parents and caregivers should also closely supervise children while seated in the highchair to prevent any potential accidents. Regularly inspect the highchair for any signs of wear or damage that may affect its safety and follow the manufacturer's guidelines for maintenance and usage.

By taking these simple yet crucial precautions, parents can help minimize the potential risks associated with highchair use and create a safe and comfortable space for their child during mealtimes. Remember, child safety is a priority in every aspect of daily life, and using a highchair correctly is an important step in ensuring a child's well-being and preventing unnecessary accidents.

- *According to CPSC. Increase in Injuries: In 2023, U.S. emergency departments treated **14,484 high chair-related injuries, a 47.8% increase from 9,803 cases in 2014.***

- *Common Age Group:* **Children aged 7 to 23 months** *are most frequently injured, with high chairs being the leading cause of nursery equipment injuries in this age group.*

- *According to Nationwide Children's Hospital. Nature of Injuries:* **Approximately 94% of injuries result from falls, often due to climbing or standing in the chair.**

Kitchen
Infant/Non-mobile: (Birth - 6 months)
Infant crawl/roll: (5 months - 1 year)
→ **Toddler/Pre-school: (1 year - 4 years)**
→ **School-age: (5 years - 6+ years)**

Kitchen Counters

Let's discuss the potential dangers of children sitting on counters. While it might seem like a harmless activity, it can pose serious risks.

Falling: Children can easily lose their balance while sitting on a counter, and the height of the counter can make a fall even more dangerous. They could hit their head or suffer other injuries, which is why it's important to discourage them from sitting on counters.

Access to dangerous objects: Depending on what's on the counter, children may be able to reach objects that could harm them, such as knives, scissors, or hot pots and pans. This can put them at risk of burns, cuts, or other injuries.

Contamination: Counters in the kitchen will have contact with food, cleaning products, or other potentially harmful substances. Allowing children to sit on counters could lead to contamination if they touch these surfaces and then put their hands in their mouths.

Damage to countertops: Sitting or standing on countertops can cause damage over time, especially if children are active or fidgety while sitting.

Encouraging bad habits: Allowing children to sit on counters can encourage them to climb onto other high surfaces, such as tables or shelves, increasing the risk of falls and other accidents.

We recommend that parents and caregivers discourage children from sitting on counters. Instead, provide them with a safe and comfortable place to sit and play, such as a child-sized table or chair. It's essential to teach children about the potential risks and the importance of using appropriate furniture for sitting and playing. Additionally, always supervise children, especially in areas where potential hazards exist, to ensure their safety and prevent accidents.

Kitchen
Infant/Non-mobile: (Birth - 6 months)
Infant crawl/roll: (5 months - 1 year)
→ **Toddler/Pre-school: (1 year - 4 years)**
→ **School-age: (5 years - 6+ years)**

Dishwasher

To ensure the safety of children in the kitchen, it's crucial to take extra precautions with dishwasher detergent pods and other cleaning supplies. These colorful, candy-like pods can be enticing to little ones, but they are hazardous if ingested. To avoid any accidents, always keep these items out of reach and store them in a secure cabinet or drawer with childproof latches.

Regarding the dishwasher itself, **installing a latch or lock** on the dishwasher door is a wise move if you have younger children. This prevents them from opening the dishwasher and potentially accessing dangerous items inside, such as sharp knives or glassware. Alternatively, using a childproofing strap to secure the door of the dishwasher can be an effective safety measure.

An additional safety tip is to **promptly unload the dishwasher** once it completes its cycle. **Leaving sharp utensils** or potentially harmful items within reach of curious children can lead to painful accidents. Ensuring that all utensils are out of reach once the dishwasher is emptied helps prevent any mishaps.

Supervising your child around kitchen appliances, including the dishwasher, is essential for their safety and to teach them proper kitchen etiquette. By providing guidance and being present during kitchen activities, you can prevent accidents and instill good habits for when they are old enough to handle these appliances independently. Safeguarding your child in the kitchen involves securely storing cleaning supplies, childproofing the dishwasher door, unloading sharp items promptly, and providing supervision during kitchen tasks. These precautions not only keep your child safe but also contribute to a clean and hazard-free kitchen environment. By following these safety measures, you can ensure that your little one explores the kitchen safely while avoiding any potential mishaps.

Kitchen
Infant/Non-mobile: (Birth - 6 months)
Infant crawl/roll: (5 months - 1 year)
→ **Toddler/Pre-school: (1 year - 4 years)**
→ **School-age: (5 years - 6+ years)**

Cabinet Locks

Childproofing your cabinets is a crucial step in creating a safe environment for your child. Annually, **more than 15,000 children** are injured by sharp edges or entrapment in kitchen cabinets and drawers. (Source: Centers for Disease Control and Prevention (CDC) – WISQARS)

    Install childproof locks or latches: Childproof locks or latches are essential for cabinets containing hazardous items like cleaning supplies, sharp objects, or medications. Various options are available in the market, including adhesive locks, sliding locks, and magnetic locks. Choose the one that suits your needs and budget while providing an effective barrier.

    Consider locks for messy items: Even non-hazardous items like flour or sugar can create a mess if your child gains access to them. Consider using childproof locks on cabinets containing such items to avoid potential choking hazards and unnecessary cleanups.

    Always keep hazardous cabinets locked: Each year, **over 100,000 children** are exposed to dangerous household chemicals, leading to numerous emergency room visits for irritation, burns, or poisoning. Source: American Association of Poison Control Centers (AAPCC) - Annual Reports Children are speedy and curious, so it's crucial to keep cabinets containing hazardous items locked at all times, even when you are in the room. Accidents can happen in the blink of an eye, and prevention is the best strategy.

    Arrange necessities within reach: Make use of lower cabinets to store items your child frequently needs, such as dishes, snacks, or toys. This way, they won't be tempted to climb or reach for items in locked cabinets, reducing the risk of accidents.

Educate your child about cabinet safety: Explain to your child why certain cabinets are off-limits. Use simple and age-appropriate language to help them understand the importance of staying away from potentially dangerous items.

Remember, childproofing your cabinets is a continuous process. As your child grows and becomes more curious, you may need to reassess and update your childproofing measures. Regularly check the locks and latches to ensure they function correctly and adjust as needed

---

Kitchen
Infant/Non-mobile: (Birth - 6 months)
Infant crawl/roll: (5 months - 1 year)
→ **Toddler/Pre-school: (1 year - 4 years)**
→ **School-age: (5 years - 6+ years)**

CHAIRS WITH WHEELS

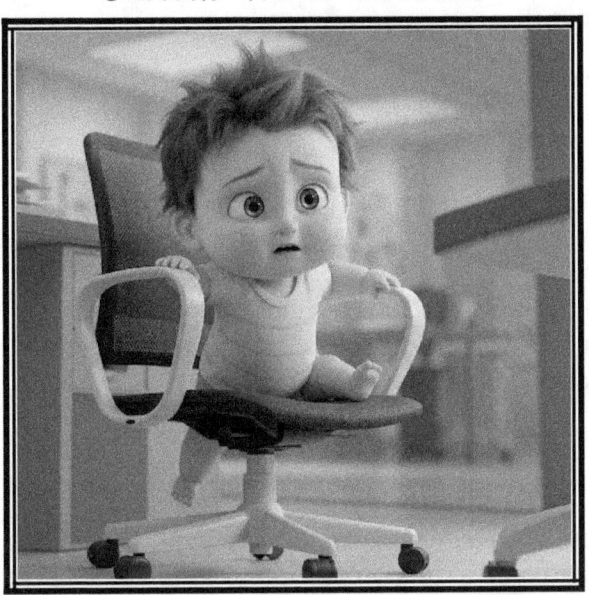

Rolling chairs can indeed pose significant dangers to young children, and as a safety expert, it's crucial to raise awareness about these risks and provide practical solutions.

Opt for child-friendly furniture: When selecting chairs for your home, consider child-friendly options that prioritize safety. Look for chairs with stable bases, rounded edges, and no moving parts that can pinch little fingers or toes. Sturdy, non-rolling chairs are generally safer for young children.

Create a designated play area: Designate specific areas in your home as safe play zones for children. Restrict rolling chairs from these spaces and ensure that they are equipped with child-friendly furniture and toys. This way, children can play freely without the risk of accidents from rolling chairs.

Supervise playtime: Active supervision is crucial when children are around rolling chairs or any potentially hazardous furniture. Parents and caregivers should closely monitor playtime and intervene if they notice any unsafe behavior or potential dangers.

Use chair stops or locking mechanisms: If you have rolling chairs in your home, consider using stops or locks to prevent them from moving freely. These devices can help keep the chairs stationary when not in use, reducing the risk of tip-overs or collisions.

Teach safe chair use: As children grow and become more independent, teach them about safe chair use. Encourage them to sit properly in chairs, avoid rocking or tilting, and be mindful of their surroundings to prevent accidents.

Clear the area: Ensure that the area around rolling chairs is free from obstacles or hazards that could cause collisions or accidents. Keep walkways clear to prevent tripping hazards and create a safe environment for children to move around.

You can minimize the risks associated with rolling chairs and provide a secure environment for children to play and explore in your home. Remember, a little foresight and proactive measures can go a long way in preventing accidents and ensuring the well-being of children.

<u>Kitchen</u>
Infant/Non-mobile: (Birth - 6 months)
Infant crawl/roll: (5 months - 1 year)
→ **Toddler/Pre-school: (1 year - 4 years)**
→ **School-age: (5 years - 6+ years)**

Install Ground Faults

Ground Fault Circuit Interrupters (GFCIs) are indispensable safety tools designed to shield households from electrical shocks. They play a pivotal role in minimizing electrical risks. Three primary GFCIs are tailored for residential use.

Receptacle Type GFCIs

Description: These are integrated into homes instead of conventional duplex outlets.

Function: They offer protection against ground faults when devices are connected to the socket. Impressively, they can also extend this protection to other outlets further along the same circuit, enhancing the safety quotient of your electrical setup.

Circuit Breaker Type GFCIs

Description: For homes equipped with circuit breakers, this GFCI variant can be incorporated into the panel box to shield selected circuits.

Function: In addition to guarding against ground faults, it also responds to short circuits or overloads. This ensures that the wiring and all electrical components linked to the protected branch circuit remain safe.

Portable Type GFCIs

Description: These are ideal when installing permanent GFCIs, which isn't practical. One design is encased in plastic, featuring plug blades at its rear and receptacle slots up front. This can be plugged into a standard outlet, offering GFCI protection to the connected device. Another design merges an extension cord with an in-built GFCI, granting flexibility for unprotected outlets.

Function: They provide temporary GFCI protection, especially useful for outlets that don't have built-in protection.

The National Electrical Code mandates GFCI protection in specific home zones. Since the 1970s, this protection has been obligatory for most exterior outlets, bathroom circuits, garage outlets, kitchen sockets, and all outlets in crawl spaces and unfinished basements. For comprehensive safety, especially in older residences, homeowners should think about integrating GFCIs even where the Code doesn't necessitate them.

GFCI circuit breakers can supplant regular circuit breakers in many older home panels for expansive coverage. If a home uses fuses, the receptacle or portable GFCIs can be incorporated in pivotal zones like bathrooms, kitchens, basements, garages, and outdoor circuits.

GFCIs are crucial when using electric garden tools or engaging in DIY tasks. They introduce an extra safety layer by promptly disconnecting power upon detecting a ground fault, averting potential harm, and safeguarding users.

Kitchen
Infant/Non-mobile: (Birth - 6 months)
Infant crawl/roll: (5 months - 1 year)
→ **Toddler/Pre-school: (1 year - 4 years)**
→ **School-age: (5 years - 6+ years)**

Garbage Disposal

Childproofing the garbage disposal is crucial to ensure the safety of young children in the kitchen.

Cover the switch: A garbage disposal switch can be easily accessed by little hands. Use a clear plastic guard to cover the switch to prevent accidental activations. This allows you to see the switch while keeping children's fingers away from it.

Install a safety switch: Consider installing a safety switch that requires a key or a unique code to operate the disposal. This additional layer of security ensures that only adults can activate the disposal, minimizing the risk of accidental use by curious little ones.

Educate your child: Take the time to teach your child about the dangers of garbage disposals. Explain that they are not toys and should only be used by adults. Reinforce the importance of staying away from them and never inserting hands or objects into them.

Use a rubber stopper: When the garbage disposal is not in use, insert a rubber stopper into it to prevent anything from accidentally falling into it. This simple measure adds an extra safety barrier and reduces the risk of small objects or utensils being inadvertently dropped into it.

Always Supervise: The most effective way to childproof the garbage disposal is to never leave your child unsupervised in the kitchen. Always keep a watchful eye on them when they are near the garbage disposal area and ensure they stay away from it.

Garbage Disposal is scary and exciting to children. They will try and find out more about this "garbage monster" Let's prevent it!

Kitchen
Infant/Non-mobile: (Birth - 6 months)
Infant crawl/roll: (5 months - 1 year)
→ **Toddler/Pre-school: (1 year - 4 years)**
→ **School-age: (5 years - 6+ years)**

Trash Compactor Safety

Childproofing the trash compactor is essential to ensure the safety of young children in the kitchen.

Use a lock: Installing a lock on the trash compactor is a reliable way to prevent children from accessing it. Choose a childproof secure lock that ensures that your little ones won't accidentally get hurt while playing with the appliance.

Place it out of reach: Whenever possible, position the trash compactor out of reach of children. Consider mounting it higher up on the wall or placing it in a locked cabinet. This will make it less accessible to curious little hands and reduce the risk of accidents.

Keep the key out of reach: If your trash compactor requires a key to operate, ensure that the key is kept out of reach of children. Store it in a safe location where children cannot access it.

Supervision is key: As with any kitchen appliance, constant supervision is crucial when children are around the trash compactor. Always watch them attentively to ensure they don't get too close or attempt to interact with the appliance.

Teach your child: Take the time to educate your child about the hazards of the trash compactor. Explain that it is not a toy and should only be used by adults. Emphasize the importance of staying away from the appliance to avoid any potential accidents.

Kitchen
→ **Infant/Non-mobile: (Birth - 6 months)**
→ **Infant crawl/roll: (5 months - 1 year)**
→ **Toddler/Pre-school: (1 year - 4 years)**
→ **School-age: (5 years - 6+ years)**

Test Water

Ensuring the purity and safety of water in your home is paramount, especially when it comes to the well-being of your children. This becomes even more critical when considering the preparation of baby formula.

Health Implications for Children: Children, especially infants, have sensitive digestive and immune systems that are more susceptible to waterborne pathogens and contaminants. Contaminants like lead can have detrimental effects on a child's cognitive development and overall growth.

Baby Formula Concerns: The purity of the water used to mix baby formula is crucial. Contaminated water can introduce harmful bacteria or chemicals to the baby's system. Certain contaminants might interfere with the absorption of essential nutrients from the formula, affecting the baby's health.

Identify Potential Sources of Contamination: Homes with older plumbing systems might have led-based pipes or fixtures, which can release harmful particles into the water. Living close to industries or farms might expose your water source to heavy metals, chemicals, pesticides, or fertilizers.

Purchase a Home Water Testing Kit: While some kits check for general water quality, others target specific contaminants. For baby formula, it's essential to ensure the absence of bacteria, lead, and harmful chemicals. Use a frequently used tap for the sample, letting the water run for a few minutes before collection. Laboratories provide an in-depth analysis of your water, ensuring it's safe for all uses, including baby formula preparation. This is critical if you're in an area with known water issues or if there's nearby construction.

Install Suitable Water Filters: These are often attached to kitchen faucets and are essential for removing specific contaminants like lead, which is especially vital for baby formula preparation. These filters ensure that all the water in your home, from the kitchen to the bathroom, is treated and safe.

Regular Maintenance of Your Water System: Clean and flush heaters and tanks regularly to prevent the buildup of minerals and the growth of bacteria or algae.

Educate Your Family: Teach older children about which taps have treated water and are safe for drinking.

Baby Formula Preparation: Ensure that anyone preparing baby formula in the home is aware of the importance of using only safe, treated water.

Ensuring the safety of water in your home is a multifaceted responsibility, especially when it concerns the health of our youngest family members. By being proactive and informed, parents can guarantee that even the most delicate tasks, like preparing baby formula, are done with the utmost care, ensuring the health and well-being of their children.

Notes:

Kitchen
Infant/Non-mobile: (Birth - 6 months)
Infant crawl/roll: (5 months - 1 year)
→ **Toddler/Pre-school: (1 year - 4 years)**
→ **School-age: (5 years - 6+ years)**

Ice Maker Safety

Lock or Disable the Ice Dispenser: Many modern refrigerators have an ice dispenser feature that can be locked or disabled. Check the user manual for your refrigerator model to find out how to activate the child lock function. This will prevent children from accessing the ice and potentially spilling it or getting injured.

Secure the Refrigerator: If your refrigerator has a separate ice maker inside the freezer compartment, make sure the freezer door has a childproof lock or latch. This will prevent children from opening the freezer and accessing the ice maker.

Educate Your Child: Explain to your child the potential dangers of playing with the ice maker and that it is not a toy. Encourage them to ask for your help when they need ice.

Keep Ice Scoops Out of Reach: If you use a separate ice scoop to dispense ice, store it in a high cabinet or drawer where children cannot reach it. This will prevent them from playing with the scoop and potentially choking on ice cubes.

Regularly Inspect the Ice Maker: Periodically check the ice maker and surrounding area for any loose or broken parts that could pose a risk to children. If you notice any issues, have them repaired or replaced promptly.

Supervise Children in the Kitchen: Always supervise young children when they are in the kitchen, especially when using appliances like the refrigerator and ice maker. This will help prevent accidents and ensure their safety.

Kitchen
Infant/Non-mobile: (Birth - 6 months)
Infant crawl/roll: (5 months - 1 year)
→ **Toddler/Pre-school: (1 year - 4 years)**
→ **School-age: (5 years - 6+ years)**

Educating Older Siblings

Ensuring sibling safety is crucial in maintaining a secure and harmonious home environment. Everyone, including older siblings, must be on the same page regarding safety. Consistency in following safety protocols and guidelines can significantly reduce the risks of accidents and injuries.

Set Clear Safety Rules: Establish clear safety rules and protocols that everyone in the family must follow. These rules may include activating safety devices, locking doors and cabinets after use, unplugging electronic items when not in use, and always supervising younger siblings.

Age-appropriate Responsibilities: Assign age-appropriate safety responsibilities to older siblings. They can play a vital role in ensuring the safety of younger siblings by helping them understand and follow the rules, keeping potentially hazardous items out of their reach, and being aware of potential dangers.

Lead By Example: Older siblings can lead by example when it comes to safety. By consistently following the safety rules and demonstrating responsible behavior, younger siblings are more likely to imitate and adopt these practices.

Communication is Key: Encourage open communication between siblings about safety concerns. Older siblings can help younger ones understand why specific safety measures are essential and how they can protect themselves and others.

Practicing Safety Drills: Conduct regular safety drills, such as fire drills or emergency evacuation plans, with all siblings. This will help them be prepared and know what to do in case of an emergency.

Foster a Supportive Environment: Create a supportive and caring atmosphere at home where siblings look out for each other's safety. Encourage older siblings to be protective and nurturing towards their younger siblings, especially in situations where safety is a concern.

Age-appropriate Supervision: While older siblings can help with supervision, it's essential for parents or caregivers to provide age-appropriate supervision based on the developmental needs and capabilities of each child.

Kitchen
Infant/Non-mobile: (Birth - 6 months)
→ **Infant crawl/roll: (5 months - 1 year)**
→ **Toddler/Pre-school: (1 year - 4 years)**
School-age: (5 years - 6+ years)

PLAYPEN IN THE KITCHEN

While it's adorable to have a little one watching and imitating us in the kitchen, safety should always be the top priority. The playpen can be a fantastic and safe place for supervision while we're busy in the kitchen. It allows us to keep an eye on our children, ensuring they are out of harm's way and away from any potential dangers.

It's important to remember that young **children are naturally curious** and may be attracted to various objects in the kitchen. By using a playpen, we can create a secure space for them to play while we focus on our kitchen tasks. This prevents them from accessing sharp objects, hot surfaces, or other potential hazards.

However, let's also consider other safety measures. When cooking, it's **crucial to use stove knob covers** to prevent little hands from accidentally turning on the burners. Keeping the playpen away from the kitchen's hot appliances is essential to avoid burns or accidents.

While our little fans enjoy watching us in the kitchen, it's vital to **maintain constant supervision**. Never leave them unattended in the playpen, especially near the kitchen. If we need to step away, it's best to take them with us or ensure another responsible adult is present to keep an eye on them.

Moreover, kitchen safety extends beyond just using the playpen. As parents, we should childproof the entire kitchen area, secure cabinets and drawers containing hazardous items, and use safety locks on
Oven doors and refrigerators. Educating our children about kitchen safety from an early age can also help them understand potential dangers and develop good safety habits.

<u>Kitchen</u>
→ **Infant/Non-mobile: (Birth - 6 months)**
→ **Infant crawl/roll: (5 months - 1 year)**
→ **Toddler/Pre-school: (1 year - 4 years)**
→ **School-age: (5 years - 6+ years)**

Mercury Concerns

Mercury, a naturally occurring heavy metal, is found in various environmental sources, but its presence in certain household items and foods can pose significant health risks, especially to children. Young children, with their developing nervous systems, are particularly vulnerable to the toxic effects of mercury. As such, childproofing against mercury exposure is a crucial aspect of ensuring a safe environment for kids.

Sources of Mercury in the Household

Thermometers and Barometers: Older thermometers and barometers often contain mercury. If they break, the mercury inside can vaporize, leading to inhalation risks.

Fluorescent Light Bulbs: These bulbs contain a small amount of mercury. If they break, proper cleanup is essential to prevent mercury exposure.

Batteries: Some older batteries, especially button batteries, may contain mercury.

Old Paints: Before the 1990s, some paints used mercury as a fungicide.

Mercury In Foods

One of the primary concerns regarding mercury exposure is its presence in certain types of fish. Mercury accumulates in aquatic food chains, leading to higher concentrations in predatory fish.

High-Risk Fish: Fish such as shark, swordfish, king mackerel, and tilefish are known to have high mercury levels and should be consumed in moderation or avoided.

Tuna: While tuna is a popular fish, it's essential to differentiate between its types. Albacore or white tuna generally has higher mercury levels than light tuna.

Protective Measures

Safe Storage: Ensure that items containing mercury are stored out of children's reach and in places where they won't easily break.

Proper Disposal: Items containing mercury, like old thermometers or fluorescent bulbs, should be disposed of at designated hazardous waste collection sites.

Dietary Choices: Limit the consumption of high-mercury fish. Adhere to recommended consumption guidelines, especially for children and pregnant women.

Educate and Inform: Teach older children about the dangers of mercury and ensure they understand the importance of not handling items that might contain it.

Mercury, while naturally occurring, can pose significant health risks when individuals, especially children, are exposed to high amounts.

Kitchen
Infant/Non-mobile: (Birth - 6 months)
Infant crawl/roll: (5 months - 1 year)
→ **Toddler/Pre-school: (1 year - 4 years)**
→ **School-age: (5 years - 6+ years)**

Risks of Raw Sprouts

The recent health advisory from the FDA has brought attention to the potential dangers of consuming raw sprouts, emphasizing the significance of food safety, particularly for those following a raw diet. The E. coli outbreak linked to alfalfa sprouts underscores that foods perceived as healthy can sometimes harbor hidden threats.

Key Concerns and Precautions

Contamination Risks: Raw foods, including sprouts, can be contaminated with harmful bacteria such as E. coli and salmonella. These bacteria might originate from fertilizers used during the growth process. While rinsing sprouts can decrease the risk of bacterial infection, it doesn't guarantee complete safety.

Cooking as a Safety Measure: Cooking sprouts effectively diminish the presence of harmful bacteria. Ensuring sprouts reach the right cooking temperature is vital to neutralizing potential pathogens.

Raw Diet Considerations: Raw diets offer certain health advantages but also have inherent risks. For raw diet enthusiasts, it's paramount to practice meticulous food handling and washing techniques.

Embracing a diet rich in raw foods, including sprouts, requires a heightened awareness of food safety. By staying updated with safety guidelines and consistently practicing safe food preparation, individuals can relish the nutritional benefits of their chosen diet, ensuring both health and safety.

Kitchen
Infant/Non-mobile: (Birth - 6 months)
Infant crawl/roll: (5 months - 1 year)
→ **Toddler/Pre-school: (1 year - 4 years)**
→ **School-age: (5 years - 6+ years)**

The Hidden Dangers in Candy: Lead Exposure

While candy is often associated with sweet indulgence, there's a lesser-known risk tied to it: lead exposure. Surprisingly, certain imported candies, especially those originating from Mexico, have been flagged due to their potentially higher lead content due to more lenient regulations compared to domestic standards. The risk doesn't end with the candy itself; even the wrappers can be a source of lead.

Key "Lead" Points to Consider

Lead's Toxicity: Lead is a potent toxin, especially harmful to young children. Their developing systems are more vulnerable, making them prone to the detrimental effects of lead exposure.

Health Implications: Lead poisoning can manifest in various ways, including developmental lags, learning challenges, and behavioral disorders.

Sources of Exposure: Imported Candies- Due to varying international standards, some imported candies may contain more lead than those made domestically.
Lead may also be present in the inks or materials used for candy wrappers. Children should be discouraged from chewing or playing with these wrappers.

Safety Measures: Always check where candies are imported from and lean towards trusted brands and sellers. Regularly check for product recalls or advisories related to lead content in candies and other consumables.

Candies: Treats loved by many, come with their set of risks when lead exposure is considered. By staying informed and practicing caution, we can enjoy these sweet delights while ensuring the safety of our loved ones.

► *Each year, U.S. poison centers receive about **102,000 calls** for candy-related exposures in kids under 6. Nearly **12,000** leading to medical treatment and **over 140 involving serious symptoms**. Imported candies, especially those with chili, tamarind, or lead-ink wrappers, have tested above FDA's safe limit (0.1 ppm), and linked to elevated blood lead levels in young children.* (Washington State Dept of Health)

Kitchen
Infant non-mobile: (Birth-6 mo.)
→ **Infant crawl/roll: (5 mo.-2 yrs.)**
→ **Toddler/Pre-School: (1 yr.-4 yrs.)**
→ **School-age: (5 yrs.-6+ yrs.)**

Nut Concerns

The rise in food allergies among children has become an increasingly pressing health concern. Data from the U.S. Food and Drug Administration (FDA) reveals that up to 6% of children under the age of three have some form of food allergy. Most concerning is the peanut allergy, notorious for its potential to trigger severe reactions, including the life-threatening condition known as anaphylaxis.

Recognizing Symptoms

Initial Indicators: The onset of an allergic reaction often begins with seemingly mild symptoms such as itching, hives, or a runny nose.

Progression to Severe Symptoms: Without timely intervention, these can rapidly escalate to more alarming manifestations like chest pain, swelling of the throat and mouth, difficulty in breathing, dizziness, and severe headaches. Seek medical attention immediately.

Speed of Onset: Anaphylaxis can develop within mere minutes of allergen exposure, underscoring the importance of swift action.

Triggers Beyond Food

Insect Stings: Certain insects, like bees or wasps, can induce allergic reactions in sensitive individuals.

Medications: Some individuals might have allergic reactions to specific drugs.

Latex: Products containing latex can also be potential allergens for some children.

Preventive Measures

Kitchen Safety: To minimize the risk of cross-contamination, use separate countertops, utensils, and storage areas for allergen-free foods.

Vigilant Label Reading: Manufacturers often list potential allergens on product labels. However, it's essential to be thorough, as some allergens might be present in trace amounts or under different names.

Dining Out: When eating out, always communicate any food allergies to the staff to ensure safe meal preparation.

Emergency Preparedness

EpiPen Training: An epinephrine auto-injector, commonly known as an EpiPen, can be a lifesaver during severe allergic reactions. Parents and caregivers should be trained to recognize when and how to administer it correctly.

Emergency Contacts: Always have a list of emergency contacts, including the child's doctor and nearby medical facilities, readily available.

The increasing prevalence of food allergies in children necessitates a comprehensive understanding and proactive approach from caregivers and society at large. By equipping ourselves with knowledge, taking preventive measures, and being prepared for emergencies, we can significantly mitigate the risks associated with food allergies, ensuring a safer environment for our young ones.

<u>Kitchen</u>
Infant/Non-mobile: (Birth - 6 months)
Infant crawl/roll: (5 months - 1 year)
→ **Toddler/Pre-school: (1 year - 4 years)**
→ **School-age: (5 years - 6+ years)**

Knife Safety

Each year, **more than 200,000 children** are treated for cuts and lacerations caused by sharp household objects like knives, scissors, and broken glass. (Source: Centers for Disease Control and Prevention (CDC) – WISQARS) Childproofing kitchen knives is of utmost importance to ensure the safety of young children in the household.

Knife Blocks or Magnetic Strips: Store knives in a knife block or on a magnetic strip that is mounted high on the kitchen wall. These methods keep the knives out of the reach of children and prevent them from accidentally accessing sharp blades.

Lockable Drawers or Cabinets: Consider using lockable drawers or cabinets to store knives and other sharp utensils. Childproofing locks and latches are available that can prevent children from opening them.

Knife Guards or Sheaths: Use knife guards or sheaths to cover the blades of knives when not in use. These protective covers help prevent accidental cuts when handling or storing the knives.

Teach Knife Safety: Educate older children about knife safety and responsible knife handling. Teach them how to properly use and store knives, emphasizing the importance of keeping knives away from younger siblings.

Supervise Young Children: Always supervise young children in the kitchen to prevent them from accessing knives or other dangerous objects. Keep them at a safe distance from the cooking area and sharp utensils.

Childproofing Gadgets: There are childproof gadgets designed specifically for kitchen knives. These may include knife edge protectors or blade covers that fit securely over the sharp edge.

Consider Child-Friendly Utensils: To minimize the risk of injuries, consider using child-friendly utensils with rounded edges and blunted tips for younger children.

Knife Locking Mechanisms: Some knife sets come with locking mechanisms that can secure the blades in the handle when not in use. This adds an extra layer of safety, especially when storing knives in drawers.

Knife Locking Straps: Like the locking mechanisms, knife locking straps can help secure the knife blade to the handle when not in use, making it more difficult for a child to accidentally open the knife.

Keep Countertops Clear: Avoid leaving knives or other sharp objects on the countertops. Always clean and put away knives immediately after use to prevent accidental contact.

Remember that childproofing measures are not a substitute for proper supervision and education. Ensuring a safe environment and teaching children about potential hazards in the kitchen are essential steps to prevent accidents and injuries.

<u>Kitchen</u>
→ **Infant/Non-mobile: (Birth - 6 months)**
→ **Infant crawl/roll: (5 months - 1 year)**
→ **Toddler/Pre-school: (1 year - 4 years)**
→ **School-age: (5 years - 6+ years)**

Bacteria Concerns

Cleaning up immediately after handling certain foods is crucial to prevent foodborne illnesses caused by harmful bacteria like Salmonella.

Meat, Poultry, and Eggs: Raw meat, poultry, and eggs can be sources of Salmonella and other harmful bacteria. After handling these foods, wash your hands thoroughly with soap and water, and clean all surfaces, utensils, and cutting boards that came into contact with them. Avoid cross-contamination by using separate cutting boards and utensils for raw meats and other foods.

Unpasteurized Foods: Unpasteurized foods, such as unpasteurized milk and cheeses, can also carry harmful bacteria. It's essential to handle these items carefully and wash your hands and surfaces after handling them.

Fruits and Vegetables: While fruits and vegetables are generally safe to eat, they can sometimes carry harmful bacteria from the soil or water they were grown in. Washing them thoroughly under running water before consumption can help reduce the risk of contamination.

Reptiles and Amphibians: Even if they appear healthy, reptiles and amphibians can carry Salmonella and other germs. Always wash your hands thoroughly with soap and water after handling these pets or their habitats. Avoid touching your face or eating while handling them.

Homemade Pet Food: If you prepare homemade food for your pets, ensure that it is properly cooked to kill any harmful bacteria. Wash your hands and surfaces after handling pet food.

Cleaning Practices: After handling potentially contaminated foods, use hot, soapy water to clean surfaces, cutting boards, and utensils. Sanitize countertops and kitchen equipment regularly to maintain a safe food preparation environment.

Proper Food Storage: Store perishable foods at the appropriate temperature to slow the growth of harmful bacteria. Keep your refrigerator at 40°F (4°C) or below and your freezer at 0°F (-18°C) or below.

Symptoms of Food Poisoning: Be aware of the symptoms of food poisoning, such as stomach cramps, diarrhea, vomiting, and fever. If you or anyone in your family experiences these symptoms after consuming food, seek medical attention promptly.

Safe Food Handling Education: Educate your family members, including children, about safe food handling practices. Teach them to wash their hands before and after handling food and to be cautious when handling raw foods.

Cutting Board Concerns

Preventing cross-contamination in the kitchen is essential for food safety, especially when dealing with allergens like salmonella and peanuts. Designating separate cutting boards for specific purposes can significantly reduce the risk of harmful bacteria and allergens spreading.

Color-Coded Cutting Boards: Consider using color-coded cutting boards to differentiate between different food groups. For example, use a red cutting board for raw meat, poultry, and seafood, and a green cutting board for fruits, vegetables, bread, and cheese. This visual distinction helps prevent accidentally using the same board for different types of foods.

Allergen Awareness: If you have a child with allergies, such as a peanut allergy, it's crucial to be extra vigilant about preventing cross-contamination. Designate a specific cutting board and utensils for preparing foods that may trigger allergies, and ensure they are thoroughly cleaned after each use.

Separate Utensils: In addition to separate cutting boards, use separate utensils (e.g., knives, forks) for handling different food groups. Avoid using the same knife to cut raw meat and then use it to slice vegetables without proper cleaning in between.

Proper Cleaning and Sanitizing: After each use, thoroughly wash cutting boards, knives, and other utensils with hot, soapy water to remove any residual bacteria or allergens. Consider using a food-safe sanitizer for an extra layer of protection.

Storage and Organization: Store cutting boards in a way that prevents them from touching each other or other surfaces that may carry contaminants. Keep them clean and dry between uses.

Educate Family Members: Teach all family members, including children, about the importance of using designated cutting boards and utensils. Explain the risks associated with cross-contamination and food allergies.

Avoid Overusing Cutting Boards: If you are preparing a meal with multiple ingredients, try to avoid using the same cutting board for different foods. If possible, use one board for slicing and dicing raw ingredients and another for assembling the final dish.

Maintain a Clean Kitchen: Regularly clean and sanitize your kitchen surfaces, including countertops and kitchen tools, to prevent the buildup of bacteria and allergens.

You can create a safer and more allergen-friendly kitchen environment, reducing the risk of cross-contamination and ensuring the well-being of all family members, especially those with allergies.

<u>Kitchen</u>
Infant/Non-mobile: (Birth - 6 months)
Infant crawl/roll: (5 months - 1 year)
→ **Toddler/Pre-school: (1 year - 4 years)**
→ **School-age: (5 years - 6+ years)**

Pots and Pans

Childproofing your pots and pans in the kitchen is important to prevent accidents and keep your child safe.

Use Rear Burners: If possible, always use the rear burners on your stove when cooking. This will keep the hot pots and pans away from the front, where your child can reach them.

Turn Handles Inward: When cooking on the stove, turn the handles of the pots and pans inward, away from the front of the stove. This prevents your child from accidentally grabbing the handle and pulling the hot contents onto themselves.

Secure Cabinets: Install childproof locks or latches on all lower kitchen cabinets where pots and pans are stored. This prevents your child from accessing the cookware when you're not around.

Store Heavy Items Wisely: If you have heavy pots or cast-iron pans, store them on lower shelves or in lower cabinets to avoid the risk of them falling on your child if they try to reach them.

Use Wall-Mounted Racks: Consider using wall-mounted pot racks to store your pots and pans. This keeps them out of reach and frees up cabinet space for other items.

Avoid Hanging Pots and Pans: If you have a hanging pot and pan rack, make sure it's out of your child's reach. Hanging cookware can be tempting for little hands to grab and pull.

Educate Your Child: Teach your child about kitchen safety from a young age. Explain to them that pots and pans can be hot and dangerous, and they should never touch them without your permission and supervision.

Supervise Your Child: Always supervise your child in the kitchen, especially when cooking. Avoid leaving them alone near the stove or any hot cookware.

Cool Down Safely: After cooking, make sure to let the pots and pans cool down before moving them or putting them away. Hot cookware can cause burns if touched.

Use Silicone Handle Covers: Consider using silicone handle covers on your pots and pans. These provide a heat-resistant barrier, making it safer to handle hot cookware.

You can create a safer environment for your child and reduce the risk of accidents and injuries. Remember, constant supervision and teaching your child about kitchen safety are essential aspects of keeping them safe in the kitchen.

► *According to the The U.S. Consumer Product Safety Commission (CPSC) Every year, more than **47,000 preschoolers (ages 0–6) in the U.S. are treated in emergency rooms for burns or scalds from pots, pans, or hot liquids**. Often after simply pulling a pan off the stove. Toddlers are at highest risk: studies show they pull down pots or pans more than any other cause when reaching.*

Kitchen
Infant/Non-mobile: (Birth - 6 months)
Infant crawl/roll: (5 months - 1 year)
→ **Toddler/Pre-school: (1 year - 4 years)**
→ **School-age: (5 years - 6+ years)**

Frying Food Dangers

Fried food splatters can indeed pose a risk of painful burns, especially for curious little ones in the kitchen.

Use Splatter Guards: Invest in splatter guards for your frying pans to prevent hot oil and grease from splashing out while you cook. These guards act as a protective barrier and reduce the risk of burns.

Create a Safe Zone: Designate a safe area in the kitchen where your child can stay while you're cooking. This area should be away from the stove and any potential hazards. You can set up a play area or provide toys to keep them occupied.

Keep Handles Turned Inward: When using frying pans, turn the handles inward to prevent accidental spills or your child reaching for them.

Use the Back Burner: Whenever possible, cook on the stove's back burners to keep the frying pans away from the front, where your child might be tempted to reach.

Cook with Lids: When frying, consider using lids to partially cover the pan. This will help contain the splatters and reduce the risk of hot oil escaping.

Teach Kitchen Safety: Educate your child about kitchen safety from an early age. Explain the dangers of hot surfaces and why they should stay away from the stove and frying pans.

Supervise Closely: Always supervise your child when you're in the kitchen. Never leave them unattended, especially when cooking with hot oil or frying food.

Use Long-Handled Utensils: When cooking with hot oil, use long-handled utensils, such as tongs and spatulas. This allows you to maintain a safe distance from the pan.

Wait for Oil to Cool: After frying, wait for the oil to cool down before transferring it to a storage container. Keep the container out of reach of children.

Have a Fire Safety Plan: Be prepared for any emergencies in the kitchen, including a small grease fire. Have a fire extinguisher or fire blanket accessible and know how to use them.

<u>Kitchen</u>
→ **Infant/Non-mobile: (Birth - 6 months)**
→ **Infant crawl/roll: (5 months - 1 year)**
→ **Toddler/Pre-school: (1 year - 4 years)**
→ **School-age: (5 years - 6+ years)**

Fluoride in Drinking Water

Fluoride, a naturally occurring mineral, is often added to public water supplies and dental products to help prevent tooth decay. While it has proven benefits for dental health, excessive fluoride exposure, especially in young children, can lead to potential health concerns. This is particularly relevant when considering the fluoride content in water used to prepare baby formula. As parents and caregivers, understanding and managing fluoride exposure is crucial to ensure the safety and well-being of our little ones.

Dental Products

Toothpaste: Many toothpastes contain fluoride. While beneficial for teeth, swallowing large amounts can be harmful.

Child-Safe Toothpaste: Consider using non-fluoridated toothpaste for very young children who have yet to master the art of spitting out toothpaste after brushing.

Supervision: Always supervise children while brushing to ensure they use only a pea-sized amount of toothpaste and teach them to spit it out after brushing.

Safe Storage: Store toothpaste out of children's reach and sight to prevent unsupervised access.

Water Supply

Fluoridated Water: Many municipalities add fluoride to the water supply. While this is beneficial for dental health, excessive consumption can lead to dental fluorosis in children.

Water Filters: Some water filters can reduce fluoride levels. If you're concerned about fluoride content, consider investing in a filter specifically designed to remove fluoride.

Bottled Water: Some bottled water brands are low in fluoride or fluoride-free. Check labels if you want to limit your fluoride intake.

Baby Formula Concerns

Fluoride in Tap Water: Mixing powdered or concentrated baby formula with tap water can increase fluoride intake, especially if your local water supply is fluoridated.

Alternate Water Sources: Consider using fluoride-free bottled water or filtered water for mixing baby formula.

Consultation: Discuss with your pediatrician about the best water sources for formula preparation and whether any fluoride supplements are necessary.

Food and Beverages

Processed Foods: Some processed foods might be made with fluoridated water, contributing to a child's overall fluoride intake.

Home Cooking: Preparing meals at home using non-fluoridated water can help control fluoride consumption.

Beverage Choices: Be aware that certain beverages, like tea, can naturally contain fluoride.

Fluoride Supplements

Prescriptions: Some children are prescribed fluoride supplements. Ensure these are stored safely out of children's reach and only given in the recommended doses.

Regular Check-Ups: Regular dental check-ups can help monitor fluoride levels and adjust any supplements or treatments as necessary.

Additional Tips

Educational Games: Turn teeth brushing into a fun game where kids "fight cavities" but also learn the importance of not swallowing toothpaste.

Fluoride-Free Days: Once a week, consider having a day where you consciously reduce fluoride intake, using non-fluoridated toothpaste and water.

DIY Natural Toothpaste: Children can make their own natural, fluoride-free toothpaste using baking soda, coconut oil, and essential oils.

While beneficial in the right amounts, fluoride requires careful management in homes with young children. This is especially true when considering the preparation of baby formula. By being informed, proactive, and creative, parents can strike the right balance, ensuring their children reap the dental benefits of fluoride without the associated risks.

▶ *Health Canada's expert panel reviewed evidence suggesting that fluoride levels commonly found in Canadian drinking water may be **associated with reduced IQ scores in children**. They recommended considering cognitive effects when setting health-based values for fluoride in drinking water.*

Kitchen
→ Infant/Non-mobile: (Birth - 6 months)
→ Infant crawl/roll: (5 months - 1 year)
→ Toddler/Pre-school: (1 year - 4 years)
→ School-age: (5 years - 6+ years)

Microwaved Food Hot Spots

Each year, approximately **3,500 children** suffer burns or scalds from microwave ovens, often due to mishandling hot containers or steam. (Source: American Burn Association (ABA) - Burn Statistics) According to the American Academy of Pediatrics (SAP) using microwaves for heating food is a convenient choice in many homes, but it's important to understand their impact on the food's molecular structure. This is especially vital when dealing with baby food and formula. Microwaves can cause uneven heating, leading to areas that are dangerously hot while others remain lukewarm, posing a burn risk to an infant's sensitive mouth and throat.

Key Considerations for Microwaving Infant Food

Uneven Heating: Microwaves can cause food or formula to heat unevenly, creating "hot spots" that can burn an infant.

Stirring is Crucial: If you choose to microwave, ensure you stir the food or formula multiple times during the heating process. This action helps in distributing the heat more evenly.

Temperature Test: Always test the temperature of the food or formula on your wrist before feeding the baby to ensure it's not too hot.

Alternative Heating Methods

Bottle Warmers: These devices are designed specifically for heating baby bottles to the right temperature.

Warm Water Bath: Placing the bottle in a bowl of warm water can gradually and evenly heat the formula.

Stove Top Heating: Gently heating food on the stove allows for more consistent temperature control.

While microwaves offer convenience, they come with specific challenges when heating infant food or formula. Caregivers must prioritize safety by being informed and cautious, ensuring that every meal is not only nutritious but also served at a safe temperature.

<u>Kitchen</u>
Infant/Non-mobile: (Birth - 6 months)
→ **Infant crawl/roll: (5 months - 1 year)**
→ **Toddler/Pre-school: (1 year - 4 years)**
→ **School-age: (5 years - 6+ years)**

The Danger of Kitchen Spices

The kitchen, with its array of aromatic spices, is a culinary artist's paradise. Yet, for households with young explorers, these spices can present hidden dangers. While they might appear innocuous in their containers, several spices are particularly potent and can be detrimental if consumed in large quantities by children.

Unraveling the Hidden Dangers

Highly Potent Spices: Some spices are especially powerful and can have adverse effects on a child's still-developing system. Here are some to watch out for.

Nutmeg: Even a small amount can cause hallucinations and seizures in children.

Chili Powder: Can cause severe discomfort, if ingested, inhaled, or comes in contact with the skin.

Cloves and Bay Leaves: These can be a choking hazard and, if swallowed whole, can cause internal discomfort.

Star Anise: Toxic varieties can sometimes be mistakenly sold, which can be harmful if ingested.

Fennel and Anise Seeds: In large amounts, these can cause difficulty breathing.

Irritation Concerns: Spices like black and white pepper can irritate the eyes, nose, and throat, especially if a curious child decides to sniff or taste them.

Safety Measures in the Spice Zone

Elevated Storage: Ensure that all spice containers, especially the more dangerous ones, are stored on high shelves or upper cabinets.

Childproof Locks: If you store spices in drawers, it's wise to install childproof locks.

Clear and Bold Labels: Ensure every spice container is clearly labeled. This way, if a child does access them, you can quickly identify what they might have consumed.

Education is Key: As they grow, teach children about the potential dangers of certain spices. Let them safely explore scents and flavors under close supervision.

Avoid Open Displays: While open spice racks or magnetic displays are trendy, they're also accessible to children. Opt for enclosed or out-of-reach storage solutions.

Prompt Clean-Up: Ensure no spices are left on countertops or within a child's reach after cooking.

Staying Ahead of the Curve

Emergency Contacts: Always have emergency numbers, including poison control, on hand.

First Aid Familiarity: Familiarize yourself with first aid for choking and remedies for spice-related irritations, such as using milk or yogurt for chili burns.

While spices add zest to our dishes, they present challenges in homes with young children. Recognizing the specific dangers of each spice and implementing meticulous childproofing strategies ensures the kitchen remains a safe space. Safety, after all, is the primary seasoning in the recipe for family well-being.

▶ *Astonishingly, over a quarter of imported spices, like chili powder and turmeric, used in American kitchens contain dangerous lead levels.* **Studies show that just a few bites can raise preschool children's blood lead by 25–30%, driving some toddlers above the 10µg/dL danger level.** *In one North Carolina study, nearly 29% of spices found in homes of lead-poisoned kids were contaminated. It's a hidden hazard in everyday cooking.* (National Library of Medicine)

Kitchen
Infant/Non-mobile: (Birth - 6 months)
→ **Infant crawl/roll: (5 months - 1 year)**
Toddler/Pre-school: (1 year - 4 years)
School-age: (5 years - 6+ years)

Sippy Cup Safety

Material Selection: Choose a sippy cup made from safe materials such as BPA-free plastic, stainless steel, or silicone. Avoid cups with harmful chemicals or materials that may leach into the drink.

No Small Parts: Opt for sippy cups with a simple design and no small detachable parts that could pose a choking hazard. Cups with a one-piece spout or valve are safer in this regard.

Secure Lid: Make sure the lid of the sippy cup fits tightly and securely, preventing spills and leaks. A secure lid also prevents your child from opening the cup easily and making a mess.

Easy to Use for the Child: Choose a sippy cup that is easy for your child to handle. Cups with handles or grip-friendly designs can help your child hold the cup comfortably and securely

Easy-to-clean: Select a sippy cup that is easy to disassemble and clean thoroughly. This ensures that no leftover residue or mold accumulates, promoting good hygiene.

Monitor the Condition: Regularly inspect the sippy cup for any signs of wear and tear. Replace the cup if you notice cracks, broken parts, or any other damage that could compromise its safety.

Safe Drinks: Fill the sippy cup only with appropriate drinks for your child's age. Avoid giving sugary drinks, carbonated beverages, or hot liquids in the sippy cup, as they may harm your child.

Supervision: Always supervise your child when they are using the sippy cup, especially younger children who may be more prone to accidents.

Transition to Open Cup: As your child grows and becomes more capable of handling regular cups, transition them to open cups when appropriate. This helps them develop proper drinking skills and reduces reliance on sippy cups.

Kitchen
Infant/Non-mobile: (Birth - 6 months)
→ **Infant crawl/roll: (5 months - 1 year)**
→ **Toddler/Pre-school: (1 year - 4 years)**
School-age: (5 years - 6+ years)

Doggy Door Concerns

Childproofing a doggy door located in the kitchen is essential to prevent your child from accessing unsafe areas or wandering outdoors unattended, while still allowing your pet the freedom to move freely. One effective strategy is to install a lockable pet door. This could be a manual lock that you can secure when the door is not in use or an electronic pet door that operates with a sensor on your pet's collar, unlocking only when it detects your pet and preventing your child from using it.

Adjusting the size and height of the doggy door can also enhance safety. Ensure the opening is just large enough for your dog but too small for your child to crawl through. For larger dogs, consider installing the pet door at a higher position that's accessible to your pet but out of reach for your child. Using a pet door cover is another option; a solid cover with a child-resistant locking mechanism can be placed over the doggy door when it's not in use. Some covers attach magnetically and are easy for adults to remove but challenging for children.

Installing a child safety gate at the entrance to the kitchen can restrict your child's access to the area with the doggy door. Some gates include a smaller pet door at the bottom, allowing your dog to pass through while keeping your child out. Adding door alarms or sensors can further enhance safety. An audible alarm that sounds when the doggy door is used can alert you immediately if your child tries to go through it, and motion-activated sensors near the door can notify you of any activity.

Education and supervision are crucial components of childproofing. As your child grows, explain that the doggy door is only for pets and is not safe for them to use. Keep a close eye on your child, especially when they are near the kitchen or the doggy door area. You might also consider using a one-way pet door that allows your dog to come inside from outdoors but requires manual assistance to go outside, preventing your child from exiting through it.

Regular maintenance and inspection of the doggy door are important to ensure that locks and mechanisms function properly and that there are no gaps your child could exploit. Upgrade outdated or easily bypassed pet doors with more secure, modern options when necessary. If feasible, relocating the doggy door to an area less accessible to your child, such as a laundry room or garage, can also be an effective solution. Alternatively, using a pet door that fits into a sliding door or window out of your child's reach may be suitable.

Consulting professional installers who specialize in childproofing and pet door installations can provide expert advice tailored to your home's layout. Additionally, ensure that the outdoor area accessible through the doggy door is safe for your pet and not accessible to your child. Consistency with rules and supervision reinforces safe behavior around the doggy door. Teach your child what to do if they accidentally get outside, including staying in a designated safe spot and calling for help.

Kitchen
Infant/Non-mobile: (Birth - 6 months)
→ **Infant crawl/roll: (5 months - 1 year)**
→ **Toddler/Pre-school: (1 year - 4 years)**
→ **School-age: (5 years - 6+ years)**

Kitty Litter Safety

Kitty litter is an essential component of cat care, but it's important to take measures to ensure the safety of children in households where cats are present. By following these detailed guidelines, you can maintain a clean and safe environment for both your feline friend and your little ones.

Choose the Right Type of Litter: Opt for clumping or non-clumping litter that is safe for both your cat and your children. Avoid litter with added chemicals or fragrances that could potentially irritate your child's skin or respiratory system.

Place the Litter Box Wisely: Select a suitable location for the litter box. It should be easily accessible for your cat yet out of reach of curious children. A well-ventilated, low-traffic area is ideal.

Use Covered Litter Boxes: Covered or hooded litter boxes can help prevent children from accessing the litter and reduce the chances of spills. However, ensure that the cover is easy for your cat to enter and exit.

Teach Proper Hand Hygiene: Instruct your children on the importance of proper hand hygiene after handling the cat or being in proximity to the litter box. Washing hands thoroughly with soap and water can prevent the spread of germs.

Supervise Interactions: Always supervise interactions between your child and the litter box area. Discourage your child from playing with or touching the litter and its contents.

Use Childproof Litter Box Enclosures: Consider installing childproof enclosures or gates around the litter box area to prevent curious toddlers from accessing it. This ensures that only the cat can comfortably use the box.

Avoid Litter Tracking: Choose a litter that minimizes tracking outside the box. Litter mats placed around the box can help contain any stray litter and reduce the likelihood of it being transferred to other areas of your home.

Regular Litter Box Cleaning: Maintain a consistent cleaning schedule for the litter box to minimize odors and prevent the accumulation of waste. A clean litter box reduces the risk of bacteria spreading to children.

Use Natural or Biodegradable Litters: Natural or biodegradable litter made from materials like corn, wheat, or pine can be safer alternatives for both pets and children. However, ensure they are still effective in controlling odors and clumping.

Keep Litter Storage Secure: Store extra bags of kitty litter in a secure, out-of-reach location to prevent accidental spills or ingestion by children.

Dispose of Waste Properly: Teach your children to properly dispose of litter waste by sealing it in a bag and placing it in an outdoor trash receptacle. This prevents curious hands from coming into contact with used litter.

Monitor Allergies and Sensitivities: Be vigilant for any signs of allergies or sensitivities in your children related to the cat litter. If any adverse reactions occur, consult a medical professional.

You can ensure that your cat's litter box remains a clean and safe area for both your feline companion and your children. Responsible management and proper education will help create a harmonious living environment where everyone can coexist comfortably.

Notes:

Kitchen
→ Infant/Non-mobile: (Birth - 6 months)
→ Infant crawl/roll: (5 months - 1 year)
→ Toddler/Pre-school: (1 year - 4 years)
→ School-age: (5 years - 6+ years)

Smoke Detectors

Smoke detectors are a critical component of home safety and are often the first line of defense in alerting you to fires and other emergencies. Ensuring that these devices are correctly installed and maintained can be a matter of life and death. Each year, **over 700 children** are treated for fire-related injuries, including burns and smoke inhalation, highlighting the need for smoke detectors and fire safety education. (Source: National Fire Protection Association (NFPA) - Fire Statistics)

Installation Locations

Every Level: Install smoke detectors on every level of your home, including the basement.

Near Sleeping Areas: Place detectors in hallways outside of bedrooms and inside rooms where people sleep.

Kitchen Caution: Keep detectors at least 10 feet away from cooking appliances to minimize false alarms.

High Ceilings: If you have vaulted ceilings, consult the manufacturer's guidelines for proper placement.

Battery Maintenance

Monthly Testing: Make it a habit to test the batteries in your smoke detectors every month. Most units have a 'test' button for this purpose.

Bi-Annual Replacement: Even if they appear to be working fine, replace the batteries twice a year. A good rule of thumb is to do this when you adjust your clocks for daylight saving time.

Chirping Sound: A chirping sound usually indicates a low battery. Replace the batteries immediately when you hear this sound.

Regular Cleaning

Dust and Debris: Use a vacuum cleaner to remove dust from the detector's exterior at least every six months.

Smoke Chamber: Some models allow you to clean the smoke chamber, which can help improve sensitivity.

Wired Detectors

Signal Light: Most wired detectors have a signal light that flashes periodically. This is an indicator that the unit is operational.

Battery Backup: Even wired detectors often have battery backups in case of power failures. Don't forget to check and replace these as well.

Specialized Detectors

For The Hearing Impaired: Special detectors with strobe lights and bed shakers are available to alert the hearing impaired.

Smart Detectors: Some newer models can send alerts to your phone and tell you which room the danger is in.

Additional Tips

Interconnected Systems: Some smoke detectors can be interconnected, so when one goes off, they all do, ensuring that everyone in the house is alerted.

Expiration Date: Smoke detectors don't last forever. Check the expiration date and replace the unit if it's past its useful life, generally 10 years.

A well-maintained smoke detector can save lives and prevent injuries, making it a cornerstone of home safety. Let's prioritize the well-being of our families by ensuring our homes are equipped with functional and up-to-date smoke detectors.

Kitchen
→ Infant/Non-mobile: (Birth - 6 months)
→ Infant crawl/roll: (5 months - 1 year)
→ Toddler/Pre-school: (1 year - 4 years)
→ School-age: (5 years - 6+ years)

Carbon Monoxide (CO): The Silent Danger Lurking in Your Home

Each year, there are approximately **400 cases of carbon monoxide poisoning in children** in the U.S., often due to faulty heating systems or improper use of generators. Source: Centers for Disease Control and Prevention (CDC) - Carbon Monoxide Poisoning Carbon monoxide (CO) is a hazardous gas that poses a significant threat to household safety. Invisible, odorless, and tasteless, CO can be produced by various common appliances, making it a particularly insidious danger. It disrupts the blood's ability to carry oxygen, leading to potentially severe health issues or even death. Therefore, understanding how to prevent and detect CO in your home is crucial.

One of the most effective ways to protect your household from CO is by **installing carbon monoxide detectors**. These devices should be strategically placed near sleeping areas and in communal spaces like living rooms and kitchens to ensure comprehensive coverage. It's important to regularly test these detectors—monthly checks are advisable—to confirm they are functioning correctly. Additionally, the batteries in CO detectors should be replaced at least twice a year or immediately if a low-battery warning sounds.

Proper appliance maintenance is another critical aspect of CO prevention. All fuel-burning appliances must be adequately ventilated to prevent CO buildup. It's essential to ensure that vents and flues are free from blockages. Never use outdoor appliances such as grills or generators inside the home, as these can produce dangerously high levels of CO.

The color of **the flame on your gas appliances can also provide valuable insights** into their safety. An orange flame indicates that the appliance is not burning fuel efficiently, which could be a sign of CO production. If you notice an orange flame, it's crucial to turn off the appliance and consult a certified technician immediately. Conversely, a blue flame typically signifies efficient combustion and lower CO risks, but regular maintenance checks remain essential regardless of flame color. Scheduling annual inspections with a certified technician ensures that all your appliances are in good working order and safe to use.

Flue and chimney safety is another key component of CO prevention. Regular inspections should be conducted to check for obstructions such as plants, nests, or debris, which could block ventilation and lead to CO buildup. It's also advisable to engage a qualified inspector periodically to assess the overall condition of your flue and chimney, ensuring they remain in optimal working condition.

When it comes to **grill safety**, constant supervision is vital, particularly in homes with children. Never leave a hot grill unattended, as this poses a significant risk, especially to young children. Implement additional safety measures such as installing latches and locks on nearby cabinets and securing the grill with anchors to prevent tipping. Protective bumpers on corners and edges can further reduce the risk of injury. Always place the grill at a safe distance from walls, fences, or any combustible materials to prevent fire hazards.

Ventilation plays a crucial role in preventing CO accumulation in the home. It's important to install ventilation systems tailored to specific appliances both inside and outside the home. Regular cleaning of these vents is necessary to avoid blockages and ensure efficient operation.

Routine safety checks of all household appliances are equally important. Regularly inspect electrical cords and plugs for wear and tear that could lead to malfunctions or fire. Gas-operated appliances require proper ventilation to prevent CO buildup. Routine cleaning helps prevent the accumulation of grease or dust that could ignite and produce CO.

For landlords, maintaining a safe environment in rental properties is a significant responsibility. Providing functional smoke and CO detectors is a basic requirement, along with regular inspections of electrical and gas systems. Landlords should ensure that all appliances meet local and national safety standards. Promptly addressing maintenance concerns raised by tenants is essential, and clear instructions for appliance usage, along with emergency contact information, should be provided.

Attic fan precautions are also important. Proper roof ventilation in the attic is necessary to prevent CO from entering the home. Regular checks and cleaning of the ventilation system will ensure it remains free from blockages.

Garage safety is another area that should not be overlooked. Never leave a car running in the garage, even for a brief period, as this can quickly fill the space with CO. Installing CO detectors with low-level indicators in the garage and throughout the home adds an extra layer of protection, providing early warnings of CO buildup.

<u>Kitchen</u>
→ **Infant/Non-mobile: (Birth - 6 months)**
→ **Infant crawl/roll: (5 months - 1 year)**
→ **Toddler/Pre-school: (1 year - 4 years)**
→ **School-age: (5 years - 6+ years)**

First Aid Kits Should Include...

When assembling a first aid kit, it's essential to include items that can address various injuries and emergencies. **Adhesive bandages in different sizes:** These are useful for covering minor cuts, scrapes, and blisters.

- ☐ **Sterile gauze pads and adhesive tape:** Use these for larger wounds that require more substantial coverage and protection.

- ☐ **Antiseptic wipes or solution:** For cleaning and disinfecting wounds to prevent infection.

- ☐ **Tweezers:** To remove splinters, thorns, or debris from the skin.

- ☐ **Scissors:** For cutting tape, gauze, or clothing in case of an emergency.

- ☐ **Instant cold packs:** To reduce swelling and relieve pain for sprains or strains

- ☐ **Elastic bandages:** Useful for providing support and compression for injured joints.
- ☐ **Cotton balls and swabs:** For applying antiseptic or cleaning wounds.
- ☐ **Thermometer:** To monitor body temperature and detect fever.
- ☐ **Non-latex disposable gloves:** For protecting yourself while administering first aid.
- ☐ **CPR face shield or barrier device:** To perform rescue breathing safely.
- ☐ **Pain relievers and antihistamines:** To provide relief from pain, fever, or allergic reactions.
- ☐ **Oral rehydration solution or electrolyte packets:** To treat dehydration in case of vomiting or diarrhea.
- ☐ **First aid manual or instruction booklet:** A guide to help you administer first aid correctly.
- ☐ **Emergency contact information:** Include phone numbers for your family doctor, pediatrician, and local emergency services.

Remember to check your first aid kit regularly and replace items that have expired or been used. **Additionally,** tailor the contents of your first aid kit to your family's specific needs and activities, considering any allergies or medical conditions.

Kitchen
Infant/Non-mobile: (Birth - 6 months)
→ **Infant crawl/roll: (5 months - 1 year)**
→ **Toddler/Pre-school: (1 year - 4 years)**
→ **School-age: (5 years - 6+ years)**

Medicine Safety

To ensure the safety of children, it is vital to store medicines in childproof containers and out of their reach and to supervise the intake of multivitamins or gummy supplements to prevent them from mistaking them for candies. Always adhere to the dosing instructions and avoid referring to medicine as "candy" to prevent overconsumption. In case of suspected overdose, seek immediate medical help. When it comes to honey, infants under one year should not be given any, as it can lead to infant botulism due to their underdeveloped digestive system. Symptoms like weakness and difficulty swallowing should prompt immediate medical attention. Additionally, maintain a separate storage area for medications and honey to avoid confusion, and consult with a healthcare provider before introducing any new medication or supplement to your child. Dispose of expired or unused medications responsibly. (For details refer to parent's bedroom **pg. 228**)

Kitchen
Infant/Non-mobile: (Birth - 6 months)
→ **Infant crawl/roll: (5 months - 1 year)**
→ **Toddler/Pre-school: (1 year - 4 years)**
→ **School-age: (5 years - 6+ years)**

Mealtime Safety

Mealtime is a cherished moment for families, but it also presents potential hazards for young children. Ensuring their safety requires a combination of vigilance, knowledge, and preventive measures.

Hot Dishes & Beverages: Always place hot dishes and beverages out of a child's reach. Avoid handling them while holding a child to prevent accidental spills and burns. Moreover, never pass hot items over a child's head; instead, pass them around the table or place them safely within reach.

Utensil Selection: While sporks might seem convenient, they can shatter, posing a choking risk. Opt for safer utensils, especially when dining out. When choosing plates, consider unbreakable options like paper or plastic over ceramic or Corelle to minimize the risk of injuries from shattered dishes.

Mindful Food Choices: Choking is a significant concern for young children. Adhere to guidelines from organizations like the American Academy of Pediatrics, which advises cutting high-risk foods into safe, non-round pieces. Foods like grapes, hot dogs, nuts, and popcorn should be served with caution and never to children under 4 years old. Always ensure children remain seated while eating and discourage them from walking or playing with food in their mouths.

Beware of "Free" Prizes: Small toys or trinkets that come with purchases can be enticing but dangerous. Always assess the size and age-appropriateness of these items before allowing children to play with them.

Constant Supervision: Regardless of the precautions in place, nothing replaces the importance of attentive supervision during mealtimes. Even if an older sibling is assisting, parents should remain vigilant to ensure the younger child is consuming age-appropriate and safe foods.

Mealtime safety involves proactive measures and constant supervision. By being aware of potential hazards and implementing these guidelines, parents can ensure that their children enjoy meals in a safe environment, fostering healthy eating habits and peace of mind.

▶ *Every year in the U.S., nearly 7,500 toddlers (ages 0–3) are rushed to emergency rooms after choking on foods like hot dogs, grapes, or hard candy. About 20 kids every day. Tragically, food choking also causes* **over 60 deaths** *annually in children under six. Experts say up to* **90%** *of meat- and candy-related choking injuries. Nearly all fatalities happen at the dinner table.*
(National Library of Medicine)

Kitchen
→ **Infant/Non-mobile: (Birth - 6 months)**
→ **Infant crawl/roll: (5 months - 1 year)**
→ **Toddler/Pre-school: (1 year - 4 years)**
School-age: (5 years - 6+ years)

Baby Bottle Tooth Decay

According to the American Academy of Pediatric Dentistry (AAPD), Baby Bottle Tooth Decay, also known as Early Childhood Caries (ECC), affects the teeth of young children, usually infants and toddlers. It occurs when the teeth are frequently exposed to sugary liquids, such as milk, formula, fruit juice, or sweetened drinks, especially when they are given in a bottle or sippy cup at naptime or bedtime.

Tooth Decay Risk: Baby Bottle Tooth Decay can lead to cavities and dental problems in baby teeth, which can be painful and affect the child's oral health and development.

Avoid Prolonged Bottle Feeding: Avoid letting your baby fall asleep with a bottle in their mouth. Prolonged exposure to sugary liquids during sleep can be particularly damaging to the teeth.

Use Water for Bedtime: If your baby needs a bottle or sippy cup to soothe them to sleep, fill it with water rather than sugary drinks.

Limit Juice Consumption: If you introduce fruit juice to your child's diet, do so in moderation and preferably during mealtime. Avoid giving juice in a bottle or sippy cup for extended periods.

Wipe Gums and Teeth: Even before your baby's teeth erupt, gently wipe their gums with a clean, damp cloth after feeding. Once teeth start coming in, use a soft, age-appropriate toothbrush to clean them.

First Dental Visit: Schedule your baby's first dental visit around their first birthday or within six months after their first tooth appears. Early dental visits help monitor oral health and provide preventive guidance.

Limit Sugary Snacks: As your child grows and starts eating solid foods, limit sugary snacks and drinks between meals. Opt for healthier options like fruits and vegetables.

Lead by Example: Show good oral hygiene habits by brushing and flossing your teeth regularly. Children often imitate what they see their parents or caregivers doing.

Fluoride Consideration: Discuss with your pediatrician or dentist whether fluoride supplements or fluoride toothpaste are recommended for your child based on their age and the fluoride content in your water supply.

Avoid Sharing Utensils: Avoid sharing utensils or cleaning a pacifier with your mouth, as this can transfer harmful bacteria to your baby.

By taking proactive steps to prevent Baby Bottle Tooth Decay, you can help protect your child's oral health and set them up for a lifetime of healthy teeth and smiles. If you have concerns or questions about your child's oral hygiene, don't hesitate to consult with a pediatric dentist or dental professional.

<u>Kitchen</u>
Infant/Non-mobile: (Birth - 6 months)
Infant crawl/roll: (5 months - 1 year)
→ **Toddler/Pre-school: (1 year - 4 years)**
→ **School-age: (5 years - 6+ years)**

A Deep Dive into Charcoal vs. Ipecac for Poisoning

While activated charcoal and ipecac were once both used to treat poisoning, significant advancements in medical understanding and treatment have led to a shift in preference toward charcoal.

Activated Charcoal: A Versatile Tool

Mechanism of Action: Activated charcoal's porous structure acts like a sponge, absorbing toxins and preventing them from entering the bloodstream.

Effectiveness: Charcoal is particularly effective for treating poisonings involving medications, heavy metals, and certain plant toxins.

Administration: It can be administered orally or through a nasogastric tube.

Timing: For maximum effectiveness, charcoal should be administered as soon as possible after ingestion, ideally within an hour.

Ipecac Syrup: A Historical Perspective

Past Use: Ipecac syrup was once a common home remedy for poisoning. It worked by inducing vomiting, which could help expel ingested substances.

Limitations: However, ipecac has several drawbacks, including:

Risk of aspiration: Vomiting can lead to aspiration, where stomach contents are inhaled into the lungs, potentially causing pneumonia or other complications.

Limited effectiveness: Ipecac may not be effective for certain types of poisons, and it can be difficult to induce vomiting in some individuals.

Dehydration: Repeated vomiting can lead to dehydration and electrolyte imbalances.

Modern Poison Treatment: Beyond Charcoal and Ipecac

Today, the treatment of poisoning involves a more comprehensive approach that may include:

Supportive care: This involves addressing symptoms such as nausea, vomiting, and seizures.

Antitoxins: For specific types of poisoning, antitoxins may be administered to neutralize the effects of the toxin

Dialysis: In severe cases, dialysis may be necessary to remove toxins from the blood.

It's important to note that the best course of action for a poisoning emergency is to call 911 or your local poison control center. They can provide specific advice based on the type of poison and the individual's symptoms.

Remember, do not attempt to treat poisoning at home without medical advice.

Kitchen
Infant/Non-mobile: (Birth - 6 months)
Infant crawl/roll: (5 months - 1 year)
→ **Toddler/Pre-school: (1 year - 4 years)**
→ **School-age: (5 years - 6+ years)**

Matches/Lighters

Storage: Store matches in a secure and locked location that is out of reach and sight of children. Consider using a high cabinet or a locked drawer.

Safety Matches: Opt for safety matches that can only be struck on a specific surface, such as the box they come in, and cannot ignite on other surfaces. These matches are harder for children to accidentally ignite.

Match Strikers: If you have large matchboxes with built-in strikers, keep them out of children's reach. Consider removing the striker from the box and storing it separately.

Teach Fire Safety: Educate your children about the dangers of matches and fire. Explain that matches are not toys and should only be used by adults for specific purposes.

Supervision: Always supervise children when matches are being used and ensure that they are never left unattended around matches or open flames.

Lighters: Keep lighters out of children's reach and use child-resistant lighters whenever possible. These lighters have safety mechanisms that make it harder for children to ignite them.

Model Safe Behavior: Set a good example by demonstrating responsible fire safety practices. Show your children how matches and lighters are used safely and responsibly.

No Playing with Fire: Emphasize the importance of never playing with fire or trying to light matches without adult supervision.

Fire Escape Plan: Create a fire escape plan and practice it regularly with your children. Teach them what to do in case of a fire emergency.

Keep Matches Unreachable During Parties: If you have guests or a party at home, ensure that matches and lighters are safely stored and out of children's reach.

<u>Kitchen</u>
→ **Infant/Non-mobile: (Birth - 6 months)**
→ **Infant crawl/roll: (5 months - 1 year)**
→ **Toddler/Pre-school: (1 year - 4 years)**
→ **School-age: (5 years - 6+ years)**

Fire Extinguishers

Regular Fire Extinguisher Inspection: Fire extinguishers are essential safety devices in any home. It's crucial to perform a monthly inspection. Check if the fire extinguisher is easily accessible, fully charged, and has the correct pressure. Examine the nozzle and other parts for any obstructions that may hinder its functionality. Verify that the pin and tamper seals are intact, and look for any signs of wear, such as dents, leaks, rust, or chemical deposits.

Maintenance and Cleaning: Keeping your fire extinguisher clean and free from corrosive chemicals, oils, or debris is essential for its proper operation. Regularly wipe off any substances that may have landed on it to ensure its effectiveness during emergencies.

Hydrostatic Testing: Fire extinguishers should undergo hydrostatic testing after a certain number of years to ensure their safety and reliability. This testing involves pressurizing the cylinder to check for any weaknesses or flaws. Consult your fire extinguisher owner's manual, label, or the manufacturer's guidelines to determine when your extinguisher requires this testing.

Fire Safety Training: Having a fire extinguisher is crucial, but knowing how to use it correctly is equally important. Consider taking a fire safety training course to learn how to operate a fire extinguisher effectively and safely. Teach all family members how to use it properly, and practice fire safety drills regularly to ensure everyone is prepared in case of an emergency.

By being proactive with fire extinguisher maintenance and knowing how to use it correctly, you can increase your home's safety and be better equipped to handle small fires effectively, preventing them from escalating into major emergencies.

Baking Soda: The Versatile Firefighter! Did you know that besides being an essential ingredient in baking, baking soda can also help you tackle grease fires in the kitchen? In the event of a small grease fire on the stove, don't panic! Simply grab a box of baking soda and pour it directly over the flames to smother them quickly and effectively.

Fire Blankets: A fire blanket can slow down or even put out small kitchen fires. However, it is not suitable for large or intense fires.

<u>Kitchen</u>
→ Infant/Non-mobile: (Birth - 6 months)
→ Infant crawl/roll: (5 months - 1 year)
→ Toddler/Pre-school: (1 year - 4 years)
→ School-age: (5 years - 6+ years)

Emergency Phone Numbers

For a child's safety, it's essential to have the following phone numbers saved in your cell and home phone:

Emergency Services: The most critical number to know is the emergency services number for your country. In the United States, it's 911. This number should be used in life-threatening situations, such as accidents, medical emergencies, or fires.

Pediatrician or Doctor: Save the number of your child's pediatrician or primary care doctor in case you need to reach them for medical advice or appointments.

Poison Control Center: Have the number for your local Poison Control Center saved. They can provide immediate guidance in case your child ingests something harmful.

Trusted Family Members or Emergency Contacts: Save the phone numbers of trusted family members, friends, or neighbors who can be contacted in case of an emergency or if you need assistance when you can't be reached.

School or Childcare Facility: Save the phone number of your child's school or childcare facility so you can easily reach them or get information if needed.

Home Address: It's a good idea to save your home address on your phone, especially if you have young children who may not know it yet.

Nearest Hospital: Save the phone number and address of the nearest hospital or medical facility in case of emergencies.

Non-Emergency Police Line: In addition to the emergency services number, you might want to save the non-emergency police line for situations that require police assistance but are not immediate emergencies.

Trusted Babysitters or Caregivers: If you frequently have babysitters or caregivers for your child, save their contact information in your phone for easy access.

Having these important phone numbers saved in your cell phone can provide peace of mind and quick access to help in case of any emergencies or unexpected situations involving your child's safety. Make sure that your child also knows how to call for help in an emergency and understands the importance of these numbers.

<u>**Kitchen**</u>
Infant/Non-mobile: (Birth - 6 months)
→ **Infant crawl/roll: (5 months - 1 year)**
→ **Toddler/Pre-school: (1 year - 4 years)**
→ **School-age: (5 years - 6+ years)**

Plastic Bags

Plastic bags pose significant suffocation hazards to children and should be handled with utmost caution. It's crucial to be aware of the potential dangers and take preventive measures to ensure child safety.

Keep Plastic Bags Out of Reach: Store plastic bags in a secure place out of the reach of young children. Avoid leaving them lying around in areas accessible to kids, such as on countertops, tables, or the floor.

Proper Disposal: After use, promptly dispose of plastic bags in a designated recycling bin or trash can with a secure lid. Do not leave them within reach of curious children.

Avoid Using Plastic Bags as Mattress Covers: Never use plastic bags as makeshift mattress covers or bedding protectors. Plastic bags are not breathable and can create a suffocation risk if they accidentally cover a child's face. Unintentional suffocation causes **1,200 child deaths each year**, frequently due to unsafe sleep environments or household items like pillows and blankets.
(Source: Centers for Disease Control and Prevention (CDC) - Safe to Sleep Campaign)

Educate Your Child: Teach your child about the dangers of plastic bags and the importance of not playing with or putting them over their heads or faces. Encourage open communication so they feel comfortable discussing any safety concerns.

Use Reusable Bags: Instead of relying on single-use plastic bags, consider using reusable bags made from cloth or other eco-friendly materials. Reusable bags are safer, sturdier, and better for the environment.

Childproof Storage Areas: If you have plastic bags in storage areas, such as cabinets or closets, ensure that these spaces are childproofed with safety latches or locks to prevent children from accessing them.

Supervise Playtime: Always supervise young children during playtime and be vigilant about keeping plastic bags and other potential hazards out of their reach.

Be Mindful of Dry-Cleaning Bags: Be cautious with dry-cleaning bags that come with your clothes. After removing your garments, immediately dispose of the bags safely or keep them out of reach of children.

By taking these preventive measures and being mindful of the potential risks, you can help protect your child from suffocation hazards associated with plastic bags. Safety awareness and proper disposal practices are essential to creating a safe environment for your little ones.

<u>Kitchen</u>
→ **Infant/Non-mobile: (Birth - 6 months)**
→ **Infant crawl/roll: (5 months - 1 year)**
→ **Toddler/Pre-school: (1 year - 4 years)**
→ **School-age: (5 years - 6+ years)**

Green Cleaning Benefits

Thinking about cleaning cleaner and greener is not only beneficial for the environment but also for the health and safety of your family, especially young children. Many household cleaning products contain harsh chemicals that can pose risks to indoor air quality and contribute to various health issues.

Indoor Air Quality: Indoor air can be two to five times more contaminated than outdoor air, largely due to the use of chemical-laden cleaning products. Opting for natural and eco-friendly alternatives can help improve indoor air quality and create a healthier living environment for your family.

Childhood Asthma: The prevalence of childhood asthma has increased significantly in the past two decades, and some cleaning products may act as triggers for asthma attacks. Switching to non-toxic cleaning brands and avoiding products with strong fragrances or volatile organic compounds (VOCs) can reduce potential asthma triggers.

Hazardous Chemicals: The average home contains approximately 25 gallons of hazardous chemicals, with a significant portion found in household cleaning products. These chemicals can pose risks to children who are more susceptible to exposure due to their curious nature and tendency to put objects in their mouths.

Poisoning Incidents: According to the Centers for Disease Control and Prevention (CDC), about 70% of all poisonings occur in the home. This includes poisonings from medications, cleaning products, and other household chemicals. Children are at a higher risk of poisoning than adults, and most poisonings in children happen in the home.

Non-Toxic Brands: Make a conscious effort to choose non-toxic and eco-friendly cleaning brands. Read the labels carefully to verify their safety and look for products with simple and natural ingredients like vinegar and baking soda, which can be just as effective for cleaning.

DIY Cleaning Solutions: Consider making your own cleaning solutions using simple and safe ingredients like vinegar, baking soda, lemon, and essential oils. These DIY solutions are not only cost-effective but also eliminate the need for harmful chemicals in your home.

Proper Ventilation: When using cleaning products, ensure proper ventilation by opening windows and doors. This helps dissipate any fumes or odors and reduces the concentration of chemicals in the air.

By adopting greener cleaning practices and using non-toxic cleaning products, you can create a safer and healthier living environment for your family. These small changes can make a significant difference in reducing exposure to harmful chemicals and promoting overall well-being for you and your children.

Secure Cleaning Supplies

Locking Cabinets: Store all cleaning supplies, including detergents, bleaches, and other chemicals, in locked cabinets or drawers that are out of reach of children. Consider installing childproof locks on cabinet doors to prevent curious little hands from accessing the dangerous contents.

High Shelves: Keep cleaning supplies on high shelves where children cannot reach them. Avoid storing them on open shelves or counter tops, as children can easily climb or reach for them.

Childproof Latches: Install childproof latches on closet doors or storage areas where cleaning supplies are kept. This adds an extra layer of protection to prevent children from accessing hazardous substances.

Safe Storage: Never transfer cleaning supplies into containers that resemble food or drink containers, as children may mistake them for something safe to consume.

Use Child-Resistant Packaging: Choose cleaning products that come in child-resistant packaging. These containers are designed to be more challenging for children to open.

Safe Alternatives: Consider using child-safe and eco-friendly cleaning products that are free from harsh chemicals. Many natural and non-toxic cleaning options are available on the market and can be safer for both your child and the environment.

Supervision: Never leave cleaning supplies unattended, especially when cleaning. Keep a close eye on your child and ensure they stay away from the area where you are cleaning.

Proper Disposal: Dispose of empty or unused cleaning supply containers properly. Rinse empty containers before recycling or discarding them to reduce the risk of accidental exposure.

Educate Older Siblings: If you have older children, educate them about the importance of keeping cleaning supplies out of reach of younger siblings.

Store Wisely: Avoid storing cleaning supplies near food items, dishes, or utensils to prevent accidental contamination.

You can minimize the risk of accidental ingestion or exposure to harmful cleaning supplies, ensuring a safer environment for your children. Always remember to read and follow the safety instructions on cleaning product labels and keep the Poison Control Center number easily accessible in case of emergencies.

Kitchen
Infant/Non-mobile: (Birth - 6 months)
Infant crawl/roll: (5 months - 1 year)
→ **Toddler/Pre-school: (1 year - 4 years)**
→ **School-age: (5 years - 6+ years)**

The Dangers of Switching Containers and Labels

One of the most crucial aspects of childproofing a home is the proper storage and labeling of household items, especially cleaning supplies and medications. Transferring contents from their original containers to different ones or altering labels can pose significant risks to children.

Confusion and Misidentification

Original Labels Provide Information: Original containers come with labels that provide essential information, including usage instructions, ingredients, and warnings. Switching containers can lead to a loss of this vital information.

Children's Curiosity: Children are naturally curious and might be attracted to a container that looks familiar or safe, not knowing that it contains a hazardous substance.

Risk Accidental Ingestion

Medications: Transferring pills or liquid medicines to unmarked or incorrectly labeled containers can lead to overdoses or adverse reactions if consumed by mistake.

Cleaning Supplies: Many cleaning agents are toxic when ingested. Storing them in food or drink containers can be especially misleading for children.

Loss of Child-Resistant Packaging

Safety Mechanisms: Many medications and toxic household products come in child-resistant packaging. Transferring these items to other containers can bypass these safety features.

Ease of Access: Without child-resistant features, young children can easily open containers and access their contents.

Potential for Cross-Contamination

Residue Issues: Even if a container is emptied, it might still have residues of its original contents. Mixing substances can lead to dangerous chemical reactions or increased toxicity.

Allergic Reactions: Unintentional mixing of products can expose children to allergens, leading to unexpected allergic reactions.

Difficulty in Emergency Situations

Lack of Information: In case of accidental ingestion, having the original container can provide crucial information to poison control centers or medical professionals.

Delayed Treatment: Misidentification can lead to delays in treatment, as time is spent trying to determine the ingested substance.

Additional Considerations

Storage: Always store cleaning supplies, medications, and other potentially harmful substances in a locked cabinet or out of reach of children.

Education: Teach children about the dangers of consuming unknown substances and the importance of not touching items without adult supervision.

Regular Checks: Periodically review and declutter storage areas to ensure that all items are in their original containers and that no potentially harmful substances are within a child's reach.

Clear Disposal: When disposing of empty containers, ensure they are rinsed and rendered unusable, especially if they once held toxic substances.

Maintaining products in their original containers with intact labels is a fundamental aspect of childproofing. It ensures safety by preventing confusion, reducing the risk of accidental ingestion, and providing essential information in emergencies. By being diligent and detail-oriented in our storage practices, we can create a safer environment for our children.

> ► *Each year in the U.S., more than **4,500 poisoning incidents involve dangerous household chemicals mistakenly stored in unmarked or food/beverage containers.** These errors result in almost **9,400 ER visits** and nearly **1,900 hospitalizations** annually. In one notable example, 94 children were exposed in just four months to brightly colored cleaners decanted into juice-like bottles.* (The American Association of Poison Control Centers (AAPCC))

Kitchen
Infant/Non-mobile: (Birth - 6 months)
Infant crawl/roll: (5 months - 1 year)
Toddler/Pre-school: (1 year - 4 years)
School-age: (5 years - 6+ years)→

Duct Tape

Ah, childproof duct tape. The superhero of childproofing materials! Before we start using it, let's clarify what it can and can't do. Childproof duct tape isn't a magical solution for every child safety challenge, but it does have its clever uses.

Secure Cords: Use duct tape to keep cords and cables neatly fastened and out of reach. This prevents potential tripping hazards and keeps little hands away from electrical items.

Cover Sharp Edges: While not as cushioned as purpose-built edge protectors, you can apply layers of duct tape to temporarily soften sharp edges. Just remember, it's a quick fix, not a permanent solution.

Temporary Locks: In a pinch, you can use duct tape to temporarily secure cabinets or drawers. However, for long-term childproofing, investing in proper childproof locks is a smarter choice.

Block Access: Attach duct tape to temporarily block off certain areas to create makeshift barriers. This clever way to deter little explorers from reaching off-limits zones is a good one.

Repair Broken Items: Sometimes, childproof duct tape can work wonders in fixing broken toys or baby-proofing equipment. It's like a versatile tool in your childproofing utility belt.

It's crucial to keep in mind that duct tape should never be used as a permanent childproofing solution. While it's handy in some situations, it's not designed for long-term safety needs.

For comprehensive childproofing, always rely on purpose-built safety products that adhere to safety standards. Baby gates, outlet covers, cabinet locks, and corner protectors are essential items that should be a part of your childproofing arsenal.

Remember, child safety is no laughing matter! So, let's mix a little humor with a whole lot of thoughtfulness to keep those tiny explorers safe and sound. Happy childproofing!

Kitchen
Infant/Non-mobile: (Birth - 6 months)
→ **Infant crawl/roll: (5 months - 1 year)**
→ **Toddler/Pre-school: (1 year - 4 years)**
→ **School-age: (5 years - 6+ years)**

Magnet Concerns

While fascinating and useful, magnets can pose significant risks to children if ingested or misused. Their strong attraction can cause serious internal injuries if multiple magnets are swallowed.

Toy Magnets

Supervision: Always supervise children when they are playing with toys that contain magnets.

Age-Appropriate Toys: Ensure that toys with magnets are age-appropriate. Many toys' packaging will have age recommendations.

Regular Inspection: Frequently inspect toys for wear and tear. If a toy is broken or if a magnet is loose, repair it immediately or discard the toy.

Refrigerator Magnets

High Placement: Place refrigerator magnets high up where young children can't reach them.

Avoid Small Magnets: Opt for larger, child-friendly magnets that can't be easily swallowed.

Magnetic Jewelry

Storage: Store magnetic jewelry in a locked jewelry box or a location out of children's reach.

Awareness: Educate older children about the dangers of swallowing magnets if they have magnetic jewelry or accessories.

Magnetic Locks and Latches

High Placement: If magnetic locks are being used for cabinets, ensure they are placed high up and out of children's reach.

Regular Checks: Periodically check to ensure the magnetic mechanism is working correctly and hasn't come loose.

Magnetic Desk Toys and Gadgets

Storage: Store these in a locked drawer or high shelf when not in use.

Education: If you have older children or teenagers, educate them about the risks and ensure they don't leave these items within reach of younger siblings.

Electronics with Magnets

Secure Placement: Ensure devices like speakers, which contain magnets, are securely placed on shelves or stands.

Cord Management: Use cord organizers or ties to keep cords out of reach, as some charging cables use magnetic connectors.

DIY and Craft Magnets

Dedicated Storage: Store craft supplies, including magnets, in dedicated containers with secure lids.

Workspace Cleanliness: After using magnets for DIY projects or crafts, ensure the workspace is cleaned up immediately to prevent any magnets from being left out.

Magnetic Tools

Toolbox Storage: Store magnetic tools like magnetic screwdrivers or pick-up tools in a locked toolbox.

Workspace Safety: If using magnetic tools for home projects, ensure the workspace is off-limits to children or is closely supervised.

General Safety Tips

Emergency Plan: Be aware of the symptoms of magnet ingestion, such as abdominal pain, nausea, or vomiting. If you suspect a child has swallowed a magnet, seek medical attention immediately.

Education: Regularly remind children of the dangers associated with swallowing or misusing magnets.

Regular Home Checks: Periodically inspect your home for any loose or stray magnets that might have been overlooked.

Magnets, due to their unique properties, can be particularly enticing to children. By being proactive and detail-oriented in our approach to magnet safety, we can ensure that our homes remain safe environments for curious young minds.

Kitchen
Infant/Non-mobile: (Birth - 6 months)
Infant crawl/roll: (5 months - 1 year)
→ **Toddler/Pre-school: (1 year - 4 years)**
→ **School-age: (5 years - 6+ years)**

Purse/Handbags

A purse can be a treasure trove of fascination for little hands, but it can also hide potential dangers. Many everyday items we carry from cosmetics to medications can pose risks to children.

Secure Medications: Use child-resistant pill cases for any medications or supplements. Remember that child-resistant doesn't mean childproof. Always keep your purse out of reach.

Cosmetic and Personal Care Items: Store cosmetics in a zippered pouch in your purse, especially items like nail polish, perfume, or makeup removers that can be harmful if ingested. Some lipsticks can contain elements that shouldn't be ingested in large amounts. Ensure caps are secure and consider a lipstick holder.

Sharp Objects: Items like scissors, nail files, or tweezers should be stored in protective sheaths or cases. Consider a separate zippered pouch for sharp items.

Coins and Small Items: Use a secure coin purse for loose change, as coins can be a choking hazard. Small brooches, pins, or other decorative items should be securely fastened or stored in a pouch.

Choking Hazards: Store necklaces, earrings, and other small jewelry items in a jewelry pouch or zippered compartment. Ensure all buttons or decorative elements on the purse are secure.

Toxic Substances: These often contain high levels of alcohol. Use a childproof bottle or keep it in a zipped compartment. Store in a sealed bag or pouch to prevent accidental ingestion or spillage.

Electronics and Batteries: Store electronics in zipped compartments. Ensure battery compartments on devices are securely closed. Wrap cords securely and store them in a pouch to prevent strangulation hazards.

Snacks and Edibles: If you carry snacks, ensure they are age-appropriate and not a choking hazard. Ensure any beverages have secure caps to prevent spills and access.

Keys and Keychains: Use a key holder or pouch to prevent sharp edges from being accessible. Avoid having too many small or detachable keychains, which can be choking hazards.

Emergency Items: If you carry a mini first aid kit, ensure items like antiseptics are sealed and out of reach. Keep a list of emergency contacts in your purse. While this isn't a childproofing tip, it's essential for emergencies.

Purse Placement: When at home, store your purse in a consistent, out-of-reach location.

Regular Cleanouts: Periodically empty and clean out your purse to remove expired items, potential hazards, or unnecessary objects.

Educate: As children grow, educate them about the dangers of certain items in a purse, teaching them not to go through anyone's bag without permission.

A purse can often be overlooked as a potential danger zone. By being proactive and detail-oriented, you can ensure that your purse is not just organized but also safe from curious little explorers.

Kitchen
Infant/Non-mobile: (Birth - 6 months)
Infant crawl/roll: (5 months - 1 year)
→ **Toddler/Pre-school: (1 year - 4 years)**
→ **School-age: (5 years - 6+ years)**

Aluminum Foil, Plastic Wrap, Wax paper, and Parchment Paper

Childproofing concerns with aluminum foil, plastic wrap, wax paper, and parchment paper mainly revolve around the risk of suffocation and choking. These materials are thin and can pose hazards to young children if not handled properly.

Storage: Keep these materials out of reach of children in a locked or high cabinet. Avoid storing them in low drawers or on easily accessible countertops.

Cut Safely: When using these materials, be cautious while cutting or tearing. Keep sharp edges and blades out of reach of children.

Discard Carefully: After use, promptly dispose of used aluminum foil, plastic wrap, wax paper, and parchment paper in a secure trash bin. Do not leave them lying around where children can grab them.

Supervision: Always supervise children when using these materials in food preparation or other activities. Avoid letting children play with them, as they can pose choking hazards.

Avoid Wrapping Food with Small Objects: Do not wrap small objects or toys in these materials, as children might mistake them for edible items and attempt to consume them.

Educate Older Children: If you have older children in the household, educate them about the potential hazards of these materials and the importance of keeping them away from younger siblings.

Childproof Cabinets: If these materials are stored in cabinets within a child's reach, consider using childproof locks to prevent curious hands from accessing them.

<u>Kitchen</u>
→ **Infant/Non-mobile: (Birth - 6 months)**
→ **Infant crawl/roll: (5 months - 1 year)**
→ **Toddler/Pre-school: (1 year - 4 years)**
→ **School-age: (5 years - 6+ years)**

Fuse Box Concerns

Childproofing a fuse box may sound odd, but it is crucial.

Install a Lockable Cover: Invest in a lockable fuse box cover or panel. These covers come with a lock and key, ensuring that only adults can access the fuses and electrical components.

Relocate Exposed Fuse Boxes: If possible, consider relocating the fuse box to an area that is out of reach of children, such as a locked utility room or basement.

Use Warning Labels: Place warning labels on or near the fuse box to remind adults of its importance and to keep it secure from children.

Educate Children: Teach children about the dangers of playing with electrical components and the importance of leaving the fuse box alone. Explain that it is an adult-only area.

Secure Cords and Wires: Ensure that any cords or wires around the fuse box are securely fastened and out of reach of children to prevent them from tampering with electrical connections.

Regular Maintenance: Periodically check the fuse box for any loose or damaged components and promptly address any issues to maintain its safety and functionality.

Supervise Access: If there are instances where adults need to access the fuse box, ensure that children are supervised and kept away during this time.

Professional Inspection: If you are unsure about the safety of your fuse box or electrical system, consider having a professional electrician inspect it to identify any potential hazards.

Notes:

Kitchen
Infant/Non-mobile: (Birth - 6 months)
Infant crawl/roll: (5 months - 1 year)
→ **Toddler/Pre-school: (1 year - 4 years)**
→ **School-age: (5 years - 6+ years)**

Pantry Concerns

Childproofing a kitchen pantry is essential to keep children safe from potential hazards and ensure that food items and cleaning products are out of their reach. **Install Childproof Locks:** Use childproof cabinet locks on pantry doors to prevent easy access by little hands. These locks will require adult dexterity to open, keeping hazardous items secure.

Reorganize: Store potentially dangerous items, such as cleaning products, chemicals, sharp utensils, and breakable items, on higher shelves, out of the reach of children.

Use High Shelves: To prevent children from reaching non-child-friendly items, place them on the highest shelves of the pantry.

Secure Heavy Items: Make sure heavy items, like large kitchen appliances or bulk containers, are stable and cannot be pulled down by curious children.

Childproof Storage Bins: Use childproof storage bins or containers for small items like snacks, grains, and baking ingredients. Ensure they are tightly closed and placed on higher shelves.

Lock Away Harmful Items: Keep potentially toxic or harmful substances, like medicine or alcohol, in a locked storage area separate from the pantry.

Remove Choking Hazards: Check for small items that can pose choking hazards, such as small candies or nuts, and store them in childproof containers or avoid keeping them in the pantry.

Educate Children: Teach children about pantry safety and explain why certain items are off-limits. Encourage them to seek an adult's help if they need something from the pantry.

Store Cleaning Supplies Safely: If you store cleaning supplies in the pantry, ensure they are in child-resistant containers and placed on higher shelves.

Regular Maintenance: Regularly inspect the pantry for any potential hazards, damaged containers, or expired products. Dispose of expired items promptly.

<u>Kitchen</u>
Infant/Non-mobile: (Birth - 6 months)
Infant crawl/roll: (5 months - 1 year)
→ **Toddler/Pre-school: (1 year - 4 years)**
→ **School-age: (5 years - 6+ years)**

Grocery Bags

Plastic and paper grocery bags are sneaky hazards! From suffocation risks to strangulation.

Keep them high and out of sight. Store bags in a high, locked cupboard or a pantry organizer mounted on the inside of a door. Out of sight, out of mind!

Use a designated bag holder: A wall-mounted bag holder keeps them organized and hard to pull out.

Use reusable cloth bags: If you're using plastic bags, consider switching to reusable cloth bags. They are less likely to cause harm and don't pose a suffocation risk.

Teach safety early: Get ahead by explaining that grocery bags are not toys and should be left alone. It's always good to reinforce with a little humor so they remember!

Kitchen
Infant/Non-mobile: (Birth - 6 months)
→ **Infant crawl/roll: (5 months - 1 year)**
→ **Toddler/Pre-school: (1 year - 4 years)**
School-age: (5 years - 6+ years)

Shopping Cart Handle Covers (Bonus non-home tip)

Use a Cart Seat Cover: Consider using a cart seat cover with safety straps to secure your child in the cart. These covers can help protect them from germs and keep them securely seated during shopping.

Check for Sturdiness: Before placing your child in the cart, inspect it for any broken or loose parts. Make sure the cart is sturdy and stable to prevent accidents.

Avoid Leaving Children Unattended: Never leave your child unattended in the shopping cart. Always keep them within your sight and reach.

Secure Belongings: Use the cart's safety straps to secure your child in the seat. Also, secure your belongings and shopping bags to prevent them from falling on your child.

Watch for Sharp Edges: The cart should be inspected for sharp edges or rough surfaces that could potentially harm your child. If necessary, use a cart liner or cushion.

Avoid Placing Infants in the Cart: For infants who cannot sit up independently, it's safer to use a baby carrier or car seat that attaches to the shopping cart or opt for alternative shopping options.

Inspect for Sanitization: If available, use sanitizing wipes to clean the cart handle and seat before placing your child in it.

► *According to the Royal Society for the Prevention of Accidents (RoSPA), parents and caregivers are generally aware of the dangers posed by plastic bags, **but may not recognize similar risks from other items like grocery bags and nappy sacks.***

|Ch. 4| Dining Room

Introduction: Childproofing a dining room is crucial to ensuring a safe environment for young children. Often bustling with activity, this space contains several elements that might pose risks to curious little ones. To initiate childproofing, it is essential to identify and mitigate potential hazards, which could include securing unstable objects and restricting access to certain areas. Employing safety measures such as using child-friendly furniture and installing protective barriers can be beneficial. It is important to approach childproofing as an ongoing task, adapting strategies as children grow and their abilities evolve. This proactive approach helps in fostering a safe and enjoyable dining space for the entire family.

Testimonial: *I never thought the dining room, a place where we gather to enjoy meals as a family, could turn into a site of such distress. Just last week, our little one, who is always bustling with energy and curiosity, managed to pull a tablecloth, causing a hot cup of tea to spill over. The seconds it took for this to happen were enough to cause her minor burns. It was a heart-wrenching sight, one that I wouldn't wish upon any parent.*

Looking back, I realize this could have been easily prevented if we had properly childproofed our dining room. Simple measures like securing the tablecloth or placing hot beverages well out of reach could have made a world of difference. I urge all parents not to overlook the potential hazards that lie in the most familiar of places. Please take the time to assess and secure your dining area, considering the little explorers who might venture there. It's about preventing accidents and fostering a safe space where your children can grow and learn without fear. Let's make our homes the safe havens they are meant to be.

Steve C. (Father or 3)

Dining room
Infant/Non-mobile: (Birth - 6 months)
→ **Infant crawl/roll: (5 months - 1 year)**
→ **Toddler/Pre-school: (1 year - 4 years)**
→ **School-age: (5 years - 6+ years)**

Place mats vs Tablecloths

Placemats and tablecloths both have their pros and cons. Placemats offer stability, easy cleaning, and less risk of pulling, while tablecloths provide comprehensive coverage, soften impacts, and enhance the aesthetic appeal of your dining area. However, tablecloths are more prone to stains and require more maintenance. The best choice between the two depends on your family's specific needs, including the age of your children, the layout of your dining area, and your personal preferences. (For details refer to kitchen **pg. 96**)

Dining room
Infant/Non-mobile: (Birth - 6 months)
→ **Infant crawl/roll: (5 months - 1 year)**
→ **Toddler/Pre-school: (1 year - 4 years)**
→ **School-age: (5 years - 6+ years)**

Unfinished Furniture

The rough and uneven surfaces typical of unfinished furniture can be a source of splinters, potentially causing painful wounds and infections in tender young skin. Moreover, these pieces of furniture may lack the stability and robustness found in finished products, increasing the risk of tipping or collapsing under the weight of a climbing child, leading to serious injuries. Additionally, unfinished furniture can be more susceptible to harboring bacteria and mold, as the lack of a protective sealant allows for the easier penetration of moisture and germs, creating an unhealthy environment for little ones who are prone to putting their mouths on surfaces. Furthermore, the materials used in the construction of such furniture might contain harmful chemicals or toxins that can be easily ingested or inhaled by children, posing a risk to their developing systems. Therefore, when considering the safety of a child-friendly home, it's prudent to meticulously evaluate the potential hazards associated with unfinished furniture. (For details refer to living room **pg. 30**)

Dining room
Infant/Non-mobile: (Birth - 6 months)
Infant crawl/roll: (5 months - 1 year)
→ **Toddler/Pre-school: (1 year - 4 years)**
→ **School-age: (5 years - 6+ years)**

Secure Pictures to the Wall

Securing pictures and other wall hangings is a critical aspect of childproofing. Brimming with curiosity and energy, little ones may be tempted to tug at or climb on protruding frames, risking damage to the artwork and potentially serious injuries from falls or broken glass. Moreover, the heavy weight of some frames can cause substantial harm if they were to fall on a child. To mitigate these risks, it's advisable to use sturdy wall anchors and hooks that can bear significant weight, ensuring a firm hold. Additionally, placing pictures out of the reach of children and opting for shatterproof acrylic glass instead of traditional glass can further enhance safety. Regular checks to ensure the stability of these hangings can prevent accidents, maintaining a safe and harmonious home environment. In summary, securing pictures on the wall is a simple yet crucial step in childproofing, safeguarding young children from potential hazards, and fostering a safe space for them to grow and explore.

Dining room
Infant non-mobile: (Birth-6 mo.)
Infant crawl/roll: (5 mo.-2 yrs.)
→ **Toddler/Pre-School: (1 yr.-4 yrs.)**
→ **School-age: (5 yrs.-6+ yrs.)**

Secure China and Utensils

Securing China

High Shelves and Cabinets: Elevate your china storage to higher shelves or cabinets, making them inaccessible to young children. Ensure that these elevated storage areas are sturdy and can bear the china's weight without collapsing.

Cabinet Locks: Invest in high-quality childproof cabinet locks. These locks should be robust enough to withstand tugging or pulling. Regularly inspect the locks to ensure they're functioning correctly and haven't loosened over time.

Non-slip Mats: Line the shelves with non-slip mats. These mats will prevent the china from shifting if the cabinet is accidentally bumped. Opt for thicker mats that provide cushioning, reducing the risk of china chipping or breaking if jostled.

Glass-fronted Cabinet Precautions: If your cabinet has a glass front, ensure the glass is tempered to prevent shattering. Consider adding a safety film to the glass, which holds the glass together if broken.

Anchor Freestanding Cabinets: For cabinets that aren't built into the wall, use furniture straps or brackets to anchor them to the wall, preventing tipping hazards.

Securing Utensils

Drawer Locks: Equip drawers containing utensils with childproof locks. Ensure these locks are durable and regularly inspected for wear and tear. Consider double-locking systems for drawers containing particularly sharp utensils.

Utensil Organizers: Use organizers with tight compartments to segregate utensils. This organization makes it harder for small hands to grasp dangerous items and keeps sharp edges contained. Opt for organizers with locking features or lids for added security.

Magnetic Strips: Consider using magnetic strips for knives or sharp utensils. Mount these strips high on a wall, out of a child's reach, and ensure the magnetic strip's strength is adequate to hold the weight of the utensils securely.

Separate Storage for Sharp Utensils: Dedicate specific drawers or compartments solely for sharp utensils. This separation ensures that children can't accidentally access them when reaching for other utensils. Label these storage areas and educate older children about the dangers within.

Blunt End First: When storing utensils in organizers or holders, ensure that the sharp or pointed ends are facing downwards. This orientation ensures that if a child does manage to reach, they touch the blunt end first.

Dining Room
Infant/Non-mobile: (Birth - 6 months)
Infant crawl/roll: (5 months - 1 year)
→ **Toddler/Pre-school: (1 year - 4 years)**
→ **School-age: (5 years - 6+ years)**

Ensuring Mealtime Safety for Children

Mealtime safety for children involves a series of precautionary measures and vigilant supervision. Keeping hot dishes and beverages away from children is essential to prevent burns and spills. Choosing safe utensils and unbreakable plates can minimize the risk of injuries from broken dishes. Parents should be cautious about the food choices they make for their children, avoiding high-risk foods or cutting them into safe, non-round pieces to prevent choking. It's also important to scrutinize the small toys or trinkets that often come with purchases, ensuring they are age-appropriate to prevent choking hazards. Despite taking these precautions, constant supervision during mealtimes is irreplaceable to guarantee the safety of young children and foster healthy eating habits and peace of mind.

Dining room
Infant/Non-mobile: (Birth - 6 months)
→ **Infant crawl/roll: (5 months - 1 year)**
→ **Toddler/Pre-school: (1 year - 4 years)**
→ **School-age: (5 years - 6+ years)**

Plant Safety

Having plants in the home poses some risks that require childproofing attention. Many common houseplants like philodendrons, pothos, and dieffenbachia contain harmful toxins that can cause nausea, mouth irritation, and other symptoms if ingested, especially by kids and pets. Cacti and succulents have painful thorns. Heavy pots can tip and crush fingers. The safest approach is to keep all plants entirely out of reach of children on high shelves or in locked planters. Also, ensure hanging plants cannot be pulled down and isolate plants with thorns. Supervise closely when children are near plants and teach them not to touch them. *(For details refer to living room* **pg. 71**)

Dining room
Infant/Non-mobile: (Birth - 6 months)
Infant crawl/roll: (5 months - 1 year)
Toddler/Pre-school: (1 year - 4 years)
School-age: (5 years - 6+ years)

Secure Throw Rugs

Throw rugs pose safety risks for young children, which require attention when childproofing a home. Loose rugs are tripping hazards and can cause falls and injuries. The best approach is to remove small throw rugs altogether. If using rugs, choose those with non-slip backing or use rug pads and double-sided tape to firmly secure rugs against slipping. Do not place rugs on top of each other. Inspect edges regularly to ensure they remain flat. For high-traffic areas, tightly woven low-pile rugs are best. Taking precautions with throw rugs by anchoring them firmly or removing them creates a safer play environment for kids. The goal is to minimize hazards. (For details refer to living room **pg. 29**)

Dining room
Infant/Non-mobile: (Birth - 6 months)
→ **Infant crawl/roll: (5 months - 1 year)**
→ **Toddler/Pre-school: (1 year - 4 years)**
→ **School-age: (5 years - 6+ years)**

Floor Lamps

To childproof a floor lamp, make sure it has a heavy base and is placed in a corner or against a wall. You can also secure it to the wall with a lamp anchor or cable tie and use a childproof lamp cord cover to prevent children from chewing on the cord. If you have a cordless floor lamp, keep it out of reach of children or place it in a playpen or gated area. (For details refer to living room **pg. 20**)

Dining room
Infant/Non-mobile: (Birth - 6 months)
→ **Infant crawl/roll: (5 months - 1 year)**
→ **Toddler/Pre-school: (1 year - 4 years)**
→ **School-age: (5 years - 6+ years)**

Outlet Covers

You can use outlet plugs, outlet covers, or tamper-resistant outlets to childproof an electric outlet. Outlet plugs are inserted into the outlet and block access to the prongs. Outlet covers fit over the entire outlet and is more difficult for children to remove. Tamper-resistant outlets have built-in shutters that prevent children from inserting objects into the outlet. (For details refer to living room **pg. 51**)

> ▶ *According to the Electrical Safety Foundation International (ESFI),* ***approximately 2,400 children in the United States are treated for electrical outlet-related injuries each year.***

|Ch. 5| Hallways/Stairways

Introduction: These areas can often be overlooked, yet they harbor potential hazards that can lead to slips, trips, and falls, especially for children between the ages of 0-6 who are just learning to navigate their surroundings. From securing loose rugs to installing safety gates at the top and bottom of staircases, taking precautionary measures in these transitional spaces is vital. Additionally, ensuring that the hallways are well-lit and free from clutter, as well as installing sturdy handrails, can further safeguard your children from potential accidents. Let's delve into the specifics of making your hallways and stairs a safe zone for your little explorers.

Testimonial: *In the midst of our hectic days, a single moment of distraction led to a nightmare we'll never forget. Our little Jack, just starting to explore the world on his own two feet, found himself in a dangerous situation we never imagined. It was just an ordinary afternoon; I was busy in the kitchen when I heard a horrifying sound. Rushing to the stairs, I found Jack at the bottom, his face twisted in pain.*

The sight of him there, injured and scared, sent a wave of guilt and fear crashing over me. I'd always thought accidents like this happened to other people, but now I was living it. We should have installed a safety gate at the top of the stairs and kept the hallway clear of toys and clutter. Simple precautions that could have prevented this.

As I sat in the hospital, holding my injured son, I realized the importance of childproofing. It's not just about protecting our kids; it's about giving ourselves peace of mind. Since then, we've taken action: safety gates, secured rugs, a clutter-free hallway, and teaching Jack about safe zones.

I share our story not to dwell on the past, but to prevent others from making the same mistakes. Childproofing isn't just a checklist; it's a commitment to our children's safety. Let's make sure our homes are safe havens, not potential danger zones.

- Patrick D. (Father of 3)

Hallways/Stairways
Infant/Non-mobile: (Birth - 6 months)
Infant crawl/roll: (5 months - 1 year)
→ **Toddler/Pre-school: (1 year - 4 years)**
→ **School-age: (5 years - 6+ years)**

Doorknob Concerns

Childproofing all possible doors in a house is a critical step in ensuring the safety of young children. From the main entryways to interior room doors, each type presents unique risks that require proactive solutions. A secure home begins with thoughtful planning and the right safety tools to prevent accidents and give caregivers peace of mind.

Front and back doors, being the primary entry and exit points, require especially stringent safety measures. **Installing high-placed deadbolts** that are well out of a child's reach is one of the most effective ways to prevent them from unlocking doors and wandering outside. **Door alarms** are also essential—they alert you immediately if a door is opened, giving you time to respond before a child exits unnoticed. If your doors have glass panels, make sure they are made of **safety glass**, which is designed to resist shattering and minimize injury in case of breakage.

Interior doors, such as those to bedrooms, bathrooms, and laundry rooms, also need attention. Children can access hazardous items, fall into water, or accidentally lock themselves in. To mitigate these risks, use **doorknob covers** that are difficult for small hands to twist and open. **Finger pinch guards** are a must to protect tiny fingers from getting caught in the door hinge. **Door stoppers** can also help by preventing doors from slamming shut, which could cause injury.

Sliding doors, often found leading to patios or balconies, require different childproofing strategies. Install **sliding door locks** at the top of the frame to prevent young children from opening them. To improve safety further, **apply shatter-resistant window film** to the glass. This minimizes injury if the door is broken. Additionally, **installing safety bars** ensures the door cannot be forced open, adding an extra layer of security.

Garage doors pose another serious hazard, as garages often contain tools, chemicals, and vehicles. **Store remote controls** for garage doors out of reach to avoid unintentional operation. It's also vital to install **safety sensors** that detect obstructions and reverse the door's motion to prevent injury. For extra protection, **use childproofing straps on emergency release levers** so that children can't operate them manually.

Closet doors, though seemingly harmless, can pose hidden risks. Children may attempt to climb or play inside closets, leading to potential injury or entrapment. For bi-fold closet doors, **install bi-fold door locks** to prevent pinching or unintended access. **Magnetic locks** are another great option; they can only be opened with a magnetic key, keeping dangerous contents out of reach.

In addition to these physical measures, don't overlook general safety practices. Teach children early about the dangers of unsupervised access to certain areas—awareness is a powerful tool in preventing accidents. And, most importantly, **supervise young children closely**, especially around doors that could lead to hazards.

By taking the time to secure every door in your home, you can create a **safe and secure environment** where your children are free to explore without unnecessary risk. **The goal is not to restrict their**

curiosity, but to channel it safely—turning your home into a secure, joyful place to grow and discover.

Hallways/Stairways
Infant/Non-mobile: (Birth - 6 months)
Infant crawl/roll: (5 months - 1 year)
→ **Toddler/Pre-school: (1 year - 4 years)**
→ **School-age: (5 years - 6+ years)**

Night Lights

There are various hallway nightlight options available to suit different preferences and needs.

Plug-In Nightlights: Plug-in nightlights are simple and easy to use. They plug directly into a wall outlet and provide gentle illumination. Many plug-in nightlights come with sensors that automatically turn the light on when it gets dark and off when it's bright.

LED Nightlights: LED nightlights are energy-efficient and long-lasting. They come in various shapes and designs, including ones that resemble stars, animals, or decorative elements, adding a touch of fun and aesthetics to the hallway.

Motion-Activated Nightlights: Motion-activated nightlights turn on when they detect movement, making them ideal for hallways used primarily at night. They conserve energy by only activating it when needed.

Battery-Operated Nightlights: Battery-operated nightlights offer flexibility in placement since they don't require an electrical outlet. They are convenient for areas without easy access to outlets.

Wall-Mounted Nightlights: Wall-mounted nightlights can be permanently fixed to the wall, providing a stable and constant source of light in the hallway.

Rechargeable Nightlights: Rechargeable nightlights are eco-friendly and cost-effective. They can be charged using a USB cable or a docking station and provide illumination without the need for disposable batteries.

Projector Nightlights: Projector nightlights create a soothing ambiance by projecting patterns or images on the walls or ceiling. Some projectors also include lullabies, or nature sounds to help children sleep peacefully.

Smart Nightlights: Smart nightlights can be controlled through smartphone apps or voice commands, allowing you to adjust brightness, color, and scheduling according to your preferences.

Glow-in-the-Dark Nightlights: Glow-in-the-dark nightlights absorb light during the day and emit a soft glow at night. They can be beneficial during power outages or for a subtle glow without using electricity.

Portable Nightlights: Portable nightlights are small and lightweight, making them easy to carry around the house. They are handy for children who might need extra light in the hallway or their bedroom.

When choosing a hallway nightlight, consider factors such as brightness levels, energy efficiency, ease of use, and safety features. Select a nightlight that complements your hallway decor and meets your family's specific needs.

Hallways/Stairways
Infant/Non-mobile: (Birth - 6 months)
Infant crawl/roll: (5 months - 1 year)
→ **Toddler/Pre-school: (1 year - 4 years)**
→ **School-age: (5 years - 6+ years)**

The Gate Keeper (Gate Safety)

Staircase-related injuries account for **over 300,000 emergency room visits annually for children** in the U.S., often due to falls or entrapment. (Source: Centers for Disease Control and Prevention (CDC) – WISQARS) Childproofing with a gate for the stairs is crucial in creating a safe environment for young children and pets. Stair gates act as protective barriers to prevent access to staircases.

Choose the Right Gate: Select a stair gate that fits the width of your staircase and is appropriate for your specific needs. There are two main types of stair gates: pressure-mounted gates and hardware-mounted gates. Pressure-mounted gates are convenient for easy installation, while hardware-mounted gates offer a more secure and permanent solution.

Measure the Staircase Opening: Measure the width of the staircase opening where you plan to install the gate. Ensure that the gate you choose is adjustable to fit the width of your stairs.

Install at the Top and Bottom: It's essential to install gates at both the top and bottom of the staircase to completely childproof the area.

Follow Manufacturer's Instructions: Read and follow the manufacturer's installation instructions carefully. Improper installation can compromise the gate's effectiveness and safety.

Position the Gate Correctly: Place the gate at the top or bottom of the stairs, depending on where you want to restrict access. Ensure the gate is securely attached and leveled to function properly.

Use Hardware-Mounted Gates for the Top of Stairs: For added safety, use hardware-mounted gates for the top of the stairs. Pressure-mounted gates may not be suitable for this area as they could potentially dislodge under pressure.

Check Latching Mechanism: Ensure that the gate's latching mechanism works correctly and is child resistant. It should be easy for adults to open and close but challenging for young children to figure it out.

Regularly Inspect the Gate: Periodically inspect the gate for signs of wear, damage, or loose components. Address any issues immediately to maintain the gate's effectiveness.

Supervision and Education: Even with stair gates in place, always supervise children and pets when they are near the stairs. Educate family members and caregivers about the importance of always using the gate and keeping it closed.

Remove Clutter: Remove the stairway area of clutter and objects that could pose a tripping hazard.

Consider Extra-Wide Gates: If your staircases are wider, consider using extra-wide gates that can extend to cover larger openings.

Properly installing a gate for the stairs and implementing these childproofing measures can significantly reduce the risk of accidents and provide a safer environment for your little ones to explore and play. Stair gates are just one part of a comprehensive childproofing strategy, so be vigilant in identifying and addressing other hazards in your home.

Hallways/Stairways
Infant/Non-mobile: (Birth - 6 months)
Infant crawl/roll: (5 months - 1 year)
→ **Toddler/Pre-school: (1 year - 4 years)**
→ **School-age: (5 years - 6+ years)**

Stairway Traction

Childproofing stairs includes ensuring they are safe and secure to prevent slips and falls, especially for young children. Making stairs anti-slip is an essential step in enhancing stair safety.

Non-Slip Treads or Stair Mats: Install non-slip treads or stair mats on each step. These adhesive mats provide a textured surface that improves traction and reduces the risk of slipping.

Carpeting or Runners: Covering the stairs with carpeting or runners can add an extra layer of slip resistance. For optimal safety, choose a carpet with a low pile and a non-slip backing.

Secure Handrails: Ensure that handrails are securely attached on both sides of the staircase. Handrails provide support and stability while climbing the stairs, reducing the risk of accidents.

Adequate Lighting: Proper lighting in the stairway is essential for visibility. Install bright and energy-efficient lighting to ensure that each step is well-illuminated, even at night.

Remove Clutter: Keep the stairway area free from clutter, toys, and other items that could become tripping hazards.

Use Slip-Resistant Paint or Coatings: Apply slip-resistant paint or coatings to wooden or concrete stairs to improve traction.

Keep Stair Edges Clearly Marked: Mark the edges of the stairs with contrasting colors or reflective strips to make them more visible, especially for young children.

Teach Safe Stair Habits: Educate children about safe stair habits, such as using the handrail, walking instead of running, and paying attention while climbing or descending.

Regular Maintenance: Regularly inspect the stairs for any loose or damaged treads, handrails, or carpeting. Repair or replace any worn-out or damaged parts promptly.

Use Stair Gates: Install stair gates at the top and bottom of the stairs to prevent young children from accessing the staircase unsupervised.

Supervision: Always supervise children when they are near the stairs, especially if they are not yet confident in their stair-climbing abilities.

Consider Stair Nosing: Stair nosing, which is a protruding edge that provides additional grip, can be installed on the front of each stair to enhance slip resistance.

You can create a safer stairway environment for children and other family members. Prioritizing stair safety can significantly reduce the risk of accidents and injuries, providing peace of mind for parents and caregivers.

Hallways/Stairways
Infant/Non-mobile: (Birth - 6 months)
Infant crawl/roll: (5 months - 1 year)
→ **Toddler/Pre-school: (1 year - 4 years)**
→ **School-age: (5 years - 6+ years)**

Banisters

Childproofing the banister is essential to create a safe environment for children, especially toddlers and young explorers.

Install a Safety Gate: Use a safety gate at the top and bottom of the stairs to prevent children from accessing the banister and staircase when unsupervised. Choose a gate that is specifically designed for use with banisters.

Add Baluster Guards or Netting: Baluster guards or netting can be attached to the banister to create a barrier that prevents children from sticking their arms or legs between the balusters. This helps to prevent entrapment or climbing.

Secure Loose Balusters: Regularly inspect the banister for any loose or wobbly balusters. Secure them firmly to prevent accidents.

Padding and Cushioning: Use cushioned padding on the banister to soften any potential impact if a child accidentally bumps into it.

Childproofing Covers: Consider using childproofing covers or guards designed specifically for banisters. These covers are typically made of durable materials and prevent children from easily dislodging or tampering with the banister.

Remove Climbing Hazards: Keep furniture or other items away from the banister that could act as a climbing aid for children to access higher areas.

Check for Splinters: Regularly check the banister for any splinters or rough edges. Sand down any rough areas to prevent injuries.

Educate Children: Teach children about the banister's purpose as a safety feature and instruct them not to play or climb on it.

Secure Handrails: Ensure that handrails are securely attached on both sides of the staircase to provide stability and support while climbing or descending.

Supervision: Always supervise children when they are near the banister and stairs, especially if they are not yet confident in using the stairs independently.

Secure Loose Carpeting or Rugs: If you have carpeting or rugs on the stairs, make sure they are securely fastened to the steps to prevent tripping hazards.

Regular Maintenance: Periodically inspect the banister for any signs of wear or damage and address any issues promptly.

Hallways/Stairways
Infant/Non-mobile: (Birth - 6 months)
Infant crawl/roll: (5 months - 1 year)
→ **Toddler/Pre-school: (1 year - 4 years)**
→ **School-age: (5 years - 6+ years)**

Rails on Both Sides of Stairs

Having handrails on both sides of stairs is not only a safety measure for general use but also an important aspect of childproofing your home. Childproofing stairs with handrails on both sides offer additional safety and support for children as they learn to navigate the staircase.

Enhanced Stability for Children: Children, especially toddlers and young kids, are still developing their balance and coordination. Having handrails on both sides of the stairs provides them with enhanced stability and support, reducing the risk of slips and falls.

Guidance for Safe Use: Handrails help guide children along the staircase, preventing them from veering off the steps or losing their footing.

Ease of Climbing and Descending: With handrails on both sides, children can use both hands to hold onto the rails while climbing up or down the stairs. This enables them to move more comfortably and confidently.

Promotes Independent Use: As children become more confident in using the stairs independently, the presence of handrails on both sides gives them the freedom to navigate the staircase with minimal assistance.

Supplement to Stair Gates: While stair gates are essential to block access to stairs when not supervised, having handrails on both sides provides an added layer of protection when children are using the stairs under adult supervision.

Safety During Emergencies: In emergencies, children can rely on the handrails to help them safely evacuate the building, providing additional support and guidance.

Prevents Cluttering on Stairs: With handrails on both sides, children are less likely to place toys or other objects on the stairs, reducing the risk of tripping hazards.

Adaptable for All Ages: Handrails on both sides benefit not only children but also adults and elderly individuals, making the staircase safer for everyone in the household.

When childproofing stairs, ensure that the handrails are securely attached to the wall or balustrade. Regularly inspect the handrails for any signs of wear or damage, and promptly address any issues to maintain their effectiveness in providing a safe and child-friendly staircase. Additionally, educate children about the importance of using the handrails while using the stairs and supervise them when they are near the staircase until they are confident in using it independently.

Hallways/Stairways
Infant/Non-mobile: (Birth - 6 months)
Infant crawl/roll: (5 months - 1 year)
→ **Toddler/Pre-school: (1 year - 4 years)**
→ **School-age: (5 years - 6+ years)**

Install a "Jr. Handrail"

Adding a lower stair handrail specifically designed for children is a great way to further enhance safety on the staircase and encourage their independence. A lower handrail allows children to have a secure grip and support while climbing or descending the stairs, making the stairway more accessible and less intimidating for them.

Measure and Mark: Measure the height at which you want to install the lower handrail. The ideal height is around 24 to 28 inches from the ground, suitable for children's reach. Use a level and a pencil to mark the height on the staircase wall.

Select the Handrail: Choose a child-friendly handrail that is sturdy, smooth, and appropriately sized for small hands. You can find handrails made of wood, metal, or plastic, depending on your preference and decor.

Prepare the Handrail: Cut the handrail to the desired length using a saw, making sure it fits the width of the staircase.

Attach Mounting Brackets: Install mounting brackets to the wall at the marked height. Use screws and anchors suitable for your wall type (drywall, wood, etc.) to secure the brackets firmly.

Install the Handrail: Slide the handrail into the mounted brackets and ensure it is level. Use a level to double-check its horizontal alignment.

Secure the Handrail: Use screws to secure the handrail to the brackets, ensuring it is firmly attached.

Smooth the Edges: If necessary, sand down any rough edges or corners of the handrail to ensure it is safe for children to hold.

Paint or Finish (optional): If you want to add a decorative touch or match the handrail with your decor, paint or finish it according to your preference.

Educate Children: Teach children how to use the lower handrail safely and encourage them to hold onto it while going up and down the stairs.

Supervise: Always supervise children when they are using the stairs, especially when they are still learning to climb independently.

Adding a lower stair handrail for children promotes safety and independence, allowing them to navigate the stairs with confidence. It is an excellent addition to childproofing measures in your home, ensuring a safe and child-friendly environment for your little ones.

<u>Hallways/Stairways</u>
Infant/Non-mobile: (Birth - 6 months)
Infant crawl/roll: (5 months - 1 year)
→ **Toddler/Pre-school: (1 year - 4 years)**
→ **School-age: (5 years - 6+ years)**

Banister Guard on the Outside of Stairs to Prevent Climbing

Adding a banister guard to the portion of the staircase ending in a newel post is an important safety precaution, especially if young children can use the newel post as a foothold to climb over the banister. A banister guard serves as an additional barrier that prevents children from accessing the space between the newel post and the banister, reducing the risk of climbing and potential falls.

Measure the Area: Measure the length and height of the space between the newel post and the banister where you plan to install the guard.

Choose the Banister Guard: Select a banister guard that is designed to fit the measurements of the area and is made of sturdy, child-safe materials.

Install the Banister Guard: Attach the banister guard to the banister and newel post securely using screws or other provided fasteners. Make sure the guard is firmly in place and cannot be easily dislodged.

Check for Gaps: Ensure that there are no gaps or openings between the banister guard and the newel post or banister where a child's foot or hand could get caught.

Smooth Edges: If the banister guard has any sharp edges or rough surfaces, consider sending them down to ensure it is safe for children.

Regular Maintenance: Periodically inspect the banister guard to ensure it remains securely attached and free from any damage or wear.

Educate Children: Teach children about the purpose of the banister guard and instruct them not to climb on or over the banister.

Supervision: Always supervise children when they are near the stairs, even with the banister guard in place.

By adding a banister guard to the portion of the staircase ending in a newel post, you create an extra layer of safety to prevent climbing and keep children from accessing potentially hazardous areas. It complements the safety measures of using stair gates and other childproofing techniques, ensuring a secure stairway environment for children to explore and play without unnecessary risks.

<u>**Hallways/Stairs**</u>
Infant/Non-mobile: (Birth - 6 months)
→ **Infant crawl/roll: (5 months - 1 year)**
→ **Toddler/Pre-school: (1 year - 4 years)**
→ **School-age: (5 years - 6+ years)**

Beaded Curtains

Beaded curtains can pose a significant safety hazard to young children. Their small size and colorful appearance make them highly attractive to curious toddlers and infants. However, the beads can be easily pulled and ingested, leading to choking or other serious injuries.

Choose Shorter Curtains: Opt for shorter curtains that hang well out of reach of young children. This prevents them from accessing the beads and reduces the risk of accidents.

Replace Beads with Fabric Strands: Consider replacing the beads with soft, fabric strands. These are less enticing to pull and less dangerous if a child becomes tangled.

Add a Latch or Hook: Install a latch or hook to tie the curtain out of the way when not in use. This prevents children from accidentally pulling on the curtain and becoming entangled.

▶ *According to American Journal of Emergency Medicine's available data,* **approximately 1,076,558 people in the US suffer from staircase-related injuries each year, with young children and elderly people being the most vulnerable.** *Specifically, a child under 5 years old is treated for a stair-related injury approximately every six minutes.*

|Ch. 6| Children's Bedroom

Introduction: A man's house is his castle; that makes the child's room the tower. Or the Great Hall. Or the dungeon. It depends on the child. Anyway, young toddlers have little say in their environment, but as they grow, their wants and needs are going to change. We're going to address the beginning phases and let you guys take it from there.

Testimonial: *The memory of that day is etched into my mind, a stark reminder of the importance of childproofing every inch of our home. My precious three-year-old was happily playing in her room, a space I had thought was entirely safe. But in a blink of an eye, a horrifying accident unfolded. A heavy bookshelf, left unsecured, toppled over, narrowly missing her.*

The sound of the crash sent chills down my spine. Rushing into the room, I found her so frightened. Thankfully, her injuries were minor, but the shock and fear were palpable. It was a wake-up call. I realized that accidents could happen anywhere, even in the most familiar of places.

A simple act of securing the bookshelf to the wall could have prevented this ordeal. It's a lesson I'll never forget. Childproofing isn't just about protecting our children from obvious dangers; it's about anticipating potential risks and taking proactive steps to minimize them.

Since then, we've transformed our home into a safe haven. Every corner, every drawer, every outlet has been scrutinized. We've secured furniture, covered outlets, and removed any potential choking hazards. It's a labor of love, but it's worth every effort.

I urge all parents to prioritize childproofing. It's a small investment with immense rewards. By taking these preventive measures, we can create a safe and nurturing environment where our children can thrive.

-Tanya J. (Mother of 2)

Children's Bedroom
Infant/Non-mobile: (Birth - 6 months)
Infant crawl/roll: (5 months - 1 year)
→ **Toddler/Pre-school: (1 year - 4 years)**
School-age: (5 years - 6+ years)

Kiddo's First Bed

Transitioning a child from a crib to their first real bed is an exciting milestone, but it's essential to childproof the new bed to ensure their safety.

Guardrails: Install sturdy guardrails on both sides of the bed to prevent the child from accidentally rolling off during sleep.

Low-Height Bed: Choose a low-profile bed frame to reduce the risk of injury in case of accidental falls.

Secure the Mattress: Ensure the mattress fits snugly within the bed frame, leaving no gaps that could pose an entrapment hazard.

Soft Bedding: Use appropriately sized and firm bedding to reduce the risk of suffocation. Avoid pillows and heavy blankets for children under the age of one.

Child-Friendly Bedding: Opt for child-friendly and age-appropriate bedding designs without small parts that could detach and become a choking hazard.

Remove Clutter: Keep the area around the bed clear of toys, cords, and other potential tripping hazards.

Night Light: Place a night light in the room or hallway to provide a dim glow and reduce the risk of trips and falls during nighttime visits to the bathroom.

Secure Furniture: Make sure any nearby furniture, such as dressers or shelves, is securely anchored to the wall to prevent tipping hazards.

Outlet Covers: Cover electrical outlets near the bed with childproof outlet covers to prevent the child from inserting objects into them.

Window Safety: If the bed is near a window, install window guards or use window stops to prevent the child from falling out or accessing cords or blinds.

Cord Safety: Secure cords from window blinds or curtains out of the child's reach to prevent strangulation hazards.

Educate About Safe Behavior: Teach your child about safe behavior in their new bed, such as not jumping on it, not using it as a play area, and staying in bed during bedtime.

Supervision: Especially during the initial transition period, supervise your child during naptime and bedtime to ensure they are adjusting well to the new bed.

Childproof the Room: Childproof the entire bedroom by using outlet covers, securing furniture, and removing or securing any potential hazards.

Remember that childproofing is an ongoing process, and you may need to adjust safety measures as your child grows and their needs change. Regularly inspect the bed and the bedroom for any potential safety risks and make necessary adjustments to maintain a safe sleeping environment for your child.

Children's Bedroom
Infant/Non-mobile: (Birth - 6 months)
Infant crawl/roll: (5 months - 1 year)
Toddler/Pre-school: (1 year - 4 years)
→ **School-age: (5 years - 6+ years)**

Bunk bed Concerns

Using a bunk bed comes with certain safety considerations, and it's generally recommended that children be at least 6 years old before using one.

- **Age and Development:** Children under 6 years old may not have the physical coordination and cognitive skills needed to safely navigate a bunk bed, especially the top bunk.
- **Top Bunk Safety:** The top bunk is not recommended for children under 6 due to the risk of falls and injuries. Older children using the top bunk should be mature enough to understand safety rules and follow them.
- **Guardrails:** Both the top and bottom bunks should have sturdy guardrails on all sides to prevent accidental falls during sleep.
- **Mattress Fit:** Ensure that the mattress fits snugly within the bed frame, with no gaps between the mattress and the guardrails.
- **Sturdy Construction:** Choose a bunk bed with sturdy and durable construction to prevent the risk of collapse or other structural failures.
- **Safe Ladder or Stairs:** If the bunk bed has a ladder or stairs for access to the top bunk, make sure it is secure, slip-resistant, and properly attached to the bed frame.
- **Bunk Bed Position:** Place the bunk bed away from ceiling fans, light fixtures, or any other potential hazards.
- **No Jumping:** Teach children that bunk beds are not for jumping or playing on, as rough play can lead to injuries.
- **Proper Assembly:** Follow the manufacturer's instructions carefully when assembling the bunk bed to ensure it is stable and safe.
- **Mattress Quality:** Use high-quality, appropriately sized mattresses with good support for growing bodies.
- **No Hanging Items:** Avoid hanging items such as ropes, belts, or cords from the bunk bed, as they can pose strangulation hazards.
- **Regular Inspection:** Regularly inspect the bunk bed for any signs of wear, loose parts, or damage. Make the necessary repairs promptly.
- **Solo Sleeping on Top Bunk:** Encourage children to sleep alone on the top bunk and avoid allowing multiple children to sleep on the same level.
- **Familiarize with Emergency Procedures:** Teach children how to safely evacuate from the top bunk in case of an emergency.

Always supervise children around bunk beds, especially during playtime, to ensure their safety. Consider the individual child's maturity, physical abilities, and understanding of safety rules before allowing them to use a bunk bed. If your child shares a bunk bed with a sibling or friend during sleepovers, ensure that both children are aware of the safety rules and guidelines.

Children's Bedroom
Infant/Non-mobile: (Birth - 6 months)
Infant crawl/roll: (5 months - 1 year)
→ **Toddler/Pre-school: (1 year - 4 years)**
→ **School-age: (5 years - 6+ years)**

Clutter Concerns

Removing clutter from bedroom floors regularly is essential to keep your child safe. Here are several reasons why.

Safety: Clutter on the bedroom floor can create tripping hazards, leading to falls and injuries. Regularly cleaning and organizing the floor space minimizes the risk of accidents.

Hygiene: Keeping the bedroom floor clean helps maintain a hygienic living environment. Clutter can collect dust, dirt, and allergens, which can trigger allergies or respiratory issues.

Organization and Productivity: A clean and organized bedroom fosters better focus and productivity for children. It allows them to find their belongings easily, reducing distractions.

Promotes Responsibility: Encouraging children to clean their bedroom floors helps instill a sense of responsibility for their personal space and belongings.

Pride in their Space: A clean and tidy bedroom can boost a child's self-esteem and create a sense of pride in taking care of their space.

Good Habits for the Future: Teaching children to keep their bedroom floors clean instills good habits that they can carry into adulthood, leading to a more organized and clutter-free life.

More Space to Play: Clearing clutter from the floor creates more play space, allowing children to engage in activities without obstacles.

Better Sleep Environment: A clutter-free bedroom promotes a relaxing and peaceful sleep environment, which is crucial for a child's physical and emotional well-being.

Improved Room Air Quality: Removing clutter and regularly cleaning the floor reduces dust accumulation, leading to better indoor air quality and fewer allergens.

Teach Prioritization: Cleaning their bedroom floor requires children to decide what items are essential and what can be put away or donated. This teaches them valuable prioritization skills.

Encourage children to clean their bedroom floors

Set a regular cleaning schedule to make it a routine part of their daily or weekly chores. Make cleaning fun by turning it into a game or playing music while they tidy up. Offer praise and positive reinforcement when they complete the task. Provide storage solutions such as shelves, bins, and drawers to help keep belongings organized.

Lead by example and maintain a clean and clutter-free environment in shared living spaces.

By emphasizing the importance of a clean and clutter-free bedroom floor, parents can teach children valuable life skills, promote a healthier living space, and create a positive and organized living environment for the whole family.

Children's Bedroom
Infant/Non-mobile: (Birth - 6 months)
Infant crawl/roll: (5 months - 1 year)
→ **Toddler/Pre-school: (1 year - 4 years)**
→ **School-age: (5 years - 6+ years)**

Flashlight Importance

Having a flashlight in the bedroom can be beneficial for children for various reasons.

Safety During Power Outages: In the event of a power outage, a flashlight can provide a reliable source of light, ensuring that the child feels safe and secure during a potentially scary situation.

Comfort During Nighttime: Some children may feel uneasy or afraid of the dark. Having a flashlight nearby can offer a sense of comfort and control, allowing them to turn on the light whenever they feel anxious.

Ease of Movement at Night: A flashlight allows the child to move around the bedroom or go to the bathroom without turning on the main room light, which could disrupt their sleep or wake up other family members.

Entertainment during Playtime: A flashlight can add an element of fun during playtime or imaginative play in the bedroom, allowing the child to create shadow puppets or explore different lighting effects.

Emergency Preparedness: Teaching children about the purpose and proper use of a flashlight can be part of emergency preparedness education. They can learn how to use it during power outages or other emergencies.

Problem-Solving Skills: Having a flashlight encourages problem-solving skills as children learn to handle and use the device responsibly.

Learning About Light and Shadows: A flashlight can be used as an educational tool to teach children about light, shadows, and how light travels.

When introducing a flashlight to a child's bedroom, Choose a child-friendly, durable, and easy-to-use flashlight suitable for their age. Ensure the flashlight is always in working order by regularly checking and changing the batteries.

Discuss the proper use of the flashlight and when it's appropriate to use it (e.g., during power outages or when moving around the room at night). Establish clear rules, such as not shining the light directly into someone's eyes or using it as a toy. Encourage responsible use of the flashlight and emphasize safety measures.

Overall, having a flashlight in the bedroom can provide children with a sense of security, enhance their bedtime routines, and offer practical benefits in various situations. It can also present an opportunity for educational exploration and learning.

<u>Children's Bedroom</u>
Infant/Non-mobile: (Birth - 6 months)
Infant crawl/roll: (5 months - 1 year)
→ **Toddler/Pre-school: (1 year - 4 years)**
→ **School-age: (5 years - 6+ years)**

Escape Plan

Having an emergency plan is of utmost importance for the safety and well-being of individuals and families.

Safety Preparedness: An emergency plan ensures that everyone in the household knows what to do in case of a crisis, reducing panic and confusion during high-stress situations.

Quick Response: With a well-thought-out plan, individuals can respond promptly and take appropriate actions, potentially preventing injuries or further damage.

Evacuation Strategy: An emergency plan includes an evacuation strategy, indicating safe routes and assembly points in case the family needs to leave the home quickly.

Communication Guidelines: The plan outlines how family members will communicate with each other during an emergency, ensuring everyone is accounted for.

Contact Information: The plan includes important contact information for emergency services, neighbors, relatives, and other relevant individuals who can assist.

Medical Considerations: For families with specific medical needs, an emergency plan can include information about necessary medications, medical equipment, and contact details for healthcare providers.

Identification of Safety Equipment: The plan identifies the location of safety equipment such as fire extinguishers, first aid kits, and flashlights, enabling swift access when needed.

Practice and Familiarity: Regularly reviewing and practicing the emergency plan with all family members ensures everyone is familiar with the procedures and can act confidently during an actual emergency.

Adaptability: An emergency plan can be adapted to address unique challenges and response measures based on the type of emergency (fire, natural disaster, etc.).

Peace of Mind: Having an emergency plan in place provides peace of mind, knowing that everyone in the family is prepared for unforeseen circumstances.

Create an Effective Emergency Plan

Involve all family members in the planning process and make sure they understand their roles and responsibilities.

Establish meeting points and communication methods in case family members are separated during an emergency.

Review and update the plan regularly, especially as family dynamics change or new risks emerge.

Practice evacuation drills and other emergency procedures to reinforce preparedness.

Keep important documents, such as identification, insurance policies, and medical records, in a safe and easily accessible place.

Remember that each family's emergency plan may vary based on their unique needs and circumstances. The goal is to be proactive and prepared to handle emergencies calmly and effectively, minimizing potential risks and ensuring the safety of everyone involved.

Children's Bedroom
Infant/Non-mobile: (Birth - 6 months)
Infant crawl/roll: (5 months - 1 year)
→ **Toddler/Pre-school: (1 year - 4 years)**
→ **School-age: (5 years - 6+ years)**

Nightlights

Nightlights come in various types to cater to different needs and preferences. Some popular choices include plug-in nightlights, which are straightforward to use and often feature sensors for automatic operation, and LED nightlights, known for their energy efficiency and decorative designs. Motion-activated nightlights are energy-saving as they light up only upon detecting movement, while battery-operated ones offer placement flexibility. Wall-mounted nightlights provide constant illumination, and rechargeable ones are an eco-friendly option. Projector nightlights create a calming atmosphere with visual projections and sometimes include soothing sounds. Smart nightlights allow customization through apps or voice commands, and glow-in-the-dark variants offer a gentle, electricity-free glow, useful during power outages. Portable nightlights are convenient for children who need a movable light source. When selecting a nightlight, consider its brightness, energy efficiency, user-friendliness, safety features, and how well it matches your hallway decor and meets your family's needs. (For details refer to living room **pg. 174**)

Children's Bedroom
Infant/Non-mobile: (Birth - 6 months)
Infant crawl/roll: (5 months - 1 year)
→ **Toddler/Pre-school: (1 year - 4 years)**
→ **School-age: (5 years - 6+ years)**

Electric Blankets

Each year, over **1,500 children** suffer burns or electrical injuries from electric blankets. (Source: American Burn Association (ABA) - Burn Statistics)

Age and Supervision: Avoid using electric blankets for infants and very young children. If used for older children, make sure they are old enough to understand and follow safety guidelines.

Inspect and Maintain: Regularly inspect the electric blanket for signs of wear, damage, or frayed cords. Follow the manufacturer's guidelines for maintenance and care.

Approved Products: Purchase electric blankets from reputable manufacturers and look for safety certifications or approval from recognized organizations.

Safe Use and Temperature Settings: Follow the manufacturer's instructions regarding safe usage and temperature settings. Never turn an electric blanket on when not in use or while sleeping.

Avoid Wet Conditions: Keep the electric blanket away from water or liquids, and never use the blanket if it is wet.

Secure Cords and Controllers: Ensure that cords and controllers are securely attached to the blanket and out of reach of young children.

Check for Safety Features: Some electric blankets have safety features like automatic shut-off timers, which can provide added protection.

Supervision: If using an electric blanket for an older child, supervise them during its use, especially if they are using it for the first time.

Remove Before Bedtime: Remove the electric blanket from the bed before bedtime or naps to avoid accidental overheating or entanglement during sleep.

Educate Children: Teach older children about the safe and responsible use of electric blankets, emphasizing the importance of turning them off when not needed.

Remember that electric blankets are not recommended for cribs or toddler beds due to the risk of suffocation, overheating, and entanglement. Always prioritize safety when using electric blankets and consider alternative heating methods for young children or infants.

<u>**Children's Bedroom**</u>
Infant/Non-mobile: (Birth - 6 months)
Infant crawl/roll: (5 months - 1 year)
→ **Toddler/Pre-school: (1 year - 4 years)**
→ **School-age: (5 years - 6+ years)**

Toy Chest Safety

Childproofing a toy chest is essential to ensure the safety of children who interact with it.

Electric Toys: Over 50,000 children suffer minor to severe injuries each year from overheating toys and electronic devices, such as handheld gaming consoles and battery-operated gadgets.
(Source: U.S. Consumer Product Safety Commission (CPSC) - Toy Safety)

Safe Material and Design: Choose a toy chest made of sturdy, non-toxic materials with smooth edges and no sharp corners. Ensure there are no small parts or choking hazards on the chest's exterior.

Safety Hinges: Opt for a toy chest with safety hinges that prevent the lid from slamming shut. These hinges should hold the lid in an open position, allowing for safe access to toys.

Slow-Close Lid: If possible, choose a toy chest with a slow-close lid feature that gently closes the lid without sudden movements, reducing the risk of accidental finger pinching.

No Locking Mechanism: Avoid toy chests with locks that can accidentally trap a child inside. The chest should be easy for a child to open from the inside.

Ventilation: Ensure the toy chest has holes or gaps to allow for airflow and prevent suffocation if a child climbs.

Anchor to the Wall: If the toy chest is tall or top-heavy, anchor it securely to the wall to prevent tipping over if a child tries to climb on it.

Childproof Latch: If the toy chest has a latch or lock, install a childproof latch that prevents young children from opening it without adult assistance.

Weight Limit: Be mindful of the toy chest's weight limit. Don't overload it with too many heavy items, as this could cause instability.

Safe Location: To avoid accidental collisions, place the toy chest in a safe location away from heavy furniture or areas where children run and play.

Keep it Tidy: Regularly clean and organize the toy chest, removing broken or unsafe toys and ensuring that all toys are age-appropriate and free of hazards.

Educate Children: Teach children about the proper use of the toy chest, such as avoiding climbing inside and closing the lid gently.

Remove the Lid: If you have concerns about lid safety, consider removing the lid altogether and using the toy chest as an open storage container.

You can help make the toy chest a safe and enjoyable storage solution for children's toys while minimizing potential hazards.

- *According to the CPSC **In 2022, there were 11 toy-related fatalities among children aged 1-14 years old in the US.***

- ***Approximately 209,500 toy-related injuries** were treated in US hospital emergency departments in 2022. 38% of the injuries involved children aged 4 or younger.*

Children's Bedroom
→ Infant/Non-mobile: (Birth - 6 months)
→ Infant crawl/roll: (5 months - 1 year)
→ Toddler/Pre-school: (1 year - 4 years)
→ School-age: (5 years - 6+ years)

Recalled Toys

Consumer Product Safety Commission (CPSC) Website: The CPSC is the primary authority responsible for monitoring and issuing recalls for unsafe products, including toys. Visit their official website at cpsc.gov to find up-to-date information on toy recalls.

Email Subscriptions: Sign up for email subscriptions from the CPSC or other reputable consumer safety organizations. They often send out alerts and notifications about product recalls, including toys.

Manufacturer Websites: Check the websites of toy manufacturers regularly for announcements and recall information. Reputable manufacturers will often publish recall notices on their websites to inform consumers.

Retailer Notifications: Some retailers may notify customers if they have purchased a recalled product. Ensure the retailer has your contact information when making purchases.

Safety Organizations and Nonprofits: Stay connected with nonprofit organizations focusing on child safety and consumer product recalls. They may share recall information through their websites, newsletters, or social media channels.

Government Agencies and Health Departments: Local government agencies and health departments may share information about product recalls, including toys, through their official websites or social media accounts.

Social media: Follow reputable safety organizations, consumer protection agencies, and the CPSC on social media platforms. They often share recall information and safety tips with their followers.

News Outlets: Watch news outlets for reports about toy recalls. Major news networks often cover significant product recalls to alert the public.

Online Forums and Parenting Groups: Join online forums and parenting groups where parents discuss child safety topics. Members may share recall information and safety tips with the community.

Apps and Mobile Alerts: Some mobile apps and services offer alerts and notifications for product recalls. Check if there are any apps specifically dedicated to child safety and product recalls.

Remember that prompt action is crucial if you learn about a toy recall. Follow the instructions provided by the CPSC or the manufacturer on safely returning or disposing of the recalled toy.

Child's Bedroom
Infant/Non-mobile: (Birth - 6 months)
Infant crawl/roll: (5 months - 1 year)
→ **Toddler/Pre-school: (1 year - 4 years)**
→ **School-age: (5 years - 6+ years)**

Headphone Safety

Headphone use among children can raise several concerns related to their safety, hearing health, and overall well-being.

Hearing Damage: Children's ears are more sensitive and prone to damage from loud sounds. Prolonged exposure to high-volume levels through headphones can lead to hearing loss and other auditory issues.

Volume Control: Children may not be aware of the appropriate volume levels when using headphones. They may inadvertently expose themselves to dangerously loud sound levels without proper supervision or volume-limiting features.

Distraction: Wearing headphones can make children less aware of their surroundings, leading to safety risks, especially when crossing streets, playing near traffic, or participating in outdoor activities.

Social Isolation: Overusing headphones can lead to social isolation, as children may become less engaged with their immediate environment and interactions with others.

Unsuitable Content: Children may access inappropriate or harmful content through headphones, especially if not properly monitored by parents or caregivers.

Physical Discomfort: Ill-fitting or poorly designed headphones can cause discomfort or pressure on a child's ears, leading to pain or irritation.

Tangled Cords: Headphone cords can pose a strangulation risk, especially for younger children or those who are not aware of the potential hazard.

Sleep Disturbances: Listening to music or other audio content through headphones before bedtime can disrupt sleep patterns and impact the quality of rest.

Promote Safe Headphone Use: Encourage responsible headphone use and set clear guidelines regarding volume levels and content access. Consider using headphones with built-in volume-limiting features to protect children's hearing. Choose well-fitting, comfortable headphones designed specifically for children to minimize physical discomfort. Supervise younger children when using headphones and limit their usage time. Educate children about the importance of taking breaks from headphone use to rest their ears. Opt for wireless or cordless headphones to reduce the risk of entanglement and strangulation. Encourage children to be aware of their surroundings, especially when wearing headphones in public places. Use parental controls and content filters on devices to restrict access to age-appropriate content.

Children's Bedroom
Infant/Non-mobile: (Birth - 6 months)
Infant crawl/roll: (5 months - 1 year)
→ **Toddler/Pre-school: (1 year - 4 years)**
→ **School-age: (5 years - 6+ years)**

Hang Things Up on the Wall Properly

When hanging things in a kids' bedroom, using tacks and nails should be done with caution and consideration for safety.

Choking Hazard: Small tacks or nails can be a choking hazard for young children. Avoid using small tacks or nails that can be easily removed and swallowed.

Sharp Points: To prevent accidental injuries, ensure that any tacks or nails used have their sharp points fully embedded in the wall or surface.

Securely Anchor: Make sure the tacks or nails are securely anchored into the wall to prevent items from falling and causing potential harm.

High Placement: Hang items out of the reach of young children to prevent them from pulling or playing with the objects.

Weight Limit: Consider the weight of the items being hung and use appropriate tacks or nails that can support the load securely.

Alternative Hanging Methods: Instead of using tacks or nails, consider using removable adhesive hooks or wall-mounted organizers specifically designed for kids' rooms. These alternatives are less likely to damage the walls and can be easily repositioned.

Childproof Wall Coverings: If using tacks or nails on the walls, ensure that the wall coverings are childproof and do not pose any health risks if accidentally ingested.

Supervision: If you have older children who want to hang things themselves, supervise them to ensure they safely handle the tacks or nails.

Consider Soft Surfaces: If possible, hang items on soft surfaces such as bulletin boards or fabric-covered walls, which are less likely to cause injuries if accidentally bumped.

Check for Safety Recalls: Before using any hanging products, check for any safety recalls or warnings related to their use.

Inspect Regularly: Periodically inspect the items hung in the kids' bedroom to ensure that tacks or nails are still securely in place and that the objects are not damaged or worn.

By being mindful of these concerns and taking appropriate safety measures, you can ensure that the kids' bedroom remains a safe and enjoyable space for children to express themselves and display their favorite items.

Children's Bedroom
→ Infant/Non-mobile: (Birth - 6 months)
→ Infant crawl/roll: (5 months - 1 year)
→ Toddler/Pre-school: (1 year - 4 years)
→ School-age: (5 years - 6+ years)

When NOT to Share

Separating toys by age group is a great way to ensure that children have access to appropriate and safe toys for their developmental stage. Here's a simple guide to help you organize toys based on age groups:

Infants (0-12 months)
- Soft, plush toys without small parts that can be detached.
- Rattles and teethers are designed for young infants.
- High-contrast toys for visual stimulation.
- Activity mats and mobiles for sensory development.

Toddlers (1-3 years)
- Stacking toys and building blocks.
- Shape sorters and puzzles with large pieces.
- Push and pull toys for early walkers.
- Play kitchen and food toys for pretend play.
- Musical instruments designed for toddlers.
- Soft and safe ride-on toys.

Preschoolers (3-5 years)
- Arts and crafts materials (non-toxic and age-appropriate).
- Playsets for imaginative play (e.g., dollhouses, action figures)
- Simple board games and puzzles with more pieces.
- Sports equipment for gross motor development.
- Educational toys for learning numbers, letters, and basic concepts.

Bonus: School-age Children (6-12 years)
- More complex board games and strategy games.
- Building sets with smaller pieces (e.g., LEGO sets).
- Science kits and educational toys exploring STEM concepts.
- Art supplies for more detailed artwork and creativity.
- Outdoor toys like bicycles, scooters, and sports gear.

Bonus: Teenagers (13+ years)
- Age-appropriate video games and gaming consoles.
- Hobby-related items, such as musical instruments or craft supplies.
- Books and educational materials catering to their interests.
- Sports equipment or gear for more advanced sports activities.

Keep in mind that children develop at different rates, so the age groups provided here are general guidelines. Some children may show an interest in toys intended for older age groups, while others may prefer toys designed for younger children. Always supervise playtime and ensure that toys are free from small parts or choking hazards, regardless of the child's age. Regularly inspect toys for wear and tear and replace or repair any damaged items to maintain a safe play environment for all age groups.

Children's Bedroom
Infant/Non-mobile: (Birth - 6 months)
Infant crawl/roll: (5 months - 1 year)
→ **Toddler/Pre-school: (1 year - 4 years)**
School-age: (5 years - 6+ years)

Board game Concerns

Board games and other toys designed for older siblings can pose potential choking hazards for younger siblings. Parents and caregivers need to be vigilant and take appropriate precautions when introducing toys or games with small parts into a household with children of different age groups.

Age Recommendations: Always follow the age recommendations provided by the manufacturer on the toy's packaging. These recommendations are based on safety and developmental considerations.

Supervision: Ensure that younger children are supervised closely when older siblings are playing with toys that have small parts. Older siblings should be reminded to keep small game pieces away from younger siblings.

Designated Play Areas: Consider creating designated play areas for older and younger children, where toys appropriate for their respective age groups are kept.

Storage Solutions: Store small game pieces and other choking hazards out of the reach of younger children in storage containers with secure lids.

Educational Opportunities: Take the opportunity to educate older siblings about the importance of keeping small parts and toys away from younger siblings to keep them safe.

Separate Playtimes: If possible, encourage older siblings to play with their small-piece toys during times when younger siblings are not present or are engaged in age-appropriate activities.

Teach Safe Play: Teach older siblings how to play responsibly and safely with their toys, emphasizing the importance of keeping small parts and game pieces in designated play areas.

Check for Loose Parts: Regularly inspect board games and toys for loose or broken parts that could pose a choking hazard. Repair or replace any damaged items promptly.

<u>**Children's Bedroom**</u>
→ **Infant/Non-mobile: (Birth - 6 months)**
→ **Infant crawl/roll: (5 months - 1 year)**
Toddler/Pre-school: (1 year - 4 years)
School-age: (5 years - 6+ years)

No Strings on Toys Longer than 6 Inches

Removing or avoiding strings longer than 6 inches on toys is an essential childproofing measure to prevent potential strangulation hazards. Strings, cords, or ribbons that are too long can pose significant risks to young children, especially infants and toddlers, who may accidentally become entangled in them.

Inspect Toys: Regularly inspect toys for any long strings or cords and trim them to a safe length if necessary. Be cautious of toys with pull cords, such as pull-along toys, and ensure they are kept out of reach when not in use.

Secure Attachments: Ensure that any strings or cords attached to toys are securely fastened to prevent accidental detachment.

Age-Appropriate Toys: For younger children who are at risk of entanglement, choose age-appropriate toys that do not have long strings or cords.

Crib Safety: Suffocation Risks Are Underestimated. Unintentional suffocation causes **around 1,200 child deaths each year**, frequently due to unsafe sleep environments or household items like pillows and blankets. (Source: Centers for Disease Control and Prevention (CDC) - Safe to Sleep Campaign)

Avoid hanging toys with strings or cords on a crib or playpen, as they can pose a strangulation hazard for infants.

Keep Strings Away: Toys with long strings or cords should be kept away from areas where children sleep or play and avoided near cribs, beds, or playpens.

Supervision: Always supervise young children during playtime to ensure their safety and intervene if they encounter toys with long strings.

Educate Older Siblings: Teach older siblings about the potential risks associated with toys that have long strings and encourage them to keep such toys away from younger siblings.

Safe Alternatives: Consider using toys with short, safely attached strings, or opt for toys without strings altogether for added peace of mind.

You can create a safer environment for children to play and explore without the risk of entanglement or strangulation from toy strings. Toy safety is a critical aspect of childproofing, and it's essential to remain vigilant and mindful of potential hazards as children grow and develop.

<u>Children's Bedroom</u>
Infant/Non-mobile: (Birth - 6 months)
→ **Infant crawl/roll: (5 months - 1 year)**
→ **Toddler/Pre-school: (1 year - 4 years)**
→ **School-age: (5 years - 6+ years)**

Never Lock a Child in a Bedroom

Locking a child in their bedroom is not safe and should never be done under any circumstances. It can be extremely dangerous and poses severe risks to the child's safety and well-being.

Fire Safety: In the event of a fire or emergency, locking a child in their bedroom can prevent them from escaping quickly and safely.

Access for Caregivers: Locking the child's bedroom may hinder access for parents or caregivers in case the child needs assistance or medical attention.

Anxiety and Fear: Being locked in a room can cause anxiety, fear, and distress for the child, leading to emotional trauma.

Security Risks: Locking a child in their bedroom can pose security risks, as they may be unable to leave the room if an intruder or dangerous situation arises.

Potential Injury: A child locked in their bedroom may try to escape by climbing out of a window or attempting other risky behaviors, leading to potential injuries.

Violation of Rights: Locking a child in their bedroom can be considered a violation of their rights and may be illegal in some jurisdictions.

Childproof the Room: Childproof the child's bedroom by securing furniture, covering electrical outlets, and removing any potential hazards.

Supervision: Always supervise young children to ensure their safety, especially during playtime or activities that may involve potential risks.

Accessible Exits: Ensure that the child's bedroom has accessible exits and is not obstructed by furniture or other items.

Night Lights: Use night lights to provide gentle illumination during the night, which can help alleviate the fear of the dark.

Open Communication: Establish open communication with the child and address any fears or concerns they may have about their bedroom or sleep environment.

Safe Sleeping Arrangements: Ensure that the child's crib or bed meets safety standards and is free from suffocation hazards.

Remember, creating a safe and nurturing environment for children is essential for their physical and emotional well-being. If you have concerns about your child's safety or behavior, consider seeking guidance from pediatric professionals or child development experts.

Children's Bedroom
Infant/Non-mobile: (Birth - 6 months)
Infant crawl/roll: (5 months - 1 year)
→ **Toddler/Pre-school: (1 year - 4 years)**
School-age: (5 years - 6+ years)

No Plastic Insulation Over Windows

Plastic insulation or any plastic covering should not be used over windows in a child's bedroom or any living space, especially if young children are present.

Suffocation Hazard: Plastic insulation can pose a suffocation hazard for young children, who may accidentally come into contact with it and risk getting entangled or trapped.

Potential for Overheating: If not installed correctly, plastic insulation can interfere with proper air circulation and heating/cooling systems, leading to potential overheating in the room.

Fire Hazard: Plastic is highly flammable, and if it gets near heat sources like candles or heaters, it can quickly catch fire and spread throughout the room.

Restricted Visibility and Emergency Exit: Covering windows with plastic can obstruct visibility and make it difficult to see outside, potentially hindering escape in case of an emergency like a fire.

Condensation and Mold: Improperly installed plastic insulation may lead to condensation build-up, trapping moisture and potentially causing mold growth, which can be harmful to children's health.

Curtains and Drapes: Install curtains or drapes made of non-toxic, child-safe materials that can provide insulation and keep the room cozy.

Weather Stripping: Use weather stripping around the window frames to prevent drafts and improve energy efficiency without obstructing visibility.

Window Caulking: Apply caulk around the window frames to seal any gaps and prevent drafts from entering the room.

Thermal Blinds or Shades: Invest in thermal blinds or shades that provide insulation and help regulate the room's temperature without compromising safety.

Window Insulation Kits: If necessary, window insulation kits should be specifically designed for safe indoor use, and the manufacturer's instructions should be followed carefully.

Window Safety Locks: Install window safety locks to prevent young children from opening the window too wide and ensure childproofing.

You can create a comfortable and secure environment for your child without compromising their safety. As always, prioritizing child safety and considering age-appropriate childproofing measures is essential for a child's well-being.

<u>**Children's Bedroom**</u>
Infant/Non-mobile: (Birth - 6 months)
Infant crawl/roll: (5 months - 1 year)
→ **Toddler/Pre-school: (1 year - 4 years)**
→ **School-age: (5 years - 6+ years)**

Closets Must Unlock from the Inside

Ensuring that closets can be unlocked from the inside is an important safety measure, especially in children's bedrooms or playrooms. Children, especially young ones, may accidentally lock themselves inside a closet while exploring, and it's crucial to provide them with a means to open the door and exit safely.

Childproof Locks: If you use locks on closet doors, make sure to use childproof locks that can be easily opened from the inside. These locks should be accessible for a child's reach and simple to operate.

No Locks: Consider avoiding locks altogether on closet doors in children's rooms. If privacy is not a significant concern, leaving the closet doors without locks can provide easy access and prevent accidental entrapment.

Doorknob with Keyhole: If the closet has a traditional doorknob with a keyhole, ensure the key can be removed from the outside when the closet is not in use. This way, children won't be able to accidentally lock themselves inside with the key left in the keyhole.

Sliding or Bi-Fold Doors: If the closet has sliding or bi-folding doors, make sure they are easy to slide or open from the inside. Avoid any mechanisms that could be difficult for a child to operate.

Test from Inside: Periodically test the closet door from the inside to ensure a child can easily unlock or open it.

Educate Children: Teach children how to unlock or open the closet door from the inside if they accidentally lock themselves in. Empowering them with this knowledge can help them stay calm and respond appropriately in such situations.

Supervision: Always supervise young children while they are in their bedrooms or playrooms to prevent accidental locking in closets.

By taking these precautions and making sure closets can be unlocked from the inside, you can create a safer environment for children and reduce the risk of accidents or entrapment. Safety should always be a top priority when childproofing living spaces.

Children's Bedroom
Infant/Non-mobile: (Birth - 6 months)
Infant crawl/roll: (5 months - 1 year)
→ **Toddler/Pre-school: (1 year - 4 years)**
School-age: (5 years - 6+ years)

Remove Door Stoppers that Can be Disassembled

Removing door stoppers that can be disassembled is an important childproofing measure. Door stoppers with small parts that can be taken apart pose a choking hazard for young children who may explore and put objects in their mouths. **Check Door Stoppers:** Inspect all door stoppers in the house to identify if any of them have small parts that can be disassembled. Look for screws, nuts, bolts, or other removable components.

Replace with Childproof Options: If you find any door stoppers with small, removable parts, consider replacing them with childproof door stoppers that are designed to prevent accidental disassembly.

Secure Existing Stoppers: If replacing the door stoppers is not immediately possible, secure the existing stoppers with solid adhesive or sealant to prevent small parts from coming loose.

Keep Small Parts Out of Reach: If you are unable to replace or secure the stoppers right away, ensure that any small parts that might come loose are kept out of reach of young children.

Supervise Children: Always supervise young children to prevent them from accessing areas where door stoppers or small parts are present.

Toy Safety: Ensure that toys and other household objects are free from small parts or choking hazards.

Educate Older Siblings: If you have older children, educate them about the importance of keeping small parts and potential hazards away from younger siblings.

Notes:

Children's Bedroom
Infant/Non-mobile: (Birth - 6 months)
Infant crawl/roll: (5 months - 1 year)
→ **Toddler/Pre-school: (1 year - 4 years)**
→ **School-age: (5 years - 6+ years)**

Finger Pinch Guards

A "finger pinch guard" or "door pinch guard." is designed to prevent fingers from getting caught or pinched in the gap between the door and the door frame when the door is being closed. These devices are a valuable addition to childproofing measures and can help prevent painful finger injuries.

Here's how a finger pinch guard typically works.

Design: A finger pinch guard is usually made of soft, flexible, and durable material, such as foam or rubber. It comes in various shapes and designs, but the most common type is a long strip that attaches to the edge of the door.

Installation: The finger pinch guard is installed on the edge of the door, either on the hinged side or the closing side, where fingers are most likely to get caught. Some models are designed to be easily adjustable or removable, making them convenient to use.

Prevention: When the door is being closed, the finger pinch guard acts as a cushion or barrier between the door and the frame. If a child's fingers are accidentally in the way, the guard absorbs the pressure, preventing fingers from being pinched.

Universal Fit: Many finger pinch guards are designed to fit various door sizes and can be used on most standard household doors.

Colorful and Child-Friendly: Some models are bright and attractive, making them visually appealing to children. This can also remind kids to keep their fingers away from the door's closing edge.

Easy to Clean: Finger pinch guards are generally easy to clean, as they can be wiped down with a damp cloth if they get dirty.

It's important to note that finger-pinch guards are not a substitute for adult supervision. While they can help prevent accidental finger-pinching, it's crucial to always supervise children around doors, especially when they are being closed or opened. Finger-pinch guards are just one part of a comprehensive childproofing plan to ensure the safety of children in the home.

Children's Bedroom
Infant/Non-mobile: (Birth - 6 months)
Infant crawl/roll: (5 months - 1 year)
→ **Toddler/Pre-school: (1 year - 4 years)**
→ **School-age: (5 years - 6+ years)**

Window Stoppers

Falls from windows result in **over 500 fatalities and 10,000 non-fatal injuries among children** annually in the U.S. frequently occurring in multi-story homes and apartments. Source: Centers for Disease Control and Prevention (CDC) Installing window stops is an effective childproofing measure to limit the opening of windows and prevent full access to children. Window stops are designed to restrict the movement of the window sash, reducing the risk of falls or other accidents.

Choose the Right Window Stops: Select window stops that are suitable for the type of window you have. There are various types of window stops available, including sliding window locks, sash stops, and wedge-style stops.

Measure the Window: Measure the window's opening to determine the appropriate placement of the window stops. The stops should be installed in a position that allows for proper ventilation while preventing full access.

Follow Manufacturer's Instructions: Read and follow the manufacturer's instructions that come with the window stops. Different types of stops may have specific installation procedures.

Install on Both Sides: For windows that slide horizontally, install window stops on both sides of the window frame to prevent the sash from being opened too wide.

Secure Installation: Ensure that the window stops are securely attached to the window frame and cannot be easily dislodged by a child.

Regular Inspection: Periodically check the window stops to ensure they are still in place and functioning properly.

Accessible for Adults: While window stops are designed to prevent children from opening the window too wide, they should be easily accessible and operable by adults in case of an emergency or for regular cleaning and maintenance.

Supervision: Always supervise children around windows, even with window stops installed. Window stops are an added safety measure but do not replace the need for adult supervision.

Remove When No Longer Needed: When appropriate, the window stops can be removed if they are no longer needed or if the child has outgrown the risk.

Window stops are essential for window safety in homes with young children. Properly installing and maintaining these devices can help reduce the risk of window-related accidents and create a safer living environment for your family.

► *According to the CDC, falls from windows result in **over 500 fatalities and 10,000 non-fatal injuries** among children annually in the U.S. frequently occurring in multi-story homes and apartments.*

Children's Bedroom
Infant/Non-mobile: (Birth - 6 months)
Infant crawl/roll: (5 months - 1 year)
→ **Toddler/Pre-school: (1 year - 4 years)**
School-age: (5 years - 6+ years)

Place Gates on Windows

Placing gates on windows is an effective childproofing measure to enhance window safety and prevent young children from accessing or falling out of open windows.

Window gates, also known as window guards, are designed to create a protective barrier over the window opening while still allowing for proper ventilation.

Choose the Right Window Gates: Select window gates specifically designed for window safety. Look for gates that meet safety standards and are appropriate for the size and type of windows in your home.

Measure the Window Opening: Accurately measure the dimensions of the window opening to ensure that the window gate fits securely. The gate should cover the entire opening without any gaps that a child could slip through.

Follow Manufacturer's Instructions: Read and follow the manufacturer's instructions that come with the window gates. Different types of window gates may have specific installation procedures.

Secure Installation: Properly install the window gate using the provided mounting hardware or brackets. Ensure that the gate is securely attached to the window frame or wall to prevent it from being dislodged by a child.

Accessible for Adults: Window gates should be easily operable by adults in case of emergency or for regular cleaning and maintenance. Some gates come with quick-release mechanisms or swing-open features for easy adult access.

Regular Inspection: Periodically inspect the window gates to ensure they are still in place and functioning properly.

Safe Distance Between Bars: Check that the gaps between the window gate's bars are small enough to prevent a child from squeezing through.

Supervision: Always supervise children around windows, even with window gates installed. Window gates are an added safety measure but do not replace the need for adult supervision.

Emergency Escape Routes: Ensure that window gates do not impede emergency escape routes in case of a fire or other emergencies. Make sure that adults can quickly remove the gates if needed.

Remove When No Longer Needed: When appropriate, the window gates can be removed if they are no longer needed or if the child has outgrown the risk. Window gates provide an added layer of protection for children's safety and peace of mind for parents or caregivers. Installing and maintaining these gates correctly can help reduce the risk of window-related accidents and create a safer living environment for your family.

Children's Bedroom
Infant/Non-mobile: (Birth - 6 months)
Infant crawl/roll: (5 months - 1 year)
→ **Toddler/Pre-school: (1 year - 4 years)**
→ **School-age: (5 years - 6+ years)**

Teach Children How to Call 911

Teaching a child how to call 911 is a crucial life skill that can help them in emergencies.

Explain the Purpose of 911: Start by explaining to your child what 911 is and why it is essential. Emphasize that 911 is a special number to call for help during emergencies, such as when someone is hurt, a fire, or a dangerous situation.

Know Child's Readiness: Assess the child's age, maturity level, and ability to comprehend the concept of an emergency. Generally, children around age 4 or 5 can start learning about 911 but remember that each child is different.

Practice Emergency Situations: Role-play various emergency scenarios with your child. For example, pretend that there is a fire, someone is injured, or a stranger is causing trouble. Practice what they should say to the 911 operator in each situation.

Memorize Basic Information: Teach your child essential information they should share with the 911 operator, such as their full name, home address, and phone number. Ensure they know how to spell their name and address correctly.

Demonstrate the Process: Show your child how to use a phone and dial 911. Explain that they should stay calm and speak clearly when talking to the operator.

Explain When to Call: Make sure your child understands that 911 is only for real emergencies, not for playing or non-urgent situations. Give them examples of when to call and when not to call.

Show How to Hang Up: Teach your child to stay on the line until the 911 operator tells them it's okay to hang up. Explain that the operator may need additional information or instructions.

Reinforce Safety Messages: Continually reinforce safety messages, such as not talking to strangers or playing with matches and emphasize that calling 911 is for serious situations.

Supervision and Practice: Always supervise the child when practicing calling 911. Repeat the process occasionally to reinforce their understanding.

Positive Reinforcement: Praise and reward the child for learning and demonstrating responsible behavior in practicing 911 calls.

Remember, teaching a child how to call 911 is vital, but it is equally important to stress the importance of using this emergency service responsibly. Children should understand that calling 911 unnecessarily can divert resources from real emergencies. With proper guidance and practice, children can become responsible and confident in knowing how to seek help in critical situations.

Children's Bedroom
Infant/Non-mobile: (Birth - 6 months)
Infant crawl/roll: (5 months - 1 year)
→ **Toddler/Pre-school: (1 year - 4 years)**
→ **School-age: (5 years - 6+ years)**

Small Pets: Gerbils, Rabbits, Etc.

To create a safe and harmonious environment for children and small pets like gerbils, rats, and rabbits, follow these guidelines: Before acquiring a pet, research to find a suitable match considering the animal's temperament and care requirements. Always supervise children during their interactions with pets, teaching them gentle handling and avoiding loud noises to prevent startling the animals. Ensure cages are secure, escape-proof, and free of sharp edges, with safe bedding materials. Emphasize hand washing before and after handling pets and instruct children on proper food handling to avoid sharing human food with pets. Schedule regular vet check-ups and adhere to vaccination guidelines. Set up a designated play area for supervised interactions and teach children empathy and respect for the animals, assigning them age-appropriate responsibilities for pet care. These measures will foster a positive and safe relationship between your family and the new furry members. (For details refer to the yard for details **pg. 468**)

> ▶ *Though these bites make up less than 1% of all pediatric animal bites, they can nonetheless cause painful punctures and carry infection risks.* **In rare documented instances, rabbits have transmitted Pasteurella infections.** *Parents often underestimate this: one caregiver noted, 'My daughter was petting her and bunny bit her and drew blood... no, your daughter does not need to see a doctor or be concerned about rabbit-borne infections.' However, even minor bites may require stitches or care, and one parent recalled winding up in the ER from a rabbit bite. It's a reminder that even small pets need supervised interaction with preschoolers."* (Veterian Key)

|Ch. 7| Children's Bathroom

Introduction: In the bustling journey of parenthood, the bathroom can often be overlooked as a potential danger zone for young explorers. Yet, this space, brimming with slippery surfaces, sharp corners, and an array of chemicals and cosmetics, harbors numerous hazards for little ones. As we venture into this critical chapter, we will guide you through comprehensive strategies to transform your child's bathroom into a haven of safety. From securing potentially harmful products to installing preventative measures against slips and falls. We aim to equip you with the knowledge and tools to create a bathroom environment where your child can safely grow and learn. Let's embark on this essential step in childproofing, ensuring peace of mind each time your child enters the bathroom.

Testimonial: *I still remember that terrible moment when I heard a loud thud followed by my child's cries coming from the bathroom. My child had managed to climb onto the bathroom counter, only to lose balance and fall. The sharp edge of the counter had left a big cut and a nasty bruise on his forehead. Looking back, I realize that this accident could have been prevented with some simple childproofing measures. I should have installed safety locks on the bathroom cabinets that would have deterred him from attempting to climb up in the first place. Also, adding soft corner protectors to the sharp edges of the counter could have minimized the impact of the fall. I now understand the importance of always supervising young children, even if it's just a quick trip to the bathroom.*

This incident was a wake-up call for me. Since then, I have made our bathroom safer for my child, including installing non-slip mats to prevent falls and keeping potentially hazardous items out of reach. I share my story in the hope that it encourages other parents to take the time to childproof their homes to protect their children from the hidden dangers that lurk in the most unexpected places. It's always better to be safe than sorry.

-Chris C. (Father of 2)

Children's Bathroom
→ Infant/Non-mobile: (Birth - 6 months)
→ Infant crawl/roll: (5 months - 1 year)
→ Toddler/Pre-school: (1 year - 4 years)
→ School-age: (5 years - 6+ years)

Bathing a Child

Each year, approximately **5,000 children** are injured by falls or drownings in overfilled bathtubs, stressing the importance of bath supervision and water level control. (Source: Safe Kids Worldwide - Drowning Prevention)

Bath time is an important part of a child's day. Splashing and playing in the water can be fun and enjoyable for your child. It is essential to keep the slippery tub a safe spot for your child to get clean and have fun.

> **Drowning Prevention:** The most significant concern during bath time is drowning. Even a small amount of water can pose a significant risk to a young child. Never leave a child unattended in the bath, even for a moment. Always stay within arm's reach of the child during bath time. If you need to leave the bathroom for any reason, take your child with you or wrap them in a towel and bring them along.
>
> **Slips and Falls:** The bathroom floor can be slippery, leading to slips and falls during bath time. Use non-slip bathmats both inside and outside the bathtub to provide secure footing. Consider placing non-slip stickers on the bathtub floor to reduce slipping. Install grab bars in the bathroom to provide additional support and stability.
>
> **Hot Water Scalds:** Hot water can cause severe burns to a child's delicate skin. Set your water heater temperature to 120°F (49°C) or below to prevent scalding. Always test the water temperature with your wrist or elbow before placing the child in the bath. Consider using a bathtub spout cover to prevent accidental contact with hot faucets.

Install a Safety Valve Cover Over the Hot Valve: To effectively prevent burns or other injuries, it's imperative to choose a cover that is durable and compatible with your specific valve. Moreover, frequently checking the integrity of the cover ensures that it remains a reliable safety feature in your home.

Electrical Appliances: Keep electrical appliances like hairdryers, curling irons, and electric razors away from the bathtub to avoid the risk of electrocution. Use electrical appliances in a different area of the bathroom, away from water sources. Unplug electrical devices after use and store them out of the child's reach.

Cord Safety: Be cautious of cords from devices like radios, phones, or other electronic gadgets in the bathroom. Keep cords away from the water and out of the child's reach—store electronic devices outside the bathroom or in a secure location.

Toiletries and Medications: To prevent accidental ingestion, store toiletries and medications out of the child's reach in a high cabinet away from the child's reach. Lock all medications away in a secure medicine cabinet.

Overflow Protection: To prevent overflowing water in the bathtub, never leave the water running without supervision. Be mindful of the water level while filling the tub.

Child-Friendly Products: Use child-friendly bath products that are free from harmful chemicals. Choose mild and hypoallergenic bath products designed for children's sensitive skin.

Proper Drainage: Ensure that the bathtub drains properly to avoid standing water and reduce the risk of slips. Clean the bathtub drain regularly to prevent clogs.

Educate Older Siblings: If you have older siblings, educate them about the importance of keeping the bathroom safe during bath time.

Use a Baby Bathtub or Bath Seat: For infants and younger babies, consider using a bathtub or seat that provides additional support and stability during bath time.

Secure Toilet Seat Locks: Install toilet seat locks to prevent young children from accessing the toilet during bath time. Children can be curious and might try to play with the water or objects inside the toilet, which can be hazardous.

Keep Bathroom Doors Closed: When the bathroom is not in use, keep the doors closed and secure with childproof doorknob covers. This prevents children from entering the bathroom without supervision.

Supervise Water Play: If your child enjoys playing with toys during bath time, ensure the toys are safe, free from small parts, and non-toxic. Also, supervise water play closely to avoid any potential choking or ingestion risks.

Avoid Slippery Bathrobes: Be cautious about using slippery bathrobes or towels, as they can make it challenging for a child to stay stable when stepping out of the bathtub.

Encourage Sitting Positions: To reduce the risk of slips and falls, encourage children to sit in the bathtub instead of standing.

Check Water Temperature Regularly: Throughout the bath, continue to check the water temperature to ensure it remains comfortable for the child. Water can cool down or heat up over time.

Emergency Preparedness: Always have emergency numbers (including poison control) readily available in the bathroom or nearby in case of accidents.

Teach Water Safety Rules: As children grow older, teach them water safety rules, such as not diving or running near water and how to call for help in case of an emergency.

Empty the Bathtub After Use: After bath time, ensure the bathtub is empty and the drain is closed. Remove toys or bath accessories that could pose a hazard when not used.

Stay Calm and Positive: Make bath time a positive and enjoyable experience for your child. Stay calm, patient, and reassuring; this will help build their confidence and make them feel safe during baths.

Following these childproofing measures and being vigilant during bath time can create a safe and enjoyable bathing experience for your child while minimizing potential hazards. Always prioritize safety and take appropriate precautions to prevent accidents in the bathroom.

Children's Bathroom
Infant/Non-mobile: (Birth - 6 months)
Infant crawl/roll: (5 months - 1 year)
→ **Toddler/Pre-school: (1 year - 4 years)**
→ **School-age: (5 years - 6+ years)**

Shower Curtain

Shower curtains seem harmless, but they can pose risks of strangulation or entanglement.

Use Weighted Shower Curtains: Opt for shower curtains with weighted hems. This reduces the likelihood of your child grabbing and pulling the curtain down or getting tangled.

Magnetic Closures: Attach magnets to the bottom corners of the shower curtain and tub to keep them closed and less accessible.

Consider a Glass Door: If you're in full childproofing mode, replace the curtain with a glass shower door for zero curtain access.

Remove Shower Hooks: Ensure shower hooks are not within reach, as they can be a choking hazard. Use hidden or snap-on hooks for a cleaner, safer look.

► *Shower curtains and rods may seem harmless, but they can present surprising dangers to toddlers.* **Plastic liners can wrap around little ones, leading to suffocation or strangulation.** *Loose tension rods are equally risky. There've been real cases where a collapsing rod fell onto a child's face, leaving a deep tear. It shows that even everyday bathroom fixtures need secure installation and careful oversight.*

Children's Bathroom
→ **Infant/Non-mobile: (Birth - 6 months)**
→ **Infant crawl/roll: (5 months - 1 year)**
→ **Toddler/Pre-school: (1 year - 4 years)**
→ **School-age: (5 years - 6+ years)**

Antibacterial Soap Concerns

There are several concerns about children using antibacterial soaps, even after the FDA banned chemicals like triclosan and triclocarban. Some remaining antibacterial agents, such as benzalkonium chloride, may still pose risks. These chemicals can be harsh on a child's sensitive skin, causing irritation or allergic reactions. Frequent use of antibacterial products may also disrupt the skin's natural microbiome, which plays a key role in immune system development. Overuse of antibacterial soaps can strip the skin of natural oils and beneficial bacteria, weakening the skin's protective barrier and making it more susceptible to dryness and infections.

Additionally, there is concern about how antibacterial soaps contribute to antimicrobial resistance. Overuse may promote the growth of bacteria that are resistant to antibiotics, making infections harder to treat in the future. This is especially concerning for children, who are more vulnerable to infections. Some antibacterial agents may also be absorbed through the skin, potentially impacting a child's developing immune system.

Environmental concerns also exist, as some antibacterial chemicals do not fully break down and may enter water systems, affecting wildlife and ecosystems. Given these risks, healthcare professionals often recommend using regular soap and water for children, which is both effective in reducing germs and safer than antibacterial alternatives.

Children's Bathroom
Infant/Non-mobile: (Birth - 6 months)
Infant crawl/roll: (5 months - 1 year)
→ **Toddler/Pre-school: (1 year - 4 years)**
→ **School-age: (5 years - 6+ years)**

Bathroom Garbage Can

Garbage cans can be an irresistible treasure trove for curious little hands.

Get a Can with a Locking Lid

Choose a garbage can with a pedal-operated, locking lid. The lock will prevent tiny fingers from accessing whatever's inside, whether it's bathroom waste or more dangerous items like razors.

Keep it Out of Reach: Store the garbage can in a locked cabinet or under the sink with childproof cabinet locks.

Use a Motion-Sensor Can: While it sounds futuristic, some cans have motion sensors that close before your child can dive in.

Secure the Can: If you cannot keep the garbage can out, use adhesive strips or anti-tip devices to prevent your toddler from tipping it over in a moment of playful curiosity.

Children's Bathroom
Infant/Non-mobile: (Birth - 6 months)
Infant crawl/roll: (5 months - 1 year)
→ **Toddler/Pre-school: (1 year - 4 years)**
→ **School-age: (5 years - 6+ years)**

No In-toilet Cleaning Supplies

Childproofing bathroom cleaning supplies is crucial to prevent accidental poisoning or harm to young children who may be curious and explore their surroundings.

Secure Storage: Keep all cleaning supplies, including toilet bowl cleaners, disinfectants, bleach, and other chemicals, in a locked cabinet or high out of the child's reach. Choose a storage location that is not easily accessible to young children.

Childproof Cabinet Locks: Install childproof cabinet locks on bathroom cabinets that contain cleaning supplies to prevent curious children from opening them.

Separate Storage: Store cleaning supplies separately from personal care items and food items. This reduces the risk of accidental ingestion if a child mistakes cleaning products for something else.

Childproof Bottles: Use childproof bottles for cleaning supplies whenever possible. These bottles require a specific action (like pressing and turning) to open, making it difficult for young children to access the contents.

Label Clearly: Label all cleaning supplies clearly with their contents and warning labels. This helps adults identify the products easily and reminds them of potential hazards.

Properly Dispose of Empty Containers: Dispose of empty cleaning supply containers safely and promptly. Rinse them thoroughly before recycling or discarding them to eliminate any residual product.

Use Safer Alternatives: Consider using non-toxic and eco-friendly cleaning products that are safer for both children and the environment.

Keep Products in Original Containers: Avoid transferring cleaning supplies into other containers, as this can lead to confusion and accidental misuse.

Child-Free Zone During Cleaning: Keep children out of the bathroom or in a separate room when cleaning is in progress. This reduces the risk of accidental exposure to cleaning products.

Proper Handling: Use cleaning supplies carefully, following instructions and safety guidelines. Always close containers tightly after use.

Educate Older Siblings: If you have older siblings, educate them about the importance of keeping cleaning supplies out of reach of younger siblings.

Childproof Trash Bins: Use childproof trash bins with secure lids to prevent children from accessing discarded cleaning supply containers.

Store Tools Safely: If you use cleaning tools like scrub brushes or sponges with cleaning products, store them out of the child's reach when not in use.

You can help ensure that bathroom cleaning supplies are safely stored and out of the reach of young children, reducing the risk of accidents and injuries.

Children's Bathroom
Infant/Non-mobile: (Birth - 6 months)
Infant crawl/roll: (5 months - 1 year)
→ **Toddler/Pre-school: (1 year - 4 years)**
→ **School-age: (5 years - 6+ years)**

Toilet Seat Closed and Secured

Keeping the toilet seat closed and installing safety measures are essential steps in childproofing the bathroom.

Keep Toilet Seat Closed: Always keep the toilet seat and lid closed when not in use. This prevents young children from accessing toilet water, which can be hazardous and unhygienic.

Toilet Locks or Latches: Install toilet locks or latches to secure the toilet seat and lid. These locks prevent young children from lifting the seat and accessing the toilet bowl.

Childproof Toilet Paper Dispenser: A toilet paper dispenser is essential to prevent young kids from creating a mess or potentially clogging the toilet. Opt for dispensers with covers or controlled dispensing mechanisms to limit access and waste. Consider mounting the dispenser higher on the wall or using childproof locks to keep it out of children's reach. Alternatively, a free-standing dispenser placed in a less accessible spot can also help. Store extra rolls out of reach and always supervise young children in the bathroom. Educate and model proper toilet paper usage to older kids, emphasizing the importance of not wasting. Some dispensers even come in child-friendly designs to promote responsible use.

Educate Older Siblings: If you have older children, teach them the importance of keeping the toilet seat closed and using the toilet locks to prevent accidents.

Supervision: Always supervise young children in the bathroom to ensure they don't access the toilet or play with toilet paper.

Safe Toilet Cleaners: Use toilet cleaners that are safe, non-toxic, and labeled as child friendly. Store these cleaning products securely out of your child's reach.

Childproof Trash Bins: Use childproof trash bins in the bathroom to prevent children from accessing and handling discarded toilet paper or other bathroom waste.

Explain Toilet Rules: As children grow older, explain the rules about toilet safety, such as not playing in or near the toilet and not flushing toys or objects down the toilet.

Lock Bathroom Doors: To prevent unsupervised access to the bathroom, consider using childproof doorknob covers or installing locks on the doors.

Encourage Hand washing: Teach children proper hand washing techniques after using the toilet to maintain good hygiene.

Avoid Clutter: Keep the bathroom free from clutter to reduce the risk of accidents and provide a safe space for children.

Childproofing the toilet area is crucial to prevent drowning hazards and keep the bathroom safe for children. By following these childproofing measures, you can create a secure environment in the bathroom and minimize potential risks associated with the toilet and toilet-related products. Remember that childproofing is an ongoing process, and it's essential to adapt safety measures as children grow and develop new abilities and interests.

Children's Bathroom
Infant/Non-mobile: (Birth - 6 months)
Infant crawl/roll: (5 months - 1 year)
→ **Toddler/Pre-school: (1 year - 4 years)**
→ **School-age: (5 years - 6+ years)**

Toilet Paper

Childproofing toilet paper in a child's bathroom is important to prevent waste, clogged toilets, and unnecessary messes. One of the simplest solutions is **using a toilet paper guard or dispenser with a controlled-release mechanism** to limit how much paper can be pulled at once. Placing the toilet paper holder slightly higher or reversing the roll so it unravels from the back can also make it more challenging for little hands to unroll large amounts. **Teaching your child the proper amount to use** and explaining that too much can clog the toilet helps reinforce good habits. For younger children, replacing the roll with a tissue box can provide better control over usage. Additionally, securing the roll with a Velcro strap or a simple latch can slow down excessive unrolling. Until your child fully understands how to use toilet paper properly, supervising their bathroom habits can prevent unnecessary waste and ensure they develop good practices. By implementing these simple strategies, you can keep the bathroom tidy while allowing your child to gain independence responsibly.

Children's Bathroom
Infant/Non-mobile: (Birth - 6 months)
Infant crawl/roll: (5 months - 1 year)
→ **Toddler/Pre-school: (1 year - 4 years)**
School-age: (5 years - 6+ years)

Potty Training Safety

Potty training is an important milestone for children, and ensuring their safety during this period is important.

Supervision: Always supervise your child during potty training. Accidents can happen, and being nearby ensures you can provide immediate assistance.

Childproof the Bathroom: Childproof the bathroom to minimize potential hazards. Keep cleaning supplies, medications, and other hazardous items out of the child's reach in locked cabinets or on high shelves.

Safe Step Stool: Use a stable and sturdy step stool to help your child reach the potty or the sink for hand washing. Make sure the step stool has a non-slip surface.

Handwashing Practice: Encourage proper hand washing after using the potty to instill good hygiene habits. Provide child-friendly soap and teach them how to thoroughly lather and rinse their hands.

Safe Potty Chairs: If using a standalone potty chair, choose one with a stable base and secure handles to help the child feel comfortable and safe while using it.

Close Supervision Near Water: If you're using a regular toilet with a potty seat or training seat, always keep your child within arm's reach near water to prevent accidents or falls.

Soft-Close Toilet Seat: To prevent pinched fingers, consider using a soft-close toilet seat, which slowly lowers the seat and lid without slamming.

Slip-Resistant Floors: Use slip-resistant bathmats or rugs in the bathroom to reduce the risk of slipping and falling.

Dress for Success: Dress your child in clothing that is easy to remove quickly during potty training. Elastic waistbands or pull-up pants can make it easier for them to undress independently.

Safety during Nighttime Potty Trips: For nighttime potty training, use a nightlight in the bathroom and along the path from the child's bedroom to the bathroom to help them navigate safely in the dark.

Praise and Encouragement: Use positive reinforcement and praise when your child successfully uses the potty. This positive reinforcement helps build confidence and encourages them in the process.

Patience and Understanding: Potty training can be a challenging time for both the child and the parent. Be patient, understanding, and supportive during this learning phase.

Remember, every child is unique, and the potty-training process may vary for everyone. The key is to create a safe and encouraging environment that fosters independence and confidence. Potty training is a significant developmental milestone, and with a focus on safety and patience, it can be a successful and positive experience for both parent and child.

Children's Bathroom
→ **Infant/Non-mobile: (Birth - 6 months)**
→ **Infant crawl/roll: (5 months - 1 year)**
→ **Toddler/Pre-school: (1 year - 4 years)**
School-age: (5 years - 6+ years)

Keep Baby Oil Out of Reach

Baby oil, while a common household item for skin care, can pose a significant safety risk to young children. Due to its slippery texture and potential for accidental spills, it's essential to store baby oil in a secure location.

Here's how to keep baby oil out of reach and prevent accidents

Lockable Storage: Store baby oil in a locked cabinet or shelf that is well out of reach of children. This prevents them from accessing the bottle and reduces the risk of accidental ingestion or spills.

Tightly Closed Bottle: Always ensure the bottle is tightly closed before placing it away. A loose lid can allow the oil to leak out, making it more accessible to children.

Out of Reach During Use: When using baby oil during massage or skincare routines, dispense only the necessary amount and keep the bottle away from the baby's reach. This prevents the baby from grabbing the bottle and potentially spilling or ingesting the oil.

Educate Caregivers: Educate all caregivers, including babysitters and nannies, about the potential hazards of baby oil and the importance of storing it securely. Ensure they are aware of the proper handling and storage procedures.

Parents and caregivers can create a safer environment for their children and prevent accidents related to baby oil. Remember, even a tiny amount of baby oil can be harmful if ingested or used improperly.

Children's Bathroom
→ **Infant/Non-mobile: (Birth - 6 months)**
→ **Infant crawl/roll: (5 months - 1 year)**
→ **Toddler/Pre-school: (1 year - 4 years)**
School-age: (5 years - 6+ years)

Baby Powder Concerns

Baby powder is talcum powder which is often used to keep babies' skin dry and prevent diaper rash. However, there are some dangers associated with baby powder.

Asbestos Contamination: Talcum powder is mined from the ground, and there is a risk that it can be contaminated with asbestos. Asbestos is a known carcinogen, and exposure to asbestos can increase the risk of developing lung cancer, mesothelioma, and other respiratory diseases.

Inhalation: Talcum powder can be inhaled, and this can irritate the lungs. In some cases, inhalation of talcum powder can lead to a condition called Talcosis, which is a type of lung scarring.

Skin Irritation: Talcum powder can irritate the skin, especially in sensitive babies. In some cases, skin irritation from talcum powder can lead to a condition called contact dermatitis.

Because of these dangers, the FDA has advised consumers to avoid using talcum powder on babies and to use alternatives.

Here are some alternatives to baby powder

Cornstarch: Cornstarch is a natural powder that is often used as an alternative to talcum powder. Cornstarch is not as absorbent as talcum powder, but it is still effective at keeping skin dry.

Arrowroot Powder: Arrowroot powder is another natural powder that can be used as an alternative to talcum powder. Arrowroot powder is just as absorbent as cornstarch, and it is also gentle on the skin.

Baby Oil: Baby oil is a liquid that can be used to keep skin dry. Baby oil is not as absorbent as talcum powder, but it can help to prevent chafing and irritation.

Petroleum Jelly: Petroleum jelly is a thick, oily substance that can be used to keep skin dry. Petroleum jelly is not as absorbent as talcum powder, but it can help to prevent chafing and irritation.

If you are looking for an alternative to baby powder, talk to your doctor or a pharmacist. They can help you choose a product that is safe and effective for your needs.

Children's Bathroom
Infant/Non-mobile: (Birth - 6 months)
Infant crawl/roll: (5 months - 1 year)
→ **Toddler/Pre-school: (1 year - 4 years)**
→ **School-age: (5 years - 6+ years)**

Children's Toothpaste Concerns

Fluoride: Fluoride is a mineral that helps to strengthen teeth and prevent cavities. However, too much fluoride can be harmful, especially for young children. The American Dental Association (ADA) recommends that children under the age of 6 use toothpaste that contains no more than 500 parts per million (ppm) of fluoride.

Artificial Sweeteners: Some children's toothpaste contains artificial sweeteners like xylitol and sorbitol. While these sweeteners can be beneficial for oral health, they may cause digestive issues, such as stomach upset or diarrhea, in some children.

Artificial Flavorings: Many children's toothpastes feature artificial flavors like bubble gum or fruit. These flavors can make brushing more enjoyable for kids but can also be irritating to the mouth, especially if used excessively.

Artificial Colorings: Artificial colorings are often added to children's toothpaste to make it visually appealing. However, these coloring's can be irritating to the mouth and may contribute to allergies or sensitivities in some children.

If you are concerned about the safety of children's toothpaste, talk to your dentist. They can recommend a toothpaste that is safe and effective for your child.

Choosing a Safe Toothpaste

Choose a toothpaste that is specifically designed for children. These toothpastes typically **contain less fluoride** and artificial sweeteners than adult toothpastes.

Look for a toothpaste that is labeled as **"kid friendly."** These toothpastes are typically free of artificial flavors and colors.

Read the label carefully. Make sure that the toothpaste you choose does not contain any ingredients that your child is allergic to.

Start with **a pea-sized amount of toothpaste**. This is enough to clean your child's teeth without too much fluoride.

Rinse your child's mouth thoroughly after brushing. This will help to remove any toothpaste that may have been swallowed.

Children's Bathroom
Infant/Non-mobile: (Birth - 6 months)
Infant crawl/roll: (5 months - 1 year)
→ **Toddler/Pre-school: (1 year - 4 years)**
→ **School-age: (5 years - 6+ years)**

Never Call Medicine "Candy"

One rule that should be non-negotiable is to never refer to medicine as candy. Children, especially at a very young age, can easily be confused by this and may seek out medicine unsupervised, thinking it's a treat. This miscommunication can lead to dangerous and potentially life-threatening situations. Therefore, always store medicine in a secure place and educate children about the potential dangers of consuming it without adult supervision.

▶ *Medication Error Statistics: Over 7 million patients in the US are impacted by medication errors annually. More than 100,000 reports of medication errors are received by the FDA each year. Medication errors injure over 1.3 million people annually in the US.*

▶ *Pediatric Medication Errors: As many as 30% of medication errors reported to US Poison Control Centers involve pediatric patients. Dosage errors are common, with 7.8% of caregivers reporting insufficient doses and 6.6% reporting overdoses. Over 50% of parents have given incorrect acetaminophen doses to their children.*

|Ch. 8| Parents and Guest Bedrooms

Introduction: In the sanctuary where parents retreat for relaxation, the nuances of childproofing often go overlooked. Yet, the parents' bedroom harbors a myriad of potential hazards for little explorers. From securing heavy furniture to ensuring that small, swallowable items are out of reach, this chapter guides you through creating a safe haven that doesn't compromise on its comforting appeal. As we delve deeper, we'll explore innovative and simple strategies to childproof your bedroom, ensuring that curious little hands and nimble little feet navigate a space that is as safe as it is serene. Let's embark on this journey to foster a home where safety meets tranquility, beginning with the cornerstone of adult sanctuaries - the parents' bedroom.

Testimonial: Where should I even begin with the great "Guest Room Expedition"? My little superhero wanna be, armed with nothing but a vivid imagination and a pair of superhero pajamas, decided to head into our seldom-used guest room. In his adventurous spirit, he managed to turn the bed into a mountain using every decorative pillow and blanket he could find.

In scaling his man made "Pillow Mountain" tragedy struck! Our brave superhero took quite the tumble. Unfortunately, before he knew it, there was a mini avalanche, and our little hero found himself tumbling down the mountain and right off the bed where he rolled into the dresser. Bumping into the dresser knocked over several items including a small mirror.

Thank heavens, his trusty sidekicks (mom and dad) were nearby to rescue him. Luckily the broken mirror didn't cause any major damage, but he did end up with a bump on his head and a bruised ego. He vowed to conquer the mountain another day.

Looking back, simple childproofing could have prevented this fiasco. A childproof gate to restrict access to the adventurous lands of the guest room. Securing items like mirrors so they can't tip over is important as well. We learned our lesson: never underestimate the adventurous spirit of a child *armed with imagination and a set of superhero pajamas! From now on, the "Great Pillow Mountain" will be off-limits until further notice, or at least until our little superhero learns the art of safe climbing!*

-Mary Ann P. (Mother of 2)

Parent's and Guest Bedroom
→ **Infant/Non-mobile: (Birth - 6 months)**
→ **Infant crawl/roll: (5 months - 1 year)**
→ **Toddler/Pre-school: (1 year - 4 years)**
School-age: (5 years - 6+ years)

Never Allow Children Under 2 Years to Sleep in an Adult Bed

It is essential to prioritize the safety and well-being of young children, and one crucial aspect of this is sleep safety. As a childproofing expert, I strongly advise against allowing children under 2 years old to sleep on an adult bed. Adult beds are not designed with the same safety features as cribs or toddler beds, and this can pose significant risks to young children.

Children under 2 years old have **limited mobility** and are at higher risk of accidental falls from an adult bed. Additionally, adult beds typically have soft mattresses and pillows, which can increase the risk of suffocation or entrapment for infants and young toddlers. The gaps between the mattress and the bed frame or headboard can also pose a potential risk for entrapment.

Instead of allowing young children on adult beds, it is essential to **provide a safe sleeping environment**, such as a crib or a toddler bed with appropriate safety features. Cribs should meet safety standards, have a firm mattress, and be free from blankets, pillows, stuffed animals, and other potential suffocation hazards.

Always follow the American Academy of Pediatrics (AAP) guidelines

For safe sleep practices, including placing infants on their backs to sleep and ensuring a clutter-free sleep area. If co-sleeping is a preferred option, parents should use a co-sleeper bassinet or bedside crib that provides a separate sleep space for the baby while still keeping them close.

By adhering to these guidelines and creating a safe sleep environment, parents can significantly reduce the risk of sleep-related accidents and provide the best possible care and protection for their young children. As children grow older and gain more mobility and awareness, they can transition to a toddler bed or age-appropriate sleeping arrangements under appropriate supervision.

Notes:

Parent's and Guest Bedroom
Infant/Non-mobile: (Birth - 6 months)
Infant crawl/roll: (5 months - 1 year)
→ **Toddler/Pre-school: (1 year - 4 years)**
→ **School-age: (5 years - 6+ years)**

Install Safety Netting on Balconies and Decks

Installing safety netting on balconies and decks is a crucial step in childproofing and ensuring the safety of young children, especially if you live in a multi-story building or have a raised deck. Safety netting provides a physical barrier that prevents children from falling through gaps, can catch falling toddlers, or prevent climbing over railings. They significantly reduce the risk of accidents and injuries.

Preventing Falls: The primary purpose of safety netting is to prevent falls from balconies or decks, which can be life-threatening, particularly for young children who are not yet aware of the dangers.

Child Safety: Safety netting acts as a childproof barrier, keeping young children from accessing the edge of the balcony or deck, where they could be at risk of falling.

Curiosity Management: Young children are naturally curious and may be drawn to explore balconies and decks. Safety netting helps manage their curiosity by creating a secure barrier.

Balcony and Deck Designs: Some balcony and deck designs may have gaps or open spaces between railings that can pose a hazard. Safety netting fills in these gaps, creating a continuous barrier.

Temporary or Permanent Use: Safety netting can be installed temporarily for specific events or permanently as a childproofing solution.

Material and Visibility: Safety netting is typically made of durable, weather-resistant materials that are see-through or transparent, maintaining the aesthetic appearance of the balcony or deck.

Easy Installation: Many safety netting products are designed for easy installation, and they can be adjusted to fit various balcony or deck sizes.

Supervision: While safety netting provides an additional layer of protection, it is essential to remember that it does not replace adult supervision. Always supervise children on balconies and decks, even with safety netting in place.

Compliance with Building Codes: Some regions or building regulations may require safety measures, including safety netting, for balconies and decks, especially in homes with young children.

Regular Inspection: Regularly inspect the safety netting to ensure it remains in good condition and properly secured.

By installing safety netting on balconies and decks, you create a safer environment for children to play and enjoy outdoor spaces while giving parents peace of mind knowing that their little ones are protected from potential falls and accidents. Always choose high-quality safety netting and follow the manufacturer's installation instructions for the best results. If you have specific concerns or questions about childproofing your balcony or deck, consider consulting a child safety expert or professional installer for personalized guidance.

Parent's and Guest Bedroom
Infant/Non-mobile: (Birth - 6 months)
Infant crawl/roll: (5 months - 1 year)
→ **Toddler/Pre-school: (1 year - 4 years)**
→ **School-age: (5 years - 6+ years)**

Gun Safety

Child gun safety is a critical aspect of responsible gun ownership and parenting. It involves taking proactive measures to prevent children from gaining access to firearms and educating them about the potential dangers associated with guns.

Safe Storage: Store firearms in a securely locked gun safe or a gun cabinet with a reliable locking mechanism. The safe should be inaccessible to children and unauthorized individuals. Keep the keys or combination to the safe away from children's reach. If a gun safe is not available, use a cable lock or trigger lock to secure the firearm. These locks prevent the gun from being fired while in place.

Ammunition Storage: Store ammunition separately from firearms in a locked container or a separate gun safe. Keep the ammunition locked away from children to prevent them from accessing bullets even if they gain access to a firearm.

Education and Communication: Educate children about gun safety from an early age, using age-appropriate language and concepts. Teach them that guns are not toys and are dangerous when mishandled. Explain that they should never touch a gun they find and should immediately inform an adult if they come across one.

Zero Tolerance Rule: Establish a strict zero-tolerance policy regarding playing with guns or pretending to use them as toys. Ensure that children understand the seriousness of the rule and the consequences of breaking it.

Adult Supervision: Always supervise children when firearms are present, even if they have received gun safety education. Never leave guns unattended and within reach of children, even for a short time.

Unload Guns When Not in Use: Whenever firearms are not in use, unload them and keep them in a securely locked storage. Double-check that the gun is unloaded before storing it.

Proper Handling: Teach older children and teenagers about proper gun handling, including how to check if a gun is loaded, how to point it safely, and how to store it securely. Ensure they understand that they should never handle a firearm without adult supervision.

Gun Safety Courses: If you have firearms in your home, enroll in a reputable gun safety course to improve your knowledge and skills. These courses often cover safe gun handling, storage, and shooting practices.

Discussing Gun Safety with Other Parents: If your child visits other homes, ask if there are guns in the house and how they are stored. Politely and respectfully discuss gun safety practices with other parents and encourage them to secure firearms responsibly.

Lead by Example: Be a responsible gun owner and parent. Follow all safety protocols and handle firearms with care. Model responsible behavior to teach children the importance of gun safety.

Parents can create a safe environment for their children and reduce the risk of accidents involving firearms. Responsible gun ownership and child gun safety education are crucial steps in safeguarding children from potential harm related to firearms.

Parent's and Guest Bedroom
Infant/Non-mobile: (Birth - 6 months)
Infant crawl/roll: (5 months - 1 year)
→ **Toddler/Pre-school: (1 year - 4 years)**
→ **School-age: (5 years - 6+ years)**

Jewelry Dangers

When it comes to jewelry, there are several child concerns that parents and caregivers should be aware of to ensure the safety and well-being of children.

Choking Hazard: Small jewelry pieces, such as earrings, necklaces, bracelets, and rings, can pose a choking hazard for young children, especially those under the age of 3. Children are naturally curious and may put jewelry in their mouths, increasing the risk of choking.

Ingestion: Young children might accidentally swallow small jewelry components, such as beads or gemstones, which can lead to choking or internal injuries.

Allergic Reactions: Some children may have allergies or sensitivities to certain metals, like nickel, which is commonly found in costume jewelry. Allergic reactions can cause skin irritation, redness, and discomfort.

Strangulation Risk: Long necklaces, cords, or chains can become entangled around a child's neck or other body parts, leading to strangulation hazards.

Swallowing Magnets: Magnetic jewelry or jewelry with detachable magnetic components can be dangerous if swallowed, as multiple magnets can attract each other within the child's body, causing intestinal complications.

Sharp Edges: Jewelry with sharp edges or points can cause injuries or scratches, especially if your child accidentally falls while wearing or handling the jewelry.

Chemicals and Lead Content: Some jewelry items may contain harmful substances like lead or toxic chemicals. Children may be more susceptible to the adverse effects of such substances.

Loss or Damage: Children may lose or damage valuable or sentimental jewelry, causing distress to them or their parents.

Precautions

Age-Appropriate Jewelry: Choose age-appropriate jewelry for children. Avoid giving small or dangling jewelry to young children who may not understand the risks.

Supervision: Always supervise young children when they are wearing jewelry. Be vigilant to prevent choking or accidents.

Avoid Magnetic Jewelry: Refrain from giving magnetic jewelry to young children or those prone to putting objects in their mouths.

Hypoallergenic Options: Opt for hypoallergenic jewelry made from materials less likely to cause allergic reactions.

Secure Closures: Ensure that jewelry items have secure closures or clasps to reduce the risk of loss or entanglement.

Check for Safety Standards: When buying jewelry for children, check for safety certifications and compliance with safety standards.

Remove Jewelry During Play: Encourage children to remove jewelry during physical activities or playtime to avoid accidents.

Regular Inspections: Regularly inspect jewelry items for any signs of damage or wear and tear.

Parent's and Guest Bedroom
Infant/Non-mobile: (Birth - 6 months)
Infant crawl/roll: (5 months - 1 year)
→ **Toddler/Pre-school: (1 year - 4 years)**
→ **School-age: (5 years - 6+ years)**

Keep All Sleep Medication Out of Reach

Childproofing medication is crucial to ensure the safety of young children who might be curious and unaware of the potential dangers of medications. Accidental ingestion of medication can lead to serious health issues.

Secure Storage: Keep all medications, including over the counter and prescription drugs, in a securely locked medicine cabinet or a high and inaccessible location. If needed, use childproof locks on cabinets.

Original Containers: Store medications in their original containers with child-resistant caps. Avoid transferring pills to other containers, as children may mistake them for candies.

Proper Labeling: Ensure all medication containers have clear and accurate labels, including the name of the medication, dosage instructions, and any warnings.

Childproof Bottles: Choose products in childproof bottles whenever possible when purchasing medications. These bottles have safety caps that require a specific squeezing and turning motion to open, making it more challenging for young children to access the contents.

Educate Children: Teach children about the dangers of medications and the importance of never taking any medication without adult supervision. Emphasize that medications are not toys and should only be taken by adults or under adult supervision.

Out of Sight, Out of Reach: Keep medications out of sight and reach of children. Avoid leaving medication bottles on countertops, nightstands, or easily accessible places.

Time-Lock Medication Dispensers: If necessary, use time-lock medication dispensers to prevent unauthorized access to medication. These devices dispense medications only at specified times, controlled by a timer or code.

Childproof Travel Containers: Use childproof containers designed for this purpose when carrying medication in a purse or travel bag. Avoid carrying medications loose in a bag where children can access them easily.

Dispose of Expired Medications: Regularly check and discard expired or unused medications safely, according to local guidelines.

Medication During Travel: When traveling with medication, ensure it is safely stored in the original containers and out of reach of children.

Be a Role Model: Set a good example by taking medications responsibly and following proper dosage instructions.

Keep Medications Separate: Keep medications separate from vitamins and supplements to avoid confusion.

Emergency Information: Save emergency contact numbers, including Poison Control Center, in your phone and post them in a visible place at home.

By implementing these childproofing strategies and taking a watchful stance on medication safety, parents and guardians can lessen the likelihood of unintentional ingestion and foster a secure space for youngsters. If you believe your child has consumed any medication or hazardous material, promptly seek medical assistance and contact your nearest Poison Control Center.

► *According to the CPSC, each year in the U.S., roughly **65,000 to 75,000 young children** (ages 0–6) are treated in emergency rooms after finding and ingesting medications left within reach. In 2022 alone, data show **68,600 unintentional pediatric poisonings** among under-fives, many due to easy access to pills or flavored supplements. For instance, **melatonin was involved in nearly 11,000 annual poisoning visits** during 2019–2022. These numbers reveal a hidden but consistent risk—everyday adult medications can rapidly turn into serious hazards when left unsecured.*

Parent's and Guest Bedroom
Infant/Non-mobile: (Birth - 6 months)
Infant crawl/roll: (5 months - 1 year)
→ **Toddler/Pre-school: (1 year - 4 years)**
→ **School-age: (5 years - 6+ years)**

Walk-in Closet Safety

It is important to consider both immediate and long-term strategies to create a safe environment for toddlers. One of the first steps is to control access by installing childproof locks or knob covers on the door. This prevents unsupervised entry and ensures that children cannot wander into potentially hazardous spaces when not under supervision.

Closet organization plays a critical role in minimizing risks. Keeping items off the floor not only reduces tripping hazards but also prevents children from accessing objects that could fall. Heavy or dangerous items such as shoes, bags, or sharp objects like scissors should be stored on higher shelves, well out of reach. Shelving units should always be secured to the wall with appropriate anchors to prevent tipping. This is especially important if the child may attempt to climb shelves or pull-on objects stored at higher levels.

Childproof containers are another valuable tool. Small items like jewelry, buttons, or other choking hazards should be stored in secure, child-resistant boxes or bins. These containers not only keep small objects organized but also protect children from accessing items that could pose a choking risk. Electronics and cords present additional dangers, so organizing cables with cable ties or cord covers ensures they are out of reach and do not create any tripping hazards.

The closet's structural elements, such as **hanging rods and shelves**, should also be adjusted with child safety in mind. Hanging rods should be placed at heights that are inaccessible to young children, preventing them from pulling down clothes or getting entangled. Sharp corners of furniture or shelves can be padded to reduce the risk of injury, and drawer latches should be installed to prevent access to items inside.

Furthermore, it is essential to ensure **proper lighting** in the closet. LED lighting is an excellent option, as it does not heat up like traditional bulbs, reducing the risk of burns. Adequate lighting also allows both adults and children to clearly see potential hazards, making it easier to navigate the space safely.

Storing cleaning supplies or other hazardous chemicals in closets should be strictly avoided unless they are securely locked in childproof cabinets. Toddlers are naturally curious and may try to explore areas where such items are kept. In addition to securing hazardous materials, laundry baskets should be placed in elevated areas to prevent toddlers from becoming trapped or tangled.

Regular inspections of the closet space should be part of the ongoing childproofing process. As children grow and become more mobile, new risks may arise, and it is important to adapt the closet's organization and safety features to meet those changes. Educating children about safe behaviors in the closet, while always supervising their access.

|Ch. 9| Parents Bathroom

Introduction: In this chapter, we delve into the critical task of childproofing the parent's bathroom, a place often laden with potential hazards for your little ones. As parents, we must transform this space into a safe space where the risk of accidents is minimized. From securing potentially harmful substances found in cabinets to ensuring the safe use of electrical appliances, we will guide you step-by-step to create a bathroom environment that combines safety with functionality. As we navigate through this chapter, you will be equipped with practical tips and insights to foster a secure and child-friendly bathroom without compromising its adult-oriented utilities. Let's embark on this journey to safeguard our children while preserving the sanctity of our personal retreat.

Testimonial: *My son Gordon is a little bundle of boundless energy. Just the other day I found that he has developed a fascination for the toilet paper roll. It seems to him like the most entertaining toy in the house, a never-ending waterfall of soft, white paper.*

I was preparing dinner when I heard a series of thuds and giggles emanating from the bathroom. As I rushed to the scene, I found Gordon, an aspiring mummy, wrapped from head to toe in toilet paper, having a grand old time. Unfortunately, during his mummification process, he had slipped on the unraveled paper and bumped his little noggin on the bathroom floor.

It was nothing more than a minor bump, but it served as an eye-opening lesson for us. We decided that it was time to invest in a childproof toilet paper dispenser to save our precious rolls and prevent Gordon from hurting himself more severely.

Looking back, we can't help but chuckle at our little mummy's antics, and we've made sure to document this adventure in the family album. Remember, fellow parents, childproofing is not just about safety, it's about saving your bathroom supplies from the clutches of tiny, curious hands!

-Stacy T. (Mother of 2)

Parents Bathroom
→ **Infant/Non-mobile: (Birth - 6 months)**
→ **Infant crawl/roll: (5 months - 1 year)**
→ **Toddler/Pre-school: (1 year - 4 years)**
→ **School-age: (5 years - 6+ years)**

Tips on How to Use the Bathroom Alone

Using the bathroom without a child can provide a moment of much-needed privacy and relaxation.

Communicate: Let your child know where you are going and that you will be back shortly. Inform them of any safety rules they need to follow while you are away.

Set Expectations: If your child is old enough, discuss with them the importance of giving you privacy when using the bathroom. Encourage them to play or engage in quiet activities while you are away.

Lock the Door: If possible, lock the bathroom door to prevent unexpected intrusions. Make sure your child knows not to disturb you while the door is locked.

Engage in Distractions: Before heading to the bathroom, set up your child with an engaging activity or toy to keep them occupied while you are away.

Time it Right: Choose a moment when your child is engaged in an activity or when they are more likely to be content and less likely to need immediate attention.

Use Visual Cues: For younger children who may not fully understand time concepts, use visual cues like an hourglass or a timer to let them know when you will be back.

Practice Independence: Encourage your child's independence by teaching them how to engage in solo play or allowing them to explore safe areas of the house while you are in the bathroom.

Prepare Essentials: Before heading to the bathroom, ensure you have everything you need within reach to minimize your time away.

Create a Safe Environment: Ensure that the bathroom environment is childproofed and safe for your child to explore if they happen to wander in while you are using it.

Plan Ahead: If you know you will need some time alone in the bathroom, plan ahead and set

Remember, young children may still need occasional supervision, so try to keep your bathroom trips relatively short. Setting clear boundaries and providing engaging activities can help your child understand the importance of giving you privacy while you use the bathroom. As they grow older and more independent, they will become better at respecting your need for some personal space.

Parents Bathroom
Infant/Non-mobile: (Birth - 6 months)
Infant crawl/roll: (5 months - 1 year)
→ **Toddler/Pre-school: (1 year - 4 years)**
→ **School-age: (5 years - 6+ years)**

Secure Razors, Nail Clippers, Tweezers, Makeup...

Annually, approximately **2,500 children** are injured by hair accessories such as clips, bands, and elastics, including choking and strangulation risks. (Source: U.S. Consumer Product Safety Commission (CPSC) - Hair Accessory Safety) Securing razors, nail clippers, tweezers, and makeup is essential for childproofing your home and ensuring the safety of young children. If these items are accessible to curious little ones, they can pose potential risks.

Razors: Switch to Electric Razors: Consider using electric razors instead of traditional razors with removable blades. Electric razors are generally safer because they have built-in safety features, and there are no sharp blades that can be easily accessed by children. Store Razors Safely: If you must use traditional razors, store them in a securely locked drawer or a high cabinet, out of children's reach. Use Razor Guards: When using disposable razors, use razor guards or blade covers to prevent accidental cuts when not in use.

Nail Clippers: Store Securely: Keep nail clippers in a locked or childproof container, drawer, or cabinet. Make sure the storage location is not accessible to young children. Use Childproof Nail

Clippers: Consider using childproof nail clippers that have safety features, such as rounded edges and locking mechanisms, to reduce the risk of accidents.

Tweezers: Store Out of Reach: Keep tweezers in a childproof drawer or cabinet that is inaccessible to young children. Choose Child-Friendly Tweezers: If you have sharp tips, consider switching to child-friendly tweezers with rounded edges for safety.

Makeup: Store Makeup Securely: Store all makeup products, including lipsticks, eyeliners, and powders, in a locked makeup case or organizer that can be kept out of children's reach. Avoid leaving makeup unattended. Never leave makeup products unattended on countertops or other accessible surfaces, as children may be tempted to play with them. Childproof Makeup Containers. Some makeup brands offer childproof containers with secure closures that can help prevent accidental spills or exposure.

Supervision and Education: Always supervise children when you are using these items and keep them out of children's reach when not in use. Educate older children about the potential dangers of these items and the importance of using them responsibly.

Regular Inspection: Regularly inspect storage areas to ensure that these items remain securely stored and that no hazards are present.

Additionally, over 15,000 children sustain burns or electrical injuries each year from hair dryers, curling irons, and other styling tools in the U.S. (Source: American Burn Association (ABA) - Burn Incidence Statistics) Store properly!

<u>Parents Bathroom</u>
Infant non-mobile: (Birth-6 mo.)
Infant crawl/roll: (5 mo.-2 yrs.)
→ **Toddler/Pre-School: (1 yr.-4 yrs.)**
→ **School-age: (5 yrs.-6 yrs.)**

Mouthwash Concerns

If mouthwash is not used properly or if the wrong type is used, it can pose several dangers for children.

Swallowing Mouthwash: One of the most significant dangers is the risk of children accidentally swallowing mouthwash. Young children, especially those under the age of 6, may not have the coordination or understanding to spit out the mouthwash properly after use. Swallowing mouthwash can lead to poisoning and cause symptoms such as gastrointestinal distress, nausea, vomiting, and, in severe cases, alcohol poisoning if the mouthwash contains alcohol.

Alcohol Content: Many mouthwash products, particularly those designed for adults, contain alcohol as an antimicrobial agent. Alcohol-based mouthwashes can be harmful if ingested in significant amounts. Children's smaller body size makes them more susceptible to the effects of alcohol, including drowsiness, dizziness, and other potential health risks.

Fluoride Overdose: Some mouthwashes contain fluoride, which is beneficial for preventing tooth decay. However, excessive swallowing of fluoride-containing mouthwash can lead to fluoride toxicity. This can result in dental fluorosis, a cosmetic issue that affects tooth enamel, or other health issues related to high fluoride levels in the body.

Sensitivity and Irritation: Some children may have sensitivities or allergies to certain ingredients found in mouthwash, such as alcohol, menthol, or other flavoring agents. Using mouthwash with irritating ingredients can cause mouth or gum irritation in sensitive individuals.

Child-Friendly Alternatives: Adult mouthwash may be too strong for children, and they may find the taste too intense or unpleasant. This can discourage children from using mouthwash properly or regularly.

Choking Hazard: Younger children may not have the motor skills or understanding to use mouthwash correctly. Accidental spills or misuse can lead to choking hazards or injuries.

Flavor Preferences: Children may not enjoy the strong mint flavors commonly found in mouthwash, which can deter them from using it effectively.

Age Appropriate: Do not give mouthwash to children under the age recommended by dental professionals or the mouthwash manufacturer. Some mouthwash products are specifically designed for children with age-appropriate ingredients and flavors.

Supervision: Always supervise older children when they use mouthwash to ensure proper use and prevent swallowing.

Limit Quantity: Use mouthwash sparingly and according to the manufacturer's recommendations.

Educate: Teach children about the correct use of mouthwash, the importance of spitting it out after use, and the potential dangers of swallowing it.

It is best to consult with a pediatric dentist or healthcare professional before introducing mouthwash into a child's oral care routine. Regular brushing, flossing, and routine dental check-ups are sufficient for children's oral hygiene needs.

▶ *Each year, around* **3,000 preschoolers** *(under 6) in the U.S. are reported to poison control centers after ingesting mouthwash. Nearly* **170 cases per 100,000 kids**. *Between 1987 and 1993,* **1,670 emergency visits** *were recorded, and three toddlers died when they swallowed alcohol-rich rinses. Even dessert-like formulas can be toxic at minor dosages in young children. In 2024, over 100,000 bottles of hydrogen-peroxide mouthwash were recalled for lacking child-resistant lids, proof that this everyday hygiene product can be deadly when left within reach.*

Parents Bathroom
Infant/Non-mobile: (Birth - 6 months)
Infant crawl/roll: (5 months - 1 year)
→ **Toddler/Pre-school: (1 year - 4 years)**
→ **School-age: (5 years - 6+ years)**

Don't Store Medicine in the Medicine Cabinet

You should always avoid storing medicine in the medicine cabinet. This is crucial for the safety of your children.

Child Access Prevention: Medicine cabinets are typically within easy reach of children, especially curious toddlers. Children may be tempted to explore and ingest medications, leading to accidental poisoning or ingestion.

Non-Locking Cabinets: Most medicine cabinets do not come with childproof locks, making it easy for children to open and access the contents inside.

Visibility and Organization: Medicine cabinets can become cluttered and disorganized, making it challenging to find the right medication when needed. Poor organization can lead to accidental misuse or taking the wrong medication.

Humidity and Heat: Bathrooms, where medicine cabinets are often located, can have higher humidity levels and fluctuations in temperature due to showers and baths. Exposure to humidity and heat can degrade the effectiveness of medications and reduce their shelf life.

Moisture and Spills: Bathrooms are prone to moisture, and there's a risk of water spills or splashes in the medicine cabinet. Moisture can seep into pill bottles, dissolve tablets, and affect the integrity of medications.

Accessibility to Guests: If guests or visitors use the bathroom, they may have access to the medicine cabinet, which could lead to accidental misuse or confusion about the medication's contents.

Alternative Childproof Storage Options

Locked Cabinet: Store medications in a locked cabinet in a cool, dry, and elevated place, out of children's reach. Lockable cabinets offer an added layer of safety and security.

Bedroom or Hallway Cabinet: Consider storing medications in a cabinet located in the bedroom or hallway, away from moisture and heat typically found in bathrooms. If possible, choose a cabinet with childproof locks.

Dedicated Storage Container: Use a dedicated, airtight container or a pill organizer designed for medication storage. Keep this container out of children's reach and in a secure location.

High Shelves: Place medications on high shelves, away from the reach of children but still within easy access for adults. Make sure the shelf is sturdy and not easily accessible to curious children.

Original Packaging: Store medications in their original packaging with clear labels to avoid confusion and ensure proper dosages. If necessary, store medications in a secure, childproof container.

Medication Drawer: Designate a specific drawer in a secure location for storing medications. Use a drawer with a childproof lock or install childproof latches on the drawer.

Temperature-controlled Space: Store temperature-sensitive medications in a cool, dark, and temperature-controlled area, away from direct sunlight and extreme temperatures.

Inform Guests: If you have guests or visitors in your home, inform them about the importance of keeping medications out of reach of children and instruct them not to use the medicine cabinet.

Remember to regularly check the expiration dates of medications and dispose of any expired or unused medications properly. Proper childproof storage and organization of medications ensure their efficacy and prevent accidental ingestion or misuse by young children.

Parents Bathroom
Infant/Non-mobile: (Birth - 6 months)
→ **Infant crawl/roll: (5 months - 1 year)**
→ **Toddler/Pre-school: (1 year - 4 years)**
→ **School-age: (5 years - 6+ years)**

Talk to Guests About Their Contents

Childproofing is not just about securing your own home; it also involves ensuring the safety of children when guests visit. It is essential to have open and clear communication with guests about potential hazards, especially regarding items like medication.

Welcoming Communication: When guests arrive, warmly welcome them and express your appreciation for their visit. Setting a positive tone will make the conversation more comfortable.

Mention Childproofing: Politely let guests know that your home is childproofed to ensure the safety of any young children who may be present. Assure them that you take precautions to create a secure environment.

Ask about Medications: When appropriate, inquire if any of your guests carry medication. Some guests may be on specific medications and may need to access them during their visit.

Storage Options: Offer to provide a secure and childproof location for their medications. Suggest using a lockable drawer or a designated container out of children's reach. Assure them that their belongings will be safe in these storage options.

Safety Tips: Share general safety tips with your guests regarding keeping medication out of reach of children. Remind them to close medication containers after use securely and not to leave them unattended.

Guest's Responsibility: Politely remind guests that they also have a role in ensuring the safety of children during their visit. Encourage them to be vigilant about their belongings and to keep an eye on young children when using personal items.

Emergency Information: Share emergency contact numbers, including the Poison Control Center, with your guests. This ensures everyone is prepared in case of any accidental ingestion or emergency.

Non-Judgmental Approach: Approach the conversation with understanding and empathy. Some guests might not be aware of childproofing measures or the potential dangers. Educate them have with them)without making them feel uncomfortable or judged.

Lead by Example: Demonstrate childproofing measures in your home. Show guests how medications are securely stored and emphasize the importance of being cautious with personal belongings.

Thank Them: Thank your guests for their cooperation and understanding in keeping the environment safe for children.

Remember that some guests may have unique medical needs, and respecting their privacy and personal choices is essential. However, when it comes to child safety, open communication is crucial. By talking to guests about potential hazards, including medication, and offering secure storage options, you can create a welcoming environment while prioritizing the safety of young children in your home.

Notes: (You probably can guess what your guests may have on them)

|Ch. 10| Nursery

Introduction: As the nursery is undoubtedly the most important room in your house, we will dedicate significant time to ensuring that the space where your baby spends most of their early life is exceptionally safe. We understand that you might have already taken some safety measures when setting up the nursery, such as reading safety manuals and choosing appropriate window treatments. However, that won't deter us from meticulously detailing every aspect of this room to maximize its safety and security from top to bottom. Your baby's well-being is our top priority, and we want to create a nurturing environment where they can thrive and explore with confidence. Let's go through the nursery step by step to implement the best safety practices and give you peace of mind knowing that your little one is protected in every possible way.

Testimonial: *I definitely consider my childproofing testimonial as a series of unfortunate events! I now consider my little guy a magician, who seems to have inherited Houdini's knack for escapology.*

It all started with the great "Crib Escape." For the first time my little munchkin figured out how to scale the crib walls, which I swear were designed to rival Fort Knox. Before I knew it, he was out and about, exploring the great, unknown territories of the nursery.

After toddling around, he quickly figured out how to climb up the changing table. With the agility of a seasoned mountaineer, he managed to reach the summit, only to find himself in a bit of a pickle, unable to get down.

While he was stuck up there my little artist managed to get his hands on a tube of diaper cream and decided that the nursery walls were his canvas. I must admit, his handiwork was nothing short of a masterpiece, albeit a very sticky one.

Now, here's where I could have prevented the entire fiasco. First, I should have lowered the mattress to thwart his escape attempts. Second, a childproof lock on the diaper cream drawer would have saved our walls from becoming an abstract art exhibit. We also realized that securing the changing table to the wall was super important after seeing how quickly he was able to scale it. We were lucky he didn't tip it over.

Looking back, I can't help but chuckle at the entire episode. My little adventurer sure knows how to keep us on our toes! Lesson learned: never underestimate the exploratory prowess of a toddler. Time to up our childproofing game!

-Sharron (Mother of 2)

Nursery
→ **Infant/Non-mobile: (Birth - 6 months)**
→ **Infant crawl/roll: (5 months - 1 year)**
Toddler/Pre-school: (1 year - 4 years)
School-age: (5 years - 6+ years)

Crib Information

According to the **Consumer Product Safety Commission** (CPSC) and the **American Academy of Pediatrics** (SAP)

Crib Construction: Check that the crib slats are spaced no more than 2.375 inches apart to prevent the baby's head from getting trapped between them. Ensure no decorative cutouts or designs are on the crib's headboard or footboard, as they could pose entrapment hazards. Inspect the crib for rough or sharp edges that could harm the baby.

Stability and Sturdiness: Ensure that the crib is sturdy and well-constructed, with no wobbling or instability. Tighten all screws and bolts securely according to the manufacturer's instructions. Check for any signs of wear, damage, or loose parts, and repair or replace them promptly.

Safe Crib Location: Place the crib away from electrical outlets, cords, and other potential hazards. Avoid positioning the crib near heating sources or direct sunlight to prevent overheating. Keep the crib away from curtains or blinds to avoid strangulation risks.

Crib Mattress Fit: Ensure that the crib mattress fits snugly within the crib frame, leaving no gaps between the mattress and the crib walls. Test the mattress by pressing firmly on the edges and corners to check for any spaces where the baby's fingers could get caught.

Safe Bedding Practices: Use a fitted crib sheet made for the specific mattress size. It should fit tightly and securely around the corners of the mattress. Avoid using soft or loose bedding, such as pillows, comforters, and stuffed animals, as they can pose suffocation hazards.

Unintentional suffocation from bedding, pillows, and soft toys leads to approximately **500 child deaths** annually in the U.S., underscoring the importance of safe sleep practices. (Source: National Center on Sleep Disorders Research (NCSDR) - Safe Sleep)

Crib Mobiles and Toys: If you use a crib mobile, ensure it is securely attached to the crib and positioned out of the baby's reach. Remove mobiles and toys once the baby can sit up on their own to prevent them from pulling them down onto themselves.

Monitor Baby's Growth and Development: Regularly monitor your baby's development milestones, especially when they roll over or climb. Adjust the crib mattress height accordingly to prevent falls once the baby becomes more mobile.

Safe Sleep Position: Always place your baby to sleep on their back, as this reduces the risk of SIDS. Avoid using sleep positioners or any additional devices that claim to keep the baby in a specific position while sleeping.

Follow Manufacturer's Guidelines: Follow the manufacturer's guidelines and instructions for assembling, using, and maintaining the crib.

Regular Maintenance: Routinely inspect the crib for wear and tear, loose parts, or any safety concerns. Clean the crib regularly and ensure it remains free from any hazards.

By paying attention to these detailed crib safety measures, you can create a secure and comfortable sleep environment for your baby. Regular vigilance and maintenance are essential to ensure the crib remains safe as your baby grows and reaches various developmental milestones. Prioritizing crib safety contributes significantly to your baby's overall well-being and provides you with peace of mind as a caring and responsible parent.

► *According to Pediatrics Journal, Nationwide Children's Hospital,* ***approximately 9,561 children under 2 years old are injured in crib-related accidents annually in the US.***

Nursery
→ **Infant/Non-mobile: (Birth - 6 months)**
→ **Infant crawl/roll: (5 months - 1 year)**
Toddler/Pre-school: (1 year - 4 years)
School-age: (5 years - 6+ years)

Mesh-sided Crib

Mesh-sided cribs are popular with many parents due to their breathable and transparent design. However, like any crib, ensuring its safety is essential for your baby's well-being.

Mesh Quality: Choose a mesh-sided crib with sturdy, tightly woven mesh that meets safety standards. To prevent entrapment hazards, the mesh should be free from tears, holes, or loose threads.

Visibility and Breathability: Mesh-sided cribs provide excellent visibility, allowing you to see your baby from various angles. This can be beneficial for monitoring your little one while they sleep. The breathable nature of the mesh allows for better air circulation within the crib, reducing the risk of overheating.

Mattress Fit: Ensure that the crib mattress fits snugly within the crib frame, leaving no gaps between the mattress and the crib's sides or corners. A properly fitting mattress helps prevent entrapment and suffocation risks.

Safe Bedding Practices: Use a fitted crib sheet made for the specific mattress size. Avoid using additional bedding, such as pillows, comforters, or blankets, to reduce the risk of suffocation or SIDS.

Check Mesh Tension: Regularly inspect the mesh to ensure it remains securely attached to the crib frame. Check for any loose or sagging areas and adjust or repair them promptly.

Weight Limits: Follow the manufacturer's weight limits for the crib. Consider transitioning to a toddler bed once your baby exceeds the weight limit or can climb out of the crib.

No Gap Between Mattress and Sides: Make sure there are no gaps between the mattress and the mesh sides where the baby's fingers or limbs could get stuck.

Safe Corner Fasteners: Check that the mesh is properly secured to the crib corners and that the fasteners are in good condition. Loose or broken fasteners could pose a safety risk.

Supervision: Always supervise your baby when they are in the crib, especially when they are very young or unable to roll over independently.

Transition to a Toddler Bed: When your baby begins to show signs of attempting to climb out of the crib or exceeds the weight limit, it's time to transition them to a toddler bed for their safety.

As with any crib, regularly inspect the mesh-sided crib for any signs of wear, damage, or safety concerns. Address any issues promptly to maintain a safe sleeping environment for your baby. Following these safety guidelines ensures that your mesh-sided crib provides a secure and comfortable place for your baby to rest and grow.

Nursery
→ **Infant/Non-mobile: (Birth - 6 months)**
Infant crawl/roll: (5 months - 1 year)
Toddler/Pre-school: (1 year - 4 years)
School-age: (5 years - 6+ years)

Bassinet Safety

Bassinets provide a cozy and convenient sleeping space for newborns and young infants. Ensuring bassinet safety is crucial to creating a secure and comforting sleep environment for your baby.

Sturdy and Stable Design: Choose a bassinet with a sturdy and stable frame that is unlikely to tip over. Check that all components, such as legs, wheels, and locking mechanisms, are securely attached and functioning correctly.

Safe Sleep Surface: Use a firm and flat mattress specifically designed for the bassinet. Ensure that the mattress fits snugly within the bassinet frame, leaving no gaps between the mattress and the sides to prevent entrapment hazards.

Age and Weight Limitations: Follow the manufacturer's recommendations regarding age and weight limitations for the bassinet. Once your baby exceeds the weight limit or can roll over independently, it's time to transition them to a crib.

Ventilation: Check that the bassinet's sides have sufficient ventilation to allow for proper air circulation.

Safe Bedding Practices: Use a fitted bassinet sheet made for the specific mattress size. Avoid using additional bedding, such as blankets, pillows, or crib bumpers, to reduce the risk of suffocation or SIDS.

Safe Bassinet Location: Place the bassinet in a safe location away from cords, curtains, and other potential hazards. To prevent overheating, avoid placing the bassinet near heating sources or direct sunlight.

Mobility and Locking Mechanism: If the bassinet has wheels, ensure they have a locking mechanism to prevent unintended movement.

Stability and Safety Standards: Ensure that the bassinet meets safety standards and regulations set by relevant authorities. Look for certification labels, such as JPMA (Juvenile Products Manufacturers Association) or ASTM (American Society for Testing and Materials).

Supervision: Always supervise your baby when they are in the bassinet, especially during sleep.

Check for Wear and Tear: Regularly inspect the bassinet for any signs of wear, damage, or loose parts. Repair or replace any damaged or missing parts immediately.

No Extra Accessories: Avoid using additional accessories, such as toys or hanging mobiles, inside the bassinet as they could pose a strangulation or choking hazard.

Safe Use of Canopy: If the bassinet has a canopy or cover, ensure it is securely attached and does not pose any suffocation risks.

Regularly inspect the bassinet for any safety concerns and address them promptly to provide your baby with a secure and restful sleep. As your baby grows and reaches developmental milestones, be prepared to transition them to a crib when it is appropriate for their safety and well-being.

<u>Nursery</u>
→ **Infant/Non-mobile: (Birth - 6 months)**
→ **Infant crawl/roll: (5 months - 1 year)**
Toddler/Pre-school: (1 year - 4 years)
School-age: (5 years - 6+ years)

Location, Location, Location (Crib location)

The placement of the crib is an important consideration for your baby's safety and comfort.

Proximity to Caregiver: Place the crib in your bedroom for the first six months to a year, especially for newborns. Having your baby close to you makes nighttime feedings and comfort more accessible.

Away from Hazards: Keep the crib away from windows, curtains, cords, and blinds to prevent strangulation hazards and to avoid direct exposure to sunlight and drafts. Position the crib away from heaters, radiators, air vents, or any other potential sources of heat that could cause overheating.

Safe Distance from Furniture: To prevent items from falling into the crib, make sure the crib is placed at a safe distance from other furniture, such as dressers or shelves.

Avoid Wall Hangings and Decorations: Do not place the crib under wall hangings, heavy pictures, or decorations that could potentially fall onto the crib.

Easy Accessibility: Ensure the crib is easily accessible so you can reach and tend to your baby comfortably. If you prefer to have your baby sleep near your bed during the first few months, use a bassinet or co-sleeper.

Avoid High-Traffic Areas: Do not place the crib in high-traffic areas, as this could disturb your baby's sleep and pose safety risks.

No Cord Hazards: To prevent accidental entanglement, keep the crib away from cords, such as blinds or curtains.

Safe from Pets: If you have pets, consider placing the crib in a location where they cannot access or jump into it.

Follow Manufacturer's Recommendations: Adhere to the manufacturer's guidelines and instructions for crib placement and assembly.

Accessibility to Baby Monitor: Ensure that the baby monitor can be easily positioned to monitor your baby while they are in the crib.

Remember, for the first six months to a year, the American Academy of Pediatrics (SAP) recommends room-sharing without bed-sharing to reduce the risk of sudden infant death syndrome (SIDS). Once your baby is older and begins to roll over, you can consider transitioning them to their room and crib, following the same safety guidelines. Always supervise your baby while they are in the crib and promptly address any safety concerns to create a safe sleep environment for your little one.

Nursery
→ **Infant/Non-mobile: (Birth - 6 months)**
Infant crawl/roll: (5 months - 1 year)
Toddler/Pre-school: (1 year - 4 years)
School-age: (5 years - 6+ years)

Teething

Preventing a child from chewing on the crib is essential to ensure their safety and avoid potential hazards.

Use Crib Rail Covers: Cover the crib rails with crib rail covers made of non-toxic and safe materials. These covers can act as a barrier, preventing direct access to the crib's wooden rails and discouraging chewing behavior.

Provide Teething Toys: Offer your child safe and appropriate teething toys to redirect their chewing behavior. Teething toys designed for babies to chew on can help soothe their gums and satisfy their urge to chew.

Keep Crib Area Free from Objects: Remove any items or objects from the crib that could encourage chewing, such as loose crib bumpers, blankets, or stuffed animals.

Offer Positive Reinforcement: Praise and reward your child when they refrain from chewing on the crib. Positive reinforcement can help them associate not chewing with positive outcomes.

Address Teething Discomfort: If your child is teething and experiencing discomfort, provide appropriate teething remedies, such as chilled teething rings, to alleviate their discomfort.

Check for Unsafe Paint or Finishes: Ensure that the crib's paint or finish is safe and non-toxic. If you notice any peeling or chipping paint, address it immediately and consider using a crib rail cover to prevent contact with the affected area.

Supervise Crib Time: Always supervise your child when they are in the crib to intervene if they attempt to chew on the crib rails.

Distract with Other Activities: Engage your child in other age-appropriate activities to divert their attention from the crib and reduce the likelihood of chewing.

Address Underlying Causes: If your child's crib chewing persists or becomes a frequent behavior, consider consulting with a pediatrician. Excessive chewing can sometimes be associated with sensory issues or other underlying causes.

By implementing these strategies, you can discourage your child from chewing on the crib and provide them with a safe sleep environment. Always prioritize your child's safety and well-being and seek professional advice if you have concerns about their behavior or teething discomfort.

Nursery
→ **Infant/Non-mobile: (Birth - 6 months)**
→ **Infant crawl/roll: (5 months - 1 year)**
Toddler/Pre-school: (1 year - 4 years)
School-age: (5 years - 6+ years)

Prevent Overheating

Preventing a child from overheating in a crib or bed is crucial for their safety and well-being.

Appropriate Room Temperature: Maintain a comfortable room temperature between 68°F to 72°F (20°C to 22°C). Use a room thermometer to monitor the temperature and adjust accordingly.

Dress for the Temperature: Your child should wear light and breathable sleepwear suitable for the room temperature. Avoid heavy or thick clothing that can lead to overheating.

Use Breathable Bedding: Choose breathable crib sheets and blankets made from natural materials like cotton. Avoid using heavy comforters, duvets, or quilts, especially for infants.

Layering: Layer your child's sleepwear and bedding so you can easily adjust to the room temperature without overheating or chilling them.

Avoid Bundling: Ensure your child is not overly bundled or swaddled while sleeping, as this can cause overheating. Swaddling should only be used in the first few months and should be stopped as the baby starts to roll over.

Fan or Air Circulation: To maintain a comfortable sleep environment, use a fan or ensure proper air circulation in the room.

Keep the Room Dark: Use blackout curtains or blinds to block out excessive sunlight and heat on hot days.

Check for Signs of Overheating: Regularly check your child's skin to see if they feel hot to the touch. Look for signs of sweating, flushed skin, or rapid breathing, which may indicate overheating.

Regular Monitoring: Always supervise your child while they are in their crib or bed to ensure their comfort and safety.

Safe Sleep Guidelines: Follow safe sleep guidelines, such as placing your baby on their back to sleep and using a firm, flat mattress in the crib.

Avoid Sleep Positioners and Loose Bedding: Do not use sleep positioners or additional loose bedding, as they can increase the risk of suffocation and overheating.

Each child is different, and their comfort levels may vary. It's essential to pay attention to your child's cues and adjust their sleep environment accordingly. If you notice any signs of discomfort or overheating, make the necessary adjustments to keep them safe and comfortable during sleep. Reevaluate their sleep environment as the seasons change, as room temperatures may fluctuate.

<u>Nursery</u>
→ **Infant/Non-mobile: (Birth - 6 months)**
→ **Infant crawl/roll: (5 months - 1 year)**
→ **Toddler/Pre-school: (1 year - 4 years)**
School-age: (5 years - 6+ years)

Crib Tents

A crib tent is a product designed **to prevent a child from climbing or falling out of the crib**. It consists of a mesh covering that securely fits over the top of the crib, creating a canopy-like enclosure. The crib tent is attached to the crib frame or mattress and typically has a zippered opening to allow easy access to the child when needed.

When using a crib tent, it is crucial to f**ollow the manufacturer's recommendations** regarding the appropriate age and weight range for its use. The crib tent should be properly and securely installed according to the instructions, with close attention to the fasteners and attachments to ensure a secure fit.

While a crib tent can effectively prevent climbing and falling incidents, it is **essential to continue supervising the child even with the tent in place**. Regularly check the crib tent for any signs of wear, tears, or loose parts and promptly address any issues to maintain its safety.

As with any safety product, consider alternatives and evaluate the overall sleep environment. Ensuring that the crib itself meets safety standards, such as having a firm mattress and properly fitting crib sheets, is crucial for the child's safety.

Once the child reaches the appropriate age or shows signs of attempting to climb out of the crib, **consider transitioning them to a toddler bed** for their safety and comfort.

Remember, prioritizing the child's safety and well-being is paramount, so consult with a pediatrician or a child safety expert if you have any concerns or questions about using a crib tent or other safety measures. By taking these precautions, you can provide a safe and comfortable sleep environment for your child during their crib years.

<u>Nursery</u>
→ **Infant/Non-mobile: (Birth - 6 months)**
→ **Infant crawl/roll: (5 months - 1 year)**
→ **Toddler/Pre-school: (1 year - 4 years)**
School-age: (5 years - 6+ years)

Crib Mounting Attachments

While mounting crib attachments on the wall side to prevent a child from climbing out of the crib may seem logical, it is essential to consider safety guidelines and manufacturer instructions when using crib attachments. Not all crib attachments are designed or intended to be mounted on the wall side, and improper installation could pose safety risks.

Follow Manufacturer's Instructions: Always follow the manufacturer's guidelines and instructions for using crib attachments. Manufacturers design and test their products based on specific safety standards; proper usage is crucial for your child's safety.

Crib Attachment Compatibility: Some cribs may come with specific attachments designed to prevent climbing or facilitate safe use. Ensure that any attachments you use are compatible with your crib model and that they are installed correctly.

Wall Mounting Safety: If you plan to mount anything on the wall side of the crib, ensure that it is securely anchored to the wall and does not pose a risk of falling or tipping onto the crib.

Crib Slats and Design: Check the spacing between the crib slats to ensure they meet safety standards and prevent the risk of entrapment or climbing.

Use Crib Mattress at the Correct Height: Ensure that the crib mattress is at the appropriate height based on the child's age and developmental stage. Lower the mattress as the child grows and becomes more mobile to prevent climbing out.

Supervision: Always supervise your child when they are in the crib, especially as they reach the age where climbing attempts are more likely.

Transition to a Toddler Bed: Once your child shows signs of attempting to climb out of the crib or reaches the recommended age, consider transitioning them to a toddler bed for their safety and comfort.

The primary goal is to create a safe sleep environment for your child. While crib attachments can offer additional safety features, they must be used correctly and according to the manufacturer's guidelines. If you have any doubts or questions about using crib attachments or ensuring crib safety, consult with a pediatrician or a child safety expert to ensure you are taking appropriate measures for your child's well-being.

Nursery
→ **Infant/Non-mobile: (Birth - 6 months)**
→ **Infant crawl/roll: (5 months - 1 year)**
→ **Toddler/Pre-school: (1 year - 4 years)**
School-age: (5 years - 6+ years)

Crib Sleep Safety

Placing a child in a crib to sleep safely is essential for their well-being.

Choose a Safe Crib: Make sure the crib meets safety standards and has no missing or broken parts. Avoid using cribs with drop-sides, as they have been deemed unsafe. Used cribs are not recommended, as parts could be worn or damaged.

Clear the Crib: Remove all soft bedding, pillows, toys, and loose blankets from the crib. These items can pose suffocation hazards for young infants.

Use a Firm Mattress: The mattress should be firm and fit snugly in the crib without gaps between it and the crib's sides.

Positioning: Always place your baby on its back to sleep. This position is the safest and reduces the risk of sudden infant death syndrome (SIDS). Once your child can roll over both ways independently, they can choose their sleep position.

Dress Appropriately: Dress your baby in light, comfortable sleepwear suitable for room temperature. Overheating can increase the risk of SIDS.

Avoid Overcrowding: Do not place additional items like stuffed animals, bumper pads, or wedges in the crib. These can create potential hazards.

Check the Surroundings: Ensure that the crib is placed away from windows, blinds, cords, and any other potential strangulation or choking hazards.

Monitor the Temperature: Keep the room at a comfortable temperature and avoid using electric blankets or heating pads in the crib. **Over 1,500 children** are injured annually by electrical heating pads, including burns and electrical shocks. (Source: U.S. Consumer Product Safety Commission (CPSC) - Heating Pad Safety)

Stay Smoke-Free: Never smoke around your baby or allow anyone else to do so. Secondhand smoke is harmful and increases the risk of SIDS.

Supervise Naps: Experts recommend placing the crib in your room for newborns and young infants for the first six months. This makes it easier for you to monitor your baby while they sleep.

Regularly Check the Crib: Periodically inspect the crib to ensure it remains in good condition and that there are no loose screws or sharp edges.

Remember, a well-prepared and safe sleep environment is vital for your child's healthy development. If you have any doubts or concerns about placing your child in a crib, consult your pediatrician or a child safety expert for personalized advice.

<u>Nursery</u>
→ **Infant/Non-mobile: (Birth - 6 months)**
→ **Infant crawl/roll: (5 months - 1 year)**
→ **Toddler/Pre-school: (1 year - 4 years)**
School-age: (5 years - 6+ years)

Install Crib Sheet Security Clips

Installing crib sheet security clips can provide an added layer of safety to keep the fitted sheet securely in place on the crib mattress. These clips, also known as sheet savers or sheet fasteners, help prevent the fitted sheet from coming loose, bunching up, or slipping off the mattress, which can reduce the risk of suffocation or entanglement for your baby.

Secure Fit: Babies are active sleepers and can move around a lot during the night. Crib sheet clips keep the fitted sheet snugly fitted to the mattress, reducing the chances of it getting loose and creating potential hazards.

Prevent Suffocation Risks: A loose sheet can accidentally cover the baby's face during sleep, increasing the risk of suffocation. Security clips help keep the sheet taut and properly positioned.

Ease of Use: Crib sheet clips are easy to install and remove when it's time to change the sheets. They typically come in sets and can be attached to the corners of the fitted sheet.

Peace of Mind: For parents or caregivers, using crib sheet security clips offers peace of mind, knowing that the baby's sleep environment is safer and more secure.

When using crib sheet security clips, it's essential to follow the manufacturer's instructions for proper installation. Additionally, always ensure that the clips are placed in a way that doesn't create any additional hazards or discomfort for the baby.

Remember that while crib sheet security clips can be helpful, they are not a substitute for maintaining a safe sleep environment. Always follow safe sleep guidelines, keep the crib free from loose bedding, and place the baby on their back to sleep. Regularly check the crib and sheets for wear and tear and replace them if needed.

As with baby-related products, if you have any doubts or concerns about using crib sheet security clips, consult your pediatrician or a childproofing expert for guidance. Safety should always be the top priority when it comes to your little one's sleeping environment.

Nursery
→ **Infant/Non-mobile: (Birth - 6 months)**
→ **Infant crawl/roll: (5 months - 1 year)**
→ **Toddler/Pre-school: (1 year - 4 years)**
School-age: (5 years - 6+ years)

Sleep Positioning Pads are Not Recommended

Sleep positioning pads, also known as sleep positioners or anti-roll pillows, are not recommended for use with infants. They have been deemed unsafe and are not endorsed by any reputable child safety organizations.

The American Academy of Pediatrics (SAP) and other health authorities strongly advise against using sleep positioning pads or any other sleep positioners due to the risk of suffocation and **sudden infant death syndrome (SIDS)**. These products claim to help keep babies in a specific sleep position, but they can pose serious hazards, including:

Suffocation Risk: Sleep positioning pads can restrict a baby's movement and potentially lead to suffocation if the baby rolls into a position where their face is pressed against the pad or a soft surface.

Overheating: Some positioning pads are made of materials that may cause a baby to overheat, which is another risk factor for SIDS.

Potential Entrapment: A baby's head or limbs could get trapped between the positioning pad and the crib mattress.

To reduce the risk of SIDS and ensure a safe sleep environment for your baby, it is essential to follow these guidelines:

Back to Sleep: Always place your baby on their back to sleep, both for naps and nighttime sleep, until they can roll over on their own.

Firm Mattress: Use a firm, flat sleep surface, such as a crib mattress that fits snugly inside the crib.

Clear the Crib: Remove all soft bedding, toys, pillows, and crib bumpers. Dress your baby in appropriate sleepwear for the room temperature.

Sleep in Your Room: The SAP recommends room-sharing with your baby for the first six to twelve months to reduce the risk of SIDS.

Avoid Smoking: Keep your home smoke-free, as exposure to secondhand smoke increases the risk of SIDS.

Breastfeed if Possible: Breastfeeding has been associated with a reduced risk of SIDS.

Always consult with your pediatrician if you have any questions or concerns about safe sleep practices for your baby. Your child's safety is of the utmost importance, and following these guidelines can help reduce the risk of sleep-related incidents.

Nursery
→ Infant/Non-mobile: (Birth - 6 months)
→ Infant crawl/roll: (5 months - 1 year)
→ Toddler/Pre-school: (1 year - 4 years)
School-age: (5 years - 6+ years)

Remove Crib Bumper Pads

The Consumer Product Safety Commission (CPSC) recommends against using bumper pads in cribs and playpens. Bumper pads are the padded linings traditionally placed around the inside of the crib to prevent the baby from bumping its head or getting its limbs caught between the crib slats.

However, extensive research and safety evaluations have shown that bumper pads pose significant risks to infants, including:

Suffocation and Entrapment: Babies can get their faces pressed against the bumper pad, leading to suffocation. They may also get their heads, limbs, or bodies caught between the bumper pad and the crib slats, potentially causing injury.

Overheating: Bumper pads can contribute to overheating, which is a risk factor for sudden infant death syndrome (SIDS).

Reduced Airflow: Bumper pads can obstruct fresh air flow into the crib, leading to decreased ventilation.

Climbing Hazard: As babies grow, bumper pads may provide a foothold for them to climb out of the crib, leading to falls and injuries.

Due to these safety concerns, the CPSC and other health organizations recommend using a bare and empty crib to create a safe sleep environment for infants. The crib should have a firm mattress with a fitted sheet, and there should be no soft bedding, pillows, toys, or other loose items in the crib.

To promote a safe sleep environment for your baby, remember to:

Follow Safe Sleep Guidelines: Always place your baby on their back to sleep on a firm, flat sleep surface in their crib.

Use a Properly Fitted Sheet: Ensure the crib mattress has a fitted sheet that fits securely without any bunching or sagging.

Keep the Crib Empty: Remove all soft bedding, bumper pads, stuffed animals, and pillows from the crib.

Room-Sharing: The American Academy of Pediatrics (SAP) recommends room-sharing with your baby for the first six to twelve months to facilitate nighttime feeding and monitoring.

Notes:

Nursery
→ **Infant/Non-mobile: (Birth - 6 months)**
→ **Infant crawl/roll: (5 months - 1 year)**
Toddler/Pre-school: (1 year - 4 years)
School-age: (5 years - 6+ years)

If your child is under 12 months: Be Aware of SIDS (Sudden Infant Death Syndrome)

Sudden Infant Death Syndrome (SIDS) is crucial for the safety and well-being of infants under 12 months old. SIDS is the sudden, unexplained death of an otherwise healthy baby during sleep, typically occurring in infants under one year of age, with the highest risk occurring between 1 and 4 months.

Back to Sleep: Always place your baby on their back to sleep for naps and nighttime sleep. This position has been shown to reduce the risk of SIDS.

Firm Sleep Surface: Use a firm and flat sleep surface, such as a crib mattress, covered with a fitted sheet that fits snugly around the mattress.

Room-Sharing: The American Academy of Pediatrics (SAP) recommends room-sharing with your baby for at least the first six months and ideally up to one year. Place the baby's crib or bassinet in your room, close to your bed.

Bare is Best: Keep the crib free from soft bedding, blankets, pillows, bumper pads, and stuffed animals. A bare crib reduces the risk of suffocation and entrapment hazards.

Avoid Overheating: Dress your baby in light sleepwear suitable for room temperature to prevent overheating.

No Smoking: Keep your home and car smoke-free, as exposure to smoke is a risk factor for SIDS.

Breastfeeding: If possible, consider breastfeeding, as it has been associated with a reduced risk of SIDS.

Regular Check-ups: Attend regular well-baby check-ups and vaccinations, as these are essential for your child's health and development.

Tummy Time: Encourage supervised tummy time when the baby is awake and alert, as it helps with their motor development and reduces the risk of flat spots on the head.

Pacifier Use: Consider offering a pacifier at naptime and bedtime, as it has been associated with a reduced risk of SIDS. However, if you are breastfeeding, wait until breastfeeding is well-established before introducing a pacifier.

By following these guidelines and creating a safe sleep environment, you can help reduce the risk of SIDS and provide your baby with the best possible care. Always consult with your pediatrician if you have any concerns or questions about safe sleep practices for your child.

Nursery
→ **Infant/Non-mobile: (Birth - 6 months)**
→ **Infant crawl/roll: (5 months - 1 year)**
→ **Toddler/Pre-school: (1 year - 4 years)**
School-age: (5 years - 6+ years)

Hanging Toy Concerns

For safety reasons, it is not recommended to hang toys, mobiles, or other objects over a child's crib.

Strangulation Hazard: Hanging toys or objects can pose a strangulation risk to the baby if they become entangled in the strings, cords, or ribbons. Babies have limited mobility and may accidentally grab or pull on these items, which can lead to dangerous situations.

Choking Hazard: Small parts or loose pieces of hanging toys can detach and become choking hazards if they fall into the crib. Babies explore their surroundings with their mouths, and anything within reach may end up in their mouths.

Risk of Falls: As babies grow and become more mobile, they may attempt to reach for or grab hanging toys, increasing the risk of falls or injuries.

Remove Hanging Toys: Remove any hanging toys, mobiles, or objects from the crib. These items are better suited for playtime when the baby is awake and under supervision.

Bare Crib: Keep the crib free from any loose items, such as blankets, pillows, stuffed animals, or bumpers. A bare crib is the safest sleeping environment for babies.

Safe Sleep Practices: Follow safe sleep practices, including placing your baby on their back to sleep on a firm, flat surface with a fitted sheet.

Avoid Wall Hangings: Also, avoid hanging anything on the walls above the crib. Decorations or pictures can accidentally fall into the crib and pose a hazard.

Use Crib Toys Safely: If you want to provide toys for your baby to play with while awake, choose toys specifically designed for cribs and attach them securely to the crib rails, ensuring they are out of the baby's reach when lying down.

Nursery
→ **Infant/Non-mobile: (Birth - 6 months)**
→ **Infant crawl/roll: (5 months - 1 year)**
→ **Toddler/Pre-school: (1 year - 4 years)**
School-age: (5 years - 6+ years)

Pillow Concerns

Children do not need pillows in their cribs or beds until they are at least one year old and, in some cases, even older. Pillows pose certain risks to infants, especially those under one year of age, and it's essential to provide a safe sleep environment for young children.

Suffocation Risk: Babies have limited control over their movements, and placing a pillow in the crib can increase the risk of suffocation if the baby's face becomes pressed against it.

Neck Support: Infants' neck muscles are not fully developed in the first few months of life. A pillow can push their head forward, interfering with their breathing or neck alignment.

Overheating: Pillows can contribute to overheating, which is a risk factor for sudden infant death syndrome (SIDS).

Crib Safety: For children who can move around, pillows can become an obstacle. They might use them to try to climb out of the crib, increasing the risk of falls and injuries.

Once your child reaches one year old and transitions to a toddler bed, you can consider introducing a small, firm pillow specifically designed for toddlers. It's essential to choose a pillow that is the right size and thickness for their age and development.

In the meantime, providing a safe sleep environment for your baby includes:

Back to Sleep: Always place your baby on their back to sleep for both naps and nighttime sleep until they can roll over on their own.

Firm Mattress: Use a firm, flat sleep surface, such as a crib mattress, covered with a fitted sheet.

Bare Crib: Keep the crib free from soft bedding, including blankets, pillows, and stuffed animals.

Room-sharing: The American Academy of Pediatrics (SAP) recommends room-sharing with your baby for at least the first six months.

Appropriate Sleepwear: Dress your baby in light, comfortable sleepwear suitable for room temperature to prevent overheating.

Always consult with your pediatrician if you have any questions or concerns about your child's sleep environment or when it's appropriate to introduce certain bedding items. Safety is paramount, and following guidelines helps reduce the risk of sleep-related accidents.

> ► *A recent CDC report (May 2025) analyzing Georgia data from 2013-2022 found that **nursing pillows were present in the sleep space of 84 (5%) of 1,685 Sudden Unexpected Infant Deaths (SUIDs)**. Most of these infants were under 4 months old.*

Nursery
→ **Infant/Non-mobile: (Birth - 6 months)**
Infant crawl/roll: (5 months - 1 year)
Toddler/Pre-school: (1 year - 4 years)
School-age: (5 years - 6+ years)

Changing Table Guards

Changing table guards, also known as changing table safety rails or changing table straps, are designed to provide additional safety and security for infants during diaper changes. They can be attached to the changing table to prevent the baby from rolling or sliding off the surface, reducing the risk of falls and injuries. While changing table guards can be helpful, there are some concerns and considerations to keep in mind.

Proper Installation: It's essential to install the changing table guard correctly, following the manufacturer's instructions. Make sure the guard is securely attached to the changing table to ensure it functions effectively.

Supervision: Even with a changing table guard in place, it's crucial never to leave the baby unattended on the changing table. Babies can be quick and unpredictable, and accidents can happen in seconds.

Age and Weight Limits: Check the product specifications to ensure that the changing table guard is appropriate for your child's age and weight. Some guards may have specific weight limits, so ensure the product suits your child's size.

Secure Attachment: Regularly inspect the changing table guard to ensure it remains securely attached and shows no signs of wear or damage.

Avoid Distractions: During diaper changes, focus solely on the baby and avoid any distractions, such as reaching for supplies or taking phone calls.

Use a Safety Strap: Many changing tables come with safety straps designed to secure the baby to the changing table. Always use the safety strap to prevent the baby from rolling or sliding off.

Safe Changing Area: Ensure that the changing table is in a safe location and away from any hazards, such as cords, windows, or furniture edges.

Proper Height: The changing table's height should be comfortable for the caregiver to avoid strain while changing the baby.

Use a Non-Slip Pad: To prevent the baby from sliding, consider using a non-slip changing pad or mat on the changing table's surface.

While changing table guards can offer an added layer of safety during diaper changes, they are not a substitute for adult supervision and responsible caregiving. Always follow safe diaper-changing practices, and never leave the baby unattended on the changing table, even for a moment. As with any baby-related product, it's essential to use changing table guards responsibly and in accordance with the manufacturer's guidelines to ensure the baby's safety during diaper changes.

Nursery
→ **Infant non-mobile: (Birth-6 mo.)**
→ **Infant crawl/roll: (5 mo.-2 yrs.)**
Toddler/Pre-School: (1 yr.-4 yrs.)
School-age: (5 yrs.-6 yrs.)

Breast Milk Safety

Breast milk is a vital source of nutrients for infants, offering numerous health benefits. To maintain its safety, mothers should adhere to certain guidelines. These include washing hands, using clean containers for storing milk, and labeling them with the date and time of expression. The milk can be refrigerated for up to four days or frozen for an extended period but should never be microwaved to prevent nutrient loss and uneven heating. When using frozen milk, avoid shaking it vigorously and refrain from adding fresh milk to a frozen batch. Always check the milk's temperature before feeding and use it within two hours if kept at room temperature. Maintain hygiene with breast pumps and be cautious about alcohol consumption and medication use, as these can transfer to the baby through the milk. In case of illness, consult a healthcare provider for guidance on breastfeeding. If in doubt, seek advice from a lactation consultant or healthcare provider. (Refer to Kitchen for details **pg. 105**)

Nursery
Infant/Non-mobile: (Birth - 6 months)
→ **Infant crawl/roll: (5 months - 1 year)**
→ **Toddler/Pre-school: (1 year - 4 years)**
School-age: (5 years - 6+ years)

Baby Bottle Tooth Decay

Baby Bottle Tooth Decay (ECC) is a dental condition affecting young children caused by prolonged exposure to sugary liquids like milk, formula, or juice, especially during sleep. To prevent ECC, avoid letting your child fall asleep with a bottle, limit juice consumption, and regularly clean their gums and teeth. Schedule regular dental visits, encourage healthy eating habits, and lead by example with good oral hygiene practices. Discuss fluoride supplements or toothpaste with a healthcare provider and avoid sharing utensils or cleaning pacifiers with your mouth to prevent bacteria transfer. Taking these proactive steps can help protect your child's oral health and prevent ECC. (For details refer to kitchen **pg. 148**)

Nursery
→ **Infant/Non-mobile: (Birth - 6 months)**
→ **Infant crawl/roll: (5 months - 1 year)**
→ **Toddler/Pre-school: (1 year - 4 years)**
School-age: (5 years - 6+ years)

Dangers of Baby Wipes and Baby Lotions

While baby wipes are convenient and often seen as a safe way to clean babies' skin, some potential dangers are associated with their use.

Skin irritation: Baby wipes can contain harsh chemicals, such as fragrances, dyes, and alcohol, which can irritate babies' delicate skin. This can lead to redness, dryness, and itching.

Allergic reactions: Some babies may be allergic to the ingredients in baby wipes. This can cause a range of reactions, from mild skin irritation to more severe symptoms, such as hives, swelling, and difficulty breathing.

Clogged pores: Baby wipes can leave residue on the skin, clogging pores and leading to breakouts.

Increased risk of infection: Baby wipes can harbor bacteria, which can increase the risk of infection, especially if they are not used properly. For example, if a wipe is used to clean a dirty diaper and then used to clean the baby's face, the bacteria from the diaper could be transferred to the baby's face.

Dangers of Baby Lotion: Baby lotion is generally safe for most babies, but there are a few potential dangers to be aware of.

Skin irritation: Some baby lotions contain fragrances, dyes, and other chemicals that can irritate babies' skin.

Allergic reactions: Some babies may be allergic to the ingredients in baby lotion. This can cause a range of reactions, from mild skin irritation to more severe symptoms, such as hives, swelling, and difficulty breathing.

Clogged pores: Baby lotion can leave residue on the skin, clogging pores and leading to breakouts.

Increased risk of infection: If baby lotion is not applied properly, it can create a moist environment on the skin, which can increase the risk of infection.

Precautions: Store baby wipes and baby lotion out of reach of children. This will help to prevent them from accidentally ingesting or getting the products in their eyes. Choose baby wipes and baby lotions that are fragrance-free, dye-free, and alcohol-free. This will help to reduce the risk of skin irritation and allergic reactions. Apply baby lotion sparingly and avoid applying it to areas of the skin that are prone to breakouts, such as the back and chest. Clean baby wipes thoroughly after each use. This will help to prevent the spread of bacteria.

Additional Tips

Use water and a washcloth to clean your baby's bottom whenever possible. This is the safest and most effective way to clean your baby's skin.

If you do use baby wipes, avoid using them on your baby's face. The skin on the face is more delicate and more prone to irritation.

If you notice any signs of skin irritation or allergic reaction after using baby wipes or lotion, stop using the product and **consult a doctor**.

Nursery
→ **Infant/Non-mobile: (Birth - 6 months)**
→ **Infant crawl/roll: (5 months - 1 year)**
Toddler/Pre-school: (1 year - 4 years)
School-age: (5 years - 6+ years)

No Bibs and Crib

Bibs can pose a suffocation risk to babies if not used correctly or if certain types of bibs are used in specific situations.

Safety Considerations When Using Baby Bibs

Supervision: Always supervise your baby when they are wearing a bib. Never leave them unattended, especially when they are lying down or sleeping.

Bib Size: Choose bibs that fit properly and are appropriate for your baby's age and size. Avoid bibs with long strings or ties that could become entangled or pose a choking hazard.

Sleeping and Napping: Do not let your baby wear a bib while sleeping or napping. The bib could get caught on something or cover the baby's face, potentially leading to suffocation.

Material: Choose bibs made of breathable materials, such as cotton, which allow air to circulate around the baby's neck.

Secure Fastening: If the bib has a fastening mechanism, make sure it is safe but not too tight. Avoid using bibs with tight elastic or neck openings that could restrict airflow.

No Loops or Drawstrings: Avoid bibs with loops or drawstrings around the neck area, as they could pose a strangulation risk.

Remove After Feeding: Remove the bib immediately after feeding or when it becomes wet to avoid skin irritation or potential hazards.

Remember, baby bibs are intended to protect your baby's clothing during mealtime and can be a useful tool for managing spills and messes. However, safety precautions should be taken to minimize any risks associated with their use.

As with all baby products, it's essential to follow the manufacturer's instructions and use bibs responsibly to ensure the safety and well-being of your little one. If you have concerns or questions about using baby bibs safely, consult your pediatrician or a child safety expert.

Nursery
→ **Infant/Non-mobile: (Birth - 6 months)**
Infant crawl/roll: (5 months - 1 year)
Toddler/Pre-school: (1 year - 4 years)
School-age: (5 years - 6+ years)

Toy Rattle Concerns

Rattles are popular toys for babies, providing both entertainment and sensory stimulation. However, there are some concerns.

Choking Hazard: Some rattles may have small parts that could pose a choking hazard if they become detached. Always choose rattles that are age-appropriate and do not have small parts that can fit into a baby's mouth.

Securely Assembled: Before giving a rattle to your baby, inspect it to ensure that it is securely assembled and that there are no loose or broken parts.

Non-Toxic Materials: Choose rattles made from non-toxic materials, free from harmful chemicals. Look for rattles labeled as BPA-free and meeting safety standards.

Age Appropriateness: Pay attention to the age recommendations on the rattle's packaging. Some rattles may be suitable for older babies, while others are designed specifically for younger infants.

Size and Shape: Ensure that the rattle is appropriate for your baby's age and development. It should be easy for your baby to hold and manipulate.

Supervision: Always supervise your baby when they are playing with a rattle. Do not leave them unattended, as accidents can happen quickly.

No Strings or Cords: Avoid rattles with strings, cords, or ribbons that could pose a strangulation risk. These items should be securely attached and out of reach of the baby.

Cleaning and Maintenance: Regularly clean and inspect the rattle to ensure it remains in good condition. Avoid submerging electronic or battery-operated rattles in water.

Use for Playtime Only: Rattles are designed for playtime and should not be used as sleep aids or left in the crib with the baby during sleep. **Rotate Toys:** To keep your baby engaged and prevent overuse of a particular rattle, rotate toys regularly to introduce new stimuli.

<u>**Nursery**</u>
→ **Infant/Non-mobile: (Birth - 6 months)**
→ **Infant crawl/roll: (5 months - 1 year)**
→ **Toddler/Pre-school: (1 year - 4 years)**
School-age: (5 years - 6+ years)

Plush Toy Concerns

Plush toys, also known as stuffed animals or soft toys, can pose several dangers when placed in a crib with a baby. It's essential to prioritize safety and create a safe sleep environment.

Suffocation Hazard: Plush toys have soft, fluffy surfaces that can accidentally cover a baby's face during sleep. This poses a suffocation risk if the baby is unable to move the toy away.

Risk of Overheating: Plush toys can trap heat, leading to overheating, which is a risk factor for sudden infant death syndrome (SIDS).

Choking Hazard: Some plush toys may have small parts, loose threads, or accessories like buttons or eyes that can become detached. If the baby puts them in their mouth, these items pose a choking hazard.

Crib Clutter: Placing plush toys in the crib adds to the clutter and increases the risk of entanglement, especially when the baby becomes more mobile.

Interference with Sleep Surfaces: Plush toys can create uneven surfaces in the crib, making providing a firm and safe sleep environment challenging.

Create a Safe Sleep Environment for Your Baby

Bare is Best: Keep the crib free from plush toys, blankets, pillows, and other soft items. A firm, flat sleep surface is the safest for your baby.

Use Sleep Sacks: To keep your baby warm during sleep, consider using sleep sacks or wearable blankets instead of loose blankets.

Separate Playtime from Sleep Time: Keep playtime and sleep time separate. Remove all toys and distractions from the crib when it's time for sleep.

Room-sharing: Consider room-sharing with your baby for the first six to twelve months. Room-sharing allows you to monitor your baby easily while they sleep.

Offer Toys for Playtime: Instead of placing plush toys in the crib, give them to your baby during supervised playtime when they can interact with them safely.

Always consult with your pediatrician or a child safety expert if you have any questions or concerns about creating a safe sleep environment for your baby. By prioritizing safety and following these guidelines, you can reduce the risk of sleep-related incidents and make a secure space for your little one to rest and grow.

Nursery
→ **Infant/Non-mobile: (Birth - 6 months)**
→ **Infant crawl/roll: (5 months - 1 year)**
→ **Toddler/Pre-school: (1 year - 4 years)**
School-age: (5 years - 6+ years)

Shower/Wash Your Hands First (Hygiene Importance)

It is essential to shower or wash up before handling a child, especially a newborn or young infant.

Preventing the Spread of Germs: Babies and young children have developing immune systems and are more susceptible to infections and illnesses. Washing your hands before handling them reduces the risk of transferring germs and bacteria.

Diaper Changing: Diaper changing is routine when caring for a baby. Thoroughly washing your hands before and after changing a diaper helps prevent the spread of bacteria and reduces the risk of diaper rash and infections.

Feeding: Whether you are breastfeeding or bottle-feeding, clean hands are vital to avoid contamination of the baby's feeding area and prevent infections.

Comfort and Bonding: A clean and fresh caregiver provides a comfortable and hygienic environment for the baby, promoting a positive bonding experience.

Preventing Skin Irritation: Babies' delicate skin can be sensitive to substances like lotions, perfumes, or other products. Washing up before handling them can help minimize the risk of skin irritation.

Postpone Handling if Unwell: If you are feeling unwell, especially if you have symptoms like coughing, sneezing, or fever, it is best to have someone else take care of your child to prevent the spread of illness. If no one is available to help wear a mask and wash your hands frequently.

Maintaining a Safe Environment: Ensuring that caregivers, family members, and visitors wash their hands before touching the baby helps maintain a safe and clean environment.

To ensure proper hygiene when handling a child, wash your hands thoroughly with soap and water for at least 20 seconds, especially after using the bathroom, changing diapers, or handling food. If soap and water are not available, use an alcohol-based hand sanitizer with at least 60% alcohol. Avoid smoking or handling anything with a strong odor before handling the baby, as babies can be sensitive to smells. Regularly clean and sanitize frequently touched surfaces and items, such as toys and baby equipment.

Nursery
→ **Infant/Non-mobile: (Birth - 6 months)**
→ **Infant crawl/roll: (5 months - 1 year)**
→ **Toddler/Pre-school: (1 year - 4 years)**
School-age: (5 years - 6+ years)

Baby Monitors

Annually, approximately **200 children** are injured by baby monitors, including electrical shocks and choking hazards from small parts. (Source: U.S. Consumer Product Safety Commission (CPSC) - Baby Monitor Safety) Baby monitors can be incredibly helpful tools for parents to keep an eye on their babies, especially when they are in a different room. However, there are some concerns associated with their use.

Privacy and Security: Some baby monitors operate on wireless networks, making them susceptible to potential hacking or unauthorized access. It's essential to choose a monitor with strong encryption and take measures to secure your home network.

Interference: Some baby monitors may experience interference from other wireless devices, such as cordless phones or Wi-Fi routers. This interference could affect the quality of the video or audio transmission.

Range Limitations: Baby monitors have a limited range, and the signal strength may weaken as you move farther from the monitor's base unit. This could be an issue if you need to move around the house or go outside while monitoring the baby.

False Alarms: Some baby monitors with motion or sound detection may trigger false alarms, causing unnecessary worry or disturbance to the parents.

Reliance on Technology: While baby monitors are useful tools, parents should avoid relying solely on them for baby supervision. Nothing can replace direct supervision and interaction with the baby.

Health Concerns: While studies have not shown conclusive evidence of harm, some parents may have concerns about the potential health effects of prolonged exposure to the radio frequency radiation emitted by wireless baby monitors.

To address these concerns and ensure the safe use of baby monitors, Choose a reputable baby monitor brand with good reviews and safety features. Use monitors with secure and encrypted connections to protect your privacy. Avoid sharing sensitive or personal information through the baby monitor's features. Regularly update the monitor's firmware to ensure it has the latest security patches. Test the monitor's range within your home to ensure it meets your needs. Position the baby monitor at a safe distance from the baby's sleep area, ensuring it does not come into direct contact with the baby. Use the baby monitor as a supplemental tool for baby supervision, not a replacement for direct supervision. Follow the manufacturer's instructions and safety guidelines for the baby monitor's setup and usage.

If you have specific concerns about using a baby monitor or questions about its safety, consider discussing them with your pediatrician or a child safety expert for guidance tailored to your situation.

Nursery
Infant/Non-mobile: (Birth - 6 months)
Infant crawl/roll: (5 months - 1 year)
Toddler/Pre-school: (1 year - 4 years)
School-age: (5 years - 6+ years)

Nursery Care Kit Should At Least Contain:

A Nursery Care Kit is a handy collection of essential items to help parents and caregivers care for their baby's basic needs. While the specific contents may vary depending on the brand and type of kit, a comprehensive Nursery Care Kit typically includes the following items:

☐ **Digital Thermometer:** A digital thermometer to measure the baby's temperature accurately. Opt for a rectal or forehead thermometer explicitly designed for infants.

☐ **Nasal Aspirator or Bulb Syringe:** Used to clear a baby's nasal passages from mucus and congestion, helping them breathe more comfortably.

☐ **Nail Clippers or Scissors:** These are specially designed to trim babies' tiny nails safely and prevent scratching.

- ☐ **Baby Brush and Comb:** Soft-bristled brush and comb to gently groom and style the baby's hair.

- ☐ **Medicine Dispenser:** A device to administer liquid medication in precise doses to the baby.

- ☐ **Medicine Spoon or Dropper:** This is used to give oral medication accurately to the baby.

- ☐ **Emery Boards:** Gentle emery boards can be used to file baby's nails, offering an alternative to nail clippers or scissors.

- ☐ **Gauze Pads or Cotton Balls:** These are used for various cleaning purposes, such as applying ointments or wiping sensitive areas.

- ☐ **Baby Lotion:** A mild, hypoallergenic baby lotion for moisturizing the baby's skin.

- ☐ **Petroleum Jelly:** Protects baby's sensitive skin from moisture and prevents diaper rash.

- ☐ **Diaper Cream or Ointment:** To soothe and protect the baby's skin from diaper rash.

- ☐ **Alcohol Swabs:** These are used to clean items like thermometers before use.

- ☐ **Safety Nail File:** A gentle nail file as an alternative to nail clippers or scissors.

- ☐ **Teething Toy or Gel:** An item to soothe the baby's gums during teething.

- ☐ **Baby Pacifier:** A pacifier can help soothe a fussy baby and promote self-soothing.

- ☐ **Organizing Case:** A convenient case to keep all the items neatly organized and easily accessible.

Remember that every baby is different, and some items in the Nursery Care Kit may be more useful than others, depending on your baby's needs. Always follow the manufacturer's instructions for using each item and prioritize your baby's safety and comfort when caring for them.

Notes: (What are you missing?)

Nursery
→ **Infant/Non-mobile: (Birth - 6 months)**
→ **Infant crawl/roll: (5 months - 1 year)**
Toddler/Pre-school: (1 year - 4 years)
School-age: (5 years - 6+ years)

Infant Carrier Safety

The U.S. Consumer Product Safety Commission (CPSC) provides important guidelines and recommendations for the safe use of infant carriers, also known as baby carriers or baby slings.

These guidelines aim to ensure the safety and well-being of infants and caregivers while using these products.

Follow Manufacturer's Instructions: Always read and follow the manufacturer's instructions and guidelines for the specific infant carrier you are using. Different carriers may have unique features and usage instructions.

Choose Age-Appropriate Carriers: Make sure the carrier is suitable for your baby's age and size. Some carriers are designed for newborns, while others are more appropriate for older infants.

Proper Positioning: Ensure your baby is positioned in an upright position with their face visible and clear of fabric or any obstructions. The baby's chin should not be pressed against the chest, as it can restrict airflow.

Keep Airway Open: Make sure the baby's nose and mouth are free from any fabric or material, allowing for easy breathing. Check on your baby frequently to ensure their airway remains open.

Support Baby's Head and Neck: For young infants, ensure the carrier provides adequate support for their head and neck. A newborn's neck muscles are not fully developed and may need extra support.

Check for Fabric and Strap Tightness: Ensure the carrier is snug, with the fabric and straps adjusted securely. However, it should not be too tight to restrict the baby's circulation or cause discomfort.

Stay Alert and Supervise: Always keep your baby within your line of sight and be attentive to their needs while using the carrier.

Take Breaks: Take breaks from using the carrier to allow your baby to change positions and to give yourself some rest.

Stay Cool: Avoid overheating by keeping the baby's face and head uncovered and ensuring good airflow.

Consider the Weather: Dress your baby appropriately for the weather conditions. In hot weather, choose lightweight and breathable clothing.

Inspect for Wear and Tear: Regularly inspect the carrier for any signs of wear and tear, loose seams, or broken parts. If the carrier shows signs of damage, discontinue its use.

Use on Stable Ground: Be cautious when bending or leaning while wearing the carrier. Make sure you are on stable ground and use your hands to support the baby's weight.

You can ensure the safe use of an infant carrier and provide a comfortable and secure experience for both the baby and the caregiver. If you have any questions or concerns about using an infant carrier, consult with the manufacturer or a baby wearing educator for guidance.

Nursery
→ **Infant/Non-mobile: (Birth - 6 months)**
→ **Infant crawl/roll: (5 months - 1 year)**
Toddler/Pre-school: (1 year - 4 years)
School-age: (5 years - 6+ years)

Diaper Pail Concerns

Diaper pails are designed to provide a convenient and hygienic way to dispose of soiled diapers. However, parents should be aware of some concerns associated with diaper pails to ensure they are used safely and effectively.

Odor Control: Diaper pails are designed to trap and contain odors from soiled diapers. However, some pails may not effectively seal in the odors, leading to unpleasant smells in the nursery or changing areas.

Hygiene and Cleaning: Diaper pails need to be cleaned regularly to prevent the buildup of bacteria and odors. Failure to clean the pail properly may compromise its effectiveness in controlling odors.

Bag Replacement: Many diaper pails require the use of special disposable bags or refills. The cost of these refills can add up over time and may be a consideration for some parents.

Child Safety: Some diaper pails have a foot pedal or a lid opening mechanism, which may be accessible to curious older children. Ensure that the pail has safety features to prevent accidental access by children.

Bag Waste: Disposable diaper pail bags contribute to plastic waste. Some parents may choose more eco-friendly options, such as reusable diaper pail liners.

Size and Capacity: Consider the size and capacity of the diaper pail, especially if you have twins or multiple children in diapers. A larger capacity pail may be more suitable for families with multiple babies.

Ventilation: Some diaper pails may not have adequate ventilation, leading to increased humidity and potential bacterial growth. Ensure the pail has proper ventilation to maintain a hygienic environment.

Proximity to Baby's Sleeping Area: If using a diaper pail in the nursery, ensure it is placed at a safe distance from the baby's sleeping area to minimize any potential odors that could disturb sleep.

Choose a diaper pail with good reviews for odor control and ease of use. Follow the manufacturer's instructions for proper cleaning and maintenance. Consider using eco-friendly diaper pail liners or reusable cloth liners if reducing plastic waste is a concern. Ensure the diaper pail is placed in a safe location away from the children's reach. Regularly empty the diaper pail to prevent excessive buildup of soiled diapers. Use a diaper pail with proper ventilation to reduce humidity and odors. If the diaper pail becomes less effective at controlling odors over time, consider replacing it or exploring alternative odor control solutions. Ultimately, every family's needs and preferences may vary, and finding the right diaper pail solution involves considering these concerns and choosing a diaper disposal method that works best for your family.

Nursery
→ **Infant/Non-mobile: (Birth - 6 months)**
→ **Infant crawl/roll: (5 months - 1 year)**
→ **Toddler/Pre-school: (1 year - 4 years)**
→ **School-age: (5 years - 6+ years)**

Air Purifier Importance

Air purifiers are especially important for children due to their developing respiratory systems and increased vulnerability to airborne pollutants.

Respiratory Health: Children's respiratory systems are still developing, making them more sensitive to air pollutants. Air purifiers can remove allergens, dust, pet dander, pollen, mold spores, and other irritants, reducing the risk of respiratory issues and allergies.

Asthma and Allergy Relief: Air purifiers can significantly benefit children with asthma or allergies, as they can help reduce triggers and symptoms.

Protection from Infections: Air purifiers equipped with HEPA filters can capture and remove bacteria, viruses, and other germs from the air, helping reduce the risk of respiratory infections.

Reduced Secondhand Smoke Exposure: Air purifiers can help minimize exposure to secondhand smoke, which can be particularly harmful to children's developing lungs and overall health.

Better Sleep Quality: Cleaner air can lead to better sleep for children, as they may experience fewer disruptions from allergies or respiratory issues.

Preventing Air Pollution Effects: Children spend more time indoors than adults, and indoor air pollution can be higher than outdoor air pollution. Air purifiers help mitigate the effects of indoor pollutants, providing a healthier living environment.

Promoting Healthy Growth: Cleaner air can lead to improved overall health, which is essential for a child's growth and development.

Enhanced Concentration: Air purifiers can help children concentrate better by reducing allergens and pollutants in their homes and learning environments.

Creating a Safe Nursery: Air purifiers can be particularly useful in nurseries, where infants spend a significant amount of time. They help maintain a clean and healthy space for babies to thrive.

Pet Allergy Management: If children have pet allergies, air purifiers can help remove pet dander and other allergens, allowing them to coexist more comfortably with family pets.

Preventing Exposure to Harmful Chemicals: Air purifiers with activated carbon filters can help remove harmful VOCs and indoor air pollutants from cleaning products, paints, and household chemicals, keeping children safe from their adverse effects.

Reduced Risk of Airborne Diseases: During flu seasons or when there are respiratory outbreaks, air purifiers can help reduce the transmission of airborne viruses and bacteria.

Overall, air purifiers are valuable tools for promoting a healthy living environment for children, providing cleaner air, and reducing their exposure to allergens and pollutants. To maximize their effectiveness, choosing the right air purifier with an appropriate filtration system and proper room size coverage is important. Additionally, regular filter replacement and maintenance are essential. However, **each year, over 1,200 children are injured by air purifiers and humidifiers, including electrical shocks and burns.** (Source: U.S. Consumer Product Safety Commission (CPSC) - Appliance Safety) Secure properly.

Nursery
→ **Infant/Non-mobile: (Birth - 6 months)**
→ **Infant crawl/roll: (5 months - 1 year)**
→ **Toddler/Pre-school: (1 year - 4 years)**
→ **School-age: (5 years - 6+ years)**

Mist Humidifiers

A mist humidifier is a device that increases the humidity level in the air by emitting a fine mist of water droplets. It helps maintain a comfortable and healthy humidity level in the environment, which can be particularly beneficial for children.

Safety: Mist humidifiers are generally considered safer for children because they do not produce hot steam like vaporizers. The mist is cool or at room temperature, reducing the risk of burns or accidental contact with hot water.

Comfortable Breathing: A mist humidifier can add moisture to the air, soothing and relieving dry nasal passages and irritated throats. This makes breathing easier for children, especially during dry weather or when they have a cold or respiratory congestion.

Allergy and Asthma Relief: Humidifiers can help reduce airborne allergens such as dust mites and pet dander, providing relief for children with allergies or asthma.

Preventing Dry Skin: Maintaining optimal humidity levels can help prevent dry and itchy skin, which is common in dry indoor environments, especially during the winter.

Restful Sleep: Improved air quality and comfortable breathing can promote better sleep for children and promote overall health and well-being.

Reduced Risk of Overheating: Vaporizers produce hot steam, which may increase room temperature. Mist humidifiers do not significantly affect room temperature, reducing the risk of overheating in a child's room.

Bacterial Growth Prevention: Many modern mist humidifiers have built-in features to prevent bacterial growth and ensure that the mist is clean and safe to inhale.

When Using a Mist Humidifier for Children: Ensure that the humidifier is cleaned regularly according to the manufacturer's instructions to prevent the growth of mold or bacteria. Use distilled or demineralized water in the humidifier to minimize mineral deposits and white dust. Place the humidifier in a safe location, out of reach of young children, to prevent accidental spills or tampering. Monitor the humidity levels in the room and adjust the humidifier settings as needed to maintain a comfortable and healthy humidity level (ideally between 30% to 50%). Use the humidifier in moderation, especially if the child shows any signs of discomfort or if the humidity level becomes too high, as excessive humidity can lead to other issues.

Overall, a properly maintained mist humidifier can provide many benefits for children by creating a comfortable and healthier indoor environment. However, using the device responsibly and following safety guidelines is essential to ensure its effective and safe use.

<u>Nursery</u>
→ **Infant/Non-mobile: (Birth - 6 months)**
→ **Infant crawl/roll: (5 months - 1 year)**
→ **Toddler/Pre-school: (1 year - 4 years)**
→ **School-age: (5 years - 6+ years)**

Ear Piercing Safety

Ear-piercing for children is a personal and cultural decision that many parents consider for various reasons. However, there are several concerns and considerations to keep in mind before deciding to pierce a child's ears:

Age and Consent: Consider the child's age and whether they can provide informed consent. Infants and very young children will not understand the procedure, or the potential pain involved. Some parents prefer to wait until their child is older and can express their desire to have their ears pierced.

Pain and Discomfort: Ear-piercing can be painful, even with the use of numbing creams. The child will experience discomfort during and after the procedure.

Infection and Aftercare: There is a risk of infection after ear piercing if proper aftercare is not followed. Parents must diligently clean the pierced area and follow the aftercare instructions provided by the piercer.

Allergies and Hypersensitivity: Some children may have allergies or sensitivities to certain metals used in ear studs. To reduce the risk of adverse reactions, it's essential to choose hypoallergenic materials.

Healing Time: Pierced ears take time to heal fully. During this time, the child should avoid touching or twisting the earrings to prevent irritation or infection.

Impact on Activities: If the child participates in sports or activities that require the removal of earrings, consider the practicality and potential disruption of the piercing.

Risks of DIY Piercing: It's crucial to avoid DIY (do-it-yourself) ear-piercing kits, as they may not be sterile and can lead to infections or complications.

Piercing Location and Professionalism: Choose a reputable, experienced piercer who practices proper hygiene and uses sterile equipment. Ensure they use piercing studs with a pointed post for easier insertion.

Potential Regret: As children grow older, their preferences may change. Some children may later regret having their ears pierced, which can be difficult to reverse.

Cultural and Family Considerations: In some cultures, ear-piercing is a common practice at a young age. Consider your family's cultural traditions and beliefs before making a decision.

If you decide to proceed with ear-piercing for your child, be well-informed about the process and ensure it is done in a safe and professional environment. Talk to the piercer about the type of earrings used, aftercare instructions, and any potential risks involved. Ultimately, the decision should prioritize the child's well-being and comfort.

> ▶ *Up to **35% of ear piercings** result in complications, ranging from infections and allergic reactions to keloid scarring and embedded earrings, according to family practice literature (parents.com) Infections occur in **20–30%** of cases, with the risk increasing when spring-loaded "piercing guns" are used and aseptic technique is lacking (PubMed) A 2011 study highlighted higher rates of infection and complication when piercings were done at very young ages. Beyond infection, nickel allergy and permanent ear deformities are well-documented outcomes, particularly in children pierced before age 11 Even professional studios sometimes see complications: about **13% of piercing-associated ED visits** involve infections, and **3% require hospitalization.***

|Ch. 11| Children with Diverse Needs

Childproofing a home is like crafting the ultimate safety zone, especially when it comes to children with special needs. These kids are superheroes in their own right, and just like superheroes, they need a space that caters to their unique abilities and challenges. Your home should be their safe space, whether it's mobility issues, sensory sensitivities, behavioral tendencies, or medical conditions. This chapter is your guide to making sure you've got every angle covered, with a sprinkle of humor to keep things light!

Children with Diverse Needs
→ **Infant/Non-mobile: (Birth - 6 months)**
→ **Infant crawl/roll: (5 months - 1 year)**
→ **Toddler/Pre-school: (1 year - 4 years)**
→ **School-age: (5 years - 6+ years)**

Understanding Children with Diverse Needs

Every child is a unique puzzle, and it's important to figure out which pieces require extra attention when it comes to special needs. Before padding corners and anchoring furniture, take a step back and consider your child's particular needs. Mobility? Sensory overload? Behavior that rivals a mini stuntman? Let's dive in! (This is just an overview. Each situation is unique)

Physical Mobility Challenges
Some kids zoom around in wheelchairs or use walkers; others need extra help getting from point A to point B. The goal is to ensure that they can move around quickly while keeping hazards at bay.

> **Ramps and broader doorways** are must-haves for children in wheelchairs. No one wants to get stuck in the hallway trying to make a sharp turn!
>
> Keep your home **trip-hazard-free** by ditching slippery rugs and taming those wandering electrical cords.
>
> Add **non-slip mats** and **padding on corners** for those "oops" moments when "Balance" decides to take a vacation.

Sensory Processing Disorders
These kids experience the world like it's on max volume or, conversely, like they're trying to crank the dial-up. Whether they're sensory seekers or avoiders, their environment must strike the right balance.

> **Hypo-sensitive kids** might look for excitement in all the wrong places, bright lights, loud sounds, deep pressure. Give them **safe zones** to channel that sensory craving.
>
> **Hypersensitive kids** might want to hide from all the chaos, so create calm, low-stimulation environments with soft lights and noise control. It's like a mini spa for their senses!

Behavioral and Cognitive Delays
For kids who have trouble grasping danger, your home needs to be a step ahead of their curiosity.

Children with autism or ADHD may be as unpredictable as a cat chasing a laser pointer climbing, touching, and wandering where they shouldn't.

For children with **severe cognitive delays**, danger is like an abstract concept. They need heightened supervision and extra layers of childproofing to keep them safe.

Medical

Needs Some children come with extra equipment think feeding tubes, oxygen tanks, or other medical devices. These things are lifesaving, but they also need to be out of reach of curious little fingers.

Lock up medical devices like they're the crown jewels! Keep them accessible for you but safely tucked away from any siblings who might see them as new toys.

Children with Diverse Needs
→ **Infant/Non-mobile: (Birth - 6 months)**
→ **Infant crawl/roll: (5 months - 1 year)**
→ **Toddler/Pre-school: (1 year - 4 years)**
→ **School-age: (5 years - 6+ years)**

General Safety Measures

All right, let's get into the real nitty-gritty. The basics of childproofing are universal, but we need to up the ante for special needs kids. Think of this as childproofing 2.0.

Furniture Anchoring and Fall Prevention

Let's face it, kids see furniture as jungle gyms, and if your child has mobility issues or an adventurous streak, you'll want to batten down the hatches.

Anchor everything! Dressers, bookcases, TVs, if they can tip, they should be attached to the wall like it's auditioning to be part of the house's foundation. *(For details refer to Living Room pg. 32)*

Got stairs? Add **extra-wide, reinforced gates** at the top and bottom. Some kids push and test every boundary (both literal and metaphorical).

For good measure, **pad those sharp corners** on tables and countertops because no one needs a trip to the ER during snack time.

Electrical and Fire Safety

Oh, the magnetic pull of outlets and wires! For some kids, they're like shiny objects just waiting to be explored.

Sliding outlet covers are your new best friends. They snap shut when not in use, preventing little fingers from exploring where they shouldn't.

Keep electrical cords **hidden and secured and** unplug appliances like toasters or coffee makers when they're not in use. For fire safety, ensure you have **smoke detectors** on every level, and consider **vibrating or visual alarms** if your child is sensitive to loud noises. No one wants the fire alarm to cause more stress than the actual fire!

Safe Rooms and Sensory Retreats

Think of a safe room as a sensory sanctuary where your child can escape the overload of everyday life.

> Equip it with **soft pillows, weighted blankets, dimmable lights,** and anything that helps your child feel calm. This room should be as inviting as a pillow fort but twice as safe.

> Keep the area **minimal and clutter-free** so they don't trip over something while seeking peace.

> If your child tends to bang their head or limbs, **padded walls** can be a lifesaver, literally!

Children with Diverse Needs
→ **Infant/Non-mobile: (Birth - 6 months)**
→ **Infant crawl/roll: (5 months - 1 year)**
→ **Toddler/Pre-school: (1 year - 4 years)**
→ **School-age: (5 years - 6+ years)**

Childproofing for Sensory Processing Issues

Children with sensory processing disorders need spaces that respond to their unique sensory needs. Creating the right environment is key, whether they're craving more input or trying to block it all out.

Lighting Adjustments
Harsh lighting can feel like being under interrogation for kids with light sensitivity.

> **Dimmable lighting** lets you adjust brightness levels based on what your child needs at any given moment. Goldilocks would approve, make it just right.

> **Blackout curtains** help in bedrooms and sensory rooms, turning down the sun's volume when it's time to calm down or rest.

Noise Management
Whether your child loves noise or can't stand it, the home environment can make or break their day.

> Add **acoustic panels** to the walls or use plush rugs to dampen the sound. Your home will be quieter and more soothing.

> For the particularly noise-sensitive, have **noise-canceling headphones** or **earplugs** handy for situations that could get loud. Your child will thank you, possibly silently.

Tactile and Textural Considerations
For some kids, touching is believing. Others might recoil at certain textures. It's all about balance.

> Offer **safe sensory materials**, soft blankets, smooth toys, and textured walls are all great options. Make sure everything is non-toxic because, let's be honest, it'll end up in their mouths.

Steer clear of materials that might be irritating, like shag rugs or rough upholstery. If it's something you wouldn't want to rub against your cheek, your child probably doesn't either!

Children with Diverse Needs
Infant/Non-mobile: (Birth - 6 months)
Infant crawl/roll: (5 months - 1 year)
→ **Toddler/Pre-school: (1 year - 4 years)**
→ **School-age: (5 years - 6+ years)**

Behavioral Safety Concerns

Childproofing goes beyond the usual cabinet locks and corner guards for kids with behavioral challenges. You need to plan for everything from impulsive wandering to self-injury prevention.

Locking Mechanisms for Safety

If your child has a knack for wandering off, you need to step up your lock game.

- Install **high locks or deadbolts** on exterior doors, and make sure they're out of reach but easy for adults to operate in an emergency.
- Consider **alarms or motion sensors** for doors and windows to alert you if your child decides to become an escape artist.

Self-Injury Prevention

If your child is prone to self-injury, padding becomes a top priority.

- **Soft padding** on walls, floors, and sharp furniture is essential in rooms where your child spends a lot of time. Think of it as creating a giant safety net.
- Offer **sensory gloves** or **chewable jewelry** for children who bite or scratch, giving them a safer way to manage their behaviors.

Medication and Hazardous Substance Security

If your child sees medicine as candy or likes to explore cleaning products, it's time to lock those things up tight.

- Use **tamper-proof locks** on cabinets where medications and hazardous substances are stored. Your child may be clever, but these locks are sneakier!

Children with Diverse Needs
→ **Infant/Non-mobile: (Birth - 6 months)**
→ **Infant crawl/roll: (5 months - 1 year)**
→ **Toddler/Pre-school: (1 year - 4 years)**
→ **School-age: (5 years - 6+ years)**

Mobility and Accessibility Adjustments

Creating a safe and accessible environment for a child with mobility challenges involves removing obstacles and making movement easy and smooth.

Removing Mobility Barriers

It's all about clearing the runway for your child to move freely.

Remove tripping hazards like rugs and electrical cords. Keep floors clear so there's no unintentional obstacle course.

Make sure **doorways and hallways** are wide enough for wheelchairs, walkers, or other mobility aids. The last thing your child needs is to get stuck in a corner.

Adding Handrails and Grab Bars

Handrails and grab bars are like extra hands helping your child keep their balance.

Install grab bars in bathrooms, near beds, and along hallways for extra support. Even the slightest handhold can make a world of difference.

Installing Lifts and Elevators

If you have multiple floors, consider a stairlift or home elevator so your child can get around easily. Because, let's face it, no one wants to be stuck on the first floor all day.

Make sure lifts are **well-maintained** and include **safety features** like seatbelts and secure footrests to prevent falls.

Conclusion: A Superhero's Sanctuary

Childproofing a home for a child with special needs is like building a fortress of safety and comfort. It's about creating a space that not only protects but also empowers. By understanding your child's unique challenges and tailoring the environment accordingly, you can ensure they have the freedom to explore and grow without fear. **Remember, every child deserves a comfortable safe space.** With a bit of creativity, patience, and a sprinkle of humor, you can transform your home into a superhero sanctuary where your child can thrive.

Notes:

|Ch. 12| Laundry Room

Introduction: In the bustling heart of every home lies a room often overlooked in the childproofing process - the laundry room. This seemingly innocuous space, brimming with the fragrance of fresh linen and fabric softener, holds a myriad of hidden dangers for our little explorers. As we venture into this chapter, we will unearth the secrets to transforming this bustling hub into a safe haven devoid of the perils that lurk in laundry baskets and behind laundry cupboard doors. From securing hazardous cleaning agents to ensuring the washing machine remains an appliance rather than a playground, we will guide you step-by-step to foster a safe and secure environment. Let's embark on this journey to create a laundry room where little dreams can't be dampened, and tiny adventurers play safely under the watchful eyes of their guardians.

Testimonial: *A sunny afternoon turned into a whirlwind of bubbles and giggles, with a sprinkle of panic. My sweet little Jacob, who is as curious as a cat with nine lives, decided to embark on a journey to the mystical land of the laundry room.*

Jacob has a knack for turning the most mundane places into realms of wonder and excitement. On this particular day, he transformed into a brave knight, ready to conquer the "Tower of Laundry". But alas, his trusty steed, the laundry basket, was not as sturdy as he thought. The basket tipped in his valiant effort to scale the mountain of clothes, sending him tumbling into a fortress of detergent bottles and fabric softeners.

I wish I had foreseen this laundry room expedition! A simple child safety lock on the laundry room door could have prevented Sir Jacob's tumble. Relocating the detergent fortress to higher ground, beyond the reach of little knights on daring quests, was a wise move. Thankfully, aside from a minor bruise and a slightly dented ego, Jacob emerged victorious, with tales of his brave conquest echoing through the halls (or at least until bedtime). As for me, I've learned a valuable lesson in childproofing and have since transformed the laundry room into a less enticing and much safer place for little explorers.

- Sue T. (Mother of 2)

Laundry Room
Infant non-mobile: (Birth-6 mo.)
Infant crawl/roll: (5 mo.-2 yrs.)
→ **Toddler/Pre-School: (1 yr.-4 yrs.)**
→ **School-age: (5 yrs.-6 yrs.)**

Washer and Dryer Safety

Annually, approximately **2,000 children** are injured by laundry machines, including entrapment and mechanical injuries. (Source: Centers for Disease Control and Prevention (CDC) – WISQARS) Childproofing the washing machine and dryer is important to prevent accidents and keep young children safe.

Install Childproof Locks: Use childproof locks on the doors of both the washer and dryer. These locks will prevent children from opening the doors and accessing the machines when they are not in use.

Elevated Placement: If possible, elevate the washer and dryer to a height that is out of reach for young children. Consider using a laundry pedestal or placing them on a secure platform.

Store Laundry Supplies Safely: Keep laundry detergents, fabric softeners, and other laundry supplies out of children's reach. Store them in a locked cabinet or on a high shelf.

Secure Power Cords: Ensure that the power cords are securely tucked away and not dangling where children can reach them.

Educate Older Children: If you have older children who may help with laundry tasks, educate them about the potential risks and safe operation of the washer and dryer.

Supervise Laundry Time: Always supervise children when you are using the washer and dryer, especially if they are curious or want to help.

Teach Safe Operation: If your children are old enough to use the washer and dryer, teach them how to operate the machines safely and responsibly.

Unplug When Not in Use: Unplug the washer and dryer when they are not in use, especially if they are located in an accessible area.

Regular Maintenance: Keep your washer and dryer well-maintained to ensure safe and efficient operation. Check for any signs of wear or damage and address them promptly.

Keep the Laundry Area Tidy: Keep the laundry area clean and tidy to prevent tripping hazards and discourage children from playing around the machines.

You can create a safe environment around the washer and dryer and minimize the risk of accidents or injuries. Always prioritize safety when it comes to household appliances and children.

<u>Laundry Room</u>
Infant/Non-mobile: (Birth - 6 months)
Infant crawl/roll: (5 months - 1 year)
→ **Toddler/Pre-school: (1 year - 4 years)**
→ **School-age: (5 years - 6+ years)**

Iron and Ironing Board Safety

Childproofing an ironing board and iron is essential to prevent accidents and ensure the safety of young children.

Ironing Board

Secure Storage: When not in use, store the ironing board in a locked closet or a room that is inaccessible to children. If the ironing board is collapsible, make sure it is fully collapsed and locked when stored.

Sturdy Design: Choose an ironing board with sturdy legs and a secure locking mechanism to prevent it from collapsing accidentally while in use.

Elevated Placement: Whenever possible, store the ironing board in an elevated position, out of the reach of young children.

Set Up a Child-Free Zone: Designate an ironing area as a child-free zone and enforce this rule with your children.

Supervise Usage: Always supervise children when using the ironing board, especially if they want to "help." Avoid leaving the ironing board unattended, even for a short period.

Avoid Overloading: Do not overload the ironing board with heavy items, as this can cause it to become unstable and tip over.

Use a Safety Cover: Consider using an ironing board cover with a childproof drawstring or fastener to prevent children from accessing the ironing board when not in use.

Iron

Each year, **more than 50,000 children** sustain burns from hot surfaces and objects like irons, curling irons, and heaters in the U.S. (Source: American Burn Association (ABA) - Burn Incidence Statistics)

Safe Storage: When not in use, keep the iron out of the reach of children. Store it on a high shelf or in a locked cabinet with a childproof lock.

Use a Cord Holder: If the iron has a cord, use a cord holder or clip to keep it secured and out of the way, preventing tripping hazards.

Educate Older Children: If you have older children who may use the iron, educate them about the potential risks and the importance of handling the iron responsibly.

Set Up a Cooling Area: After use, designate a safe cooling area for the iron. Use a heat-resistant iron rest or pad if the iron doesn't have a built-in rest.

Unplug After Use: Always unplug the iron after use and allow it to cool down before storing.

Avoid Leaving Water Inside: If using a steam iron, be cautious with the water reservoir. Do not leave the iron with water inside when not in use, as children may be tempted to play with it.

Regular Maintenance: Inspect the iron regularly for signs of wear or damage. Address any issues promptly to ensure safe and proper functioning.

You can create a safer environment, reduce the risk of accidents and injuries, and protect children from potential hazards associated with ironing tasks by always prioritizing safety when using any household appliances, especially when children are present.

Laundry Room
Infant/Non-mobile: (Birth - 6 months)
Infant crawl/roll: (5 months - 1 year)
→ **Toddler/Pre-school: (1 year - 4 years)**
→ **School-age: (5 years - 6+ years)**

Clothing Steamers

Due to the high heat and steam they produce; clothing steamers can pose a significant safety risk to children. If not handled and stored correctly, they can cause burns or scalds.

To Minimize the Risk of Accidents

Lockable Storage: When not in use, store the clothing steamer in a locked cabinet or out of reach on a high shelf. This prevents children from accessing the device and potentially turning it on.

Unplug Immediately: Unplug the steamer immediately after use and store the cord out of reach. Cords can be tempting for children to pull or chew on, leading to electrical hazards or injuries.

Automatic Shutoff and Safety Lock: Choose a clothing steamer with automatic shutoff and a safety lock to prevent accidental activation. These features can help reduce the risk of burns or scalds.

Laundry Room
Infant/Non-mobile: (Birth - 6 months)
Infant crawl/roll: (5 months - 1 year)
→ **Toddler/Pre-school: (1 year - 4 years)**
→ **School-age: (5 years - 6+ years)**

DRYING RACK SAFETY

Childproofing a clothing drying rack is essential to prevent accidents and ensure the safety of young children.

Elevated Placement: Whenever possible, place the clothing drying rack in an elevated position, out of the reach of young children. Use a wall-mounted drying rack or put it on a high surface.

Sturdy Design: Choose a clothing drying rack with a sturdy and stable design that is less likely to tip over easily.

Secure Wall Mounting: If you opt for a wall-mounted drying rack, make sure it is securely attached to the wall using appropriate hardware and anchors.

Avoid Sharp Edges: Ensure that the drying rack does not have sharp edges or protruding parts that could pose a risk to children.

Supervise Usage: Always supervise children when using the drying rack, especially if they are helping with hanging or removing clothes.

Avoid Overloading: Do not overload the drying rack with too many clothes, as this can make it unstable and increase the risk of tipping over.

Set Up a Child-Free Zone: Designate an area around the drying rack as a child-free zone and enforce this rule with your children.

Secure Drying Rack Legs: If the drying rack has folding legs, make sure they are securely locked in place when in use.

Store Safely When Not in Use: When the drying rack is not in use, store it in a locked closet or room inaccessible to children.

Educate Older Children: If you have older children who may use the drying rack, educate them about the potential risks and the importance of handling it responsibly.

Avoid Hanging Heavy Items: Do not hang heavy or sharp items on the drying rack, as they can create additional risks.

Keep Drying Rack Tidy: Encourage children to tidy the area around the drying rack to prevent tripping hazards.

Laundry Room
Infant/Non-mobile: (Birth - 6 months)
Infant crawl/roll: (5 months - 1 year)
→ **Toddler/Pre-school: (1 year - 4 years)**
→ **School-age: (5 years - 6+ years)**

Detergent and Bleach Safety

Detergent and bleach safety is crucial, as both of these household cleaning products can be hazardous if not used and stored properly.

Read and Follow Instructions: Always read and follow the manufacturer's instructions on the detergent and bleach labels. Pay attention to usage guidelines, dilution ratios, and safety precautions.

Detergent Pods: Although easy to use detergent pods can be dangerous. Childproofing detergent pod containers are essential to prevent accidental ingestion and ensure the safety of young children in the home. Make sure the container has a childproof top and is stored high up or in a locked cabinet.

Use in a Well-Ventilated Area: When using detergent or bleach, ensure the area is well-ventilated to avoid inhaling fumes. Open windows or use exhaust fans to improve ventilation.

Wear Protective Gear: If you need to handle concentrated bleach, wear protective gear such as gloves and eye protection to prevent skin and eye irritation.

Keep Out of Reach of Children and Pets: Store detergent and bleach in a high, locked cabinet, out of reach of young children and pets. Never leave these products unattended where they can be accessed easily.

Store Separately: Keep bleach and detergent containers separate, and never mix the two products together, as this can create hazardous chemical reactions.

Never Mix with Ammonia or Acids: <u>Never</u> mix bleach with ammonia or any acidic cleaners, as it can produce toxic fumes. Also, avoid mixing bleach with other cleaning agents, especially those containing hydrogen peroxide.

Use Appropriate Amounts: Use the recommended amount of detergent or bleach for each laundry or cleaning task load. Using excessive amounts can be wasteful and increase the risk of accidents.

Clean Up Spills Promptly: If detergent or bleach spills, clean it up immediately using proper safety precautions. Wear gloves and avoid direct skin contact.

Keep Original Containers: Always keep detergents and bleach in their original containers with proper labels to prevent confusion.

Dispose of Properly: Dispose of empty or unused containers properly, following local waste disposal guidelines. Do not pour bleach or detergent down drains or toilets unless instructed to do so on the product label.

Childproof Laundry Areas: Childproof the laundry area by securing the detergent and bleach containers and keeping the laundry appliances out of children's reach.

Teach Children About Dangers: Educate children about the potential dangers of cleaning products, including detergent and bleach. Teach them to avoid touching.

<u>Laundry Room</u>
Infant/Non-mobile: (Birth - 6 months)
Infant crawl/roll: (5 months - 1 year)
→ **Toddler/Pre-school: (1 year - 4 years)**
→ **School-age: (5 years - 6+ years)**

Standing Water Concerns

Standing water in a laundry room can pose various dangers and risks, affecting both the occupants and the property.

Slip and Fall Hazards: Standing water on the floor can create slippery surfaces, increasing the risk of slip and fall accidents for anyone in the area. This is particularly dangerous for young children, the elderly, or individuals with mobility issues.

Electrical Hazards: If water comes into contact with electrical outlets, appliances, or wiring in the laundry room, it can lead to electrical shocks or fires. Water and electricity do not mix, and any contact between the two must be avoided.

Damage to Flooring and Property: Prolonged exposure to standing water can damage flooring material, especially if it is not water-resistant. Water can also seep into walls, cabinets, and other structures, leading to water damage, mold growth, and costly repairs.

Appliance Damage: Water leaking into electrical appliances such as washing machines, dryers, or water heaters can cause malfunctions or render them unsafe to use.

Potential Health Hazards: Standing water can become a breeding ground for bacteria, mold, and mildew. Prolonged exposure to these contaminants can lead to health issues, particularly for individuals with allergies or respiratory conditions.

Water Contamination: If the standing water is from a sewage backup or contains contaminants, it can pose health risks to anyone who comes into contact with it. In such cases, professional cleanup and disinfection are necessary.

Structural Damage: If the standing water persists, it can weaken the laundry room's structural integrity, leading to more severe damage over time.

Immediately address any leaks or water spills in the laundry room to prevent standing water from forming. Ensure proper drainage in the laundry room to direct water away from appliances and other areas where it can accumulate. Regularly inspect the laundry room for leaks, water damage, or any signs of standing water. Promptly address any plumbing issues that may lead to water leaks or flooding. Use water-resistant flooring and materials in the laundry room to reduce the risk of water damage. Install water leak detectors or flood sensors to provide early warning in case of water-related emergencies.

Laundry Room
Infant/Non-mobile: (Birth - 6 months)
Infant crawl/roll: (5 months - 1 year)
→ **Toddler/Pre-school: (1 year - 4 years)**
→ **School-age: (5 years - 6+ years)**

Laundry Basket Concerns

Childproofing a laundry basket is an important step in preventing accidents and ensuring the safety of young children. Laundry baskets can pose potential risks, such as tipping over, falling on children, or becoming a dangerous play object. By taking the necessary precautions, you can significantly reduce these hazards and create a safer environment for your home.

Choose a Child-Safe Design: When selecting a laundry basket, opt for one with rounded edges and no sharp or protruding parts to minimize the risk of injuries. Additionally, consider a lightweight material like plastic or fabric to reduce the potential harm if the basket falls.

Lid with Safety Lock: If your laundry basket has a lid, ensure it comes equipped with a childproof safety lock or latch. This will prevent young children from opening the basket and potentially climbing inside, which can be dangerous.

Store Out of Reach: When the laundry basket is not in use, store it in a locked closet or a room inaccessible to children. Alternatively, place it on a high shelf that young children cannot reach. This will prevent them from accessing and playing with the basket unsupervised.

Avoid Heavy Loads: To prevent strain on the laundry basket and reduce the risk of tipping over, avoid overloading it with heavy items. A heavier basket is more likely to fall, potentially causing injuries.

Supervise Usage: Always supervise young children when they are playing near or with the laundry basket. This will allow you to intervene if they attempt to climb inside or misuse it.

Teach Proper Use: Educate older children on the proper use of the laundry basket and discourage them from using it as a toy. Explain to them that the laundry basket is intended for carrying laundry and should not be used for other activities.

Remove Tripping Hazards: To prevent accidents, keep the laundry area tidy and free of tripping hazards. Ensure that there are no loose items or cords on the floor that children could stumble over.

Teach Children About Risks: Educate children about the potential dangers associated with the laundry basket. Explain to them why handling the basket safely is important and why climbing inside or playing with it is not recommended.

|Ch. 13| Home Office/Den

Introduction: In the modern home, the home office often stands as a sanctuary of productivity and creativity, a place where great ideas come to life. However, to the curious eyes of a child, it transforms into a wonderland of intriguing gadgets, colorful stationery, and mysterious nooks. As we delve into this chapter, we will guide you in crafting a space that nurtures both your professional aspirations and your child's safety. From securing heavy furniture to organizing cords and electrical outlets, we will explore comprehensive strategies to foster a child-friendly environment without compromising your workspace aesthetics. Join us in sculpting a home office that harmoniously blends safety and functionality, allowing peace of mind to fuel your productivity while nurturing the budding curiosity of the little ones.

Testimonial: *It was a typical busy morning, and I was trying to juggle work while keeping an eye on my toddler, Benny. In a blink, he climbed onto my office chair, exploring my desk and navigating through all the stationery. Before I could react, he was drawn to the paper shredder and tried to feed it his drawing book. He ended up pinching his finger, and his scream brought me rushing over. Thankfully, he wasn't seriously hurt, but it was a wake-up call. If I had taken the time to childproof the office, covering the shredder and keeping it out of reach, Benny's little adventure wouldn't have ended in tears. Since then, I've made my office a safer space for him, allowing him to explore while I work without worrying about any hidden dangers. It's been a learning experience, but one that has helped create a better balance between safety and productivity.*

-John D. (Father of 3)

Home Office/Den
Infant/Non-mobile: (Birth - 6 months)
Infant crawl/roll: (5 months - 1 year)
→ **Toddler/Pre-school: (1 year - 4 years)**
→ **School-age: (5 years - 6+ years)**

Home Office Doorknobs

Childproofing doorknobs is an important safety measure to prevent young children from accessing certain areas or leaving the safety of a room.

Doorknob Covers: Use doorknob covers or childproof locks designed to fit over the existing doorknobs. These covers are typically made of durable materials that are difficult for young children to manipulate.

Door Lever Locks: If your doors have lever-style handles, consider installing door lever locks specifically designed to prevent children from operating them.

Height Adjustment: Adjust the height of the doorknob cover or lock to ensure that it is out of your child's reach. The higher the placement, the more challenging they will be to access.

Secure External Doors: Install childproof locks on external doors to prevent young children from wandering outside unsupervised.

Educate Older Children: If you have older children in the house who can open the doors, educate them about the importance of securing the doorknob covers or locks.

Consistent Use: Always remember to use the doorknob cover or lock whenever you leave a room.

Keep Keys Out of Reach: If your door has a key lock, keep the keys out of children's reach to prevent them from unlocking the door.

Regular Maintenance: Inspect the doorknob covers or locks regularly for signs of wear or damage and replace them promptly if needed.

You can create a safer environment for your child and have peace of mind knowing that certain areas are securely off-limits. As with all childproofing efforts, vigilance and consistency are key to maintaining a safe home for your little ones.

Home Office/Den
Infant/Non-mobile: (Birth - 6 months)
→ **Infant crawl/roll: (5 months - 1 year)**
→ **Toddler/Pre-school: (1 year - 4 years)**
→ **School-age: (5 years - 6+ years)**

Office Supplies

Childproofing office supplies is essential to create a safe workspace, especially when young children are around.

Store in Locked Cabinets: Keep office supplies like pens, scissors, staplers, and paper clips in locked cabinets or drawers that are out of children's reach.

Use Childproof Containers: Utilize childproof containers or storage boxes for smaller office supplies like paper clips, rubber bands, and push pins. Ensure these containers have secure lids that little hands can't open easily.

Secure Cords and Wires: Use cord organizers and cable clips to keep cords and wires out of the way and prevent children from pulling on them or tripping over them.

Organize Cables: Use cable sleeves or wraps to bundle cords together and avoid a tangled mess, reducing the risk of accidents.

Keep Sharp Objects Out of Reach: Store sharp objects such as scissors, letter openers, and utility knives in secure drawers or containers with childproof features.

Childproof Electronics: If your office contains electronic devices like computers or printers, ensure they are placed in a stable position and out of reach from children.

Secure Heavy Items: Ensure that heavy office equipment, such as printers or monitors, is stable and cannot be easily tipped over.

Educate Older Children: If you have older children who may use office supplies, educate them about the potential hazards and encourage responsible usage.

Keep Chemicals Separate: If your office includes cleaning supplies or other chemicals, store them in a separate locked cabinet away from office supplies and out of children's reach.

You can create a safer office environment and reduce the risk of accidents for curious children. Remember to keep the workspace organized and tidy to maintain a child-friendly, hazard-free office space.

▶ ***Accoring to Nationwide Childrens Hospital,** everyday items like scissors, staples, and paper clips frequently lead to eye injuries and puncture wounds in young children. And with office desks or shelves toppling over, youngsters account for 70% of furniture-tip-over injuries, happening as often as **one child every 46 minutes in ERs**. Together, these risks show that even quiet office areas need childproofing.*

Home Office/Den
Infant/Non-mobile: **(Birth - 6 months)**
Infant crawl/roll: **(5 months - 1 year)**
→ **Toddler/Pre-school: (1 year - 4 years)**
→ **School-age: (5 years - 6+ years)**

Paper Shredder Safety

Childproofing a paper shredder is crucial to prevent accidents and injuries, as its sharp blades can be dangerous for young children.

Unplug When Not in Use: Always unplug the paper shredder when it's not in use and keep the power cord out of reach of children.

Use a Childproof Lock: If your paper shredder has a safety lock feature, make sure to engage it whenever the shredder is not in use. This will prevent children from accidentally activating the shredder.

Store the Shredder Safely: When not in use, store the paper shredder in a locked cabinet or a room that is inaccessible to children.

Educate Older Children: If you have older children who may need to use the paper shredder, educate them about the potential dangers and how to operate it safely. Always supervise their usage.

Keep Hands and Objects Clear: Teach everyone in the household to keep their hands and any objects (such as toys or utensils) away from the shredder's opening, even when it's not in use.

Use Safety Features: Some paper shredders come with safety features, such as sensors that automatically shut off the shredder if hands get too close to the opening. Make sure these features are functioning properly.

Secure Waste Bin: If the paper shredder has a waste bin, ensure it is securely attached to the shredder and cannot be accessed by children.

Monitor Usage: Always supervise the usage of the paper shredder when it's in operation, even if it has safety features.

Regular Maintenance: Inspect the paper shredder regularly for signs of wear or damage. Replace or repair any damaged parts promptly.

Following these childproofing measures can help prevent accidents and ensure that the paper shredder is used safely in your home or office. Safety should always be the top priority when it comes to potentially hazardous office equipment.

Home Office/Den
Infant/Non-mobile: (Birth - 6 months)
Infant crawl/roll: (5 months - 1 year)
→ **Toddler/Pre-school: (1 year - 4 years)**
→ **School-age: (5 years - 6+ years)**

Ink and Toner Concerns

Childproofing ink and toner safety is essential to prevent children from accidentally ingesting or spilling these potentially hazardous substances.

Store in Childproof Containers: Keep ink bottles, toner cartridges, and any other printing supplies with secure lids or caps in childproof containers. Ensure that these containers are labeled properly for easy identification.

Elevated Storage: Store ink and toner supplies on high shelves or in locked cabinets that are out of children's reach.

Educate Older Children: If you have older children who may handle ink or toner, educate them about the potential hazards and the importance of using these supplies responsibly.

Clean Up Spills Immediately: If you spill something, clean it up immediately and thoroughly. Keep children away from the area until it's cleaned up properly.

Monitor Usage: Always supervise the usage of ink and toner supplies, especially when children are nearby.

Avoid Decanting: Do not transfer ink or toner into other containers, as this may increase the risk of accidental spills or exposure.

Proper Disposal: When disposing of empty ink cartridges or toner containers, follow the manufacturer's instructions and local guidelines for safe disposal.

Keep Caps Secure: After using ink or toner, make sure to close the caps or lids securely to prevent leakage.

Store away from Food and Drink: Avoid storing ink and toner supplies near food or drink to prevent accidental contamination.

Lock Printer Trays: Some printers have trays that contain ink cartridges or toner. If possible, lock or secure these trays to prevent children from accessing them.

By always prioritizing safety when handling office supplies or equipment, especially when young children are present, you can create a safer environment and reduce the risk of accidents or exposure to these potentially hazardous substances.

Home Office/Den
Infant/Non-mobile: (Birth - 6 months)
Infant crawl/roll: (5 months - 1 year)
→ **Toddler/Pre-school: (1 year - 4 years)**
→ **School-age: (5 years - 6+ years)**

Copier and Printer Safety

Childproofing a copier and printer is essential to ensure the safety of children and prevent accidents or damage to the equipment.

Elevated Placement: Place the copier and printer on a stable surface, such as a sturdy desk or a stand, which is out of children's reach. Avoid placing them on low furniture or near the floor where little hands can access them easily.

Secure Cables: Use cable organizers or clips to secure cords and cables, keeping them out of the way and reducing the risk of tripping or accidental pulling.

Childproof Covers: If your copier or printer has removable parts, such as ink cartridges or toner, consider using childproof covers or locks to prevent children from tampering with them.

Use Child Lock Features: Many modern copiers and printers have child lock features in their settings. Activate these features to limit access to certain functions or settings.

Educate Older Children: If you have older children who may use the copier or printer, educate them about its proper usage and the importance of handling it responsibly.

Supervise Usage: Always supervise the usage of the copier and printer when children are around, especially if they are curious about the equipment.

Store Supplies Securely: Keep ink cartridges, toner, paper, and other supplies in a locked cabinet or drawer, out of children's reach.

Secure Paper Trays: If the copier or printer has paper trays, consider locking or securing them to prevent children from accessing the paper.

Regular Maintenance: Inspect the copier and printer regularly for signs of wear or damage. Address any issues promptly to ensure safe and proper functioning.

Proper Disposal: When disposing of empty ink cartridges or toner containers, follow the manufacturer's instructions and local guidelines for safe disposal.

You can create a safer environment around the copier and printer, reducing the risk of accidents and ensuring the equipment is used responsibly. Safety should always be a priority when it comes to office equipment, especially when children are present.

Home Office/Den
Infant/Non-mobile: (Birth - 6 months)
Infant crawl/roll: (5 months - 1 year)
→ **Toddler/Pre-school: (1 year - 4 years)**
→ **School-age: (5 years - 6+ years)**

Computer Equipment

Each year, **over 5,000 children** are injured by personal computers and laptops, including electrical hazards and falls. (Source: National Electronic Injury Surveillance System (NEISS) – CDC) Childproofing computer equipment is important to protect both the equipment and the safety of children.

Elevated Placement: Place your computer, monitor, and other equipment on a sturdy desk or table that is out of children's reach. Avoid placing them on low furniture where kids can access them easily.

Secure Cords: Use cable organizers or clips to secure cords and cables, keeping them out of the way and reducing the risk of tripping or accidental pulling.

Use Childproof Covers: If your computer tower or other equipment has removable parts, consider using childproof covers or locks to prevent children from accessing internal components.

Keep Accessories Secure: When not in use, store computer accessories such as keyboards, mice, and headphones in a locked cabinet or drawer.

Childproof Power Strips: Use childproof power strips or surge protectors to prevent children from unplugging or playing with cords.

Educate Older Children: If you have older children who use the computer, educate them about proper usage, responsible internet browsing, and the importance of taking care of the equipment.

Set Up Parental Controls: Implement parental controls on your computer to restrict access to inappropriate content and limit screen time for younger children.

Monitor Usage: Always supervise computer usage when children are around, especially if they are using the internet.

Use Child-Friendly Software: Install child-friendly software that offers educational content and safe online activities for kids.

Regular Maintenance: Inspect your computer equipment regularly for signs of wear or damage. Address any issues promptly to ensure safe and proper functioning.

Lock the Screen: When leaving the computer unattended, lock the screen or set up a password to prevent children from accessing it.

Reduce the risk of accidents and ensure that children use the computer responsibly. Safety should always be a top priority, especially when it comes to technology and children.

Home Office/Den
Infant/Non-mobile: (Birth - 6 months)
Infant crawl/roll: (5 months - 1 year)
→ **Toddler/Pre-school: (1 year - 4 years)**
→ **School-age: (5 years - 6+ years)**

Manual and Electric Stapler Safety

Manual Staplers

Store in a Secure Location: Keep manual staplers stored in a locked drawer or cabinet that is out of children's reach when not in use.

Educate Older Children: If you have older children who may use the stapler, educate them about proper stapler usage and the importance of handling it responsibly.

Supervise Usage: Always supervise children when they are using a manual stapler, especially younger children.

Teach Safe Usage: Instruct children on properly using the stapler, emphasizing the importance of keeping fingers away from the stapling area.

Use Safety Guards: Consider using manual staplers with safety guards or covers that prevent access to the stapling mechanism when not in use.

Electric Staplers

Unplug When Not in Use: Always unplug electric staplers when they are not in use and keep the power cord out of children's reach.

Store Safely: When not in use, store the electric stapler in a locked drawer or cabinet that is inaccessible to children.

Educate Older Children: If older children need to use the electric stapler, educate them about its proper usage and the importance of responsibly handling it.

Use Safety Features: Some electric staplers have safety features, such as automatic shut-off when not in use for a certain period. Make sure these features are functioning properly.

Monitor Usage: Always supervise the usage of the electric stapler when children are nearby.

Keep Hands Clear: Teach everyone to keep their hands away from the stapling area, even when the electric stapler is not in use.

Regular Maintenance: Inspect the electric stapler regularly for signs of wear or damage. Address any issues promptly to ensure safe and proper functioning.

Home Office/Den
Infant/Non-mobile: (Birth - 6 months)
Infant crawl/roll: (5 months - 1 year)
→ **Toddler/Pre-school: (1 year - 4 years)**
→ **School-age: (5 years - 6+ years)**

Laser Pointer Concerns

Laser pointers can be dangerous for children's eyes. The light from a laser pointer can damage the retina, the light-sensitive tissue at the back of the eye. This can lead to vision problems, including blindness.

Children are more likely to be injured by laser pointers than adults because their eyes are still developing and are more vulnerable to damage. Children are also more likely to point laser pointers at their own eyes or the eyes of others.

If you have a laser pointer, it is important to keep it out of the reach of children. You should also teach children about the dangers of laser pointers and how to use them safely.

Here are some tips for keeping children safe from laser pointers.
- Keep laser pointers out of the reach of children.
- Teach children about the dangers of laser pointers and how to use them safely.
- Never point a laser pointer at anyone's eyes, including your own.
- If you use a laser pointer for presentations, ensure the beam is always directed away from the audience.
- Be aware of the laws in your area regarding laser pointers. Some states have banned the sale of laser pointers with a power output of more than five milliwatts.

If you think that your child has been injured by a laser pointer, you should take them to the doctor immediately.

Notes:

Home Office/Den
Infant/Non-mobile: (Birth - 6 months)
Infant crawl/roll: (5 months - 1 year)
→ **Toddler/Pre-school: (1 year - 4 years)**
→ **School-age: (5 years - 6+ years)**

Door Security

Childproofing every door in your home is vital in safeguarding young children from potential hazards. This involves securing various types of doors, including front and back doors, by installing high-placed deadbolts and door alarms and using safety glass to prevent breakage. Interior doors, such as those in bedrooms and bathrooms, should have knob covers, finger pinch guards, and door stoppers to prevent injuries and accidental lock-ins. Sliding doors, often leading to patios, require top locks, window films, and safety bars to deter children from opening them and to prevent shattering. Garage doors should have remote controls stored safely, safety sensors installed, and childproofing straps on emergency levers to avoid unauthorized access. Closet doors need special attention, with bi-fold door locks and magnetic locks to prevent children from getting trapped or accessing unsafe items. Educating children about the potential dangers and supervising them closely are general safety practices that should be adopted. These measures help in fostering a safe and secure home environment for children to explore without risks. (For details refer to Hallway/Stairs **pg. 173**)

Home Office/Den
Infant/Non-mobile: (Birth - 6 months)
Infant crawl/roll: (5 months - 1 year)
→ **Toddler/Pre-school: (1 year - 4 years)**
→ **School-age: (5 years - 6+ years)**

Emergency Distraction Kit

Creating a distraction kit to keep kids busy when they are next to you is a great way to provide entertainment and engagement while you focus on other tasks.

Coloring Books and Crayons: Add coloring books or activity pads and a set of washable crayons to spark their creativity.

Sticker Sheets: Include sticker sheets with various themes or characters that they can stick on paper or create fun scenes.

Puzzle Books: Add age-appropriate puzzle books, such as mazes or crossword puzzles, to challenge their minds.

Storybooks: Include a few of their favorite storybooks to encourage reading and quiet time.

Play-Doh or Modeling Clay: Provide a small container of Play-Doh or modeling clay for sensory play and imaginative sculpting.

Small Toys: To keep their hands busy, add a few small, quiet toys like fidget spinners, mini figurines, or squishy toys.

Activity Cards: Create activity cards with simple games or challenges they can do independently.

Snacks: Include some healthy and non-messy snacks to keep their tummies satisfied.

Travel Games: Consider small travel-sized board games or card games suitable for their age.

Flashcards: Include educational flashcards with numbers, letters, shapes, or colors to promote learning.

Water Wow Books: These reusable water-reveal activity books are mess-free and perfect for on-the-go entertainment.

Headphones and Audiobooks: If you're comfortable with screen time, you can include headphones and an audio story or educational content.

Pipe Cleaners and Beads: For older kids, provide pipe cleaners and beads so they can create their own jewelry or crafts.

Scavenger Hunt Lists: Create simple scavenger hunt lists for them to find objects around the room or outdoors.

Notebooks and Gel Pens: Include blank notebooks and colorful gel pens for drawing or journaling.

Remember to customize the distraction kit based on your child's age and interests. Rotating the items regularly and introducing new surprises can also help keep their curiosity piqued.

Notes: (What do you currently have?)

|Ch. 14| Sunroom/Patio

Introduction: In the blissful embrace of your home's sunroom or patio, where sunlight filters through, and laughter echoes, the safety of your little ones remains paramount. This chapter is dedicated to transforming your sunroom or deck into a haven where curiosity meets safety, allowing your children to explore without encountering hazards. From securing railings to ensuring the safety of outdoor furniture, we will guide you through comprehensive strategies to childproof these spaces. Let's embark on this journey of creating a sunroom or patio that harmonizes the joyous melodies of childhood with the comforting embrace of safety, fostering a space where memories are made with peace of mind.

Testimonial: *Our patio has always been one of my kiddos favorite spots to explore, with all the potted plants to navigate and the patio furniture to climb and hide behind. But one sunny afternoon, his exploring took a turn for the worse.*

As I was sipping my tea, I heard a small yet determined voice declare, "I'm the king of the world!" followed by a not-so-royal tumble. My heart raced as I rushed outside to find Logan on the ground, his paper crown sadly crumpled beside him. It seems his royal throne (the patio chair) wasn't quite stable enough for his kingly endeavors.

With a few tears and a slightly bruised ego, we realized that our patio wasn't exactly Logan-proof. If we had secured the patio furniture to prevent it from tipping over, our little king's reign would not have been so short.

Our patio is now equipped with child-friendly furniture, and all potential hazards are kept at bay, ensuring that King Logan's next royal proclamation will be met with cheers, not tears. Let this be a gentle reminder to all fellow parents to childproof your patios because you never know when a little king or queen might decide to hold court there!

-Kelly M. (Mom of 4)

Sunroom/Patio
Infant/Non-mobile: **(Birth - 6 months)**
→ Infant crawl/roll: **(5 months - 1 year)**
→ Toddler/Pre-school: **(1 year - 4 years)**
→ School-age: **(5 years - 6+ years)**

Remove Chairs with Rubber-Striped Seats and Backs

One area that demands immediate attention is the removal of chairs with rubber-striped seats and backs. These chairs pose **a significant choking hazard for children**, particularly those in the toddler stage who tend to put objects in their mouths.

First and foremost, thoroughly inspect the chairs to identify any loose or detachable rubber strips, which can quickly come off and become lodged in a child's throat. Bear in mind that this inspection should not just be a one-time event; **regular checks are essential** to catch any wear and tear that might occur over time. It's crucial to be methodical in this process, scrutinizing each crevice and component to ensure no small parts are overlooked.

After the potential risks have been identified, **the next step should be to remove these chairs entirely from areas where the child has access**. If complete removal is not feasible immediately, a temporary solution could be to store these chairs in a locked room, ensuring that the child cannot reach them under any circumstances.

Taking it a step further, it would be prudent to replace these chairs with safer alternatives, ones that do not have small parts or materials that can come off and cause harm. When choosing new chairs, **opt for ones with solid backs and seats**, avoiding those with any kind of detachable elements.

In addition, while focusing on these chairs, take the opportunity to extend the detail-oriented approach to other areas of your home. This includes **anchoring furniture** to prevent tip-overs, checking for sharp edges or corners that could cause injury, and educating all family members and frequent visitors about the safety measures in place and the reasons behind them.

Furthermore, **consider taking a first aid course that teaches handling choking incidents** and keeping emergency numbers readily accessible. This comprehensive approach to childproofing, focusing on the detailed inspection and removal of hazardous chairs along with a broader safety strategy, will ensure a safer environment for your child, allowing peace of mind for everyone involved.

<u>Sunroom/Patio</u>
Infant/Non-mobile: (Birth - 6 months)
Infant crawl/roll: (5 months - 1 year)
→ **Toddler/Pre-school: (1 year - 4 years)**
→ **School-age: (5 years - 6+ years)**

Wicker Safety

Given its distinct features, such as intricate weaves and sometimes sharp edges, childproofing wicker furniture requires a detail-oriented approach.

Inspection

Identify Loose Fibers: Wicker furniture tends to have loose fibers that can easily come off. Inspect the furniture minutely to identify any protruding or loose fibers that can be a potential hazard.

Check Stability: Ensure the furniture is stable and does not wobble to prevent tipping over, which could injure a child.

Modifications

Sand Sharp Edges: If the wicker furniture has sharp edges, use sandpaper to smooth them down to prevent injuries.

Secure Loose Fibers: Secure any loose fibers by weaving them back into the main structure or trimming them to prevent choking hazards.

Padding: Add padding or cushions to cover gaps or openings in the wicker furniture that could trap a child's fingers or limbs.

Maintenance

Regular Maintenance: Schedule regular maintenance to check for wear and tear and to ensure that any new loose fibers or sharp edges are addressed promptly.

Cleaning: Clean the furniture regularly to prevent the accumulation of dust and small particles that a child might ingest.

Additional Safety Measures

Furniture Positioning: Position the wicker furniture away from windows and other hazardous areas where a child might climb and risk falling.

Corners and Edges: Consider installing corner protectors to prevent injuries if the furniture has sharp corners.

Education and Preparedness

Educating Family Members: Educate family members and visitors about the precautions taken and supervise children when they are around the furniture.

Emergency Readiness: Be prepared for emergencies by having a first aid kit readily available and keeping emergency numbers at hand.

First Aid Training: Consider enrolling in a first aid training course to learn how to handle potential injuries effectively.

Sunroom/Patio
Infant/Non-mobile: (Birth - 6 months)
Infant crawl/roll: (5 months - 1 year)
→ **Toddler/Pre-school: (1 year - 4 years)**
→ **School-age: (5 years - 6+ years)**

INSTALL SECURITY WINDOW LOCKS

Installing security window locks in your Sunroom or Patio is a vital step in childproofing your home. They serve the dual purpose of keeping your little ones safe while enhancing the security of your living space. To embark on this project, first, conduct a comprehensive assessment of all the windows in the Sunroom or Patio to identify their specific vulnerabilities and areas that need immediate attention.

Next, select high-quality, child-resistant window locks designed to withstand considerable force, thus deterring potential intruders. These locks should be installed at a height out of reach of children to prevent them from unlocking them accidentally. In addition, consider integrating alarms into the window locks, which would alert you immediately if any attempt is made to open the window from either inside or outside.

Ensure that the chosen window locks allow for a quick-release mechanism, a crucial feature that facilitates easy and rapid egress in case of emergencies, thereby ensuring the safety of all family members. Make sure to educate everyone in the household about the functioning and benefits of these new locks, fostering a family-wide culture of safety and vigilance.

Incorporating these strategies in your childproofing plan will not only safeguard your children from potential accidents but also elevate the overall security of your home, fostering a safe and secure environment for your family to thrive. It is not just an investment in security equipment but a significant stride towards fostering a safe haven for your children to grow and flourish.

Notes:

Sunroom/Patio
Infant/Non-mobile: (Birth - 6 months)
Infant crawl/roll: (5 months - 1 year)
→ **Toddler/Pre-school: (1 year - 4 years)**
→ **School-age: (5 years - 6+ years)**

BEWARE OF EXPOSED METAL
(Heat Concerns)

To childproof a Sunroom/Patio against heat hazards posed by exposed metal elements, it's essential to take a multifaceted approach. Begin by identifying areas with metals that heat up significantly, which could be metal frames or furniture. Implement strategies such as installing shades to control sunlight and possibly replacing metal items with non-conductive materials. Cover exposed metal areas with heat-resistant materials like insulating foam or silicone to prevent direct contact. Establish a child-friendly zone away from these areas and educate children about the dangers of touching hot surfaces. Also, ensure a first-aid kit equipped to treat burns is readily available in the Sunroom/Patio. Supervision is key to preventing accidents and cultivating a sense of caution in children towards these hazards.

► *A study from **Children's Hospital Colorado (2012–2017)** documented **58 children** (median age 17 months) who suffered **contact burns** from sun-heated surfaces around the home—think metal thresholds, toilet lids, or other surfaces heated by sunlight.*

|Ch. 15| Attic

Introduction: Due to its specific characteristics, childproofing an attic requires a combination of traditional techniques and unique considerations.

Testimonial: *Our attic, once just a storage space for forgotten relics, became a tempting adventure spot for my five-year-old, Rachel. One afternoon, while I was making lunch, I heard a series of thuds followed by a loud crash. My heart nearly stopped as I ran upstairs, only to find Rachel among a pile of old boxes, her little face a mix of shock and awe. She'd managed to climb into the attic, but her quest led to a small avalanche of stored memories. Thankfully, she only had a few scrapes, but that was the moment I realized the attic, while mysterious and exciting, wasn't the safest place for our curious explorer.*

Now, we've installed a childproof lock on the attic door, turning it into a no-go zone. Rachel's adventures are now limited to the backyard, where she can climb without fear of falling boxes! Lesson learned: no space is too hidden or too high for a determined five-year-old. Secure those tempting spots, fellow parents—our little explorers are more resourceful than we think!

-Norman R. (Father of 3)

Attic
Infant/Non-mobile: (Birth - 6 months)
Infant crawl/roll: (5 months - 1 year)
→ **Toddler/Pre-school: (1 year - 4 years)**
→ **School-age: (5 years - 6+ years)**

Attic Access Control

Lockable Door/Gate: Install a childproof lock or gate at the entrance to prevent unsupervised access.

Stair Safety: If the attic is accessed via stairs, consider installing safety gates at both the top and bottom. Non-slip pads can also be added to each step to prevent slips.

Window Locks: Install childproof locks to prevent children from opening them.

Window Guards: If the windows are low or significant, consider adding window guards to prevent falls.

Attic
Infant/Non-mobile: (Birth - 6 months)
→ **Infant crawl/roll: (5 months - 1 year)**
→ **Toddler/Pre-school: (1 year - 4 years)**
→ **School-age: (5 years - 6+ years)**

Floor Security

Childproofing an attic floor is critical to ensuring the safety of children. Attics often house numerous hazards, especially when it comes to flooring.

Floor Stability: Carry out a meticulous inspection of the attic floor. Repair any weak or rotten spots to prevent the risk of falling through. Ensure **no nails or screws are protruding** from the floor that could cause injuries. If the floor is made of rough material that might cause splinters, consider covering it with child-friendly material like carpeting or rugs.

Trip Hazards: Remove any clutter from the floor that might cause tripping hazards. If rugs are used, ensure they are secured properly to prevent children from tripping over them.

Safe Play Area: Create a designated play area on the floor with safe toys and materials, away from potential hazards like stairs or windows. Consider adding padding to the play area to prevent injuries in case of falls.

Electrical Safety: Ensure that there are no loose cords on the floor that children might trip over or pull down. Install protective covers on any floor-level electrical outlets to prevent children from inserting objects or fingers.

Chemicals and Harmful Substances: Ensure that any harmful substances stored in the attic are securely locked away, far from the reach of children.

Supervision and Education: Children should always be supervised when spending time in the attic to prevent accidents. Educate children about the potential hazards in the attic and the importance of safe behavior.

Emergency Preparedness: Make sure there are clear paths to exits in case of an emergency.

Attic
- → Infant/Non-mobile: (Birth - 6 months)
- → Infant crawl/roll: (5 months - 1 year)
- → Toddler/Pre-school: (1 year - 4 years)
- → School-age: (5 years - 6+ years)

Childproofing Electricity in the Attic

Secure Electrical Outlets

Outlet Covers: Install tamper-resistant outlet covers that are difficult for children to remove but easy for adults. These covers should snugly fit into the outlets, preventing tiny fingers from prying them open.

Safety Caps: Safety caps can also be used to block unused electrical outlets. Ensure they are large enough to prevent choking hazards if accidentally removed.

Conceal Electrical Cords

Cord Organizers: Use cord organizers or cable management boxes to bundle and hide electrical cords. This prevents tripping hazards and discourages children from playing with or chewing on the cords.

Secure Loose Cords: Fasten loose cords to the wall or floor using adhesive cord clips or cable ties, keeping them out of children's reach and pathway.

Install GFCI Outlets

Safety Feature: Ground Fault Circuit Interrupter (GFCI) outlets automatically cut off power when they detect an imbalance, protecting against electrical shocks. Replace standard outlets in the attic with GFCI outlets for enhanced safety.

Light Fixture Safety

Secure Light Bulbs: Ensure all light bulbs are tightly screwed in and consider using safety cages or covers to prevent children from touching hot bulbs.

Opt for LED: Choose LED bulbs that stay cool to the touch, reducing the risk of burns if a child manages to touch them.

Limit Access to Electrical Panels

Lockable Panel Cover: If the attic houses the home's electrical panel, install a lockable cover or door to restrict access. Only adults should have the keys or access codes.

Educate and Supervise

Safety Education: Teach older children basic electrical safety rules, like not inserting objects into outlets and avoiding wet hands when touching electrical devices.

Constant Supervision: Always supervise children when they are in the attic, ensuring they stay away from electrical hazards.

Regular Safety Inspections

Routine Checks: Regularly inspect the attic's electrical components for wear and tear, frayed cords, or damaged outlets. Promptly replace or repair any faulty items to maintain a safe environment.

Childproofing the electricity in the attic requires a combination of safety devices, education, and supervision. Taking these proactive steps can create a secure space that allows children to explore without risking electrical accidents or injuries. Always stay updated on the latest childproofing products and technologies to enhance the safety measures in place.

Attic
→ Infant/Non-mobile: (Birth - 6 months)
→ Infant crawl/roll: (5 months - 1 year)
→ Toddler/Pre-school: (1 year - 4 years)
→ School-age: (5 years - 6+ years)

Insects and Pests
(For more details refer to Living Room **pg. 59**)

Natural Repellents: Use natural repellents like peppermint oil or cedarwood to deter pests without introducing harmful chemicals.

Check for Pests: Regularly inspect the attic for signs of pests like rodents or insects and address any infestations promptly.

Attic
→ Infant/Non-mobile: (Birth - 6 months)
→ Infant crawl/roll: (5 months - 1 year)
→ Toddler/Pre-school: (1 year - 4 years)
→ School-age: (5 years - 6+ years)

Temperature

Addressing temperature control in the attic is a crucial aspect of childproofing, especially since extreme temperatures can pose a risk to children's health and safety.

Insulation
Ensure the attic is well-insulated to maintain a stable temperature. This will prevent the space from becoming too hot in summer or too cold in winter. If the attic has windows, make sure they are insulated to prevent drafts and heat loss or gain

Ventilation
Install an efficient ventilation system that helps regulate the temperature, drawing out hot air during summer and moist air during winter. If possible, install roof vents to allow hot air to escape during summer.

Heating and Cooling Systems
Install a safe heating system for the winter months to prevent the attic from getting too cold. Make sure heating elements are safeguarded to prevent burns. Set up a cooling system, like a window air conditioner or fan, for the summer months. Ensure cords are secured to prevent tripping hazards.

Monitoring Temperature
Install a reliable temperature monitoring system to keep an eye on the attic's temperature and adjust as needed. Use thermal curtains to help maintain the desired temperature in the attic.

Safe Play Area
A designated area for children to play that is well-regulated in terms of temperature. Consider installing flooring that remains at a neutral temperature to prevent cold or hot surfaces that could be uncomfortable or even harmful to children.

Education and Supervision
Teach children the importance of staying away from potential heat sources or cold drafts. Ensure that children are always supervised during their time in the attic to monitor their well-being.

Regular Maintenance
Conduct regular maintenance checks to ensure all temperature control systems are functioning properly and safely. Have professional inspections performed periodically to ensure that insulation and ventilation are adequate and up to code.

You will create a safer and more comfortable environment for children in the attic, promoting well-being and preventing potential hazards associated with temperature extremes.

Attic
Infant/Non-mobile: (Birth - 6 months)
Infant crawl/roll: (5 months - 1 year)
→ **Toddler/Pre-school: (1 year - 4 years)**
→ **School-age: (5 years - 6+ years)**

Attic Play Zone

Creating a dedicated and safe play area in the attic is an excellent way to utilize space while providing children with a secure zone to explore and enjoy. Start by meticulously inspecting the floor, ensuring it is free of splinters and uneven surfaces that could cause trips and falls.

Opt for soft flooring solutions such as plush carpets or play mats to cushion potential impacts and provide a comfortable playing surface. Also, consider installing soft wall coverings to minimize injuries in case of bumps and collisions.

Equally crucial is the **establishment of a temperature control system** to maintain a comfortable and stable environment year-round. Ensure the attic is well-insulated and possesses adequate heating and cooling facilities. Implementing child-friendly furniture with rounded edges and corners helps prevent injuries, and securing any heavy furniture to the wall is vital to avoid tipping accidents. Keeping the area well-lit is another priority, with the installation of sufficient lighting fixtures and perhaps even night lights. to guide children safely during the evening hours. For window safety, **window locks and guards** can be installed to prevent falls and unauthorized openings. All nearby electrical outlets should be securely covered, and cords should be managed proficiently to avoid tripping hazards. It's essential to keep the play area tidy, with dedicated, secure storage units for toys and play materials to prevent clutter and associated accidents.

Ensuring easy and clear access to exits in case of emergencies is vital. Having a well-stocked first-aid kit can be a lifesaver for promptly addressing minor injuries. To supplement the physical safety measures, it is essential to maintain a vigilant eye on the children playing in the area and to educate them about the safety rules to adhere to while playing in the attic. Regular maintenance checks and a clean, hygienic environment will round off your efforts in establishing a safe, secure, and delightful attic play area for children.

► *Studies show that falls from elevated spots like attics are nearly **seven times more likely** to cause skull fractures or brain injuries compared to low-level trips and slips. Each year, over **10,000 preschoolers are hospitalized from falls.** And when they happen in attics, the injuries are often the most severe. A tragic recent incident saw a child fall 25 feet through attic flooring in an unsupervised moment, showing how quickly exploration turns to peril in unfinished spaces.* (PubMed)

"No adventure should lead to danger. Childproof the attic play space before little ones make it their kingdom." – Artemis

|Ch. 16| Panic/Safe Room

Introduction: In the modern home, a panic room stands as a fortress of safety, a haven designed to shield its occupants from unforeseen dangers and emergencies. Yet, in the eyes of a child, this secure space can morph into a realm of mystery and adventure, beckoning them with the lure of the unknown. As we venture into this chapter, we delve deep into the essential strategies to transform your panic room into a zone that safeguards not only against external threats but also the curious and ever-adventurous spirits of little ones. From installing child-resistant locks to securing potential tripping hazards, we will guide you step-by-step to ensure that your fortress of safety remains impenetrable to young explorers, keeping them safe from both external dangers and the bumps and bruises of unintended adventures.

Testimonial: *Jaxon, our fearless four-year-old, transformed into a master locksmith, equipped with nothing but his toy screwdriver and endless determination. His latest conquest? The panic room. One afternoon, while I was deep in work mode, Jaxon managed to unlock the door and turn our panic room into his playground. Of course, it didn't take long for the fun to end with a little trip over the rug and a minor bump on the head. Cue the tears, and a frantic dad rushing to the rescue!*

In hindsight, a childproof lock on the panic room door and securing that loose rug would've spared us the drama. Now, our panic room is once again a no-kid zone, safe for emergencies but off-limits for tiny adventurers. The lesson? Never underestimate the ingenuity of a child with a toy tool kit. Childproof even the unexpected spaces!

-Micheal S. (Father of 2)

Panic/Safe Room
Infant/Non-mobile: (Birth - 6 months)
Infant crawl/roll: (5 months - 1 year)
→ **Toddler/Pre-school: (1 year - 4 years)**
→ **School-age: (5 years - 6+ years)**

Control Access

Biometric Locks: Install fingerprint or retina scan locks that can be programmed to recognize only adult family members. This prevents children from accidentally locking themselves inside.

Secondary Manual Lock: In case of electronic failures, ensure there's a manual lock that children can't easily manipulate.

Panic/Safe Room
Infant/Non-mobile: (Birth - 6 months)
Infant crawl/roll: (5 months - 1 year)
→ **Toddler/Pre-school: (1 year - 4 years)**
→ **School-age: (5 years - 6+ years)**

Floor and Wall Concerns

Non-slip Flooring: Use non-slip mats or tiles to prevent falls.

Wall Padding: Consider adding padded walls not just for soundproofing but also to prevent injury if a child falls or bumps into them.

Panic/Safe Room
Infant/Non-mobile: (Birth - 6 months)
Infant crawl/roll: (5 months - 1 year)
→ **Toddler/Pre-school: (1 year - 4 years)**
→ **School-age: (5 years - 6+ years)**

Furniture Preferences

When setting up a childproof panic room, the primary focus should be on blending safety with functionality and comfort. Opting for furniture with rounded corners can prevent injuries while securing heavy furniture pieces firmly to the walls helps in minimizing the risk of tipping accidents. In addition, choosing soft materials for seating and avoiding glass elements are critical steps to ensure child safety. Essential furniture pieces include a lockable storage cabinet stocked with emergency supplies, comfortable padded seating, a foldable cot or bed for resting, and a small desk equipped with communication devices. Incorporating carpeted or rubber-matted flooring can offer added comfort and noise reduction. Setting aside a designated play area stocked with soft toys and non-toxic materials can help keep children engaged and less stressed. Moreover, including an air purifier or a proper ventilation system would be beneficial for extended stays in the room, ensuring a comfortable and safe sanctuary during emergencies.

Panic/Safe Room
→ Infant/Non-mobile: (Birth - 6 months)
→ Infant crawl/roll: (5 months - 1 year)
→ Toddler/Pre-school: (1 year - 4 years)
→ School-age: (5 years - 6+ years)

Intercom Communication

Intercom System: The incorporation of an intercom system in a childproofed panic room cannot be overstated. In the event of an emergency, quick and clear communication is a critical element for ensuring the safety and well-being of everyone, especially children. First, an intercom system allows for direct communication with the outside world, facilitating contact with emergency services if necessary. Second, it can serve to communicate with other members of the household in different parts of the home, ensuring their safety or directing them to join the panic room.

From a childproofing perspective, it's vital to select an intercom system that is easy to use, possibly featuring large, clear buttons that can be easily operated by a child in case an adult is incapacitated or unable to operate the system. The intercom should be installed at a height that is accessible to both adults and children, allowing for easy access in critical situations. Investing in a system that comes with features like a video display can help keep a vigilant eye on the surroundings or identify individuals outside the panic room before opening the door, adding an extra layer of security and peace of mind.

An intercom system in a panic room is a vital tool that synergizes safety and communication, thereby playing an indispensable role in fostering a secure environment where children and adults can stay safe and connected during emergencies. It should be easy to operate to ensure that even children can use it effectively if the situation demands, enhancing the overall safety profile of your childproofed panic room.

Panic/Safe Room
→ Infant/Non-mobile: (Birth - 6 months)
→ Infant crawl/roll: (5 months - 1 year)
→ Toddler/Pre-school: (1 year - 4 years)
→ School-age: (5 years - 6+ years)

Separate Air Source

Integrating a separate air source in a childproofed panic room is indeed an astute decision. The necessity stems from emergencies such as fires or chemical hazards where the regular ventilation system could potentially bring in contaminated air, posing serious health risks, especially to children with more vulnerable respiratory systems.

Having a separate, **sealed air source** ensures that the occupants, including children, have access to clean and uncontaminated air for breathing during emergencies. This system would be independent of the home's main ventilation system and would be capable of filtering out smoke, chemicals, and other hazardous substances, thereby safeguarding the respiratory health of everyone inside. From a childproofing perspective, this separate air source should be designed to be foolproof and easy to activate, even by a child, in case adults are unable to do so. **Clear**

instructions should be displayed near the unit to guide older children on how to operate it if necessary. Safety features should be in place to prevent young children from tampering with the system during non-emergency times.

It is **beneficial to include an oxygen supply unit within** this separate air source, to ensure sufficient oxygen levels are always maintained, especially if there are infants in the house, as they are particularly vulnerable to low oxygen levels.

Establishing a separate air source in a childproofed panic room not only guarantees a safe haven during emergencies but also empowers children with a layer of protection that can be potentially lifesaving, hence fostering an environment where the young ones can stay safe and breathe easily, no matter the circumstance.

Panic/Safe Room
- **Infant/Non-mobile: (Birth - 6 months)**
- **Infant crawl/roll: (5 months - 1 year)**
- **Toddler/Pre-school: (1 year - 4 years)**
- **School-age: (5 years - 6+ years)**

Needed Supplies

Creating a childproof panic room requires meticulous planning to ensure that it is equipped with all the necessary supplies to ensure children's safety and well-being during an emergency.

Food and Water: Stock up on a variety of non-perishable food items that are easy to prepare and consume. Include baby food and formula if there are infants in the house. Ensure a sufficient supply of bottled water for drinking and possibly for hygiene purposes. Have child-friendly utensils, including bottles and sippy cups for little ones.

Health and Hygiene: A well-equipped first aid kit with essential medicines, antiseptics, bandages, and a digital thermometer. Ensure that child-specific medications and baby wipes include stock personal hygiene items like toothbrushes, toothpaste, sanitary products, and infant diapers.

Comfort and Accommodation: Comfortable bedding options like sleeping bags or foldable mats are easy to set up and store. Keep a set of spare clothes for children, including warm clothing and blankets.

Entertainment and Engagement: Include a small collection of toys and books to keep children entertained and distracted. Choose soft toys to avoid injuries. Have board games and activity kits to engage older children and keep them occupied.

Communication and Safety: As discussed, an easy-to-use intercom system to maintain communication with the outside world. A charging station with multiple ports to ensure that communication devices remain powered.

Special Supplies: A separate air source to maintain air quality, masks, and air purifiers. Emergency lighting options like flashlights, battery-operated lanterns, and night lights to comfort children. Keep a file with essential documents, including identification and medical records, easily accessible in the panic room.

Panic/Safe Room
→ Infant/Non-mobile: (Birth - 6 months)
→ Infant crawl/roll: (5 months - 1 year)
→ Toddler/Pre-school: (1 year - 4 years)
→ School-age: (5 years - 6+ years)

Surveillance

Considering children, incorporating a surveillance system needs to strike a balance between high-level security and child safety.

Camera Installation

Camera Placement: Cameras should be installed strategically to monitor the panic room's main access routes. To prevent tampering, they should be mounted high and out of the reach of children.

Infrared Capabilities: Cameras with infrared capabilities can be monitored even in low-light conditions, always ensuring the safety of the occupants.

Covered Wiring: All wiring connected to the surveillance system should be concealed and secured to prevent tripping hazards and to stop curious children from playing with them.

Monitoring Screens

Secured Screens: The monitoring screens should be securely mounted on the wall at a height that is accessible to adults but not reachable by young children.

Password Protected: The system should be password-protected to prevent unauthorized access, especially by children who might accidentally alter settings.

Simple User Interface: Despite being secure, the system should have a simple user interface that older children can navigate easily under adult supervision in case they need to use it during emergencies.

Alert Systems

Silent Alarms: Install silent alarms that can be activated to alert authorities without alerting intruders, thus maintaining a secure environment within the panic room.

Panic Buttons: Install panic buttons at various heights, some accessible to adults and others that older children can reach, to allow them to alert authorities in case of an emergency.

Child Safety Protocols

Education: Educate the children about the importance of the surveillance system and instruct them on the do's and don'ts to prevent mishandling and ensure their safety.

Safety Covers: Use safety covers on outlets and secure any power strips to prevent electric shock hazards for children exploring.

Emergency Drills: Conduct regular emergency drills with the children to familiarize them with the system and the steps to follow in case of an emergency, including how to use the surveillance system appropriately.

Panic/Safe Room
Infant/Non-mobile: (Birth - 6 months)
Infant crawl/roll: (5 months - 1 year)
→ **Toddler/Pre-school: (1 year - 4 years)**
→ **School-age: (5 years - 6+ years)**

Proper Lighting

Ensuring appropriate and safe lighting in a childproofed panic room is paramount to guarantee young occupants' safety and comfort during an emergency.

Lighting Type and Installation

Soft Lighting: Utilize soft lighting options to prevent eye strain, especially for children. LED lights with dimmable features could be a great choice for adjusting the brightness according to the time of day and the occupants' comfort.

Secure Installations: Ensure that all lighting fixtures are securely installed and recessed into the ceiling or walls, where they cannot be easily reached or tampered with by children.

Diffused Lighting: Install diffused lighting fixtures to prevent harsh glares that can be uncomfortable or even harmful to children's sensitive eyes.

Emergency Lighting

Battery-Powered Lights: Incorporate battery-powered emergency lights that can automatically turn on in case of power failures, providing a continuous source of illumination.

Night Lights: Plug-in night lights provide gentle illumination during the night, comforting children and preventing accidents in the dark.

Control Systems

Remote Controls: Integrate remote-controlled lighting systems so that the lighting can be adjusted without physical contact, preventing potential hazards with switches and wiring.

Childproof Switches: If switches are to be used, they should be childproof, meaning they should be installed at a height unreachable by young children and have safety covers to prevent mishaps.

Safety Measures

No Exposed Wires: To prevent potential electrical hazards, make sure that there are no exposed wires that children might trip over or pull on.

Heat-Resistant Covers: Employ heat-resistant covers on lighting fixtures to prevent burns in case a child comes in contact with the light source.

Notes:

Panic/Safe Room
Infant/Non-mobile: (Birth - 6 months)
Infant crawl/roll: (5 months - 1 year)
→ **Toddler/Pre-school: (1 year - 4 years)**
→ **School-age: (5 years - 6+ years)**

Educate and Support Children

Helping a child to deal with the potentially distressing experience of being in a panic room involves both preparation before any emergency occurs and supportive actions during an actual event.

Preparation Phase

Age-appropriate Conversations: Start with age-appropriate conversations about the purpose of the panic room without instilling fear. Make sure to use language that they can understand and relate to.

Emergency Drills: Conduct regular emergency drills so that the children are familiar with the process and know exactly what to expect. Make it a routine yet non-threatening activity.

Safety Education: Teach them basic safety knowledge, such as how to use the intercom, when to use the panic buttons, and the importance of staying quiet during certain emergencies.

Comfort Items: Encourage them to choose a few comfort items (like a favorite toy or blanket) that can be kept in the panic room to provide a sense of security and familiarity.

During the Emergency

Stay Calm: As an adult, try to remain calm. Children often take cues from the adults around them, and your calm demeanor can help them stay calm as well.

Comforting Presence: Ensure that you offer a comforting presence through physical contact, such as hugs, holding hands, or reassuring pats on the back.

Distraction and Engagement: Engage them in quiet activities to distract them. This could be reading books, drawing, or playing with toys kept in the panic room.

Open Communication: Maintain a line of communication where they can express their fears or concerns and respond to them with reassurance and empathy.

Post Emergency Phase

Debriefing: After the event, have a gentle conversation with them about what happened, allowing them to express their feelings and thoughts.

Professional Support: If necessary, don't hesitate to seek professional support to help them process the event.

Notes:

Panic/Safe Room
Infant/Non-mobile: (Birth - 6 months)
Infant crawl/roll: (5 months - 1 year)
Toddler/Pre-school: (1 year - 4 years)
School-age: (5 years - 6+ years)

Practice

Drills: Regularly conduct drills with all family members, including children, so they know how to behave in the safe room during emergencies.

Escape Plan: Even in a safe room, there should be a way out in case of unforeseen circumstances. Ensure this escape route is childproofed to prevent unsupervised access but can be used with guidance during emergencies.

By combining security measures with childproofing techniques, a panic or safe room can be both a fortress against external threats and a safe haven for the family's youngest members. Regular reviews and updates to the safety protocols are essential.

► *Panic or safe rooms are designed to protect, but for toddlers they can feel more like cages. Enclosed spaces with reinforced doors can cause acute fear and anxiety. Sometimes triggering panic or dissociation. Young children may trip over emergency supplies, head-butt reinforced walls, or trap their fingers in door hinges. In the chaos of an actual crisis, a locked door can be terrifying if they can't quickly release it themselves.* ***That's why safe rooms meant for families must be intentionally child-safe, equipped with simple exits, soft edges, and comforting input from caregivers.***

|Ch. 17| Prayer/Meditation Room

Introduction: In the journey of spiritual growth, a prayer and meditation room serves as a sanctuary, a place of solace and introspection. As we invite the younger members of our family into this sacred space, it becomes imperative to ensure their safety without compromising the room's spiritual essence. Childproofing such a room requires a delicate balance, ensuring that the space remains conducive to spiritual practices and safe for curious little souls.

Testimonial: *It was a serene Sunday morning; the sun shone, and the birds sang melodious tunes. Our prayer room, usually a sanctuary of peace and tranquility, was transformed into a playground for Lily's boundless imagination. Lily has a penchant for turning the most serene places into stages for her fun adventures.*

Lily decided that the prayer cushions were perfect steppingstones across a raging river (our polished oak floor), and the incense holder was a magic wand capable of conjuring dragons. In her fervor, she tripped on a meditation mat and took a tumble, the "magic wand" following suit and landed right on her little toe. Her laughter quickly turned to tears.

Looking back, I realize that a simple rearrangement could have prevented Lily's painful encounter with the "wand". Perhaps placing the fragile and potentially hazardous items on higher shelves, out of reach of tiny hands, would have been wise. Additionally, securing the mats to the floor to prevent slips and trips could have saved Lily from her fall.

As I nursed her little toe with a cold pack, amidst tears and sobs, she managed to say, "Mommy, the dragon got me, but I'll be brave next time." I couldn't help but laugh. Lesson learned: childproofing the prayer room has now become a priority in our household to ensure that future dragon-slaying adventures end with smiles rather than tears.

-Tonia W. (Mother of 1)

Prayer/Meditation Room
Infant/Non-mobile: (Birth - 6 months)
Infant crawl/roll: (5 months - 1 year)
→ **Toddler/Pre-school: (1 year - 4 years)**
→ **School-age: (5 years - 6+ years)**

Your Spiritual Haven

Childproofing a prayer and meditation room requires a fine balance between maintaining the space's sanctity and tranquility and ensuring it is safe and secure for children. First and foremost, any candles or incense should be kept out of the reach of children to prevent burns or fire hazards; consider using battery-operated candles or diffusers as safer alternatives. **Ensure that the room is equipped with soft furnishings that don't have sharp edges to prevent injuries from bumps and falls.**

If the room contains small items or decorative pieces, such as beads or statues, these should be securely placed on high shelves or in locked cabinets to prevent choking hazards. The flooring should be non-slip to avoid accidents, and any rugs or mats should be secure to prevent tripping. If windows are present, they should have secure locks and possibly window guards to prevent falls. Moreover, consider installing gentle lighting with protective covers to maintain a serene atmosphere without risking burns or electrical shocks.

When it comes to the storage of books, prayer materials, or meditation accessories, ensure they are stored in a manner that is both accessible and safe, avoiding any high stacks that might topple over. Lastly, educate children on the importance of the room, fostering a sense of respect and understanding, which will naturally encourage them to navigate the space with caution and reverence. This way, the prayer and meditation room can remain a haven of peace and spirituality, conducive to quiet reflection for both adults and children alike.

> ▶ *Meditation and prayer rooms are often seen as peaceful retreats. But for toddlers and preschoolers, even peaceful spaces can hide surprising dangers. Items like candles, incense, beaded decor, hanging fabrics, or electrical diffusers can quickly become choking, burn, or strangulation hazards. In fact, child safety experts say that most home injuries happen within just five minutes of unsupervised play, no matter how "calm" the room seems.* ***That's why even your quietest room deserves childproofing attention.***

|Ch. 18| Game/Recreation/Fitness Room

Introduction: In the heart of every home, the game, recreation, or fitness room pulsates with laughter, energy, and the spirit of family bonding. It's a sanctuary where fun meets fitness, children cultivate a love for physical activity, and cherished memories are created. However, amidst the joyous chaos, our guardians must weave a safety net that guards the youthful zest yet shields the tender limbs from potential hazards. This chapter is dedicated to helping you foster a space that nurtures both fun and safety in equal measure. From securing heavy equipment to creating zones that encourage safe play, we guide you in crafting a stimulating and secure environment. Let us embark on this mission to create a haven where little feet can run, little hands can explore, and little hearts can enjoy, all under the watchful eyes of safety and precaution.

Testimonial: *Our game room is filled with all sorts of toys, a mini basketball hoop, and even a toddler-friendly treadmill. Mason my little bundle of energy, decided that he was going to scale new heights—literally! He quickly climbed the treadmill and spread his arms, pretending to be a superhero. Of course, even superheroes stumble, and down he went.*

As I sat there, ice pack in hand, tending to his scraped knees , I couldn't help but laugh at the drama that unfolded. Looking back, a soft play mat around the treadmill and a good sturdy barrier would have turned that fall into a gentle landing. Lesson learned: the game room is getting a safety makeover so Mason can continue his superhero adventures with fewer bumps and more fun. Safety first, fellow parents - it's our job to keep the drama low and the fun high!

- Ava R (mother of 4)

Game/Recreation/ Fitness Room
Infant/Non-mobile: (Birth - 6 months)
Infant crawl/roll: (5 months - 1 year)
→ **Toddler/Pre-school: (1 year - 4 years)**
→ **School-age: (5 years - 6+ years)**

Game Console

Childproofing a game console is important to ensure the safety of children and prevent potential issues related to excessive screen time or access to age-inappropriate content.

Parental Controls: Most modern game consoles come with built-in parental control features. You can activate these controls to limit access to certain games, online content, or features that may not be suitable for children.

Set Time Limits: Use the console's time management features to set daily or weekly playtime limits. This helps prevent excessive screen time and encourages a healthy balance between gaming and other activities.

Secure Location: Place the game console in a safe location, such as a family room or living room, where you can easily monitor your child's gaming activities. Avoid placing it in a child's bedroom, as this may lead to unsupervised and excessive gaming.

Password Protection: Set up a secure password to access the console's settings and parental controls. Make sure the password is not easy for children to guess.

Age-Appropriate Games: Choose age-appropriate games for your child and review their content ratings. Avoid games with mature or violent content that may not be suitable for their age.

Physical Safety: Ensure that the game console and its accessories are safely stored and not in a position where they could be tripped over or damaged.

Wired Controllers: If the game console uses wired controllers, make sure the cords are artfully arranged and secured to prevent tripping hazards.

Internet Connectivity: If the game console has internet connectivity, be cautious about enabling online features. Monitor your child's online interactions and set up restrictions for online gaming and communication.

Regular Monitoring: Regularly check your child's gaming activities and progress in games. Engage in conversations about their gaming experiences and interests.

Educate Your Child: Teach your child about responsible gaming, including taking breaks, being respectful to others while playing online, and avoiding sharing personal information.

Consider Age-Appropriate Accessories: Some game consoles offer age-appropriate accessories, such as motion controllers designed for young children. These can provide a safer and more engaging gaming experience.

Parental Involvement: Play games with your child to learn about their interests and experiences. Playing together can be a fun way to bond and ensure that your child is engaged in age-appropriate content.

Regular Updates: Keep the game console's software and firmware updated to ensure it has the latest security features and improvements.

Remember that childproofing a game console goes beyond simply limiting access. Communicating openly with your child about gaming habits, setting boundaries, and encouraging responsible gaming practices is essential. By taking these steps, you can create a safe and enjoyable gaming environment for your child.

▶ *Game consoles may seem harmless, but they can cause real injuries even in preschoolers. Anecdotal cases of 'Nintendo thumb' (tendonitis and swelling) have appeared in young children after repetitive play. NEISS data shows* **roughly 6,800 gaming-related injuries yearly in kids under 10**. *Mostly to fingers, hands, and wrists, including strains and sprains. These findings highlight the need for younger gamers to take breaks, use proper posture, and limit extended play.*

Game/Recreation/ Fitness Room
Infant/Non-mobile: (Birth - 6 months)
Infant crawl/roll: (5 months - 1 year)
→ **Toddler/Pre-school: (1 year - 4 years)**
→ **School-age: (5 years - 6+ years)**

Pool Table

Childproofing a pool table is a crucial step in ensuring the safety of little ones while maintaining the sanity of the adults in the household. Not only is a pool table a hotspot for potential accidents but it can also be transformed into a child-friendly zone with a sprinkle of creativity and a dash of safety precautions.

Corner Cushions and Edge Guards

First and foremost, the sharp corners of a pool table are potential hazards that can cause injuries.

Install Corner Cushions: To prevent bumps and bruises, cushion the sharp corners of the pool table with corner guards. Opt for ones made of soft yet durable material to ensure longevity.

Edge Guards: Install edge guards along the sides of the pool table. These guards will protect little heads from getting hurt if they bump into the sides while playing around it.

Secure the Pool Balls

Children are naturally drawn to colorful and shiny pool balls. Pool Balls are heavy and can easily hurt little fingers. They can be quite a dangerous weapon if someone, especially a child, gets hit with one. When the pool table is not in use, store the balls in a locked cabinet or somewhere out of reach of children.

Safety Measures for Pool Cues

Pool cues can be heavy and may cause injuries if improperly handled. They can become a weapon in the hands of a small child.

Store Pool Cues Securely: Store the pool cues in a secure place, preferably a locked cabinet, to avoid children mishandling them.

Provide Alternative Cues: Offer children lightweight, harmless alternatives to play with, such as pool noodles or soft foam sticks, eliminating the risk of injuries.

Creating a Child-Friendly Zone

Creating a child-friendly zone around the pool table can prevent accidents and provide an engaging space for children.

Creating a Play Zone: Designate an area near the pool table where children can play with toys or engage in other activities. This will distract them from the pool table.

Educational Posters: Put up posters or charts near the pool table that encourage learning and creativity, shifting their focus from the pool table to the educational materials.

Turning a pool table area into a child-safe zone requires a detailed approach that focuses on cushioning sharp edges, securing pool equipment, and creating an engaging and safe environment around the pool table. Installing corner cushions and edge guards can prevent injuries from sharp corners and edges, which is the first step towards childproofing the area.

Securing the pool balls and cues in a safe storage area prevents the risk of choking hazards and other injuries. If the children want to play a game, providing them with safe alternatives like soft balls and foam sticks can prevent accidents while keeping them entertained.

Creating a child-friendly zone with a designated play area and educational posters can shift their focus from the pool table to more engaging and learning-focused activities. This way, the pool table area becomes not only safe but also a space for learning and fun for the children. Through detailed planning and implementation, the pool table area can be transformed into a haven of safety and entertainment for little ones.

► *According to Library of Medicine, from 2000 to 2020, U.S. emergency departments treated an **estimated 78,500 billiards-related injuries, including cuts, bruises, and strikes from pool cues.***

Game/Recreation/ Fitness Room
Infant/Non-mobile: (Birth - 6 months)
Infant crawl/roll: (5 months - 1 year)
→ **Toddler/Pre-school: (1 year - 4 years)**
→ **School-age: (5 years - 6+ years)**

Ping-Pong Table

Childproofing a ping-pong table requires a keen eye for potential hazards and a creative mind to maintain the game's fun while ensuring the safety of young children.

Secure the Table Structure

The physical structure of a ping-pong table can pose certain risks for kids, especially when it comes to the table's sharp edges and corners. Here are some steps to mitigate those risks:

Table Corners: Install soft corner protectors on the table's sharp corners to prevent injuries from accidental bumps and falls.

Stable Setup: Ensure that the table's setup is stable to prevent it from collapsing or tipping over. If necessary, add additional support.

Ping Pong Ball Safety

Ping-pong balls are small and lightweight, which could be a choking hazard for very young children.

Storage of Balls: Store the ping-pong balls in a secure place where young children cannot access them.

Supervised Play: Children should be allowed to play with the balls only under adult supervision to prevent choking hazards and other injuries.

Paddle Precautions

Though not extremely dangerous, the paddles could be used in a way that could cause injury.

Paddle Storage: Store paddles in a place that is not easily accessible to children to prevent potential misuse.

Softer Alternatives: Offer children softer alternatives to traditional paddles for play, such as foam paddles, which are smoother and lighter.

Creating a Safe Play Environment

The surroundings of the ping-pong table should also be considered when childproofing.

Safe Flooring: To prevent falls during play, ensure that the flooring around the table is non-slip. Consider adding a rubber mat or carpet with a good grip.

Clear Surrounding Area: Maintain a clear area around the table, removing any objects that kids might trip over while playing.

Childproofing a ping-pong table starts with securing the table structure itself, ensuring that sharp corners are covered with protectors to prevent injuries and that the table is stable and won't tip over. Additional support could be added to enhance stability, if necessary.

The next step involves taking precautions with the ping-pong balls, which could be a choking hazard for younger children due to their small size. Properly storing these balls in a secure place and allowing children to play with them only under adult supervision can help prevent any mishaps.

Furthermore, paddles should also be stored securely to prevent potential misuse by children. Offering them softer alternatives like foam paddles can be a safer option for play, reducing the risk of injuries.

Lastly, creating a safe play environment is crucial. This includes ensuring that the flooring around the table is non-slip to prevent falls and maintaining a clear area around the table to avoid tripping hazards. Through a meticulous approach, you can transform the ping-pong table area into a safe and enjoyable space for children to play and have fun, without any worries of potential hazards.

▶ *Ping-pong tables and accessories may look harmless, but they hide risks for toddlers. Even a quick game can cause repetitive strains in wrists and shoulders, while unstable folding tables have collapsed under light pressure, resulting in falls and bruises. Tiny ping-pong balls are also swallowing hazards for little ones.* ***In one U.S. recall, a table's sudden collapse injured four people.*** *That's why young children need close supervision, use age-appropriate gear, and safe, stabilized table setups, even for fun backyard rallies."* (Rethink Childhood)

Game/Recreation/ Fitness Room
Infant/Non-mobile: **(Birth - 6 months)**
Infant crawl/roll: **(5 months - 1 year)**
→ **Toddler/Pre-school: (1 year - 4 years)**
→ **School-age: (5 years - 6+ years)**

Foosball Safety

Childproofing a foosball table is vital to ensure the safety of younger family members while maintaining a playful environment. The table's moving parts and solid structure could potentially pose risks to children.

Securing Sharp Edges and Corners

Foosball tables often have sharp corners and edges, which can be hazardous for children.

Corner Protectors: Install soft corner protectors on the table's sharp corners to avoid injuries from accidental bumps.

Edge Guards: Attach edge guards along the sides of the table to prevent children from getting hurt when they run around the table.

Rod Safety Measures

The rods of a foosball table can cause injuries if not handled properly.

Rod Bumpers: Add rod bumpers to the ends of each rod to prevent them from protruding too much and causing injury.

Handle Grips: Install handle grips on the rods to ensure that children have a secure grip while playing and prevent hand injuries.

Rod Locks: If possible, install rod locks to prevent the rods from being pulled out entirely, which could be a potential hazard.

Ball Safety Precautions

The balls used in foosball are small and could be considered a choking hazard.

Secure Ball Storage: When not in use, store the foosball balls in a secure location to avoid choking hazards for smaller children.

Supervised Play: To prevent accidents, children should play with the balls only under the supervision of an adult.

Creating a Safe Play Environment

The area surrounding the foosball table should also be organized to promote children's safety.

Spacious Play Area: Ensure that there is enough space around the table for children to move freely without tripping or bumping into things.

Floor Safety: Implement non-slip flooring around the area to prevent falls and accidents during an energetic game.

Game/Recreation/ Fitness Room
Infant/Non-mobile: (Birth - 6 months)
Infant crawl/roll: (5 months - 1 year)
→ **Toddler/Pre-school: (1 year - 4 years)**
→ **School-age: (5 years - 6+ years)**

Dartboard Safety

Childproofing a dartboard area requires meticulous attention to detail to prevent potential accidents and injuries, especially considering the sharp objects involved.

Location and Height of the Dartboard
Ensuring that the dartboard is hung at an appropriate location and height can mitigate a lot of potential risks.

Height of Installation: Install the dartboard at a height that is not easily accessible to young children, preventing them from reaching the darts or the board itself.

Isolated Area: Place the dartboard in an isolated area where children do not frequently play, reducing the risk of accidents.

Safety Dart Options Considering that traditional darts have sharp tips, it might be worth exploring safer alternatives for children.

Magnetic Darts: Use magnetic darts, which are safer as they do not have sharp tips but still stick to the board.

Rubber-Tipped Darts: Another safe alternative is darts with rubber tips, which prevent injuries while maintaining the fun of the game.

Storage of Darts Safe and secure storage of darts is essential in preventing accidents.

Locked Storage: Store the darts in a locked cabinet or container to prevent children from accessing them unsupervised.

Out of Reach: Ensure that the storage area is out of reach for younger children, adding an extra layer of safety.

Supervised Play Ensuring that children only play with the dart set under supervision can prevent many potential accidents.

Adult Supervision: Always ensure that an adult is present when children are playing darts and guides them on safe practices.

Educate on Safe Play: Educate children on the potential hazards of playing with darts and emphasize the importance of safe play.

- *In the UK Paediatric Ocular Trauma Study (POTS2), **31.4% of blunt and sharp implement-related eye injuries in children occurred at home, often involving things like darts***

- *This means nearly 1 in 3 pediatric ocular traumas from sharp objects happen indoors. **Showing the hidden risk of a dartboard in the home.***

Game/Recreation/ Fitness Room
Infant/Non-mobile: (Birth - 6 months)
→ **Infant crawl/roll: (5 months - 1 year)**
→ **Toddler/Pre-school: (1 year - 4 years)**
→ **School-age: (5 years - 6+ years)**

Slot Machines

Childproofing a slot machine requires meticulous attention, given the electronic components, movable parts, and sometimes the coin or token systems involved.

Physical Components of the Slot Machine: The exterior and interior components of the slot machine can be fascinating for children.

  Secure the Machine: To prevent the slot machine from tipping over, secure it to the wall or a stable base.

  Cover Sharp Edges: Use corner protectors to cover any sharp edges or corners to prevent injuries to children.

Coin/Token Slot: The coin or token slot can be a curious spot for children. Here are ways to ensure their safety:

  Block the Slot: Utilize a cover or block to prevent children from inserting foreign objects or their fingers into the slot.

  Lockable Access: If possible, make the slot lockable to prevent children from accessing it.

Buttons and Levers: Buttons and levers are often the most attractive components for children.

  Disable Buttons: If possible, disable the buttons when the machine is not in use to prevent children from tampering with them.

Lever Safety: If the machine has a lever, consider installing a lever that can be removed when not in use.

Electrical Safety: Slot machines are electrical devices, and safeguarding children from electrical hazards is vital.

Cord Management: Ensure cords are appropriately managed, with no exposed wires that might pose a risk of electrical shocks.

Surge Protection: Use a surge protector to prevent electrical mishaps and to protect the machine.

Game/Recreation/ Fitness Room
Infant/Non-mobile: (Birth - 6 months)
Infant crawl/roll: (5 months - 1 year)
→ **Toddler/Pre-school: (1 year - 4 years)**
→ **School-age: (5 years - 6+ years)**

BOARDGAMES

Various elements must be addressed when childproofing board games to ensure safe and enjoyable playtime for children.

Game Pieces and Accessories: Most board games contain small pieces that could pose choking hazards.

Organized Storage: Store small pieces in containers with secure lids, which prevents young children from accessing them unsupervised.

Age-Appropriate Alternatives: Consider purchasing or creating age-appropriate versions of the game with larger, non-choke hazard pieces for young children to use.

Board and Game Surfaces: The board itself can have some areas of concern, primarily related to its corners and potential pinching points.

> **Corner Cushions:** Apply corner cushions to board game corners to prevent injuries from sharp points.
>
> **Smooth Edges:** Ensure that the board's edges are smooth and free of splinters or rough areas that could cause injuries.

Card Safety

> **Card Protectors:** Use card protectors to prevent young children from bending, tearing, or attempting to ingest parts of the cards.
>
> **Teaching Careful Handling:** Educate older children on carefully handling cards to prevent damage and potential hazards.

Game Storage: Proper storage of board games can prevent many hazards.

> **High Shelving:** Store board games on high shelves where young children cannot reach them without adult assistance.
>
> **Secure Storage:** Consider storing games, especially those with many small parts, in secure cabinets or containers with childproof locks.

Game/Recreation/ Fitness Room
Infant/Non-mobile: (Birth - 6 months)
Infant crawl/roll: (5 months - 1 year)
→ **Toddler/Pre-school: (1 year - 4 years)**
→ **School-age: (5 years - 6+ years)**

Popcorn Maker

Hot Surfaces

Large popcorn makers often have surfaces that can get quite hot. To prevent burns:

Safety Gates: Install safety gates to keep children at a safe distance from the popcorn maker.

Heat-Resistant Covers: Use heat-resistant covers on handles and other parts that may become hot to the touch.

Electrical Concerns

Electrical components can be hazardous for children.

Safety Plugs: Use safety plugs to cover any unused electrical outlets on the popcorn maker.

Cord Management: Ensure cords are properly managed, avoiding any hanging parts that children could pull or get tangled in.

Moving Parts

Moving parts in a popcorn maker can pose a risk of injury.

Guard Rails: Install guard rails or screens around the moving parts to prevent children from sticking their hands or fingers in them.

Locking Mechanisms: Use locking mechanisms to prevent children from being able to open doors or lids where there are moving parts.

Cleaning Agents

Cleaning agents used to clean popcorn makers can be toxic.

Non-Toxic Cleaners: Use only non-toxic cleaners to clean the popcorn maker, avoiding any potential poisoning hazards.

Secure Storage: Ensure cleaning agents are stored in a secure location that is out of reach of children.

► *Although there's no national tally, only one confirmed incident has been documented: **a 21-month-old child suffered serious burns** on his thigh when a kernel from a domestic popcorn machine 'missile-popped' into his leg. It highlights how seemingly innocuous joys can hide unsuspected hazards."*

Game/Recreation/ Fitness Room
Infant/Non-mobile: (Birth - 6 months)
Infant crawl/roll: (5 months - 1 year)
→ **Toddler/Pre-school: (1 year - 4 years)**
→ **School-age: (5 years - 6+ years)**

Bar or Wet Bar

Childproofing a bar or wet bar area in your home is essential to ensure the safety of young children. Here, we will focus on various aspects, including securing alcoholic beverages, glassware, sharp utensils, and potential spill areas. Here's how to proceed in a detail-oriented manner.

Alcohol and Beverage Service: Alcohol and other beverages should be stored securely to prevent children from accessing them.

Lockable Cabinets: Install cabinets that can be locked to store alcoholic beverages.

Out-of-Reach Shelves: Utilize shelves that are out of the reach of children for storing liquors and other beverages.

Glassware and Utensils: Glassware and utensils can be hazardous if accessible to children.

Secure Storage: Store glassware and sharp utensils in secure cabinets that are either locked or equipped with childproof latches.

Plastic Alternatives: Consider using plastic alternatives to glassware to prevent breakage and related injuries.

Spills and Wet Areas: Spills and wet areas can be slipping hazards.

Non-Slip Mats: Use non-slip mats in areas where spills are likely to occur.

Prompt Clean-Up: Ensure prompt clean-up of any spills to prevent slipping and falling accidents.

Electrical Appliances: Wet bars can contain small appliances, which can be hazardous. Here's how to secure them:

Safety Covers: Use safety covers on any electrical outlets to prevent electrocution hazards.

Appliance Locks: Use appliance locks to prevent children from being able to operate appliances.

Game/Recreation/ Fitness Room
Infant/Non-mobile: (Birth - 6 months)
Infant crawl/roll: (5 months - 1 year)
→ **Toddler/Pre-school: (1 year - 4 years)**
→ **School-age: (5 years - 6+ years)**

Fitness Room Safety

Childproofing a home fitness room demands meticulous planning and careful implementation. A fitness room usually contains various equipment and accessories that could potentially be hazardous to children. Here, we will focus on securing heavy equipment, managing loose accessories, and ensuring the safety of flooring and electrical components.

Safety Locks: Install safety locks on treadmills and other machines to prevent children from operating them.

Equipment Positioning: Ensure heavy equipment is positioned against the wall to prevent children from getting behind them and risking injury.

Loose accessories like dumbbells and resistance bands can be hazards.

Secure Storage: Store all loose accessories in cabinets equipped with childproof locks to prevent access.

Organize Wisely: Keep smaller accessories in bins or baskets out of children's reach.

Exercise Resistance Bands: Exercise bands are stretchy and fun to pull—but dangerous when they snap back.

Store the bands in a high, locked cabinet when not in use.

Opt for bands with safety covers or built-in safety cords.

Use a storage rack that makes them less accessible to children.

Exercise Ball

Store it high or in a closet: Keep exercise balls in a high closet or invest in a rack to suspend them off the ground. If the ball is out of reach, it's out of play.

Use a deflation plug: If the exercise ball isn't in use, deflate it! It's an easy way to remove the temptation entirely.

Create a designated play area: Sometimes, letting your child play with a small, safe ball in a controlled area distracts them from the exercise ball. "This is mommy's bouncy ball, and you get this fun one!"

Game/Recreation/ Fitness Room
Infant/Non-mobile: (Birth - 6 months)
Infant crawl/roll: (5 months - 1 year)
→ **Toddler/Pre-school: (1 year - 4 years)**
→ **School-age: (5 years - 6+ years)**

Fitness Room Flooring and Electrical Components

The flooring and electrical components in a fitness room must also be secured.

Soft Flooring: Install soft flooring such as foam mats to prevent injuries from falls.

Outlet Covers: Use safety outlet covers to prevent children from inserting objects or fingers into electrical outlets.

Childproofing a home fitness room involves a detailed strategy that encompasses various aspects. One critical area to address is the presence of heavy equipment, such as treadmills and weight machines, which could pose a significant danger to children. **Installing safety locks on these machines will prevent children from being able to operate them,** thus averting potential accidents. Moreover, positioning such heavy equipment against the wall will deter children from going behind them, minimizing the risk of injury.

Furthermore, loose accessories common in fitness rooms, like dumbbells and resistance bands, can be hazardous to children. Establishing secure storage systems for these accessories is essential. **Cabinets equipped with childproof locks** can effectively prevent children from accessing these potentially dangerous items. Additionally, maintaining a high degree of organization by storing smaller accessories in bins or baskets, preferably out of children's reach, can be another safety layer.

The safety of flooring and electrical components within the fitness room is also a pivotal concern.

Installing soft flooring options such as foam mats can be instrumental in preventing injuries resulting from falls. Also, the use of safety outlet covers can prevent curious children from inserting objects or their fingers into electrical outlets, thus averting potential electrocution hazards.

Implementing these detail-oriented strategies can transform your home fitness room into a space that is safe for children and conducive for adults to focus on their fitness goals, fostering a safe and healthy environment for the entire family.

Notes:

▶ *U.S. National Electronic Injury Surveillance System (1990–2008) recorded an average of **12,714 annual injuries** to children (0–18) involving home exercise equipment. **71%** of these were in kids under 10, meaning roughly **9,000 injuries per year in preschool-aged children.***

▶ *The **CPSC reports approximately 8,700 children under age 5**, and an additional 16,500 children aged 5–14, are treated yearly in U.S. emergency rooms for exercise-equipment injuries.*

|Ch. 19| Theater/Entertainment Room

Introduction: Childproofing a home theater or entertainment room is essential to keep little ones safe while allowing the family to enjoy movies, music, and other entertainment without worry. From securing heavy furniture and electronics to managing cords and small components, here's a detail-oriented plan to make your entertainment room child-friendly.

Testimonial: *We were all watching a movie, and I didn't notice my child trying to climb the bookshelf where we kept our DVDs. Suddenly, the shelf wobbled, and a speaker fell, narrowly missing him. We were all shaken by how close he had come to being hurt. Looking back, it was preventable. We should have secured the furniture to the wall with anti-tip brackets and kept the DVDs out of his reach to remove the temptation. We've since taken childproofing more seriously, installing furniture anchors and keeping attractive items like DVDs out of sight. I encourage other parents to do the same childproofing isn't just about making your home safer, it's about creating peace of mind, and knowing your kids can explore safely.*

-Chris P (father of 3)

Theater/Entertainment Room
Infant/Non-mobile: (Birth - 6 months)
Infant crawl/roll: (5 months - 1 year)
→ **Toddler/Pre-school: (1 year - 4 years)**
→ **School-age: (5 years - 6+ years)**

Heavy Furniture and Electronics

The Home Theater Room: This type of room typically contains heavy furniture and electronic appliances that can cause injuries if not secured properly. Here's how you can ensure safety:

When it comes to creating a fun and cozy home theater or entertainment room, safety should always be top of mind, especially when little ones are around. One of the biggest concerns is heavy furniture and electronic appliances that can tip over and hurt someone. But don't worry, we've got some super helpful solutions! Using furniture anchors to secure big items like shelves and cabinets to the walls can give you peace of mind. And, TV straps can keep those flat-screen TVs safe and sound. Plus, corner protectors on sharp furniture edges can help prevent bumps and boo-boos.

Now, let's talk about cords and wires - they can be a real trip hazard! A cord management system can keep everything tidy and secure, which is a big win for safety. And, safety outlet covers can keep curious kids from poking around in electrical outlets. We can also stash power strips in cord management boxes to keep little hands away from them.

Those tiny remote batteries and media disks can be a choking hazard, so let's keep them out of reach! Storing remote controls in a closed cabinet or a holder up high can be a great idea. And, closed media storage units can keep CDs and DVDs safe from little ones. They may hold nostalgic memories.

By taking these simple steps, we can create a safe and happy space for our whole family to enjoy. So, let's get started and make our home theater a place where everyone can relax and have fun - safely!

Furniture Anchors: Use furniture anchors to secure heavy furniture to the walls to prevent tipping. (For more details refer to Living Room for **pg. 31**)

TV Straps: Secure flat-screen TVs with anti-tip straps/metal cords to prevent them from falling over.

Corner Protectors: Install corner protectors on sharp furniture edges to prevent injuries from bumps and falls. (For more details refer to living room table edges **pg. 24**)

Cords and Wires: Cords and wires can be tripping hazards or pose strangulation risks.

Cord Management: Use cord management systems to bundle and secure loose wires and cords. (For more details refer to Living Room for details **pg. 53**)

Outlet Covers: Install safety outlet covers to prevent children from playing with electrical outlets. (For more details refer to Living Room for details **pg. 51**)

Hide Power Strips: Hide power strips in cord management boxes to prevent children from accessing them. (For more details refer to Living Room **pg. 54**)

Small Components

Remote Control Storage: Store remote controls in a closed cabinet or container out of the reach of children.

Media Storage: Use closed media storage units to prevent children from accessing CDs, DVDs, and other small items.

Notes:

Theater/Entertainment Room
Infant/Non-mobile: (Birth - 6 months)
Infant crawl/roll: (5 months - 1 year)
→ **Toddler/Pre-school: (1 year - 4 years)**
→ **School-age: (5 years - 6+ years)**

Projector TVs

Childproofing a projector TV is essential to prevent accidents and ensure both the safety of your child and the longevity of the device. One of the most effective ways to childproof a projector is **by mounting it on the ceiling or a high shelf**, keeping it out of reach of curious hands. Securing all cables and wires with cord covers or organizers helps eliminate tripping hazards and prevents children from pulling on them. If your projector uses a screen, make sure it is securely mounted or rollable so that it can be stored away when not in use.

Protecting the projector's lens with a cover or using a model with a built-in protective casing can prevent fingerprints and potential damage. If the projector is placed on a table or stand, it should be on a sturdy surface to prevent tipping Anchor to wall!

- ► *11,500 emergency room visits per year in the U.S. involve children injured by furniture or TV tip-overs. 70% of those are kids under age 6, with peak risk at around 2 years old.*

- ► *On average, a child is treated in the ER **every 46 minutes** due to tip-overs* (Consumer report)

- ► *Tragically, **about one child dies every 2–3 weeks** from a television tip-over in the U.S.* (ABC News)

|Ch. 20| Hobby/Scrapbooking/ Sewing Room

Introduction: In the vibrant world of hobby rooms, where creativity knows no bounds, and every corner is a treasure trove of artistic potential, safeguarding our little artists becomes paramount. This chapter is dedicated to transforming your hobby, scrapbooking, or sewing room into a haven where creativity and safety coexist harmoniously. From organizing an enticing yet secure space for children to explore their artistic inclinations to selecting child-friendly tools and materials, we will guide you through comprehensive strategies to foster their creativity while keeping those precious fingers and curious minds safe. Dive into this chapter to craft a nurturing environment where your child's imagination can soar, free from the worries of potential mishaps, allowing the seeds of creativity to blossom safely and splendidly.

Testimonial: *The vibrant chaos of the hobby room, where creativity blossoms and where, unfortunately, my little artist had her first art-related mishap. Imagine a room sprinkled with colorful pieces of scrapbook papers, a kaleidoscope of threads, and the ever-so-enticing sparkle of sequins and glitter. It's a paradise for any budding artist, including my little one, who has an affinity for bright and shiny things.*

On this particular day, my daughter decided to embark on a secret mission to create the "world's most beautiful dress" for her teddy bear. Armed with an unyielding determination and a pair of scissors that were not so child-friendly, she started snipping away at her favorite piece of fabric. As her grand design was taking shape, those sharp scissors slipped and nipped her tiny finger. A yelp of surprise was followed by a river of tears.

As I rushed to her side, I couldn't help but feel a pang of guilt. My little seamstress was only trying to bring a sprinkle of beauty into the world, a task that should never end in tears. I scooped her up, her finger now adorned with a princess band-aid, and we vowed to make the hobby room a safer place for little creators.

Looking back, I realize that a simple drawer with child-safe crafting supplies could have saved the day. Scissors with rounded tips, non-toxic glues, and perhaps a little crafting table just her size would have been the perfect setup for her artistic endeavors.

Fellow parents let's not curb the enthusiasm of our little creators. Instead, create a space where their imagination can soar without the fear of boo-boos. After all, every artist deserves a safe canvas, and every parent deserves to see their child's creations come to life without any hiccups, or in our case, little nicks and cuts!

-Samantha R. (Mother of 3)

Hobby/Scrap booking/Sewing Room
Infant/Non-mobile: (Birth - 6 months)
Infant crawl/roll: (5 months - 1 year)
→ **Toddler/Pre-school: (1 year - 4 years)**
→ **School-age: (5 years - 6+ years)**

Tools and Sharp Objects

Each year, **more than 50,000 children** are treated for injuries related to arts and crafts supplies like scissors, glue guns, and sharp tools. (Source: National Electronic Injury Surveillance System (NEISS) – CDC)

Tool Storage: Store all sharp tools, such as scissors, needles, and rotary cutters, in locked drawers or cabinets.

Safety Caps: Use safety caps on sharp tools to prevent injuries.

Table Corners: Install soft corner protectors on tables to prevent injuries from sharp edges.

Small Accessories: Small accessories like beads, buttons, and pins can be choking hazards.

Organized Storage: Use containers with secure lids to store small accessories like beads and buttons.

High Shelving: Store items that could be a choking hazard on high shelves out of reach of children.

Secure Trash Bins: Ensure trash bins are secured to prevent children from accessing discarded items.

Safe and Healthy Environment: Maintaining a safe environment involves considering ventilation and chemicals.

Ventilation: Ensure proper ventilation in the room to prevent inhalation of fumes from glues and markers.

Chemical Storage: Store potentially harmful chemicals in locked cabinets, like certain glues and paints.

Safe Flooring: Consider installing soft flooring to prevent injuries from falls.

|Ch. 21| Unfinished Basement Furnace/Water Heater

Introduction: In the hidden corners of our homes, where the furnace hums and the water heater stands sentinel, lies an area often overlooked in the childproofing process - the unfinished basement. This chapter is your guiding light in transforming this space, often brimming with potential hazards, into a secure zone that keeps the little adventurers at bay. From securing heavy appliances and shielding hot surfaces to creating barriers around potentially dangerous zones, we will walk you through meticulous steps to ensure safety without compromising the functionality of these vital home systems. As you turn the pages, you'll find insightful tips and innovative solutions that will help you foster a home where curiosity can flourish without fear and where every nook and cranny echoes with the laughter of safe and happy children.

Testimonial: *Our basement, full of storage and utilities, became Griffin's mystical cave one day. Armed with his toy sword, he transformed into a knight ready to slay the "dragons," which were, in reality, our furnace and water heater. But in his quest, he got a little too close to the furnace and ended up with a minor burn on his arm. My heart dropped; I should have anticipated that Griffin's wild imagination would turn even the basement into a battleground.*

Since that day, we've childproofed the basement with gates and barriers, and we've shielded the furnace to keep our little knight safe. Now, the dragons in his stories are friends, and the furnace is just another gentle giant in his world of make-believe. Fellow parents, let our experience be a reminder: always childproof, even the most unexpected corners of your home. Because with kids, adventure is everywhere!

-Chris P. (Father of 3)

Unfinished Basement/Furnace/Water Heater
Infant/Non-mobile: (Birth - 6 months)
Infant crawl/roll: (5 months - 1 year)
Toddler/Pre-school: (1 year - 4 years)
→ **School-age: (5 years - 6+ years)**

Window Fire Escapes

Childproofing a window fire escape demands meticulous attention, as it involves maintaining a delicate balance between safety and accessibility. Here's a structured guide on how to effectively childproof a window fire escape without compromising its intended functionality.

Window Locks and Guards: Secure the windows but ensure they can be easily opened in case of an emergency.

- **Window Guards:** Install window guards that prevent children from falling but can be quickly released by an adult in case of an emergency.

- **Locks and Latches:** Use child-safe locks and latches that are sturdy enough to prevent falls but can be quickly opened by adults.

- **Window Alarms:** Install window alarms to be alerted if the window is opened unexpectedly.

Education and Drills: Education about the importance and proper use of the fire escape is vital. Here's how you can implement this:

- **Fire Safety Education:** Educate children on the importance of the fire escape and that it is not a play area.

- **Emergency Drills:** Conduct regular emergency drills with children to safely practice using the fire escape.

- **Emergency Numbers:** Teach children about emergency numbers and how to use them.

Accessible Tools: Ensure that tools required during an emergency are accessible and easy to use.

- **Fire Escape Ladder:** Store a fire escape ladder near the window and teach adults and older children how to use it properly.

- **Emergency Toolkit:** Keep an emergency toolkit nearby, including necessary items like a flashlight, whistle, and first-aid kit.

- **Escape Plan:** Develop a clear escape plan and ensure that all family members are familiar with it.

Notes:

Unfinished Basement/Furnace/Water Heater
→ Infant/Non-mobile: (Birth - 6 months)
→ Infant crawl/roll: (5 months - 1 year)
→ Toddler/Pre-school: (1 year - 4 years)
→ School-age: (5 years - 6+ years)

Uncovered Doors and Vents

Keeping the doors and vents in an unfinished basement uncovered can indeed have some benefits, especially when considering ventilation, moisture control, and easy access to various utilities.

Ventilation and Air Circulation

Improved Airflow: Leaving vents uncovered can facilitate better airflow, which can help reduce the buildup of stale or moist air, which is often a problem in basements.

Preventing Mold: Increased airflow can also help prevent mold and mildew growth, which thrive in damp, stagnant environments.

Easy Access to Utilities

Quick Access: Not having door covers allows for fast and easy access to utilities and storage areas, which is often necessary in a basement where many home utilities are located.

Safety: In case of emergencies, such as gas or water leaks, having uncovered doors can facilitate a quicker response time as you can easily spot and address the issue.

Cost Effectiveness

Saving Money: Leaving the basement unfinished, including not adding door or vent covers, can save a considerable amount of money, which might be preferable if the basement is primarily used for storage or utilities.

Flexibility: Without permanent fixtures, you retain the flexibility to make changes or upgrades to the basement layout without the additional cost of removing and replacing doors and vents.

► *Unfinished basements with exposed furnaces and water heaters can hide serious burn hazards. In the U.S. alone,* **nearly 3,800 scald injuries from hot water are treated annually.** *Often near water heater systems, with* **over 30 deaths.** *Altogether,* **about 435 children per day end up in emergency rooms** *due to burns from hot equipment, making supervision and protective barriers around utility zones essential.* (The American Burn Association (ameriburn.org) and the CDC)

Unfinished Basement/Furnace/Water Heater
Infant/Non-mobile: (Birth - 6 months)
Infant crawl/roll: (5 months - 1 year)
→ **Toddler/Pre-school: (1 year - 4 years)**
→ **School-age: (5 years - 6+ years)**

Water Heater Area

Each year, **more than 1,000 children** are injured by hot water heaters, including scald burns and electrical hazards. (Source: U.S. Consumer Product Safety Commission (CPSC) - Water Heater Safety) Childproofing the water heater area in an unfinished basement requires careful planning to ensure safety while maintaining the space's functionality.

Creating a Barrier

Safety Gates: To restrict access, install safety gates around the water heater area. These gates should be sturdy and tall enough that a child cannot climb over them.

Locked Doors: If the water heater is enclosed, ensure that the door is equipped with a child-proof lock to prevent unauthorized access.

Clear Perimeter: Maintain a clear perimeter around the water heater to prevent children from hiding or playing around it.

Temperature Settings

Lower the Temperature: To prevent scalding accidents, adjust the water heater's temperature to below 120°F (48.9°C).

Thermal Insulation: Install thermal insulation around the water heater to prevent burns from the hot surface.

Securing Components and Utilities

Anchor the Water Heater: Anchor the water heater to the wall to prevent it from tipping over in case a child manages to reach it.

Cover Pipes: Cover exposed pipes with insulation to prevent burns.

Secure Gas Lines: If the water heater is gas-powered, ensure that gas lines are secured and not accessible to children.

Emergency Protocols

Install Smoke and CO Detectors: Install smoke and carbon monoxide detectors near the water heater to alert you to potential dangers.

Emergency Shut-Off Instructions: Post clear instructions on how to shut off the water heater in an emergency.

First-Aid Kit: Keep a first-aid kit nearby to treat minor injuries immediately.

Childproofing the water heater in an unfinished basement demands foresight and meticulousness. Creating a barrier around the water heater area is essential. Installing safety gates that are sturdy and high enough to prevent a child from climbing over them can offer a robust first line of defense. Fitting the door with a child-proof lock can further restrict unauthorized access if the water heater is housed within an enclosure. Maintaining a clear perimeter around the water heater is also prudent to prevent children from playing or hiding in the vicinity.

Adjusting the settings of the water heater is vital. Lowering the temperature to below 120°F (48.9°C) can prevent potential scalding incidents. Installing thermal insulation around the water heater can also prevent burns from accidental contact with the hot surface.

In addition, securing the components and utilities is crucial. **Anchoring the water heater to the wall** can prevent it from tipping over, which would be dangerous if a child managed to access the area. Covering exposed pipes with insulation can also prevent burns. If the water heater operates on gas, securing gas lines to make them inaccessible to children is vital.

Establishing emergency protocols is an important aspect of childproofing. This involves installing smoke and carbon monoxide detectors near the water heater to provide alerts in case of potential dangers. Furthermore, implementing clear instructions on how to shut off the water heater in emergencies and keeping a first-aid kit nearby to address minor injuries immediately are important measures.

Through these detailed steps, you can effectively childproof the water heater area in an unfinished basement, ensuring safety without compromising the space's functional aspects.

Notes:

Unfinished Basement/Furnace/ Water Heater
→ **Infant/Non-mobile: (Birth - 6 months)**
→ **Infant crawl/roll: (5 months - 1 year)**
→ **Toddler/Pre-school: (1 year - 4 years)**
→ **School-age: (5 years - 6+ years)**

Furnace Concerns

Childproofing the furnace area in an unfinished basement is crucial, especially since furnaces can pose significant risks due to their heat and associated components.

Creating a Secure Barrier

Safety Gates: Erect sturdy, childproof gates around the furnace area. Ensure these gates are tall enough so children cannot climb over them.

Locked Doors: Use a door with a childproof lock if the furnace is in a specific room or closet.

Fence or Plexiglass Barrier: As an added measure, you can enclose the furnace within a fenced area or use a plexiglass barrier.

Temperature and Burn Prevention

Guard Hot Surfaces: Use heat-resistant guards or barriers around hot surfaces to prevent direct contact.

Insulate Exposed Pipes: Furnaces often have hot water pipes running from them. Ensure they are insulated to prevent burns upon contact.

Avoiding Fire Hazards

Keep Flammables Away: Ensure no flammable materials or liquids are stored near the furnace.

Regular Maintenance: Regularly maintain the furnace to prevent malfunctions that could lead to fires.

Securing Components and Utilities

Secure Gas Lines: If gas lines are present, ensure they are safely out of reach and secured to prevent tampering.

Filter Access: Filters might be of interest to kids. Ensure they can't be easily removed or tampered with.

Cord Management: Bundle and secure any electrical cords associated with the furnace, keeping them out of reach.

Air Quality

Carbon Monoxide Detector: Install a carbon monoxide detector near the furnace area to alert you of any leaks or malfunctions.

Proper Ventilation: Ensure the furnace area is well-ventilated, preventing the build-up of harmful gases.

Educating Children

Hazard Awareness: As kids grow, teach them about the dangers associated with the furnace. Making them aware can sometimes be the best deterrent.

While essential for the comfort of our homes, a furnace can be a danger zone in an unfinished basement, especially for curious children. Start by establishing a clear barrier using safety gates or doors with childproof locks, ensuring children cannot access the furnace area. For additional security and visibility, consider using a plexiglass barrier.

Hot surfaces are a significant concern. Using heat-resistant guards or barriers can prevent accidental burns. Likewise, insulate any exposed hot water pipes associated with the furnace.

A major concern with furnaces is the risk of fire. Ensure the area is free of any flammable materials and undergo regular maintenance checks to ensure the furnace functions correctly. If your furnace operates on gas, secure the gas lines and ensure they are out of a child's reach. Cords should also be managed effectively to prevent tripping or tampering hazards.

Air quality is a silent concern. Furnaces can sometimes leak carbon monoxide, a deadly gas. Install detectors to alert you to any leaks. Proper ventilation also prevents harmful gases from accumulating.

Finally, educate your children about the furnace's risks as they grow. This awareness can act as a deterrent, as kids often avoid things they know are dangerous.

Unfinished Basement/Furnace/ Water Heater
→ Infant/Non-mobile: (Birth - 6 months)
→ Infant crawl/roll: (5 months - 1 year)
→ Toddler/Pre-school: (1 year - 4 years)
→ School-age: (5 years - 6+ years)

Provide Good Ventilation

Childproofing an unfinished basement while ensuring good ventilation is a meticulous process that aims to create a safe and healthy environment for children.

Install Quality Ventilation Systems

Air Purifiers: Set up air purifiers to remove impurities and allergens.

Dehumidifiers: Utilize dehumidifiers to control humidity levels and prevent mold growth.

Exhaust Fans: Install exhaust fans to eliminate stale air and bring in fresh air.

Open Windows

Window Guards: Install window guards to prevent children from falling or climbing out.

Window Screens: Incorporate window screens to keep insects and debris out.

Natural Ventilation

Vented Doors: Use vented doors to facilitate air circulation.

Ventilation Grills: Install ventilation grills at strategic points to enhance airflow.

Chemical and Fume Control

Chemical Storage: Store any chemicals, paints, or solvents in a secured cabinet, inaccessible to children.

Safety Latches: Install safety latches on storage cabinets to prevent children from accessing potentially harmful substances.

Heating and Cooling Systems

HVAC Maintenance: Regular maintenance of heating and cooling systems to ensure they function properly and do not emit harmful substances.

Carbon Monoxide Detectors: Install carbon monoxide detectors to alert in case of gas leaks or harmful emissions.

Education and Supervision

Education: Educate children about the importance of not playing near windows or ventilation systems.

Supervision: Always supervise children when they are in the basement to prevent accidents.

|Ch. 22| Rooftop Terrace

Introduction: In the bustling embrace of urban living, a rooftop terrace stands as a serene oasis, offering a breath of fresh air and a slice of the sky amidst concrete jungles. Yet, as parents, we must remember that this elevated paradise comes with its own set of challenges when it comes to ensuring the safety of our little explorers. This chapter delves deep into the nuances of childproofing your rooftop terrace, transforming it into a haven where your children can play and explore without any looming dangers. From securing the railings to creating a safe play zone, we guide you in crafting a space that combines safety with the joyous freedom a rooftop terrace can provide. Let's embark on this journey of creating a secure yet enchanting kingdom in the sky for our little ones, where adventures await at every corner, sans the perils.

Testimonial: *The rooftop terrace, our little slice of heaven in the bustling city, turned into the scene of a mini heart attack for me as a parent. It was a breezy afternoon, and my little adventurer, Bella, decided it was the perfect setting for her to become a "Sky Princess." With my favorite scarf as her cape, she was ready to conquer her lofty kingdom.*

Her journey met a hiccup. In her excitement, she didn't notice the uneven tile near the flowerpots. With a grand swoosh of her cape, she tripped and took a tumble, resulting in a scraped knee, bruised elbows and a few tears. My heart raced as I rushed to her side, cursing myself for not foreseeing the potential hazards that lay in her path.

Reflecting on the incident, I realized that a few preventative measures could have averted Bella's fall from grace. Ensuring that the flooring on the terrace was even and free of potential tripping hazards would have been a step in the right direction. Setting up a designated play area, away from the edges and potential hazards, could have provided a safer environment for my Princess to rule over her kingdom.

As I cuddled her, nursing her wounded knee, she declared, "Mommy, even Sky Princesses fall sometimes, but they always get up." Her resilience made me smile, but I knew it was time to make our rooftop terrace safer for my little Sky Princess. With a few adjustments, Bella can rule her sky kingdom with all the grace and safety a Sky Princess deserves.

-Jennifer Y. (Mother of 6)

Rooftop Terrace
Infant/Non-mobile: (Birth - 6 months)
Infant crawl/roll: (5 months - 1 year)
→ **Toddler/Pre-school: (1 year - 4 years)**
→ **School-age: (5 years - 6+ years)**

Railing Concerns

High Railings: Ensure railings are at least 4 feet high, if not higher. This height is typically above the reach of most toddlers and young children.

Dense Railings: The spaces between the railings should be less than 4 inches. This prevents children from attempting to squeeze through or getting limbs stuck.

Reinforced Materials: Opt for railings made of sturdy materials like wrought iron or thick wood. Regularly inspect for wear, rust, or rot.

Rooftop Terrace
Infant/Non-mobile: (Birth - 6 months)
Infant crawl/roll: (5 months - 1 year)
→ **Toddler/Pre-school: (1 year - 4 years)**
→ **School-age: (5 years - 6+ years)**

Anti-Climbing

Smooth Railings: Railings should be vertical and smooth, with no horizontal bars or decorative elements that can act as footholds.

Furniture Positioning: Place furniture, especially the climbable types, centrally and away from the edges. This reduces the temptation for children to climb and reach the railings.

Rooftop Terrace
Infant/Non-mobile: (Birth - 6 months)
Infant crawl/roll: (5 months - 1 year)
→ **Toddler/Pre-school: (1 year - 4 years)**
→ **School-age: (5 years - 6+ years**

Floor Concerns

Non-slip Surface: Choose tiles with a rough texture or specifically designed outdoor non-slip tiles. Wet conditions can make surfaces slippery, increasing the risk of falls.

Cushioned Areas: Consider areas with outdoor play mats or cushioned tiles, especially if children play there frequently.

Splinters and Nails: Sand down those splinters and remove those nails that can be reached.

Rooftop Terrace
Infant/Non-mobile: (Birth - 6 months)
Infant crawl/roll: (5 months - 1 year)
→ **Toddler/Pre-school: (1 year - 4 years)**
→ **School-age: (5 years - 6+ years)**

Limit Roof Access

High Locks: Install locks or latches high up on the access doors, out of children's reach.

Alarm Systems: Consider installing alarms that notify you when the door to the terrace is opened.

Rooftop Terrace
Infant/Non-mobile: (Birth - 6 months)
Infant crawl/roll: (5 months - 1 year)
→ **Toddler/Pre-school: (1 year - 4 years)**
→ **School-age: (5 years - 6+ years)**

Sturdy and Stable Furniture

Heavy-Duty Furniture: Choose heavy furniture to prevent tipping over but not too hard or rigid, which could cause injury.

Low-Centered Gravity: Furniture with a low center of gravity will be less likely to tip over if a child attempts to climb on it.

Non-Tipping Chairs: Choose chairs that have a broad base to prevent tipping, avoiding high stools or chairs that can easily tip over.

Safety Features: Furniture with rounded edges and non-toxic finishes are preferable. Avoid glass tables or fragile items.

Rooftop Terrace
Infant/Non-mobile: (Birth - 6 months)
Infant crawl/roll: (5 months - 1 year)
→ **Toddler/Pre-school: (1 year - 4 years)**
→ **School-age: (5 years - 6+ years)**

Plant Safety

Safe Plants: Research plants to ensure they aren't toxic. Common plants like oleander can be poisonous if ingested. (For more details refer to Living Room and Yard **pg. 71 & 377**)

Stable Planters: Heavy or anchored planters prevent children from tipping them over.

Rooftop Terrace
Infant/Non-mobile: (Birth - 6 months)
Infant crawl/roll: (5 months - 1 year)
→ **Toddler/Pre-school: (1 year - 4 years)**
→ **School-age: (5 years - 6+ years)**

Terrace Electricity Concerns

Elevated Outlets: Have outlets installed at a higher level that is out of the reach of children.

Childproof Covers: Use safety covers on all outlets to prevent curious fingers from poking inside.
(For more details refer to Living Room **pg. 50**)

Rooftop Terrace
Infant/Non-mobile: (Birth - 6 months)
Infant crawl/roll: (5 months - 1 year)
→ **Toddler/Pre-school: (1 year - 4 years)**
→ **School-age: (5 years - 6+ years)**

Standing Water Concerns

Childproofing a rooftop terrace to address water concerns is a comprehensive process that necessitates close attention to numerous details to prevent accidents and maintain a safe environment.

Non-Slip Flooring: Install non-slip flooring to prevent accidents from slips and falls, especially in wet conditions. This could be tiled with a rough texture or wooden decking with adequate grip.

Drainage Systems: Ensure that a proper drainage system is in place to prevent water accumulation and puddle formation, which could lead to slips and falls.

Water-Alert Sensors: Consider installing water-alert sensors that notify you if there's water accumulation in certain areas, allowing for timely intervention.

Routine Inspections: Carry out regular inspections, especially during the rainy season, to check for water stagnation and clear it promptly to prevent accidents.

Water Features and Pools

Drowning Remains a Silent Threat. Drowning is the leading cause of injury-related death for children aged 1 to 4 years, with **over 3,500 fatalities worldwide each year.** (Source: World Health Organization (WHO) – Drowning)

Fenced Water Features: If the terrace has water features or a small pool, make sure it is fenced off properly to prevent unsupervised access by children.

Anti-Slip Mats: Place anti-slip mats near water features or pools to provide additional traction and prevent slips.

Covered Water Features: To prevent drowning hazards, ensure that water features can be covered securely when not in use.

Safety Equipment: Keep life-saving equipment like life rings or ropes near water features, even if they are shallow.

Rainwater Harvesting and Plants

Secure Rain Barrels: If rainwater is harvested on the terrace, ensure that the collection barrels are securely covered to prevent children from falling in.

Safe Plant Watering Systems: Set up safe plant watering systems that do not create puddles or slippery areas. Consider drip irrigation systems for water efficiency and safety.

Education and Supervision: Educate children on the dangers of water bodies and ensure constant supervision when they are near water features or pools.

Rooftop Terrace
Infant/Non-mobile: (Birth - 6 months)
Infant crawl/roll: (5 months - 1 year)
→ **Toddler/Pre-school: (1 year - 4 years)**
→ **School-age: (5 years - 6+ years)**

Storage Concerns

Locked Containers: All gardening tools, fertilizers, or chemicals should be stored in locked containers or cabinets.

Organized Play Area: Designate specific areas for toys and play items. This not only keeps the area tidy but reduces tripping hazards.

Rooftop Terrace
→ Infant/Non-mobile: (Birth - 6 months)
→ Infant crawl/roll: (5 months - 1 year)
→ Toddler/Pre-school: (1 year - 4 years)
→ School-age: (5 years - 6+ years)

Environmental Concerns

UV-Protected Areas: Use UV-protected umbrellas or shades to protect children from harmful sun rays.

Wind Safety: Anchor items that might blow away in strong winds, such as lightweight chairs or toys.

Rooftop Terrace
→ Infant/Non-mobile: (Birth - 6 months)
→ Infant crawl/roll: (5 months - 1 year)
→ Toddler/Pre-school: (1 year - 4 years)
→ School-age: (5 years - 6+ years)

Inspect Frequently

Monthly Checks: Dedicate time each month to inspect the entire terrace. Check for loose screws, wobbly railings, or other potential hazards.

Immediate Repairs: Address any wear and tear immediately. A small issue can quickly become a significant hazard if left unattended.

Rooftop Terrace
Infant/Non-mobile: (Birth - 6 months)
Infant crawl/roll: (5 months - 1 year)
→ Toddler/Pre-school: (1 year - 4 years)
→ School-age: (5 years - 6+ years)

Educate and Supervise

Safety Rules: Establish and consistently enforce rules, such as no running on the terrace or no climbing on furniture.

Constant Supervision: Even with all safety measures, always supervise children. It's the best way to ensure their safety.

|Ch. 23| Garage

Introduction: In the journey of making every nook and cranny of your home a safe haven for your little ones, the garage should not be overlooked. Often considered a storage spot for tools, automobiles, and miscellaneous items, a garage harbors potential dangers that are sometimes underestimated. As we venture into this chapter, we will guide you through the essential steps of childproofing your garage, a place where safety measures are as crucial as in any other part of your home. From securing hazardous materials to ensuring the safe storage of tools and machinery, we aim to help you create a space that is not only functional but also child friendly. Let's embark on this vital aspect of home safety together, fostering a secure environment where your children can grow and explore without bounds.

Testimonial: *I'll never forget the moment my heart skipped a beat in the garage. What's usually a space for tools and the car quickly turned into a place of panic. Our youngest, in all his curious glory, managed to sneak in unsupervised and found a tool we had left within reach, something I still kick myself about. Next thing you know, there were tears, frantic calls, and a blur of guilt as I held him, wishing I could turn back time. Luckily, his injuries weren't too bad, but the sight of his wounded little hand is something that sticks with me.*

That day was a huge wake-up call. We realized a simple childproof lock on the garage door would've kept him out, and securing all the tools and hazardous materials in locked cabinets would have made all the difference. We immediately went into full-on safety mode and childproofed every inch of the garage. Now, I tell every parent not to overlook the garage! It's not just a spot for your car; it can hide some serious dangers for little ones. Childproof it before curiosity leads to a situation you'll regret. Trust me, a few extra safety measures go a long way!

- Steve C. (Father of 3)

Garage
Infant/Non-mobile: (Birth – 6 months)
Infant crawl/roll: (5 months – 1 year)
→ **Toddler/Pre-school: (1 year – 4 years)**
→ **School-age: (5 years – 6+ years)**

Garage Tool Storage

More than 10,000 children are injured each year by improperly stored tools such as hammers, screwdrivers, and power tools. (Source: U.S. Consumer Product Safety Commission (CPSC) - Tool Safety) Childproofing a tool cabinet in the garage is crucial to prevent accidents and ensure the safety of children.

Lockable Cabinet: Choose a tool cabinet with lockable doors or drawers to prevent children from accessing sharp or dangerous tools.

Store Tools Properly: Ensure that all tools are stored properly in their designated places within the cabinet, with sharp edges and blades secured or covered.

Keep Keys Out of Reach: If the tool cabinet has a lock, keep the keys out of children's reach, ideally in a secure location.

Childproof Latches: If the tool cabinet doesn't have a built-in lock, consider adding childproof latches to keep it securely closed.

Elevated Placement: To keep the tool cabinet out of the reach of young children, mount it on the wall or in an elevated position.

Organize and Label: Organize the tools in the cabinet neatly and consider labeling the drawers or shelves to make it easier for adults to find and put away tools, reducing the time the cabinet is left open.

Safe Tool Handling: Teach older children about the safe handling of tools and the importance of not using them without adult supervision.

Use Tool Guards: For hand tools with sharp edges, consider using tool guards or blade covers to protect against accidental injuries.

Secure the Garage: Keep the garage door locked and ensure that children cannot access the garage without adult supervision.

Regular Inspection: Regularly inspect the tool cabinet and its contents to ensure that everything is stored safely and securely.

Install Garage Safety Devices: Consider installing safety devices in the garage, such as garage door sensors and motion detectors, to alert you if a child enters the area.

Proper Disposal: Properly and safely dispose of old or damaged tools, keeping them out of the reach of children.

You can create a safer environment in the garage and prevent children from accessing dangerous tools. Always prioritize safety and take appropriate measures to protect children from potential hazards in the garage.

Garage
Infant/Non-mobile: (Birth - 6 months)
Infant crawl/roll: (5 months - 1 year)
→ **Toddler/Pre-school: (1 year - 4 years)**
→ **School-age: (5 years - 6+ years)**

Booster Seat

Child safety is of the utmost importance when it comes to booster seats, and choosing and using them correctly is crucial.

Check for expiration dates: Like car seats, booster seats have expiration dates. Be sure to check the manufacturer's label or manual for the expiration date and replace the booster seat if it has passed. Expired seats may not provide the necessary protection in case of an accident.

Proper positioning of the seatbelt: Ensure that the seatbelt fits your child correctly when using a booster seat. The shoulder belt should lie across the chest and shoulder, not the neck or arm, and the lap belt should fit low and snug across the hips, not the stomach.

Backless vs. High-back Boosters: There are two main types of booster seats - backless boosters and high-back boosters. Backless boosters are suitable for vehicles with headrests and provide a lift to ensure proper seatbelt positioning. High-back boosters offer additional head and neck support and are ideal for vehicles without headrests or for children who need extra support.

Use in the Rear Seat: Booster seats should always be used in the vehicle's back seat. The rear seat is the safest place for children to ride, and using a booster seat in the front seat may expose them to unnecessary risks from airbags.

Set a Good Example: As a parent or caregiver, it's essential to lead by example. Always wear your seatbelt when driving and ensure that all vehicle passengers are buckled up. Children are more likely to adopt safe behaviors when they see adults following the rules.

Remember, booster seats play a crucial role in protecting children during car rides and using them correctly can significantly reduce the risk of injuries in the event of an accident. By following these tips and prioritizing child safety, you can ensure that your child is safe and secure on every journey.

<u>Garage</u>
Infant/Non-mobile: (Birth - 6 months)
Infant crawl/roll: (5 months - 1 year)
→ **Toddler/Pre-school: (1 year - 4 years)**
→ **School-age: (5 years - 6+ years)**

Toolbox

Lock It Down: Get a sturdy, lockable toolbox. If it can't be locked, you might as well leave the garage door open, allowing all the tools to come to life like a toy story gone wrong.

Keep it Out of Reach: Keep it on a high shelf or locked in a cabinet. Unless your child is Spider-Man, they're unlikely to climb that high.

Tool Covers: Sharp tools? Put covers on anything pointy, stabby, or capable of unscrewing your sanity.

Magnetic Tool Holders: Tools that stick to the wall with magnets are fantastic for adults but might look like magic to kids. Ensure they are high up or inside a closed area.

No Power-Play: If there are power tools, unplug them! Even better, store them in a separate, locked cabinet. A kid with a drill is a disaster movie waiting to happen.

<u>Garage</u>
Infant/Non-mobile: (Birth - 6 months)
Infant crawl/roll: (5 months - 1 year)
→ **Toddler/Pre-school: (1 year - 4 years)**
→ **School-age: (5 years - 6+ years)**

Kid-Free Zone

To create a childproof area in the garage that a child can't access, follow these steps:

Install Safety Gates: Place sturdy safety gates or barriers at the entrance of the designated area to prevent children from entering.

Elevated Shelving: Utilize high and secure shelving to store items that could be hazardous or easily reached by children.

Lockable Cabinets: Store tools, chemicals, or any potentially dangerous items out of children's reach in lockable cabinets or drawers.

Childproof Latches: Install childproof latches on any cabinets, drawers, or storage containers within the area.

Secure Doors and Windows: Ensure that any doors or windows leading to the childproof area have secure locks to prevent unauthorized access.

Store Ladders Safely: If ladders are in the garage, store them vertically or hang them on wall hooks high above children's reach.

Organize Cords and Wires: Tuck away and secure any cords or wires, especially those connected to power tools or equipment, to avoid tripping hazards and potential accidents.

Hazardous Materials: Store dangerous materials, such as chemicals or flammable substances, in a locked cabinet or a separate area inaccessible to children.

Label Danger Zones: Use clear signage or labels to indicate areas that are off-limits to children.

Keep Floor Clean and Tidy: Remove any small objects or debris from the floor that children could potentially pick up and put in their mouths.

Properly Store Garden Tools: securely Store Garden tools such as rakes, shovels, and shears in designated racks or wall hangers.

Provide Safe Play Areas: Create a separate play area for children in the garage with age-appropriate toys and activities away from potential hazards.

<u>Garage</u>
Infant/Non-mobile: (Birth - 6 months)
Infant crawl/roll: (5 months - 1 year)
→ **Toddler/Pre-school: (1 year - 4 years)**
→ **School-age: (5 years - 6+ years)**

Garage Freezer Concerns

Childproofing the freezer in the garage is essential to prevent accidents and ensure the safety of children.

Lock or Secure the Freezer: Secure the freezer door with a childproof lock or latch to prevent young children from opening it without adult supervision.

Elevate the Freezer: If possible, elevate the freezer to a height that is out of reach of young children. This can be achieved by placing it on a sturdy stand or platform.

Store Hazardous Items Safely: If the freezer contains items that could be hazardous to children, such as alcoholic beverages or medications, store them in a separate locked compartment or higher shelf within the freezer.

Organize Contents: Keep the freezer organized and tidy so children are less likely to be tempted to explore its contents.

Teach Safe Habits: Educate older children about the potential dangers of the freezer and the importance of not playing with the appliance.

Store Cleaning Products Separately: If you store cleaning products or chemicals in the garage, ensure they are kept in a locked cabinet or a high shelf away from the freezer.

Supervise Children: Always supervise children when they are in the garage or near the freezer to prevent accidents.

Use Warning Signs: Consider placing a warning sign on the freezer to remind children that it is off-limits without adult permission.

Secure Power Cord: Ensure that the freezer's power cord is securely tucked away and not dangling where children can reach it.

Regular Maintenance: Regularly inspect the freezer for any signs of wear or damage and address them promptly.

Proper Disposal: If you decide to replace the freezer, dispose of the old one properly, making sure it is inaccessible to children.

You can create a safer environment in the garage, especially around the freezer, and reduce the risk of accidents or injuries. Always prioritize safety and take appropriate measures to protect children from potential hazards in the garage.

<u>Garage</u>
Infant/Non-mobile: (Birth - 6 months)
Infant crawl/roll: (5 months - 1 year)
→ **Toddler/Pre-school: (1 year - 4 years)**
→ **School-age: (5 years - 6+ years)**

Install Automatically Reversing Garage Door
(Or make sure yours comes with one)

<u>**Installation and Maintenance**</u>

Sensor Height: To detect small children effectively, the sensors should be installed no higher than 6 inches above the floor.

Regular Testing: Frequently test the sensors to ensure they are functioning correctly. A simple test involves placing an object, like a roll of paper towels, under the door and then attempting to close it. The door should reverse upon sensing the object.

Professional Inspection: Have the system inspected by a professional annually to ensure all components are working correctly.

Education and Supervision

Teach Safety: Educate children about the dangers associated with garage doors and instruct them never to play near or under the door.

Supervision: Always supervise children when they are in or around the garage to prevent accidents.

Remote Control Safety: Keep remote controls out of children's reach and teach them not to play with them.

Additional Safety Measures

Emergency Release: Familiarize yourself with your garage door opener's emergency release feature and teach older children how to use it in case of emergencies, but only under adult supervision.

Anti-Entrapment Features: Ensure your garage door system has anti-entrapment features that cause the door to reverse if it encounters an obstruction.

Visual Inspection: Regularly inspect the garage door for signs of wear and tear, paying special attention to the springs, cables, rollers, and pulleys. Do not attempt to repair these yourself; instead, call a professional.

By ensuring proper installation, conducting regular maintenance, and educating children about the potential dangers, you can significantly reduce the risk of accidents and injuries associated with garage doors. Always prioritize safety by supervising children in the garage area and keeping remote controls out of their reach.

Garage
Infant/Non-mobile: (Birth - 6 months)
Infant crawl/roll: (5 months - 1 year)
→ **Toddler/Pre-school: (1 year - 4 years)**
→ **School-age: (5 years - 6+ years)**

Emergency Release Rope

Tying up the emergency release rope on a garage door is not recommended as it can compromise the safety of the garage door system.

The emergency release rope is an essential safety feature designed to allow manual garage door operation in case of power outages or other emergencies. Tying up the emergency release rope can prevent it from functioning correctly when it's needed most and could also lead to safety hazards in an emergency.

Instead of tying up the emergency release rope, **consider educating household members** about its purpose and proper usage. Teach them how to operate the emergency release correctly and safely in case of emergencies.

If there are concerns about the emergency release rope being accidentally pulled or causing inconvenience, consider **adjusting its placement** or securing it in a way that is accessible during emergencies but less prone to accidental activation.

Always prioritize safety and follow the manufacturer's guidelines and recommendations for the proper use of garage door features, including the emergency release rope. If you have any concerns or questions about your garage door's safety features, it's best to consult a professional garage door technician.

Garage
Infant/Non-mobile: (Birth - 6 months)
Infant crawl/roll: (5 months - 1 year)
→ **Toddler/Pre-school: (1 year - 4 years)**
→ **School-age: (5 years - 6+ years)**

Never Tie Anything to the Garage Door Handle

Tying anything to the garage doorknob or handle on the outside of the door is not recommended and can lead to safety hazards and damage to the door. Tying objects on the garage doorknob can **interfere with the door's proper operation** and may prevent it from closing or opening correctly. It can also unnecessarily stress the door mechanism and hardware, leading to potential malfunctions or damage.

Furthermore, tying anything to the garage door from the outside can be seen as an **invitation to potential intruders,** as it may indicate that the garage is not secured correctly.

To ensure the safety and security of your garage and belongings, avoid tying anything to the garage doorknob or handle on the outside. Instead, use appropriate locks and security measures to protect your garage and its contents.

If you have specific needs or concerns regarding your garage security, consider consulting a professional locksmith or garage door technician who can provide expert advice, and solutions tailored to your situation.

Garage
Infant/Non-mobile: (Birth - 6 months)
Infant crawl/roll: (5 months - 1 year)
→ **Toddler/Pre-school: (1 year - 4 years)**
→ **School-age: (5 years - 6+ years)**

Water Bucket Concerns

Keeping buckets out of reach of young children is an important safety measure. Buckets can pose various risks to children, especially if they contain liquid or other materials.

Drowning Hazard: Buckets filled with water, cleaning solutions, or any other liquid can be a drowning hazard for young children. Even a tiny amount of water in a bucket can be dangerous if a child accidentally falls into it headfirst.

Suffocation Risk: An empty bucket can become a suffocation risk if a child places it over their head and gets stuck inside. This is especially true for small children who may not have the strength to remove the bucket themselves.

Ingestion of Harmful Substances: If a bucket contains chemicals, paints, or any toxic substances, a child may accidentally ingest them if they get access to the bucket.

Store Buckets Upside Down: Store buckets upside down to prevent them from collecting water or other liquids, reducing the risk of drowning.

Keep Buckets in Locked Cabinets: Store buckets in locked cabinets or on high shelves where young children cannot reach them.

Empty Buckets Promptly: Empty any buckets used for cleaning or other purposes immediately after use and store them out of reach.

Toppling Over: Children may use buckets as stepping stools or try to climb on them, which can cause the bucket to tip over and cause injuries.

Supervise Children: Always supervise young children and keep them away from areas where they store buckets or potentially hazardous items.

Educate Older Children: If you have older children, educate them about the potential risks of buckets and the importance of keeping them out of reach of younger siblings.

<u>Garage</u>
Infant/Non-mobile: (Birth - 6 months)
Infant crawl/roll: (5 months - 1 year)
→ **Toddler/Pre-school: (1 year - 4 years)**
→ **School-age: (5 years - 6+ years)**

Designated Toy Area

Having a designated box in the garage or a shed for children's toys is a fantastic idea to keep the play area organized and create a safe and easily accessible space for children to enjoy their toys.

Choose the Right Location: Select a suitable garage or yard location for the toy box or shed. Ensure it is easily accessible to children but also protected from the elements, especially if it's an outdoor shed.

Toy Box or Shed: Decide whether a designated toy box or a dedicated shed is more appropriate depending on the number of toys and available space. Both options work well, but a shed provides additional protection from the weather and more storage capacity.

Child-Friendly Design: Whether it's a toy box or a shed, make sure the design is child-friendly and safe. Avoid sharp edges, choose childproof locks if needed, and ensure proper ventilation in the shed.

Organize and Label: Organize toys in the box or shed by categories or age-appropriateness. Use labels or pictures to help children identify where each type of toy belongs.

Involve Children: Involve your children in the setup process. Let them choose the organization and decorations for their toy box or shed, making it a fun and engaging project.

Rotate Toys: If space is limited, consider rotating toys periodically. Keep some toys in storage while others are available for play. This helps to keep the play area fresh and encourages creativity.

Regular Clean-up: Encourage children to clean up and put their toys back in the designated area after playtime. Make it a routine, and they will develop good habits.

Safety Precautions: Ensure that the toy box or shed is secure and childproofed. Lock the shed if it contains items that may be hazardous to children.

Regular Maintenance: Regularly inspect and maintain the toy box or shed to ensure it remains safe and in good condition. Having a designated box in the garage or a shed for children's toys helps with the organization and fosters a sense of responsibility and ownership in children. It creates a safe and enjoyable play environment, making playtime more fun for kids and less stressful for parents.

Garage
Infant/Non-mobile: (Birth - 6 months)
Infant crawl/roll: (5 months - 1 year)
→ **Toddler/Pre-school: (1 year - 4 years)**
→ **School-age: (5 years - 6+ years)**

Golf Clubs

Childproofing golf clubs is important to keep children safe and prevent accidents. Golf clubs can have sharp edges and heavy heads, making them potentially dangerous if not properly stored. Each year, approximately **4,000 children** are injured by improperly stored sporting goods, such as bats, hockey sticks, and balls. (Source: National Safety Council (NSC) - Injury Facts)

Secure Storage: Store golf clubs in a locked or secured area, such as a golf bag with a zipper or a locked closet. When not in use, keep them out of the reach of children.

Use Golf Club Covers: Invest in golf club headcovers to protect the clubs' sharp edges and prevent scratching or damage.

Remove Grips: Remove the grips from the clubs when not in use. This will make them less appealing to children and deter them from trying to play with them.

Educate Children: Teach children about the potential dangers of golf clubs and explain that they are not toys. Let them know that golf clubs are for adults to use responsibly.

Supervise Play: If you allow children to be near golf clubs or play with plastic toy golf clubs, always supervise their activities to ensure their safety.

Lock the Golf Bag: If you keep your golf clubs in a bag, consider using a padlock or a bag with a lockable compartment to prevent unauthorized access.

Store Out of Sight: To minimize children's curiosity, keep golf clubs out of sight and out of reach.

Use Childproof Locks: If you store your golf clubs in a cabinet or closet, consider using childproof locks to prevent children from opening them.

Golf Club Organizer: If you have a golf club organizer or stand, ensure it is stable and securely attached to prevent tipping over.

Set a Good Example: Always model responsible behavior with golf clubs when children are around. Demonstrating safe handling will teach them to treat the clubs with respect.

You can ensure that golf clubs are safely stored and handled, reducing the risk of accidents and injuries to children. Remember, child safety should always be a priority, and taking proactive measures can prevent potential hazards.

<u>Garage</u>
Infant/Non-mobile: (Birth - 6 months)
Infant crawl/roll: (5 months - 1 year)
→ **Toddler/Pre-school: (1 year - 4 years)**
→ **School-age: (5 years - 6+ years)**

Garage Floor

Childproofing a garage floor is essential to create a safe environment for children. The garage floor can pose various hazards, especially if it's made of concrete or contains oil stains and other substances.

Clean and Seal: Thoroughly clean the garage floor to remove any oil stains, chemicals, or debris that could be hazardous. Consider sealing the floor with a non-slip sealant to reduce the risk of slips and falls.

Use Rubber Mats: Place rubber mats or interlocking foam tiles on the garage floor to provide a softer and more forgiving surface for children to play on. These mats also offer insulation against cold floors.

Cover Cracks: If the garage floor has cracks or uneven areas, consider repairing them or covering them with epoxy or rubber patches to avoid tripping hazards.

Avoid Slippery Surfaces: Avoid using glossy or polished coatings on the garage floor, as they can become slippery and increase the risk of accidents.

Keep Chemicals Secure: Store any chemicals, paints, or other hazardous materials in locked cabinets or high shelves, out of reach of children.

Clear the Floor: Remove the garage floor from clutter and unnecessary items to reduce tripping hazards and provide more space for safe play.

Childproof Cabinets and Shelves: If you have cabinets or shelves in the garage, use childproof latches to prevent children from accessing potentially dangerous tools or items.

Create Designated Play Areas: Designate specific garage floor areas as play zones for children. Mark these areas with colored tape or floor mats to make it clear where they can play safely.

Supervise Playtime: Always supervise children when they are in the garage to ensure their safety and guide them in appropriate play activities.

Childproof Garage Door: Install safety sensors on the garage door to prevent accidental closing while children are playing in the garage.

Store Sports Equipment Safely: If you store sports equipment in the garage, use designated racks or hooks to keep them organized and out of the way when not in use.

<u>Garage</u>
Infant/Non-mobile: (Birth - 6 months)
Infant crawl/roll: (5 months - 1 year)
→ **Toddler/Pre-school: (1 year - 4 years)**
→ **School-age: (5 years - 6+ years)**

Vehicle Lighter/Outlet Concerns

Childproofing a car lighter/outlet is essential to prevent children from accidentally engaging or playing with it, as car lighters can get hot and cause burns or other injuries.

Use a Safety Plug: Consider using a safety plug or cover specifically designed for car lighters. These plugs will prevent children from inserting objects into the lighter socket and engaging the heating element.

Educate Children: Teach children about the car's interior components and explain to them that the car lighter is not a toy and should never be touched or played with.

Keep Lighter Away: Store lighters and any other potentially hazardous items out of children's reach, such as in the glove compartment or other secure compartments.

Child Locks: If your car model has child safety locks, activate them to prevent children from accessing the front console or lighter area without adult supervision.

Supervise: Always supervise children in the car to ensure they don't engage with the lighter or any other controls.

Use the Lighter with Caution: If you must use the car lighter to charge devices or for other purposes, do so with caution and keep it out of children's reach when not in use.

Regular Maintenance: Ensure that the lighter socket is in good working condition. If it becomes loose or malfunctioning, have it repaired or replaced promptly.

Teach Emergency Procedures: If you have older children, teach them about the car's emergency procedures, including the use of the car lighter for emergency purposes only.

Keep a Spare: If possible, keep a spare car lighter plug or cover in case the original one gets lost or damaged.

Garage
Infant/Non-mobile: (Birth - 6 months)
Infant crawl/roll: (5 months - 1 year)
→ **Toddler/Pre-school: (1 year - 4 years)**
→ **School-age: (5 years - 6+ years)**

Lock Vehicle Doors

Prevent Unwanted Access: Locking the garage doors ensures that children cannot enter the vehicle without adult supervision, preventing potential accidents and injuries.

Avoid Trapped Children: Children may be curious and inadvertently climb into an unlocked car while playing in the garage, putting them at risk of being trapped inside.

Prevent Accidental Engaging: Locking car doors helps prevent children from accidentally engaging controls or equipment inside the car, such as activating the windows or playing with the gearshift.

Carbon Monoxide Safety: If the car is running, locking the doors helps prevent children from entering the car and being exposed to carbon monoxide, a dangerous and potentially fatal gas.

Avoid Car Rolling: Locking the car doors prevents children from accidentally releasing the parking brake or shifting gears, which could cause the car to roll in the garage.

Garage Safety: Locking the car doors adds an extra layer of security to the garage, minimizing the risk of unauthorized individuals gaining access to the car.

Supervision: While in the garage, always supervise children and make sure they are away from the car. Locking the car doors is an additional safety measure, but proper supervision is crucial.

Prevent Theft: Locking the car doors also helps protect the vehicle from theft, ensuring it remains secure in the garage.

Childproofing is not limited to the home interior, and the garage is an important area to consider. Always prioritize safety and establish good habits, such as locking car doors when in the garage, to keep children safe from potential dangers.

Notes:

Garage
→ **Infant/Non-mobile: (Birth - 6 months)**
→ **Infant crawl/roll: (5 months - 1 year)**
→ **Toddler/Pre-school: (1 year - 4 years)**
→ **School-age: (5 years - 6+ years)**

Car Seat Safety

Car seats play a crucial role in keeping children safe while traveling in vehicles.

Choose the Right Seat: Select a car seat or booster seat appropriate for your child's age, weight, and height. Follow the manufacturer's guidelines and local regulations to ensure proper fit and safety.

Rear-Facing Seats for Infants: Infants should ride in a rear-facing car seat until they are at least two or until they reach the maximum height and weight limit recommended by the car seat manufacturer.

Forward-Facing Seats for Toddlers: Use a forward-facing car seat with a harness once your child outgrows the rear-facing seat. Continue using this seat until your child is ready for a booster seat.

Booster Seats for Older Children: Transition your child to a booster seat when they outgrow the forward-facing car seat. A booster seat positions the seatbelt correctly over their lap and shoulder.

Proper Installation: Ensure that the car seat or booster seat is correctly installed in your vehicle. Follow the installation instructions provided by the car seat manufacturer and your vehicle's owner's manual.

Tighten Straps Securely: When using a car seat with a harness, make sure the straps are snug and properly adjusted. The harness should fit snugly against your child's body.

Position of the Harness: When using a forward-facing car seat, the harness straps should be at or just above your child's shoulders.

Secure the Booster Seat: If you use a booster seat, ensure it is securely installed in the vehicle and that the seatbelt passes correctly through its guides.

Use the Right Seatbelt: Ensure that your child uses the vehicle's seatbelt correctly when in a booster seat. The seatbelt should properly fit across their lap and shoulder without crossing the neck or face.

Check for Recalls: Regularly check for recalls on your car seat or booster seat to ensure they meet current safety standards.

Keep Children in the Back: Always place children in the vehicle's back seat. This is the safest place for them to ride until they reach the appropriate age and size to use a seatbelt without a booster seat.

Set a Good Example: Always wear your seatbelt when driving with children to set a positive example for safe behavior.

You can significantly reduce the risk of injuries and ensure that your child is properly protected during car rides. Remember that car seats save lives; using them correctly and consistently is essential.

<u>Garage</u>
→ **Infant/Non-mobile: (Birth - 6 months)**
→ **Infant crawl/roll: (5 months - 1 year)**
→ **Toddler/Pre-school: (1 year - 4 years)**
→ **School-age: (5 years - 6+ years)**

What to Put in a Travel Safety Kit

A car safety kit is essential to have in your vehicle, especially when traveling with children.

First Aid Kit: A well-stocked first aid kit should include bandages, adhesive tape, antiseptic wipes, gauze pads, tweezers, scissors, pain relievers, and any necessary medications specific to your family's needs.

Emergency Contact Information: Keep a list of emergency contact numbers, including local emergency services, your pediatrician, and family members or friends who can be reached in case of an emergency.

Bottled Water and Non-Perishable Snacks: Include bottled water and non-perishable snacks, like granola bars or dried fruit, to keep everyone hydrated and nourished during unexpected delays or emergencies.

Blankets or Extra Clothing: Have blankets or extra clothing, including jackets or sweaters, in case of cold weather or if you need to stay warm during an emergency.

Flashlight and Extra Batteries: A flashlight will be useful at night in case of car trouble or to search for items in the car. Make sure you have extra batteries for the flashlight.

Reflective Triangles or Flares: These can alert other drivers if your car breaks down on the side of the road, making your vehicle more visible and promoting safety.

Jumper Cables: Carry jumper cables in case your car battery dies, and you need a jump-start from another vehicle.

Tire Jack and Spare Tire: Ensure your car has a tire jack and a properly inflated spare tire in case of a flat tire.

Multi-Tool or Swiss Army Knife: A multi-tool with a knife, screwdriver, and other functions can be handy in various situations.

Roadside Assistance Information: Keep information about your roadside assistance coverage and contact numbers accessible.

Paper Towels and Trash Bags: Have paper towels and trash bags to clean up spills and keep the car tidy.

Car Phone Charger: Keep a car phone charger to ensure your phone is always charged. This allows you to make emergency calls or access navigation.

Child-Friendly Items: If you have children, consider adding items like baby wipes, diapers, and children's entertainment (books, toys) to keep them comfortable during a car journey.

Make sure to periodically check and update the items in your car safety kit, especially the first aid supplies and emergency contact information. Being prepared with a well-stocked car safety kit can provide peace of mind and assistance during unexpected situations while traveling with children.

Garage
Infant/Non-mobile: (Birth - 6 months)
Infant crawl/roll: (5 months - 1 year)
→ **Toddler/Pre-school: (1 year - 4 years)**
→ **School-age: (5 years - 6+ years)**

Garage Wall Concerns

Cover Sharp Edges: Inspect the garage walls for any sharp edges or protruding nails. Use edge protectors or corner guards to cover these areas and prevent injuries if children accidentally bump into them.

Lock Hazardous Items: Store hazardous items, such as tools, chemicals, and sharp objects, in locked cabinets or on high shelves that are out of children's reach.

Secure Heavy Items: Ensure that heavy items, such as bicycles, ladders, or gardening equipment, are securely stored and properly anchored to prevent them from toppling over.

Install Safety Mirrors: If the garage has blind spots, consider installing safety mirrors to improve visibility and prevent accidents.

Use Non-Slip Flooring: If the garage floor is slippery, consider using non-slip flooring or placing anti-slip mats in areas where children are likely to walk or play.

Childproof Garage Door: Install safety sensors and use childproof locks on the garage door to prevent accidental closing while children are near it.

Create a Designated Play Area: If you have space in the garage for play, designate a safe play area away from hazardous items and ensure it is well-supervised.

Check for Mold or Mildew: To maintain a healthy environment, regularly inspect the walls for signs of mold or mildew and address any issues promptly.

Secure Electrical Outlets: If there are electrical outlets in the garage, use childproof outlet covers to prevent children from inserting objects into them.

Proper Lighting: Ensure that the garage is well-lit to avoid trips and falls, especially during nighttime use.

Install a Fire Extinguisher: Keep one in the garage and teach older children how to use it in case of emergencies.

Supervise Children: Always supervise children when they are in the garage to ensure their safety and guide them away from potential hazards.

You can help create a safer garage environment for children by regularly assessing the garage for potential risks and taking appropriate actions to minimize them. Remember, child safety should be a top priority in every area of the home, including the garage.

<u>Garage</u>
Infant/Non-mobile: (Birth - 6 months)
Infant crawl/roll: (5 months - 1 year)
→ **Toddler/Pre-school: (1 year - 4 years)**
→ **School-age: (5 years - 6+ years)**

Ladders

Childproofing ladders are essential to prevent accidents and injuries, as ladders can be dangerous for children if not properly secured or supervised.

- **Store Ladders Safely:** When not in use, store ladders in a locked shed, garage, or other secure area where children cannot access them.
- **Use Childproof Locks:** If you have a retractable or foldable ladder, consider using childproof locks to prevent children from extending or opening the ladder.
- **Secure Non-Retractable Ladders:** For non-retractable ladders, such as extension ladders, secure them in an upright position and use a ladder lock or strap to keep them closed.
- **Keep Ladders Out of Reach:** Store ladders in a location that is out of children's reach, such as high shelves or hanging from the ceiling.
- **Supervise Children:** Always supervise children when ladders are in use or accessible, ensuring they do not climb on or play with the ladder.
- **Teach Ladder Safety:** If you have older children, teach them ladder safety rules and proper ladder usage, emphasizing that ladders are not toys.
- **Anchor Ladders Securely:** When using a ladder, ensure it is placed on a stable and level surface and anchored securely to prevent tipping.
- **Use Anti-Slip Feet:** Install anti-slip feet on the ladder to provide better stability and reduce the risk of sliding.
- **Check for Damage:** Regularly inspect the ladder for any signs of damage, wear, or loose parts. Repair or replace any damaged components promptly.
- **Properly Lock Hinges and Spreader Bars:** Before using the ladder, ensure that all hinges and spreader bars are securely locked in place.
- **Demonstrate Safe Ladder Use:** Set a good example by using ladders safely and responsibly in front of children.

You can significantly reduce the risk of ladder-related accidents and create a safer environment for children by always prioritizing safety and ensuring that ladders are properly stored, secured, and used under appropriate supervision.

<u>Garage</u>
Infant/Non-mobile: (Birth - 6 months)
Infant crawl/roll: (5 months - 1 year)
→ **Toddler/Pre-school: (1 year - 4 years)**
→ **School-age: (5 years - 6+ years)**

Chemical Concerns

Childproofing the garage and ensuring the safety of children involves carefully managing and securing all chemicals and hazardous substances.

Storage of Chemicals: Store all chemicals, including cleaning solutions, pesticides, fertilizers, paints, and automotive fluids, in locked cabinets or on high shelves that are out of children's reach.

Secure Lids and Caps: Ensure that all containers with hazardous substances have secure lids and caps and double-check that they are tightly closed after use.

Labeling: Clearly label all chemical containers with their contents and potential hazards. When possible, use childproof and waterproof labels.

Organize and Separate: Store chemicals separately from other items in the garage and organize them so that they are easily accessible only to adults.

Childproof Locks: Install childproof locks on cabinets containing hazardous substances, making it difficult for young children to open them.

Dispose of Unused Chemicals: Properly dispose of any old or expired chemicals following local guidelines and hazardous waste disposal regulations.

Educate Older Children: If you have older children, educate them about the potential dangers of chemicals and the importance of not handling them without adult supervision.

Regular Inspection: Regularly inspect the garage to ensure that no chemicals or hazardous materials are left unattended or within your children's reach.

Locking the Garage Door: Keep the garage door locked when not in use and ensure that children cannot access the garage without adult permission.

Safety Data Sheets (SDS): Keep safety data sheets for all chemicals in the garage. These sheets provide essential information on handling, storage, and emergency procedures.

Childproof Outlets: If there are electrical outlets in the garage, use childproof outlet covers to prevent children from inserting objects into them.

Remove Toxic Plants: If you have plants in the garage, ensure they are non-toxic and safe for children. Remove any poisonous plants from the area.

Lock Up Tools: When not in use, keep tools, especially sharp or heavy ones, in locked toolboxes or cabinets.

Maintain Fire Safety: Install a fire extinguisher in the garage and teach older children how to use it in case of emergencies.

Supervision: Always supervise children when they are in the garage and guide them away from potential hazards.

Childproofing the garage requires vigilance and attention to detail, but it is essential for creating a safe environment for children. To maintain a child-safe garage, regularly review and update safety measures as needed.

Garage
Infant/Non-mobile: (Birth - 6 months)
Infant crawl/roll: (5 months - 1 year)
→ **Toddler/Pre-school: (1 year - 4 years)**
→ **School-age: (5 years - 6+ years)**

Garage Lighting Concerns

Ensuring good garage lighting is crucial for childproofing and overall safety.

Install Adequate Lighting: Make sure the garage has sufficient lighting to provide clear visibility throughout the space. Consider installing overhead, wall-mounted, or LED strip lights to brighten the area.

Motion-Activated Lights: Consider installing motion-activated lights near the garage entrance and key areas. These lights automatically turn on when someone enters the garage, providing enhanced safety and energy efficiency.

LED Bulbs: Use energy-efficient LED bulbs in the garage. They provide bright illumination while consuming less energy and lasting longer.

Light Switch Accessibility: Ensure that light switches are easily accessible and conveniently placed, allowing for quick lighting adjustments when entering or exiting the garage.

Night Lighting: If the garage is frequently used at night, install night lighting with a lower intensity to provide visibility without disturbing others nearby.

Task Lighting: Add task lighting in specific areas, such as workbenches or tool storage areas, to provide focused and adequate illumination for specific activities.

Clean Light Fixtures: Regularly clean the light fixtures to remove dust and debris, as dirty fixtures can reduce the effectiveness of the lighting.

Reflective Surfaces: Consider using reflective surfaces like white walls or mirrors to bounce light around the garage and improve overall brightness.

Bright Paint: If feasible, consider painting the garage walls and ceiling with light-colored, reflective paint to enhance the overall brightness.

Skylights or Windows: Add skylights or windows to allow natural light into the garage during the daytime.

Regular Maintenance: Regularly inspect and maintain the lighting system, promptly replacing any faulty bulbs or fixtures.

Emergency Lighting: Install battery-operated emergency lights or keep flashlights handy in case of power outages.

You create a safer and more child-friendly environment. Proper lighting helps reduce the risk of accidents and allows for better supervision and organization of the space. Regularly assess the lighting needs and adjust as necessary to maintain a well-lit and safe garage area.

Garage
Infant non-mobile: (Birth-6 mo.)
Infant crawl/roll: (5 mo.-2 yrs.)
→ **Toddler/Pre-School: (1 yr.-4 yrs.)**
→ **School-age: (5 yrs.-6 yrs.)**

Lookout as You Pull In or Out of a Garage

Being aware of your children's whereabouts when pulling in and out of the garage is crucial for their safety.

Check Surroundings Before Moving: Always check around and behind your vehicle before moving it. Walk around the car to ensure there are no children or pets nearby.

Use Rearview Cameras and Sensors: Many modern vehicles are equipped with rearview cameras and parking sensors. Utilize these technologies to better view the area behind your car.

Supervise Children: Always supervise children when they are in or near the garage. Make sure they are a safe distance away from moving vehicles.

Teach Children About Garage Safety: Educate your children about the potential dangers of playing near cars and the importance of staying away from moving vehicles.

Designate Safe Areas: Establish specific safe areas in the driveway or garage where children can play, away from moving cars.

Keep the Garage Door Closed: Keep the garage door closed when not in use to prevent children from running into the garage unexpectedly.

Use Visual Aids: If necessary, use visual aids such as colorful flags or markers in the driveway to remind children to stay away from moving vehicles.

Teach Children Traffic Safety: Teach older children about traffic safety, including staying clear of vehicles, looking both ways before crossing driveways, and using designated sidewalks.

Limit Distractions: Avoid distractions while driving in the driveway or garage, such as using a cell phone or adjusting the radio.

Use Reflective Gear: If children play outside during low-light conditions, have them wear reflective clothing or accessories to be easily visible to drivers.

Backup Safely: If you need to exit the garage, do so slowly and cautiously, checking all mirrors and using rearview cameras.

Keep Keys Out of Children's Reach: Never leave car keys accessible to children. Store keys in a secure location to prevent them from accidentally starting the vehicle.

Recent data (2018–2022) shows: (According to Consimer Affairs)

▸ ***10.4% of all reported garage door injuries occurred in children 10 and under, totaling 22 injuries in that age group during the period.***

▸ *Garage door injuries overall have declined from 61 to 34 annual cases (2018 → 2022), but safety risks remain, especially for young kids.*

▸ *Despite CPSC-mandated safety features (automatic reverse, sensors), finger and head injuries still make up 50% of all incidents*

|Ch. 24| The Yard

Introduction: Playground-related injuries account for **over 300,000 emergency visits annually** in the U.S., with fractures and concussions being the most common types of injuries. (Source: U.S. Consumer Product Safety Commission (CPSC) - Playground Safety) The family yard metamorphoses into a vast realm of endless adventures, from pirate-infested seas to jungles brimming with wildlife. As parents, our role is to foster this rich playground of imagination while ensuring it remains a sanctuary of safety. This chapter guides you through the essential steps to transform your yard into a haven where little explorers can embark on their adventures without any peril. From securing potentially hazardous areas to selecting child-friendly plants and materials, we'll help you craft a yard where children can grow, play, and explore, enveloped in the comforting embrace of safety. Let's embark on this journey to create a yard that harmonizes the spirit of adventure with the peace of mind that comes from knowing your child is safe. Also, I chose to put this statistic in this section, but it applies to the whole house. Each year, **over 100,000 children in the U.S. suffer eye injuries** caused by household objects such as toys, tools, and cleaning supplies. (Source: Centers for Disease Control and Prevention (CDC) - Eye Injury Statistics)

Testimonial: *The adventures Sammy has in our backyard never cease to amaze me! Just the other day, he turned our yard into an Amazon jungle, complete with a garden gnome sidekick. With his makeshift cape billowing behind him, Sammy ventured into every corner, his imagination running wild. But in the midst of his jungle exploration, he decided to climb the rockery in the corner of our yard. Unfortunately, the rocks were still slick from a recent rain, and Sammy took a small tumble, leaving him with a few scrapes, a sore wrist, and a bit of a scare.*

As I comforted him and cleaned his scrapes, it struck me how easily this could have been avoided. A softer play area or fencing off the rockery could have kept his adventures just as fun, but a bit safer.

This was a real wake-up call for us, showing that even in the familiar comfort of our backyard, there are potential hazards that a creative and adventurous child-like Sammy might overlook.

Now, we're taking steps to make sure our yard is both a place to foster his imagination and a safe space for him to explore. I hope our experience serves as a reminder to other parents—don't forget to childproof your outdoor spaces too. Every little adventurer deserves a safe base camp to return to after their grand backyard expeditions!

-John W. (Father of 2)

<u>Yard</u>
→ **Infant/Non-mobile: (Birth - 6 months)**
→ **Infant crawl/roll: (5 months - 1 year)**
→ **Toddler/Pre-school: (1 year - 4 years)**
→ **School-age: (5 years - 6+ years)**

Bee Safety

Bee safety is important to ensure that children can enjoy the outdoors and learn about nature while minimizing the risk of bee stings. Bees play a crucial role in pollination and are generally not aggressive unless provoked.

Educate Children: Teach children about bees, their importance in nature, and how to observe them from a safe distance. Explain that bees are not interested in stinging unless they feel threatened.

Avoid Swatting or Agitating Bees: Instruct children not to swat at bees or try to catch them. Sudden movements may provoke a defensive response from the bees.

Wear Light-Colored Clothing: Bees are attracted to dark colors, so encourage children to wear light-colored clothing when spending time outdoors.

Avoid Fragrances: Scented products like perfumes, scented lotions, and heavily scented soaps may attract bees. Encourage children to avoid using such products when going outside.

Choose Appropriate Play Areas: Avoid setting up play areas near beehives or flowering plants where bees are actively foraging.

Inspect Play Areas: Before allowing children to play outside, regularly inspect play areas, treehouses, and outdoor toys for signs of bee activity.

Cover Food and Drinks: During picnics or outdoor activities, cover food and drinks to deter bees from being attracted to them.

Stay Calm: Teach children to remain calm if a bee comes near them. Panicking or running can increase the likelihood of a bee sting.

Use Bee Repellents with Caution: Avoid using bee repellents or insecticides on children unless recommended by a healthcare professional.

Keep Gardens and Lawns Maintained: Regularly maintain gardens and lawns to reduce bee nesting sites and minimize bee activity close to play areas.

Create Bee-Friendly Gardens: Plant bee-friendly flowers away from play areas to attract bees away from high-traffic zones.

Supervise Play: Always supervise young children when they are playing outdoors, especially in areas with flowering plants.

Avoid Attracting Bees during Feeding: If bottle-feeding infants outdoors, keep the bottles covered to avoid attracting bees.

Be Prepared/Know Allergies: If your child has known bee sting allergies, keep a bee sting kit or other relevant medications on hand.

You can promote bee safety, allowing children to explore and appreciate nature while minimizing the risk of bee stings. Educating children about bees and their behavior is key to fostering respect for these important pollinators and ensuring peaceful coexistence.

<u>**Yard**</u>
Infant/Non-mobile: (Birth - 6 months)
Infant crawl/roll: (5 months - 1 year)
→ **Toddler/Pre-school: (1 year - 4 years)**
→ **School-age: (5 years - 6+ years)**

Tree and Plant Concerns

Each year, **more than 500 children** are injured near chemical plants and industrial areas due to accidental exposure to hazardous substances. (Source: Centers for Disease Control and Prevention (CDC) - Environmental Health) Ensuring the safety of children in a yard filled with nature's greenery involves being aware of the potentially dangerous plants and trees that could cause harm to the little ones.

Dangerous Plants and Trees

Oleander (Oleander Nerium)

Description: A beautiful shrub with glossy leaves and vibrant flowers, usually pink, red, or white.
Danger: Every part of this plant is toxic and can cause severe poisoning, resulting in symptoms such as nausea, vomiting, abdominal pain, heart irregularities, and even death.

Castor Bean Plant (Ricinus Communis)

Description: A plant with large, glossy leaves and clustered flowers, producing beans that contain seeds.

Danger: The seeds are highly toxic if ingested, causing severe abdominal pain, vomiting, diarrhea, and potentially fatal organ damage.

Foxglove (Digitalis Purpurea)

Description: A tall plant with a spike of bell-shaped flowers, usually in purple or white.

Danger: All parts of the plant are poisonous, leading to symptoms like diarrhea, headache, and convulsions. It affects the heart and can be fatal in high doses.

Poison Ivy (Toxicodendron Radicans)

Description: A plant with leaves grouped in threes exhibiting a glossy surface. It can grow as a vine or shrub.

Danger: Contact can cause skin irritation, intense itching, and blisters due to an oily resin called urushiol present in the leaves. Wash off your skin immediately after contact and wash clothes that were in contact as well.

Angel's Trumpet (Brugmansia)

Description: A shrub or small tree with large, pendulous flowers that resemble trumpets, typically yellow, pink, or white.

Danger: All parts are toxic, causing symptoms like confusion, hallucinations, and potentially fatal respiratory depression if ingested.

Rosary Pea (Abrus Precatorius)

Description: A vine with slender stems, light green leaves, and seeds encased in bright red pods.

Danger: The seeds are highly toxic if ingested, causing severe nausea, vomiting, and abdominal pain, and can lead to death due to organ failure.

Daphne (Daphne spp.)

Description: A small shrub with clusters of fragrant, tubular flowers, usually pink or white.

Danger: The berries are poisonous, causing symptoms like diarrhea, headache, and even coma in severe cases.

Child Safety Measures: Remove or fence off these dangerous plants from areas where children play. Educate children about the dangers of touching or ingesting unknown plants. Supervise children closely while they are playing in the yard.

Notes:

Yard
Infant/Non-mobile: (Birth - 6 months)
Infant crawl/roll: (5 months - 1 year)
Toddler/Pre-school: (1 year - 4 years)
→ **School-age: (5 years - 6+ years)**

Limit Tree Climbing

Childproofing your yard by trimming trees to prevent unwanted climbing is critical. Children are naturally curious and may be tempted to climb trees, which can lead to falls and injuries.

Identifying Risk Factors

Low Branches: Identify and trim branches that are low enough for children to reach and attempt to climb.

Weak Limbs: Remove weak or rotting limbs, as they can easily break under a child's weight.

Nearby Structures: Note any structures near trees, like fences or playsets, that children might use to access higher branches.

Trimming Techniques

Professional Consultation: Consult with a professional arborist to identify the best methods for trimming your trees without damaging them.

Regular Maintenance: Regularly trim the trees to prevent the growth of low, accessible branches.

Proper Tools: Use the correct trimming tools, such as pruners for small branches and chainsaws for larger limbs, to ensure clean cuts and prevent disease.

Safe Tree Varieties

Choosing Safe Trees: Consider planting trees that don't readily encourage climbing, such as those with smooth bark or densely packed branches.

Thorny Plants: If possible, avoid having trees with thorns or spiky leaves that can cause injuries.

Educational Measures

Teaching Safety: Teach children about the dangers of climbing trees and explain why certain trees are off-limits.

Supervision: Always supervise young children when they are playing outside to prevent unwanted climbing attempts.

Creating Safe Play Areas

Separate Play Areas: Create designated play areas away from tempting trees to discourage climbing.

Ground-Level Play: Encourage ground-level play by providing play equipment like swings and slides, which are safer alternatives to tree climbing.

To ensure children's safety, you must first identify the risk factors, such as low branches and weak limbs that may invite climbing. You must also notice any nearby structures that children might use to gain access to higher branches. Once identified, employ the right techniques for trimming trees.

It is advisable to consult with a professional arborist for guidance on trimming without damaging the trees. Regular maintenance is key to preventing the growth of accessible branches.

Furthermore, you should consider planting tree varieties that do not encourage climbing and avoid trees with thorns or spiky leaves to prevent injuries. At the same time, it's crucial to educate children about the dangers associated with tree climbing and constantly supervise them to prevent unwanted climbing attempts. Creating separate play areas and encouraging ground-level play with safe play equipment can also discourage children from climbing trees.

► *According to Nationwide Children, each year, approximately 2,800 children (up to age 19) are treated in U.S. emergency departments for treehouse-related injuries, with most injuries involving falls, fractures, and head trauma.* ***Children under 5 years old are particularly likely to suffer head injuries from these falls.***

Yard
Infant/Non-mobile: (Birth - 6 months)
Infant crawl/roll: (5 months - 1 year)
→ **Toddler/Pre-school: (1 year - 4 years)**
→ **School-age: (5 years - 6+ years)**

Slip and Slide

Supervision: Always ensure that children are supervised by an adult when using the slip-and-slide. Active supervision can prevent accidents.

Surface Check: Before setting up the slip-and-slide, check the ground for sharp objects, rocks, or uneven surfaces that could cause injury. Choose a soft, grassy area free of potential hazards.

Water Control: Ensure the water source used to keep the slide slippery is at a safe pressure. Too much water pressure can cause more dangerous slips and falls.

Age Appropriateness: Ensure the slip and slide is suitable for the child's age. Some slides have size or age limits, so it's important to follow those guidelines.

End Padding: Place a padded surface, like soft mats or inflatable barriers, at the end of the slip and slide to prevent children from sliding into hard surfaces or obstacles like fences or trees.

No Rough Play: Establish rules for safe use, such as no running before jumping onto the slide and limiting the number of children using it at once to avoid collisions.

Sun Protection: Ensure children wear sunscreen and wear hats or clothing that provides sun protection. A slip-and-slide can keep kids in the sun for long periods.

Hydration: Ensure children drink enough water, as outdoor play in the sun can lead to dehydration.

Yard
Infant/Non-mobile: (Birth - 6 months)
Infant crawl/roll: (5 months - 1 year)
→ **Toddler/Pre-school: (1 year - 4 years)**
→ **School-age: (5 years - 6+ years)**

Hedges and Bushes Concerns

Keeping hedges and bushes trimmed is crucial for ensuring children's safety in and around the yard. Overgrown vegetation can pose various hazards, from hiding potential dangers to providing easy access to climbing or tripping risks.

Visibility: Trim hedges and bushes to maintain clear sightlines throughout the yard. This ensures that hazards, such as toys left out, uneven ground, or sharp objects, are easily visible, reducing the risk of accidents.

Accessibility: Overgrown hedges can become inviting hiding spots for children, which may lead to them getting stuck or injured. Regular trimming eliminates such hiding spots and discourages children from venturing into confined areas.

Thorny or Poisonous Plants: If you have hedges or bushes with thorns or poisonous berries, it's essential to trim them regularly and keep them at a safe distance from play areas to prevent accidental contact.

Prevent Overgrowth: Regular trimming prevents hedges and bushes from becoming overgrown, which could encroach on walkways, play areas, or structures, posing tripping or entanglement hazards.

Maintain Pathways: Trim hedges along pathways and walkways to keep them clear and prevent obstruction or potential injuries.

Prevent Nesting Areas: Untrimmed hedges may become nesting spots for insects or animals, increasing the risk of stings or bites. Regular maintenance helps reduce this risk.

Avoid Climbing Risks: Overgrown bushes with sturdy branches may tempt children to climb. Keeping them trimmed discourages climbing and reduces the risk of falls.

Avoid Spider Webs: Trim bushes away from doorways and play areas to reduce the likelihood of encountering spider webs that may cause discomfort or surprise.

Use the Right Tools: Use appropriate gardening tools, such as hedge trimmers or pruning shears, to ensure clean and precise cuts while trimming.

Safety Gear: When trimming hedges and bushes, wear appropriate safety gear, such as gloves and eye protection.

Regular Trimming Schedule: Establish a regular trimming schedule for the hedges and bushes in your yard, usually once or twice a year, depending on the plant's growth rate.

Proper Disposal: Dispose of trimmed branches and debris safely to prevent tripping hazards or the risk of children playing with the waste.

Educate Children: Explain to children the importance of avoiding hedges and bushes and the potential risks involved.

Supervision: Always supervise children when they are playing outdoors, especially in areas with hedges and bushes.

Keeping hedges and bushes trimmed creates a safer outdoor environment for children to play and explore. Regular maintenance of vegetation contributes to a well-maintained yard that minimizes potential hazards and ensures children's safety while enjoying outdoor activities.

<u>Yard</u>
Infant/Non-mobile: (Birth - 6 months)
Infant crawl/roll: (5 months - 1 year)
→ **Toddler/Pre-school: (1 year - 4 years)**
→ **School-age: (5 years - 6+ years)**

Moss Concerns

Moss is generally not harmful to children and can add a natural and charming element to outdoor spaces. However, some child safety concerns are associated with moss, especially in specific situations.

Slippery Surfaces: Moss can make surfaces, such as rocks, stones, or pathways, slippery when it's wet or damp. This may lead to slips and falls, especially for young children who may not have fully developed their balance and coordination. To address this concern, regularly inspect areas with moss and remove it from high-traffic pathways or play areas to reduce the risk of slipping.

Allergies: Some children may be allergic to moss or may develop skin irritation after contact with it. If you notice any signs of allergic reactions or skin irritation in your child after contact with moss, avoid direct exposure and seek medical advice if necessary.

Choking Hazard: Moss, particularly small and loose pieces, may pose a choking hazard if young children put it in their mouths. Always supervise young children when they are playing in areas with moss to prevent them from doing so.

Ingestion Concerns: Ingesting large quantities of moss could cause stomach upset or other gastrointestinal issues. Educate children about the importance of not eating or putting moss in their mouths and regularly remind them to avoid doing so.

Bacteria and Contaminants: Moss can sometimes grow in damp and shady areas, possibly accumulating bacteria or contaminants. Regularly inspect areas with moss, especially if it's growing in stagnant water, and promptly address any potential contamination concerns.

Habitat for Insects: Moss can provide a habitat for insects, some of which may bite or sting. Inspect areas with moss for insect activity and take measures to control or remove insects, especially those that may pose a threat to children.

Falling Moss: Moss may detach and fall in certain situations, particularly on trees or other structures. To prevent injury, keep children away from areas where moss is likely to fall.

Respiratory Concerns: Although rare, inhaled spores from certain types of moss may cause respiratory issues in some individuals. If your child has a respiratory condition, consult with a healthcare professional about potential risks and whether precautions are necessary.

While moss can be a beautiful part of the outdoor environment, addressing these child safety concerns and taking appropriate measures to ensure a safe and enjoyable play experience for children in areas where moss is present is essential. Regular maintenance, supervision, and education about potential hazards are key to promoting child safety around moss. This applies equally to algae, which is more likely to be found around ponds and permanent waterways, like drainage ditches or sprinkler systems. Some bleach water and a good blast from the hose should remedy the problem.

Yard
Infant/Non-mobile: (Birth - 6 months)
→ **Infant crawl/roll: (5 months - 1 year)**
→ **Toddler/Pre-school: (1 year - 4 years)**
→ **School-age: (5 years - 6+ years)**

Chemically Treated Lawn Concerns

Chemically treated lawns can present several child safety concerns due to the potential exposure to harmful chemicals. Lawn care products, such as herbicides, pesticides, and fertilizers, often contain toxic substances that can be hazardous to children's health.

Toxic Exposure: Children may come into direct contact with chemically treated lawns while playing or crawling on the grass, leading to skin irritation, eye irritation, or more severe health issues if they accidentally ingest or inhale the chemicals. Avoid using chemical lawn care products in areas where children play frequently. Opt for organic or natural lawn care alternatives that are safer for children and pets.

Accidental Ingestion: Young children may inadvertently put their hands in their mouths after playing on chemically treated lawns, leading to the ingestion of harmful chemicals.

Keep children away from chemically treated lawns for at least 24-48 hours after application to allow the chemicals to dry or dissipate. Encourage children to wash their hands thoroughly after playing outdoors, especially on chemically treated lawns.

Contaminated Play Equipment: Chemicals used on the lawn may transfer to play equipment, toys, or other outdoor items, increasing the risk of exposure to children. Clean and rinse play equipment regularly to remove any chemical residues. Store toys and play equipment away from chemically treated areas when not in use.

Runoff and Water Contamination: Rainwater or irrigation can wash chemicals from the lawn into nearby water sources, such as ponds, streams, or storm drains, contaminating the water. Follow application instructions carefully and avoid overusing lawn care products. Water lawns conservatively to minimize runoff and prevent chemicals from leaching into the soil.

Respiratory Irritation: Children with respiratory conditions like asthma may be more sensitive to airborne chemical particles from chemically treated lawns. To minimize the risk of chemical particles becoming airborne, avoid applying lawn care products on windy days. Consider using natural lawn care methods that reduce the potential for respiratory irritation.

Educate and Post Warnings: If you use chemical lawn care products, post visible warnings to keep children and pets away from treated areas until it's safe. Educate children about the potential hazards of chemically treated lawns and the importance of not touching or playing on treated grass.

Switch to Safer Alternatives: Consider switching to non-toxic and eco-friendly lawn care products that are safer for children, pets, and the environment.

You can minimize child safety concerns associated with chemically treated lawns and create a healthier and safer outdoor environment for children to enjoy. Always prioritize the safety of children when choosing lawn care products and methods.

<u>Yard</u>
Infant/Non-mobile: (Birth - 6 months)
Infant crawl/roll: (5 months - 1 year)
→ **Toddler/Pre-school: (1 year - 4 years)**
→ **School-age: (5 years - 6+ years)**

Garden Safety

Each year, **over 5,000 children** are injured by garden tools such as rakes, shovels, and hoes. (Source: U.S. Consumer Product Safety Commission (CPSC) - Garden Tool Safety) Gardens can be beautiful places for children to explore, learn about nature, and develop a love for plants and outdoor activities. However, specific child safety concerns in gardens need attention to ensure a safe and enjoyable experience.

Plant Selection: Choose plants carefully, avoiding toxic or poisonous varieties that may pose a risk if ingested. Research plant toxicity and opt for child-friendly plants.

Garden Layout: Plan the garden layout with safety in mind. Consider creating designated play areas away from potentially hazardous plants or gardening tools.

Fencing: Install a childproof fence around the garden or specific areas to prevent children from accessing areas with potential dangers, such as thorny plants or water features.

Sharp Tools: To avoid accidents, store garden tools like pruners, shears, and shovels in a locked shed or out of children's reach.

Chemical-Free Gardening: To reduce the risk of exposure to chemicals, avoid using harmful pesticides and herbicides in the garden. Opt for organic and natural gardening methods.

Water Safety: If there are water features, such as ponds or fountains, install a safety fence or barrier to prevent accidental drowning.

Container Gardens: Secure heavy or unstable containers to prevent tipping. Avoid using containers that could be a choking hazard for young children.

Garden Décor: Be cautious with garden decorations, such as sculptures or garden gnomes, as they may have sharp edges or small parts that could be dangerous.

Avoid Tripping Hazards: Regularly inspect the garden for potential tripping hazards, like loose paving stones or hoses, and address them promptly.

Supervision: Always supervise young children when they are in the garden. Teach them about safe gardening practices and potential hazards.

Plant Labels: Label plants that may have thorns, cause skin irritation, or be potentially harmful if ingested.

Garden Paths: Ensure garden paths are clear and well-maintained to avoid trips and falls.

Garden Furniture: Check garden furniture for sharp edges or potential pinch points. Secure furniture to prevent tipping.

Garden Wildlife: Teach children about garden wildlife, like bees and spiders, to encourage understanding and respect.

Educate Children: Educate children about safe gardening practices, such as wearing gloves, washing hands after gardening, and not eating plants or fruits without adult supervision.

First Aid Kit: Keep a well-stocked first aid kit handy in case of minor cuts, scrapes, or insect bites.

Sun Protection: Provide shade or encourage children to wear sun hats and sunscreen when spending extended periods in the garden.

You can create a safe and enriching outdoor space where children can explore, play, and develop a love for nature without undue risks. Regular maintenance, supervision, and age-appropriate education about garden safety are essential for fostering a positive and safe gardening experience for children.

Notes:

Yard
Infant/Non-mobile: (Birth - 6 months)
Infant crawl/roll: (5 months - 1 year)
→ **Toddler/Pre-school: (1 year - 4 years)**
→ **School-age: (5 years - 6+ years)**

Deck/Patio Safety

Deck and patio areas can be enjoyable spaces for families to spend time together outdoors. However, they also present specific child safety concerns that need to be addressed to ensure a safe environment for children.

Railings and Balustrades: Ensure that deck or patio railings are at least 36 inches high to prevent falls. The gap between balusters or railing slats should be less than 4 inches to prevent children from slipping through.

Secure Furniture and Equipment: To prevent tipping or accidental injuries, secure patio furniture, grills, and other equipment.

Sturdy Construction: Regularly inspect the deck or patio for any loose boards, nails, or splinters. Repair and maintain the structure to ensure its sturdiness.

No-Climb Zone: Establish a "no-climb zone" to prevent children from attempting to climb over the railing. Use visual markers or signs to remind them of this boundary.

Gate and Latch: If the deck has stairs leading down to the yard, install a gate with a self-closing and self-latching mechanism to prevent unsupervised access.

Slip-Resistant Surface: Choose a slip-resistant surface material for the deck or patio to reduce the risk of slips and falls, especially when wet.

Avoid Overcrowding: Avoid overcrowding the deck or patio with furniture and decor to create ample space for children to move around safely.

Safe BBQ Area: Keep the grill and any open flames away from play areas and consider using a grill guard to prevent accidental contact.

No Glassware: Avoid using glassware or fragile dishes on the deck or patio, as broken glass can cause serious injuries.

Electrical Safety: Cover outdoor outlets with weatherproof covers to prevent children from inserting objects into them.

Supervision: Always supervise young children when they are on the deck or patio. Never leave them unattended.

Secure Umbrellas and Canopies: Ensure that umbrellas and canopies are securely anchored to avoid tipping over in windy conditions.

Proper Lighting: Install adequate lighting on the deck or patio to improve visibility during the evening and prevent accidents.

Pool Safety: If there is a pool nearby, ensure that it is securely fenced with a self-closing gate to prevent unsupervised access.

Educate Children: Teach children about deck and patio safety rules, such as no running, no leaning on railings, and using furniture appropriately.

First Aid Kit: Keep a well-stocked first aid kit in a convenient location in case of minor injuries.

Regular Maintenance: Regularly inspect the deck or patio for any hazards, such as loose boards or damaged railings, and address them promptly.

You can create a secure and enjoyable outdoor space for your family. Remember that parental supervision, child education, and regular maintenance are essential for promoting a safe environment for children to play and relax outdoors.

<u>Yard</u>
→ Infant/Non-mobile: (Birth - 6 months)
→ Infant crawl/roll: (5 months - 1 year)
→ Toddler/Pre-school: (1 year - 4 years)
→ School-age: (5 years - 6+ years)

Allow your Home Address to be Seen (Lighting)

Ensure the Home Address is Visible to Emergency Responders. Having a marked home address is crucial for emergency responders to locate your home quickly during an emergency.

Use large, reflective numbers that are a contrasting color from your home. Dark numbers on a light background are ideal.

Position address numbers near the street on your home, mailbox, or driveway entrance should be easily seen from the road.

Make sure address numbers are not obstructed by trees, shrubs, decorations, or anything else. Trim back any foliage blocking visibility.

Install adequate lighting to illuminate your address at night. Use spotlights or solar-powered numbers.

Add reflective address stickers on your mailbox to identify it from both directions. Post your address number at the end of your driveway if your home is not visible from the road.

Childproofing extends beyond the interior of your home; it also involves ensuring that help can reach you swiftly in case of emergencies. Making sure your home address is easily visible both during the day and at night is a critical part of this.

Visibility During the Day

Contrasting Colors: Use large numbers in a color that contrasts sharply with the background. This will make the numbers stand out clearly. For example, if your home is painted in a light color, use dark numbers and vice versa.

Proper Placement: Place the numbers where they are easily visible from the road. This could be near the street, your home's facade, the mailbox, or the driveway entrance.

Unobstructed View: Ensure that the view of the numbers is not obstructed by trees, shrubs, or decorations. Regular trimming of foliage and prudent placement of decorations can help maintain clear visibility.

Weather-Resistant Materials: Use materials that can withstand various weather conditions without fading or wearing out.

Visibility at Night

Illumination: Install adequate lighting to illuminate the numbers during the night. This could be in the form of spotlights or light fixtures directed at the numbers. Solar-powered numbers that glow in the dark can also be a great option.

Reflective Materials: Use reflective materials for the numbers so they can be seen easily under the beam of headlights.

Additional Markings: In addition to the main display, add reflective stickers to the mailbox or other noticeable areas that can be seen from both directions of the street.

Driveway Posting: If the house is not visible from the road, consider placing a sign with the house number at the end of the driveway.

Regular Maintenance

Routine Checks: Perform routine checks to ensure that the numbers are always clean and visible.

Updates after Renovation: Ensure that the numbers' visibility has not been compromised after any renovation or landscaping activity.

Multi-directional Visibility: Ensure the numbers can be seen from multiple directions, enhancing the chances of quick identification.

In an emergency, every second counts. A visible home address can ensure that help arrives without unnecessary delays, potentially safeguarding the lives and well-being of your children.

Yard
Infant/Non-mobile: (Birth - 6 months)
Infant crawl/roll: (5 months - 1 year)
→ **Toddler/Pre-school: (1 year - 4 years)**
→ **School-age: (5 years - 6+ years)**

Water Well Concerns

Install a weatherproof cover over the window well. Look for heavy-duty metal or fiberglass covers that can be locked or screwed in place. This prevents kids from falling in or climbing into the well.

Consider installing vertical bars or grates over the window well opening. Space the bars no more than 4 inches apart to prevent children from slipping through, and the bars need to be securely installed.

Use a sturdy grate or mesh screen over the window well. The openings should be too small for a child's head to fit through, and the screens should be tightly fastened.

Plant thorny bushes like roses or pyracantha around the inside perimeter of the window well. The thorns will deter kids from climbing down into the space.

Place large rocks, gravel, or wood chips in the bottom of the well to make the area uninviting for play and provide safer footing.

Check that the window well cover is locked and secure at all times. Conduct regular inspections and maintenance.

Keep toys, chairs, etc., away from window wells so kids are not tempted to stand on them to look inside.

Attach a safety ladder inside the window well so anyone who falls in can climb out.

Talk to children and explain the dangers of window wells so they understand to stay away.

Taking proper precautions with covers, barriers, and signage can help prevent tragic window well accidents involving curious kids. Be vigilant!

<u>Yard</u>
Infant/Non-mobile: (Birth - 6 months)
Infant crawl/roll: (5 months - 1 year)
→ **Toddler/Pre-school: (1 year - 4 years)**
→ **School-age: (5 years - 6+ years)**

Fence Concerns

Childproofing your yard fence requires meticulous planning and execution to ensure the safety of your children.

Material and Structure

Smooth Surface: Choose fencing materials with smooth surfaces to prevent splinters and other injuries. Avoid fences with sharp edges or points.

Sturdy Construction: The fence should be constructed with solid materials to withstand pressure or force, preventing it from collapsing or being easily climbed.

Non-Toxic Materials: Ensure that the materials used are non-toxic and do not have the potential to harm children if they happen to chew or lick the fence.

Design and Layout

Visibility: While privacy is important, consider having sections of the fence where you can easily see through to monitor your children as they play.

Height: The fence should be tall enough to prevent children from climbing over it. Generally, a height of 4 feet or more is recommended.

Gaps and Openings: Make sure that there are no gaps or openings where children can squeeze through. Any slats should be spaced closely to prevent kids from getting their heads or limbs stuck.

Gate and Locking Mechanism

Self-Closing and Self-Latching Gates: Install self-closing and self-latching gates to prevent children from accidentally leaving the yard unsupervised.

Locks and Alarms: Consider installing locks and alarms on the gates that notify you if they are opened.

Surrounding Area

Climbable Objects: Ensure that no climbing objects are near the fence that children can use to scale it.

Vegetation: Be cautious about the type of vegetation near the fence. Avoid thorny or poisonous plants that could harm children.

Maintenance

Regular Inspections: Conduct regular inspections to check for any damage or wear and tear that might create a safety hazard.

Quick Repairs: Address any issues promptly to maintain the safety of the fence.

Education and Supervision

Educate Your Children: Teach your children about the importance of staying inside the fence and not attempting to climb it.

Supervision: Always supervise your children while they are playing in the yard, especially if they are very young.

Childproofing your yard fence is an ongoing process that requires regular checks and maintenance to ensure it remains safe and secure.

According to the CPSC

- *From 1990–2010, about **37,673 children under age 7 were treated in U.S. emergency departments yearly due to injuries from gates and barriers**—averaging roughly 1,800 cases per year.*

- ***Children ages 2–6** were more likely injured by gate contact (e.g., pinches, cuts), whereas toddlers under 2 more often suffered falls due to gate collapses*

- *Between 2008–2018, the CPSC **recorded 436 incidents involving gates or enclosures**. Including 19 fatalities and 108 nonfatal injuries. Many involving children under age 5 .*

Yard
Infant/Non-mobile: (Birth - 6 months)
Infant crawl/roll: (5 months - 1 year)
→ **Toddler/Pre-school: (1 year - 4 years)**
→ **School-age: (5 years - 6+ years)**

Picnic Table Safety

Secure the table to the ground. This will prevent it from tipping over if a child climbs on it.

Ground Anchors: These are metal spikes that you drive into the ground and then attach the table to them.

Tiedowns: These are straps that you can wrap around the table legs and secure to a tree or other solid object.

Remove loose Items: Remove loose items when they are not being used like tablecloths, placemats, and chairs. Make sure small items are not left on the table which could be a choking hazard for young children.

Block Access to Sharp Edges: If the table has any sharp edges, you can cover them with tape or rubber edging.

Install Corner Guards: These are plastic or rubber bumpers that you can attach to the corners of the table to prevent children from getting hurt if they bump into them.

Keep the Table Clean and Free of Debris: This will help to prevent children from tripping or slipping.

Always Supervise Children: Even if you have taken all of these precautions, it is still important to supervise children closely when they are near the table.

Here are Some Additional Tips

If you have a very young child, consider storing the table away when it is not in use.

If you have a dog, make sure that the table is not accessible to them. Dogs can knock over tables and injure children.

If you have a pool or other water feature nearby, make sure that the table is not located too close to it. Children could climb on the table and fall into the water.

<u>Yard</u>
Infant/Non-mobile: (Birth - 6 months)
Infant crawl/roll: (5 months - 1 year)
→ **Toddler/Pre-school: (1 year - 4 years)**
→ **School-age: (5 years - 6+ years)**

Yard Tool Safety

Yard tools can be very dangerous, and childproofing is essential in preventing accidents and ensuring the safety of your children.

Dangers

Sharp Edges: Tools like saws, pruners, and shears have sharp edges that can cause cuts and severe injuries.

Heavy Objects: Heavy tools such as hammers and axes can cause bruises or more severe injuries if dropped or mishandled.

Chemical Exposures: Tools like sprayers may contain residues of harmful chemicals that can be dangerous if ingested or come in contact with skin.

Tripping Hazards: Tools left lying around can create tripping hazards, leading to falls and injuries.

Electrical Tools: Electric yard tools can cause electrocution if not handled correctly or if they are faulty.

Precautions

Designated Storage Area: Create a designated storage area for all yard tools, ideally locked to prevent children from accessing them.

Tool Covers: Use tool covers to shield sharp edges and prevent accidents when tools are not in use.

Secure Heavy Tools: Store heavy tools so that they cannot be pulled down or tipped over.

Supervision: Never use potentially dangerous yard tools when children are around without another adult supervising them.

Safety Gear: When children are old enough to use yard tools, ensure they are wearing appropriate safety gear, including gloves, eye protection, and helmets as necessary.

Education: From an early age, teach children about the dangers associated with yard tools and instruct them never to touch these tools without adult supervision.

Demo Safety Measures: As children grow, demonstrate the correct way to handle tools safely, instilling good habits early on.

Maintenance

Regular Maintenance: Ensure all tools are well maintained to prevent accidents due to malfunction or breakage.

Electric Tool Safety: When it comes to electrical tools, teach children the importance of keeping them away from water and the proper way to handle them to avoid electrocution.

First Aid

First Aid Kit: Keep a first-aid kit readily accessible in the yard to immediately address minor injuries.

Emergency Plan: Have an emergency plan in place, and ensure children know what to do if they see someone getting hurt with a yard tool.

By being meticulous about storage, usage, and education, you can substantially reduce the risks associated with yard tools and create a safer environment for your children.

▶ *According to Stanford Medicine Children's Health,* **over 5,900 young children (ages 0–5) are injured every year in the U.S. by yard tools.** *About 4,800 from lawn mowers alone, and another 1,100+ from trimmers, rakes, shovels, and other equipment. Among toddlers (under 5), nearly 42% of mower injuries are burns, and lawn mowers cause around 600 amputations annually. It's a chilling reminder. Even simple yard chores carry serious risks for little ones.*

Yard
Infant/Non-mobile: (Birth - 6 months)
Infant crawl/roll: (5 months - 1 year)
→ **Toddler/Pre-school: (1 year - 4 years)**
→ **School-age: (5 years - 6+ years)**

Lawnmower Safety

Children should never be in the yard or on a riding mower while it is being operated. According to the U.S. Consumer Product Safety Commission (CPSC). **More than 800 young children are run over or backed over by riding mowers each year**. This can happen when children fall off the mower while being given rides or when they approach the operating mower and are not seen until it is too late.

Riding mowers can be very dangerous, even for adults. They can weigh hundreds of pounds and have blades that can rotate at high speeds.

Children are especially vulnerable to riding mower injuries. They are small and may not be seen by the operator, and they may not be able to get out of the way of the mower in time.

Even if you are not using the mower, children should not be allowed in the yard while it is running. Even if it is not moving, the mower can still be a hazard.

It is Important to Take Steps to Keep Children Safe Around Riding Mowers

- **Never give children rides on a riding mower.**
- **Never allow children to operate a riding mower.**
- **Keep children away from the mower when it is running.**
- **Be aware of your surroundings** when you are mowing. Ensure no children or pets are in the area before you start mowing.
- **If you see a child** or pet in the area, stop the mower immediately. Do not start mowing again until the child or pet is safely away.

Many children suffer severe burns to their hands and arms when they touch the hot muffler of running or recently running engines. Keep children away from power equipment.

This also applies to hedge trimmers, where the noisy motor blocks out the sound of an approaching child.

Yard
Infant/Non-mobile: (Birth - 6 months)
Infant crawl/roll: (5 months - 1 year)
→ **Toddler/Pre-school: (1 year - 4 years)**
→ **School-age: (5 years - 6+ years)**

Yard Toy Safety

Childproofing yard toys is important for creating a safe outdoor environment where children can play freely without the risk of injury. By understanding potential hazards and implementing preventive measures, you can ensure that your yard is a secure space for children to enjoy.

Choking Hazards

Small Parts: Yard toys with small, detachable components, like building blocks or action figures, can pose a significant choking risk, especially for younger children who are prone to putting objects in their mouths.

Balloons: Broken balloon pieces can be particularly dangerous as they can easily get lodged in a child's throat, leading to choking.

Strangulation Hazards

Strings & Ropes: Toys that include long strings, ropes, or cords, such as jump ropes or pull toys, can be a strangulation risk if they become wrapped around a child's neck.

Bike Helmets: While helmets are crucial for safety when riding, children should not wear them during other play activities as the straps can get caught on playground equipment or branches, posing a strangulation hazard.

Tip and Fall Hazards

Uneven Surfaces: Toys that create an uneven playing surface, like toy trucks or wagons left on the ground, can cause children to trip and fall.

Wet Toys: Toys that become slippery when wet, such as plastic slides or inflatable pools, increase the risk of falls and injuries.

Chemical Hazards

Toxic Paints & Materials: Some older or cheaply made toys may contain harmful chemicals or toxic paints, which can be hazardous if ingested or absorbed through the skin.

Batteries: Battery-operated toys can pose a risk if the batteries leak harmful chemicals or if small batteries like button cells are swallowed.

Projectile Hazards: Toys that shoot projectiles, such as darts, arrows, or balls, can cause serious injuries, particularly to the eyes.

Heat-Related Hazards: Toys with metal components can absorb heat from the sun and become hot enough to cause burns, especially in warm climates.

Prevention Strategies

Proper Storage: Use weather-resistant storage bins to keep toys organized and prevent them from becoming tripping hazards. Proper storage also protects toys from weather damage. Store toys with metal parts in shaded areas to keep them cool and prevent burn injuries.

Supervision: Always supervise children, especially when they are playing with toys that have small parts, long strings, or can shoot projectiles. This ensures immediate intervention if a dangerous situation arises.

Safe Toy Selection: Choose toys suitable for your child's age and developmental level. This helps reduce the risk of choking, strangulation, and other injuries. Select toys made from non-toxic, BPA-free materials, and ensure any paints or finishes are lead-free and safe for children.

Regular Inspections: Regularly check toys for wear and tear, such as cracks, sharp edges, or loose parts. Discard or repair any damaged toys immediately. Routinely inspect battery-operated toys to ensure batteries are intact and not leaking. Replace worn-out batteries promptly.

Education: Educate children on the importance of safe play. Teach them not to put toys in their mouths, to be mindful of others when playing with projectiles, and to play cautiously to avoid trips and falls. Make sure children know how to seek help in an emergency, such as finding an adult if they or another child are hurt.

Surface Safety: Install soft surfaces like grass, mulch, or rubber mats in play areas to cushion falls and reduce the severity of injuries. Regularly clear the play area of debris, toys, and other obstacles that could cause trips and falls.

First Aid: Keep a well-stocked first aid kit easily accessible in the yard. Include bandages, antiseptic wipes, and other essentials to quickly address any minor injuries.

Being vigilant and proactive about yard toy safety can significantly reduce the risk of accidents and ensure that outdoor playtime is both fun and safe. By following these guidelines, you can create a secure environment where children can explore, play, and grow with confidence.

- *U.S. Consumer Product Safety Commission (CPSC). In backyards across America, an estimated **208,000 young children** (ages 0–6) are treated in emergency rooms every year for injuries caused by yard toys. Everything from trampolines and ride-on scooters to playsets and bounce houses. That's over **22 kids every hour, injured while doing something as innocent as playing outside.***

Yard
Infant/Non-mobile: (Birth - 6 months)
Infant crawl/roll: (5 months - 1 year)
→ **Toddler/Pre-school: (1 year - 4 years)**
→ **School-age: (5 years - 6+ years)**

Sandbox Safety

A sandbox can provide endless fun and sensory play for children, but it also comes with some child safety concerns that need to be addressed.

Sandbox Location: Choose a suitable location away from direct sunlight to prevent overheating during hot weather. Also, avoid placing it under trees or near overhanging branches that could drop debris into the sandbox.

Cover When Not in Use: When not in use, cover the sandbox with a secure and well-fitting lid or tarp to prevent animals from using it as a litter box and keep it free from debris and rainwater.

Inspect for Hazards: Before allowing children to play, regularly inspect the sandbox for broken glass, sharp objects, or other potential hazards.

Clean Sand: Use clean and washed play sand without any contaminants, chemicals, or harmful substances.

Sun Protection: Provide shade or use a sun umbrella to protect children from the sun's harmful UV rays while playing in the sandbox.

Proper Clothing: Encourage children to wear appropriate clothing, such as hats and closed-toe shoes, to protect them from the sun and sand.

No Eating or Drinking: Teach children not to eat or drink while playing in the sandbox to prevent the ingestion of sand and potential health issues.

Supervision: Always supervise young children while they play in the sandbox to prevent them from engaging in unsafe behaviors or sharing sand toys that may pose choking hazards.

Insect Control: Take measures to control insects in the sandbox to avoid stings or bites.

Allergies: Be aware of any allergies to sand or outdoor elements that your children may have and take appropriate precautions.

Clean Hands: Encourage children to wash their hands thoroughly after playing in the sandbox, especially before eating.

Keep Cats Away: To prevent cats from using the sandbox as a litter box, consider using natural deterrents or placing physical barriers around it.

Size and Depth: Ensure the sandbox is appropriate in size and depth, allowing enough room for children to play comfortably without overcrowding.

Regular Maintenance: Regularly rake and maintain the sand to keep it clean and free from debris.

Sand Toy Safety: Provide age-appropriate and safe sand toys that are free from sharp edges or small parts that could pose choking hazards.

You can create a safe and enjoyable sandbox experience for children. Regular maintenance, proper supervision, and age-appropriate education about sandbox safety are essential to ensure a fun and safe outdoor playtime.

<u>Yard</u>
Infant/Non-mobile: **(Birth - 6 months)**
Infant crawl/roll: **(5 months - 1 year)**
→ **Toddler/Pre-school: (1 year - 4 years)**
→ **School-age: (5 years - 6+ years)**

Hide 'N Seek

Hide and Seek is a classic and enjoyable game that children love to play. However, to ensure a fun and risk-free experience, it's essential to consider child safety while playing this game.

Choose Safe Hiding Places: Encourage children to hide in safe and visible areas. Avoid places with potential hazards, such as near traffic, bodies of water, or sharp objects.

Set Boundaries: Establish clear boundaries for the game to ensure that children do not wander too far from the play area.

Supervision: Always have adult supervision during the game, especially for younger children. The supervisor can ensure that all participants are safe and following the rules.

Avoid Enclosed Spaces: To prevent accidental lock-ins or entrapment, discourage children from hiding in enclosed spaces, such as locked rooms, large containers, or small cabinets.

Communication: Teach children to communicate clearly and calmly if they are in distress or need help during the game.

Avoid Darkness: Avoid playing hide-and-seek in dark or poorly lit areas to reduce the risk of falls and injuries.

Check Before Seeking: Before counting and seeking, ensure that all children are in safe hiding spots, not dangerous areas.

Play with Familiar Playmates: Play Hide and Seek with children who are familiar with the game's rules and safety guidelines.

Age-Appropriate Boundaries: Set different boundaries for older and younger children to ensure a safe level of challenge for each age group.

Emergency Plan: Have an emergency plan in place in case a child gets hurt or lost during the game. Make sure all participants know what to do in case of an emergency.

Inclusive Play: Consider the abilities and limitations of all players to ensure that the game is inclusive and accessible for everyone.

Respect Private Areas: Teach children to respect private areas or spaces that are off-limits for hiding.

Be Mindful of Furniture: Avoid hiding behind or inside furniture that may tip over or cause injury.

No Climbing: Discourage children from climbing on structures or trees during the game.

Fair Play: Encourage fair play and sportsmanship among participants.

Ensuring adult supervision, setting clear boundaries, and teaching children about safe hiding places are essential elements for promoting child safety during this popular game.

<u>Yard</u>
Infant/Non-mobile: (Birth - 6 months)
Infant crawl/roll: (5 months - 1 year)
→ **Toddler/Pre-school: (1 year - 4 years)**
→ **School-age: (5 years - 6+ years)**

Well-drained Yard Play Area

A well-drained play area is crucial for child safety, especially during outdoor activities.

Preventing Puddles and Water Accumulation: A well-drained play area ensures that rainwater and other liquids do not accumulate, preventing the formation of puddles that could pose slipping hazards for children.

Reducing Trip and Fall Hazards: Proper drainage helps keep the play area dry and free from mud, reducing the risk of trips and falls.

Preventing Mosquito Breeding: Standing water can become a breeding ground for mosquitoes carrying diseases. A well-drained play area minimizes the risk of mosquito infestations.

Maintaining Play Equipment Integrity: Water accumulation around play equipment can lead to rust and deterioration, compromising its safety and longevity.

Site Selection: Choose a location that naturally allows water to flow away from the play area. Avoid areas with poor drainage, low spots, or places prone to flooding.

Grading and Sloping: Grade the play area to slope slightly away from the play structures. This allows water to drain away naturally.

Install Drainage Systems: For areas with more significant drainage challenges, consider installing drainage systems such as French drains, swales, or catch basins to direct water away from the play area.

Use Permeable Materials: For the playing surface, opt for permeable materials such as rubber tiles, mulch, or gravel. These materials allow water to pass through, reducing runoff and promoting better drainage.

Regular Maintenance: Keep the play area clear of debris, leaves, and other materials that can clog drainage systems or impede water flow.

Inspect and Repair: Regularly inspect the play area for any drainage issues and promptly address any problems, such as clogged drains or erosion.

Ensuring proper drainage in the play area creates a safer and more enjoyable environment for children to play and explore without concerns about water accumulation or slipping hazards.

Notes:

Yard
Infant/Non-mobile: (Birth - 6 months)
Infant crawl/roll: (5 months - 1 year)
→ **Toddler/Pre-school: (1 year - 4 years)**
→ **School-age: (5 years - 6+ years)**

Swing Set Safety

Play area safety is paramount to protect children while they engage in outdoor play. Let's address the specific safety concerns related to tubes on swing sets and sand underneath swings.

Tubes on Swing Sets

Entrapment Hazards: Ensure that the tubes on swing sets have appropriate openings or are designed to prevent the entrapment of children's heads, limbs, or clothing.

Secure Installation: Check that the tubes are securely fastened to the swing set frame to prevent them from loosening or detaching during play.

Sand Underneath Swings

Depth and Cushioning: Ensure that the sand under the swings is of an adequate depth to provide sufficient cushioning in case of falls. A depth of at least 12 inches is recommended to help absorb impact.

Maintain Sand Level: Regularly inspect and maintain the sand surface to ensure it remains at the appropriate depth. Rake and level the sand as needed to prevent uneven surfaces.

Free of Debris: Keep the sand area free from any debris, sharp objects, or rocks that could cause injuries during play.

Impact Zones: Establish a clear zone around the swings where children should not be standing or playing to avoid collisions with other swinging children.

General Play Area Safety Tips

Supervision: Always provide adult supervision during playtime to quickly respond to any emergencies or potential hazards.

Age-Appropriate Play: Ensure that the play area and equipment are suitable for the children's age and developmental level.

Regular Inspections: Regularly inspect the play area, including swing sets and other equipment, for signs of wear, damage, or potential hazards. Address any issues promptly.

Soft Surfaces: Consider using soft surfaces like rubber tiles, wood chips, or rubber mulch under play equipment to provide cushioning in case of falls.

Sun Protection: Provide shade or use sun umbrellas to protect children from excessive sun exposure during outdoor play.

Proper Use: Educate children on how to use play equipment safely and enforce rules to promote safe play behaviors.

Clear Space: Ensure there is ample clear space around play equipment to avoid collisions with other children or nearby objects.

<u>Yard</u>
Infant/Non-mobile: (Birth - 6 months)
Infant crawl/roll: (5 months - 1 year)
→ **Toddler/Pre-school: (1 year - 4 years)**
→ **School-age: (5 years - 6+ years)**

Building a Better Play Area

Choose a Safe Location: Select a flat and level area away from traffic, water features, and potential hazards. Ensure there are no overhanging branches or obstacles that could pose a risk.

Proper Ground Surface: Under play equipment, use a soft and impact-absorbing ground surface like rubber tiles, wood chips, or rubber mulch to cushion falls and reduce the risk of injuries.

Age-Appropriate Equipment: Install age-appropriate play equipment that suits the children's developmental level and abilities.

Sturdy and Well-Maintained Equipment: Ensure that all play equipment is sturdy, properly anchored, and free from sharp edges or protruding parts. Regularly inspect and maintain the equipment to keep it safe.

No Trip Hazards: Keep the play area free from tripping hazards such as rocks, tree roots, or debris.

Fence the Play Area: Consider fencing the play area to prevent unauthorized access and to keep children safely contained.

Safe Entry and Exit Points: Install easy-to-use entry and exit points for children, such as ramps or steps with handrails, to ensure secure access to the play area.

Shade and Sun Protection: Provide shade structures or use sun umbrellas to protect children from sunburn and overheating during hot weather.

Water Safety: If there is a water play feature, ensure proper supervision and age-appropriate safety measures to prevent drowning.

Supervision: Always have adult supervision during playtime to monitor children's activities and quickly respond to any emergencies.

Age-Appropriate Rules: Teach children the rules of safe play and enforce them consistently.

Safe Swings: If including swings, make sure they have appropriate seat restraints, and provide enough space between swings to prevent collisions.

Avoid Toxic Materials: Use non-toxic and child-safe materials for construction and avoid any chemicals that could be harmful to children.

Accessibility: To promote inclusive play, consider making the playground accessible to children of all abilities, including those with physical disabilities.

Emergency Plan: Establish an emergency plan and ensure that all caregivers and supervisors are aware of it.

To create a safe play area, choose a suitable location and use proper ground surfaces. Install age-appropriate equipment, maintain equipment regularly, and eliminate trip hazards. The area should be fenced with safe entry and exit points. It should offer shade and sun protection. Ensure water safety, avoid toxic materials, and use safe swings and equipment. Always supervise children, enforce age-appropriate rules, and consider accessibility. Make sure you have an emergency plan in place.

Yard
Infant/Non-mobile: (Birth - 6 months)
Infant crawl/roll: (5 months - 1 year)
→ **Toddler/Pre-school: (1 year - 4 years)**
→ **School-age: (5 years - 6+ years)**

Bicycle/Scooter/Skateboard Safety

Outdoor play is essential for children's physical development and overall well-being. Activities such as riding bicycles, scooters, inline skates, and skateboards provide excellent opportunities for fun and exercise. However, these activities come with inherent safety risks that must be carefully managed to prevent accidents and injuries.

Bicycles

They require strict adherence to safety measures. Bicycle related injuries lead to more than **100,000 emergency visits each year for children**, many of which could be prevented with proper helmet use and safety measures. (Source: Centers for Disease Control and Prevention (CDC) - Bicycle Safety)

Helmet Use: The most crucial safety gear for cycling is a helmet. A properly fitted helmet should always be worn while riding a bike. Ensure the helmet meets recognized safety standards; this is the best defense against head injuries in case of falls or collisions.

Bike Size: The bicycle must be the correct size for the child. A bike that is too large or too small can be challenging to control. The seat height should be adjusted so that the child's feet can comfortably touch the ground when seated. This adjustment enhances stability and control, particularly when stopping.

Traffic Rules: Teaching children about traffic rules is essential for their safety on the roads. They should understand how to interpret traffic signals and use hand signals to indicate turns and stops. Knowledge of these rules is crucial for navigating roads safely, especially in areas with vehicular traffic.

Safe Riding Areas: Encourage children to ride in safe, designated areas such as bike lanes, parks, or sidewalks where permitted. Avoid allowing them to ride in areas with heavy traffic or on busy streets, as these environments pose significant risks.

Supervision: Young children, particularly those who are still learning to ride, should always be supervised. Adult supervision is critical near roads, intersections, and unfamiliar areas to ensure that they adhere to safety practices.

Reflectors and Lights: Visibility is key to safety, especially during early morning or evening rides. Ensure that bicycles are equipped with reflectors and lights to make the child visible to other road users. This precaution is essential in low-light conditions.

Electric Bikes (E-bikes)

Electric bikes are gaining popularity for their convenience, but they present additional safety challenges, particularly for children.

Battery Hazards: E-bikes are powered by batteries, which can pose several risks. If damaged, batteries may leak hazardous chemicals or overheat, potentially leading to fires. It is also important to prevent children from tampering with or removing batteries, as this could expose them to electric shocks or other dangers.

Increased Weight: E-bikes are generally heavier than regular bicycles, which makes them more prone to tipping over. The added weight can also result in more severe injuries in the event of a fall. Children may struggle to manage or stabilize these bikes due to the extra weight.

Speed Concerns: One of the main attractions of e-bikes is their ability to accelerate quickly and reach higher speeds than traditional bikes. However, this feature can catch children off guard, increasing the risk of accidents. Higher speeds also mean that crashes or falls will likely result in more severe injuries.

Complexity of Operation: E-bikes often come with multiple modes and settings, confusing children. This complexity can lead to unintended acceleration or improper use of the bike's features, increasing the likelihood of accidents.

Electrical Components: The electrical components of an e-bike, such as wires and battery connections, can be tempting for curious children. Tampering with these parts can lead to electric shocks or damage to the bike. Additionally, unlike regular bikes, e-bikes have electrical parts that should not get wet, which may not be apparent to children.

Charging Concerns: Charging e-bikes presents its own set of risks. If left unattended, charging cables can create tripping hazards, and batteries can overheat if left to charge for too long. Monitoring the charging process and keeping cables out of children's reach is crucial.

Prevention Tips: To minimize risks, store e-bikes in a secure location where children cannot access them. If the e-bike has adjustable speed settings, set it to the lowest speed when it is used by or near children. Educate children about the differences between e-bikes and regular bikes, emphasizing the specific risks involved. Regular professional maintenance is also essential to ensure the e-bike remains in safe working condition.

Scooters, Inline Skates, and Skateboards

These wheeled devices are beloved by children for their fun and excitement, but they also come with specific safety risks.

Annually, approximately **10,000 children** are injured using electric scooters and skateboards, including fractures and head injuries. (Source: National Electronic Injury Surveillance System (NEISS) – CDC)

Protective Gear: Just like with bicycles, wearing protective gear is essential when using scooters, inline skates, or skateboards. Children should wear helmets, knee pads, elbow pads, and wrist guards to protect against injuries in case of falls or collisions.

Skill Level: Ensure children only attempt tricks or maneuvers matching their skill level. Beginners should start with basic movements in a safe environment before progressing to more advanced techniques. This gradual approach helps build confidence and skill while minimizing the risk of accidents.

Safe Surfaces: Wheeled devices should be used on smooth, flat surfaces free of traffic and obstacles. Avoid using them on uneven or cracked surfaces, as these can lead to falls. It is also important to keep these activities away from areas where vehicular traffic is present.

Avoid High-Speed Areas: High speeds increase the likelihood of losing control, which can lead to severe accidents. Children should avoid using scooters, skates, or skateboards on steep hills or in areas where high speeds are likely to be reached.

Watch for Hazards: Teach children to stay alert for potential hazards such as cracks, gravel, or debris that could cause them to trip or fall. Awareness of their surroundings is crucial for avoiding accidents.

Supervision and Age Limits: Younger children should always be supervised while using these devices. Age-appropriate restrictions should be considered, as younger children may not have the coordination or judgment needed to operate scooters, skates, or skateboards safely.

Additional Tips for Safe Riding

Teach Safe Riding Techniques: Educate children on how to stop, turn, and maintain control while using their wheeled devices. Knowing how to execute these basic maneuvers safely is essential for avoiding accidents.

No Riding at Dusk or in the Dark: Riding at dusk or in the dark when visibility is poor is particularly dangerous. If riding at these times is unavoidable, ensure that children are equipped with proper lighting and reflective gear.

Ride in Open Areas: Encourage the use of open spaces, such as parks or playgrounds, where there is plenty of room to maneuver safely. These areas are generally free of vehicles and other hazards, making them ideal for riding.

Traffic Awareness: Children should be taught to be aware of their surroundings, including pedestrians and vehicles. This is especially important when riding near roads or in shared spaces where they may encounter others.

Avoid Distractions: Discourage the use of mobile phones, headphones, or other distractions while riding. Staying focused on the activity is crucial for maintaining control and avoiding accidents.

Parents and caregivers can significantly reduce the risks associated with outdoor wheeled activities. Ensuring that children are properly supervised, equipped with the right gear.

Yard
Infant/Non-mobile: (Birth - 6 months)
Infant crawl/roll: (5 months - 1 year)
→ **Toddler/Pre-school: (1 year - 4 years)**
→ **School-age: (5 years - 6+ years)**

Trampoline Safety

Each year, approximately **100,000 children** in the U.S. are treated for injuries related to trampolines and bounce houses, including fractures, sprains, and head injuries. (Source: Centers for Disease Control and Prevention (CDC) - Trampoline Safety) Trampolines are a popular source of fun and exercise for children, but they also come with significant safety risks.

Supervision: Always have adult supervision when children are using the trampoline. A responsible adult should be present at all times to monitor the children's activities and enforce safety rules. This supervision is crucial in preventing accidents and ensuring that safety protocols are followed.

Age and Size Restrictions: When allowing children to use a trampoline, it's important to adhere to the manufacturer's age and size guidelines. Trampolines designed for older children or adults may not be safe for younger children, who are at a higher risk of injury due to their smaller size and less developed motor skills.

One Jumper at a Time: To minimize the risk of collisions and injuries, only allow one child to jump on the trampoline at a time. Multiple jumpers can cause unpredictable movements, leading to accidents such as falls, bumps, and even more severe injuries.

No Flips or Somersaults: Discourage children from attempting flips, somersaults, or other complex maneuvers on the trampoline. These actions significantly increase the risk of head, neck, and spinal injuries. Even experienced jumpers can misjudge a flip and land awkwardly, leading to severe consequences.

Use Safety Enclosures: Install a safety enclosure or netting around the trampoline to prevent children from accidentally bouncing off the edge. These enclosures are essential safety features that help keep the child within the trampoline area, reducing the risk of falls.

Proper Setup: Ensure that the trampoline is set up on a level surface and that it is properly anchored to the ground. A secure setup prevents the trampoline from tipping over or shifting during use. Follow all manufacturer instructions carefully during assembly.

Soft Landing Surface: Place the trampoline on a soft surface, such as grass or safety mats, to help cushion falls and reduce the risk of impact injuries. Hard surfaces like concrete or asphalt can cause serious injuries if a child falls off the trampoline.

Clear Area Around Trampoline: Keep the area surrounding the trampoline free from obstacles, toys, or furniture that could cause tripping or collisions. A clear area ensures that children can safely enter and exit the trampoline and reduces the risk of injury if they fall or jump off unexpectedly.

Regular Inspection and Maintenance: Regularly inspect the trampoline for any signs of wear, tears, or damage, such as frayed springs, torn netting, or rusted frames. Damaged parts should be repaired or replaced immediately to maintain the trampoline's safety and functionality.

No Jumping from Height: Teach children to enter and exit the trampoline safely using the provided entrance rather than jumping off from high positions. Jumping from a height can lead to severe injuries, including broken bones and sprains.

Use Ladders Safely: If your trampoline has a ladder for access, ensure that children use it properly and do not play on it. The ladder should be securely attached and used only for getting on and off the trampoline, not as a toy or play structure.

Weather Conditions: Do not allow children to use the trampoline during inclement weather, such as rain, strong winds, or storms. Wet surfaces can be slippery, increasing the risk of falls, while strong winds can make the trampoline unstable and dangerous.

Educate on Safe Jumping: Teach children to jump in the center of the trampoline, avoid the springs and frame, and keep their jumps controlled and low. This practice helps maintain balance and reduces the risk of injury from landing on the hard parts of the trampoline.

No Horseplay: Discourage rough play, pushing, or other forms of horseplay on the trampoline. Such behavior increases the likelihood of accidents and injuries, particularly when children do not notice their surroundings.

Set Time Limits: Limit the amount of time children spend on the trampoline to reduce the risk of fatigue-related accidents. Tired children are more likely to lose their balance or fail to follow safety rules, leading to potential injuries.

Yard
Infant/Non-mobile: (Birth - 6 months)
Infant crawl/roll: (5 months - 1 year)
→ **Toddler/Pre-school: (1 year - 4 years)**
→ **School-age: (5 years - 6+ years)**

Garden Hose Concerns

Childproofing a garden hose is important for preventing accidents and ensuring that children are kept safe while in outdoor spaces. Key precautions include storing the hose properly, using a hose reel or wall-mounted holder to keep it neatly coiled and off the ground, which minimizes tripping hazards. Elevating the hose using hooks or hangers also helps to keep it out of children's way. Regularly inspecting the hose for sharp edges, kinks, and wear and tear is crucial, as damaged areas can cause injuries or disruptions in water flow. Additionally, removing nozzles and spray attachments when not in use prevents children from accidentally turning on the water, which could lead to soaking or injury. Reducing water pressure around children adds another layer of safety by preventing high-pressure accidents.

Further steps involve teaching children not to drink from the garden hose due to potential contaminants or water temperature issues. Using childproof hose bib attachments ensures that children cannot turn the water on unsupervised. It is also important to store watering tools such as sprinklers or spray nozzles out of reach when not in use and opt for child-friendly designs. Always supervise children during use and keep them at a safe distance when watering plants. Additionally, regularly inspecting and maintaining the hose, as well as educating children on safe usage, reinforces the importance of safety around garden hoses. Note: **Annually, approximately 1,000 children are injured by lawn sprinklers and irrigation systems**, including trips and falls. (Source: U.S. Consumer Product Safety Commission (CPSC) - Outdoor Equipment Safety)

Yard
Infant/Non-mobile: (Birth - 6 months)
Infant crawl/roll: (5 months - 1 year)
→ **Toddler/Pre-school: (1 year - 4 years)**
→ **School-age: (5 years - 6+ years)**

Bird Bath Concerns

Elevate the Bird Bath: Consider elevating the bird bath on a sturdy pedestal or platform to keep it out of reach of young children. This will help prevent accidental falls or splashing.

Smooth Edges: Ensure that the edges of the bird bath are smooth and rounded to minimize the risk of cuts or injuries.

Safe Material: Choose a bird bath made of child-safe materials, such as non-toxic resin, stone, or ceramic, to avoid any potential harm from harmful chemicals.

Stability and Weight: The bird bath should be stable and heavy enough to prevent tipping or toppling over if a child tries to climb on it.

Secure Placement: To minimize the risk of children colliding with it, place the birdbath away from play areas or high-traffic zones.

No Deep Water: Avoid filling the bird bath with deep water, which may pose a drowning risk to young children. Keep the water level shallow, allowing birds to bathe safely without creating a hazard for kids.

Keep It Clean: Regularly clean the bird bath to prevent the growth of algae or bacteria that could be harmful if children come into contact with the water.

No Chemicals: Do not use chemical additives or treatments in the bird bath water, as children might accidentally touch or ingest them.

Cover when Not in Use: When the bird bath is not in use, consider covering it with a childproof cover or net to prevent curious children from exploring it.

Supervision: Always supervise children around the bird bath to ensure their safety and to prevent them from touching the water or any decorative elements.

Educate About Birds: Teach children about the importance of bird baths and the significance of leaving them undisturbed to attract and nurture birds.

Inspect for Hazards: Regularly inspect the bird bath for any signs of wear, damage, or potential hazards. Repair or replace any issues promptly.

Secure Surrounding Area: To prevent accidents, keep the area around the bird bath free of tripping hazards, such as toys or garden tools.

Use Child-Friendly Bird Baths: If possible, choose bird baths with child-friendly designs, smooth surfaces, and no small parts that might pose choking hazards.

You can make the bird bath area safer for children and create a welcoming environment for both birds and kids to enjoy the outdoors responsibly.

<u>Yard</u>
Infant/Non-mobile: (Birth - 6 months)
Infant crawl/roll: (5 months - 1 year)
→ **Toddler/Pre-school: (1 year - 4 years)**
→ **School-age: (5 years - 6+ years)**

Water Feature Concerns

Fencing around water features is a critical child safety measure to prevent accidents and protect young children from potential hazards.

Drowning Prevention: The most significant concern is drowning, which is a leading cause of accidental death in young children. Fencing creates a physical barrier between children and the water, reducing the risk of accidental entry and drowning incidents.

Curiosity and Exploration: Children are naturally curious and may be drawn to the water feature, unaware of its dangers. Fencing acts as a deterrent, limiting access and discouraging unsupervised exploration.

Fast Access to Water: Children can move quickly and reach a water feature before parents or caregivers intervene. Fencing provides an additional layer of protection and buys valuable time to react and prevent accidents.

Unpredictable Behavior: Young children can exhibit unpredictable behavior, such as climbing or reaching for objects near the water feature. A fence can prevent them from accidentally falling in or getting too close to the water.

Preventing Climbing: Fencing should be designed to avoid climbing. Children might try to climb over the fence, so it's crucial to ensure it is tall enough and doesn't have any footholds or objects nearby that could aid climbing.

Protection from Accidental Falls: Water features like ponds or waterfalls may have slippery surfaces or uneven terrain surrounding them, increasing the risk of accidental falls. Fencing keeps children at a safe distance away from such areas.

Supervision Limitations: Even with diligent supervision, accidents can happen. A fence provides an additional safety measure, reducing the reliance solely on adult supervision.

Unsupervised Access: In settings like public parks or community areas, a fence helps prevent unauthorized or unsupervised access to water features, ensuring they are enjoyed responsibly.

Compliance with Regulations: In many jurisdictions, installing fencing around certain types of water features is required by law to meet safety standards.

Education and Awareness: Fencing also serves as a visual reminder for children and adults about the potential dangers of the water feature and the importance of staying away when unsupervised.

Fencing helps keep children safe by creating a physical barrier and allows for worry-free enjoyment of water features under appropriate supervision. It is a responsible and effective way to protect young children and ensure they can explore and play safely in their surroundings.

<u>Yard</u>
→ **Infant/Non-mobile: (Birth - 6 months)**
→ **Infant crawl/roll: (5 months - 1 year)**
→ **Toddler/Pre-school: (1 year - 4 years)**
→ **School-age: (5 years - 6+ years)**

Septic Tanks and Water Well Security

Child safety concerns related to wells and septic tanks are significant due to their potential dangers to young children.

Water Wells

Water Well Caps and Covers: Ensure wells have secure and child-resistant caps or covers. The cover should be durable, lockable, and capable of withstanding a child's weight to prevent accidental falls into the well.

Regular Inspections: Conduct regular inspections of the well cover to check for damage or wear. If any issues are identified, repair or replace the cover immediately.

Fencing and Barriers: Install a fence or barrier around the well to restrict access and prevent children from getting too close to the opening. The fence should be at a safe distance from the well to avoid accidents.

Supervision: Always supervise young children when they are playing outside to prevent them from wandering near the well.

Educate Children: Teach children about the dangers of wells and the importance of staying away from them. Create clear rules about not playing around wells.

No Play Equipment Near Wells: Keep play equipment, such as swings or slides, away from the well area to prevent children from accidentally falling into the well.

Septic Tanks

Tank Covers and Lids: Ensure that septic tank covers and lids are secure and child resistant. Consider using lockable covers to prevent unauthorized access.

Clear Signage: Display clear and visible warning signs near the septic tank area to indicate the presence of a hazardous site.

Fencing and Barriers: Install a fence or barrier around the septic tank area to prevent children from accessing it.

Regular Inspections: Regularly inspect the septic tank covers and lids to check for any signs of damage or wear. Repair or replace them promptly if needed.

Supervision: Supervise young children when they are playing outside to ensure they do not go near the septic tank area.

No Digging: Instruct children not to dig or play in the ground near the septic tank area, as this could damage the tank or cause accidents.

Safe Landscaping: Choose landscaping materials, such as thorny bushes or gravel, that deter children from playing near the septic tank area.

Proper Maintenance: Ensure the septic tank is properly maintained and emptied regularly to reduce the risk of overflows or leaks.

Educate Children: Teach children about the potential dangers of septic tanks and the importance of staying away from them.

Overall, taking these safety measures seriously is crucial to protect children from potential hazards associated with wells and septic tanks. Regular maintenance, proper covers and barriers, and constant supervision are crucial to ensuring child safety around these areas.

► *Septic tanks and wells can hide lethal dangers right in your backyard. While no U.S. data isolates toddlers, legal records estimate about* **50 child fatalities per year from unsecured septic tanks. In one Florida county, a child under 5 lost their life in such a tank.** *Add wells and cisterns, and you're looking at an under reported but unmistakable threat to young children.* (House Digest)

Yard
Infant/Non-mobile: (Birth - 6 months)
Infant crawl/roll: (5 months - 1 year)
Toddler/Pre-school: (1 year - 4 years)
School-age: (5 years - 6+ years)

Teach Your Child to Swim

Start your child's water safety journey early by introducing them to swimming at a young age. Some believe that newborns have an innate ability to swim to the surface, and many community centers offer swim lessons tailored for infants, toddlers, and school-aged children. Seize this opportunity to instill a love for swimming and ensure your kids are equipped for a lifetime of summer fun.

However, it's essential to remember that even proficient swimmers are not entirely safe when alone in a pool. Shockingly, **according to the U.S. Consumer Product Safety Commission (CPSC) swimming pools rank as the second-leading cause of death in children under five years old.** It takes less than four minutes for a person to drown, emphasizing the critical importance of constant supervision and vigilance around water.

If your child ever goes missing, always **check the pool first** in case of an accident. Never underestimate the potential risks of water, even if your child appears confident in swimming. Enroll them in formal swimming lessons but remember that adult supervision and proper pool safety measures are equally indispensable in ensuring your child's safety in and around water.

Notes:

Yard
Infant/Non-mobile: (Birth - 6 months)
Infant crawl/roll: (5 months - 1 year)
→ **Toddler/Pre-school: (1 year - 4 years)**
→ **School-age: (5 years - 6+ years)**

PFD's (Life Jacket) Information

Personal Flotation Devices (PFDs) are essential for child safety in and around water.

Proper Fit: Choosing a PFD that fits the child properly is crucial. PFDs that are too loose may not provide adequate buoyancy, while those that are too tight can be uncomfortable and restrict movement.

Age and Weight Recommendations: When selecting a PFD for a child, follow the manufacturer's age and weight recommendations. Different sizes and styles are designed to support various age groups and weights.

US Coast Guard Approved: Ensure that the PFD is approved by the US Coast Guard or the appropriate regulatory authority. Approved PFDs meet specific safety standards and offer reliable buoyancy.

Check for Damage: Regularly inspect the PFD for any signs of damage, wear, or tear. Replace or repair damaged PFDs immediately to maintain their effectiveness.

Comfort and Freedom of Movement: Children are more likely to wear a PFD if it is comfortable and allows them to move freely. Look for PFDs with adjustable straps and secure buckles to achieve a snug yet comfortable fit.

Supervision: Even when a child is wearing a PFD, they should never be left unsupervised near water. PFDs are not a substitute for adult supervision.

Water Activities: Match the type of PFD to the specific water activity. Different PFDs are designed for various water sports, such as boating, kayaking, or swimming.

Proper Use: Educate children on how to wear and use the PFD correctly. Teach them how to fasten the straps securely and understand the purpose of the PFD.

Regular Practice: Encourage children to practice wearing their PFDs in a controlled environment, such as a pool, to become familiar and comfortable with them.

Replacement: As children grow, their PFDs may no longer fit properly. Regularly assess the fit of the PFD and replace it as needed to ensure continued safety.

Respect Water Safety Rules: Reinforce water safety rules with children, emphasizing that wearing a PFD is only one part of staying safe in and around water.

Parents and caregivers can significantly enhance child safety during water activities and provide children with the necessary protection and confidence to enjoy water sports responsibly.

<u>Yard</u>
Infant/Non-mobile: (Birth - 6 months)
→ **Infant crawl/roll: (5 months - 1 year)**
→ **Toddler/Pre-school: (1 year - 4 years)**
→ **School-age: (5 years - 6+ years)**

Don't Be Overconfident!

Swimmies and floaties are fantastic aids for beginners, ensuring those little smiling faces have help staying afloat and visible in the water. However, it's crucial to remember that these floatation devices are not a substitute for vigilant supervision. While they provide valuable support, they should never replace the watchful eye of an adult.

Arm floaties, rubber duckies, or even life jackets are not enough to ensure a child's safety without proper supervision. These accessories are designed to assist in swimming but should always be accompanied by responsible adult supervision. Even the most proficient swimmers need someone to watch over them to prevent accidents.

So, don't rely solely on floatation devices when enjoying water activities with your little ones. Be the lifeguard they need by always keeping a close eye on them. Together with the right safety gear and vigilant supervision, you can create a safe and enjoyable water experience for your children.

Notes:

Yard
Infant/Non-mobile: (Birth - 6 months)
Infant crawl/roll: (5 months - 1 year)
→ **Toddler/Pre-school: (1 year - 4 years)**
→ **School-age: (5 years - 6+ years)**

Pool Gates

Gating a pool is of utmost importance for child safety and is essential in preventing accidents and potential tragedies.

Drowning Prevention: Drowning is a significant risk for young children, especially those under the age of five. Gating a pool acts as a physical barrier that keeps children from accessing the pool area unsupervised, significantly reducing the risk of accidental drowning.

Preventing Unsupervised Access: Children are naturally curious and may be drawn to water without understanding the dangers it poses. A pool gate with a secure latch ensures that children cannot access the pool area without adult supervision.

A Layer of Protection: A pool gate is an additional layer of protection that complements adult supervision. Even with vigilant monitoring, a moment of distraction can occur, and a closed and locked gate provides an extra barrier to prevent unsupervised entry.

Safety Compliance: In many jurisdictions, installing a pool gate is required by law to meet safety standards. Failure to comply with these regulations can result in legal consequences and, more importantly, jeopardize the safety of children.

Types of Pool Gates: Pool gates come in various designs, including self-closing and self-latching options. Choose a gate at least four feet high with a latch that children cannot open easily.

Gating Additional Water Features: If your pool has additional water features, such as fountains or spas, make sure to gate these areas as well to prevent access when not in use.

Fence Material: To deter children from attempting to scale the fence, consider using a fence material that is difficult to climb, such as smooth vinyl or metal.

Education and Rules: Educate children about pool safety and establish clear rules regarding pool access. Teach them never to attempt to open the gate without adult permission.

Supervision Reminders: Never leave children unattended around the water, even with a pool gate. Constant adult supervision is vital, and the gate should serve as an added safety measure, not a substitute for supervision.

Regular Maintenance: Inspect the pool gate regularly to ensure it is in good condition. Check for damage, loose parts, or malfunctioning latches and address issues promptly.

Gating a pool is a critical safety measure to protect children from the risks associated with water. By providing a physical barrier, gating ensures that children can only access the pool area under adult supervision, significantly reducing the chances of accidents and providing parents and caregivers with peace of mind. Always prioritize water safety and remember that a pool gate is just one piece of the comprehensive safety measures needed to create a safe and enjoyable swimming environment for children.

<u>Yard</u>
→ Infant/Non-mobile: (Birth - 6 months)
→ Infant crawl/roll: (5 months - 1 year)
→ Toddler/Pre-school: (1 year - 4 years)
→ School-age: (5 years - 6+ years)

CPR (Cardiopulmonary Resuscitation)

Child safety and the importance of CPR (Cardiopulmonary Resuscitation) go hand in hand, as CPR can be a life-saving skill in emergencies.

Rapid Response in Emergencies: Accidents and medical emergencies can happen at any time, and children, in particular, are vulnerable to injuries. Knowing CPR enables adults to provide immediate assistance while waiting for professional medical help to arrive.

Preventing Brain Damage and Death: In critical situations like drowning, choking, or cardiac arrest, CPR can help maintain blood flow to vital organs, especially the brain, until emergency services arrive. Early initiation of CPR increases the chances of a positive outcome and reduces the risk of permanent brain damage or death.

Common Childhood Emergencies: Children are prone to various accidents and medical emergencies, such as choking on small objects, near-drowning incidents, or sudden cardiac events. Being trained in CPR empowers caregivers to respond appropriately.

Immediate Action Matters: In cardiac arrest cases, the survival rate drops by approximately 10% for every minute that passes without CPR. Quick and effective CPR can make a significant difference in the outcome.

Peace of Mind: Knowing CPR provides parents, caregivers, and teachers with confidence and a sense of empowerment to handle emergencies effectively, creating a safer environment for children.

Safety at Home and in Public Places: CPR skills are valuable both at home and in public spaces. Children spend considerable time in various environments, and CPR-trained individuals can respond effectively in any setting.

Complementing Professional Help: While waiting for emergency medical services to arrive, CPR acts as a bridge to maintain blood circulation and oxygen supply, improving the child's chances of survival.

Standard First Aid Training: CPR training is a standard in first aid courses, which also teach participants how to manage injuries and medical emergencies specific to children.

Community Awareness: Widespread knowledge of CPR within a community increases the likelihood that someone nearby can assist in an emergency, making communities safer for children.

Empowerment for Teenagers: Teaching CPR to teenagers can empower them to respond effectively in emergencies and even become responsible babysitters or caregivers for younger siblings.

CPR is a critical skill that plays a significant role in child safety. Being trained in CPR enables adults to respond promptly and effectively during emergencies, improving the chances of positive outcomes and reducing the severity of potential injuries. CPR education should be accessible to all caregivers, parents, teachers, and older children to create a safer environment for children and foster a community that is well-prepared to handle emergencies.

<u>Yard</u>
→ **Infant/Non-mobile: (Birth - 6 months)**
→ **Infant crawl/roll: (5 months - 1 year)**
→ **Toddler/Pre-school: (1 year - 4 years)**
→ **School-age: (5 years - 6+ years)**

Life-Saving Education

Taking a child life-saving course is a proactive and responsible step to ensure the safety of children in various situations. These courses typically cover essential skills, techniques, and knowledge necessary to respond effectively to emergencies involving children.

CPR and First Aid Skills: Child life-saving courses teach essential CPR, and first aid skills explicitly tailored to respond to emergencies involving infants, toddlers, and older children. Participants learnhow to provide immediate assistance in critical situations, such as choking, drowning, or cardiac arrest.

Accident Prevention: Child life-saving courses often include valuable information on accident prevention, highlighting potential hazards at home, at school, and in public spaces. Understanding and addressing these risks can significantly reduce the likelihood of accidents.

Quick and Confident Response: Knowing how to respond promptly and confidently in emergencies can make a life-saving difference for a child. Child life-saving courses help build the necessary skills and boost participants' confidence in handling challenging situations.

Preparedness for Caregivers: Parents, grandparents, teachers, babysitters, and anyone responsible for children can greatly benefit from child life-saving courses. Being prepared to handle emergencies increases children's safety and provides caregivers with peace of mind.

Specialized Techniques: Child life-saving courses often cover specialized techniques, such as caring for children with specific medical conditions, dealing with allergic reactions, or managing pediatric injuries.

Emergency Scenarios Practice: These courses often include practical exercises and simulations of emergency scenarios involving children. This hands-on experience helps participants apply their knowledge and skills in a controlled setting.

Community Safety: Widespread participation in child life-saving courses enhances overall community safety. The more people trained in life-saving skills mean that there is a higher likelihood of someone nearby being able to respond effectively in an emergency.

Certification: Many children's life-saving courses offer certification upon successful completion, which can be valuable for certain professions or when seeking babysitting or caregiving opportunities.

Individuals can actively promote child safety and well-being within their families and communities by taking a child life-saving course. Being prepared to respond effectively in emergencies involving children can save lives and make a positive difference in critical situations.

<u>Yard</u>
→ **Infant/Non-mobile: (Birth - 6 months)**
→ **Infant crawl/roll: (5 months - 1 year)**
→ **Toddler/Pre-school: (1 year - 4 years)**
→ **School-age: (5 years - 6+ years)**

Keep Rescue Equipment and a Phone Near the Pool

Life jackets should be U.S. Coast Guard approved and the correct type/size for each child's weight. Check straps and buckles periodically for adjustments as needed.

To prevent electric shock, the reaching pole should be made of non-conductive materials like fiberglass or plastic. Aim for 12-16 feet long with a securely attached Shepherd's Crook to hook swimmers.

To prevent damage, keep the phone in a waterproof pouch or container well away from the pool. Make sure it is charged and clearly labeled "**EMERGENCY PHONE.**"

The first-aid kit should be a marked waterproof/weather-resistant container stored in the same secure spot as the phone. It should include bandages, gauze, tape, antiseptic wipes, antibiotic ointment, medical gloves, a CPR mask, an emergency blanket, trauma pads, tweezers, scissors, and instant cold packs.

Safety signs should be made of durable materials and placed prominently around the pool area. They should include depth markers, NO DIVING warnings, pool rules, emergency numbers, CPR instructions, etc.

Fencing should be at least 4 feet high and have self-closing, self-latching gates. Inspect the gates regularly for proper function and maintenance and consider installing an alarm.

Actively **watch children** when they are in the pool. Never leave them unsupervised, even for a moment. Adults should avoid distractions like phones.

<u>Yard</u>
Infant/Non-mobile: (Birth - 6 months)
→ **Infant crawl/roll: (5 months - 1 year)**
→ **Toddler/Pre-school: (1 year - 4 years)**
→ **School-age: (5 years - 6+ years)**

Proper Pool Cover

A proper pool cover is an essential safety measure to prevent accidents and protect children around pools. By providing a physical barrier between children and the pool, a pool cover can significantly reduce the risk of accidental drownings.

Benefits of Using a Pool Cover

Prevents Unsupervised Access: A pool cover effectively prevents children from accessing the pool without adult supervision, eliminating the risk of accidental drownings.

Maintains Water Quality: By covering the pool, you can help keep the water clean and free of debris, such as leaves, insects, and dirt. This reduces the need for frequent cleaning and chemical treatments, saving you time and money.

Reduces Evaporation: A pool cover can significantly reduce water evaporation, leading to lower water loss and decreased operating costs. This is especially beneficial during dry seasons or when the pool is not in use.

Improves Water Temperature: Pool covers can help insulate the pool, keeping the water warmer in the winter and cooler in the summer. This allows you to enjoy swimming for a longer period throughout the year.

Types of Pool Covers

There are two primary types of pool covers: **safety covers** and **solar covers**.

Safety Covers: Safety covers are designed to prevent children from accessing the pool. They are typically made of a strong material like vinyl or mesh and engineered to be difficult for children to climb or crawl through, providing a secure barrier.

Solar Covers: Primarily used to maintain water temperature, solar covers are transparent or translucent materials that allow sunlight to pass through. This helps to warm the pool water, reducing the need for heating systems.

Choosing the Right Pool Cover

Safety coverage is highly recommended if you have young children. It provides the most robust protection against accidental drownings. However, a solar cover might be suitable if water temperature is your primary concern, and you have fewer safety concerns.

Proper Installation and Maintenance

Regardless of the type of pool cover you choose, **ensure it is properly installed and maintained**. A loose or damaged cover can compromise its safety features and become a potential hazard. Regular inspections and maintenance are crucial to ensure optimal performance and safety.

Yard

Infant/Non-mobile: (Birth - 6 months)
Infant crawl/roll: (5 months - 1 year)
→ **Toddler/Pre-school: (1 year - 4 years)**
→ **School-age: (5 years - 6+ years)**

Remove the Ladder from Above Ground Pool

One key area that demands meticulous attention is the setup around an above-ground pool, specifically concerning the ladder that grants access to the pool. It is **vitally important to remove or secure the ladder to prevent unsupervised access by children** to the pool area, which can potentially lead to dangerous situations, including drowning incidents.

To implement this safety measure efficiently, **always ensure that the ladder is removed immediately after use and securely stored in a place inaccessible to children.** When removing the ladder, double-check that there are no residual steps or platforms that a child might climb onto. If your ladder is retractable, ensure it is fully retracted and locked in a position children cannot reach or manipulate.

Additionally, **it would be prudent to incorporate a safety cover or fence around the pool area as a supplementary security measure, creating a dual barrier system that would further deter unsupervised access**. Coupled with constant adult supervision during pool usage times, the removal of the ladder should be a fundamental part of your childproofing routine. This routine should be reinforced with education on pool safety for older children, teaching them never to try and access the pool without adult supervision.

It is a good practice to conduct regular checks to ensure that the ladder removal protocol is being followed consistently, making this a habitual part of your safety measures. This measure, although simple, can be a lifesaver, emphasizing prevention as a key component in childproofing efforts surrounding an above-ground pool.

Yard
Infant/Non-mobile: (Birth - 6 months)
Infant crawl/roll: (5 months - 1 year)
→ **Toddler/Pre-school: (1 year - 4 years)**
→ **School-age: (5 years - 6+ years)**

Separate Play and Pool Areas

Separating play areas and pool areas is an essential child safety measure that helps prevent accidents and ensures a safer environment for children.

Drowning Prevention: Separating play areas from the pool area reduces the risk of accidental drowning incidents. It creates a physical barrier between children engaged in other activities and the pool, minimizing the chances of unsupervised access.

Focused Supervision: When play areas and the pool area are distinct, parents and caregivers can focus their attention solely on the children in the pool, ensuring constant and vigilant supervision.

Avoiding Distractions: Children can easily get caught up in play and may not realize the potential dangers of the pool. Separating the areas can minimize distractions and encourage children to stay in designated play zones.

Establish Boundaries: Clearly define the play areas' and pool areas' boundaries using fences, hedges, or other physical barriers. This helps children understand where they are allowed to play and reinforces the rule that the pool area requires adult supervision.

Childproofing the Pool Area: Implement safety measures specifically for the pool area, such as installing a fence with self-closing and self-latching gates, using pool safety covers, and having pool alarms. This further enhances pool safety while keeping the play areas separate.

Age-Appropriate Activities: Designate play areas based on age-appropriate activities. Younger children may have a separate play zone with toys and games suitable for their age, while older children can have a different area with activities that match their interests and abilities.

Educate Children: Teach children about the importance of staying in designated play areas and the rules surrounding pool safety. Reinforce the idea that the pool area is off-limits without adult supervision.

Visual Cues: Use signs or visual markers to indicate the boundaries of the pool and play areas. These visual cues can serve as a reminder for children and adults alike.

Regular Maintenance: Regularly inspect fences and barriers to ensure they are in good condition and functioning as intended. Repair or replace any damaged or compromised elements promptly.

Supervision and Communication: Responsible adults should always supervise the children in the play and pool areas. Establish clear communication protocols between adults to ensure a watchful eye is always present.

Separating play areas and the pool area creates a safer space for children to enjoy their activities while minimizing the risk of accidents and promoting water safety.

Yard
Infant/Non-mobile: (Birth - 6 months)
Infant crawl/roll: (5 months - 1 year)
→ **Toddler/Pre-school: (1 year - 4 years)**
→ **School-age: (5 years - 6+ years)**

Batteries over Pool Outlets

If any of the pool equipment is not working properly, keep everyone out of the water. This includes underwater lights, pumps, and filters. If any of these device's malfunction, they could create a stray electrical current that could be fatal.

> **Use only battery-operated appliances in and around the swimming pool.** This includes radios, fans, and water toys. If you must use an electrical appliance, make sure it is plugged into a GFCI outlet. GFCI outlets have built-in safety features that will cut off the power if there is a problem.

> **Designate a Water Watcher** to supervise children in the swimming pool. The Water Watcher should be an adult who is not distracted by anything else and can always pay attention to the children.

> **Teach children about the dangers of electricity and swimming pools.** They should know not to touch electrical equipment near the pool and never swim alone.

Have your pool professionally inspected and maintained every year. This will help ensure that all of the electrical equipment is in good working order. Keep the pool area clear of clutter. This will help prevent people from tripping over objects and falling into the water. Post warning signs around the pool. These signs should alert people to the dangers of electricity and swimming pools.

Yard
Infant/Non-mobile: (Birth - 6 months)
Infant crawl/roll: (5 months - 1 year)
→ **Toddler/Pre-school: (1 year - 4 years)**
→ **School-age: (5 years - 6+ years)**

Toys Near the Pool Concerns

It is important to be aware when children play with toys in or near the pool, especially riding toys.

These toys can be fun but can also be dangerous if not used properly.

Never leave children unattended while they are playing with riding toys in or near the pool. Even if they are good swimmers, they can still drown if they fall off the toy and are not rescued quickly.

Make sure the riding toy is the right size for the child. A toy that is too big or too small can be unstable and lead to a fall.

Only use riding toys in shallow water. Deep water can be dangerous, especially if the child falls off the toy.

Teach children how to get off the toy if they fall in the water. They should know how to swim to the edge of the pool and climb out.

Be aware of the weather conditions. Do not use riding toys in windy or stormy weather.

Check the toys for damage before each use. The toy should not be used if there are any holes or tears.

Store the toys away from the pool when they are not in use. This will help prevent children from tripping over them or falling into the pool.

Teach children about the dangers of running around near the pool. They should know to walk slowly and carefully so that they do not trip and fall in.

<u>Yard</u>
Infant/Non-mobile: (Birth - 6 months)
Infant crawl/roll: (5 months - 1 year)
→ **Toddler/Pre-school: (1 year - 4 years)**
→ **School-age: (5 years - 6+ years)**

Secure Pool Chemicals

Securing pool chemical supplies is critical to child safety around the pool area. While pool chemicals are essential for maintaining water quality, they can pose significant risks if not stored and handled properly. By following these guidelines, you can create a safer environment for your children while enjoying the benefits of a swimming pool.

Lockable Storage: Invest in a lockable cabinet or storage container specifically designed for hazardous materials. This will prevent children from accessing pool chemicals and reduce the risk of accidental exposure. Ensure that only authorized adults have access to the key or combination.

High and Dry Storage: Store pool chemicals on a high shelf or elevated surface that is well out of reach of children. Avoid placing them on the floor or at a level where children can quickly grab them.

Separation and Organization: Keep different types of pool chemicals separate from each other and other household items. Use designated containers for each chemical and clearly label them to avoid confusion. This prevents accidental mixing, which can create dangerous substances.

Original Containers: Always store pool chemicals in their original containers with the labels intact. This helps ensure that you have accurate information regarding the chemical, its intended use, and any necessary safety precautions.

Ventilation: Store pool chemicals in a well-ventilated area to prevent the buildup of fumes. Avoid storing them in a confined space or near heat sources.

Dry and Cool Storage: Keep pool chemicals in a dry, cool, and shaded area. Excessive heat, moisture, or direct sunlight can cause chemicals to degrade or become unstable, potentially increasing their toxicity.

Childproof Latches: Use childproof latches or locks on storage cabinets to further prevent access by curious children. This provides an extra layer of security and reduces the risk of accidental ingestion or exposure.

Read Labels and Instructions: Familiarize yourself with the handling and storage instructions provided on the chemical containers. Follow the manufacturer's guidelines for safe storage and usage.

Personal Protective Equipment: When handling pool chemicals, always wear appropriate personal protective equipment, such as gloves and eye protection. This minimizes the risk of skin and eye contact, which can cause irritation or burns.

Secure Waste Disposal: According to local regulations, empty chemical containers and unused or expired chemicals should be disposed of. Do not leave them accessible to children.

Educate Children: Teach older children about the potential dangers of pool chemicals and the importance of never touching or handling them without adult supervision. Explain to them the risks associated with accidental ingestion or exposure.

Emergency Preparedness: Have a first aid kit and emergency contact information readily available in case of accidental exposure to pool chemicals. This will allow you to respond quickly and effectively in case of an emergency.

Notes:

Yard
Infant/Non-mobile: (Birth - 6 months)
→ **Infant crawl/roll: (5 months - 1 year)**
→ **Toddler/Pre-school: (1 year - 4 years)**
→ **School-age: (5 years - 6+ years)**

Kiddie Pools

Childproofing a kiddie pool involves implementing safety measures to ensure a secure and enjoyable water play experience for children.

Supervision: Never leave children unattended near the kiddie pool. Continuous adult supervision is essential to prevent accidents.

Secure Location: Place the kiddie pool in a safe, level area away from hazards like fences, sharp objects, or direct sunlight.

Fencing and Barriers: Erect a childproof fence or barrier around the pool area to prevent unauthorized access by young children or pets.

Water Depth: Fill the pool to an appropriate water depth for the child's age and height, ensuring they can comfortably touch the bottom.

Empty After Use: Always empty the pool immediately after use to prevent accidental drowning and avoid water accumulation.

Cover Drainage: Ensure the pool's drainage area is covered or secured to prevent entrapment or entanglement.

Anti-Slip Surface: Place a non-slip mat or padding around the pool to prevent slips and falls on wet surfaces.

No Running: To reduce the risk of accidents, enforce a "no running" rule around the pool area.

Safe Toys Only: Use age-appropriate and safe water toys without small parts that can be a choking hazard.

Sun Protection: Provide adequate sun protection with shade structures or umbrellas to prevent sunburn.

Water Quality: Regularly change and clean the water to maintain proper hygiene and prevent skin irritations.

Childproof Latches: If the kiddie pool has a cover or lid, ensure it has childproof latches to prevent unauthorized access.

Educate Children: Teach children about water safety rules, the importance of not entering the pool without adult permission, and how to use the kiddie pool safely.

Emergency Preparedness Have a first aid kit and emergency contact information nearby in case of accidents.

Childproofing a kiddie pool ensures that children can enjoy water play in a secure environment, reducing the risk of accidents and promoting a positive water experience. Always prioritize safety and supervision to create lasting memories of safe and enjoyable water play.

Yard
Infant/Non-mobile: (Birth - 6 months)
Infant crawl/roll: (5 months - 1 year)
→ **Toddler/Pre-school: (1 year - 4 years)**
→ **School-age: (5 years - 6+ years)**

Winter Safety

Never Allow Children to Play on a Snowbank by the Road

It's important to prioritize child safety at all times, including during winter activities. Playing on a snowbank near the road can pose significant risks, so it's essential to take precautions to ensure the safety of children.

Traffic Hazards: Snowbanks near the road can obstruct drivers' visibility, making it difficult for them to see pedestrians, especially small children. Playing near the road increases the chances of accidents and collisions.

Unpredictable Behavior: Children's behavior can be unpredictable. They may suddenly run onto the road while playing, which can lead to dangerous situations, especially in areas with moving vehicles.

Slippery Surfaces: Snowbanks can be slick, and children playing on them may accidentally slip and fall onto the road or into the path of vehicles.

Limited Reaction Time: Vehicles traveling on the road may not have sufficient time to react and stop if a child suddenly enters the road from a snowbank.

Distractions for Drivers: Children playing near the road can be a distraction for drivers, diverting their attention away from the road and increasing the risk of accidents.

Snow Removal Equipment: Snow removal equipment, such as plows and snow blowers, may be operating near snowbanks, posing additional hazards to children playing in the area.

Unknown Road Conditions: Children may not be aware of road conditions under the snow, such as potholes or uneven surfaces, which can lead to trips and falls.

To Ensure Child Safety

Designated Play Areas: Encourage children to play in designated and safe areas away from the road, such as yards, parks, or playgrounds.

Supervision: Always supervise children when they are playing outdoors and guide safe play practices.

Educate Children: Teach children about the dangers of playing near the road and the importance of staying away from snowbanks that are close to traffic.

Communication: Talk to children about road safety and the potential hazards of playing near roads, helping them understand the risks involved.

Install Barriers: If feasible, use physical barriers, such as fences or caution tape, to prevent children from accessing snowbanks near the road.

Yard
Infant/Non-mobile: (Birth - 6 months)
Infant crawl/roll: (5 months - 1 year)
→ **Toddler/Pre-school: (1 year - 4 years)**
→ **School-age: (5 years - 6+ years)**

Frostbite and Frostnip

Protecting children from frostbite and frostnip is crucial during cold weather conditions. These conditions occur when the skin and underlying tissues freeze due to prolonged exposure to cold temperatures. By taking appropriate precautions and educating children about the risks, you can help prevent these painful and potentially dangerous conditions.

Dress Appropriately

Layer Up: Wearing multiple layers of clothing helps trap warm air close to the body. Start with a moisture-wicking base layer to prevent excessive sweating and keep the skin dry.

Insulation: Use insulating materials like fleece or wool for the middle layer to provide ample warmth without restricting movement.

Waterproof Outer Layer: A waterproof and windproof outer layer protects against moisture and cold wind, helping to maintain body heat.

Protect Extremities: Don't forget to cover your child's hands, feet, and head with gloves, mittens, socks, and a hat. Consider using a neck gaiter or scarf to protect the face.

Stay Dry

Moisture Management: Adjust clothing layers as needed to avoid excessive sweating. Wet clothing can quickly accelerate heat loss and increase the risk of frostbite.

Change Wet Clothes: If your child's clothing becomes wet, change into dry clothes promptly. Wet clothing can significantly increase the risk of frostbite.

Keep Moving

Stay Active: Encourage your child to stay active and keep moving to generate body heat. Avoid prolonged periods of inactivity in cold weather.

Wiggle Toes and Fingers: Teach your child to wiggle their toes and fingers regularly to improve blood circulation and prevent numbness.

Stay Hydrated and Nourished

Stay Hydrated: Ensure your child drinks plenty of fluids to avoid dehydration, which can increase the risk of frostbite.

Eat Nutritious Foods: Provide your child with warm and nutritious meals to fuel their body's energy production and maintain warmth.

Time Outdoors: Limit your child's time outdoors in extremely cold conditions. Check weather forecasts for wind chill warnings.

Seek Shelter: Encourage your child to seek shelter if they feel too cold or experience numbness.

Avoid Frostnip and Frostbite

Know the Signs: Teach your child to recognize the early signs of frostnip, such as cold, pale skin, or tingling sensations.

Act Promptly: If you suspect frostnip, warm the affected area using body heat (e.g., tucking hands under armpits). For frostbite, seek medical attention immediately.

Use Protective Measures

Sunscreen: Apply sunscreen to exposed skin, as sunburn can increase the risk of frostbite.

Lip Balm: Use a lip balm with SPF to protect your child's lips from chapping.

Warm Footwear: Ensure your child is wearing insulated and waterproof footwear to protect against cold and moisture.

Warm Sleeping Gear: Provide your child with warm and dry sleeping gear during camping or outdoor activities.

Educating your child about the risks of frostbite and frostnip, you can help them stay safe and comfortable in cold weather.

Yard
Infant/Non-mobile: (Birth - 6 months)
Infant crawl/roll: (5 months - 1 year)
→ **Toddler/Pre-school: (1 year - 4 years)**
→ **School-age: (5 years - 6+ years)**

Sledding Safety

When childproofing sledding for a toddler, several safety concerns need to be addressed to minimize the risk of injury. First, it's important to **ensure the sledding hill is appropriate for toddlers.** Look for a gentle slope without obstacles like trees, rocks, fences, or other hazards that could cause a collision. **Ensure that the area is far from roads or bodies of water**, as toddlers may lack the ability to steer or stop effectively. It's also important to choose a hill that isn't too crowded, as older children may sled too quickly and pose a danger to smaller, less coordinated toddlers.

Safety gear is another essential consideration. Toddlers should wear a helmet to protect against head injuries, as sledding accidents can lead to falls or collisions. Dress them in warm, layered clothing that is water-resistant to prevent hypothermia, and ensure gloves, boots, and hats are secure. The sled itself should be toddler-appropriate, with a wide, stable base and steering controls if possible. Avoid sleds that are difficult to control or overly fast. Additionally, always supervise closely standing at the bottom of the hill to help guide or stop the sled if necessary. If the toddler appears tired or cold, take frequent breaks to avoid accidents caused by fatigue or discomfort.

Yard
Infant/Non-mobile: (Birth - 6 months)
Infant crawl/roll: (5 months - 1 year)
Toddler/Pre-school: (1 year - 4 years)
School-age: (5 years - 6+ years)

Ice Skating Safety

Oh, the joy of gliding on a smooth sheet of ice with twinkling holiday lights reflecting on the surface! Ice skating is a quintessential holiday activity, transforming the colder months into a winter wonderland of fun and laughter.

Choosing the Right Venue

Holiday Atmosphere: Choose a rink that is decked in festive decorations, enhancing the joyful holiday spirit.

Quality of Ice: Ensure the ice is smooth and well-maintained to prevent trips and falls.

Safe Surroundings: The surrounding area should be well-lit and festively decorated, maintaining a cheerful atmosphere while prioritizing safety.

Dressing Up for the Occasion

Festive Attire: Dress the little ones in festive yet warm clothing. Think of cute holiday sweaters that are also snug and comfortable.

Protective Gear: For a fun yet essential holiday present, gift them protective gear wrapped in holiday-themed wrappers. Include items like helmets, knee pads, and elbow pads.

Warm Accessories: To keep them warm and festive, don't forget the cute mittens and hats, perhaps in a Holiday theme.

On the Ice

Holiday Spirit: Begin the session with a little holiday jingle to get them in the festive mood.

Supervised Skating: Ensure children are always supervised by an adult, perhaps dressed as a friendly holiday elf, to keep the mood light and festive.

Skating Lessons with a Twist: Enroll them in skating lessons where they can learn to skate to their favorite holiday tunes.

Safety Elf: Designate a "Safety Elf" who watches over the children and ensures they follow safety rules while skating.

Post Skating

Warm Cocoa Treats: Set up a little booth offering warm cocoa, a perfect treat to warm them up after their fun-filled skating session.

Holiday Gift Bags: Reward their safe skating with small holiday gift bags filled with goodies and a safety star for being safety-conscious on the ice.

Emergency Preparedness

First Aid with a Holiday Flair: Have a first-aid station decked in holiday cheer, ready to treat any minor injuries with a sprinkle of holiday spirit.

Contact List: Maintain a contact list with a festive touch, noting all emergency contacts with little holiday stickers next to them.

You'll ensure not only the safety of the little ones but also a holiday ice skating experience filled with joy, laughter, and the magical spirit of the season. Happy holidays and happy skating!

Yard
Infant/Non-mobile: (Birth - 6 months)
Infant crawl/roll: (5 months - 1 year)
→ **Toddler/Pre-school: (1 year - 4 years)**
→ **School-age: (5 years - 6+ years)**

Snowmobile Concerns

Snowmobiling can be thrilling yet potentially dangerous, especially for children. Therefore, it's imperative to adopt meticulous safety measures. Here, we will outline various concerns and precautionary steps that should be taken when it comes to childproofing for snowmobiling.

Equipment and Gear

Helmets: Ensure children are equipped with DOT-approved helmets that fit snugly, protecting their heads from potential impacts.

Eye Protection: Equip children with clear eye shields or goggles to protect their eyes from flying debris and the glare from the snow.

Proper Clothing: Ensure children wear layers of water-resistant clothing to prevent hypothermia. The clothing should also be brightly colored to enhance visibility in the snow.

Gloves and Boots: Invest in good-quality gloves and boots that offer warmth and adequate grip and protection.

Snowmobile Suitability and Maintenance

Age-Appropriate Snowmobiles: Choose snowmobiles that are suitable for children's age and physical capabilities.

Routine Checks: Before letting children on a snowmobile, conduct a thorough check to ensure brakes, lights, and other safety features are working properly.

Speed Limiter: If possible, install a speed limiter on the snowmobile to ensure that the children cannot exceed a safe speed.

Education and Supervision

Safety Courses: Enroll children in snowmobile safety courses, where they can learn the rules of safe snowmobiling.

Supervised Rides: Always supervise children while they are snowmobiling and never let them ride alone.

Safe Routes: Educate children on choosing safe, designated routes for snowmobiling, avoiding areas with thin ice, open water, or obstacles like trees and rocks.

Emergency Preparedness

Emergency Kit: Equip the snowmobile with a child-friendly emergency kit, including items like band-aids, warm blankets, and a whistle.

Communication Device: Provide children with a communication device and educate them on how to use it in case of emergencies.

Safe Stop and Start: Teach children the secure way to stop and start the snowmobile, emphasizing the importance of doing so in open, clear areas where visibility is high.

Behavioral Guidelines

No Stunts: Clearly state that performing stunts or reckless driving is strictly prohibited.

Distance Maintenance: Teach children to maintain a safe distance from other snowmobiles to prevent collisions.

Wildlife Respect: Instruct children to respect wildlife and avoid areas where animals are present to prevent startling them or causing accidents.

Parents and guardians can significantly reduce the risk of accidents, ensuring children's safe and enjoyable snowmobiling experience. It's all about combining fun with safety for a memorable snow season!

Yard
→ Infant/Non-mobile: (Birth - 6 months)
→ Infant crawl/roll: (5 months - 1 year)
→ Toddler/Pre-school: (1 year - 4 years)
→ School-age: (5 years - 6+ years)

Sunscreen Protection
(It's especially Serious!)

Understanding SPF

SPF Range: Choose sunscreens with a minimum SPF of 30 to a maximum of 50 to provide adequate protection against harmful UV rays.

Broad Spectrum: Ensure the sunscreen is labeled as "Broad Spectrum," which means it can protect against both UVA and UVB rays.

Ingredient Check

Chemical vs. Mineral Sunscreens: Understand the difference between chemical and mineral sunscreens and choose mineral-based ones for children, as they are gentler on their sensitive skin.

Avoid Oxybenzone: Avoid sunscreens containing oxybenzone, a chemical that can cause skin irritations and allergies.

Fragrance-Free: Choose fragrance-free sunscreens to prevent potential skin irritations.

Proper Application

Generous Application: Teach children to apply sunscreen generously on all exposed parts of the skin, including the neck, ears, and the back of the hands.

Reapplication: Instill a habit of reapplying sunscreen every two hours or immediately after swimming or sweating.

Before Sun Exposure: Apply sunscreen at least 20-30 minutes before stepping out in the sun to allow the skin to absorb it properly.

Complimentary Protections

Sunglasses: Encourage children to wear sunglasses with UV protection to shield their eyes from harmful rays.

Hats and Cover-ups: Provide them with wide-brimmed hats and cover-ups to protect their head, neck, and shoulders.

Seek Shade: Teach children to seek shade during the peak sun hours (10 AM to 4 PM) to avoid excessive sun exposure.

Special Considerations

Infants and Sunscreen: Avoid using sunscreen on babies younger than six months. Instead, keep them shielded from the sun with protective clothing and shade.

Test for Allergies: Before using a new sunscreen, do a patch test to ensure the child doesn't have any allergic reactions to it.

Lip Balm with SPF: Don't forget the lips; use a lip balm with SPF to protect the child's lips from sunburn.

Education

Importance of Sun Protection: Teach children about the importance of sun protection and the potential dangers of sunburn and heatstroke.

Self-Application: As they grow, teach them how to apply sunscreen themselves to cultivate a lifelong sun-protection habit.

You can ensure a safe and fun time under the sun for children, minimizing the risk of sunburns and other sun-related skin issues. It's all about forming habits that guarantee a lifetime of skin health and safety!

Yard
Infant/Non-mobile: **(Birth - 6 months)**
→ **Infant crawl/roll: (5 months - 1 year)**
→ **Toddler/Pre-school: (1 year - 4 years)**
→ **School-age: (5 years - 6+ years)**

Pet Waste Concerns

(Hygiene and Infection Prevention)

Frequent Hand Washing

Hand Washing for Children: Encourage children to wash their hands thoroughly with soap and water after playing in areas where pets have been.

Supervision: Always supervise young children to ensure they are washing their hands properly.

Proper Disposal of Pet Waste

Timely Clean-Up: Clean up pet waste promptly to prevent children from coming into contact with it.

Use of Gloves: While cleaning, use gloves to prevent any contact with the skin.

Safe Disposal: Dispose of pet waste in a secure bin to avoid attracting pests or spreading bacteria.

Safe Play Areas

Separate Play Areas: Establish separate play areas for children and pets to minimize the contact children have with areas where pets relieve themselves.

Garden Concerns: If children are playing in the garden, ensure pet waste is clear to prevent potential ingestion of parasites or bacteria.

Pet Litter Boxes

Placement of Litter Boxes: Place pet litter boxes in areas that are inaccessible to children to prevent them from handling or ingesting feces.

Daily Cleaning: Clean pet litter boxes daily to maintain hygiene and prevent the breeding of parasites and bacteria.

Education and Awareness

Understanding Dangers: Teach children about the potential dangers associated with pet waste and why they should avoid contact with it.

Report Concerns: Encourage children to inform an adult if they notice pet waste in their play areas.

Health Concerns

Parasite Control: Ensure that pets are regularly treated for worms and parasites to reduce the risk of transmission through waste.

Vet Visits: Regular vet visits can help maintain the pet's health and prevent diseases that can be transmitted through waste.

Allergies and Respiratory Concerns

Air Quality: Be cautious about indoor air quality, as dried feces can contribute to respiratory concerns, especially in children with asthma or allergies.

You can create a safe environment for children, reduce the potential risks associated with pet waste, and foster a healthy relationship between your children and pets by implementing preventive measures and fostering education and awareness!

Yard
Infant/Non-mobile: (Birth - 6 months)
Infant crawl/roll: (5 months - 1 year)
→ **Toddler/Pre-school: (1 year - 4 years)**
→ **School-age: (5 years - 6+ years)**

Help Prevent Lyme Disease

Preventing Lyme disease, especially in children, is of paramount importance.

Understanding Lyme Disease

Educational Materials: Use age-appropriate educational materials to teach children about Lyme disease and the dangers of tick bites.

Recognizing Ticks: Teach children to recognize different types of ticks and to avoid areas where ticks are commonly found.

Prevention Strategies

Dress Smartly: Encourage children to wear long sleeves and pants when playing in wooded or grassy areas to minimize skin exposure. They should also wear light-colored clothing to easily spot ticks.

Use of Repellents: Use child-safe tick repellents on skin and clothing, strictly following the product's guidelines.

Application by Adults: Ensure that an adult is responsible for the application of repellents on children.

Yard Safety

Regular Mowing: Maintain your yard by regularly mowing the lawn and removing tall grasses and brush, which are potential tick habitats.

Play Area: Establish a tick-safe play area in the yard, possibly with wood chips separating it from wooded areas.

Post Play Precautions

Tick Checks: Perform routine tick checks on children after they have played outdoors, focusing on the head, neck, and skin folds. Use bath time as an opportunity to check for ticks.

Proper Tick Removal: Keep a tick-removal kit handy and be knowledgeable about the safe removal of ticks to prevent Lyme disease transmission. If a tick is found embedded, seek medical advice or assistance for proper removal and monitoring for signs of Lyme disease.

Pets and Lyme Disease

Pets and Ticks: Regularly check pets for ticks as they can bring ticks into the home.

Veterinary Advice: Seek veterinary advice on tick control products for pets.

Community Education

School Programs: Advocate for school programs that educate children on Lyme disease and its prevention.

Community Engagement: Engage with the community to create awareness and collective prevention strategies against Lyme disease.

Implementing these strategies can significantly reduce the risk of Lyme disease in children. The combination of preventive measures, education, and community engagement can foster a safer environment for children both at home and in the wider community.

Yard
Infant/Non-mobile: (Birth - 6 months)
Infant crawl/roll: (5 months - 1 year)
→ **Toddler/Pre-school: (1 year - 4 years)**
→ **School-age: (5 years - 6+ years)**

Filling Holes in the Yard

The backyard often serves as a primary play area for children to explore, play, and connect with nature. However, it can also house certain dangers, especially if it is not well-maintained. One such danger is the presence of holes in the yard, which can pose several risks to children. Here, we explore why it's vital to fill up these holes with an eye for detail.

Potential Risks

Tripping Hazards: Holes can create uneven ground, increasing the risk of tripping and falling. Children often run around without paying full attention to the ground, making them more prone to accidents caused by holes.

Pest Infestation: Holes can act as breeding grounds for pests like rodents and insects. These pests can potentially carry diseases and infections which can be harmful to children.

Water Accumulation: Holes can accumulate water and create puddles, encouraging mosquito breeding. Puddles can turn into messy, muddy pits and can be a slipping hazard.

Preventive Measures

Regular Yard Maintenance: Conduct routine inspections of the yard to identify and fill up any holes. Once identified, take immediate action to fill the holes to prevent any accidents.

Proper Filling Materials: Use appropriate material to fill the holes, ensuring that it is compacted well to prevent recurrence. Make sure the ground is leveled properly to prevent tripping hazards.

Education and Supervision: Educate children about the dangers of playing near or in holes. Ensure that children are supervised by an adult while playing in the yard.

Engaging a Professional: If the yard has multiple holes or more significant depressions, engaging a professional landscaping service might be beneficial to ensure the yard is safe and well-maintained.

Ensuring a yard is free of holes is a critical step in childproofing your outdoor space. It prevents potential physical injuries and keeps pests and related diseases at bay. A level, well-maintained yard provides a safe and enjoyable environment where children can play without risks. By taking the steps outlined above, you can create a fun and safe yard for children.

Yard
Infant/Non-mobile: (Birth - 6 months)
Infant crawl/roll: (5 months - 1 year)
→ **Toddler/Pre-school: (1 year - 4 years)**
→ **School-age: (5 years - 6+ years)**

Fire Pit/Bonfire Safety

Annually, approximately 700 children are injured by portable fire pits, including burns and smoke inhalation. (Source: National Fire Protection Association (NFPA) - Fire Pit Safety) Ensuring the safety of children around a fire is of utmost importance. Here, I will explain the concerns surrounding open fires, and bonfires, and how to effectively childproof these areas. Fire is an element that holds a certain fascination, especially for children. However, it is also potentially very dangerous. Whether it's a fireplace inside the home or a bonfire in the yard, it is essential to childproof these areas to prevent accidents and injuries. Here, we will explore the various concerns associated with fires and how to mitigate them effectively, focusing on details that might be overlooked but are vital in childproofing.

Potential Dangers

Burns and Scalds: Children may get too close and touch the flames or hot embers. Certain types of children's clothing can catch fire easily.

Inhalation of Smoke and Fumes: Prolonged exposure to smoke can cause respiratory issues. Burning certain materials can release toxic fumes that are harmful to children. Fire can easily spread to nearby flammable objects. Without proper supervision, fires can get out of control quickly.

Take These Measures

Creating a Safety Perimeter: Install a physical barrier, such as a fence or gate, to prevent children from getting too close to the fire. Create a clear zone around the fire area where no flammable materials are allowed.

Supervision and Education: Ensure that children are under constant supervision when near a fire. Have talks with children about the dangers of fire and establish rules for safe behavior.

Emergency Preparations: Have fire extinguishers readily available and know how to use them. Ensure that emergency numbers are easily accessible.

Safe Materials for Burning: Avoid burning materials that can release toxic fumes. Use safe fire starters instead of gasoline or other dangerous accelerates.

You can create a safe environment where children can enjoy the warmth and fascination of a fire without being at risk of the associated dangers. Vigilance and proactiveness are key to preventing accidents and ensuring the safety of children around fires.

<u>Yard</u>
→ **Infant/Non-mobile: (Birth - 6 months)**
→ **Infant crawl/roll: (5 months - 1 year)**
→ **Toddler/Pre-school: (1 year - 4 years)**
→ **School-age: (5 years - 6+ years)**

Apply Insect Repellent During Proper Seasons

In the delightful journey of childhood, where every stone unturned is a new adventure, it's crucial to safeguard children from the potential hazards of bug bites. Bug bites are not just itchy and uncomfortable—they can also pose significant health risks. Some insects carry serious diseases, and for children with sensitive skin or allergies, a simple bite can lead to severe reactions. That's why using bug repellent is not just a matter of comfort, but a vital step in ensuring children's health and safety. Let's explore why bug repellent is important and how to use it wisely.

Understanding the Risks

Bug bites can lead to both immediate discomfort and long-term health issues. Children are naturally curious and tend to spend time exploring gardens, parks, and outdoor trails—all of which increase their exposure to insects.

Disease Transmission is a primary concern.

Mosquitoes are more than just a nuisance; they can transmit **malaria, dengue, West Nile virus, and Zika virus.**

Ticks, often found in grassy or wooded areas, are known carriers of **Lyme disease and Rocky Mountain spotted fever.**

Flies, though often overlooked, can spread diseases such as **leishmaniasis**, especially in certain regions.

Allergic Reactions are another important risk.

Some children may experience **intense allergic responses**, which can range from mild swelling to more severe complications like hives or even anaphylaxis.

Scratching bug bites can lead to secondary infections, especially if the skin is broken and bacteria enter the wound. These infections can require antibiotics or other treatments, further stressing a child's immune system.

Choosing the Right Bug Repellent

When selecting a bug repellent, it's important to choose products that are both safe and effective for children. Not all repellents are created equal, and some ingredients may not be suitable for younger age groups.

Age Appropriateness should always be the first consideration.

For infants under two months, avoid repellents altogether. Instead, use protective clothing, mosquito nets, and stroller covers to keep insects away.

For older children, choose repellents that are specifically labeled as safe for pediatric use, and always check the recommended age range on the label.

Ingredients also play a key role in safety and effectiveness.

DEET is one of the most effective repellents but should be used in **concentrations of 10–30% for children**. Higher concentrations do not offer better protection, just longer duration.

Picaridin is a **gentle, non-greasy alternative to DEET**, and is considered safe for children when used as directed.

Oil of Lemon Eucalyptus, although natural, **should not be used on children under 3 years old** due to its potency.

Proper Application

Correct application is just as important as choosing the right product.

Ensure even coverage on all exposed skin, avoiding broken or irritated skin.

For facial application, spray the repellent into your hands first, then gently rub it onto the child's face, steering clear of the eyes and mouth.

Avoid overapplication More product does not mean better protection. Follow the instructions on the label carefully.

Apply repellent to clothing (especially socks and cuffs) for additional protection, but avoid treating undergarments. After outdoor play, wash treated skin with soap and water to reduce the risk of irritation or residue buildup.

Understanding the significance of bug repellent in protecting children from insect-borne illnesses is a key part of responsible parenting. Taking the time to select the right repellent and apply it correctly ensures children can enjoy the outdoors with minimal risk. In the grand adventure of growing up, preventing a bug bite is far easier—and healthier—than treating one. So let's nurture children's curiosity and spirit of exploration by prioritizing their safety and well-being with thoughtful use of bug repellent.

<u>Yard</u>
Infant/Non-mobile: (Birth - 6 months)
Infant crawl/roll: (5 months - 1 year)
→ **Toddler/Pre-school: (1 year - 4 years)**
→ **School-age: (5 years - 6+ years)**

Install "Watch for Children" Signs in the Front Yard

Setting up kid warning signs is an indispensable safety measure when it comes to childproofing a yard, particularly in homes close to roads. These signs alert drivers to slow down and be extra vigilant, as children could be playing nearby.

Selection of the Correct Signs

Visual Appeal: Opt for signs in bright colors such as fluorescent yellow or green to catch drivers' attention easily. Choose signs made with reflective materials to ensure visibility even in low light conditions.

Message Conveyed: The wording on the sign should be clear and direct, like "Caution: Children at Play." Signs with pictures of children playing can visually communicate the message swiftly.

Strategic Placement of Signs: Set up the signs at a distance, visible to oncoming traffic but not too close to the road where children might venture out.

Height and Angle: Ensure the signs are installed at an appropriate height, where they are clearly visible to the driver. The signs should also be angled so that drivers can read them from a distance and have ample time to slow down.

Maintenance of the Signs: Regularly check the signs for any wear and tear and replace them as necessary. Keep the signs clean so that they remain visible and their message clear.

Safety Education: Teach children the importance of staying within the boundaries of the yard. Educate children on the purpose of the signs and why they should adhere to safety rules.

Additional Tips

Fencing: Consider installing fencing around the yard to provide an additional layer of safety.

Supervision: Ensure that children are always supervised while playing in the yard, particularly when close to a road.

Setting up a kids' warning signs near the road is a vital aspect of childproofing a yard. It involves choosing visually appealing and clear signs, placing them strategically for maximum visibility, and maintaining them well. Coupled with educating children on road safety and implementing other complementary safety measures, these signs can significantly enhance the safety of a yard where children play, fostering a secure and worry-free play environment for them.

Notes:

Yard
Infant/Non-mobile: (Birth - 6 months)
Infant crawl/roll: (5 months - 1 year)
→ **Toddler/Pre-school: (1 year - 4 years)**
→ **School-age: (5 years - 6+ years)**

Retractable Driveway Guard

Childproofing demands attention to every potential risk factor in a child's environment. One important aspect that often goes unnoticed is securing the driveway, and this is where retractable driveway guards come into play. Let us delve into the multifaceted benefits and importance of installing a retractable driveway guard in homes with children.

Understanding a Retractable Driveway Guard

A retractable driveway guard is a barrier, often made of durable netting or similar material, that can be extended across the driveway to prevent children from running into the street and deter vehicles from entering the play area.

Advantages of Installing a Retractable Driveway Guard

Child Safety

Preventing Accidents: Children often get engrossed in play and may not notice an approaching vehicle. A guard acts as a physical barrier, preventing kids from accidentally running onto the road.

Defining Play Zones: Helps demarcate safe play areas and teach children boundaries early on.

Driver Awareness
Visual Alert: This signal acts as a visual cue for drivers to slow down and be alert as they approach your residence.

Preventing Driveway Turnarounds: Deters drivers from using your driveway as a turnaround, ensuring the safety of playing children.

Easy to Use
Retractability: Can be easily retracted when not in use, which does not obstruct driveway access for family vehicles.

Ease of Installation: These guards are relatively easy to install and do not require any specialized equipment or expertise.

Selecting the Right Driveway Guard

Consider the Following
Width: Ensure the guard is wide enough to cover the entire width of your driveway.

Height: The height should be sufficient to act as a visual and physical barrier for children and vehicles alike.

Material: This should be made of durable, weather-resistant materials to ensure longevity.

Additional Features
Reflective Strips: Opt for guards with reflective strips for better visibility during nighttime.

Lockable Feature: A guard with a lockable feature would prevent unauthorized removal or tampering.

Maintenance and Upkeep

Regular Inspection
Inspect Regularly: Regular inspection to check for any wear and tear is essential to ensure its effectiveness.

Cleanliness: Keeping the guard clean ensures visibility and functionality over time.

Educating the Family

Informing Family Members
Usage: Educate family members, especially children, on the importance and proper use of the driveway guard.

Emergency Protocols: Establish protocols for quick removal in case of emergencies.

A retractable driveway guard is a significant addition to your childproofing measures, offering both a physical barrier and a visual cue to enhance safety in the driveway area. It assists in preventing accidents, delineating play zones, and fostering a safer environment for children. Making a choice based on width, height, and material, coupled with regular maintenance, can help optimize its efficacy for a long time. Moreover, educating family members, especially children, about its usage and importance can go a long way in ensuring a safer play area.

Yard
Infant/Non-mobile: (Birth - 6 months)
Infant crawl/roll: (5 months - 1 year)
→ **Toddler/Pre-school: (1 year - 4 years)**
→ **School-age: (5 years - 6+ years)**

Barbecue/Grill Safety

When enjoying outdoor gatherings and delicious grilled meals, it's essential to prioritize child safety around barbecues and grills.

> **Location Matters:** Set up the barbecue or grill in a safe and well-ventilated area away from high foot traffic, play zones, and flammable materials like dry leaves or paper. Keep a minimum distance of 10 feet from any structure or overhanging branches.
>
> **Stable Surface:** To prevent tipping, ensure the grill is placed on a level and stable surface. Use a grill pad or heat-resistant mat underneath to protect the ground from heat and grease.
>
> **Supervision is Key:** Always have a responsible adult present when grilling. Children should never be left unattended near a hot grill, even for a moment.
>
> **Keep Kids Away:** Establish a "no-play" zone around the grill. Use physical barriers like a safety fence or cones to mark the area where kids are not allowed.
>
> **Proper Attire:** Encourage everyone, especially children, to wear appropriate clothing while near the grill. Loose sleeves, flowing clothes, and long apron strings can easily catch fire.
>
> **Utensil Safety:** Teach kids to use long-handled utensils to avoid getting too close to the heat. Keep grilling tools out of their reach when not in use.
>
> **Hot Surfaces:** Emphasize the importance of not touching any part of the grill, as it gets extremely hot during and after cooking. Use oven mitts or heat-resistant gloves.

Fire Safety: Keep a fire extinguisher or a bucket of sand nearby in case of flare-ups or emergencies. Educate children on how to use them if necessary.

Gas Cylinder Safety: Before using a gas grill, check the gas cylinder for leaks. Keep cylinders upright, secure, and away from direct sunlight or heat sources.

Charcoal Safety: If using a charcoal grill, ensure the charcoal is completely cool before disposing of ashes. Store unused charcoal in a dry, cool place.

Lighting Precautions: Teach children to stay away from the grill when it's being lit. Use long-reach lighters to ignite the grill and avoid lighter fluid if possible.

Cleanliness Matters: Regularly clean grease and food build-up from the grill's grates and trays. Empty grease trays after each use to prevent flare-ups.

Safe Food Handling: Educate children about the importance of proper food handling and cooking temperatures to avoid foodborne illnesses.

After Grilling: Once grilling is done, turn off the gas and let the coals cool down. Ensure that the grill is properly extinguished before leaving the area.

Storage Safety: Store grilling equipment, utensils, and fuel sources out of children's reach in a locked storage area.

Model Safe Behavior: Set an example by following all safety practices and rules yourself. Children are more likely to adopt safe habits if they see adults prioritizing safety.

<u>Yard</u>
→ **Infant/Non-mobile: (Birth - 6 months)**
→ **Infant crawl/roll: (5 months - 1 year)**
→ **Toddler/Pre-school: (1 year - 4 years)**
→ **School-age: (5 years - 6+ years)**

Best Age to Get a Dog... 8-10

According to the American Society for the Prevention of Cruelty to Animals (ASPCA) and The Humane Society of the United States, waiting until a child reaches around 8 to 10 years of age before considering getting a dog is advisable. This age range ensures that children have developed the cognitive, emotional, and physical abilities needed to responsibly care for and interact with a pet. Younger children might have difficulty understanding the responsibilities that come with pet ownership and may not be able to handle specific tasks involved in caring for a dog. Waiting until they are older allows for a better match between the child's capabilities and the needs of a pet, ensuring a positive and safe experience for both the child and the dog.

Notes:

Yard
Infant/Non-mobile: (Birth - 6 months)
Infant crawl/roll: (5 months - 1 year)
→ **Toddler/Pre-school: (1 year - 4 years)**
→ **School-age: (5 years - 6+ years)**

Doghouse Safety

When it comes to a doghouse, it's essential to create a safe environment for both your furry friend and your child.

Location Selection: Choose a doghouse location that is away from high-traffic areas and play zones. Ensure it's situated in a well-ventilated and shaded spot, protecting your child and dog from excessive heat or harsh weather conditions.

Secure Construction: Choose a sturdy, well-built doghouse that can withstand weather conditions and provide adequate shelter for your pet. Make sure there are no sharp edges, protruding nails, or splinters that could potentially harm your child.

Proper Sizing: Select a doghouse appropriate for your pet's size. An overly large doghouse may pose safety hazards for smaller children, while a cramped space could lead to accidental injuries.

Raised Flooring: Choose a doghouse with raised flooring to keep your pet dry and comfortable. This also helps prevent water from entering and minimizes the risk of pests or insects.

Entry and Exit: Teach your child to respect the dog's space by not blocking the entrance or exit of the doghouse. This ensures that your pet can move in and out freely without any obstacles.

Supervised Interaction: Always supervise your child's interactions with the dog inside the doghouse. Teach your child that it's a private space for the pet and should be entered only when necessary.

No Climbing or Sitting: Instruct your child not to climb onto or sit atop the doghouse. This prevents any accidental falls or damage to the structure.

Regular Cleaning: Maintain cleanliness by regularly cleaning the doghouse and the surrounding area. This helps prevent the accumulation of dirt, debris, or potential health hazards.

Safe Materials: Ensure that the materials used in the construction of the doghouse are non-toxic and safe for both pets and children. Avoid materials that may cause allergies or skin irritations.

Secured Roof: If the doghouse has a hinged or removable roof, make sure it's properly secured to prevent accidental collapses or injuries.

Educate About Pet Behavior: Educate your child about dog behavior, especially signs that indicate when the dog wants to be left alone. This helps your child understand when it's appropriate to approach the doghouse.

Respectful Boundaries: Teach your child to approach the doghouse gently and respectfully. Encourage them to avoid sudden movements or loud noises that may startle the dog.

Pet and Child Interaction: Foster positive interactions between your child and the dog within the doghouse area. This can include supervised play sessions and teaching your child to offer treats or toys to the pet.

Regular Maintenance: Conduct routine maintenance on the doghouse, such as checking for loose parts, ensuring proper ventilation, and addressing any repairs promptly.

<u>Yard</u>
Infant/Non-mobile: (Birth - 6 months)
Infant crawl/roll: (5 months - 1 year)
→ **Toddler/Pre-school: (1 year - 4 years)**
→ **School-age: (5 years - 6+ years)**

Beware of Dog Leashes Both Outside and Inside

Ensuring your child's safety around dog leashes, whether inside or outside, is paramount to a harmonious coexistence between the home, your family, and your furry friend.

Inside the House

Supervised Interactions: When your dog is indoors and leashed, always supervise interactions between your child and the dog. This prevents any unexpected tugging or entanglement.

Proper Storage: When not in use, store dog leashes out of your child's reach. Hanging them on hooks or keeping them in designated areas helps avoid accidental entanglement.

Teaching Boundaries: Teach your child to respect the dog's space when it's leashed indoors. Encourage them not to pull, play with, or tug on the leash.

Cord Management: Keep dog leashes away from blind cords, curtain ties, or other cords that could pose a strangulation risk to a curious child.

Outside the Home

Leash Control: Always control the dog's leash when outside. Avoid allowing the leash to dangle loosely, as this can become a tripping hazard for both you and your child.

No Wrapping: Instruct your child not to wrap the leash around their hands, arms, or body. This prevents accidental injuries if the dog suddenly pulls or moves.

Walking Etiquette: Teach your child the proper way to hold the leash during walks. Usually, this is with both hands, avoiding excessive slack or tension.

No Tugging: Emphasize that your child should never tug on the leash or try to lead the dog independently. An adult needs to guide the dog's movements.

Be Mindful of Surroundings: When in public areas, ensure that the leash doesn't become entangled with objects like benches, poles, or playground equipment.

Avoiding Strangulation Risks: If possible, use a leash without a loop handle. This reduces the risk of a child accidentally putting their head through the loop and getting stuck.

Safety Conversations: Have age-appropriate discussions with your child about the importance of being cautious around leashed dogs and the need to ask permission before interacting with unfamiliar dogs.

Dog Training: Properly train your dog to walk on a leash without excessive pulling or sudden movements, which can help prevent unexpected situations.

Notes:

Yard
Infant/Non-mobile: (Birth - 6 months)
→ **Infant crawl/roll: (5 months - 1 year)**
→ **Toddler/Pre-school: (1 year - 4 years)**
→ **School-age: (5 years - 6+ years)**

Teach Children that a Pet Isn't a Toy

Each year, approximately **50,000 children** are bitten or scratched by pets, leading to injuries that require medical attention. (Source: Centers for Disease Control and Prevention (CDC) - Pet-Related Injuries) Instilling proper pet interaction etiquette in a child is essential for fostering a safe, respectful, and loving relationship between your child and your furry companions.

Educational Conversations: Begin by having age-appropriate conversations with your child about treating pets with kindness and respect. Explain that pets have feelings and sensations just like humans, and their ears, tails, and bodies are sensitive.

Gentle Touch: Demonstrate and encourage your child to use a gentle touch when petting animals. Show them how to stroke a pet's fur without sudden movements softly.

Role-Modeling: Model appropriate behavior by interacting gently with the pets yourself. Let your child observe how you approach and handle animals.

Supervised Interactions: Always supervise your child's interactions with pets, especially when they are young and still learning how to interact safely.

Using Visual Aids: Use children's books, videos, or online resources depicting respectful pet interactions. These resources can visually reinforce the concept for your child.

Positive Reinforcement: Praise your child when they exhibit gentle behavior around pets. Positive reinforcement helps them associate good behavior with positive outcomes.

Teaching Boundaries: Teach your child that pets have personal space like humans do. Explain that they should respect a pet's space and not invade it.

Recognizing Signs: Educate your child on how to recognize signs that a pet is uncomfortable or stressed. Explain that a pet may move away, lower its ears, or show other signs of distress.

Empathy Training: Cultivate empathy in your child by asking how they would feel if someone pulled their ears or tail. This will help them understand the importance of being kind to animals.

Introducing Gentle Play: Encourage your child to engage in gentle play activities with pets, such as using toys or tossing treats, instead of physically pulling on them.

Positive Associations: Teach your child that pets should associate them with positive experiences. Show them how to offer treats or rewards when the pet behaves well during interactions.

Redirecting Behavior: If your child displays inappropriate behavior towards a pet, calmly redirect their attention to a different activity or explain why their action is not suitable.

Supervising Friends' Interactions: When friends visit, ensure they also understand the importance of treating pets gently. Supervise their interactions to ensure everyone follows proper pet etiquette.

Consistency: Consistency is key. Continuously reinforce the importance of treating pets kindly and promptly correct any misbehavior.

You'll empower your child to develop a deep understanding of respectful pet interactions. Your guidance will help create a loving bond between your child and your pets while ensuring the safety and well-being of both parties.

<u>**Yard**</u>
Infant/Non-mobile: (Birth - 6 months)
Infant crawl/roll: (5 months - 1 year)
→ **Toddler/Pre-school: (1 year - 4 years)**
→ **School-age: (5 years - 6+ years)**

Keep Dog Food Dishes Out of Reach

Ensuring child safety around dog food dishes is vital to fostering a harmonious and secure environment for both your child and your furry companion.

Choking Hazard: Dog bowls often contain small kibbles or food particles that can pose a choking risk to young children if ingested.

Unwanted Interaction: Children may unknowingly disturb or agitate a dog while it's eating, which can lead to defensive behavior.

Hygiene Concerns: Young children may touch the dog's food, potentially transferring germs or contaminants from their hands to the dog's meal.

Preventing Food Sharing: Children might try to share their food with the dog, introducing potential hazards if the food isn't suitable for the dog's diet.

Steps to Keep Dog Food Dishes Out of Reach

Designated Feeding Area: Set up a designated feeding area that is not easily accessible to young children. Choose a spot that is away from play areas or high-traffic zones.

Elevated Feeding Stations: Invest in elevated feeding stations or wall-mounted holders for dog bowls. This raises the bowls to a level that children cannot reach.

Pet-Only Zone: Create a "pet-only zone" where dog food dishes are placed. Teach your child that this area is off-limits to them.

Scheduled Feedings: Establish a feeding schedule for your dog. This helps children know when it's mealtime for the dog, reducing the chances of unwanted interactions.

Supervised Feedings: When your dog is eating, ensure that feedings are supervised to prevent children from approaching or disturbing the dog.

Teach Respectful Behavior: Educate your child about the importance of letting the dog eat in peace. Explain that just like humans, dogs need privacy during meals.

Positive Reinforcement: Praise and reward your child for respecting the dog's feeding space. Positive reinforcement encourages them to follow this practice.

Pet-Proof Gates or Barriers: Use pet-proof gates or barriers to create a physical separation between the dog's feeding area and play areas.

Storage Solution: Store dog food and treats in a secure, child-resistant container. This prevents curious children from accessing the food on their own.

Mealtime Routine: Incorporate the dog's mealtime into a consistent routine so children are aware and can avoid the feeding area during those times.

Hygiene Habits: Teach your child about proper hygiene around pets and their belongings, including not touching or playing near the dog's feeding dishes.

Role Modeling: Lead by example. Demonstrate respectful behavior around the dog's feeding area, reinforcing the importance of boundaries.

Keeping dog food dishes out of reach prevents potential hazards and helps nurture a positive relationship between your child and your furry friend based on mutual respect and understanding.

Yard
Infant/Non-mobile: (Birth - 6 months)
→ **Infant crawl/roll: (5 months - 1 year)**
→ **Toddler/Pre-school: (1 year - 4 years)**
→ **School-age: (5 years - 6+ years)**

Do Not Bother a Dog When They are Resting, Sleeping, or Eating

Teaching children to respect a dog's rest, sleep, and mealtime is crucial for ensuring their safety and your furry friend's well-being.

Importance of Respecting a Dog's Rest, Sleep, and Mealtime

Health and Stress: Interrupting a dog's rest or sleep can lead to stress and anxiety, affecting their overall well-being.

Preventing Aggression: Dogs can become startled or defensive if suddenly woken up or disturbed while eating, potentially leading to aggressive behavior.

Bond and Trust: Allowing a dog to rest, sleep, and eat peacefully fosters a stronger bond of trust and respect between the child and the pet.

Steps to Teach Children Respect for a Dog's Rest, Sleep, and Mealtime

Educational Conversations: Have age-appropriate conversations with your child about the importance of not bothering a dog during specific times. Explain that just like people, dogs need their rest, sleep, and uninterrupted mealtime.

Recognize Signs: Teach your child to recognize signs of a resting or sleeping dog, such as closed eyes, relaxed body, and quiet demeanor. Explain that these are indications that the dog needs privacy.

Create Resting Zones: Designate specific resting areas for the dog, such as a comfortable bed or cushion. Teach your child that when the dog is in this area, it's time for rest.

Mealtime Etiquette: Educate your child about mealtime etiquette for dogs. Explain that dogs may need space to eat without disturbances, just like humans.

Supervised Interaction: Always supervise interactions between the child and the dog, especially during mealtime and when the dog is resting or sleeping.

Set Boundaries: Teach your child to respect boundaries by not approaching the dog when it's resting or sleeping. To remind them, create a visual indicator, such as a "Do Not Disturb" sign.

Positive Reinforcement: Praise and reward your child when they exhibit respectful behavior around the dog's rest, sleep, and mealtime. Positive reinforcement encourages consistent behavior.

Interactive Playtimes: Schedule playtimes with the dog when it's awake and energetic. Engage your child in interactive play sessions to appropriately channel the dog's energy.

Gentle Wakeups: If the dog is resting or sleeping and needs to be awakened, demonstrate and encourage a gentle approach. Teach your child to call the dog's name softly and wait for it to wake up on its own.

Understanding Personal Space: Explain the concept of personal space to your child and how it applies to both humans and pets. Teach them to give the dog space during certain times.

Modeling Behavior: Lead by example by showing your child how to approach and interact with the dog respectfully during different times of the day.

Consistency: Consistency reinforces the importance of respecting a dog's rest, sleep, and mealtime. Over time, this will become a natural and respectful habit for your child.

You're fostering a safe and harmonious environment where your child and dog can coexist with mutual respect and understanding. Teaching children to avoid bothering a dog during rest, sleep, and mealtimes contributes to a positive and nurturing relationship between the two.

<u>Yard</u>
Infant/Non-mobile: (Birth - 6 months)
→ **Infant crawl/roll: (5 months - 1 year)**
→ **Toddler/Pre-school: (1 year - 4 years)**
→ **School-age: (5 years - 6+ years)**

Train Your Dog to Tolerate Kids

Teaching your dog to tolerate and interact positively with children is a valuable skill that fosters a safe environment for both your pet and your family.

Benefits of Training a Dog to Behave Around Children

Safety: A dog that is comfortable around children is less likely to exhibit aggressive or fearful behavior, reducing the risk of accidents.

Positive Interactions: Positive interactions between your dog and children enhance their overall bond and relationship.

Stress Reduction: Proper training helps your dog feel more at ease around children, reducing stress and anxiety for both parties.

Steps to Train Your Dog to Behave Around Children

- **Basic Obedience Training:** Start with basic obedience training, including commands like "sit," "stay," "come," and "leave it." A well-trained dog is more responsive and manageable around children.

- **Positive Associations:** Associate positive experiences with children by offering treats, toys, or praise whenever your dog interacts calmly or tolerates the presence of children.

- **Gradual Exposure:** Introduce your dog to children gradually and in controlled settings. Begin with calm and older children before progressing to more energetic or younger ones.

- **Supervised Encounters:** Always supervise interactions between your dog and children, especially during the initial stages of training. This ensures safety and provides opportunities for intervention if needed.

- **Body Language Education:** Teach children to recognize and respect your dog's body language. Explain signs of stress or discomfort, such as growling, lip licking, or stiff posture.

- **Desensitization Exercises:** Gradually expose your dog to common child-related sights and sounds, such as children playing, laughing, or running—reward calm behavior during these exposures.

- **Positive Reinforcement:** Reward your dog for calm and tolerant behavior around children. Use treats, toys, or praise to reinforce positive interactions.

- **Redirecting Attention:** Teach your dog to focus on you when children are around. Use commands like "look at me" or "watch me" to divert their attention away from potential triggers.

- **Teach "Go to Place":** When children are around, train your dog to go to a designated spot, such as a mat or bed. This will give your dog a safe space and teach it self-control.

- **Crate Training:** If your dog becomes overwhelmed or needs a break, use crate training as a positive and calming retreat.

- **Socialization Opportunities:** Expose your dog to various child-friendly environments, such as parks or family gatherings, where they can gradually learn to interact with different children.

- **Model Gentle Behavior:** Demonstrate gentle and calm interactions with children, serving as your dog's role model.

- **Teach "No Jumping":** Train your dog not to jump on children by rewarding them when they keep all four paws on the ground during greetings.

- **Consistency:** Consistency is key to successful training. Regular practice and reinforcement help solidify your dog's positive behavior around children.

- **Professional Guidance:** If your dog shows signs of aggression or fear towards children, seek the guidance of an experienced dog trainer or behaviorist.

You're laying the foundation for a harmonious relationship between your dog and children. Training your dog to tolerate children promotes safety, positive interactions, and a nurturing environment where both can coexist happily and comfortably.

Yard
→ Infant/Non-mobile: (Birth - 6 months)
→ Infant crawl/roll: (5 months - 1 year)
→ Toddler/Pre-school: (1 year - 4 years)
→ School-age: (5 years - 6+ years)

Beware of Mixed Breed Dogs

Understanding the mix of breeds in a dog is crucial in ensuring safety, especially when children are involved. Begin by conducting research and observing the dog's physical attributes, size, coat type, and behavior to get an idea of its heritage. If possible, inquire about the known or suspected breeds in its lineage. Additionally, delve into the temperament traits associated with these breeds to better understand potential behaviors. While certain breeds may have inclinations toward herding or protective instincts, remember that each dog is unique and can display a range of characteristics. This knowledge helps foster informed and secure interactions.

Yard
 Infant/Non-mobile: (Birth - 6 months)
→ Infant crawl/roll: (5 months - 1 year)
→ Toddler/Pre-school: (1 year - 4 years)
→ School-age: (5 years - 6+ years)

Beware of Dogs that Bite Frequently

Ensuring child safety around dogs is of utmost importance, and being aware of dogs with frequent biting incidents is crucial for preventing potential harm.

Recognize Warning Signs: Be aware of warning signs that a dog may bite, such as growling, baring teeth, raised hackles, stiff body posture, and intense staring. Teaching your child to recognize these signals can help them stay safe.

Ask Owners for Information: When you encounter a dog you're unfamiliar with, ask the owner about the dog's behavior and any history of biting incidents. Honest communication can provide valuable insights.

Maintain Distance: If you're uncertain about a dog's behavior, keep a safe distance and avoid approaching it. Teach your child to do the same, especially if the dog displays signs of aggression.

Avoid Unsupervised Interactions: Never allow your child to interact with a dog prone to biting without proper supervision. Ensure an adult monitors the interaction and steps in if needed.

Respect the Dog's Space: Teach your child to respect a dog's personal space and not to approach or touch the dog without the owner's permission. Even friendly dogs can become agitated if their space is invaded.

Teach Gentle Interaction: Instruct your child on gently interacting with dogs, using slow movements and calm voices. Sudden movements or loud noises can startle a dog and lead to defensive reactions.

Avoid Aggravating Situations: Be cautious around dogs that are eating, chewing on a toy, or caring for puppies. These situations can trigger protective instincts and increase the risk of a biting incident.

Seek Professional Help: If you encounter a dog with a known history of biting, consider seeking advice from a professional dog trainer or behaviorist. They can provide guidance on safe interactions and ways to prevent incidents.

Report Aggressive Dogs: If you encounter a dog that displays aggressive behavior, report it to local animal control or authorities. This helps protect not only your child but also others in the community.

Educate Children: Educate your child about the importance of caution around unfamiliar dogs and the potential risks associated with dogs that have a history of biting. Encourage open communication so they feel comfortable sharing any concerns.

Promote Responsible Ownership: Advocate for responsible dog ownership within your community. Encourage proper training, socialization, and responsible confinement of dogs to prevent aggressive behaviors.

By being cautious around dogs with a history of frequent biting incidents and teaching your child to do the same, you're taking proactive steps to ensure child safety. A combination of awareness, education, and respectful interaction can contribute to a safer environment for both children and dogs.

► *In the U.S., **roughly 50,000 children under age 6 visit emergency rooms each year after being bitten by dogs.** About half of all pediatric dog-bite cases. With bite injuries often focused on the head and neck and over 70% of serious bites happening to kids under five, this is a major hazard even in familiar settings.* (DogsBite.org)

Yard
→ **Infant/Non-mobile: (Birth - 6 months)**
→ **Infant crawl/roll: (5 months - 1 year)**
→ **Toddler/Pre-school: (1 year - 4 years)**
→ **School-age: (5 years - 6+ years)**

Better Dog Breeds for Children

When it comes to choosing a dog breed for families with children, certain breeds are known for their compatibility, gentle nature, and suitability for young ones.

Golden Retriever: Golden Retrievers are renowned for their friendly and tolerant nature. They're patient, loyal, and great with children, making them an excellent choice for families. They are also intelligent and trainable, which can lead to positive interactions between kids and dogs.

Labrador Retriever: Labradors are known for their playful and outgoing personalities. They have a gentle disposition and are particularly patient with children. Labradors thrive on human companionship and often form strong bonds with family members.

Beagle: Beagles are energetic and friendly dogs that get along well with kids. Their smaller size makes them suitable for indoor living, and their curiosity and affectionate nature make them a good choice for families.

Bulldog: Bulldogs, with their calm and gentle demeanor, are excellent companions for children. They have a loving nature and are less prone to high-energy antics, making them a good fit for families seeking a more relaxed dog.

Poodle (Standard or Miniature): Poodles are highly intelligent and versatile dogs that come in different sizes. They are typically easy to train, and their hypoallergenic coats can be a bonus for families with allergies.

Boxer: Boxers are known for their boundless energy and playful spirit. They form strong bonds with children and are protective without being aggressive. Their playful nature can provide hours of entertainment for active kids.

Collie: Collies are gentle and loyal dogs that often-become devoted family members. They are good with children and are known for their strong herding instincts, which can lead to playful interactions.

Newfoundland: Newfoundlanders are affectionate giants with a calm and patient demeanor. They are known for being excellent with children and can even act as natural lifeguards due to their strong swimming abilities

Cavalier King Charles Spaniel: These small and affectionate dogs are great companions for kids. They are gentle, adaptable, and thrive on human interaction, making them suitable for families with varying activity levels.

Pug: Pugs are known for their charming personalities and love of companionship. They are affectionate and easygoing, making them a popular choice for families seeking a smaller breed.

Important Considerations

Temperament: Look for breeds with friendly, patient, and gentle temperaments that are well-suited to a family environment.

Size: Consider the size of the breed concerning your living space and the ages of your children.

Energy Level: Match the breed's energy level with your family's activity level to ensure a harmonious fit.

Trainability: Breeds that are easy to train and socialize can lead to positive interactions and obedience.

Allergies: If family members have allergies, consider hypoallergenic breeds to minimize allergic reactions.

Regardless of breed, each dog is an individual, so proper socialization, training, and supervision are essential to fostering a positive relationship between children and dogs. Always take the time to assess the dog's specific needs and characteristics and ensure a safe and loving environment for both your children and your new furry friend.

Yard
→ **Infant/Non-mobile: (Birth - 6 months)**
→ **Infant crawl/roll: (5 months - 1 year)**
→ **Toddler/Pre-school: (1 year - 4 years)**
→ **School-age: (5 years - 6+ years)**

Declaw your cat?

Declawing a cat is a significant decision that requires careful consideration for both the children's safety and the cat's well-being. While declawing may seem like a solution to prevent scratching-related injuries, it's essential to understand the procedure, its potential consequences, and alternative approaches to ensure a safe and loving environment for both your child and your feline friend.

Understand the Procedure: Declawing, known as onychectomy, involves the surgical removal of a cat's claws and is often done to prevent scratching-related issues. However, the procedure is not a simple nail trim; it involves amputation of the last bone of each toe, which can be painful and have lasting effects on the cat's behavior and comfort.

Consider Alternatives: Instead of declawing, consider alternative strategies to manage scratching behavior. Regular nail trimming, providing scratching posts, and using soft nail caps are humane ways to address the issue without harming the cat.

Consult a veterinarian: If scratching is a concern, consult a veterinarian or a professional cat behaviorist. They can provide guidance on behavior modification techniques and recommend appropriate scratching posts and deterrents.

Education and Supervision: Educate your child about appropriate ways to interact with the cat. Teach them not to provoke or handle the cat roughly, which can reduce the likelihood of scratching incidents.

Nail Trimming Routine: Establish a regular nail trimming routine for your cat. This helps keep the claws at a manageable length and reduces the risk of unintentional scratches.

Provide Scratching Outlets: Cats scratch to mark territory and maintain their claws. To satisfy this natural behavior, provide multiple scratching posts made of different materials and placed strategically around the house.

Use Soft Nail Caps: Soft nail caps, also known as nail covers, can be applied to a cat's claws to prevent scratching-related injuries. These caps are safe, and comfortable, and do not require surgical intervention.

Supervise Interactions: Always supervise interactions between your child and the cat, especially if the cat is known to scratch. This ensures that both parties remain safe and can develop a positive relationship.

Positive Reinforcement: Reward and praise your cat for using scratching posts and exhibiting desirable behavior. This encourages the cat to engage in positive scratching habits.

Regular Vet Check-ups: Schedule regular veterinary check-ups to monitor your cat's health and behavior. Discuss any concerns with your vet and seek their advice on managing scratching behavior.

Create Safe Spaces: Provide your cat with safe spaces where they can retreat and rest peacefully, away from children's activities.

After exhausting all alternative options, declawing should be considered a last resort. It's important to prioritize the well-being of your cat while also ensuring the safety of your children. By understanding your cat's behavior, providing appropriate outlets for scratching, and promoting positive interactions, you can create a harmonious environment where both your child and your cat can thrive.

Notes:

Yard
Infant/Non-mobile: (Birth - 6 months)
→ **Infant crawl/roll: (5 months - 1 year)**
→ **Toddler/Pre-school: (1 year - 4 years)**
→ **School-age: (5 years - 6+ years)**

Gerbils/Rats/Rabbits Safety

Introducing small pets like gerbils, rats, and rabbits into your household can be a rewarding experience for children. However, it's important to prioritize the safety of both your little ones and the furry members of your family.

Choosing the Right Pet: Before bringing a small pet into your home, consider the temperament, care requirements, and potential health risks associated with gerbils, rats, and rabbits. Research each animal's specific needs to ensure a suitable match for your family.

Proper Handling and Interaction

Supervise All Interactions: Always supervise children when they are interacting with these pets to prevent accidental harm to both the child and the animal.

Gentle Handling: Teach your children to handle gerbils, rats, and rabbits gently and calmly. Quick movements or rough handling can startle or stress these animals.

No Sudden Loud Noises: Avoid sudden loud noises or shouting around the pets, as it can cause stress or fear.

Cage and Habitat Safety

Secure Cages and Enclosures: Ensure that cages and enclosures are securely locked and properly closed to prevent accidental escapes or tampering by curious children.

Escape-Proof Design: Choose cages with escape-proof designs, as small pets can squeeze through tiny openings. Rats, in particular, are skilled at escaping, so select an appropriate enclosure.

Avoid Sharp Edges: Check the cage for sharp edges, protruding wires, or rough surfaces that could harm pets or children.

Safe Substrate: Use appropriate bedding materials that are safe for the animals and free from chemicals. Be cautious if using materials that can cause allergies or respiratory issues in children.

Feeding and Hygiene

Hand Washing: Teach children to wash their hands before and after handling the pets or cleaning their habitats to prevent the spread of germs.

Food Handling: Instruct children not to share their food with pets, as some human foods can be harmful to small animals.

Health and Hygiene

Regular Vet Check-ups: Schedule regular veterinary check-ups for your pets to ensure their health and well-being.

Vaccinations and Preventive Care: Follow your veterinarian's recommended vaccination and preventive care guidelines.

Safe Playtime and Interaction

Designated Play Area: Create a designated play area where children can interact with the pets under supervision. This helps prevent pets from wandering into areas where they may encounter hazards.

Teaching Empathy and Responsibility

Respect for Animals: Teach children to respect the pets' boundaries and signals. Encourage empathy and understanding of the pets' needs and behaviors.

Age-Appropriate Responsibilities: Assign age-appropriate responsibilities to children, such as feeding, cleaning, and interacting with pets. Supervise and guide them in these tasks.

You can ensure a harmonious and safe environment for your children and small pets by teaching responsible pet ownership, empathy, and proper handling.

Yard
→ **Infant/Non-mobile: (Birth - 6 months)**
→ **Infant crawl/roll: (5 months - 1 year)**
→ **Toddler/Pre-school: (1 year - 4 years)**
→ **School-age: (5 years - 6+ years)**

Exotic Pets Safety

Introducing exotic animals into your home can be an exciting and unique experience for your family.

However, it's crucial to prioritize safety when caring for these special pets.

Research and Choose Wisely: Before acquiring an exotic pet, thoroughly research its specific needs, behaviors, and potential risks. Consider your family's lifestyle and the age of your children to ensure a suitable match.

Secure and Appropriate Enclosures: Select a sturdy, escape-proof enclosure appropriate for the size and type of exotic animal you have. Ensure the enclosure is designed to prevent accidental openings or tampering.

Escape Prevention: Examine the enclosure regularly for gaps, holes, or weak points the animal could exploit to escape. Choose enclosures with secure locks and latches that children cannot easily open.

Child-Free Zones: Designate specific areas where the exotic animal's enclosure is placed as child-free zones. This helps prevent unsupervised interactions between children and the pet.

Childproof the Enclosure: Cover any sharp edges or corners within the enclosure to prevent injuries to both the pet and children. Remove or secure any small parts that children could potentially ingest.

Safe Substrate and Bedding: Use appropriate bedding or substrate that is safe for the exotic pet and does not pose a choking hazard if accidentally ingested by a child.

Feeding Safety: Establish a routine for feeding the exotic animal and ensure that children are not present during feeding times. Store food securely and keep it out of reach of children.

Supervise Interactions: Always supervise interactions between children and exotic animals closely. Teach children to approach the pet calmly and avoid sudden movements that could startle or stress the animal.

Educational Sessions: Educate your children about the exotic animal's characteristics, behavior, and proper handling. Instill a sense of responsibility and empathy for the pet's well-being.

Hygiene and Handwashing: Teach children to wash their hands thoroughly after handling the exotic pet or cleaning its enclosure. This helps prevent the spread of germs and potential diseases.

Healthcare and Veterinary Care: Schedule regular veterinary check-ups for the exotic pet to ensure its health and well-being. Discuss any health concerns or potential risks with the veterinarian.

Escape Plan: Create an escape plan in case the exotic pet was to escape its enclosure. Teach children not to chase or approach the pet but to alert an adult immediately.

Emergency Supplies: Keep a designated emergency kit for the exotic pet, including any necessary medications, tools, and contact information for a veterinarian familiar with exotic animals.

No Unsupervised Contact: Emphasize that children should never attempt to handle or interact with the exotic pet without adult supervision, even if the animal appears docile.

Respect Boundaries: Teach children to respect the exotic animal's boundaries. Avoid touching the animal when it is sleeping, eating, or showing signs of stress.

Encourage Observation: Encourage children to observe the exotic pet's behavior from a safe distance. This will help them better understand the animal's needs and habits.

You can create a safe and enriching environment for both your exotic pet and your children. Education, supervision, and proper care will ensure a positive and rewarding experience for your family while prioritizing the well-being of the exotic animal.

Yard
Infant/Non-mobile: (Birth - 6 months)
Infant crawl/roll: (5 months - 1 year)
→ **Toddler/Pre-school: (1 year - 4 years)**
→ **School-age: (5 years - 6+ years)**

Farm Animals

Living on a farm provides unique opportunities for children to interact with a variety of animals. However, it's essential to prioritize safety and teach children how to interact with farm animals responsibly.

Educational Farm Tour: Begin by giving your children an educational tour of the farm. Teach them about the different types of animals, their behaviors, and how to approach and interact with each species safely.

Supervision and Boundaries: Always supervise children's interactions with farm animals closely. Set clear boundaries and designated areas where children can safely interact with animals under adult supervision.

Teach Animal Behavior: Educate children about the behavior of each farm animal. Explain how to recognize signs of stress, aggression, or discomfort in animals and the appropriate responses.

Hands-On Learning: Encourage children to participate in age-appropriate farm chores and animal care tasks under adult guidance. This helps them learn responsibility and respect for animals.

Safe Feeding Practices: Teach children the proper way to feed farm animals, including using appropriate feeding tools and keeping hands out of animals' mouths to prevent accidental bites.

Animal-Specific Safety: Provide specific safety guidelines for different animals. For example, teach children to approach horses from the side and avoid standing directly behind them.

Safety Gear: When interacting with larger animals, such as horses or cows, ensure children wear appropriate safety gear, such as helmets or gloves, to reduce the risk of injury.

Fencing and Enclosures: Install secure fencing and enclosures to keep farm animals contained and prevent unauthorized access by children. Regularly inspect and maintain fencing to prevent gaps or weak spots.

No Rough Play: Teach children to avoid rough play or teasing of farm animals, as it can agitate or stress the animals, leading to unpredictable behavior.

Proper Handling Techniques: Train children in proper handling techniques for various farm animals. This includes how to approach, lead, and secure animals safely.

Hygiene and Handwashing: Emphasize the importance of handwashing after handling farm animals. This helps prevent the spread of germs and potential diseases.

Emergency Protocol: Develop an emergency plan for dealing with potential incidents involving farm animals. Teach children how to respond calmly and seek help if needed.

Animal Health Checks: Involve children in routine health checks for farm animals, such as observing signs of illness, checking for injuries, and reporting any concerns to adults.

Respect for Personal Space: Teach children to respect farm animals' personal space and not to approach them suddenly or unexpectedly.

Safe Interaction with Young Animals: Instruct children on how to interact safely with young farm animals, such as chicks, piglets, or lambs. Teach gentle handling to avoid causing stress or harm.

Appropriate Play: Encourage children to play safely and appropriately with farm animals, such as using toys or participating in supervised activities that promote bonding and understanding.

Supervised Feeding: Children should feed farm animals under adult supervision to ensure the animals are not accidentally overfed or given inappropriate food.

Animal Socialization: Socialize farm animals with children from a young age to help the animals become accustomed to human interaction and reduce the risk of fear or aggression.

You can create a safe and enriching environment for children to learn and interact responsibly with farm animals. Building a strong foundation of knowledge, respect, and care will ensure a positive and educational experience for both children and the animals they encounter on the farm.

|Ch. 25| Wild Animals

Yard
→ **Infant/Non-mobile: (Birth - 6 months)**
→ **Infant crawl/roll: (5 months - 1 year)**
→ **Toddler/Pre-school: (1 year - 4 years)**
→ **School-age: (5 years - 6+ years)**

Keeping Little Ones Safe from Wild Animals

As a parent or caregiver, it's natural to worry about the safety of your little ones when it comes to wild animals. Children aged 0-6 are curious and may not understand the risks, making it essential to take proactive steps to childproof against wild animal encounters.

Understanding the Risks

Wild animals can be unpredictable, and their behavior can be influenced by various factors such as habitat, food, and human interaction. While most wild animals will avoid humans, some may feel threatened or territorial, leading to defensive behavior. It's crucial to be aware of the types of wild animals that may visit your yard or neighborhood.

Common Wild Animals That May Visit Your Yard

Some common wild animals that may visit your yard include:

- Raccoons
- Skunks
- Snakes
- Squirrels

- Coyotes (in some areas)
- Opossums
- Rats and mice

These animals may be attracted to food sources, shelter, or water, and can pose a risk to your child's safety.

Securing Your Yard

To prevent wild animals from visiting your yard, consider the following:

Secure trash cans: Use animal-proof trash cans or secure regular cans with tight-fitting lids.

Remove food sources: Keep pet food and bird seed in secure containers.

Seal entry points: Block holes around pipes and vents to prevent animals from entering your yard or home.

Keep your yard clean: Regularly clean up debris, leaves, and weeds, which can attract wild animals.

Install fencing: Consider installing fencing around your yard to prevent wild animals from entering.

Teaching Older Children About Wild Animals

For children aged 4-6, you can start teaching them about wild animals in a way that's both fun and safe. Here are some key points:

Stay away from wild animals: Teach your child to stay away from animals they don't know.

Don't feed wild animals: Explain why feeding wild animals can be bad for them and for us.

What to do if they see a wild animal: Teach your child to stay calm and slowly back away from the animal, then find a trusted adult.

Supervising Younger Children

For children under 4, it's essential to provide close supervision when they're playing outside. Here are some tips:

Always supervise: Never leave your child unattended in the yard or near areas where wild animals may be present.

Watch for potential hazards: Be aware of potential hazards such as holes in the fence, open gates, or animal tracks.

Keep your child close: Keep your child within arm's reach when playing outside.

What to Do in Case of a Wild Animal Encounter: If you encounter a wild animal with your child:

Stay calm: Keep your child close and stay calm to prevent the situation from escalating.

Back away slowly: Slowly back away from the animal with your child.

Seek shelter: If necessary, quickly move to a safe location.

Call for help: If the animal appears aggressive or threatening, call 911 or your local animal control service.

Additional Tips

Be aware: Know what wild animals are common in your area and take steps to prevent encounters.

Keep your child informed: As your child gets older, continue to teach them about wild animal safety and the importance of respecting wildlife.

Prepare for emergencies: Make sure you have a plan in place in case of a wild animal encounter, including knowing who to call and what to do.

By taking these steps, you can help keep your little ones safe from wild animals and create a secure outdoor environment for them to play and explore.

|Ch. 26| Holidays

Introduction: Holidays are a time of joy, celebration, and family gatherings filled with laughter and love. Homes are adorned with twinkling lights, fragrant candles, and festive decorations, creating a magical atmosphere that delights both adults and children alike. However, amidst the enchantment and excitement, the holiday season also brings unique safety challenges that parents must navigate to ensure their little ones can celebrate safely and joyously.

Testimonial: *The holiday season has always been a time of joy, laughter, and creating precious memories with my family. However, last Christmas brought a sobering reminder that amidst the festivities, we must never let our guard down when it comes to the safety of our children.*

On a chilly December evening, our living room was aglow with our Christmas tree's warm and inviting lights. The air was filled with the scent of pine and the sound of holiday carols. My five-year-old daughter, Emma, was captivated by the sparkling ornaments and decided to reach for a shiny glass bauble. In her enthusiasm, she lost her balance and fell into the tree, causing it to topple over. The glass ornaments shattered, and one of the broken pieces caused a deep cut on Emma's arm.

The joy of the evening quickly turned into panic. We rushed Emma to the emergency room, where she received stitches for her wound. As I sat beside her hospital bed, I couldn't help but reflect on how this accident could have been prevented.

In hindsight, several childproofing measures we overlooked were. First, we should have secured the Christmas tree to prevent it from tipping over. A sturdy tree stand and possibly anchoring the tree to the wall would have provided the necessary stability. Second, opting for shatterproof ornaments would have been a safer choice for decorating the lower branches of the tree, keeping the fragile glass ornaments out of reach.

Additionally, creating a designated play area away from the tree where Emma could play safely would have been wise. This space could have been set up with her favorite toys and games, providing a distraction from the tempting but dangerous decorations.

This experience was a wake-up call for our family. Since then, we have proactively ensured our home is childproofed for the holidays. We share our story as a reminder to all parents that the safety of our children should always be the top priority, even during the most joyous times of the year.

- Jim S. (Father of 2)

Christmas
Infant/Non-mobile: (Birth - 6 months)
Infant crawl/roll: (5 months - 1 year)
Toddler/Pre-school: (1 year - 4 years)
School-age: (5 years - 6+ years)

Christmas Decoration Safety

During the holiday season, approximately **5,000 children** are treated for injuries related to Christmas decorations, including falls from ladders and cuts from ornaments. (Source: U.S. Consumer Product Safety Commission (CPSC) - Holiday Safety) The holiday season is a time of joy and festivity, often accompanied by beautiful decorations. However, it's important to prioritize child safety when decorating your home for Christmas.

Tree Placement: Choose a secure location for your Christmas tree, away from high-traffic areas and potential hazards. Anchor the tree properly to prevent tipping, especially if you have young children or pets.

Secure Decorations: Use shatterproof ornaments and decorations that are child friendly. Avoid fragile or sharp ornaments that could break and pose a choking or injury risk. Hang decorations securely to prevent them from falling.

Tinsel and Garlands: Keep tinsel and garlands out of reach of young children, as they can easily ingest or become entangled in them.

Lights Safety: Inspect Christmas lights for any frayed wires or damaged sockets before use. Keep lights and cords out of reach to prevent children from pulling on them.

Candles and Flames: Place candles on sturdy surfaces that are well out of reach of children. Consider using flameless candles or LED alternatives to reduce fire hazards.

Ornament Selection: Opt for non-toxic and child-safe ornaments. Avoid using ornaments that could be mistaken for food or toys, such as small, colorful objects that resemble candy.

Tree Decorations: Place larger, heavier ornaments on lower branches to prevent them from falling if touched. Hang small decorations higher up to reduce the risk of choking hazards.

Tree Skirt: Choose a tree skirt that is securely fastened and won't easily be pulled or tugged by curious children.

Artificial Snow: If using artificial snow, ensure it is non-toxic and keep it out of children's reach to prevent ingestion.

Edible Decorations: Be cautious with edible decorations like popcorn strings or gingerbread ornaments. Keep them securely attached to the tree and away from small hands.

Gift Wrapping Safety: Store wrapping paper, ribbons, and bows out of reach to prevent children from ingesting or becoming entangled in them.

Extension Cord Management: Use extension cords that are designed for outdoor use and ensure they are not a tripping hazard for children.

Plant Safety: Be cautious with holiday plants like poinsettias, holly, and mistletoe, which can be toxic if ingested. Keep them out of reach of children and pets.

Fragile Decor: Place fragile decorations or ornaments high on the tree or in areas that are inaccessible to children.

Window Decorations: Avoid using decorations that obstruct visibility from windows and doors, which could impact emergency exits.

Toy Safety: When using toy decorations, ensure they are age-appropriate and don't pose choking hazards to young children.

Stairs and Railings: Secure stair railings and banisters to prevent children from pulling on them or using them as climbing structures for decorations.

Childproofing Accessories: Consider using childproofing accessories like safety gates to keep young children away from holiday decorations.

Supervision: Always supervise children around holiday decorations, especially if they are very young or curious.

Storage Safety: When storing decorations, keep small parts, batteries, and sharp objects out of reach. Use containers with secure lids to prevent children from accessing them.

You can create a festive and magical atmosphere while keeping your children safe from potential hazards. Enjoy the holiday season with peace of mind and the joy of celebrating safely with your loved ones.

Christmas
Infant/Non-mobile: (Birth - 6 months)
Infant crawl/roll: (5 months - 1 year)
→ **Toddler/Pre-school: (1 year - 4 years)**
→ **School-age: (5 years - 6+ years)**

Christmas Stocking Safety

Christmas stockings are a delightful tradition that adds to the holiday spirit. To keep the festivities merry and safe, it's essential to consider child safety when hanging and filling stockings.

Secure Hanging: Hang stockings securely using hooks or hangers that are safely attached to the wall or mantle. Avoid using sharp or easily dislodged hooks that could pose a hazard.

Height Consideration: Hang stockings high enough to keep them out of reach of young children, especially those who might be tempted to pull on them.

Small Parts Alert: Be cautious with small decorations, trinkets, or toys that might be placed inside stockings. Avoid items that could be choking hazards for young children.

Avoid Sharp Objects: To prevent accidental injuries, avoid placing sharp objects or items with sharp edges inside stockings.

Batteries and Electronics: If you include battery-operated or electronic gifts in stockings, ensure that the battery compartments are securely closed and that children cannot easily access the batteries.

Food Safety: If you include edible treats in stockings, choose age-appropriate items without choking risk. Avoid hard candies or small snacks that could be ingested too quickly.

Supervision: Supervise young children when they are exploring their stockings to ensure they do not ingest or misuse any items.

Cords and Strings: Be mindful of cords, strings, or ribbons attached to stocking decorations. Make sure they are securely fastened to prevent entanglement hazards.

Personalized Stockings: Consider getting personalized stockings with your child's name embroidered on them. This not only adds a special touch but also prevents mix-ups.

Gift Wrapping Safety: When wrapping stocking gifts, use child-safe wrapping paper and avoid excessive tape or sharp objects.

Age-Appropriate Gifts: Tailor the contents of stockings to suit each child's age and developmental stage. Avoid items that are not suitable for their age group.

Balancing Gifts: Keep the weight of stockings balanced to prevent them from falling and potentially causing harm.

Decorative Elements: Be cautious with decorative elements like buttons, beads, or embellishments that could come loose and pose a choking hazard.

Scented Items: If you include scented items like potpourri or scented sachets, make sure they are securely enclosed and cannot be accessed by curious hands.

Emergency Exits: Ensure that stockings do not block emergency exits or pathways in case of an evacuation.

Childproofing Techniques: If you have infants or toddlers, consider using childproofing techniques such as safety gates to limit access to areas with stockings.

Regular Inspections: Periodically inspect stockings for potential hazards, such as loose decorations or shifted items.

Safe Removal: When taking down stockings, avoid dislodging any hanging items that could fall and harm children.

Christmas
Infant/Non-mobile: (Birth - 6 months)
Infant crawl/roll: (5 months - 1 year)
Toddler/Pre-school: (1 year - 4 years)
School-age: (5 years - 6+ years)

Anchor the Christmas Tree to the Wall to Prevent Falling

The holiday season brings the joy of decorating your home, and the centerpiece of many homes is the Christmas tree. To ensure the safety of your little ones, it's important to take precautions to prevent the tree from toppling over and causing harm.

- **Choose a Stable Location:** Choose a location for your Christmas tree away from high-traffic areas and heavy furniture that children might try to climb. A corner is often a good choice, as it provides additional support.

- **Secure Tree Base:** Use a sturdy and wide tree stand that provides a stable base for the tree. Ensure that the stand is appropriately sized to hold the tree's weight.

- **Anchor to Wall:** Purchase a tree anchor kit or wall hook explicitly designed for securing Christmas trees. These kits typically include an anchor strap, screws, and wall brackets.

- **Measure and Mark:** Before drilling any holes, measure the distance from the top of the tree stand to the wall. This will help you determine the appropriate height for the anchor point.

- **Wall Bracket Installation:** Install the wall bracket using the provided screws and a drill. Make sure the bracket is securely attached to the wall and aligned with the mark you made earlier.

- **Attach Anchor Strap:** Attach the anchor strap to the top of the tree stand. Some kits may include adjustable straps that can be tightened for a secure fit.

- **Secure Anchor Strap:** Extend the anchor strap and connect it to the wall bracket. Tighten the strap to ensure a snug fit, but avoid over-tightening, which could damage the tree or the wall.

- **Conceal and Cover:** If the anchor strap is visible, consider using garlands, ribbons, or other decorative elements to conceal it and blend it with the tree's decorations.

- **Maintain Balance:** As you decorate the tree, distribute ornaments and decorations evenly to maintain its balance and stability.

- **Supervise and Educate:** Teach your children the importance of not pulling, tugging, or climbing on the Christmas tree. Remind them that the tree is meant for admiration, not for play.

- **Regular Checks:** Periodically check the anchor strap, wall bracket, and tree stand throughout the holiday season to ensure they remain secure.

- **Use Extra Precautions:** If you have particularly active children or pets, you may consider using additional safety measures, such as securing heavy objects to the tree's base to lower the center of gravity.

- **Artificial Trees:** The same principles apply to artificial trees. Make sure the tree stand is stable and use an anchor kit if needed.

You're creating a safer environment for your children to enjoy the holiday festivities. This precaution ensures that the tree remains a symbol of joy and celebration without posing any risks to the well-being of your little ones. Celebrate the season with peace of mind, knowing that you've taken steps to safeguard your home and make it a joyful space for everyone.

Christmas
→ **Infant/Non-mobile: (Birth - 6 months)**
→ **Infant crawl/roll: (5 months - 1 year)**
→ **Toddler/Pre-school: (1 year - 4 years)**
→ **School-age: (5 years - 6+ years)**

Consider Getting an Artificial Tree

The holiday season is a magical time filled with joy and celebration, and one of the central elements of this festive period is the Christmas tree. When it comes to child safety, considering an artificial tree can provide numerous benefits and peace of mind.

> **Sturdy Construction:** Artificial trees are designed with stability in mind. They typically come with a sturdy base and well-balanced branches, reducing the risk of toppling over, especially in households with curious and active children.
>
> **Fire Safety:** Artificial trees are often made from flame-resistant materials, which significantly reduces the risk of fire hazards compared to natural trees. This is especially important when considering the placement of the tree near lights and decorations.
>
> **Needle Shedding:** Unlike real trees, artificial trees don't shed needles, which can pose a choking hazard for small children or pets. This eliminates the need to sweep or vacuum around the tree constantly.
>
> **Allergen-Free:** Many individuals, including children, may have tree pollen or sap allergies. Opting for an artificial tree eliminates this concern, providing a sneeze-free and comfortable environment during the holiday season.
>
> **Customizable Height and Design:** Artificial trees come in various sizes and styles, allowing you to choose the perfect fit for your home. You can also easily adjust the height to keep fragile ornaments and decorations out of the reach of little hands.
>
> **Hassle-Free Maintenance:** Artificial trees require minimal maintenance compared to real trees. There's no need to water them, and they won't dry out and become brittle over time.
>
> **Reduced Mess:** An artificial tree does not require dealing with fallen needles, sap, or water spills, contributing to a cleaner and safer environment for children to play and celebrate.
>
> **Longevity:** An artificial tree can be reused for several holiday seasons, making it a cost-effective and eco-friendly choice. This consistency can provide children with a sense of tradition and familiarity as they grow.
>
> **Easy Decoration:** Artificial trees often come with hinged branches that make decorating a breeze. You can hang ornaments securely without the risk of branches breaking or bending under the weight.

Avoiding Outdoor Hazards: Bringing an artificial tree indoors eliminates exposure to outdoor allergens, insects, and critters that might hitch a ride on a natural tree.

Personalization: You can choose an artificial tree with built-in lights, reducing the need for additional cords and outlets. This feature can enhance the safety of your holiday setup.

Child-Friendly Activities: Artificial trees are conducive to child-friendly decorating activities, such as allowing kids to hang ornaments, create handmade decorations, and showcase their creativity.

By considering an artificial Christmas tree, you're making a thoughtful choice that prioritizes child safety without compromising the festive spirit. It's a decision that offers practicality, longevity, and the opportunity to create cherished holiday memories in a safe and secure environment for your children and the entire family.

<u>Christmas</u>
→ **Infant/Non-mobile: (Birth - 6 months)**
→ **Infant crawl/roll: (5 months - 1 year)**
→ **Toddler/Pre-school: (1 year - 4 years)**
→ **School-age: (5 years - 6+ years)**

LED Decorative Lights

While generally safer than traditional incandescent bulbs, LED decorative lights can still pose risks to children.

Secure the Lights

Out of Reach: Place the lights on high shelves or fixtures that children cannot reach.

Cord Management: Secure cords against the wall or furniture with cord covers or cable clips to prevent tripping hazards.

Choose Safe Materials

Avoid Fragile Materials: Opt for lights made from sturdy materials that are less likely to break and cause injuries.

Check for Small Parts: Ensure the lights do not have small parts that children can swallow.

Consider Battery-Powered Options

Reduce Electrical Hazards: Battery-powered lights eliminate the risk of electrical shocks from cords or outlets.

Supervise and Educate

Constant Watch: Always supervise children when they are around lights, especially when the lights are turned on.

Teach Safety: Educate children about the importance of avoiding touching lights or cords.

Regularly Inspect

Check for Damage: Periodically inspect the lights for any signs of wear or damage, such as frayed cords or broken bulbs.

Christmas
→ Infant/Non-mobile: (Birth - 6 months)
→ Infant crawl/roll: (5 months - 1 year)
→ Toddler/Pre-school: (1 year - 4 years)
→ School-age: (5 years - 6+ years)

Beware of Lead Candles

Candles are a popular choice for creating a warm and inviting ambiance. However, it's important to be aware of potential hazards, especially when it comes to lead candles. Lead wicks were commonly used in candles in the past, and while regulations have significantly reduced their prevalence, it's still crucial to exercise caution.

Lead Exposure Risk: Lead is a toxic metal that can be harmful when ingested or inhaled, particularly to young children who are more susceptible to its effects. Burning candles with lead wicks can release lead into the air, putting children at risk of lead exposure.

Invisible Threat: Lead in candle wicks may not be immediately visible to the naked eye. Even if a candle looks harmless, it could still contain lead in the wick's core.

Health Impact: Lead exposure in children can lead to developmental and cognitive issues, behavioral problems, learning disabilities, and other serious health concerns. It's essential to minimize their exposure to lead as much as possible.

Deterioration: Lead wicks can deteriorate while burning, releasing even higher levels of lead into the air. This is especially true for candles with metal-core wicks.

Regulations: Many countries have imposed restrictions and regulations on lead content in candle wicks. However, imported candles or older candles may not adhere to these standards.

Protect Your Child

Check Labels: Look for candles labeled as "lead-free" or "non-toxic." Choose reputable brands and sources that prioritize safety.

Inspect Candles: Before purchasing or using candles, inspect the wicks. Avoid using the candle if you notice a metal core or suspiciously thick wick.

Opt for Alternatives: Choose candles made from safer materials such as cotton, soy, or beeswax. These candles are less likely to contain lead.

Proper Ventilation: When burning any candles, ensure proper ventilation in the room to reduce the concentration of airborne particles.

Limit Exposure: If you suspect a candle may contain lead, refrain from burning it, especially in areas frequented by children.

Supervision: Candles should always be kept out of reach of children and never left unattended, especially in a child's play area or bedroom.

Educate Children: Teach your children about the dangers of touching or playing with candles and emphasize the importance of safety.

Regular Cleaning: Dust and clean your home regularly, as lead particles can settle on surfaces and be ingested by children.

You can help protect your child from the potential risks associated with lead candles. Prioritizing their safety involves making conscious choices and opting for candles that contribute to a cozy and secure environment without compromising their health and well-being.

Halloween
- Infant/Non-mobile: (Birth - 6 months)
- Infant crawl/roll: (5 months - 1 year)
- Toddler/Pre-school: (1 year - 4 years)
- School-age: (5 years - 6+ years)

Use Flame Retardant Costumes and Reflective Components

When the spooky season of Halloween rolls around, dressing up in creative and imaginative costumes is all part of the fun. However, safety should always be at the forefront, especially when it comes to children's costumes. Incorporating flame retardant and reflective elements into Halloween attire can significantly enhance your child's safety during nighttime festivities.

Flame Retardant Costumes

Reduced Fire Risk: Flame retardant costumes are treated with special chemicals that slow down the spread of fire. This added layer of protection can help prevent costumes from accidentally catching fire.

Candlelit Environments: Halloween often involves candles, pumpkins, or other open flames. Flame retardant costumes offer peace of mind in case your child comes into contact with a lit candle or other sources of fire.

Avoiding Accidents: Children can easily brush against decorations or candles without noticing. Flame retardant costumes decrease the risk of accidental ignition, making Halloween festivities safer for everyone.

Reflective Components

Enhanced Visibility: Halloween often takes place in the evening or at night, making visibility a critical concern. Reflective elements on costumes ensure that your child remains visible to drivers and other pedestrians, reducing the risk of accidents.

Street Crossing Safety: If your child is trick-or-treating or attending Halloween events, reflective accents make them more noticeable when crossing streets or walking near roads.

Group Safety: Reflective costumes help members of a group stand out in the dark, making it easier for parents, guardians, and event organizers to keep track of children.

Incorporate Flame Retardant and Reflective Features

Costume Selection

Look for costumes labeled as "flame retardant" or "fire-resistant." These costumes are designed with safety in mind and have undergone specific testing to meet safety standards.

Choose costumes that feature reflective strips or accents. These can be strategically placed on the costume to ensure maximum visibility.

DIY Options

If you're creating a homemade costume, opt for flame-retardant fabrics and materials. Some fabrics, such as wool and polyester, naturally have flame-retardant properties.

Sew or attach reflective tape or fabric onto the costume in creative patterns. This enhances visibility without compromising the overall look.

Accessories: Incorporate reflective elements into accessories like hats, shoes, or treat bags. This adds an extra layer of visibility without altering the costume's design.

Test Flame Resistance: If you are unsure about a costume's flame resistance, you can perform a simple test. Hold a small piece of the costume fabric briefly over an open flame and observe its reaction. The costume is not flame retardant if it melts, drips, or ignites.

Be Visible in Dark Areas: Encourage your child to carry a flashlight or glow sticks to increase visibility in areas with limited lighting.

By prioritizing flame retardant and reflective elements in your child's Halloween costume, you're taking proactive steps to ensure their safety during the festive celebrations. These precautions not only provide peace of mind for parents and guardians but also contribute to a safer and more enjoyable Halloween experience for children and families alike.

► *Each holiday season, more than **3,000 children under age 15** are treated in U.S. emergency rooms for burns related to flammable costumes. And toddlers often comprise the majority of these cases. Before the 1970s, clothing ignition accounted for half of pediatric burn injuries. Thanks to today's flame-resistance rules, such incidents are now less common, but not entirely gone."*

Halloween
→ **Infant/Non-mobile: (Birth - 6 months)**
→ **Infant crawl/roll: (5 months - 1 year)**
→ **Toddler/Pre-school: (1 year - 4 years)**
→ **School-age: (5 years - 6+ years)**

Candle Lit Jack-O'-Lanterns

When it comes to Halloween traditions, carving and displaying jack-o'-lanterns is a cherished and creative activity. However, safety should always be a top priority, especially when children are involved. Using candle-lit jack-o'-lanterns can pose potential hazards, making it advisable to explore safer alternatives.

Fire Hazard: Candle-lit jack-o'-lanterns are a fire hazard, particularly in environments with nearby flammable materials like dry leaves or paper. The open flame of a candle can easily ignite these materials, posing a severe risk of fire.

Children's Curiosity: Children are naturally curious, and the allure of a flickering flame inside a jack-o'-lantern can lead them to touch or investigate. This increases the risk of burns or accidental fires.

Tipping and Accidents: Children running around or playing near jack-o'-lanterns can accidentally tip them over, potentially spreading the flame or causing burns.

Smoke and Fumes: Candle-lit jack-o'-lanterns emit smoke and fumes, which can irritate the eyes and respiratory system, especially for children with sensitivities or respiratory conditions.

Safer Alternatives

Battery-Operated Lights: Opt for battery-operated LED lights or flameless candles. These provide a similar flickering effect without the risk of an open flame; they are cool to the touch and eliminate fire hazards.

Glow Sticks: Use glow sticks to add an eerie glow to your jack-o'-lantern. They are safe, non-toxic, and do not emit heat or smoke.

String Lights: Wrap string lights around or inside the jack-o'-lantern for a magical and safe illumination effect.

Glow Paints: Apply glow-in-the-dark paints to the interior of the pumpkin for a spooky glow without any fire risk.

Supervision and Education: If you decide to use real candles for your jack-o'-lanterns, ensure that they are placed in a secure location away from children's reach. Always supervise children when they are around lit jack-o'-lanterns and educate them about the potential dangers.

Display Height: Place jack-o'-lanterns at a height where they cannot be accidentally knocked over by children or pets.

Well-Ventilated Area: If you choose to use real candles, place the jack-o'-lantern in a well-ventilated area to minimize the buildup of smoke and fumes.

Fire Safety Measures: When using real candles, keep a fire extinguisher or water source nearby, and never leave them unattended.

Dispose of Properly: After Halloween, properly dispose of your jack-o'-lantern by extinguishing any candles and placing them in a safe area away from flammable materials.

By avoiding candle-lit jack-o'-lanterns and opting for safer alternatives, you can create a festive and spooky atmosphere without compromising children's and your home's safety. Making conscious choices to prevent fire hazards during Halloween ensures that the holiday remains enjoyable, memorable, and incident-free for everyone.

<u>Halloween</u>
Infant/Non-mobile: (Birth - 6 months)
Infant crawl/roll: (5 months - 1 year)
→ **Toddler/Pre-school: (1 year - 4 years)**
→ **School-age: (5 years - 6+ years)**

When Carving a Pumpkin, Do Not Use a Knife

To ensure a fun and accident-free pumpkin carving experience.

Sharp Object Hazard: Knives are sharp objects that can cause cuts, punctures, and injuries, particularly when mishandled. Children may not have the dexterity or understanding of proper knife usage to carve a pumpkin safely.

Slip and Cut Risk: Carving a pumpkin involves applying force to cut through the tough skin and flesh. If a child's hand slips, there is a high risk of accidental cuts or injuries.

Children's Inexperience: Children's fine motor skills and understanding of safety precautions may not be fully developed. They might struggle to control a knife or underestimate the force needed for carving.

Alternate Methods

Pumpkin Decorating Kits: Purchase pumpkin decorating kits that include safe tools specifically designed for children. These tools often have blunt edges or serrated edges that are safer than traditional knives.

Pumpkin Scoopers: Use pumpkin scoopers or scrapers to remove the pumpkin's insides. These tools are less sharp and allow children to participate in the carving process without the risk of cuts.

Stencil and Poke Method: Instead of cutting through the pumpkin, use a stencil and a small poking tool to create a design by poking holes along the stencil lines. This can be followed by coloring the design with markers or paint.

Pumpkin Drills: Battery-operated pumpkin drills can create fun patterns by drilling holes into the pumpkin's surface. These drills are safer and more accessible for children to handle.

Stickers and Paint: Children can decorate pumpkins with stickers, adhesive gems, or non-toxic paint, letting their creativity flow without the need for sharp tools.

Adult Supervision: If you still opt to use a knife for more intricate designs, ensure that an adult with proper knife-handling skills is present to supervise and guide the process.

Safety Gear: If using any tools, provide children with appropriate safety gear, such as gloves and safety goggles, to protect their hands and eyes.

Educate and Demonstrate: Before starting, educate children about the potential risks of using knives and demonstrate proper pumpkin carving techniques to ensure they understand how to handle tools safely.

Pre-Carved Pumpkins: Consider purchasing pre-carved pumpkins from local stores or farms. This way, children can still enjoy the festive spirit without the need for carving.

Parental Assistance: When children are involved in pumpkin carving, parents or guardians should always be present to provide guidance, answer questions, and step in if necessary.

By avoiding the use of knives and choosing alternative methods for pumpkin carving, you can create a safe and enjoyable activity for children during the Halloween season. Emphasizing safety while fostering creativity ensures that pumpkin carving remains a memorable and injury-free experience for the whole family.

Halloween
Infant/Non-mobile: (Birth - 6 months)
Infant crawl/roll: (5 months - 1 year)
→ **Toddler/Pre-school: (1 year - 4 years)**
→ **School-age: (5 years - 6+ years)**

Costume Prop Concerns

While adding props to a Halloween costume can enhance the overall look, it's crucial to prioritize child safety and ensure that these props do not have sharp edges.

Inspect Props Thoroughly: Before purchasing or using any costume props, carefully inspect them for sharp edges, protruding parts, or any potential hazards that could cause cuts or injuries.

Avoid Metal or Hard Materials: Choose props made from lightweight, soft, and flexible materials that do not have sharp or rigid edges. Avoid props made from metal, hard plastics, or other materials that could cause harm upon impact.

Smooth and Rounded Edges: Opt for props with smooth and rounded edges that are less likely to cause cuts or scratches. Ensure that any seams or joints are securely fastened to prevent accidental detachment.

Avoid Pointed Objects: Avoid costume props with pointed ends, spikes, or sharp tips. These could pose a significant risk, especially in crowded or confined spaces.

Flexible and Bendable Props: Look for flexible or bendable props, as they are less likely to cause injury if accidentally bumped or dropped.

Secure Attachments: If the prop requires attachments or fasteners, make sure they are securely attached to the costume and will not easily come loose during wear.

Size Consideration: Choose props that are appropriately sized for your child's age and size. Oversized or heavy props could cause accidents or restrict movement.

Avoid Functional Weapons: Refrain from using costume props that resemble functional weapons, such as swords, knives, or guns. Instead, opt for props that are clearly fictional and non-threatening.

Test the Prop: Before Halloween night, have your child test the prop and practice using it safely. Teach them to be mindful of their surroundings and avoid swinging or wielding the prop recklessly.

Supervision: Always supervise your child when they are wearing the costume and using props, especially if they are interacting with other children or in crowded areas.

Remove Sharp Components: If a prop comes with any removable or detachable parts, ensure they are safely secured or remove them altogether.

Use Child-Friendly Alternatives: Instead of using potentially hazardous props, consider child-friendly alternatives such as foam replicas, soft toys, or inflatable props.

Costume Comfort: Make sure the prop does not hinder your child's ability to see, walk, or move comfortably. A well-fitted costume and prop will prevent accidents caused by tripping or falling.

Emergency Awareness: Teach your child how to handle the prop responsibly and what to do if they accidentally bump into someone or encounter a potential hazard.

<u>Halloween</u>
Infant/Non-mobile: (Birth - 6 months)
Infant crawl/roll: (5 months - 1 year)
→ **Toddler/Pre-school: (1 year - 4 years)**
→ **School-age: (5 years - 6+ years)**

Avoid Using Dry Ice

While dry ice can indeed create a captivating visual spectacle, it's essential to prioritize child safety and exercise caution, especially when using dry ice in punch bowls.

Temperature Extremes: Dry ice is extremely cold, reaching -109.3°F (-78.5°C). Placing dry ice directly into a liquid, such as a punch bowl, can lead to rapid cooling and freezing of the liquid. If a child's skin comes into contact with ice or the extremely cold liquid, this can result in cold burns or frostbite.

Ingestion Hazard: Dry ice is not edible and can release carbon dioxide gas as it sublimates (transforms from a solid to a gas). If a child accidentally ingests a piece of dry ice or consumes a drink with dissolved carbon dioxide, it can cause discomfort, bloating, and potentially more severe health effects.

Choking Hazard: Dry ice can also present a choking hazard if children unknowingly place a piece in their mouths or if small fragments break off and are ingested.

Carbon Dioxide Buildup: When dry ice sublimates, it releases carbon dioxide gas, which is heavier than air. In an enclosed or poorly ventilated area, such as indoors, excessive carbon dioxide buildup can displace breathable air and lead to difficulty breathing, dizziness, and even unconsciousness.

Spills and Splashes: Placing dry ice directly into a punch bowl can cause vigorous bubbling and splashing, increasing the risk of spills. Spilled liquid with dry ice can cause burns or discomfort if it comes into contact with skin or clothing.

Safe Alternatives: Instead of placing dry ice directly into a punch bowl, consider placing it in a separate container outside the punch bowl to create the misty effect. This way, there is no direct contact between the dry ice and the drink. Use caution when handling the dry ice and ensure it is safely out of reach of children.

Supervision and Education: If you choose to use dry ice in any capacity, make sure to educate your guests, especially children, about its potential hazards. Encourage children to observe from a safe distance and discourage them from touching or handling the dry ice.

Proper Handling: When handling dry ice, always wear protective gloves or use tongs to avoid direct contact with the ice. Store dry ice in a well-ventilated area and away from children's reach.

Emergency Preparedness: In the event of accidental ingestion, skin contact, or exposure to excessive carbon dioxide, be prepared to seek medical attention promptly. Educate yourself and your guests on the signs of distress and what to do in case of an emergency.

While dry ice can certainly create a mesmerizing effect, it's crucial to prioritize the safety of children and all guests. Avoiding the use of dry ice in punch bowls and using alternative methods to achieve the misty effect can help prevent potential hazards and ensure a worry-free and enjoyable gathering for everyone. Remember, a successful and spooktacular event is one where safety takes center stage.

Halloween
Infant/Non-mobile: (Birth - 6 months)
Infant crawl/roll: (5 months - 1 year)
→ **Toddler/Pre-school: (1 year - 4 years)**
→ **School-age: (5 years - 6+ years)**

Beware of Violent Movies

As children's imaginations develop and they become more curious about the world around them, caregivers need to be mindful of the content they are exposed to, including movies. While movies can be entertaining and educational, exposure to violent or scary content can significantly impact a child's emotional well-being and development.

Emotional Impact: Children are still developing their understanding of reality and fantasy, and their ability to differentiate between the two may not be fully developed. Violent or scary images and themes in movies can evoke strong emotions such as fear, anxiety, or confusion, which can be distressing and overwhelming for young minds.

Nightmares and Sleep Disturbances: Exposing children to frightening or intense content before bedtime, such as in scary movies, can lead to nightmares and sleep disturbances. Restful sleep is essential for a child's growth and overall well-being, and avoiding disturbing content can help ensure peaceful sleep.

Behavioral Changes: Repeated exposure to violent or frightening scenes can contribute to behavioral changes in children. They may become more irritable, anxious, or aggressive when imitating what they see on screen.

Desensitization: Frequent exposure to violence in movies can desensitize children to real-life violence, leading them to perceive aggressive behavior as normal or acceptable. This can impact their social interactions and attitudes toward conflict resolution.

Developmental Stage: Children at different ages have varying cognitive and emotional development levels. Younger children, in particular, may have difficulty processing the intense emotions and complex themes presented in violent or scary movies.

Overstimulation: Children have a limited capacity to process sensory input, and exposure to intense and frightening stimuli can lead to sensory overload, anxiety, and stress.

Positive Role Models: Movies often portray characters as heroes or villains, and children may internalize these portrayals as models for their behavior. Ensuring that the characters and behaviors depicted align with positive values and role models is important.

Open Communication: If your child expresses interest in watching a movie that may contain violent or scary content, engage in open communication. Discuss the themes, content, and potential emotional reactions with your child. Ask questions to understand their perspective and decide together whether the movie is suitable.

Content Ratings: When selecting movies for children, pay attention to content ratings and reviews. Ratings are designed to help parents and caregivers make informed choices based on age-appropriateness.

Preview Content: Whenever possible, watch movies before your child does. This allows you to assess the content and determine whether it aligns with your child's emotional and cognitive development.

Alternative Choices: Choose movies that promote positive values, teamwork, friendship, and creativity. Opt for age-appropriate animated films or family-friendly content that fosters imagination and learning.

Supervision and Discussion: If you decide to watch a movie with your child, provide supervision and be prepared to pause the film to discuss any questions or concerns that arise.

By being vigilant about children's content and making thoughtful choices about movies, you can help create a safe and nurturing media environment. Prioritizing age-appropriate and positive content supports your child's emotional development and helps them navigate the world with confidence and resilience. Remember, the stories we expose to children can shape their perceptions and beliefs, so choose wisely to promote a positive and enriching media experience.

Birthdays
Infant/Non-mobile: (Birth - 6 months)
Infant crawl/roll: (5 months - 1 year)
→ **Toddler/Pre-school: (1 year - 4 years)**
→ **School-age: (5 years - 6+ years)**

Conservatively Block all Exits from the Birthday Party

When hosting a birthday celebration for children, it's essential to prioritize their safety by creating a secure environment that prevents wandering and ensures their well-being. Children's curiosity and boundless energy can lead them to explore, making it crucial to conservatively block all exits from the birthday room.

Room Layout Evaluation: Begin by carefully assessing the birthday room's layout. Identify all potential exit points, including doors and windows, and consider any additional openings that may lead to other areas of the house or outdoors.

Entrance Supervision: Designate one entrance to the birthday room and position a responsible adult or caregiver to monitor and control access. This ensures that only authorized individuals enter and exit, reducing the risk of children wandering away unnoticed.

Childproof Door Locks: Install childproof door locks or latches on all exit doors in the birthday room. These locks should be positioned out of reach of young children, preventing them from opening the doors independently.

Safety Gates: Utilize safety gates or barriers to block off any doorways or passages that lead to areas where children shouldn't venture. These gates should be sturdy, properly installed, and difficult for children to open.

Window Locks and Guards: If the birthday room has windows, ensure they are equipped with childproof locks to prevent children from opening them. Additionally, consider installing window guards to prevent accidental falls or escapes.

Visible Signage: Place prominent and easy-to-understand signs near exit points, reminding adults to keep doors closed and secure. This serves as a visual cue for everyone attending the celebration.

Supervision Plan: Assign responsible adults or caregivers to monitor the exits and entrances throughout the event. Their role is to ensure that children remain within the designated celebration area and to intervene if any child attempts to exit.

Engaging Activities: Create a fun and engaging atmosphere within the birthday room to captivate children's attention and discourage them from trying to leave. Plan age-appropriate activities, games, and entertainment to keep them entertained and focused.

Seating Arrangements: Strategically position seating and activity stations to deter children from wandering toward exits. Keep the central area engaging and surrounded by adult supervision.

Adult-to-Child Ratio: Maintain an appropriate adult-to-child ratio to ensure enough caregivers are present to supervise and guide the children's activities.

Emergency Preparedness: While conservatively blocking exits, also consider emergency preparedness. Ensure that adults are aware of exit routes and emergency evacuation procedures in case they become necessary.

Communication: Communicate with parents or guardians attending the celebration, informing them of the safety measures in place to prevent wandering. Encourage them to be vigilant and actively supervise their children.

Keep Celebrations Indoors: If the weather permits, consider hosting the celebration indoors to eliminate the risk of children wandering into unfamiliar or potentially hazardous outdoor areas.

Regular Checks: Periodically perform visual checks of the exits and the overall room layout to ensure that safety measures remain in place and effective.

You can create a safe and secure birthday environment that allows children to enjoy the festivities while minimizing the potential for wandering. Remember that proactive planning and vigilant supervision are key to a successful and worry-free celebration that prioritizes the well-being of all young attendees.

Birthdays
Infant/Non-mobile: (Birth - 6 months)
Infant crawl/roll: (5 months - 1 year)
→ **Toddler/Pre-school: (1 year - 4 years)**
→ **School-age: (5 years - 6+ years)**

Do Not Use Sharp or Heavy Objects

When planning birthday games for children, safety should always take center stage. It is essential to create an environment that allows kids to have fun while minimizing potential risks. One crucial aspect is to avoid using sharp or heavy objects in birthday games.

Game Selection: Opt for games that involve soft, lightweight, and child-friendly objects. Choose activities that don't require the use of sharp or heavy items to prevent accidents or injuries.

Thorough Preparations: Plan games well in advance and carefully consider the materials needed. Ensure that all game props, equipment, and objects are safe for children to handle.

Inspection: Before the event, thoroughly inspect all game materials and props. Check for any sharp edges, loose parts, or potential hazards. If an item is found to be unsuitable, replace it with a safer alternative.

Artificial Props: For games that traditionally involve sharp or heavy objects, such as darts or horseshoes, consider using artificial props made from lightweight, soft materials. These props can replicate the game's essence while eliminating the risk of injury.

Soft Targets: If the game involves throwing objects, use soft and cushioned targets that pose no harm if struck. This ensures that even if the objects accidentally hit someone, they won't cause injury.

Supervision: Assign responsible adults or caregivers to supervise the games closely. Their role is to ensure that children are using the game props appropriately and safely.

Clear Instructions: Before starting a game, give the children clear and concise instructions. Emphasize the importance of handling objects gently and avoiding any rough or reckless behavior.

Age-Appropriate Games: Choose games that are suitable for the age and developmental stage of the children attending the celebration. Games that match their physical abilities and coordination reduce the risk of accidents.

Alternative Activities: If a game involves potential hazards, consider offering alternative activities that are equally engaging and safe. This way, children can enjoy the festivities without compromising their well-being.

Communication with Parents: Before the event, communicate with the parents or guardians of the attendees. Inform them about the types of games planned and assure them that safety precautions have been taken to prevent any accidents.

Safe Props: If a game requires the use of objects, opt for child-safe props made from soft materials, foam, or plastic. These items can replicate the game's concept without posing a danger to the children.

Education and Awareness: Take a moment to educate the children about safely handling objects. Use simple and relatable language to explain why sharp or heavy items should be avoided during the games.

Adaptation and Modification: To make traditional games safer, use foam balls instead of hard balls for throwing activities or replace traditional piñatas with pull-string versions.

Prioritize Fun and Safety: Remember that the primary goal of birthday games is to provide entertainment and enjoyment for the children. By prioritizing safety and avoiding sharp or heavy objects, you can ensure that everyone has a delightful and accident-free experience.

You can create a birthday celebration filled with laughter, joy, and worry-free fun. A child-safe environment ensures that all participants can engage in games and activities without the risk of harm, making the celebration a memorable and cherished experience for everyone involved.

<u>Birthdays</u>
→ **Infant/Non-mobile: (Birth - 6 months)**
→ **Infant crawl/roll: (5 months - 1 year)**
→ **Toddler/Pre-school: (1 year - 4 years)**
→ **School-age: (5 years - 6+ years)**

No Pets at Birthday Celebrations

It's important to exercise caution when including pets at parties involving children. The lively and sometimes chaotic atmosphere of a party can create potential risks for both pets and young guests. To ensure a safe and enjoyable celebration, adopting a "no pets at parties" policy is wise.

Unpredictable Reactions: Parties can be overwhelming for pets due to the increased noise, activity, and unfamiliar faces. Even well-behaved pets may react unpredictably when faced with a large group of excited children. They might become anxious, stressed, or exhibit unexpected behaviors that could lead to accidents or conflicts.

Allergies and Sensitivities: Some children may have allergies or sensitivities to pet dander, fur, or saliva. Exposure to pets during a party could trigger allergic reactions, ranging from mild discomfort to more severe symptoms that require medical attention.

Safety Concerns: Children's behavior around pets can be unpredictable. Despite their best intentions, kids may accidentally frighten, startle, or mishandle a pet, leading to bites, scratches, or other injuries. Pets may also become defensive in unfamiliar or overwhelming environments.

Food Hazards: Parties often involve a variety of foods, some of which may be harmful to pets if ingested. Accidental ingestion of human food, especially those toxins to animals, could lead to digestive issues or poisoning.

Escape Risk: Due to guests' frequent comings and goings, pets may be more likely to escape or become lost during a party. This can pose a significant risk, particularly if the pet is not accustomed to crowds or unfamiliar surroundings.

Agitation and Stress: Even well-socialized pets may become agitated or stressed by the presence of numerous people, loud noises, and unfamiliar activities. This can lead to behavioral changes and create a less enjoyable experience for both pets and guests.

Distractions and Responsibilities: Party hosts and parents have their hands full managing the festivities and ensuring the safety and enjoyment of the children. Adding the responsibility of monitoring and caring for pets can be overwhelming and potentially divert attention from other critical tasks.

Preventing Accidents: Even the most well-behaved pets can accidentally knock over decorations, presents, or even young children during a party's excitement. It's best to keep pets separate from the party area to prevent such accidents.

Guest Comfort: Some guests may have phobias or fears of animals, and their presence could make them uncomfortable or anxious. A pet-free environment ensures that all attendees can relax and enjoy the party without any concerns.

Pet's Well-Being: Ultimately, the decision to exclude pets from parties is also about ensuring their well-being. Keeping pets away from parties is a considerate choice that prioritizes their comfort, creating a calm and stress-free environment for them.

While pets bring joy and companionship to our lives, it's wise to keep their well-being and the safety of young guests in mind. By opting for a "no pets at parties" approach, you create a more controlled and secure environment, allowing children to celebrate without worrying about potential pet-related incidents or distractions.

Notes:

Birthdays
Infant/Non-mobile: (Birth - 6 months)
→ **Infant crawl/roll: (5 months - 1 year)**
→ **Toddler/Pre-school: (1 year - 4 years)**
→ **School-age: (5 years - 6+ years)**

Popped/Un-popped Balloons

Each year, **over 1,200 children** in the U.S. suffer injuries from balloons and balloon ties, including choking and strangulation incidents. (Source: U.S. Consumer Product Safety Commission (CPSC) - Balloon Safety) Balloons are a staple of celebrations, adding a festive touch to birthdays, parties, and special occasions. While they bring joy and color to any event, it's important to be mindful of both popped and un-popped balloons to ensure child safety.

Popped Balloons

Choking Hazard: Popped balloons can pose a choking hazard, especially for young children who may put balloon fragments in their mouths. The small pieces of latex or plastic can block a child's airway and lead to a choking incident.

Loud Noise: The loud noise produced by a popped balloon can startle or frighten young children, causing distress or potential injury if they fall, bump into objects, or become disoriented in their attempt to escape the noise.

Un-popped Balloons

Choking Hazard: Un-popped balloons also present a choking hazard if children put them in their mouths or attempt to inflate them without adult supervision. The act of blowing up a balloon can cause a child to accidentally inhale the balloon's contents or even the balloon itself.

Swallowing Risk: If a child accidentally swallows an inflated balloon, it can become lodged in the throat or digestive tract, leading to a medical emergency that requires immediate intervention.

Balloon Safety Tips

Supervision: Always supervise children when balloons are present. Ensure that younger children cannot access balloons without proper adult supervision.

Proper Inflation: Inflate balloons only to a safe and appropriate size for children. Over-inflated balloons are more likely to pop, while under-inflated balloons are easier to swallow or put in the mouth.

Secure Strings: Keep balloon strings short and securely tied to prevent entanglement, especially for younger children who might wrap the string around their necks or limbs.

Adult Assistance: Instruct children that balloons are not toys and should not be inflated without adult assistance. Teach them the importance of responsible balloon handling.

Discard Popped Balloons: Immediately dispose of popped balloons and their fragments in a secure trash receptacle out of reach of children.

Choose Safe Materials: Opt for balloons made of natural latex rather than metallic or plastic balloons, as natural latex is biodegradable and poses a lower risk if ingested.

Age-Appropriate Play: Ensure that balloon-related games and activities are age-appropriate and well-suited to the children's developmental level.

Educate Guests: If you're hosting a party, educate guests, especially parents and caregivers, about balloon safety and the potential hazards they may pose to young children.

By being vigilant and proactive, you can ensure that children of all ages enjoy the joy and excitement of balloon-filled celebrations safely. Remember, while balloons can add a whimsical touch to any occasion, prioritizing child safety is essential to creating a positive and worry-free experience for everyone involved.

> ► *Latex balloons are the leading cause of toy-related choking deaths among children and tragically, over 110 suffocation deaths have occurred since 1973, mostly among kids under six.* ***From 1990 to 2004 alone, at least 68 U.S. children died from choking on balloons, often in just seconds. Pediatricians describe balloon fragment asphyxia as one of the most terrifying emergencies they encounter.*** *(U.S. Consumer Product Safety Commission (CPSC))*

Birthdays
Infant/Non-mobile: (Birth - 6 months)
Infant crawl/roll: (5 months - 1 year)
→ **Toddler/Pre-school: (1 year - 4 years)**
→ **School-age: (5 years - 6+ years)**

Long Hair Near Candles

Fire Risk: Long hair can easily come into contact with an open flame, resulting in the hair catching fire. The flame can travel up the hair quickly, leading to potential burns, injuries, or even starting a fire.

Entanglement: Hair can become entangled in a burning candle, causing pain, injury, or damage to the hair itself. This entanglement can also lead to knocking over the candle or other nearby objects, creating additional hazards.

Candle Safety Tips for Long Hair

Secure Hair: When lighting candles or being around open flames, ensure that long hair is securely tied back in a bun, ponytail, or other updo. This prevents loose strands from accidentally coming into contact with the flame.

Choose Candle Placement: Place candles in areas where there is minimal risk of hair coming into contact with the flame. Avoid placing candles on low surfaces where hair might easily fall or brush against the candle.

Supervise Children: If children with long hair are present, closely supervise them around candles to ensure their hair is kept a safe distance away.

Wear Protective Styles: When near candles, consider wearing hairstyles that keep hair contained, such as braids or tucking hair under a hat or headscarf.

Keep Hair Elevated: When sitting or leaning near candles, keep hair elevated and away from the flame. Avoid leaning over candles, especially if the hair is loose.

Blow Out Candles: Before leaning over or moving close to candles, remember to blow them out to prevent accidental contact with hair.

Use Flameless Alternatives: Consider using flameless candles, LED candles, or other safe alternatives that mimic the appearance of real candles without the risk of an open flame.

Educate Children: Teach children about the importance of keeping their hair away from candles and the potential dangers associated with hair catching fire.

Stay Alert: Be attentive when moving around candles, especially in environments with multiple sources of open flame.

Adult Supervision: Ensure that young children are always supervised when candles are lit and educate them about the dangers of hair near flames.

You can enjoy the comforting glow of candles while minimizing the risk of hair-related accidents. Remember, being proactive and mindful about hair safety around candles is essential to creating a safe and enjoyable environment for everyone, especially in homes with young children or individuals with long hair.

Birthdays
Infant/Non-mobile: (Birth - 6 months)
Infant crawl/roll: (5 months - 1 year)
→ **Toddler/Pre-school: (1 year - 4 years)**
→ **School-age: (5 years - 6+ years)**

Plastic Birthday Cake Decorations

Choking Hazard: Many plastic cake decorations are small and can quickly become a choking hazard if ingested by curious little ones.

Swallowing Risk: Children might accidentally swallow small pieces of plastic cake decorations, which can lead to discomfort, potential injury, or medical complications.

Sharp Edges: Some plastic decorations may have sharp or pointed edges that can cause cuts or scratches if mishandled.

More Cake Decoration Safety Tips

Size Matters: Opt for larger plastic cake decorations that are less likely to be accidentally ingested or inhaled by young children.

Age-Appropriate Decorations: Choose cake decorations suitable for the child's age. Avoid decorations with small parts that can be easily detached.

Secure Placement: Ensure that plastic decorations are securely placed on the cake, so they won't easily come loose during cutting or handling.

Avoid Sharp Edges: Be cautious when using decorations with sharp edges. Make sure they are positioned to prevent direct contact with fingers or skin.

Remove Before Serving: Consider removing plastic decorations from the cake before serving slices to children, especially if the decorations are small or have detachable parts.

Supervision: Always supervise young children when they are around a cake with plastic decorations and educate them about the importance of not touching or playing with the decorations.

Use Edible Alternatives: Consider using edible cake decorations made from fondant, icing, or other food-safe materials.

Prevent Access: Store leftover plastic decorations out of reach of children when the cake is not being served to avoid potential risks.

Decoration Placement: If using plastic decorations on cupcakes, muffins, or other individual treats, ensure that they are securely positioned and won't easily detach.

Dispose Properly: After enjoying the cake, properly and securely dispose of plastic decorations to prevent children from accidentally finding and playing with them.

Read Labels: If you choose to use plastic decorations, read the labels or packaging to ensure they are labeled as safe for use on food items.

You can enjoy your celebratory cakes while ensuring the safety of the little ones around you. Remember, making informed choices about cake decorations adds extra joy to your festivities while keeping child safety a top priority.

<u>Easter</u>
Infant/Non-mobile: (Birth - 6 months)
Infant crawl/roll: (5 months - 1 year)
→ **Toddler/Pre-school: (1 year - 4 years)**
→ **School-age: (5 years - 6+ years)**

Beware of Lawn Chemicals During Outdoor Egg Hunts

As you gear up for a fun-filled outdoor egg hunt, keeping your child's safety a top priority is important.

One aspect that requires careful consideration is the use of lawn chemicals. While these chemicals may contribute to a lush and vibrant lawn, they can also pose potential risks to young children who will be exploring and hunting for eggs in the outdoor space.

Potential Hazards of Lawn Chemicals

Chemical Exposure: Lawn chemicals, such as fertilizers, pesticides, and herbicides, contain potentially harmful substances that can be absorbed through the skin or accidentally ingested by children who come into contact with treated areas.

Skin Irritation: Some lawn chemicals may cause skin irritation, rashes, or allergic reactions if children come into direct contact with them.

Inhalation Risk: Children may inhale fumes or particles from freshly treated lawns, which could lead to respiratory discomfort or irritation.

Outdoor Egg Hunt Safety Tips

Choose a Safe Location: Opt for an egg hunt location that is free from recent chemical treatments. Choose areas of the yard that have not been recently sprayed with lawn chemicals.

Read Labels: If you do use lawn chemicals, carefully read and follow the instructions on product labels. Keep children away from treated areas until it is safe for them to access.

Timing is Key: Schedule your outdoor egg hunt well after any lawn chemical application to ensure that children won't come into contact with treated areas.

Mark Treated Areas: If you've recently treated your lawn, mark the treated areas with clear signs or temporary barriers to prevent children from accidentally wandering into those areas.

Protective Clothing: Dress children in long sleeves, pants, and closed-toe shoes to minimize direct skin exposure to the grass, especially if lawn chemicals have been applied.

Hand Washing: Encourage children to wash their hands thoroughly with soap and water after the egg hunt to remove any potential residue from the grass.

Supervision: Assign adult supervisors to keep a watchful eye on the children during the egg hunt and ensure they stay away from any treated areas.

Use Alternative Areas: If you have concerns about lawn chemicals, consider hosting the egg hunt in a different outdoor space, such as a community park or a friend's yard.

Rinse Eggs: Before decorating or consuming the eggs, rinse them with water to remove any potential contaminants that may have come into contact with the grass.

Educate Participants: Inform parents and guardians about the importance of being cautious around lawn chemicals and share any information about recent treatments.

Natural Lawn Care: Consider using natural and organic lawn care methods that pose fewer risks to children and the environment.

You can create a safe and enjoyable outdoor egg hunt experience for children without compromising their well-being. Keeping a keen eye on lawn chemical usage and following these safety tips ensures that the festivities remain fun, memorable, and, most importantly, safe for everyone involved.

Easter
Infant/Non-mobile: (Birth - 6 months)
→ **Infant crawl/roll: (5 months - 1 year)**
→ **Toddler/Pre-school: (1 year - 4 years)**
→ **School-age: (5 years - 6+ years)**

Small Easter Treats

As Easter festivities approach, it's important to be mindful of potential choking hazards, especially when it comes to small Easter treats. While these delightful goodies add to the joy of the holiday, they can pose risks to young children who may be tempted to put them in their mouths.

Identifying Choking Factors

Size Matters: Be cautious of treats that are small enough to fit easily into a child's mouth, such as jellybeans, chocolate eggs, or small candies.

Texture and Consistency: Foods that are hard, round, or have a smooth surface are more likely to become lodged in a child's throat.

Components: Watch out for treats with small, detachable parts or decorations that could break off and become potential choking hazards.

Choking Hazard Prevention

Age-Appropriate Treats: Choose Easter treats that are age-appropriate and safe for your child's developmental stage. Opt for larger, softer treats that are less likely to cause choking.

Supervision: Always supervise young children while they enjoy their Easter treats. Encourage them to sit down while eating and discourage running or playing with food in their mouths.

Inspect Treats: Examine all treats before giving them to your child. Remove any small or potentially hazardous components that could pose a choking risk.

Cut Foods into Smaller Pieces: If you're serving larger treats, like marshmallows or cupcakes, consider cutting them into smaller, bite-sized pieces to reduce the risk of choking.

Educate Older Siblings: If you have older children, educate them about the importance of keeping small treats away from their younger siblings to prevent accidental ingestion.

Safe Alternatives: Offer alternative Easter treats that are specifically designed for young children, such as larger chocolate bunnies, soft cookies, or age-appropriate toys.

Teach Proper Eating: Teach your child to take small bites and chew their food thoroughly before swallowing. Encourage them to eat slowly and savor their treats.

Choking Rescue Knowledge: Familiarize yourself with infant and child CPR techniques and the Heimlich maneuver in case of a choking emergency.

Stay Informed: Keep up to date with information about product recalls or safety alerts related to Easter treats or toys.

Open Treats Carefully: When unwrapping treats or removing packaging, ensure that small pieces don't become loose and pose a choking hazard.

Clear Eating Area: Create a designated eating area that is free from small objects or toys that could accidentally end up in your child's mouth.

Lead by Example: Model safe eating habits for your child by sitting down, taking small bites, and chewing thoroughly.

4th of July
→ **Infant/Non-mobile: (Birth - 6 months)**
→ **Infant crawl/roll: (5 months - 1 year)**
→ **Toddler/Pre-school: (1 year - 4 years)**
→ **School-age: (5 years - 6+ years)**

Firework Concerns

Annually, **over 5,000 children** are injured by fireworks in the United States, with burns and eye injuries being the most common. (Source: U.S. Consumer Product Safety Commission (CPSC) - Fireworks Safety) The 4th of July is synonymous with vibrant celebrations, but the inclusion of fireworks necessitates heightened vigilance to safeguard children from accidents and injuries. Firework concerns primarily revolve around the potential for burns and physical injuries. Burns can vary in severity, potentially causing considerable harm to a child's sensitive skin. Furthermore, the risk of injuries extends to cuts and bruises, which can occur from being struck by firework debris or from accidents during firework displays.

To circumvent these dangers, parents and guardians must be proactive in recognizing and mitigating potential hazards. Educating children about the dangers associated with fireworks is vital, fostering a cautious approach towards these pyrotechnic devices. Maintaining a safe distance from the fireworks display area is a crucial preventative measure, which includes steering clear of crowded places where maintaining safety distances might be challenging.

Implementing **Prevention Strategies** is a proactive approach to ensuring children's safety during the 4th of July celebrations. These strategies encompass:

Choosing Safe Locations: Select locations that are sufficiently removed from the fireworks display to reduce the risk of injury from stray fireworks or debris.

Proper Supervision: Always have an adult supervising children to prevent them from wandering too close to the fireworks display area.

Protective Gear: Equip children with appropriate protective gear, such as safety glasses, to shield them from potential flying debris.

First Aid Preparedness: Keep a first aid kit accessible and stocked with necessities to address minor burns and injuries promptly.

Emergency Contacts: Maintain a list of emergency contact numbers, including the nearest medical facility, to expedite assistance in the event of serious injuries.

Parents can foster a secure and enjoyable 4th of July celebration for their children, minimizing the risks associated with fireworks and allowing the family to revel in the festivities with peace of mind.

4th of July
→ Infant/Non-mobile: (Birth - 6 months)
→ Infant crawl/roll: (5 months - 1 year)
→ Toddler/Pre-school: (1 year - 4 years)
→ School-age: (5 years - 6+ years)

Protect Children's Hearing During Fireworks

Fireworks are a dazzling spectacle that often accompanies celebrations and special occasions. While they bring joy and excitement, it's essential to be aware of the potential risks they pose, particularly to children's delicate ears. Fireworks can produce loud and sudden noises that have the potential to cause permanent damage to children's hearing.

Understanding the Risks

Decibel Levels: Fireworks produce sounds that can reach extremely high decibel levels, well above the safe range for human hearing. Prolonged exposure to loud noises can lead to hearing loss.

Vulnerable Ears: Children's ears are more sensitive than adults, making them more susceptible to hearing damage. Their auditory systems are still developing, which increases the risk of permanent harm.

Protecting Children's Hearing

Keep a Safe Distance: Watch fireworks from a safe distance, preferably where the noise levels are reduced. Consider attending public displays hosted by professionals where safety measures are in place.

Use Ear Protection: Provide children with appropriate ear protection, such as earmuffs or earplugs, designed specifically for their size. Ensure the protection fits well and is comfortable for them to wear.

Limit Exposure: If you're attending a private fireworks display, consider allowing children to watch for a short period from a safe distance before moving indoors or to a quieter area.

Explain the Dangers: Talk to children about the potential harm that loud noises from fireworks can cause to their hearing. Encourage them to communicate any discomfort or pain in their ears.

Prevent Close Proximity: Discourage children from handling fireworks or standing too close to where they are being ignited. Emphasize the importance of following safety guidelines.

Quiet Viewing Areas: If you're hosting a fireworks event, create designated quiet viewing areas where children and those who are sensitive to loud noises can enjoy the visual spectacle without the intense sound.

Alternatives: Consider enjoying the visual aspects of fireworks through televised displays or video recordings that allow you to control the volume and reduce the risk of hearing damage.

Monitor Reactions: Pay attention to children's reactions to the noise. If they cover their ears, appear uncomfortable, or express distress, it's a sign that the noise level may be too intense for them.

Education: Teach children about the importance of protecting their ears and the potential consequences of exposing themselves to loud noises. Encourage responsible habits from a young age.

Professional Displays: Choose public fireworks displays hosted by professionals who adhere to safety regulations and use appropriate noise-reducing measures.

Healthy Hearing Habits: Foster a culture of healthy hearing habits by encouraging children to keep the volume at a reasonable level when using headphones or earbuds.

Regular Check-ups: Schedule regular hearing check-ups for your child to monitor their auditory health and catch any potential issues early.

You can help safeguard your child's hearing and ensure that their enjoyment of fireworks is both safe and memorable.

Notes:

Thanksgiving
Infant/Non-mobile: **(Birth - 6 months)**
Infant crawl/roll: **(5 months - 1 year)**
→ **Toddler/Pre-school: (1 year - 4 years)**
→ **School-age: (5 years - 6+ years)**

Turkey Fryer Concerns

Turkey frying, a popular culinary endeavor, especially during festive seasons, brings with it the need for stringent childproofing measures to ensure the little ones remain safe and sound. The process involves the use of hot oil and open flames, which can pose significant risks to children if not adequately managed. Therefore, it becomes essential to create a childproof environment that considers all aspects of safety.

First and foremost, establish a **'Kid-Free Zone'** around the area where the turkey fryer is set up. This zone should be marked, and children should be educated about the importance of staying outside of this zone to avoid accidents. It might be beneficial to set up a physical barrier, such as a baby gate or a playpen, to delineate this zone.

Stable Setup: Ensure that the fryer is set up on a stable, flat surface to prevent it from tipping over.

Constant Supervision: Always have an adult supervise the fryer and watch over the children to prevent them from coming close to it.

Secure Tools and Accessories: Keep all tools, accessories, and hot liquids securely placed at a height that is out of reach for children.

Cooling Time: After the frying is done, allow sufficient time for the oil and the fryer to cool down before allowing children back into the area.

Emergency Preparedness: Be prepared for emergencies by having a fire extinguisher and a first aid kit readily available.

Furthermore, engage children in safe activities away from the frying area, possibly setting up a play area with toys and games to keep them occupied. It's also a good idea to have another adult responsible for monitoring the children, ensuring they remain entertained and far from potential hazards.

By taking these comprehensive measures, parents can ensure that the turkey frying process is conducted safely and without any accidents. This allows for a festive and joyous occasion that is enjoyed by all, including the little ones. Remember, child safety is a priority, and a little preparation goes a long way in preventing accidents and ensuring a happy, safe celebration.

Thanksgiving
Infant/Non-mobile: (Birth - 6 months)
Infant crawl/roll: (5 months - 1 year)
→ **Toddler/Pre-school: (1 year - 4 years)**
→ **School-age: (5 years - 6+ years)**

Child-Friendly Zone

To ensure a safe and enjoyable Thanksgiving celebration, create a child-friendly zone adorned with festive decorations and stocked with crafts and toys to keep the little ones engaged. Involve children in safe cooking activities, set up a cozy corner for parade viewing, and organize fun safety-related games and role-play activities. Additionally, secure heavy furniture, install stair gates and manage cords effectively to prevent accidents. These measures will foster a festive and secure environment where children can enjoy the celebrations safely.

> ► *According to the National Fire Protection Association (NFPA) and Fire Department of New York (FDNY **Deep-fryer incidents, especially from turkey fryers, cause about 60 injuries nationwide each year**, and studies show that half of pediatric hot-oil burns are linked to these appliances. That translates to roughly 10–11 children per year, most under age 6, suffering serious grease burns.*

|Ch. 27| Grandparents/Caretakers

Caretaker/Grandparents
→ Infant/Non-mobile: (Birth - 6 months)
→ Infant crawl/roll: (5 months - 1 year)
→ Toddler/Pre-school: (1 year - 4 years)
→ School-age: (5 years - 6+ years)

Grandparent Safety

Medication Safety: Ensure all medications are stored out of children's reach in a locked cabinet. Communicate any specific medication instructions or allergies to grandparents.

Small-Object Choking Hazards: Remove small toys, buttons, coins, and other choking hazards from accessible areas and store them securely.

Electrical Outlets and Cords: Cover unused electrical outlets with safety plugs and secure cords and cables to prevent tripping hazards.

Window and Door Safety: Install window locks or guards to prevent accidental falls. Ensure doors leading outside are securely locked or childproofed.

Kitchen Safety: Store sharp knives, utensils, and cleaning supplies in locked cabinets. Keep hot liquids and pans away from the edges.

Stairway and Balcony Safety: Install safety gates at the top and bottom of staircases. Secure balcony doors and ensure childproof locks are in place.

Furniture Stability: Ensure furniture is securely anchored to the wall to prevent tipping. Remove any unstable or wobbly furniture.

Fire and Burns: Childproof fireplace and stove areas with safety gates or screens. Store matches and lighters out of reach.

Bathroom Safety: Secure toilet lids with locks or close the bathroom door. Remove cleaning supplies and toiletries from accessible areas.

Pet Safety: Ensure pets are well-controlled and supervised around children. Teach children how to interact safely with pets.

Emergency Contacts and Information: Provide grandparents with emergency contact numbers, including your pediatrician. Share any allergies or medical conditions your child has.

Safe Sleep Environment: Ensure cribs, playpens, and sleeping areas meet safety standards. Communicate safe sleep guidelines, such as placing infants on their backs.

Poisonous Plants and Substances: Remove toxic plants from indoor and outdoor areas and store cleaning products and chemicals out of reach.

Safety Gear: Ensure car seats, strollers, and other gear are correctly installed and used. Provide helmets for bike rides or outdoor activities.

Supervision and Communication: Establish clear communication about routines, schedules, and any special instructions. Encourage grandparents to maintain active supervision and engage in safe activities.

Home Security: Check that home security systems are functioning properly. If available, teach children how to use alarms or emergency buttons.

Personal Items: Securely stores personal items, such as jewelry or small accessories. Keep purses, bags, and briefcases out of children's reach.

First Aid Kit: Ensure a well-stocked first aid kit is accessible, and grandparents know how to use it. Include items like bandages, antiseptic ointment, and child-safe medications.

Caretaker/Babysitter safety

Several concerns may arise when entrusting your child to a babysitter and addressing these effectively can make a significant difference in ensuring your child's safety and well-being.

Inadequate Knowledge of Emergency Procedures: Ensure that the babysitter is well-versed in basic first aid and emergency procedures. Provide them with a list of emergency contact numbers, including poison control, pediatrician, and nearest hospital.

Access to Hazardous Areas/Items: Before the babysitter arrives, secure all potential hazardous zones in your home, such as the kitchen, bathroom, or areas with heavy furniture and sharp corners. Store away cleaning agents, medicines, and other dangerous substances.

Allergic Reactions: Thoroughly communicate any allergies your child may have and make sure the babysitter knows how to respond to an allergic reaction, including administering medications if necessary.

Choking Hazards: Educate the babysitter about potential choking hazards, such as small toys and certain types of foods. Instruct them to supervise the child during meal and play times to prevent choking incidents.

Improper Sleep Supervision: Inform the babysitter about the correct sleeping positions for your child, mainly if they are infants, to prevent issues such as Sudden Infant Death Syndrome (SIDS).

Inadequate Fire Safety Measures: Ensure that the babysitter is familiar with the home's fire safety measures. Show them how to operate fire extinguishers and the quickest exit routes in case of a fire.

Additional Solutions

Open Communication Line: Keep an open line of communication with the babysitter, where they can reach out with any concerns or updates about the child.

Information Sheet: Provide a detailed information sheet containing all necessary details about your child's routines, preferences, and any other information that can assist in providing better care.

First Visit Orientation: During the babysitter's first visit, allocate time to walk them through the house, pointing out all the safety measures put in place and addressing any concerns they may have.

Feedback and Learning: After the babysitting session, talk to the babysitter to understand if they faced any difficulties and learn how to make the process smoother in the future.

Ensuring a safe and comfortable environment for both the child and the babysitter is paramount. Addressing these concerns with thorough preparation and open communication can create a safe and happy childcare experience.

Notes: (Based of your caretaker/babysitter's personality and experience.)

|Ch. 28| Child Internet Safety

Internet Safety
Infant/Non-mobile: (Birth - 6 months)
Infant crawl/roll: (5 months - 1 year)
Toddler/Pre-school: (1 year - 4 years)
→ **School-age: (5 years - 6+ years)**

Child internet safety is of utmost importance in today's digital age, as children are increasingly exposed to online platforms and content. Ensuring their safety involves a comprehensive approach that combines education, supervision, and the use of technology tools.

Educate Children about Online Risks: Discuss potential dangers such as cyberbullying, online predators, phishing scams, and inappropriate content. Teach them about the importance of privacy and the risks of sharing personal information online. Explain the concept of a digital footprint and how their online actions can have long-term consequences.

Set Clear Rules and Boundaries: Establish rules regarding screen time, online activities, and appropriate websites and apps. Create a family media plan that outlines when and how devices can be used. Set age-appropriate guidelines for social media usage and online interactions.

Use Parental Control Software: Install parental control software or apps on devices used by children to filter content and block inappropriate websites. Set up safe search filters on search engines to ensure age-appropriate search results.

Create a Safe Online Environment: Ensure that computers and devices used by children are in common areas of the home, allowing for easy supervision. Set up child accounts on devices with restricted access to certain features and content.

Teach Responsible Online Behavior: Encourage kindness and empathy in online interactions and discourage cyberbullying or harmful behavior. Teach them to think critically about online information and verify its accuracy from reliable sources.

Monitor Online Activities: Regularly check your child's internet browsing history to ensure they are using the internet responsibly. Be aware of the websites, apps, and social media platforms they are using.

Be Involved in Their Online World: Engage in online activities together, such as playing educational games or exploring age-appropriate websites. Show genuine interest in their online experiences and discuss what they encounter.

Address Cyberbullying: Teach children how to handle cyberbullying situations, including blocking bullying and reporting the incident to you or a trusted adult. Encourage them to be open about any bullying experiences they may face online.

Stay Informed and Updated: Stay updated on the latest internet trends and potential risks to better guide your children. Stay informed about the popular websites, apps, and social media platforms among children.

By combining these strategies, parents and caregivers can create a safer online environment for children, promoting responsible digital citizenship and protecting them from potential online threats. The key is maintaining open communication, establishing clear boundaries, and providing ongoing guidance as children navigate the digital world.

Notes: (Evaluate current routines)

Ch. 29 | Intruder and Child Abduction Protection

Intruder and Child Abduction Protection
→ Infant/Non-mobile: (Birth - 6 months)
→ Infant crawl/roll: (5 months - 1 year)
→ Toddler/Pre-school: (1 year - 4 years)
→ School-age: (5 years - 6+ years)

Intruder and Child Abduction Protection

Ensuring your child's safety from potential intruders and abduction threats requires a comprehensive approach that combines home security measures, education, communication, and vigilance.

Home Security

Secure Entry Points: To deter intruders, install sturdy locks, deadbolts, and security bars on all doors and windows.

Window Coverings: Use curtains or blinds to prevent outsiders from peering into your home.

Alarm System: Consider installing a monitored home security system with sensors, cameras, and motion detectors.

Outdoor Lighting: Illuminate the perimeter of your home with motion-activated lights to deter intruders and improve visibility.

Stranger Awareness

Teach Your Child: Educate your child about the dangers of talking to strangers in person and online. Emphasize the importance of never accepting rides or gifts from unknown individuals.

Safe Passwords: Establish a family password that only trusted individuals should know. Teach your child to ask for the password if someone claims to have been sent it by you.

Emergency Contacts: Ensure your child knows essential contact numbers, including your phone number, emergency services, and trusted family or friends.

Scheduled Activities

Know Your Child's Schedule: Be aware of your child's daily routine and the whereabouts of their friends and caregivers.

Designated Meeting Points: Teach your child about safe locations to go to if they feel unsafe, such as a trusted neighbor's house or a nearby store.

Home Safety Zones: Designate areas in your home where your child can go if they sense danger, such as a locked room or a neighbor's home.

Open Communication

Foster Open Dialogue: Encourage your child to share any concerns or uncomfortable situations with you. Create a safe and supportive environment where they feel comfortable expressing.

School and Activity Policies: Ensure schools and activity providers have strict authorization procedures for releasing your child to someone other than you.

Internet Safety (Details on pg. 512)

Set Rules: Establish rules for online activities, including not sharing personal information with strangers and reporting any suspicious online interactions.

Social Media Privacy: Educate your child about the importance of privacy settings and avoid sharing their location or personal details online.

Family Emergency Plan

Create a Plan: Develop a comprehensive family emergency plan that outlines escape routes, meeting points, and roles during a crisis.

Practice Drills: Regularly conduct safety drills with your child to familiarize them with the emergency plan and ensure they know how to respond to a crisis.

Community Awareness

Stay Informed: Be aware of registered sex offenders in your area and use community resources to receive alerts and updates.

Neighbors Network: Develop a network of trusted neighbors who can help watch over your child when you're not around.

Identification

Child ID Kit: Maintain an up-to-date identification kit for your child, including recent photos, fingerprints, and important details. This can be invaluable in the case of a missing child situation.

Travel Precautions

Inform Others: When traveling with your child, inform a trusted neighbor or friend of your plans and provide contact information.

Safe Accommodation: Choose accommodations with strong security measures when traveling.

Trust Your Child's Instincts

Intuition: Encourage your child to trust their instincts. If something doesn't feel right, teach them to remove themselves from the situation and seek help.

Notes:

Intruder and Child Abduction Protection
→ Infant/Non-mobile: (Birth - 6 months)
→ Infant crawl/roll: (5 months - 1 year)
→ Toddler/Pre-school: (1 year - 4 years)
→ School-age: (5 years - 6+ years)

Track your child!

Losing sight of a child, even for a moment, is every caregiver's worst fear. Young children are naturally curious and can wander off in seconds. While traditional methods like calling their name or checking common hiding spots are crucial, modern technology and creative strategies can enhance child tracking and recovery. Below are innovative ways to track a missing child both inside and outside the home.

Wearable GPS Trackers: Invest in child-friendly GPS bracelets, smartwatches, or shoe inserts that allow real-time tracking via a mobile app. Some even have geofencing alerts if the child leaves a designated area.

Sound-Activated Tags: Attach small devices to shoes or clothing that emit a sound when activated via a phone app or remote. This is useful for quickly locating a child who may be hiding or lost in a crowded space.

Temporary Tattoos with Contact Info: For outings, use dissolvable tattoos or wristbands with a phone number to help others identify and return your child quickly.

Personalized Call-and-Response Games: Teach your child a fun call-and-response phrase (e.g., "Marco!" – "Polo!") that you can use in case they wander too far.

Clothing with Reflective Patches or Colors: Dressing your child in bright or glow-in-the-dark clothing makes them easier to spot, especially in dimly lit areas.

Shoes with Light-Up Soles: Flashing or light-up shoes can help track a running child in a crowd or dim environment.

Safety Word System for Strangers: Teach your child a family "safety word" that only trusted adults know, so if someone tries to take them, they'll recognize a red flag.

Motion-Activated Door and Gate Alarms: Install alarms that beep when a door, window, or backyard gate is opened unexpectedly.

Mirror and Camera Trick: Set up baby monitors and strategically placed mirrors in blind spots like hallways and staircases to quickly check hiding places.

Hidden Tracking Stickers: Some high-tech stickers have embedded Bluetooth tracking chips that can be placed on clothing, inside backpacks, or even inside a favorite stuffed animal.

Balloon or Flag System for Play Areas: When outside at a park or event, attach a helium balloon or small flag to a stroller or backpack to create an easy visual marker.

By using a mix of these tools and techniques, parents can dramatically increase their chances of quickly finding a missing child while also instilling safety habits from an early age.

|Ch. 30| Government Agencies

Government Agencies
→ Infant/Non-mobile: (Birth - 6 months)
→ Infant crawl/roll: (5 months - 1 year)
→ Toddler/Pre-school: (1 year - 4 years)
→ School-age: (5 years - 6+ years)

Several U.S. agencies work to protect children by enforcing safety regulations, promoting injury prevention, and providing childproofing guidelines to create safer environments for young children. These agencies focus on different aspects of child safety, from product regulations to poisoning prevention and digital security.

Key Agencies & Their Responsibilities

Consumer Product Safety Commission (CPSC)
- Regulates children's products such as cribs, car seats, and safety gates.
- Issues recalls on dangerous toys, furniture, and baby products.
- Provides childproofing guidelines for home safety

Centers for Disease Control and Prevention (CDC)
- Focuses on injury prevention, including falls, burns, drowning, and poisoning.
- Promotes safe sleep practices to reduce Sudden Infant Death Syndrome (SIDS).
- Provides guidelines for preventing household accidents.

U.S. Food and Drug Administration (FDA)
- Ensures baby food, formula, and medications are safe for children.
- Regulates packaging and labeling to prevent accidental poisoning.
- Issues warnings on unsafe substances and recalled products.

National Highway Traffic Safety Administration (NHTSA)
- Enforces child car seat regulations and crash safety standards.
- Provides installation guidance and recalls defective car seats.
- Educates parents on preventing hot car deaths

Environmental Protection Agency (EPA)
- Regulates exposure to hazardous materials such as lead, asbestos, and mold.
- Promotes clean air and water for child health.
- Provides resources on household toxin reduction

U.S. Fire Administration (USFA)
- Educates families on fire prevention and emergency planning.
- Recommends installing smoke and carbon monoxide detectors.
- Provides guidance on safe use of electrical outlets and heating devices.

Poison Control Centers (AAPCC)
- Offers a 24/7 emergency hotline (**1-800-222-1222**) for poisoning incidents.
- Educates families on safe storage of medications and household chemicals.
- Provides immediate treatment advice for accidental ingestion.

Administration for Children and Families (ACF) – U.S. Department of Health and Human Services (HHS)
- Oversees child abuse prevention programs and ensures child welfare.
- Provides funding and resources to help families create safe home environments.
- Supports early childhood safety education programs.

Office of Juvenile Justice and Delinquency Prevention (OJJDP) – U.S. Department of Justice (DOJ)
- Protects children from abuse, exploitation, and endangerment.
- Funds programs aimed at preventing child trafficking and online threats.
- Works with law enforcement to enhance child safety initiatives

National Center for Missing & Exploited Children (NCMEC)
- Assists in locating missing children and preventing abductions.
- Provides digital safety resources for families and children

Operates a tip line for reporting child exploitation and suspicious activity. These agencies work together to ensure children's safety in homes, schools, vehicles, and online spaces. By following their childproofing recommendation such as securing furniture, installing smoke detectors, using baby gates, and locking away hazardous substances, parents and caregivers can create a safer environment for children from birth to six years old.

Conclusion

Congratulations!

Pat yourself on the back, diligent guardian of tiny daredevils! You have successfully navigated the perilous journey of childproofing your home, transforming it into a fortress of safety and fun for your little adventurer. Oh, the countless stubbed toes and bumped heads you've prevented! Your home is now less of a danger zone and more of a secure play paradise.

Not only have you mastered the art of spotting a choking hazard from a mile away, but you've also become fluent in the language of "Baby-ese" and can now differentiate between a cry of hunger and a cry of "I've just found another thing to get into!"

Your new eagle-eyed vigilance means that every sharp corner is cushioned, and every electrical outlet is covered. Your child might think they've got the upper hand, but little do they know, they're up against a childproofing ninja, a safety virtuoso, and a maestro of baby-proof barricades!

But remember, childproofing isn't just about keeping those little rascals safe; it's about fostering a space where their curiosity and imagination can run wild without you having to run behind them with a first-aid kit.

So, here's to you, brave protector of tiny humans! You've climbed the mountains of baby gates, sailed the seas of spill-proof sippy cups, and emerged victorious. Now, go ahead and enjoy a well-earned cup of coffee or perhaps a nap. (We won't tell if you do.) Your home is now a childproofed haven, a place where your child can explore, play, and grow under the loving watch of the world's newest childproofing champion - You!

Remember, in the grand playground of life, it's always better to be safe than sorry!

Ultimate Childproofing Checklist

(A Quick Reference Guide)

Home Entry & Exits

- ☐ Install **doorknob covers** or lever locks on doors leading outside.
- ☐ Secure **deadbolts and peepholes** out of children's reach.
- ☐ Use **door stoppers** to prevent finger pinching.
- ☐ Set up **video doorbells** or security systems.
- ☐ Keep **keys and garage openers** out of reach.
- ☐ Ensure **screens on windows** are secure and childproof.

Living Room & Common Areas

- ☐ Cover **sharp furniture corners and edges** with padding.
- ☐ Secure **TVs, bookcases, and heavy furniture** to the wall.
- ☐ Keep **cords, chargers, and electrical outlets** covered.
- ☐ Install **cordless window blinds** or secure loose blind cords.
- ☐ Store **remote controls, small objects, and choking hazards** out of reach.
- ☐ Use **fireplace screens** and store matches/lighters safely.
- ☐ Keep **houseplants out of reach** (some can be toxic).
- ☐ Secure **pet food and water bowls** (choking and drowning hazard).

Nursery & Bedroom

- ☐ Use a **firm crib mattress** with a fitted sheet (no loose blankets or pillows).
- ☐ Keep **cribs away from windows, blinds, and heaters.**
- ☐ Install **drawer and dresser anchors** to prevent tipping.
- ☐ Secure **diaper creams, lotions, and small items** in locked drawers.
- ☐ Use **nightlights with cool-to-touch bulbs** and keep lamps out of reach.
- ☐ Ensure **mobiles and wall decorations** are well secured and out of baby's reach.
- ☐ Use **cordless baby monitors** or secure monitor cords away from cribs.
- ☐ Remove **stuffed animals and bumpers** from cribs to prevent suffocation.

Kitchen

- ☐ Install **stove knob covers** and use back burners for cooking.
- ☐ Secure **cabinets and drawers** with childproof locks.
- ☐ Store **knives, sharp objects, and cleaning supplies** in locked drawers.
- ☐ Keep **hot liquids and foods** away from edges of tables and counters.
- ☐ Use **appliance locks** on the fridge, oven, and dishwasher.
- ☐ Set the **water heater to 120°F (49°C)** to prevent burns.
- ☐ Store **breakable dishes and glassware** out of reach.
- ☐ Keep **small magnets and fridge decorations** out of reach (choking hazard).
- ☐ Use **high chairs with secure straps and never leave child unattended.**
- ☐ Keep **plastic bags and cling wrap** stored safely.

Bathroom & Laundry Room
- ☐ Use **toilet locks** to prevent drowning hazards.
- ☐ Secure **medications, toiletries, and cleaning supplies** in locked cabinets.
- ☐ Install **non-slip mats** inside and outside the bathtub.
- ☐ Always **unplug hair dryers, curling irons, and electric razors** after use.
- ☐ Keep the **washer and dryer doors closed and locked** when not in use.
- ☐ Store **laundry detergent pods** in a locked cabinet.
- ☐ Use **a thermometer to test bathwater temperature** before placing a child in.
- ☐ Ensure **razors, scissors, and tweezers** are stored out of reach.

Stairs & Hallways
- ☐ Install **safety gates** at the top and bottom of stairs.
- ☐ Secure **loose rugs and carpets** to prevent tripping.
- ☐ Use **motion-sensor nightlights** in hallways and staircases.
- ☐ Ensure **banister gaps** are too narrow for a child's head to fit through.
- ☐ Keep **hallways free of clutter** to avoid tripping hazards.

Playroom & Toy Safety
- ☐ Choose **age-appropriate toys** without small, detachable parts.
- ☐ Keep **batteries, especially button batteries, locked away**.
- ☐ Store toys in **open bins (not heavy-lid toy chests)** to prevent trapped fingers.
- ☐ Regularly **inspect and clean toys** for damage or choking hazards.
- ☐ Avoid **balloons or plastic wrappers** that pose a suffocation risk.
- ☐ Anchor **bookshelves and play furniture** to the wall.
- ☐ Make sure **puzzle pieces and board game parts** are stored safely.

Outdoor & Garage Safety
- ☐ Install **fences around pools, ponds, or water features** with self-latching gates.
- ☐ Keep **garage tools, chemicals, and gas cans** in locked cabinets.
- ☐ Ensure **playground equipment** is sturdy and placed over soft ground (e.g., mulch, rubber).
- ☐ Store **bicycles, scooters, and helmets** in an organized area.
- ☐ Keep **grills, fire pits, and propane tanks** locked or covered.
- ☐ Secure **garden hoses and electrical outlets**.
- ☐ Ensure **fences and gates are properly maintained** to prevent escape.

Car Safety
- ☐ Use an **age-appropriate car seat** and install it correctly.
- ☐ Never leave a child **alone in a car, even for a minute**.
- ☐ Keep **loose items secured** to prevent them from becoming projectiles in a crash.
- ☐ Use **child safety locks** on doors and windows.
- ☐ Keep **emergency roadside supplies** (first-aid kit, flashlight, blanket, water).
- ☐ Store **car cleaning supplies and tools** in a locked trunk or cabinet.

Emergency & First Aid
- ☐ Keep a **fully stocked first-aid kit** in an accessible place.
- ☐ Install **smoke detectors and carbon monoxide detectors** on every floor.
- ☐ Test **smoke alarms monthly** and replace batteries yearly.

☐ Teach **fire escape plans** and practice them regularly.
☐ Have **emergency contact numbers** posted in a visible area.
☐ Keep **a fire extinguisher in the kitchen and know how to use it.**
☐ Create and review **a choking response plan** for all caregivers

Final Safety Reminders
☐ Always **supervise young children, especially in high-risk areas.**
☐ Regularly **inspect and update safety measures** as your child grows.
☐ Stay informed about **recalls on child safety products and toys.**
☐ Teach **older siblings and caregivers** about childproofing rules.

Notes:

EVERPRESENT
North America Inc.
Copyright © 2025

www.ingramcontent.com/pod-product-compliance
Lightning Source LLC
Chambersburg PA
CBHW081143290426
44108CB00018B/2429